VOLUME 61

SCREEN WORLD™

The Films of 2009

BARRY MONUSH

JOHN WILLIS, EDITOR EMERITUS

APPLAUSE
THEATRE & CINEMA BOOKS

An Imprint of Hal Leonard Corporation • New York

SCREEN WORLD
Volume 61Copyright © 2010 by Barry Monush

Published in 2010 by Applause Theatre & Cinema Books
An Imprint of Hal Leonard Corporation
7777 West Bluemound Road
Milwaukee, WI 53213

Trade Book Division Editorial Offices
19 West 21st Street, New York, NY 10010

Printed in the United States of America
Book design by Tony Meisel

ISBN 978-1-4234-9272-6
ISSN 1545–9020

www.applausepub.com

To **CLINT EASTWOOD**

Who reigned as modern cinema's biggest box office attraction longer than any other star and whose solid underplaying as an actor and streamlined storytelling skills as a director have made him one of the industry's most admired and truly iconic figures.

SCREEN: *Revenge of the Creature; Francis in the Navy; Lady Godiva of Coventry; Tarantula; Never Say Goodbye; Star in the Dust; Away All Boats; The First Traveling Saleslady; Escapade in Japan; Ambush at Cimarron Pass; Lafayette Escadrille; Fistful of Dollars; For a Few Dollars More; The Good the Bad and the Ugly; Hang 'em High; Coogan's Bluff; The Witches; Where Eagles Dare; Paint Your Wagon; Two Mules for Sister Sara; Kelly's Heroes; The Beguiled; Play Misty for Me* (and director); *Dirty Harry; Joe Kidd; High Plains Drifter* (and director); *Breezy* (and director); *Magnum Force; Thunderbolt and Lightfoot; The Eiger Sanction* (and director); *The Outlaw Josey Wales* (and director); *The Enforcer; The Gauntlet* (and director); *Every Which Way But Loose; Escape From Alcatraz; Bronco Billy* (and director); *Any Which Way You Can; Firefox* (and director, producer); *Honkytonk Man* (and director, producer); *Sudden Impact* (and director, producer); *Tightrope* (and producer); *City Heat; Pale Rider* (and director, producer.); *Heartbreak Ridge* (and director, producer); *The Dead Pool* (and producer); *Bird* (director, producer); *Thelonius Monk: Straight, No Chaser* (executive producer); *Pink Cadillac; White Hunter Black Heart* (and director, producer); *The Rookie* (and director); *Unforgiven* (and director, producer; Academy Awards for Best Director and Best Picture; Oscar nomination for actor); *In the Line of Fire; A Perfect World* (and director, producer); *Casper; The Bridges of Madison County* (and director, producer); *The Stars Fell on Henrietta* (producer); *Absolute Power* (and director, producer); *Midnight in the Garden of Good and Evil* (director, producer); *True Crime* (and director, producer); *Space Cowboys* (and director, producer); *Blood Work* (and director, producer); *Mystic River* (director, producer, music; Oscar nominations for Director, Picture); *Million Dollar Baby* (and director, producer, music; Academy Award Winner for Best Director; Oscar nomination for actor); *Flags of Our Fathers* (director, producer, music); *Letters from Iwo Jima* (director, producer; Oscar nominations for Director and Picture); *Grace is Gone* (music); *Changeling* (director, producer); *Gran Torino* (and director, producer); *Invictus* (director, producer); *Hereafter* (director, producer).

CONTENTS

A Not-so-Serious Man in Need of an Education

The Oscars for 2009 included a milestone, and I'm not talking about Kathryn Bigelow becoming the first female director to win the trophy (congratulations, Kathryn, nice job), but something rather less positive and definitely more irksome. The film Bigelow directed, *The Hurt Locker*, won the Academy Award that night for Best Picture as well, and do you know how far down the list it sits on the 100 highest grossing movies of 2009? It doesn't. It's not on that list. And that's because it took in a mere $14 million during its theatrical run prior to its Oscar win, meaning it did not even make as much cash as such failures as *Did You Hear about the Morgans?* or *Aliens in the Attic*. So, the milestone is, that the Academy has finally, thoroughly and completely conceded to the fact that a motion picture's theatrical impact is meaningless where voting is concerned as long as complimentary Academy screeners show up at the end of the year and the critics awards have influenced members enough to encourage them to look no further than the film's *they* have selected for *their* honors. *Variety* can crow all it wants about the gigantic grosses of *Avatar*, but the sad truth remains that there is still a huge difference out there between the pictures that fill the top box office slots and all those interesting movies that would make the year appear a whole lot better in most people's eyes, if they bothered to see them, or were even aware they existed.

It's great that such fine movies as *An Education* and *A Serious Man* ended up with Oscar nominations for Best Picture because of the controversial decision on the Academy's part to expand the category to 10 contestants, but why on earth does a bad movie starring Peter Sarsgaard, *Orphan*, still end up making so much more money than *An Education*, featuring Sarsgaard as well, when there is little doubt as to which is the superior work? I have a sneaking suspicion that most people who patronized such high money earners as *G-Force* and *Alvin and the Chipmunks: The Squeakquel* aren't even aware of the existence of *The Messenger* or *A Single Man*, both of which are outstanding films that scored major Oscar nominations. Sadly, of all the movies mentioned in this paragraph, it's the ones that did *not* gross big box office figures that weren't released by major studios. Hollywood is no doubt content with its position of ignoring most projects that deal with such complexities as human relationships. However, if you've got a script about wisecracking members of the squirrel family, you're in luck.

But I'm not here for chipmunk bashing, but to praise the resilience of meaningful movies of quality and sincerity, the ones that set out to accomplish what the best films are supposed to do: entertain and yet not condescend simply to make a cheap buck. There were a handful of films that actually harkened back to better days, when commercial-minded pictures could also pass for quality entertainment that did not insult your intelligence. And yes, some of them even brought in substantial audiences, including two from the ever-reliant Meryl Streep, *Julie & Julia* and *It's Complicated*; George Clooney's sophisticated, thought-provoking *Up in the Air*, which like Michael Moore's documentary *Capitalism: A Love Story*, pointed out with chilling insight that something has gone terribly wrong in this country as far as how we treat our workers; *The Blind Side*, which retold a remarkable true story and did so with an unforced degree of uplift; and Quentin Tarantino's deliriously

audacious World War II epic, *Inglourious Basterds* which ended the reign of the Third Reich the way we all wished it could have been wrapped up. It was also nice to see such clever animated pictures as the sweet *Up* (from Pixar, who has a reliability quotient almost as high as Meryl Streep's), the funny *Cloudy with a Chance of Meatballs*, the bleak *9*, and the quirkily hip *Fantastic Mr. Fox*, though the last did about as well with mainstream audiences as *The Hurt Locker*.

Jeff Bridges reached another in a career full of peaks with his deeply felt performance in *Crazy Heart* and at long last won an Oscar, well-deserved; Mo'Nique shattered her comical persona with her frightening work in *Precious: Based on the Novel Push by Sapphire*, which pulled no punches in showing a hellishly loveless upbringing and the possibility of escape from it; and newcomer Christian McKay gave so uncanny an impersonation of the great filmmaker-actor Orson Welles in the delightful *Me and Orson Welles*, that I'm still scratching my head as how the Academy could have overlooked this one.

The year included a good use of a starry young ensemble in a romantic comedy that did not fry the brain, *He's Just Not That into You*; a nice return to tradition for Disney with *The Princess and the Frog*, which included songs, the way animated films customarily did for decades; a whip-smart screenplay played to the hilt in *In the Loop*; one of those "small" films doomed for obscurity because they so tellingly capture the truth about second-tier show business, *The Great Buck Howard*; a bracingly exciting sci-fi film that also served as a comment on apartheid, *District 9*; a pleasing romantic match-up, *Management*, that the same people who devoured reams of newsprint about Jennifer Aniston's personal life didn't bother to notice; some fascinating show business documentaries that the Academy didn't acknowledge, *The Boys: The Sherman Brothers' Story*, *Michael Jackson's This is It*, and *Every Little Step*; an intriguing near-solo tour de force for Sam Rockwell in *Moon*; a perceptive glimpse into how nobody gets life "right" in the very funny *Away We Go*; an unsettling look into celebrity obsession in *Big Fan*; the oh-so-right coming together of Woody Allen and Larry David in *Whatever Works*; a chaotic but often disturbingly accurate expose of American homophobia in *Brüno*; a bittersweet examination of the bumpy course of relationships in a comedy for the ages, *(500) Days of Summer*; *Funny People*, which contained the first good performance ever given by Adam Sandler; the often painfully astute *World's Greatest Dad*, which examined the human habit of embracing the *un*-truths about people; a movie about roller derby that surprisingly wasn't the junk you'd expect, *Whip It*; another ideal showcase for the marvelously droll Ricky Gervais, *The Invention of Lying*; the laugh-out-loud horror send-up, *Zombieland*; and an inventive imagining of the classic love-it-or-hate-it children's book *Where the Wild Things Are*. Adding up the grosses for each of these titles probably wouldn't bring you within tens of millions of what *Avatar* took in, despite the fact that most people I spoke with reacted to James Cameron's box office behemoth with modulated interest rather than awe. Am I missing something? Maybe I need an education.

— Barry Monush

ACKNOWLEDGMENTS

Anthology Film Archives, Balcony Releasing The Cinema Guild, Cinema Libre, Columbia Pictures, Scott Denny, DreamWorks, Brian Durnin, Emerging Pictures, Film Forum, First Independent, First Look, First Run Features, Focus Features, Fox Searchlight, Freestyle Releasing, Jason Hadzinikolov, Ben Hodges, IFC Films, International Film Circuit, Tim Johnson, Marybeth Keating, Kino International, Koch Lorber Films, Lionsgate, Tom Lynch, MGM, Magnolia Films, Anthony Meisel, Miramax Films, Daniel Munro, Music Box Films, New Line Cinema, New Yorker Films, Oscilloscope, Overture Films, Palm Pictures, Paramount Pictures, Paramount Vantage, Picture This!, Picturehouse, Regent/here!, Roadside Attractions, Rogue Pictures, Greg Rossi, Screen Gems, Seventh Art Releasing, Samuel Goldwyn Films, James Sheridan, Sony Pictures Classics, Strand Releasing, Summit Entertainment, ThinkFilm, TriStar, Truly Indie, Twentieth Century Fox, United Artists, Universal Pictures, Walt Disney Pictures, Warner Bros., The Weinstein Company

Sam Worthington, Laz Alonso in Avatar © Twentieth Century Fox

Quinton Aaron, Sandra Bullock in The Blind Side © Warner Bros.

Maggie Gyllenhaal, Jeff Bridges in Crazy Heart © *Fox Searchlight*

Rosamund Pike, Carey Mulligan in An Education © Sony Pictures Classics

Joseph Gordon-Levitt, Zooey Deschanel in (500) Days of Summer © Fox Searchlight

Adam Sandler in Funny People © Universal Studios/Columbia Pictures

John Malkovich in The Great Buck Howard © *Magnolia Pictures*

Ed Helms, Bradley Cooper, Zach Galifianakis in The Hangover © *Warner Bros.*

Daniel Radcliffe in Harry Potter and the Half-Blood Prince © Warner Bros.

Ginnifer Goodwin, Justin Long in He's Just Not That into You © New Line Cinema

Heath Ledger in The Imaginarium of Doctor Parnassus
© Sony Pictures Classics

Stanley Tucci, Meryl Streep in Julie & Julia *© Columbia Pictures*

Jeremy Renner in The Hurt Locker *© Summit Entertainment*

Meryl Streep, Steve Martin in It's Complicated © *Universal Studios*

Ricky Gervais, Jonah Hill in The Invention of Lying © *Warner Bros.*

Christian McKay, Zac Efron in Me and Orson Welles *© Freestyle Releasing*

Sam Rockwell in Moon *© Sony Pictures Classics*

Molly C. Quinn, Logan Lerman in My One and Only © *Freestyle Releasing*

Taylor Lautner in New Moon © *Summit Releasing*

Judi Dench, Penélope Cruz, Marion Cotillard, Sophia Loren, Fergie, Nicole Kidman, Daniel Day-Lewis (back to camera), Kate Hudson in Nine
© *The Weinstein Company*

Kevin James in
Paul Blart: Mall Cop
© *Columbia Pictures*

Lenny Kravitz, Gabourey Sidibe in Precious: Based on the Novel Push by Sapphire © *Lionsgate*

Johnny Depp in Public Enemies
© *Universal Studios*

Julianne Moore in A Single Man © *The Weinstein Company*

Liam Neeson in Taken © Twentieth Century Fox

Russell (top), Carl Fredricksen in Up © Pixar/Walt Disney

George Clooney, Ann Kendrick in Up in the Air *© Paramount Pictures*

Malin Akerman, Billy Crudup, Jackie Earle Haley in Watchmen *© Warner Bros.*

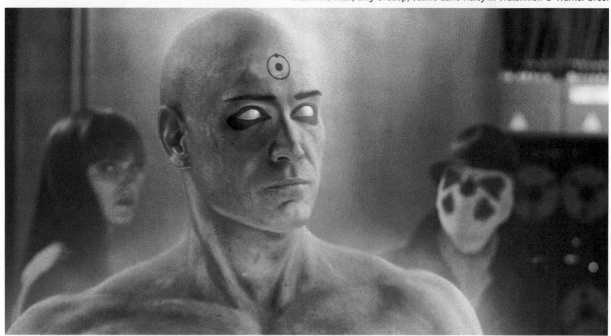

Carol, Max Records in Where the Wild Things Are © *Warner Bros.*

Alexie Gilmore, Robin Williams in World's Greatest Dad © *Magnolia Pictures*

DOMESTIC FILMS A

2009 Releases / January 1–December 31

BRIDE WARS

(20th CENTURY FOX) Producers, Julie Yorn, Kate Hudson, Alan Riche; Executive Producers, Arnon Milchan, Jay Cohen, Tony Ludwig, Matt Luber, Jonathan Filley; Director, Gary Winick; Screenplay, Greg DePaul, Casey Wilson, June Diane Raphael; Story, Greg DePaul; Photography, Frederick Elmes; Designer, Dan Leigh; Costumes, Karen Patch; Music, Edward Shearmur; Music Supervisor, Linda Cohen; Editor, Susan Littenberg Hagler; Casting, Jennifer Euston, Marcia DeBonis; a Fox 2000 Pictures and Regency Enterprises presentation of a New Regency/Birdie/Riche Ludwig production; Dolby; Deluxe color; Rated PG; minutes; 89 minutes; Release date: January 9, 2009

CAST

Liv Lerner	**Kate Hudson**
Emma Allan	**Anne Hathaway**
Nate Lerner	**Bryan Greenberg**
Fletcher Flemson	**Chris Pratt**
Daniel Williams	**Steve Howey**
Marion St. Claire	**Candice Bergen**
Deb	**Kristen Johnston**
Kevin	**Michael Arden**
Colson	**Victor Slezak**
Kathy	**Kelly Coffield Park**
John Allan	**John Pankow**
Young Liv	**Zoe O'Grady**
Young Emma	**Shannon Ferber**
Amanda	**June Diane Raphael**
Wedding DJ	**Charles Bernard**
Simmons	**Bruce Altman**
Marissa	**Hettienne Park**
Amie	**Lauren Bittner**

Emily Sarah Stikeman, Robert B. Capron, Kallie Mariah Tabor (Students), Jeremy Brothers (Nerdy Colleague), Rena Maliszewski (Female Colleague), Casey Wilson (Stacy), Sarah Kate Jackson (Salesgirl), Jason Kolotouros (Delivery Guy), Paul Scheer (Ricky Coo), Kristofer Stock (Officer "Not Your Husband"), André Holland (DJ Jazzles), Anna Madigan (Tanorexic), Daniel Raymont (Colorist), Jon C. Daly, Ryan B. Young, Hannah Yun (Head Sets), Dennis Parlato (Dance Instructor), Michael Anastasia (Geeky Neighbor), Georgia Lyman (Airbrush Technician), Ryan A. Shaw (Singer), Derek Yuen (Hair Stylist), Eryn Gruttadauria (Locker Student), Nicole Stuart (Receptionist), Kayce Brown (Bespectacled Colleague), Manuel Lopes (Miguel), Rob Wilson (Rob), Pamela Figueiredo (Pamela), Sam Pannier (Stationery Clerk), Ariel Shafir (Security Guard)

Two lifelong friends turn enemies when they realize both their upcoming nuptials at New York's Plaza Hotel have been accidentally booked on the same day.

Anne Hathaway, Kate Hudson, Steve Howey

Chris Pratt, Anne Hathaway © Twentieth Century Fox/Regency Enterprises

Kate Hudson, Anne Hathaway

Anne Hathaway, Kate Hudson

Morris Chestnut,
Taraji P. Henson

Taraji P. Henson, Jenifer Lewis, Maeve Quinlan © Screen Gems

NOT EASILY BROKEN

(TRISTAR) Producers, T.D. Jakes, Curtis Wallace, Bill Duke; Executive Producers, Morris Chestnut, Steven Brown; Director, Bill Duke; Screenplay, Brian Bird; Based on the book by T.D. Jakes; Photography, Geary McLeod; Designer, Cecil Gentry; Costumes, Diane Charles; Music, Kurt Farquhar; Music Supervisors, Alison Ball, David Lombard; Editor, Josh Rifkin; Co-Producer, Brian Bird; Casting, Kimberly R. Hardin, Michelle D. Adams; a T.D. Jakes production in association with Duke Media; Dolby; Color; Rated PG-13; 99 minutes; Release date: January 9, 2009

CAST

Dave Johnson	**Morris Chestnut**
Clarice Clark	**Taraji P. Henson**
Julie Sawyer	**Maeve Quinlan**
Tree	**Kevin Hart**
Darnell Gooden	**Wood Harris**
Brock Houseman	**Eddie Cibrian**
Mary "Mama" Clark	**Jenifer Lewis**
Michelle	**Niecy Nash**

Cannon Jay (Bryson Sawyer), Albert Hall (Bishop Wilkes), Jeff Krebs (Trauma Doctor), Nathaniel Carter (Deshawn), Brendon Terrell (Marcus), Kwame Boateng (Darius), Henry Brown (Mr. Reid), Olivia Brown (Mrs. Reid), Lee Reherman (Coach Spinello), Elizabeth Uhl (Trauma Nurse), Justin Michael Carter, Gregg Bello (Onlookers), Louis C. Simon (Police Officer), Michael Taylor Gray (Maitre d'), T.D. Jakes (Allen), Denetria Champ (Church Singer), Jesse Campbell (Wedding Singer), Terry Thomas (Funeral Singer), Baldwin Sykes (Basketball Player), Garry Guerrier (Curtis), Serita Jakes (Allen's Wife)

Unfulfilled by his career and feeling his wife drifting out of his life, Dave Johnson finds some degree of solace when he meets up with a physical therapist who enlists Dave to help coach her son and his friends in Little League baseball.

THE UNBORN

(ROGUE) Producers, Michael Bay, Andrew Form, Brad Fuller; Executive Producers, Jessika Borsiczky Goyer, William Beasley; Director/Screenplay, David S. Goyer; Photography, James Hawkinson; Designer, Craig Jackson; Costumes, Christine Wada; Music, Ramin Djawadi; Music Supervisor, Spring Aspers; Editor, Jeff Betancourt; Visual Effects Supervisors, Nathan McGuinness, & Mitchell S. Drain; Special Makeup Effects, Greg Nicotero & Howard Berger; Casting, Juel Bestrop, Seth Yanklewitz; a Platinum Dunes/Phantom Four production, presented in association with Michael Bay; Dolby; Panavision; Technicolor; Rated PG-13; 86 minutes; Release date: January 9, 2009

CAST

Casey Beldon	**Odette Yustman**
Rabbi Sendak	**Gary Oldman**
Romy	**Meagan Good**
Mark Hardigan	**Cam Gigandet**
Arthur Wyndham	**Idris Elba**
Sofi Kozma	**Jane Alexander**
Matty Newton	**Atticus Shaffer**

James Remar (Gordon Beldon), Carla Gugino (Janet Beldon), C.S. Lee (Dr. Lester Caldwell), Rhys Coiro (Mr. Shields), Michael Sassone (Eli Walker), Ethan Cutkosky (Barto), Craig Harris (Rick Hesse), Rachel Brosnahan (Lisa Shepherd), Kymberly Mellen (Gail Newton), Brian Boland (Roger Newton), Mindy Bell (Librarian), Roslyn Alexander (Evelyn), Maury Cooper (Grandfather), Mandy Schneider (Housewife), Guy Van Swearingen (Library Guard), Ericka Ratcliff (Charge Nurse), Savannah Walker (Seven-Year-Old Casey), Domenica Fisher (Gordon's Secretary), Marcella Marssie Mencotti (Mrs. Byrne), Sarah Wellington (OB/GYN Doctor), Alexis Wade (Nine-Year-Old Sofi), Tom Lowell (Library Patron), Kenya Drew (Student), Scott Lindvall (Detective), Braden Moran (Joseph Mengele), Aiden David, Connor David (Newton Baby), Lili Haydn (Singer), John Bryant, Richard Mosely, Ronni Sellers (Musicians), Joseph Luis Caballero (Chicago Cop)

Casey Beldon is haunted by visions of a demonic fetus, fearing that her twin who had died in her mother's womb is finally waiting to be born.

Gary Oldman, Odette Yustman, Cam Gigandet © Rogue Pictures

PAUL BLART: MALL COP

(COLUMBIA) Producers, Todd Garner, Kevin James, Barry Bernardi, Adam Sandler, Jack Giarraputo; Executive Producer, Jeff Sussman; Director, Steve Carr; Screenplay, Kevin James, Nick Bakay; Photography, Russ T. Alsobrook; Designer, Perry Andelin Blake; Costumes, Ellen Lutter; Music, Waddy Wachtel; Music Supervisor, Michael Dilbeck; Editor, Jeff Freeman; Casting, Jeanne McCarthy, Nicole Abellera; a Happy Madison production, presented in association with Relativity Media; Dolby; Panavision; Deluxe color; Rated PG; 91 minutes; Release date: January 16, 2009

CAST

Paul Blart	**Kevin James**
Veck Sims	**Keir O'Donnell**
Amy	**Jayma Mays**
Maya Blart	**Raini Rodriguez**
Mom	**Shirley Knight**
Stuart	**Stephen Rannazzisi**
Chief Brooks	**Peter Gerety**
Commander Kent	**Bobby Cannavale**
Sergeant Howard	**Adam Ferrara**
Leon	**Jamal Mixon**
Pahud	**Adhir Kalyan**
Vijay	**Erick Avari**
Karaoke Singer	**Gary Valentine**
Jerky Security Guy	**Allen Covert**
Rudolph	**Mike Vallely**
Blitzen	**Mike Escamilla**
Prancer	**Jason Ellis**
Comet	**Jason Packham**
Cupid	**Rick Thorne**
Donner	**Victor T. Lopez**
Vixen	**Natascha Hopkins**

Jackie Sandler (Victoria's Secret Sales Associate), Mookie Barker (Mr. Ferguson), Jackie Flynn (Officer), Richie Minervini (Bank Manager), Brie Arbaugh (Bank Teller), Bernie McInerney (Old Man on Scooter), Steffiana De La Cruz (Shopper with Kids), Dylan Clark Marshall (Jacob), Tyler Spindel (SWAT Tech), Bas Rutten (Drill Instructor), Teresa Zantua (Shopper), Dahlia Salem (Mother), Zele Ayradopoulos, Maria Arcé (Victoria's Secret Customers), Robert Harvey (SWAT Officer), Bill Concha, Michael Burton (Joe's Patrons), Carl Randall (Father Carl), Carla Antonino (Joe's Waitress), Ruby Wendell (Ruby the Waitress)

A former state trooper-turned-mall security guard is forced to save the day when a gang of high tech thieves seize control of his New Jersey shopping center.

Shirley Knight, Raini Rodriguez

Bernie McInerney, Kevin James © Columbia Pictures

Mike Vallely

Keir O'Donnell, Kevin James

Kevin Dillon, Lisa Kudrow © Paramount Pictures

Juliette, Romeo

Emma Roberts, Jake T. Austin, Don Cheadle

HOTEL FOR DOGS

(DREAMWORKS) Producers, Lauren Shuler Donner, Jonathan Gordon, Ewan Leslie, Jason Clark; Executive Producers, Ivan Reitman, Tom Pollock, Jeffrey Clifford; Director, Thor Freudenthal; Screenplay, Jeff Lowell, Bob Schooley, Mark McCorkle; Based on the book by Lois Duncan; Photography, Michael Grady; Designer, William Sandell; Costumes, Beth Pasternak; Music, John Debney; Editor, Sheldon Kahn; Visual Effects, Pixel Magic; Special Effects Coordinator, Michael Lantieri; Casting, Randi Hiller, Sarah Halley Finn; a Donners' Co./Montecito Picture Co. production, presented with Nickelodeon Movies, in association with Cold Spring Pictures; Dolby; Deluxe color; Rated PG; 100 minutes; Release date: January 16, 2009

CAST
Andi	**Emma Roberts**
Bruce	**Jake T. Austin**
Bernie	**Don Cheadle**
Lois Scudder	**Lisa Kudrow**
Carl Scudder	**Kevin Dillon**
Dave	**Johnny Simmons**
Heather	**Kyla Pratt**
Mark	**Troy Gentile**
Carol	**Robinne Lee**
ACO Jake	**Ajay Naidu**
ACO Max	**Eric Edelstein**
Ms. Camwell	**Yvette Nicole Brown**
Officer Jeff	**Andre Ware**
Evan	**Jonathan Klein**

Maximiliano Hernandez (Officer Mike), Ruben Garfias (Department Store Employee), Kenny Vibert (Jason), Stephen Liska (Desk Sergeant), Jeremy Howard (Hot Dog Man), Tiya Sircar (Marianne), Mariah Moore (Beth), Britney Christian (Girl in TV Room), Jim Doughan, Gina St. John (Reporters), Catherine Hill McCord (Mathilda Frohmann), Carina Oakland (Passerby), Susan Avalos (Mom with Kid in Car), Dwayne Swingler (Officer Clark), Gregory Sporleder (ACO Dooley), Brandon Avalos (Kid in Car), Brendan Wayne (ACO Tanner), Andrea Gold (Woman with Dog), Leslie Del Rosario (Alexa), Hira Ambrosino (Social Worker), Stefán Mávi (City Cop), Ashley Rose (Orphan)

Two orphans on the run stumble upon an abandoned hotel which they decide to turn into a residence for homeless dogs.

Kyla Pratt, Troy Gentile, Emma Roberts, Johnny Simmons

NOTORIOUS

(FOX SEARCHLIGHT) Producers, Voletta Wallace, Wayne Barrow, Mark Pitts, Robert Teitel, Trish Hofmann; Executive Producer, Sean Combs; Co-Producer, George Paaswell; Director, George Tillman Jr.; Screenplay, Reggie Rock Bythewood, Cheo Hodari Coker; Photography, Michael Grady; Designer, Jane Musky; Costumes, Paul A. Simmons; Music, Danny Elfman; Music Supervisors, Francesca Spero, Barry Cole; Editor, Dirk Westervelt; Choreographer, Tanisha Scott; Casting, Tracy "Twinkie" Byrd; Dolby; Deluxe color; Rated R; 122 minutes; Release date: January 16, 2009

CAST

Christopher Wallace (Biggie Smalls)	**Jamal Woolard**
Voletta Wallace	**Angela Bassett**
Sean "Puffy" Combs	**Derek Luke**
Tupac Shakur	**Anthony Mackie**
Lil Kim	**Naturi Naughton**
Mark	**Kevin Phillips**
Damion "D-Roc" Butler	**Dennis L.A. White**
Lil Cease	**Marc John Jefferies**
Jan	**Julia Pace Mitchell**
Sandy	**Aunjanue Ellis**
Det. Farelli	**John Ventimiglia**
Wayne Barrow	**C. Malik Whitfield**
Biggie (age 8-13)	**Christopher Jordan Wallace**

Mohamed Dione (Record Executive at Party), Menyone DeVeaux (Hot Girl), Ginger Kroll (Debbie), Ricky Smith (Wally), Amanda Christopher (Keisha), Jasper Briggs (Damion, age 8-13), Cyrus Farmer (Selwyn), David Costabile (Mr. Webber), Jermaine Denny (Primo), Naquon "Nino Brown" Jackson (Nino Brown), Jason Croasdaile (Security Thug), Valence Thomas (50 Grand), Edwin Freeman (Mister Cee), Cimone Campbell (Cute Girl Assistant), Duane Cooper (Howard Emcee), Miya Granatella (Hot Lady), Susie Da Silva (Jessica), Antonique Smith (Faith Evans), Sean Hall-Earl (Heavy Set Guy Fan), Jelani Mashariki (Rough Guy), Tony Mui (Asian Hip Hop Guy), Atalya Slater (Fan), John Hills (Justice of the Peace), Lamont "Money L" Mosley (Money L), Hisham Tawfiq (Fatique Guy), I.N. Sierros (Cop, Quad Studios), Sean Ringgold (Suge Knight), Marco Best, Erskine Bonilla, KeShauna White, Andre Roberson, Donté Kinsey, Adre'an Simms, Brandi Nicole Feemster, Corey Browne, Nina Daniels, Grant Hayes (Persons on the Street), Denae Innis (Tyanna –age 3)

The true story of how Christopher Wallace rose from a life of crime and poverty in Brooklyn to become a successful, best-selling rapper, Biggie Smalls (the Notorious B.I.G.) before being shot to death in 1997.

Dennis White, Jamal Woolard © Twentieth Century Fox

Jamal Woolard, Derek Luke

Jamal Woolard, Angela Bassett, Antonique Smith

Jamal Woolard, Antonique Smith

Kerr Smith, Tom Atkins, Jaime King © Lionsgate

MY BLOODY VALENTINE

(LIONSGATE) Producer, Jack Murray; Executive Producers, John Dunning, Andre Link, Michael Paseornek, John Sacchi; Director, Patrick Lussier; Screenplay, Todd Farmer, Zane Smith; Based on the screenplay by John Beaird, from a story by Stephen Miller; Photography, Brian Pearson; Designer, Zack Grobler; Costumes, LeeAnn Radeka; Music, Michael Wandmacher; Editors, Patrick Lussier, Cynthia Ludwig; Special Make-Up Effects, Gary J. Tunnicliffe; Stunts, Melissa Stubbs; 3-D Stereographer, Max Penner; Casting, Nancy Nayor Battino; Dolby; Technicolor; 3-D; Rated R; 101 minutes; Release date: January 16, 2009

CAST
Tom Hanniger	Jensen Ackles
Sarah Palmer	Jaime King
Axel Palmer	Kerr Smith
Irene	Betsy Rue
Deputy Martin	Edi Gathegi
Sheriff Jim Burke	Tom Atkins
Ben Foley	Kevin Tighe

Megan Boone (Megan), Karen Baum (Deputy Ferris), Joy de la Paz (Rosa), Marc Macaulay (Riggs), Todd Farmer (Frank the Trucker), Jeff Hochendoner (Red), Bingo O'Malley (Officer Hinch), Liam Rhodes (Michael), Michael Roberts McKee (Jason), Andrew Larson (Noah Palmer), Jarrod DiGiorgi (Doc Miller), Selene Luna (Selene), Cherie McClain (Commentator), Rich Walters (Harry Warden/The Miner), David Whalen (Bartender '08), Denise Dal Vera (Nurse), Sam Nicotero (Bartender '98), Tim Hartman (Eli Hanniger), Ruth Flaherty (Thelma), Annie Kitral (Desk Clerk), Jerry Johnston (Verne), Rita Gregory (Doctor), Brandi Engel (Teen Straggler), Mightie Louis Greenberg (Louis)

Years after a tragic mining accident that yielded a sole survivor, a series of grisly murders are committed in the small town of Harmony by an axe-wielding madman.

Remake of the 1981 Paramount film of the same name.

UNDERWORLD: RISE OF THE LYCANS

(SCREEN GEMS) Producers, Tom Rosenberg, Gary Lucchesi, Len Wiseman, Richard Wright; Executive Producers, Skip Williamson, Henry Winterstern, James McQuade, Eric Reid, Beth DePatie; Co-Producers, David Kern, Kevin Grevioux; Director/Creature Designer & Supervisor, Patrick Tatopoulos; Screenplay, Danny McBride, Dirk Blackman, Howard McCain; based on characters created by Len Wiseman, Kevin Grevioux, Danny McBride; Photography, Ross Emery; Designer, Dan Hennah; Costumes, Wendy Partridge; Music, Paul Haslinger; Editor, Peter Amundson; Stunts/Fight Coordinator, Allan Poppleton; a Lakeshore Entertainment production in association with Sketch Films; Dolby; Deluxe color; Rated R; 93 minutes; Release date: January 23, 2009

CAST
Lucian	Michael Sheen
Viktor	Bill Nighy
Sonja	Rhona Mitra
Tannis	Steven Mackintosh
Raze	Kevin Grevioux
Coloman	David Aston

Geraldine Brophy (Nobleman's Wife), Leighton Cardno (Fearful Lycan), Alexander Carroll (Young Lucian), Elizabeth Hawthorne (Orsova), Jason Hood (Death Dealer), Mark Mitchinson (Nobleman), Tania Nolan (Luka), Craig Parker (Sabas), Tim Raby (Janosh), Larry Rew (Kosta), Peter Tait (Gyorg), Olivia Taylforth (Young Sonja), Jared Turner (Xristo), Eleanor Williams (Teenage Girl), Edwin Wright (Death Dealer Captain), Brian Steele (Big Lycan), Kate Beckinsale (Selene), Shane Brolly (Kraven)

Lucian leads a rebellion of werewolves against their enslaving vampire masters. Third in the series following *Underworld* (2003) and *Underworld: Evolution* (2006).

Rhona Mitra, Michael Sheen

Bill Nighy © Screen Gems

Jim Broadbent, Paul Bettany

Helen Mirren

Rafi Gavron, Eliza Hope Bennett

INKHEART

(NEW LINE CINEMA) Producers, Iain Softley, Diana Pokorny, Cornelia Funke; Executive Producers, Toby Emmerich, Mark Ordesky, Ileen Maisel, Andy Licht; Director, Iain Softley; Screenplay, David Lindsay-Abaire; Based on the book by Cornelia Funke; Photography, Roger Pratt; Designer, John Beard; Costumes, Verity Hawkes; Music, Javier Navarrette; Music Supervisor, Sara Lord; Editor, Martin Walsh; Visual Effects Supervisor, Angus Bickerton; Casting, John Hubbard, Daniel Hubbard; Distributed by Warner Brothers; Dolby; Panavision; Deluxe color; Rated PG; 105 minutes; Release date: January 23, 2009

CAST

Mortimer "Mo" Folchart	**Brendan Fraser**
Dustfinger	**Paul Bettany**
Elinor Loredan	**Helen Mirren**
Fenoglio	**Jim Broadbent**
Capricorn	**Andy Serkis**
Resa	**Sienna Guillroy**
Meggie Folchart	**Eliza Hope Bennett**
Farid	**Rafi Gavron**
Cockerell	**Matt King**
Flatnose	**Steve Speirs**
Basta	**Jamie Foreman**
Fulvio	**Stephen Graham**
Darius	**John Thomson**
Mortola	**Lesley Sharp**
Rapunzel	**Tereza Srbova**
Antiquarian Bookshop Owner	**Richard Strange**
Young Meggie	**Mirabel O'Keefe**
Roxanne	**Jennifer Connelly**
Narrator	**Roger Allam**

Mo Folchart, a Silvertongue responsible for conjuring a group of characters out of the novel *Inkheart*, hopes to find his wife, who had been banished into the same book.

Steve Speirs, Brendan Fraser, Matt King, Stephen Graham, Jamie Foreman © New Line/Warner Bros.

NEW IN TOWN

(LIONSGATE) Producers, Paul Brooks, Darryl Taja, Tracey Edmonds, Peter Safran; Executive Producers, Scott Niemeyer, Norm Waitt; Co-Producer, Jeff Levine; Director, Jonas Elmer; Screenplay, Kenneth Rance, C. Jay Cox; Photography, Chris Seager; Designer, Daniel Davis; Costumes, Darena Snowe, Lee Harper; Music, John Swihart; Editor, Troy Takaki; a Lionsgate and Gold Circle Films presentation of an Epidemic Pictures/Edmonds Entertainment/Safran Co. production; Dolby; Color; Rated PG; 96 minutes; Release date: January 30, 2009

CAST

Lucy Hill	**Renée Zellweger**
Ted Mitchell	**Harry Connick Jr.**
Blanche Gunderson	**Siobhan Fallon Hogan**
Stu Kopenhafer	**J.K. Simmons**
Lars Ulstead	**Mike O'Brien**
Trudy Van Uuden	**Frances Conroy**

Ferron Guerreiro (Bobbie Mitchell), Barbara James Smith (Joan), James Durham (Rob Deitmar), Robert Small (Donald Arling), Wayne Nicklas (Harve Gunderson), Hilary Carroll (Kimberley), Nancy Drake (Flo), Stewart Zully (Wallace Miller), Marilyn Boyle (Winnie), Dan Augusta (Billy Gunderson), Jimena Hoyos (Cathy), Suzanne Coy (Kiki), Ordena Stephens-Thompson (Leslie), Devin McCracken (Maurice), Leif Lynch (Albert), Adam Cronan (Wes), Tom Wahl (Harman), Christopher Read (Officer Olafsen), Peter Jordan (Edwin Schuck), Vanessa Kuzyk (Reporter), Matt Kippen (Business Man), Benjamin Beauchemin (Waylon), Kristen Harris (Mother in Supermarket), Blane Cypurda (Boy in Supermarket)

Ambitious corporate executive Lucy Hill reluctantly agrees to travel to a tiny town in the frigid upper regions of Minnesota to oversee the restructuring of a failing food-manufacturing plant.

Harry Connick Jr., Renée Zellweger

Siobhan Fallon Hogan, J.K. Simmons © Lionsgate

Elizabeth Banks, David Strathairn, Emily Browning

THE UNINVITED

(DREAMWORKS) Producers, Walter F. Parkes, Laurie MacDonald, Roy Lee; Executive Producers, Michael Grillo, Doug Davison, Ivan Reitman, Tom Pollock; Co-Producers, Riyoko Tanaka, Casey Grant; Directors, The Guard Brothers; Screenplay, Craig Rosenberg, Doug Miro, Carlo Bernard; Based on the motion picture *A Tale of Two Sisters* written by Kim Jee-woon; Photography, Daniel Landin; Designer, Andrew Menzies; Costumes, Trish Keating; Music, Christopher Young; Editors, Christian Wagner, Jim Page; Casting, Debra Zane; a Parkes/MacDonald and Montecito Picture Co./Vertigo Entertainment production, presented in association with Cold Spring Pictures; Dolby; Color; Rated PG-13; 87 minutes; Release date: January 30, 2009

CAST

Anna	**Emily Browning**
Alex	**Arielle Kebbel**
Steven	**David Strathairn**
Rachel Summers	**Elizabeth Banks**
Mom	**Maya Massar**
Sheriff Emery	**Kevin McNulty**
Matt Hendricks	**Jesse Moss**

Dean Paul Gibson (Dr. Silberling), Don S. Davis (Mr. Henson), Lex Bunrham (Iris), Matthew Bristol (David), Danny Bristol (Samuel), Heather Doerksen (Mildred), Alfred E. Humphreys (Priest), Ryan Cowie, Troy Rudolph (Orderlies), John Prowse (Butcher)

Sent to live with her father following her mom's death, Anna receives warning from the beyond that dad's live-in girlfriend, Rachel, is up to no good.

Emily Browning, Jesse Moss © DreamWorks/Paramount

HE'S JUST NOT THAT INTO YOU

(NEW LINE CINEMA) Producer, Nancy Juvonen; Executive Producers, Drew Barrymore, Toby Emmerich, Michele Weiss, Michael Beugg; Co-Producers, Michael Disco, Gwenn Stroman; Director, Ken Kwapis; Screenplay, Abby Kohn, Marc Silverstein; Based on the book by Greg Behrendt, Liz Tuccillo; Photography, John Bailey; Designer, Gae Buckley; Costumes, Shay Cunliffe; Music, Cliff Eidelman; Music Supervisor, Danny Bramson; Editor, Cara Silverman; Casting, Justine Baddeley, Kim Davis Wagner; a Warner Brothers release of a New Line Cinema presentation of a Flower Films production; Dolby; Deluxe color; Rated PG-13; 129 minutes; Release date: February 6, 2009

Bradley Cooper, Scarlett Johansson

CAST

Neil Jones	**Ben Affleck**
Beth Murphy	**Jennifer Aniston**
Mary Harris	**Drew Barrymore**
Janine Gunders	**Jennifer Connelly**
Conor Barry	**Kevin Connolly**
Ben Gunders	**Bradley Cooper**
Gigi Phillips	**Ginnifer Goodwin**
Anna Marks	**Scarlett Johansson**
Alex	**Justin Long**
Ken Murphy	**Kris Kristofferson**
Amber	**Natasha Leggero**
Kelli Ann	**Busy Philipps**
Angela	**Angela V. Shelton**
Frances	**Frances Callier**
Jarrad	**Brandon Keener**
Bruce	**Rod Keller**
Joshua	**Leonardo Nam**
Nathan	**Wilson Cruz**
Paige	**Brooke Bloom**
Laura	**Hedy Burress**
Catherine	**Sasha Alexander**

Ginnifer Goodwin, Jennifer Aniston, Jennifer Connelly

Morgan Lily (5 Yr. Old Girl), Michelle Carmichael (Mother), Trenton Rogers (6 Yr. Old Boy), Kristen Faye Hunter (Crying 20-Something), Sabrina Revelle (Consoling Friend), Zoe Jarman, Alia Rhiana Eckerman (Sorority Girls), Julia Pennington, Renee Scott (Sous Chefs), Chihiro Fujii, Sachiko Ishida (Tokyo Girls), Claudia DiMartino (Jogger #1), Eve Curtis, Carmen Perez, Traycee King (Joggers), Délé, Eunice Nyarazdo, Anita Yombo (African Women), Niki J. Crawford, Melanie Stephens (Waitresses), Joan M. Blair (Emotionless Cashier), Anna Bugarim (Yoga Teacher), Marc Silverstein (Bartender), Cory Hardrict (Tyrone), Rene Lopez (Gregory), Annie Ilonzeh (Hot Girl), Mike Beaver (Cousin Jay), Kai Lennox (Devon), Shane Edelman (George), Stephen Jared (Steven), Nicole Steinwedell ("No Spark" Girl), Erik David (Slick Guy in Bar), Jarrett Grode ("Droopy Dog"), Alex Dodd (Skip), Bill Brochtrup (Larry), Jason Roth (Trent), Corey Pearson (Jude), Sally Nisbet (Wedding Guest), John Ross Bowie (Dan the Wiccan), Sydney Lauren (Tall Girl), Googy Gress (Cousin Dominic), Derek Waters, Nana Hill (Party Guests), Peter O'Meara (Bill), Jocelin Donahue (Cute Girl), Luiz Guzman (Javier)

A series of criss-crossing stories about the obstacles and difficulty of finding the perfect mate.

Jennifer Aniston, Ben Affleck

Drew Barrymore, Kevin Connolly

Justin Long, Kevin Connolly

Drew Barrymore, Scarlett Johansson

Jennifer Connelly, Bradley Cooper

Justin Long, Ginnifer Goodwin

Kevin Connolly, Scarlett Johansson

Wilson Cruz, Drew Barrymore, Leonardo Lam, Rod Keller © New Line Cinema

Coraline, Mr. Bobinsky

Other Father, Other Mother, Coraline

Miss Spink, Miss Forcible

CORALINE

(FOCUS) Producers, Bill Mechanic, Claire Jennings, Henry Selick, Mary Sandell; Executive Producer, Michael Zoumas; Director/Screenplay/Designer, Henry Selick; Based on the novel by Neil Gaiman; Photography, Pete Kozachik; Music, Bruno Coulais; Editors, Christopher Murrie, Ronald Sanders; Supervising Animator, Anthony Scott; Lead Animators, Travis Knight, Trey Thomas, Eric Leighton, Phil Dale; Visual Effects Supervisor, Brian Van't Hul; Casting, Kalmenson & Kalmenson; a Laika presentation in association with Pandemonium; Dolby; Color; Rated PG; 100 minutes; Release date: February 6, 2009

VOICE CAST

Coraline Jones	**Dakota Fanning**
Mother/Other Mother	**Teri Hatcher**
Miss Spink	**Jennifer Saunders**
Miss Forcible	**Dawn French**
Cat	**Keith David**
Father/Other Father	**John Hodgman**
Wybie Lovat	**Robert Bailey Jr.**
Mr. Bobinsky	**Ian McShane**

Aankha Neal (Sweet Ghost Girl), George Selick (Ghost Boy), Hannah Kaiser (Tall Ghost Girl), Harry Selick, Marina Budovsky (Photo Friends), Emerson Hatcher (Magic Dragonfly), Jerome Ranft (Mover), Christopher Murrie, Jeremy Ryder (Toys), Carolyn Crawford (Wybie's Grandmother), Yona Prost (Shakespeare Rascal)

A little girl finds a door in her home that leads to a parallel dimension.

This film received an Oscar nimination as animated feature.

Wybie, Coraline © Focus Features

THE PINK PANTHER 2

(MGM/COLUMBIA) Producer, Robert Simonds; Executive Producers, Shawn Levy, Ira Shuman; Director, Harald Zwart; Screenplay, Scott Neustadter, Michael H. Weber, Steve Martin; Story, Scott Neustadter, Michael H. Weber; Based on the *Pink Panther* films of Blake Edwards; Photography, Denis Crossan; Designer, Rusty Smith; Costumes, Joseph G. Aulisi; Music, Christophe Beck; *Pink Panther* Theme, Henry Mancini; Editor, Julia Wong; Casting, Ilene Starger; a Robert Simonds production; Dolby; Deluxe color; Rated PG; 92 minutes; Release date: February 6, 2009

CAST

Inspector Jacques Clouseau	**Steven Martin**
Ponton	**Jean Reno**
Nicole	**Emily Mortimer**
Vicenzo	**Andy Garcia**
Pepperidge	**Alfred Molina**
Kenji	**Yuki Matsuzaki**
Sonia	**Aishwarya Rai Bachchan**
Chief Inspector Dreyfus	**John Cleese**
Mrs. Berenger	**Lily Tomlin**
Avellaneda	**Jeremy Irons**

Johnny Hallyday (Milliken), Geoffrey Palmer (Joubert), Philip Goodwin (Renard), Armel Bellec (Louis), Jack Metzger (Antoine), Eugene Lazarev (The Pope), Lewis D. Wheeler (Black Beret), Richard LaFrance (Security Installer), Simon Green (British Librarian), Federico Castelluccio (Turin Guide), Abe Lee Tsunenori (Japanese Policeman), Jimmy May (Japanese Curator), Harry Van Gorkum (Ticketed Driver), Michael Allosso (Maitre D'), Zofia Moreno, Alexis Furic, Réna Kano, Jonathan Dino (Reporters), Sharon Tay (Newscaster), Thomas Derrah (Guard), Joshua R. Roberts (Cameraman), Christy Scott Cashman (Joubert's Secretary), Joe Drago (Archbishop at Wedding), Oscar Valero, Omayra Amaya, Lia Ochoa (Flamenco Dancers), Christiane Amanpour (Herself)

Inept but intrepid French police inspector Jacques Clouseau teams up with various international detectives in hopes of finding out the identity of the elusive Tornado, who has stolen some of the world's most valuable items. Second Steve Martin Clouseau film following *The Pink Panther* (MGM/Col, 2006).

Steve Martin, Emily Mortimer © Columbia/MGM

Dakota Fanning © Summit Entertainment

PUSH

(SUMMIT) Producers, Bruce Davey, William Vince, Glenn Williamson; Executive Producers, Gretchen Somerfield, David Bourla, Dave Valleau, Amy Gilliam, Michael Ohoven, Stan Wlodkowski; Co-Producers, David Richardson, Christa Vausbinder; Director, Paul McGuigan; Screenplay, David Bourla; Photography, Peter Sova; Designer, Francois Seguin; Costumes, Nina Proctor, Laura Goldsmith; Music, Neil Davidge; Music Supervisor, Liza Richardson; Editor, Nicolas Trembasiewicz; Visual Effects Supervisor, Kent Houston; Visual Effects, Digiscope, Peerless Camera Co.; Stunts, Nick Powell; Casting, Tricia Wood, Deborah Aquila, PoPing Auyeung; an Infinity Features Entertainment and Icon Productions production; Dolby; Panavision; Deluxe color; Rated PG-13; 111 minutes; Release date: February 6, 2009

CAST

Nick Gant	**Chris Evans**
Cassie Holmes	**Dakota Fanning**
Kira Hudson	**Camilla Belle**
Hook Waters	**Cliff Curtis**
Henry Carver	**Djimon Hounsou**
Emily Wu	**Ming-Na**
Pinky Stein	**Nate Mooney**

Colin Ford (Young Nick), Joel Gretsch (Nick's Father), Robert Tsonos, Brandon Rhea (Division Doctors), Neil Jackson (Victor Budarin), Kai Cheung Leung (Dice Man), Sun Nan Hung (Dice Man's Heavy), Corey Stoll (Agent Mack), Scott Michael Campbell (Agent Holden), Wai Man Tam (Cook in Fish Market), Haruihko Yamanouchi (Pop father), Xiaolu Li (Pop Girl), Kwan Fung Chi, Jacky Heung (Pop Boys), Paul Car (Wo Chiang), Maggie Siff (Teresa Stowe), Lam Wong (Gas Station Casheir), Bun Lam Shing (Taxi Driver), Hung Liu Kwok (Bouncer), Siu Yin Ming (Card Trick Woman at Club), Rain Lau (Cocktail Waitress), Sai Tang Yu (Businessman), Pancy Chan (Businessman's wife on Boat), Cheuk Shing Sum (Kwun Tong Pier Man), Lee Man Fan (Kwun Tong Pier Woman), Ming-Fai Sheung (Liquor Salesman), Wong Man Kit (Dim Sum Manager), Yuk Hing Chan (Dim Sum Waitress), Jason Wong (Chinese Agent), Tsang Tak Wah (Security Guard), Woon Ling Hau (Old Woman with Gun)

A "mover" possessed of paranormal powers reluctantly agrees to stop a "pusher" before she can help Henry Carver enhance his own psychic powers and create an army capable of destroying the world.

Jay Baruchel, Kristen Bell, Dan Fogler, Chris Marquette

Dan Fogler Jay Baruchel, Chris Marquette, Sam Huntington, Kristen Bell

Chris Marquette, Kristen Bell © The Weinstein Co.

FANBOYS

(WEINSTEIN COMPANY) Producers, Dana Brunetti, Kevin Spacey, Matthew Perniciaro, Evan Astrowsky; Executive Producers, Kevin Mann, Bob Weinstein, Harvey Weinstein; Director, Kyle Newman; Screenplay, Ernest Cline, Adam F. Goldberg; Story, Ernest Cline, Dan Pulick; Photography, Lukas Ettlin; Designer, Corey Lorenzen; Costumes, Johanna Argan; Music, Mark Mothersbaugh; Editor, Seth Flaum; Casting, Anne McCarthy, Jay Scully; an MGM release of a Trigger Street/Coalition Film production; Dolby; Color; Rated PG-13; 90 minutes; Release date: February 6, 2009

CAST
Eric	**Sam Huntington**
Linus	**Chris Marquette**
Hutch	**Dan Fogler**
Windows	**Jay Baruchel**
Zoe	**Kristen Bell**
Chaz	**David Denman**
Big Chuck	**Christopher McDonald**
Myron	**Charlie B. Brown**
Garfunkel	**Isaac Kappy**
Admiral Seasholtz/Alien/Roach	**Seth Rogen**
The Vulcan/Gruvock	**Thom Bishops**
Bartender	**Clark Sanchez**
Thick-Necked Thug	**Stanley Shunkamolah**
The Chief	**Danny Trejo**

Hugh Elliot (Ewok), Allie Grant (Rogue Leader/Kimmy), Ethan Suplee (Harry Knowles), Joe Lo Truglio (Jail Guard), Billy Dee Williams (Judge Reinhold), Jaime King-Newman (Amber), Pell James (Crystal), William Shatner, Kevin Smith, Jason Mewes (Themselves), Carrie Fisher (Doctor), Zak Knutson (Bob the Trucker), Chuck Borden, Ray Park, Peter Reinert, Will Forte, Craig Robinson (THX Security Guards), Lou Taylor Pucci (Boba Fett #1), Noah Segan (Boba Fett #2), Rachel Klein (Liz), Stephen Pina (Simon), Danny McBride (Head of Security)

Four obsessive fans travel to George Lucas' Skywalker ranch in hopes of getting a sneak peak of the newest *Star Wars* epic.

Chris Marquette, Dan Fogler, Sam Huntington

THE INTERNATIONAL

(COLUMBIA) Producers, Charles Roven, Richard Suckle, Lloyd Phillips; Executive Producers, Alan G. Glazer, Ryan Kavanaugh; Co-Producers, Gloria Fan, Henning Molfenter, Carl L. Woebcken, Christoph Fisser; Director, Tom Tykwer; Screenplay, Eric Warren Singer; Photography, Frank Greibe; Designer, Uli Hanisch; Costumes, Ngila Dickson; Music, Tom Tykwer, Johnny Klimek, Reinhold Heil; Editor, Mathilde Bonnefoy; Stunts, Glenn Boswell; Casting, Francine Maisler; an Atlas Entertainment production, a Rose Lind Productions and Siebente Babelsberg Film co-production; presented in association with Relativity Media; American-German; Dolby; Arri Widescreen; Deluxe color; Rated R; 118 minutes; Release date: February 13, 2009

CAST

Louis Salinger	**Clive Owen**
Eleanor Whitman	**Naomi Watts**
Wilhelm Wexler	**Armin Mueller-Stahl**
Jonas Skarssen	**Ulrich Thomsen**
The Consultant	**Brían F. O'Byrne**

Michel Voletti (Viktor Haas), Patrick Baladi (Martin White), Jay Villiers (Francis Ehames), Fabrice Scott (Nicolai Yeshinski), Haluk Bilginer (Ahmet Sunay), Luca Giorgio Barbareschi (Umberto Calvini), Alessandro Fabrizi (Inspector Alberto Cerutti), Felix Solis (Det. Iggy Ornelas), Jack McGee (Det. Bernie Ward), Nilaja Sun (Det. Gloria Hubbard), Steven Randazzo (Al Moody), Tibor Feldman (Dr. Isaacson), James Rebhorn (New York D.A.), Remy Auberjonois (Sam Purvitz), Ty Jones (Eli Cassel), Ian Burfield (Thomas Schumer), Peter Jordan (Berlin Doctor), Axel Milberg (Klaus Diemer), Thomas Morris (Chief Inspector Reinhard Schmidt), Oliver Trautwein (Dietmar Berghoff), Luigi Di Fiore (Carabinieri Captain), Verena Schonlau (I.B.B.C. Secretary {White}), Laurent Spielvogel (Commissioner Villon), Marita Hueber (Woman in Knit Cap), Giorgio Lupano (Milan Sniper), Loris Loddi (Calvini's Chief of Staff), Natalia Magni (1st Speaker/Politico), Emilio Dino Conti (Café Barista), Lucian Msamati (Gen. Charles Motomba), Benjamin Wandschneider (Cassian Skarssen), Alessandro Quattro (Milan Airport Security), Marco Gambino (Calvini Lawyer), Matt Patresi (Calvini Defense Security Chief), Tristana Moore (World News Reporter), Naomi Krauss (I.B.B.C. Secretary {Skarssen}), Franco Trevisi (Italian Gentleman), Antonio Santoro (Lab Technician), Hakan Boyav (Attendant/Bodyguard), Luca Calvani (Enzo Calvini), Gerolamo Fancellu (Mario Calvini), Ben Whishaw (Rene Antall), Sedat Mert (Bodyguard), Tevfik Polat (Bodyguard), Darren Pettie (Elliot Whitman), Mike Braun, Michael Bornhuetter, Heiko Kiesow, Markus Puetterich, Ronnie Paul, Gerd Grzesczak, Piet Paes, Sigo Heinisch (Hitmen), Georges Bigot (André Clement), Eric Warren Singer (Cashier), Federico Pacifici (Man in Green Fedora), Brad Holbrook (TV Reporter), Jon DeVries (New York Mayor), Chris Henry Coffey, Alex Cranmer (Museum Visitors), Robert Salerno (Little Boy Whitman), Nicole Shalhoub (Witness)

Interpol agent Louis Salinger and New York District Attorney Eleanor Whitman join forces to uncover a powerful banking organization's involvement in arms dealing.

Clive Owen, Jack McGee

Naomi Watts, Clive Owen © Columbia Pictures

Clive Owen

Clive Owen, Armin Mueller-Stahl

CONFESSIONS OF A SHOPAHOLIC

(WALT DISNEY STUDIOS) Producer, Jerry Bruckheimer; Executive Producers, Mike Stenson, Chad Oman, Ron Bozman; Director, P.J. Hogan; Screenplay, Tracey Jackson, Tim Firth, Kayla Alpert; Based on the books *Confessions of a Shopaholic* and *Shopaholic Takes Manhattan* by Sophie Kinsella; Photography, Jo Willems; Designer, Kristi Zea; Costumes, Patricia Field; Music, James Newton Howard; Music Supervisor, Kathy Nelson; Editor, William Goldenberg; Casting, Denise Chamian, Julie Schubert; a Touchstone Pictures and Jerry Bruckheimer Films presentation; Dolby; Panavision; Deluxe color; Rated PG; 104 minutes; Release date: February 13, 2009

CAST

Rebecca Bloomwood	**Isla Fisher**
Luke Brandon	**Hugh Dancy**
Suze	**Krysten Ritter**
Jane Bloomwood	**Joan Cusack**
Graham Bloomwood	**John Goodman**
Edgar West	**John Lithgow**
Alette Naylor	**Kristin Scott Thomas**

Fred Armisen (Ryan Koenig), Leslie Bibb (Alicia Billington), Lynn Redgrave (Drunken Lady at Ball), Robert Stanton (Derek Smeath), Julie Hagerty (Hayley), Nick Cornish (Tarquin), Wendie Malick (Miss Korch), Clea Lewis (Miss Ptaszinski), Stephen Guarino (Allon), Tuomas Hiltunen (Jan Virtanen), Yoshiro Kono (Ryuichi), John Salley (D. Freak), Lennon Parham (Joyce), Christine Ebersole (TV Show Host), Michael Panes (Russell), Kaitlin Hopkins (Event Planner), Katherine Sigismund (Claire), Alexandra Balahoutis (Prada Manager), Elizabeth Riley (Prada Store Shopper), Madeleine Rockwitz (8-Year-Old Rebecca), Tommy Davis (Jan's Colleague), Andy Serwer (Mr. Lewis), Kelli Barrett (Girl in Black/Talking Mannequin), Kristen Connolly (Girl in Pink), Paloma Guzmán, Ilana Levine (Svelte Manhattanites), Lenora May (Suze's Mom), Ed Crescimanni (Suze's Dad), Susan Blommaert (Charity Store Orla), Jenn Harris (Christy), Matt Servitto (Head Waiter), Jennifer Kim (Denny & George Clerk), Ginifer King (Candidate), Steve Greenstein (Hot Dog Vendor), Heidi Kristoffer, Kate Simses (Alette Girls), Claire Lautier (Sample Sale Competitor), Brandi Burkhardt (Sample Sale Worker), Denicia Marie Jefferson (Sample Sale Security #1), Renee Victor (Bag Lady), Scott Evans (Chad, the Mail Clerk), Asmeret Ghebremichael (Alette Receptionist), Chris Bachman (Mailroom Clerk), Peter Kapetan (Gin and Tonic Guy), Jim Holmes (Comintex CEO), Claudia Rocafort (Businesswoman), Molly Regan (Smeath's Assistant), Rose Rosconi, Robin E. Billson, Richard G. Batista (Swap Meet Vendors), Maeve Yore (Wedding Planner), Ptolemy Slocum, Jenny Powers (Borders Assistants), Jennifer Smith (Sara), Gonzalo Escudero (Alette's Date), Tim Ware (Fund Manager), Anjali Bhimani (Girl #1), Jonathan Tisch (Bank Lender), Shonn Wiley (Good-Looking Guy), Brad Aldous (Alicia's Friend at Party), Annie Chadwick (Mrs. Edgar West), Laurie Cole (Ryan Koenig's Girlfriend), Kara Jackson (Woman Hit with Fish), Yadira Santana (Fan Vending Lady), Charles De La Rosa (Barman), Jordyn Taylor Wilsea (Little Girl at Borders), Harvey Waldman, Howard Samuelson (Advertising Execs), Marceline Hugot (Saleswoman), Abby Lee, Caitlin McColl (Bridesmaids), Beatrice Miller, Peyton List, Isabella Palmieri (Shoestore Girls), Darly Wanatick (Sample Sale Shopper), Vinci Alonso (Prada Salesperson)

Rebecca Bloomwood, a woman with a severe addiction to shopping gets a job at a money magazine where she becomes an unexpected celebrity with her column, *The Girl in the Green Scarf*.

Joan Cusack, John Goodman, Isla Fisher

Kristin Scott Thomas, Isla Fisher, Leslie Bibb

Tim Ware, Hugh Dancy, Isla Fisher © Touchstone Pictures/ Jerry Bruckheimer Inc.

Elias Koteas, Gwyneth Paltrow, Joaquin Phoenix

Gwyneth Paltrow, Joaquin Phoenix © Magnolia Pictures

Joaquin Phoenix, Vinessa Shaw

TWO LOVERS

(MAGNOLIA) Producers, Donna Gigliotti, James Gray, Anthony Katagas; Executive Producers, Agnes Mentre, Todd Wagner, Mark Cuban, Marc Butan; Co-Producers, Mike Upton, Couper Samuelson; Director, James Gray; Screenplay, James Gray, Richard Menello; Photography, Joaquin Baca-Asay; Designer, Happy Massee; Costumes, Michael Clancy; Music Supervisor, Dana Sano; Editor, John Axelrad; Casting, Douglas Aibel; a 2929 Productions and Wild Bunch presentation of a Tempesta Films production; American-French; Dolby; Arri Widescreen; Technicolor; Rated R; 109 minutes; Release date: February 13, 2009

CAST

Leonard Kraditor	**Joaquin Phoenix**
Michelle Rausch	**Gwyneth Paltrow**
Sandra Cohen	**Vinessa Shaw**
Reuben Kraditor	**Moni Moshonov**
Ruth Kraditor	**Isabella Rossellini**
Jose Cordero	**John Ortiz**
Michael Cohen	**Bob Ari**
Carol Cohen	**Julie Budd**
Ronald Blatt	**Elias Koteas**
DJ Juice	**Shiran Nicholson**
Jeweler	**David Cale**

Kathryn Gerhardt (New Year's Eve Party Guest), Nick Gillie (Livery Driver), Samantha Ivers (Stephanie), Anne Joyce (Leonard's Ex-Fiancée), Mari Koda (Popping Dancer), RJ Konner (Upscale Opera Guest), Evan Lewis (Uncle), Marion McCorry (Nurse), David Ross (Waiter), Jeanine Serralles (Dayna), Naeem Uzimann (Cab Driver), Elliot Villar (Bystander), Mark Vincent (Ronald's Driver)

Leonard, a troubled young man suffering from a bi-polar disorder, returns to live in his parents' home where he finds himself falling in love with a manipulative, wildly unpredictable neighbor, just as his family is hoping he will instead marry a far less complicated girl, thereby solidifying a potential business merger.

Isabella Rossellini, Joaquin Phoenix

Willa Ford, Julianna Guill, Arlen Escarpeta, Aaron Yoo, Ryan Hansen

Willa Ford © New Line/Warner Bros.

Nick Mennell, Amanda Righetti

FRIDAY THE 13TH

(NEW LINE/PARAMOUNT) Producers, Michael Bay, Andrew Form, Brad Fuller, Sean S. Cunningham; Executive Producers, Brian Witten, Walter Hamada, Guy Stodel; Co-Producer, Alma Kuttruff; Director, Marcus Nispel; Screenplay, Damian Shannon, Mark Swift; Story, Damian Shannon, Mark Swift, Mark Wheaton; Based on characters created by Victor Miller; Photography, Daniel C. Pearl; Designer, Jeremy Conway; Costumes, Mari-An Ceo; Music, Steve Jablonsky; Editor, Ken Blackwell; Visual Effects Supervisors, Nathan McGuiness, Mitchell S. Drain; Casting, Lisa Fields; Distributed by Warner Brothers; a Platinum Dunes production, presented in association with Michael Bay; Dolby; Panavision; Technicolor; Rated R; 97 minutes; Release date: February 13, 2009

CAST

Clay Miller	**Jared Padalecki**
Jenna	**Danielle Panabaker**
Whitney Miller	**Amanda Righetti**
Trent	**Travis Van Winkle**
Chewie	**Aaron Yoo**
Jason Voorhees	**Derek Mears**
Wade	**Jonathan Sadowski**
Bree	**Julianna Guill**
Richie	**Ben Feldman**
Lawrence	**Arlen Escarpeta**
Nolan	**Ryan Hansen**
Chelsea	**Willa Ford**
Mike	**Nick Mennell**

America Olivo (Amanda), Kyle Davis (Donnie), Richard Burgi (Officer Bracke), Chris Coppola (Gas Station Attendant), Rosemary Knower (Old Lady), Bob King (Old Caretaker), Nana Visitor (Pamela Voorhees), Stephanie Rhodes (Camp Counselor), Caleb Guss (Young Jason), Travis Davis (Officer Lund)

Seeking revenge for the death of his mother, deranged killer Jason Voorhees stalks the campers at Crystal Lake. Remake of the 1980 Paramount film of the same name, and its many sequels.

Jared Padalecki, Derek Mears

Tyler Perry's MADEA GOES TO JAIL

(LIONSGATE) Producers, Tyler Perry, Reuben Cannon; Director/Screenplay, Tyler Perry; Co-Producers, Roger M. Bobb, Joseph P. Genier; Photography, Alexander Gruszynski; Designer, Ina Mayhew; Costumes, Keith G. Lewis; Music, Aaron Zigman; Music Supervisor, Joel C. High; Editor, Maysie Hoy; Visual Special FX/ Prosthetic Makeup, Bill "Splat" Johnson; Casting, Kimberly R. Hardin; a TPS presentation of a Reuben Cannon/Lionsgate production; Dolby; Color; Rated PG-13; 103 minutes; Release date: February 20, 2009

CAST

Madea/Uncle Joe/Brian	**Tyler Perry**
Joshua Hardaway	**Derek Luke**
Candace Washington	**Keshia Knight Pulliam**
Mr. Brown	**David Mann**
Cora	**Tamela Mann**
Chuck	**RonReaco Lee**
Linda	**Ion Overman**
Donna	**Vanessa Ferlito**
Ellen	**Viola Davis**
T.T.	**Sofia Vergara**
Big Sal	**Robin Coleman**
Tanya	**Bobbi Baker**
Fran Walker	**Aisha Hinds**
Arthur	**Benjamin Benitez**

Karan Kendrick (Guard Watson), Njema Williams, Kevin Wayne (Officers), Richard Malcolm Reed, Mark Wilson (Bailiffs), Judge Mathis, Judge Mablean Ephraim, Dr. Phil McGraw, Whoopi Goldberg, Tom Joyner, Rev. Al Sharpton, Michael Baisden, Steve Harvey, Wanda Smith, Sybil Wilkes, Shirley Strawberry, J. Anthony Brown, Joy Behar, Sherri Shepherd, Elisabeth Hasselbeck, Frank Ski (Themselves); Eric V. Williams, Nathan Standridge (Guards), Elizabeth Wells Berkes (Lady), James Sutton, Theroun Patterson (Public Defender), Tamika "Georgia Me" Harper (Prisoner), Rob Glidden (John), Constantine Varazo (Man), Jackson Walker (Mr. Brackman), Leon LaMar (Old Man), Allen Earls (Pastor), Valeria Taylor, Sheryland Neal (Prostitutes), Tony Harris (TV Reporter), Annie Cook, Trey Greene (Reporters), Robert Summe (Police Officer), Ciera Payton (Undercover Detective)

Feisty matriarch Madea ends up behind bars after an altercation over a parking dispute, placing her in close proximity with Candy, a drug addicted prostitute who is being helped by a district attorney who remembers the girl from his childhood.

Derek Luke, Keisha Knight Pulliam

Tamela Mann, Tyler Perry, David Mann

Viola Davis, Vanessa Ferlito, Keisha Knight Pulliam

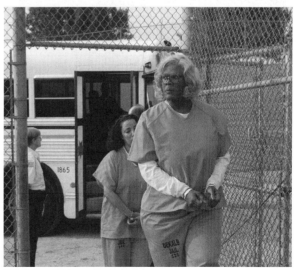

Tyler Perry © Lionsgate

CROSSING OVER

(WEINSTEIN COMPANY) Producers, Frank Marshall, Wayne Kramer; Executive Producers, Michael Beugg, Bob Weinstein, Harvey Weinstein; Co-Producer, Gregg Taylor; Director/ Screenplay, Wayne Kramer; Photography, James Whitaker; Designer, Toby Corbett; Costumes, Kristin M. Burke; Music, Mark Isham; Music Supervisor, Brian Ross; Editor, Arthur Coburn; Casting, Anne McCarthy, Jay Scully; a Kennedy/Marshall Co. and Movie Prose production; Dolby; Super 35 Widescreen; Technicolor; Rated R; 114 minutes; Release date: February 27, 2009

Jamison Haase, Harrison Ford

CAST

Max Brogan	**Harrison Ford**
Cole Frankel	**Ray Liotta**
Denise Frankel	**Ashley Judd**
Gavin Kossef	**Jim Sturgess**
Hamid Baraheri	**Cliff Curtis**
Mireya Sanchez	**Alice Braga**
Claire Sheperd	**Alice Eve**
Taslima Jahangir	**Summer Bashil**
Special Agent Phadkar	**Jacqueline Obradors**
Yong Kim	**Justin Chon**
Zahra Baraheri	**Melody Khazae**
Farid Baraheri	**Merik Tadros**
Sanjar Baraheri	**Marshall Manesh**
Minoo Baraheri	**Nina Nayebi**
Rokeya Jahangir	**Naila Azad**
Mark	**West Liang**
Munshi Jahangir	**Shelley Malil**
Steve	**Tim Chiou**
Howie	**Josh Gad**
Abul Jahangir	**Jamen Nanthakumar**
Jahanara Jahangir	**Jaysha Patel**
Juan Sanchez	**Aramis Knight**
Kwan	**Leonardo Nam**
Mireya Look-Alike	**Claudia Salinas**
Justin	**Johnny Young**
Marla	**Lizzy Caplan**
Alike	**Ogechi Egonu**
Chin Kim	**Chil Kong**
Det. Strickland	**Mahershalalhashbaz Ali**

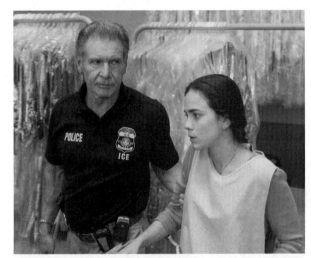

Harrison Ford, Alice Braga © The Weinstein Co.

Bailey Chase (Border Patrol Agent), Sarah Shahi (Pooneh Baraheri), Sung Hi Lee (Min Kim), Andy Kang (Seung Kim), Roger Marks (Rabbi Yoffie), Terence Bernie Hines (Immigration Adjudicator), Maree Cheatham (Judge Freeman), Esther Paik (Liquor Store Owner's Wife), Greg Joung Paik (Liquor Store Owner), Rey Valentin (Javier Pedraza), Michael Cudlitz (San Pedro ICE Processing Agent), Juan Garcia (Special Agent Howell), Christopher Murray (Special Agent Ludwig), Joaquin Garrido (Juan's Grandfather), Julia Vera (Juan's Grandmother), Deborah Puette (Mrs. Benedict), Yvette Cruise (Hispanic Woman), Ryan Gesell, David Guzzone (ICE Agents), Jamison Haase (Police Officer in Liquor Store), Kevin Sizemore (FBI Agent), Yuriana Kim (Middle-Aged Woman in Liquor Store), Jack Conley (OIG Agent Poulson), John Lafayette (OIG Agent Womack), Fia Pergera, Lavetta Cannon (Detention Officers), Judith Moreland (USCIS Worker), Tammin Sursok (Rosalyn), Don Scribner (Bartender), Kevin Alejandro (Gutierrez), Kacem Benyoucef (Imam), Phil Perry (Himself), Marque Richardson II, Chioke Dmachi (Disparaging Teens), Michael Esparza, Daniella De Rosa, Chrissie Fit, Aaron Todd Kessee, Kenny Copeland Jr., Mona Weiss (Students), Bob Rumnock (Human Resources Manager), Misha Huang (Soo Kim), Alma Martinez (Mexican Woman, Dress Factory), Gigi Rice (Hooker), Tim Coyne (Regular #3), Nancy Chidi (Dayo), George Fitch Watson (ICE Agent Watson), Jessica Tuck (Elaine)

Ray Liotta, Ashley Judd

A look into various denizens of Los Angeles who are facing difficulties with the immigration authorities and the toll it takes on them all.

Kevin Jonas, John Taylor, Nick Jonas, Greg "Garbo" Garbowsky, Joe Jonas, Ryan Liestman © Disney Enterprises

Kevin Jonas, Nick Jonas, Joe Jonas

JONAS BROTHERS:
THE 3D CONCERT EXPERIENCE

(WALT DISNEY PICTURES) Producers, Art Repola, Johnny Wright, Philip McIntyre, Kevin Jonas Sr., Alan Sacks; Executive Producer, Doug Merrifield; Director, Bruce Hendricks; Photography, Mitchell Amundsen, Reed Smoot; Editor, Michael Tronick; a Jonas Films production; Dolby; Color; HD; 3-D; Rated G; 76 minutes; Release date: February 27, 2009

WITH
Kevin Jonas, Joe Jonas, Nick Jonas, "Big Rob" Feggans, Demi Lovato, Taylor Swift, Kevin Jonas Sr.; Musicians: **John Lloyd Taylor, John Cahill Lawless, Ryan Matthew Liestman, Gregory Robert Garbowsky, Caitlin Evanson, Ben Clark**

A 3D film of the 2008 Jonas Brothers "Burning Up" concert tour, as well as documentary footage on the lives of the three brothers.

EXPLICIT ILLS

(PEACE ARCH) Producers, Sol Tryon, Liz Destro, Mark Webber; Executive Producers, Jim Jarmusch, Gary Adelman, Nick Kalikow, Jaylaan Llewellyn, Michael Morrison, Michael Wolk; Co-Producer, Seth Scher; Director/Screenplay, Mark Webber; Photography, Patrice Lucien Cochet; Designer, Michael Grasley; Costumes, Nikia Nelson; Music, Khari Mateen; Editor, Jay Rabinowitz; Casting, Mike Lemon; a Mangusta Productions/Riker Hill/Film 101 production; Super 35 Widescreen; Color; Rated R; 87 minutes; Release date: March 6, 2009

CAST
Babo's Mom	**Rosario Dawson**
Rocco	**Paul Dano**
Jacob	**Lou Taylor Pucci**
Kaleef	**Tariq Trotter**
Jill	**Naomi Harris**
Michelle	**Frankie Shaw**
Babo	**Francisco Burgos**

Martin Cepeda (Demitri), Destini Edwards (The Girl), Ross K. Kim-McManus (Heslin), Rebecca Comerford (Kelly), Jermaine Crawford (Tony), Namaiya Cunningham (Baby on Bus), Ruth DeSantis (Protester), Tim Dowlin (Chris), Joe Hansard (Bloody Towel Man), Zoe Lister Jones (Jen), Jacob Lavin (Indy Rock Guy), Anna Martemucci (Sarah), Shoha Parekh (Aisha), Peter Patrikios (Thug), Ben Rekhi (Gulab), Ronald Robertson (Thrift Store Clerk), Rocco Rosanio (Will), J. Santiago (Bodega Clerk), Noah Simmons (Little Boy), Eugene Smith (Customer), Rukiya Thomas (Maria), Brian Anthony Wilson (Demetri's Dad)

A glimpse into the lives of several Philadelphians dealing with drugs and poverty.

Lou Taylor Pucci, Frankie Shaw © Peace Arch Releasing

Paul Dano, Rosario Dawson

WATCHMEN

(WARNER BROTHERS/PARAMOUNT) Producers, Lawrence Gordon, Lloyd Levin, Deborah Snyder; Executive Producers, Herbert W. Gains, Thomas Tull; Co-Producer, Wesley Coller; Director, Zack Snyder; Screenplay, David Hayter, Alex Tse; Based on the graphic novel by Alan Moore and Dave Gibbons, published by DC Comics; Photography, Larry Fong; Designer, Alex McDowell; Costumes, Michael Wilkinson; Music, Tyler Bates; Editor, William Foy; Visual Effects Supervisor, John "DJ" DesJardin; Visual Effects and Animation, Sony Pictures Imageworks; Special Effects Makeup, Greg Cannom; Stunts/Fight Choreographer, Damon Caro; Casting, Kristy Carlson; a Lawrence Gordon/Lloyd Levin production, presented in association with Legendary Pictures; Dolby; Panavision; Technicolor; Rated R; 161 minutes; Release date: March 6, 2009

CAST

Laurie Jupiter/Silk Spectre II	**Malin Akerman**
Dr. Manhattan/Jon Osterman	**Billy Crudup**
Adrian Veidt/Ozymandias	**Matthew Goode**
Sally Jupiter/Silk Spectre	**Carla Gugino**
Walter Kovacs/Rorschach	**Jackie Earle Haley**
Edward Blake/Comedian	**Jeffrey Dean Morgan**
Dan Dreiberg/Nite Owl II	**Patrick Wilson**
Edgar Jacobi/Moloch the Mystic	**Matt Frewer**
Hollis Mason/Nite Owl	**Stephen McHattie**
Janey Slater	**Laura Mennell**
Wally Weaver	**Rob LaBelle**
John McLaughlin	**Gary Houston**
Pat Buchanan	**James Michael Connor**
Eleanor Clift	**Mary Ann Burger**
Doug Roth	**John Shaw**
Richard Nixon	**Robert Wisden**
Detective Fine	**Jerry Wasserman**
Detective Gallagher	**Don Thompson**
Henry Kissinger	**Frank Novak**

Sean Allan, Gary Chalk (Norad Generals), Ron Fassler (Ted Koppel), Stephanie Belding (Janet Black), Chris Burns (Dumb Thug), Nhi Do (Vietnamese Girl), Walter Addison (Lee Iacocca), Alison Araya, Sahar, Matthew Harrison, Bernadeta Wrobel, Youri Obryvtchenko, Heidi Iro, Kit Koon, Parm Soor, Cristina Menz, Lynn Colliar, Tony Ali, Katie Bennison, Ian Farthing, Calvin Lee, Alexander Sasha Mandra, Isabelle Champeau, Ashley O'Connell (Foreign Newscasters), Greg Armstrong-Morris (Truman Capote), Tony Bardach (John with Rorschach's Mother), Carly Bentall (Wally's Girlfriend), Jay Brazeau (News Vendor), Clint Carleton (Young Hollis Mason), Mike Carpenter (Young Moloch), Frank Cassini (Sally's Husband), Fulvio Cecere (Agent Forbes), Ron Chartier (Carnvial Photographer), Louis Chirillo (Face to Face TV Producer), Dale Wolfe, Ken Tremblett, Dawn Chubai (Keene Act Anchors), Mark Gash, Suzanne Clements-Smith, Agam Darshi (On Location Reporters), Andrew Colthart (Naked Man at Warhol Party), Bruce Crawford (Bank robber), Sahara Oasis Ashanti Davis (Young Tenement Fire Child), Mark Docherty, Clay St. Thomas (Newscasters), Matt Drake (Older Boy Bully), Greig Hospes, Danny Hospes, Ali Dunn (Tenement Fire Children), Neil Schell, Michael Eklund (Men in Riot Crowd), Glenn Ennis (Hooded Justice), Kurt Evans (Tenement Fire News Reporter), Deborah Finkel (Woman in Riot Crowd), Jeffrey Flieler (Tenement Fire Policeman), Tara Frederick (Aggressive Hooker), Ted Friend (Larry Culpepper), Chris Gauthier (Seymour), Carrie Genzel (Jackie Kennedy), Leah Gibson (Silhouette's Girlfriend), L. Harvey Gold (New Frontiersman Editor), Haley Adrianna Guiel (Laurie, 13 Years), Jaryd Heidrick (Young Jon), Alessandro Juliani (Rockefeller Military Base Technician), Terence Kelly (General West), J.R. Killigrew (David Bowie), Manuelita Kinsley (Keene Riot Reporter), John Kobylka (Fidel Castro), Carmen Lavigne (Anti War Protester), Colin Lawrence (Officer Kirkpatrick), Mi-Jung Lee (A-Bomb Test Anchorwoman), John Tench, Santo Lombardo (Knot Top Gang Members), Niall Matter (Mothman), Tom McBeath (News Analyst), Tyler McClendon (Veidt Enterprises Security Guard), Kevin

McNulty (News Anchor), Dan Payne (Dollar Bill), Marsha Regis (Face to Face TV Receptionist), Jesse Reid (Teenager at Newsstand), Martin Reiss (Brezhnev), Patrick Sabongui (Knot Top Gang Leader), Salli Saffioti (Annie Leibowitz), Sonya Salomaa (Adrian Veidt's Assistant), Darryl Scheelar (Captain Metropolis), Jason Schombing, Darren Shahlavi, Marshall Virture (NY SWAT), Daryl Shuttleworth (Jon's Father), Eli Snyder (Young Rorschach), Manoj Sood (Karnak Scientist), Salvatore Sortino (1940 Watchmen Photographer), Tamara Stanners (Vietnam 51st State Anchor), Brett Stimely (John F. Kennedy), Steve Stojkovic (Mick Jagger), Sylvesta Stuart (Destruction Firefighter), John R. Taylor (Priest), Greg Travis (Andy Warhol), Apollonia Vanova (Silhouette), Lori Watt (Rorschach's Mother), Chris Weber (Officer O'Brien), Danny Woodburn (Big Figure), Zack Snyder (Commando in Vietnam), Michael Kopsa (Paul Klein), William Taylor (Prison Psychiatrist), Malcolm Scott (Fat Thug), Danny Wattley (Huge Prisoner)

The mysterious murder of an unorthodox crime fighter known as "The Comedian," brings together a group of disparate superheroes who have been outlawed by a society that no longers seems worth fighting for.

Billy Crudup

Matthew Goode

Apollonia Vanova, Niall Mater, Dan Payne, Clint Carleton, Daryl Scheeler, Jeffrey Dean Morgan, Carla Gugino, Glenn Ennis

Malin Akerman, Billy Crudup

Jeffrey Dean Morgan, Malin Akerman, Billy Crudup, Matthew Goode, Patrick Wilson, Jackie Earle Haley

Malin Akerman, Patrick Wilson

Malin Akerman © Warner Bros.

Jeffrey Dean Morgan, Carla Gugino

Jackie Earle Haley, Patrick Wilson

Jackie Earle Haley

Amy Adams, Emily Blunt © Overture Films

Alan Arkin

Clifton Collins Jr., Jason Spevack, Amy Adams

SUNSHINE CLEANING

(OVERTURE) Producers, Peter Saraf, Marc Turtletaub, Jeb Brody, Glenn Williamson; Co-Producer, Robert J. Dohrmann; Director, Christine Jeffs; Screenplay, Megan Holley; Photography, John Toon; Designer, Joseph T. Garrity; Costumes, Alix Friedberg; Music, Michael Penn; Music Supervisors, Susan Jacobs; Editor, Heather Persons; Casting, Avy Kaufman; a Big Beach production; Dolby; Arri Widescreen; Technicolor; Rated R; 102 minutes; Release date: March 13, 2009

CAST

Rose Lorkowski	**Amy Adams**
Norah Lorkowski	**Emily Blunt**
Joe Lorkowski	**Alan Arkin**
Oscar Lorkowski	**Jason Spevack**
Mac	**Steve Zahn**
Lynn	**Mary Lynn Rajskub**
Winston	**Clifton Collins Jr.**
Randy	**Eric Christian Olsen**
Sherm	**Paul Dooley**
Carl	**Kevin Chapman**
Paula Datzman-Mead	**Judith Jones**
Heather	**Amy Redford**

Christopher Dempsey (Gun Shop Suicide), Vic Browder (Gun Shop Owner), Ivan Brutsche (Above and Beyond Worker), Arron Shiver (Detective), Ralph Jason Aukison, Cliff Garstka Sr., Charles Domenici (Gun Shop Employees), Susie Yip (Mrs. Kim), Michael L. Miller (Counselor), Sarah Hudnut (Teacher), Anya Alyassin (Mac's Daughter), Pab Schwendimann (Apartment Super), William Sterchi (Candy Store Manager), Amber Midthunder (Candy Store Girl), Angelique Midthunder (Girl's Mother), Olive Gallagher (Seminar Speaker), Lois Geary (Mrs. Davis), Frank E. Cruz (Shrimp Truck Driver), Esodie Geiger (Reporter), Kevin Wiggins (Police Officer), Epifanio Hernández (Restaurant Owner), McKenna Hutton (Young Rose), Mason Frank (Young Norah), Marya Beauvais (TV Waitress/Mother Lorkowski), Maddie Corman (Mousey Baby Shower Guest), Rebekah Wiggins (Peppy Shower Guest), Kristin Reese, Veronica Hernandez, Jourdan Reese (Hinkle's Employee Singers), Josh Berry (TV Detective)

Two sisters whose lives are seemingly going nowhere decide to start their own crime scene clean up service.

Steve Zahn, Amy Adams

RACE TO WITCH MOUNTAIN

(WALT DISNEY PICTURES) Producer, Andrew Gunn; Executive Producers, Mario Iscovich, Ann Marie Sanderlin; Director, Andy Fickman; Screenplay, Matt Lopez, Mark Bomback; Screen Story, Matt Lopez; Based on the novel *Escape to Witch Mountain* by Alexander Key; Photography, Greg Gardiner; Designer, David J. Bomba; Costumes, Genevieve Tyrrell; Music, Trevor Rabin; Music Supervisor, Lisa Brown; Editor, David Rennie; Executive Visual Effects Supervisor, David Lingenfelser; Special Character Effects Designers/Creators, Alec Gillis, Tom Woodruff Jr.; Casting, Randi Hiller, Sara Finn; a Walt Disney Pictures presentation of a Gunn Films production; Dolby; Super 35 Widescreen; Deluxe color; Rated PG; 98 minutes; Release date: March 13, 2009

Cheech Marin, AnnaSophia Robb, Alexander Ludwig

CAST

Jack Bruno	**Dwayne Johnson**
Sara	**AnnaSophia Robb**
Seth	**Alexander Ludwig**
Dr. Alex Friedman	**Carla Gugino**
Henry Burke	**Ciarán Hinds**
Matheson	**Tom Everett Scott**
Pope	**Chris Marquette**
Carson	**Billy Brown**
Dr. Donald Harlan	**Garry Marshall**
Tina	**Kim Richards**
Sheriff Antony	**Iake Eissinmann**
Eddie Cortez	**Richard "Cheech" Marin**

Chris Marquette, Ciarán Hinds, Tom Everett Scott

Tom Woodruff Jr. (Siphon), John Duff (Frank), Bob Koherr (Marty), Kevin Christy (Matt), Bob Clendenin (Lloyd), Sam Wolfson (Imperial Stormtrooper Ciardi), Bryan Fogel (Imperial Stormtrooper Gray), Robert Tori (Dominick), John Kassir (Chuck), Beth Kennedy (Steftenagel), Jonathan Slavin (Gallagher), Harry S. Murphy (Analyst D. Pleasence), Ted Hartley (Four-Star General V. Lewton), Jack Eastland (General E. Albert), Meredith Salenger (Natalie Gann), Andrew Shaifer (Casey Taylor), Suzanne Krull (Gail Ross), Steve Rosenbaum (Oren Bergman), Christine Lakin (Sunday), Corri English, Randy Dunham, Jeff LeGore, Danny Reuland, Don Ian (Brokedown Cadillac), Dave Engfer (Iscovich), Joseph Leo Bwarie (Frankie Valet), Omar Dorsey (Police Officer Hough), Paul Nygro (Teddy Tentacles), Brandon Miller (Hendricks), Andrew T. Janey (Repola), Dennis Hayden (Ray), Shengyi Huang (Shira the UFO Huntress), Hiromi Oshima, Christina Wun (Fem-Aliens), Christopher Dobler (Hansen), Garrett Marshall (Bomback), Buck (Junkyard), Whitley Strieber (Himself)

Two young extraterrestrials enlist the aide of Vegas cab driver Jack Bruno to help them recover their damaged space ship, which had been confiscated by military intelligence. Remake/re-imagining of the 1975 Disney film *Escape to Witch Mountain*, starring Kim Richards and Ike Eisenmann (Iake Eissinmann), both of whom make appearances here.

Dwayne Johnson, Carla Gugino

AnnaSophia Robb, Alexander Ludwig, Dwayne Johnson
© Disney Enterprises

THE LAST HOUSE ON THE LEFT

(ROGUE) Producers, Wes Craven, Sean Cunningham, Marianne Maddalena; Executive Producer, Ray Haboush; Co-Producers, Jonathan Craven, Cody Zwieg; Director, Dennis Iliadis; Screenplay, Adam Alleca, Carl Ellsworth; Based on the 1972 motion picture written and directed by Wes Craven; Photography, Sharone Meir; Designer, Johnny Breedt; Costumes, Katherine Jane Bryant; Music, John Murphy; Music Supervisor, Ed Gerrard; Editor, Peter McNulty; Visual Effects Supervisor, Jamison Goei; Casting, Nancy Nayor Battino, Scout Masterson; a Craven/Cunningham/Maddalena production; Dolby; Color; Rated R; 109 minutes; Release date: March 13, 2009

CAST
John Collingwood	**Tony Goldwyn**
Emma Collingwood	**Monica Potter**
Krug	**Garret Dillahunt**
Justin	**Spencer Treat Clark**
Sadie	**Riki Lindhome**
Paige	**Martha MacIsaac**
Morton	**Michael Bowen**
Mari Collingwood	**Sara Paxton**

Josh Cox (Giles), Aaron Paul (Francis), Usha Khan (Maid)

John and Emma Collingwood take revenge on the trio of thugs that assaulted their daughter.

Remake of the 1972 Hallmark Releasing film of the same name.

Tony Goldwyn, Sara Paxton, Monica Potter © Rogue Pictures

Aaron Paul, Garret Dillahunt, Spencer Treat Clark, Riki Lindhome

Bruce Dern, Aaron Stanford © Screen Media Films

Kristen Stewart, Aaron Stanford

THE CAKE EATERS

(7-57 RELEASING/SCREEN MEDIA) Producers, Mary Stuart Masterson, Elisa Pugliese, Jesse Scolaro, Allen Bain, Darren Goldberg; Executive Producer, Patrick Morris; Co-Producer/Screenplay, Jayce Bartok; Director, Mary Stuart Masterson; Photography, Peter Masterson; Designer, David Stein; Music, Duncan Sheik; Editors, Joe Landauer, Colleen Sharp; a 57th & Irving/7th Floor/Vinyl Foote production; Dolby; Color; HD-to-35mm; Rated R; 95 minutes; Release date: March 13, 2009

CAST
Georgia Kaminski	**Kristen Stewart**
Beagle Kimbrough	**Aaron Stanford**
Easy Kimbrough	**Bruce Dern**
Marg	**Elizabeth Ashley**
Guy Kimbrough	**Jayce Bartok**
Violet	**Talia Balsam**
Judd	**Jesse L. Martin**
Ceci	**Melissa Leo**

Marylouise Burke (Babe), E.J. Carroll (Vito), Tom Cavanagh (Lloyd), Miriam Shor (Stephanie), Robert Meo (Bobby), Devin Rattray (JJ), Andrew George Jr. (Young Beagle), Elizabeth Girardeau (Maggie Lynn), Zoe Hunter (Girl on the Bus), Grant Monohon (Bum), Elisa Pugliese (Stacy), Elizabeth van Meter (Hippy Chick)

A teenage girl suffering from a degenerative nervous disease connects with a simple young man who had taken care of his mother during her terminal illness.

Pugs

Valentino Garavani and his models © Truly Indie

VALENTINO: THE LAST EMPEROR

(TRULY INDIE) Producers, Matt Kapp, Matt Tyrnauer; Executive Producer, Carter Burden III; Co-Producer, Frederuc Tcheng; Co-Executive Producer, Adam Leff; Director, Matt Tyrnauer; Photography, Tom Hurwitz; Editor, Bob Eisenhardt; an Acolyte Films production; Dolby; Color; DV-to-35mm; Rated PG-13; 96 minutes; Release date: March 18, 2009

WITH
Valentino Garavani, Giancarlo Giammetti, Matteo Marzotto, Nati Abascal, Giorgio Armani, Jeannie Becker, Matthew Broderick, Michael Caine, Joan Collins, Alessandra Facchinetti, Dante Ferretti, Tom Ford, Anne Hathaway, Karl Lagerfeld, Gwyneth Paltrow, Sarah Jessica Parker, Claudia Schiffer, André Leon Talley, Uma Thurman, Donatella Versace, Diane von Fürstenberg, Alek Wek, Anna Wintour

Documentary on noted fashion designer Valentino Garavani as he and his partner Giancarlo Giammetti prepare for the 2006 Spring/Summer Collection in Paris and attend a July 2007 retropective of Valentino's 45-year career.

KNOWING

(SUMMIT) Producers, Todd Black, Jason Blumenthal, Steve Tisch, Alex Proyas; Executive Producers, Stephen Jones, Topher Dow, Norm Golightly, David Bloomfield; Co-Producer/Story, Ryne Douglas Pearson; Co-Executive Producers, Aaron Kaplan, Sean Perrone; Director, Alex Proyas; Screenplay, Ryne Douglas Pearson, Julie Snowden, Stiles White; Photography, Simon Duggan; Designer, Steven Jones-Evans; Costumes, Terry Ryan; Music, Marco Beltrami; Editor, Richard Learoyd; Special Effects Supervisor, Angelo Sahin; Visual Effects Supervisors, Andrew Jackson, Eric Durst; Stunts, Chris Anderson; Casting, Greg Apps; an Escape Artists production, in association with Mystery Clock Cinema; Dolby; HD Widescreen; Deluxe color; DV; Rated PG-13; 121 minutes; Release date: March 20, 2009

CAST
John Koestler	**Nicolas Cage**
Diana Wayland	**Rose Byrne**
Caleb Koestler	**Chandler Canterbury**
The Stranger	**D.G. Maloney**
Abby Wayland/Lucinda Embry	**Lara Robinson**
Grace Koestler	**Nadia Townsend**
Reverend Koestler	**Alan Hopgood**
Allison Koestler	**Adrienne Pickering**
Younger Caleb	**Joshua Long**
Phil Beckman	**Ben Mendelsohn**
Miss Taylor (1959)	**Danielle Carter**
Miss Taylor (2009)	**Alethea McGrath**

D.G. Maloney (The Stranger), David Lennie (Principal Clark, 1959), Tamara Donnellan (Lucinda's Mother), Travis Waite (Lucinda's Father), Gareth Yuan (Donald), Lesley Anne Mitchell (Stacey), Liam Hemsworth (Spencer), Raymond Thomas (Teacher), Jake Bradley (Boy), Joanna Hunt-Prokhovnik, Jean-Michael Tan (Carpool Mates), Rody Claude (Patrolman), Alyssa McClelland (Flight Attendant), Harli Ammouchi (Man in Duffle Coat), Giovanni Bartuccio (Transit Officer), Menik Gooneratne (Woman with Baby), Chris McLean (Commuter), Marc Lawrence (Train Driver), Terry Camilleri (Cashier), Erin Klein (Jeep Driver), Angie Diaz, Breanne Bergs, Georgie Bolton, Jo Buckley (Reporters), Archie Kirkland (Student), Sara Reed (Kid with Glasses), Ted Maynard, Anna Anderson, Tony Porter, Rob McPherson, Kate Doherty (News Anchors), David Whiteley, Miles Paras, Clare Chihambakwe (Newscasters), Michael C. Gwynne (Coast Patrol Official), Markus Hamilton (Weatherman), Brendan Bacon (Man on Sidewalk), Joel Bow, Maximillian Paul, Karen Hadfield (Strangers), Matt Boesenberg (Traffic Cop), Jim Knobeloch (Army General), Steve Mouzakis (Head Paramedic), Sonya Suares (Assistant Paramedic), Ra Chapman (Jessica), Benita Collings (John's Mother), Verity Charlton (Kim), Janet Foye (Lady on Train), Clem Maloney, Sally Anne Arnott (Rioters), Carolyn Shakespeare-Allen (Principal, 2009)

Astrophysics professor John Koestler realizes that a sheet of seemingly random numbers left in a recently-opened time capsule are clues predicting catastrophic events that are about to happen in the near future.

Nicolas Cage, Chandler Canterbury © Summit Entertainment

Paul Giamatti, Tom Wilkinson © Universal Studios

Julia Roberts, Clive Owen

Julia Roberts, Clive Owen

DUPLICITY

(UNIVERSAL) Producers, Jennifer Fox, Kerry Orent, Laura Bickford; Executive Producer, Ryan Kavanaugh; Co-Producers, Christopher Goode, John Gilroy; Director/ Screenplay, Tony Gilroy; Photography, Robert Elswit; Designer, Kevin Thompson; Costumes, Albert Wolsky; Music, James Newton Howard; Music Supervisor, Brian Ross; Editor, John Gilroy; Special Effects Coordinators, Jeff Brink, Eddie Droghan; Casting, Ellen Chenoweth; Presented in association with Relativity Media; Dolby; Panavision; Technicolor; Rated PG-13; 125 minutes; Release date: March 20, 2009

CAST

Claire Stenwick	**Julia Roberts**
Ray Koval	**Clive Owen**
Howard Tully	**Tom Wilkinson**
Richard Garsik	**Paul Giamatti**
Jeff Bauer	**Tom McCarthy**
Duke Monahan	**Denis O'Hare**
Pam Frales	**Kathleen Chalfant**
Ned Guston	**Wayne Duvall**
Barbara Bofferd	**Carrie Preston**
Boris Fetyov	**Oleg Stefan**
Dale Raimes	**Rick Worthy**
Dinesh Patel	**Khan Baykal**

Ulrich Thomsen (Big Swiss Suit), Christopher Denham (Ronny Partiz), Dan Daily (Garsik's Aide), Lisa Roberts Gillan (Tully's Assistant), David Shumbris (Turtleneck), Fabrizio Brienza (Hotel Manager), Lucia Grillo (Italian Chambermaid), Conan McCarty (Bartender), Kirby Mitchell (Realtor), Christopher Mann (Mr. Security), Seth Kirschner (Counter Sloth), Karl Bury, Happy Anderson (Physecs), James Cronin, Esther Pringle, Mary Anne Prevost (San Diego Equikroms), Annabel Seymour (Tully's Makeup Girl), Sandy Hamilton (Swiss Chemist), Helen Elswit (Swiss Executive), Samantha Stark (B&R Employee)

The announcement of a revolutionary new product guaranteed to generate huge profits prompts agents Ray Koval and Claire Stenwick to spy for rival corporations with the intention of uncovering some profitable secrets.

Oleg Stefan, Kathleen Chalfant, Denis O'Hare

I LOVE YOU, MAN

(DREAMWORKS) Producers, Donald De Line, John Hamburg; Executive Producers, Bill Johnson, Andrew Haas, Ivan Reitman, Tom Pollock, Jeffrey Clifford; co-Producer, Anders Bard; Director, John Hamburg; Screenplay, John Hamburg, Larry Levin; Story, Larry Levin; Photography, Lawrence Sher; Designer, Andrew Laws; Costumes, Leesa Evans; Music, Theodore Shapiro; Music Supervisor, Jennifer Hawks; Editor, William Kerr; a De Line Pictures/Bernard Gayle Productions/Montecito Picture Co. production; Distributed by Paramount; Dolby; Deluxe color; Rated R; 104 minutes; Release date: March 20, 2009

CAST

Peter Klaven	**Paul Rudd**
Sydney Fife	**Jason Segel**
Zooey	**Rashida Jones**
Robbie Klaven	**Andy Samberg**
Oz Klaven	**J.K. Simmons**
Joyce Klaven	**Jane Curtin**
Barry	**Jon Favreau**
Denise	**Jaime Pressly**
Tevin Downey	**Rob Huebel**
Doug	**Thomas Lennon**
Hailey	**Sarah Burns**
Himself	**Lou Ferrigno**

Greg Levine (Hailey's Date), Jean Villepique (Leanne), Colleen Crabtree, Kym Whitley, Caroline Farah (Co-Workers), Mather Zickel (Gil), Aziz Ansari (Eugene), Nick Kroll (Larry), Liz Cackowski, Kulap Vilaysack, Catherine Reitman, Carla Gallo, Vicki David (Zooey's Friends), Josh Cooke (Alan, Bench Press Guy), Jay Chandrasekhar, Seth Morris, James Engel, Jerry Minor (Barry's Buddies), Joe Lo Truglio (Lonnie, Cracked Voice Guy), Murray Gershenz (Mel Stein), Keri Safran (Jar Waitress), Greg Tuculescu, Renee Darmiento (Open House Couple), Ian Roberts (Venice Boardwalk Jogger), Robert Cicherillo (Venice Boardwalk Bodybuilder), Ethan S. Smith, Nelson Franklin, David Krumholtz (Sydney's Buddies), Ping Wu (Mr. Chu), Jill Bartlett (Woman Leaving Sydney's House), Matt Walsh (Impatient Golfer), Raquel Bell (Saks Fifth Avenue Saleswoman), Kris Edwards (Bromancer)

Socially awkward Peter Klaven realizes that his lack of close male friends means he will not have a Best Man at his upcoming wedding. Peter attempts to bond with extroverted Sydney Fife, whose crude, no-holds-barred lifestyle couldn't be further from his own.

Jaime Pressly, Rashida Jones, Sarah Burns © DreamWorks/Paramount

J.K. Simmons, Lou Ferrigno, Joe Lo Truglio, Paul Rudd, Thomas Lennon, Adam Samberg

Jason Segel, Paul Rudd

Paul Rudd, Jason Segel

THE GREAT BUCK HOWARD

(MAGNOLIA) Producers, Tom Hanks, Gary Goetzman; Executive Producers, Steven Shareshian, Marvin Acuna; Director/Screenplay, Sean McGinly; Photography, Tak Fujimoto; Designer, Gary Frutkoff; Co-Producer, Ginger Sledge; Music, Blake Neely; Editor, Myron Kerstein; Casting, Jeanne McCarthy; a Bristol Bay Productions presentation of a Playtone production; Dolby; Color; Rated PG; 90 minutes; Release date: March 20, 2009

Colin Hanks, Tom Hanks

CAST

Buck Howard	**John Malkovich**
Troy Gable	**Colin Hanks**
Valerie Brennan	**Emily Blunt**
Gil Bellamy	**Ricky Jay**
Doreen	**Debra Monk**
Alan Berkman	**Adam Scott**
Michael Perry	**Patrick Fischler**
Dan Green	**Wallace Langham**
Johnathan Finerman	**Griffin Dunne**
Kenny	**Steve Zahn**
Mr. Gable	**Tom Hanks**
Kip	**Terry Scannell**

Tom Arnold, David Blaine, Conan O'Brien, Regis Philbin, Kelly Ripa, Jon Stewart, Martha Stewart, George Takei, Jay Leno, Mary Hart, Damien Fahey, Michael Winslow, Bill Saluga, Gary Coleman, Jack Carter (Themselves), B.J. Hendricks (Burly), Jacquie Barnbrook (Sheila Heller), Nate Hartley (Teenage Kid), Matt Hoey (Charley), Dale Waddington Horowitz (Sleeping Woman), Shane Johnson (Las Vegas Producer), Katherine VanderLinden, Nate Witty (Law Students), Marni McFair (Doctor in Audience), Don Most (*Tonight Show* Producer), Norm O'Neill (Audience Member with Cash), Jill Ragan (Cincinnati Producer), Kimberly Scott (Nurse), Danica Sheridan (Wisconsin Woman), Melissa Dawn Stone, Amy Jo Traicoff (Las Vegas Women), Stacey Travis (Cindy Crown), Max Williams (Flower Delivery Guy), Casey Wilson (Charity), Wendy Worthington (Oregon Woman), Jonathan Ames (Edward Kelly)

Colin Hanks, John Malkovich, Ricky Jay

Young Troy Gable drops out of law school to take a job as the personal assistant to once-noted mentalist Buck Howard who now makes his living accepting second-rate engagements on the road.

Colin Hanks, Steve Zahn © Magnolia Pictures

Colin Hanks, Emily Blunt

Missing Link, Susan, BOB, Insectasaurus, Dr. Cockroach ©
DreamWorks/Paramount

Monger, President

Alien Robot, Susan

MONSTERS VS ALIENS

(DREAMWORKS/PARAMOUNT) Producer, Lisa Stewart; Co-Producers, Jill Hopper Descmarchelier, Latifa Ouaou; Directors/Story, Rob Letterman, Conrad Vernon; Screenplay, Maya Forbes, Wallace Wolodarsky, Rob Letterman, Jonathan Aibel, Glenn Berger; Designer, David James; Music, Henry Jackman; Editors, Joyce Arrastia, Eric Dapkewicz; Visual Effects Supervisor, Ken Bielenberg; Head of Character Animation, David Burgess; Head of Layout, Damon O'Beirne; a DreamWorks Animation presentation; Dolby; Widescreen; 3-D; Deluxe color; Rated PG; 95 minutes; Release date: March 27, 2009

VOICE CAST

Susan Murphy/Ginormica	**Reese Witherspoon**
B.O.B.	**Seth Rogen**
Dr. Cockroach, Ph.D.	**Hugh Laurie**
The Missing Link	**Will Arnett**
General W.R. Monger	**Kiefer Sutherland**
Gallaxhar	**Rainn Wilson**
Derek Dietl	**Paul Rudd**
President Hathaway	**Stephen Colbert**
Wendy Murphy	**Julie White**
Carl Murphy	**Jeffrey Tambor**
Computer	**Amy Poehler**
News Reporter	**Ed Helms**
Katie	**Renée Zellweger**
Cuthbert	**John Krasinski**

Sean Bishop (Private Bullhorn/Helicopter Pilot/Advisor Ortega), Rich B. Dietl (Commander/Advisor Smith), Stephen Kearin (Technician Ben), Rob Letterman (Secret Service Man #1/Lieutenant), Tom McGrath (Wilson), Chris Miller (Advisor Cole/Army Commander Jones), Mike Mitchell (Advisor Wedgie), Kent Osborne (Technician Jerry), Latifa Ouaou (Advisor Ouaou/Mrs. Ronson/Advisor/Panicked Guest), Geoffrey Pomeroy (Soldier #4/Pilot/Soldier #3/News Technician), David Smith (Soldier #1/Advisor Jackson), Lisa Stewart (Bridesmaid Candy), Conrad Vernon (Advisor Hawk/Advisor Dither/Minister/Secret Service Man #2/Mama Dietl)

After a meteor causes her to grow to freakish proportions, Susan joins forces with a group of outcast mutants to help battle aliens that have invaded Earth.

Gallaxhar

THE HAUNTING IN CONNECTICUT

(LIONSGATE) Producers, Paul Brooks, Andrew Trapani, Daniel Farrands, Wendy Rhoads; Executive Producers, Scott Niemeyer, Norm Waitt, Steve Whitney; Co-Producers, Brad Kessell, Jeff Levine; Director, Peter Cornwell; Screenplay, Adam Simon, Tim Metcalfe; Photography, Adam Swica; Designer, Alicia Keywan; Costumes, Meg McMillan; Music, Robert J. Kral; Editor, Tom Elkins; Visual Effects Supervisor, Erik Nordby; Prosthetics and Character Effects, Masters FX, Todd Masters, Dan Rebert; Casting, Eyde Belasco, Jim Heber; an Integrated Films production, presented with Gold Circle Films; Dolby; Color; Rated PG-13; 92 minutes; Release date: March 27, 2009

Martin Donovan

CAST

Sara Campbell	**Virginia Madsen**
Matt Campbell	**Kyle Gallner**
Reverend Popescu	**Elias Koteas**
Wendy	**Amanda Crew**
Peter Campbell	**Martin Donovan**
Mary Campbell	**Sophi Knight**
Billy Campbell	**Ty Wood**
Jonah	**Erik J. Berg**
Ramsey Aickman	**John Bluethner**

D.W. Brown (Dr. Brooks), John B. Lowe (Mr. Sinclair), Adriana O'Neil (Chemo Nurse), Will Woytowich (Cop), James Durham (Matt's Cell Mate), Darren Ross, Sarah Constible (Paramedics), Blake Taylor, Keith James, Kelly Wolfman, Jessica Burleson (1920s Séance), Matt Kippen (Strung Out Guy)

In order to be near her sickly son who is receiving cancer treatments, Sara Campbell rents a long vacated house in Connecticut only to realize that the dwelling is haunted.

Elias Koteas, Amanda Crew, Kyle Gallner

Virginia Madsen, Kyle Gallner

Virginia Madsen, Kyle Gallner © Lionsgate

Diana Franco Galindo, Souleymane Sy Savane © Roadside Attractions

GOODBYE SOLO

(ROADSIDE ATTRACTIONS) Producers, Jason Orans, Ramin Bahrani; Executive Producers, Brian Devine, Brooke Devine; Co-Executive Producer, Stephen Bannatyne; Director/Editor, Ramin Bahrani; Screenplay, Ramin Bahrani, Bahareh Azimi; Photography, Michael Simmonds; Designer, Chad Keith; Music, M. Lo; a Gigantic Pictures, Noruz Films production, in association with Lucky Hat Entertainment, Independent Television Service (ITVS); Color; Not Rated; 91 minutes; Release date: March 27, 2009

CAST
Solo	**Souleymane Sy Savane**
William	**Red West**
Alex	**Diana Franco Galindo**
Roc	**Lane "Roc" Williams**
Mamadou	**Mamadou Lam**
Quiera	**Carmen Leyva**

Peter N. Anyieth, Wel Mayom Jok (DVD Sellers), Jim Babel, Neill Fleeman, Linda Lindsly (Airline Interviewers), Sarah S. Brooks (Passenger with Hat), Lasheka Brown (Crack Passenger), Alexandra Dimopoulos (Nurse), Jamill "Peaches" Fowler (Pork Chop), Evelia Garcia (Bar Owner), Chris Greene (Thug), Viktor Hernandez (Quiera's Cousin), J. Malaak Juuk (Motel Janitor), Damian Jewan Lee (Passenger), Djibril Lo (Bank Cab Driver), Ken Lugen (Taxi Cab employee), Angus MacLachlan (Crack Passenger), Trevor Metscher (Ticket Attendant), Caleb Paul (Solo's Baby), Christian Prince, Greg Prince, Jeff Prince (Thugs), Navani Reyes (Navani), Catherine Sewell (Hospital Receptionist), Norman L. Sloan (Pharmacist), Virgilio Tix (Quiera's Cousin), Donald Wardlow (Sleeping Passenger), Pat West (Diner Hostess)

When an elderly passenger asks taxi driver Solo to drive him to destination where he can kill himself, the cabbie becomes determined to sway the man from his decision.

THE EDUCATION OF CHARLIE BANKS

(ANCHOR BAY/MYRIAD) Producer, Marisa Polvino; Executive Producers, Sam Maydew, Peter Elkoff; Senior Executive Producer, Ken Guarino; Co-Producer, Declan Baldwin; Director, Fred Durst; Screenplay, Peter Elkoff; Photography, Alex Nepomniaschy; Designer, Chad Detwiller; Costumes, Elizabeth Shelton; Music, John Swihart; Editor, Eric L. Beason; a Strongheart Pictures production; Dolby; Color; Rated R; 100 minutes; Release date: March 27, 2009

CAST
Charlie Banks	**Jesse Eisenberg**
Mick	**Jason Ritter**
Mary	**Eva Amurri**
Danny	**Chris Marquette**
Leo	**Sebastian Stan**
Nia	**Gloria Votsis**

Danny A. Abeckaser (Arresting Officer), Dennis Boutsikaris (Mr. Banks), Miles Chandler (Young Mick), Sam Daly (Owen), William DeCoff (Airport Valet), Amanda Donaghey (Glee Club Member), Alex Guarino (Buzzy Tim), Steven Hinkle (Young Charlie), Gabe Karon (Terry), Olivia Keister (Michelle), Cain Kerner (Young Danny), Nicholas Leiter Mele (Screaming Kid), Charles Parnell (Asst. DA Worsheck), Patrick Pitu (Suicide Witness), Todd Poudrier (Pilot), Josh Richman (Prof. Gersten), Vincent James Russo ('70s Rocker), Jeremy Schwartz (Bartender), Gabby Sherba (Gabby), James Zimmerman (Tim)

Charlie Banks must confront his past when a volatile teen he'd secretly turned in to the police shows up at his college, not quite making his reasons for being there clear but making Charlie's life a living hell in the process.

Eva Amurri, Jesse Eisenberg, Jason Ritter, Sebastian Stan © Anchor Bay Entertainment

Jesse Eisenberg, Jason Ritter, Eva Amurri

Don Omar, Wilmer Calderon

Vin Diesel, Michelle Rodriguez

FAST & FURIOUS

(UNIVERSAL) Producers, Neal H. Moritz, Vin Diesel, Michael Fottrell; Executive Producers, Amanda Lewis, Samantha Vincent; Director, Justin Lin; Screenplay, Chris Morgan; Based on characters created by Gary Scott Thompson; Photography, Amir Mokri; Designer, Ida Random; Costumes, Sanja Milkovic Hays; Music, Brian Tyler; Music Supervisor, Kathy Nelson; Editors, Christian Wagner, Fred Raskin; Visual Effects Supervisors, Thaddeus Beier, Michael J. Wassel; Casting, Sarah Halley Finn, Randi Hiller; an Original Film/One Race Films production, presented in association with Relativity Media; Dolby; Panavision; Technicolor; Rated PG-13; 106 minutes; Release date: April 3, 2009

CAST

Dominic Toretto	**Vin Diesel**
Brian O'Conner	**Paul Walker**
Letty	**Michelle Rodriguez**
Mia	**Jordana Brewster**
Campos	**John Ortiz**
Fenix Rise	**Laz Alonso**
Gisele Harabo	**Gal Gadot**
Penning	**Jack Conley**
Agent Ben Stasiak	**Shea Whigham**
Agent Sophie Trinh	**Liza Lapira**
Han Lue	**Sung Kang**

Don Omar (Himself), Mirtha Michelle (Cara), Greg Cipes (Dwight), Tego Calderon (Tego), Ron Yuan (David Park), Alejandro Patino (Gas Truck Driver), Joe Hursley (Virgil), Cesar Garcia (Juvenal), Brandon T. Jackson (BMW Driver), Mousa Kraish (Silvia Driver), Neil Brown Jr. (Malik), Wilmer Calderon (Tash), Joseph Julian Soria, Don Tai Theerathada (Drug Runners), Robert Miano (Braga Double), Luis Moncada (Scar Thug), Kofi Natei (Thug), McCaleb Burnett (Federal Investigator), Greg Collins (Lead Investigator), Monique Gabriela Curnen, Jimmy Lin, Roger Fan, Brendan Wayne, Lou Reyes (FBI Agents), Breon Ansley (FBI Assistant), Assaf Cohen, Loren Lazerine (Border Agents), Lou Beatty Jr. (Judge), Julian Starks (Bailiff), Christopher Gehrman (Impound Clerk), Marco Rodriguez (Mexican Priest), Naureen Zaim, Becky O'Donohue, Sharon Zeev (Hot Girls), Alexandra Castro (Woman in Hallway), Jaimie Sullivan (Girl at the Beach), Leigh Folsom (GPS Voice)

Brian O'Conner and Dominic Toretto team up to help the FBI track down an L.A. drug kingpin who is known to dwell in their world of illegal street racing. Fourth in the Universal series following *The Fast and the Furious* (2001), *2 Fast 2 Furious* (2003), and *The Fast and the Furious: Tokyo Drift* (2006).

Paul Walker © Universal Studios

BART GOT A ROOM

(ANCHOR BAY) Producers, Galt Neiderhoffer, Daniela Taplin Lundberg, Celine Rattray, Jai Stefan, Tony Shawkat; Executive Producers, Pamela Hirsch, Stephen Benedek, Ed Hart, Bruce Lunsford, Reagan Silber, Dina Burke, Mario Fallone, Michael LaFetra, Randy Simon; Co-Producers, Frank Demartini, Riva Marker; Director/Screenplay, Brian Hecker; Photography, Hallvard Braein; Designer, Regina McLarney-Crowley; Costumes, Jacqui G; Music, Jamie Lawrence; Editors, Danny Rafic, Annette Davey; Casting, Lori Wyman; a Plum Pictures production, in association with Shrink Media, Basra Entertainment, Hart-Lunsford Pictures, Benedek Films; Color; HD; Rated PG-13; 80 minutes; Release date: April 3, 2009

CAST

Ernie Stein	**William H. Macy**
Beth Stein	**Cheryl Hines**
Danny Stein	**Steven J. Kaplan**
Camille	**Alia Shawkat**
Craig	**Brandon Hardesty**
Alice	**Ashley Benson**
Bart Beeber	**Chad Jamian Williams**
Mrs. Goodson	**Dinah Manoff**
Dr. Goodson	**Michael Mantell**
Bob	**Jon Polito**
Prom Date	**Lynna Baculo**
Chauffeur	**Mike Benitez**
Makeout Kissing Students	**Estefania Crespo**
	Jean-Paul Chreky
Diane	**Carrie Drazek**
Mr. Carr	**Marshall B. Gage**
Ms. Fines	**Elena Maria Garcia**

Sam E. Goldberg (Ice Cream Customer), Kate Karpinski (Hotel Clerk), Katie McClellan (Gertie), Kate Micucci (Abby Marcus), Margot Moreland (Mrs. Hogan), Tyler O'Campo (Brittney Goodson), Brett Weiss (Young Bart), Brittney Winton (Debbie Yang), Jennifer Tilly (Melinda)

Under pressure to find a date for the senior prom, Danny Stein banks on getting a date with popular cheerleader Alice.

Alia Shawkat

Steve J. Kaplan, Cheryl Hines

Steven J. Kaplan, Brandon Hardesty

William H. Macy, Steven J. Kaplan © Anchor Bay Entertainment

ADVENTURELAND

(MIRAMAX) Producers, Ted Hope, Anne Carey, Sidney Kimmel; Executive Producers, William Horberg, Bruce Toll; Director/Screenplay, Greg Mottola; Photography, Terry Stacey; Designer, Stephen Beatrice; Costumes, Melissa Toth; Music, Yo La Tengo; Music Supervisor, Tracy McKnight; Editor, Anne McCabe; a Sidney Kimmel Entertainment presentation of a This is That production; Dolby; Deluxe color; Rated R; 106 minutes; Release date: April 3, 2009

CAST

James Brennan	**Jesse Eisenberg**
Em Lewin	**Kristen Stewart**
Joel Schiffman	**Martin Starr**
Paulette	**Kristen Wiig**
Bobby	**Bill Hader**
Mike Connell	**Ryan Reynolds**
Arlene	**Kelsey Ford**
Eric	**Michael Zegen**
Brad	**Ryan McFarland**
Mr. Brennan	**Jack Gilpin**
Mrs. Brennan	**Wendie Malick**
Tommy Frigo	**Matt Bush**
Rich	**Stephen Mast**
Velvet Touch Manager	**Todd Cioppa**
Adult Contestant	**Adam Kroloff**
Molly Hatchet T-Shirt Guy	**Kevin Breznahan**
Panda Con Dad	**Marc Grapey**

Paige Howard (Sue O'Malley), Dan Bittner (Pete O'Malley), Moe Slinger, Jesse Slinger (Loud Kids), Jack Baldwin (Barfing Kid), Barret Hackney (Munch), Margarita Levieva (Lisa P), Kimisha Renee Davis (Kelly), Russell Steinberg, Andrew Ransom, Joe Sanderson, Cliff Chen, Rob Orr, Eric Schaeffer (Foreigner Tribute Band), Vanessa Wanger (Ronnie Connell), Josh Pais (Mr. Lewin), Mary Birdsong (Francy), Gennaro DiSilvio (Nicky), Alexis Ferrante (Nicky's Girlfriend), Joe Pawlenko (Denny, Nicky's Pal), Zack Palmer (Joel's Younger Brother), Declan Baldwin (Customer), Ian Harding (Wealthy Prepster), Ashtin Petrella (Prepster's Girlfriend), Amy Landis (Mrs. Ostrow), Janine Viola (Mrs. Frigo), Alana Hixson, Erin Cappiccie (Pretty Girls)

Forced to find a summer job, James Brennan ends up joining the misfit staff at a second-rate amusement park.

Jesse Eisenberg, Martin Starr

Jesse Eisenberg, Kristen Stewart © Miramax Films

Bill Hader, Kristen Wiig

Ryan Reynolds

Paul Dano, John Goodman, Sean Dugan

Zooey Deschanel, Paul Dano © First Independent Pictures

GIGANTIC

(FIRST INDEPENDENT) Producers, Mindy Goldberg, Christine Vachon; Executive Producers, Paul Dano, Scott Ferguson, Jerry Soloman, Jeff Preiss, John Wells; Co-Producer, Charles Pugliese; Director, Matt Aselton; Screenplay, Matt Aselton, Adam Nagata; Photography, Peter Donahue; Designer, Rick Butler; Costumes, Paola Weintraub; Music, Roddy Bottum; Editor, Beatrice Sisul; Casting, Mark Bennett; an Epoch Films presentation in association with Killer Films/John Wells Productions; Dolby; Super 35 Widescreen; Technicolor; Rated R; 98 minutes; Release date: April 3, 2009

CAST
Brian Weathersby	**Paul Dano**
Harriet Lolly	**Zooey Deschanel**
Al Lolly	**John Goodman**
Mr. Weathersby	**Ed Asner**
James Weathersby	**Robert Stanton**

Ian Roberts (John Weathersby), Jane Alexander (Mrs. Weathersby), Clarke Peters (Roger), Daniel Stewart Sherman (Kevin), Zach Galifianakis (Homeless Guy), Sean Dugan (Gary Wynkoop), Brian Avers (Larry Arbogast), Louis Ozawa Changchien (Matsubara), Frank Harts (Kenyatta Folds), Tatsuo Ichikawa (Nagata), Ilana Levine (Ducky Saltinstall), Susan Misner (Melanie Lolly), Kenji Nakano (Kanagae), Leven Rambin (Missy Thaxton), Matt Walton (Conner)

Unfulfilled by his work, Brian Weathersby, a salesman at a Swedish mattress company, spends a good portion of his day pursuing his goal of adopting a baby from China. His obsession subsides when he gets swept up in a romance with the lovely but misguided Harriet Lolly when she comes in to his store.

SUGAR

(SONY CLASSICS) Producers, Paul Mezey, Jamie Patricof, Jeremy Kipp Walker; Executive Producer/Editor, Anna Boden; Directors/Screenplay, Anna Boden, Ryan Fleck; Photography, Andrij Parekh; Designer, Elizabeth Mickle; Costumes, Erin Benach; Music, Michael Brook; Music Supervisor, Lynn Fainchtein; Casting, Cindy Tolan; an HBO Films presentation of a Journeyman Pictures/Hunting Lane Films production in association with Gowanus Projections; Dolby; Color; Rated R; 119 minutes; Release date: April 3, 2009

CAST
Miguel "Sugar" Santos	**Algenis Perez Soto**
Jorge Ramirez	**Rayniel Rufino**
Johnson	**Andre Holland**
Helen Higgins	**Ann Whitney**
Anne Higgins	**Ellary Porterfield**
Osvaldo	**Jaime Tirelli**
Alvarez	**Jose Rijo**
Stu Sutton	**Michael Gaston**

Alina Vargas (Reyna), Richard Bull (Earl Higgins), Kelvin Leonardo Garcia (Salvador), Joendy Pena Brown (Marcos), Karl Bury (Rudy Hubbard), Greg D'Agostino (Gregory the Delivery Man), Larry E. Donaldson (Michael Higgins), Barbara P. Engstrom (Hilary Higgins), Brandon Gorrell (Randy), Chris Harkins (Batter – Fight Scene), Taylor Hogue, Tomas Johansson, Alyssa Simmons, Tom Sponberg, Chelsea Zeleny (Baseball fans), Rita Kurtz (Dominican Baseball Fan), Eddie Martinez (Rafael), Cesar Minaya (Pedro), Sabien Minteer (Hardy, Team Mascot), Isaac Thomas Richer Smith (Clubby), Randolph Wehofer (Jack Jeffries), Michael Robert Yeager (Fan at Spring Training Game), Antonia Molina (Wife)

Dominican baseball player Miguel "Sugar" Santos hopes to parlay his status to similar success in America.

Ellary Porterfield, Algenis Perez Soto © Sony Pictures Classics

Alec Baldwin, Rory Culkin, Kieran Culkin, Jill Hennessy

Alec Baldwin, Timothy Hutton © Screen Media Films

LYMELIFE

(SCREEN MEDIA) Producers, Steven Martini, Barbara DeFina, Jon Cornick, Alec Baldwin, Michele Tayler, Angela Somerville; Executive Producers, Martin Scorsese, Leonard Loventhal; Co-Producers, Michael G. Jefferson, Jamin O'Brien, William Baldwin, Tiffany Nishimoto; Director, Derick Martini; Screenplay, Derick Martini, Steven Martini; Photography, Frank Godwin; Designer, Kelly McGehee; Costumes, Erika Munro; Music, Steven Martini; Editors, Derick Martini, Steven Martini, Mark Yoshikawa; a Martini Brothers production, in association with El Dorado Pictures and Cappa DeFina Productions; Dolby; Panavision; Color; Rated R; 95 minutes; Release date: April 8, 2009

CAST
Mickey Bartlett	**Alec Baldwin**
Jimmy Bartlett	**Kieran Culkin**
Scott Bartlett	**Rory Culkin**
Brenda Bartlett	**Jill Hennessy**
Charlie Bragg	**Timothy Hutton**
Melissa Bragg	**Cynthia Nixon**
Adrianna Bragg	**Emma Roberts**

Adam Scarimbolo (Todd O'Leary), Phillip Pennestri (Father Pazo), Logan Huffman (Blaze Salado), Derick Martini (Photographer), Steven Martini (Taxi Driver), Matthew Martini (Jimmy's Friend), Brandon Thane Wilson (Stewart)

A troubled Long Island teen must cope with his brother's decision to serve in the military, his angry dad and his neglected mom, while the girl of his desires deals with her own family problems.

DRAGONBALL: EVOLUTION

(20th CENTURY FOX) Producer, Stephen Chow; Executive Producer, Tim Van Rellim; Co-Producers, Rodney Liber, Rich Thorne; Director, James Wong; Screenplay, Ben Ramsey; Based on the graphic novel series *Dragonball* by Akira Toriyama, original manga published by Shonen Jump; Photography, Robert McLachlan; Designer, Bruton Jones; Costumes, Mayes C. Rubeo; Music, Brian Tyler; Editors, Matthew Friedman, Chris Willingham; Visual Effects Supervisor, Ariel Velasco Shaw; Visual Effects, Frantic Films, Hybride, Zoic Studios, Soho VFX; Special Makeup Effects, Alec Gillis, Tom Woodruff Jr.; Casting, John Papsidera; a Star Overseas production, in association with Ingenious Film Partners, Big Screen Productions; presented in association with Dune Entertainment III; Dolby; Super 35 Widescreen; Deluxe color; Rated PG; 85 minutes; Release date: April 10, 2009

CAST
Goku	**Justin Chatwin**
Master Roshi	**Chow Yun-Fat**
Bulma	**Emmy Rossum**
Chi Chi	**Jamie Chung**
Lord Piccolo	**James Marsters**
Yamcha	**Joon Park**
Mai	**Eriko Tamura**
Gohan	**Randall Duk Kim**
Sifu Norris	**Ernie Hudson**

Texas Battle (Carey Fuller), Megumi Seki (Seki), Ian Whyte (Oozaru), Richard Blake (Agundes), Jon Valera (Moreno), Rafael Valdez (Butler), Mike Wilson (Hildenbrand), Freddy Bouciegues (Palmer), Shavon Kirksey (Emi), Julian Sedgwick (Mr. Kingery), Luis Arrieta (Weaver), Gabriela de la Garza (Avatar), Rich E. Cordobes (Referee)

Goku receives a dragonball on his 18th birthday, which grants unusual power to anyone who can unite it with six other existing orbs.

Eriko Tamura, James Marsters © Twentieth Century Fox

Chow Yun-Fat, Justin Chatwin

Seth Rogen, Collette Wolf

Michael Peña, John Yuan, Seth Rogen, Jesse Plemons, Matt Yuan

Seth Rogen, Ray Liotta © Warner Bros.

Anna Faris, Seth Rogen

OBSERVE AND REPORT

(WARNER BROTHERS) Producer, Donald De Line; Executive Producers, Andrew Haas, Marty Ewing, Thomas Tull, Jon Jashni; Director/Screenplay, Jody Hill; Photography, Tim Orr; Designer, Chris Spellman; Costumes, Gary Jones; Music, Joseph Stephens; Editor, Zene Baker; Casting, Sheila Jaffe; a De Line Pictures production, presented in association with Legendary Pictures; Dolby; Color; Rated R; 86 minutes; Release date: April 10, 2009

CAST

Ronnie Barnhardt	**Seth Rogen**
Detective Harrison	**Ray Liotta**
Dennis	**Michael Peña**
Brandi	**Anna Faris**
Mark	**Dan Bakkedahl**
Charles	**Jesse Plemons**
John Yuen	**John Yuan**
Matt Yuen	**Matt Yuan**
Mom	**Celia Weston**
Nell	**Collette Wolfe**
Pervert	**Randy Gambill**
Bruce	**Alston Brown**
D-Rock	**Cody Midthunder**
Saddamn	**Aziz Ansari**
Reporter	**Deborah Brown**
Angry Store Owner	**Eddie Rouse**
Toast a Bun Manager	**Patton Oswalt**

Lauren A. Miller (Employee), Rafael Herrera (Janitor), Ben Best (Det. Nichols), William Sterchi (Department Store Manager), Robbie Hill (Tyler), Marlon Cunningham (Little Kid), Danny McBride (Caucasian Crackhead), Milos Milicevic (Random Crackhead), Antonia DeNardo (Sarah), Danielle Martin (Young Girl), David House (Policeman), Fran Martone (Psychologist), Gail L. Harrington (Flashed Lady), Cody Tyler Weselis, Wyatt Tipton, Shane Habberstad, Dylan Hice (Skateboarders), Lucy Hill (Makeup Counter Lady), Parker Ewing (Young Girl Shoplifter), Ivan Kraljevic (Mall Patron)

An unhinged mall security guard makes it his mission to put a stop to a flasher who has been stalking the premises.

THE MYSTERIES OF PITTSBURGH

(PEACE ARCH ENTERTAINMENT) Producers, Jason Mercer, Thor Benander, Michael London; Executive Producers, Peter Chiarelli, Bruna Papandrea, Claus Clausen, Omar Amanat, Marina Grasic, Jan Korbelin, Vicki Dee Rock, John Woldenberg; Director/Screenplay, Rawson Marshall Thurber; Based on the novel by Michael Chabon; Photography, Michael Barrett; Designer, Maher Ahmad; Costumes, Wendy Chuck; Music, Theodore Shapiro; Editor, Barbara Tulliver; Casting, Deborah Aquila; a Groundswell production in association with Scheherezade Film and Visitor Pictures; Dolby; Panavision; Color; Rated R; 95 minutes; Release date: April 10, 2009

CAST

Art Bechstein	**Jon Foster**
Cleveland Arning	**Peter Sarsgaard**
Jane Bellwether	**Sienna Miller**
Joseph Bechstein	**Nick Nolte**
Phlox Lombardi	**Mena Suvari**
Momo	**Omid Abtahi**
Keith	**Keith Michael Gregory**

Seth Adams (Feldman), Jack Baun, Jeff Hochendoner (Cops), Don Wadsworth (Class Instructor), Christian Hand (Punk Rock Bathroom Patron), Jarid Faubel (Mohawk Man), Tim Hartman (Restaurant Manager), Jocelyn Wrzosek (Townie), Patrick Jordan (Phlox's New Boyfriend), Stephen Liska (Jimmy Breezy), Marc Macaulay (Lenny Burns), Tommy Lafitte (Precinct Officer)

Anxious to chart his own destiny rather than follow in the footsteps of his gangster father, Art Bechstein stays on in Pittsburgh after college where he meets up with free-spirit musician Jane and her enigmatic boyfriend Cleveland.

Peter Sarsgaard, Sienna Miller © Peace Arch Entertainment

Steve "Lips" Kudlow © Abramorama

ANVIL! THE STORY OF ANVIL

(ABRAMORAMA) Producer, Rebecca Yeldham; Co-Producer/Photography, Chris Soos; Director, Sacha Gervasi; Music, Mat Dennis; Music Supervisor, Dana Sano; Editors, Jeff Renfroe, Andrew Dickler; a Little Dean and Ahimsa Films production; Dolby; Color; Sony HDcam; Not rated; 80 minutes; Release date: April 10, 2009

WITH

Steve "Lips" Kudlow, Robb Reiner, Nigel Hudson, Ivan Herd, Chris Tsangarides, Tiziana Arrigoni, Lars Ulrich, Lemmy, Slash, Kevin Goocher, Glenn Gyorffy, William Howell

A documentary on Canadian metal band Anvil.

Miley Cyrus, Emily Grace Reaves, Lucas Till © Disney Enterprises

Mitchel Musso, Moises Arias

Miley Cyrus

HANNAH MONTANA: THE MOVIE

(WALT DISNEY PICTURES) Producers, Alfred Gough, Miles Millar; Executive Producers, David Blocker, Michael Poryes, Steve Peterman; Co-Producer, Billy Ray Cyrus; Director, Peter Chelsom; Screenplay, Dan Berendsen; based on characters created by Michael Poryes, Rich Correll, Barry O'Brien; Photography, David Hennings; Designer, Caroline Hanania; Costumes, Christopher Lawrence; Music, John Debney; Editor, David Moritz; Visual Effects Supervisor, John Fragomeni; Casting, Lisa Beach, Sarah Katzman; a Millar/Gough Ink production; Dolby; Deluxe color; Rated G; 102 minutes; Release date: April 10, 2009

CAST

Hannah Montana/Miley Stewart	**Miley Cyrus**
Robby Ray Stewart	**Billy Ray Cyrus**
Lilly Truscott/Lola Luftnagle	**Emily Osment**
Jackson Stewart	**Jason Earles**
Oliver Oken/Mike Standley III	**Mitchell Musso**
Rico	**Moises Arias**
Travis Brody	**Lucas Till**
Vita	**Vanessa Williams**
Ruby	**Margo Martindale**
Oswald Granger	**Peter Gunn**
Lorelai	**Melora Hardin**
Derrick	**Jared Carter**
Mr. Bradley	**Barry Bostwick**

Beau Billingslea (Mayor), Katrina Hagger Smith (Mayor's Wife), Emily Grace Reaves (Cindy-Lou), Jane Carr (Lucinda), Taylor Swift, Tyra Banks (Themselves), Gary LeVox, Jay deMarcus, JoeDon Rooney (Rascal Flats), Joshua Childs (Store Manager), Rachel Woods (Phoebe Granger), Natalia Dyer (Clarissa Granger), Jerry Foster (Elderly Gentleman), Adam Gregory (Drew), Shawn Carter Peterson (Video Director), Jamal Sims (Rodeo Drive Dancer), John Will Clay (Volleyball Captain), D. Todd Hammond (Coach), Michael Cornacchia (Security Guard), Valorie Hubbard (Ticket Clerk), Tommy Barnes (Farmer's Market Vendor), Gary Schleimer (Distinguished Man), Jaci Cordell (Distinguished Woman), Jack Hoke (Bowtie Jack), Lisa Darr (Mother on the Pier), Paul Perri (Father on the Pier), Mario Carter (Beach Security Guard), Amber Hubert, Ashley Sundberg (Hannah Fans), Travis Allen Archer (Headset Flunkie), Cole S. McKay (Pastry Chef), Ben Hatchell, Chris O'Reilly, James Alexander (Skateboarders), Shane T. Anderson (Limo Driver)

Miley Stewart's career as a moonlighting pop star has wrecked havoc with her family and friends. Fed up, her dad drags her to a small Tennessee town to subject her to a dose of reality.

Melora Hardin, Billy Ray Cyrus

Alfre Woodard, Nicole Behaire

Alfre Woodard, Will Patton

Tim Blake Nelson

AMERICAN VIOLET

(SAMUEL GOLDWYN) Producer/Screenplay, Bill Haney; Executive Producer, Peter Newman; Co-Executive Producers, Jennifer Eplett, Sean Reilly, Tom R. Camp; Director, Tim Disney; Photography, Steve Yedlin; Designer, Monroe Kelly; Costumes, Caroline Eselin-Schaefer; Music, Teddy Castellucci; Music Supervisor, Jennifer Nash; Editors, Nancy Richardson, Curtiss Clayton, Terilyn A. Shropshire; Casting, Susan Shopmaker; an Uncommon Productions presentation; Dolby; Panavision; Technicolor; Rated PG-13; 103 minutes; Release date: April 17, 2009

CAST
Dee Roberts	**Nicole Beharie**
Sam Conroy	**Will Patton**
Alma Roberts	**Alfre Woodard**
Calvin Beckett	**Michael O'Keefe**
David Cohen	**Tim Blake Nelson**
Jerry Arnold	**Scott A. Martin**
Reverend Sanders	**Charles S. Dutton**

Malcolm Barrett (Byron White), Jackson Beals (Officer Carter), Michael Beasley (Tony Flair), Samantha Beaulieu (Mrs. Lloyd), Tody Bernard (Judge Pryor), Allen Boudreaux (Lawyer), Jeanne Bourgeois, Hunter McGregor, Jessie Blake Lough (Reporters), Andrew Buchler (Deposition Videographer), Kesha Bullard (Angry Woman), J. Omar Castro (Cisco), John Will Clay (Henry Franklin), Portia Cue (Laquathia), Daurice Cummings (Pedestrian), Roslyn D. Evans (Magnolia), Jon Eyez (Bar Owner), Rodney Hebert (Cisco's Diner Patron), Louis Herthum (Officer Smith), Elton LeBlanc (Restaurant Patron), Jerry Leggio (Norman), Anthony Mackie (Eddie Porter), Christopher McCann (Joe Fisher), Lance E. Nichols (Mr. Moss), Zardis Nichols (Gayzeen), Henry Pelitire (Texas State Trooper), Lyssa Prine (Deposition Stenographer), Ryan Reinike (Audio Dude), Tarra Riggs (Lavosha), Glenn Robin (Court Bailiff), Sue Rock (Elizabeth Beckett), C. Stuart Rome, Michael Wozniak (Bailiffs), Michael Scialabba (Thomas Willis), Janet Shea (Helen), Chaz Smith (Still Photographer), Terry Lee Smith (SWAT), Lindsay Soileau (Julie Beckett), Antoine Spillers (Mr. Roberts), Defecio Stoglin (Brian Green), Paul David Story (David Higgins), Deneen Tyler (Suzzannha), Jearl Vinot (County Sheriff), Tim Ware (Mark Shelby), David Warshofsky (Robert Foster), Karimah Westbrook (Claudia Johnson), Xzibit (Darrell Hughes), Richard Zeringue (Store Manager)

A single mother living in an all-black housing project decides to fight for her rights when she is unjustly arrested and held on drug charges.

Charles S. Dutton © Samuel Goldwyn Co.

17 AGAIN

(NEW LINE CINEMA) Producers, Adam Shankman, Jennifer Gibgot; Executive Producers, Toby Emmerich, Mark Kaufman, Keith Goldberg, Jason Barrett; Co-Producer, Dara Weintraub; Director, Burr Steers; Screenplay, Jason Filardi; Photography, Tim Suhrstedt; Designer, Garreth Stover; Costumes, Pamela Withers Chilton; Music, Rolfe Kent; Music Supervisor, Buck Damon; Editor, Padraic McKinley; Visual Effects Supervisor, Kelly Bumarger; Casting, Lisa Beach, Sarah Katzman; an Offspring Entertainment production; Distributed by Warner Brothers; Dolby; Super 35 Widescreen; Deluxe color; Rated PG-13; 102 minutes; Release date: April 17, 2009

Zac Efron, Sterling Knight

CAST

Mike O'Donnell (Teen)	**Zac Efron**
Scarlet O'Donnell (Adult)	**Leslie Mann**
Ned Gold (Adult)	**Thomas Lennon**
Mike O'Donnell (Adult)	**Matthew Perry**
Ned Gold (Teen)	**Tyler Steelman**
Scarlett (Teen)	**Allison Miller**
Alex O'Donnell	**Sterling Knight**
Maggie O'Donnell	**Michelle Trachtenberg**
Principal Jane Masterson	**Melora Hardin**
Janitor	**Brian Doyle-Murray**
Dom	**Adam Gregory**
Stan	**Hunter Parrish**
Samir	**Mario Cassem**

Katerina Graham (Jaime), Tiya Sircar (Samantha), Melissa Ordway (Lauren), Josie Lopez (Nicole), Jim Gaffigan (Coach Murphy), Randy Gordon (Photographer), Collette Wolfe (Wendy), Tommy Dewey (Roger), Lorna Scott (Secretary), Kodi Kitchen (Hostess), Ellis Williams (Bailiff), Diana-Maria Riva (Judge), Jeff Snyder (Waiter), Antonio Lewis Todd (Referee, 1989), Angee Hughes (Waitress), Ed Ackerman (School Cop), Will Schaub (Referee), Loren Lester (Mike's Lawyer), Alexander Goschin (Kid in Hallway), Nicole Sullivan (Naomi), Margaret Cho (Mrs. Dell), Larry Poindexter (Dean), Bubba Lewis (Dorky Kid at Ned's Party), Chris Valenti (Syracuse Scout, 1989), G. Lane Hillman (Kevin, 1989), Hope Riley (Girl), Jeanine Jackson (Scarlett's Lawyer), Gregory Sporleder (Ohio Scout), Keith Oney (Guy in Crowd), Leonard Wu (Kid, Office), Liana Blackburn, Lindsay Taylor, Danielle E. Hawkins, Shelby Rabara, Katrina Norman, Tiana Brown, Rhapsody Violetti, Tasha Monique Clark (Cheerleaders, 1989), Vanessa Lee Chester, Amber Estrada, Chanel "Coco" Malvar, Galen Hooks, Tyne Stecklein, Kiara Ely, Mihran Kirakosian, Dres Reid (Cheerleaders), Terrance Harrison (Mascot), Rachele Brooke Smith, Christopher Scott (Hammer Dancers), Eric McCoy (Dancer), Raymond Chacon (Jazz), Megan Galiber (Girl #2), Renee Krieg (ROTC Leader), Jordan Schatz (Mr. Adams), Jaclyn Matfus (Party Girl), Justin C. Todd (Football Player), Linda Miller (Janitor)

Leslie Mann, Nicole Sullivan

Mike O'Donnell feels that his life has not gone the way he wanted it to. When he finds himself magically turned back into his teenage self, he experiences the current day high school that his kids are attending.

Matthew Perry

Thomas Lennon, Melora Hardin © New Line Cinema

STATE OF PLAY

(UNIVERSAL) Producers, Andrew Hauptman, Tim Bevan, Eric Fellner; Executive Producers, Paul Abbott, Liza Chasin, Debra Hayward, E. Bennett Walsh; Co-Producer, Eric Hayes; Director, Kevin Macdonald; Screenplay, Matthew Michael Carnahan, Tony Gilroy, Billy Ray; Based on the BBC television series created by Paul Abbott; Photography, Rodrigo Prieto; Designer, Mark Friedberg; Costumes, Jacqueline West; Music, Alex Heffes; Music Supervisor, Nick Angel; Editor, Justine Wright; Casting, Avy Kaufman; a Working Title Films presentation, in association with Studio Canal and Relativity Media, of an Andell Entertainment/Bevan-Feller production; Dolby; Panavision; Technicolor; Rated PG-13; 127 minutes; Release date: April 17, 2009

CAST
Cal McAffrey — **Russell Crowe**
Stephen Collins — **Ben Affleck**
Della Frye — **Rachel McAdams**
Cameron Lynne — **Helen Mirren**
Anne Collins — **Robin Wright Penn**
Dominic Foy — **Jason Bateman**
Rep. George Fergus — **Jeff Daniels**

Michael Berresse (Robert Bingham), Harry Lennix (Detective Bell), Josh Mostel (Pete), Michael Weston (Hank), Barry Shabaka Henley (Gene Stavitz), Viola Davis (Dr. Judith Franklin), David Harbour (PointCorp Insider), Sarah Lord (Mandi Brokaw), Tuck Milligan (PointCorp Executive), Stephen Park (Chris Kawai), Brennan Brown (Andrew Pell), Maria Thayer (Sonia Baker), Wendy Makkena (Greer Thornton), Zoe Lister Jones (Jessy), Michael Jace (Officer Brown), Rob Benedict (Milt), LaDell Preston (Deshaun Stagg), Dan Brown (Vernon Sando), Katy Mixon (Rhonda Silver), Shane Edelman (D.A. Purcell), Maurice Burnice Harcum (Ben's Cashier), Cornell Womack, Nat Benchley (Junior Detectives), Gregg Binkley (Ferris), Trula Marcus (Carol), Carolyn Barrett (Policewoman Escorting Della), Wil Love (Iowan Congressman), John Badila (Mr. James), Brigid Cleary (Mrs. James), Joy Spears, Brandi Oglesby, Stacey Walker (Waitresses/Dancers), R.B. Brenner (Globe Production Manager), Lucia Navarro (Telemundo Reporter), Chris Matthews (MSNBC Reporter), Lou Dobbs (CNN Reporter), James Vance III (Reporter), Sharon Dugan (Business Woman), Noel Werking (Business Man), Rose Coleman (Jackie), Lee von Ernst (ICU Nurse), Richard Ruyle (Karaoke Singer), Susan Stuart Brazell (Karaoke Bar Hostess), Herbert "Chris" Gordon, Keith Anthony Garvin, Julie Carey, Eun Yang, Denae D'Arcy, Natasha Chugtai (News Reporters), Greg Graham (The Wolf), Eric Hatch (Peter), Josh Rhodes (The Hunter), David Copeland Goodman (Graves), Todd A. Langenfeld (Navy Commander Garner)

Journalists Cal McAffrey and Della Frye try to piece together the mystery behind the death of a young woman with whom Congressman Stephen Collins was having an affair.

Robin Wright Penn, Ben Affleck

Helen Mirren, Russell Crowe

Rachel McAdams

Jeff Daniels, Russell Crowe © Universal Studios

Charlotte d'Amboise

A Chorus Line cast © Sony Pictures Classics

Auditioners

EVERY LITTLE STEP

(SONY CLASSICS) Producers/Directors, James D. Stern, Adam Del Deo; Executive Producers, Douglas E. Hansen, Christopher C. Chen, John Breglio; Co-Producer, Eleanor Nett; Music, Marvin Hamlisch, Jane Antonia Cornish; Editors, Fernando Villena, Brad Fuller; an Endgame Entertainment presentation of a Vienna Waits/Endgame Entertainment production; Dolby; Color; DV; Rated PG-13; 93 minutes; Release date: April 17, 2009

WITH
Bob Avian, Charlotte d'Amboise, Jacques d'Amboise, Candy Ann Brown, Mara Davi, Natascia Diaz, Ramon Flowers, Jessica Lee Goldyn, Marvin Hamlisch, Megan Larche, Baayork Lee, J. Elaine Marcos, David Marquez, Donna McKechnie, Heather Parcells, Meredith Patterson, Alisan Porter, Rachelle Rak, German Santiago, Nikki Snelson, Yuka Takara, Jason Tam, Chryssie Whitehead

A documentary about the casting process for the 2006 Broadway revival of *A Chorus Line.*

Jason Tam

Yuka Takara

Terrence Howard, Channing Tatum

Brian White

FIGHTING

(ROGUE/UNIVERSAL) Producer, Kevin Misher; Executive Producers, Lisa Bruce, Andrew Rona; Director, Dito Montiel; Screenplay, Robert Munic, Dito Montiel; Photography, Stefan Czapsky; Designer, Therese Deprez; Costumes, Kurt and Bart; Music, David Wittman, Jonathan Elias; Editors, Jake Pushinsky, Saar Klein; Fight Coordinator, Mike Gunther; Casting, Amanda Mackey, Cathy Sandrich Gelfond; a Rogue Pictures presentation of a Misher Films production; Dolby; Color; Rated PG-13; 105 minutes; Release date: April 24, 2009

CAST
Shawn MacArthur	**Channing Tatum**
Harvey Boarden	**Terrence Howard**
Zulay Velez	**Zulay Henao**
Ajax	**Michael Rivera**
Ray Ray	**Flaco Navaja**
Z	**Peter Tambakis**
Martinez	**Luis Guzman**
Christopher Anthony	**Anthony DeSando**
Jack Dancing	**Roger Guenveur Smith**
Ean Hailey	**Brian White**

Ivan Martin (Stockbroker Jerry), Danny Mastrogiorgio (Trader Jim), Altagracia Guzman (Alba Guzmán), Gabrielle Pelucco (Lila), Angelic Zambrana (Kimo's Girl), Dante Nero (Kimo), Jim Coope (Roommate Sal), Melody Herman (Fine Claudette), Doug Yasuda (Jun Seoul), Cung Le (Dragon Le), Rich Pecci (Loud Club Wannabe), Nina Poon (Questionable Asian), David John Bernardo (Strong Pete), Manuel Cabral (Screaming Man), Christopher Swift (Father), Elias Swift (Son), John Cenatiempo (Big Construction Worker), Steven Randazzo (Toll Booth Clerk), Kimelisa Chomba Dunn (Crazy Mary), Jovan U. Hernandez (Little Boy), Jessica Castro, Michelle Gottschalk, Christina Llano (Flawless Women), Michael Early (Mr. Wilson), Louis Vanaria (Driver Charles), Fernando Limonta (Cooler Kid), Aram Lumley (Sleepy), Manuel Molina (Mannie/Giovanni), Clem Cheung (Korean Grocer), Julia Garro, Misha Hasiuk (Fine Russian Girls), Yuri Foreman (Russian Fighter Yuri), Peter Mele (Doorman Renee), Kelvin Coffey (Local), Jermel Wilson (Man in Cowhide Suit), Ksyn Cason (Fine Woman Shevonne), Berto Colon (Expensive Suit Man), Eleonore Hendricks (Waitress Riley), Marilyn Raphael (Old Woman), Ann McGowan (Woman Outside, Protester), Joel Nagle (Binghampton #1), Richard DeDomenico (Sydney), Fredric Ross-Wilmoth (Greek Diner Owner), Mahindra Persaud (Doorman), Chad Thompson (Business/Suitcase Guy), André Tavarez, Antonio Gonzalez, Ibn Dixon (Thieves), James Caver (Pink Bunny Man), Boris Talis (Announcer), Janet Paparazzo (Old Religious Woman), Will Cote Kruschwitz (Irate Customer), Leonard Hollinger (Text Message Man), Keith Greaves, Robert Humphrey, Shayshahn MacPherson (The Three Drummers)

Channing Tatum © Rogue/Universal

Zulay Henao

Harvey Boarden enlists two-bit street peddler Shawn MacArthur to participate in New York's underworld of bare-knuckle fighting.

Robert Downey Jr., Nelsan Ellis

Lisa Gay Hamilton, Jamie Foxx

THE SOLOIST

(DREAMWORKS/UNIVERSAL) Producers, Gary Foster, Russ Krasnoff; Executive Producers, Tim Bevan, Eric Fellner, Jeff Skoll, Patricia Whitcher; Director, Joe Wright; Screenplay, Susannah Grant; Based on the book by Steve Lopez; Photography, Seamus McGarvey; Designer, Sarah Greenwood; Costumes, Jacqueline Durran; Music, Dario Marianelli; Editor, Paul Tothill; a Krasnoff/Foster Entertainment production in association with Working Title Films, presented in association with StudioCanal and Participant Media; Distributed by Paramount; Dolby; Color; Rated PG-13; Release date: April 24, 2009

CAST

Nathaniel Anthony Ayers	**Jamie Foxx**
Steve Lopez	**Robert Downey Jr.**
Mary Weston	**Catherine Keener**
Graham Claydon	**Tom Hollander**
Jennifer Ayers-Moore	**Lisagay Hamilton**
Nathaniel, age 13-16	**Justin Martin**
Curt Reynolds	**Stephen Root**

Kokayi Ampah (Bernie Carpenter), Lemon Anderson (Uncle Tommy), Courtney Andre (Courtney), Orlando Ashley (LAMP Homeless Guy), Hazard Banner (Hazard), Melissa Black (Melissa), Darryl Black Sr. (Darryl), Troy Blendell (New Editor), J.J. Boone (Shouting Woman), Moya Brady (Barely Dressed Woman), Russell Brown (Russell), Michael Bunin (Adam Crane), Ralph Cole Jr. (Enraged Homeless Man), Marcos De Silvas (Mayor Antonio Villaraigosa), Quiana Farrow (Quiana), Steve Foster (Steve), Will Garret (Homeless Man), Tony Genaro (Globe Lobby Guard), Vivian Teresa George (Teresa), Noel G. (Winston Street), Bronwyn Hardy (Beauty Shop Girl), Linda Harris (Linda), Rachel Harris (Leslie Bloom), Lorinda Hawkins (Singing Woman), Kenneth Henry (Simone), Myia Hubbard (Young Jennifer), Joe Hernandez-Kolski, Paul Cruz, Halbert Bernal (EMTs), Isabel Hubmann (Laid-Off Employee), Valarie Hudspeth (Mama Grouch), Teri Hughes (Detroit), Patrick Kelly (Patrick), Kevin Michael Key (Homeless Transvestite), Susane E. Lee (Marisa), Lee Anna Levin (Leeann), Wayne Lopez (Cop with Tents), Jena Malone (Cheery Lab Tech), Joyre Manuel (Ashley), Annie McKnight (LAMP Advocate), Rob Nagle (Neil), Nick Nervies (Jennifer's Son), Iyanna Newborn (Miss Little John), Michael Nowak (Juilliard Conductor), Albert Oson (Bam Bam), Eshana O'Neal (Winston Street Prostitute), Kiana Parker (Kiana), Alejandro Patino (Construction Worker), Gladys Peters (Reception Nurse), Patricia Place (Cello Donor), Palma Lawrence Reed (ER Nurse), Octavia Spencer (Troubled Woman), Karole Selmon, Bonita Jefferson (Homeless Women), Bernadette Speakes (Homeless Lady), Octavia Spencer (Troubled Woman), Patrick Tatten (Paul Jr.), David Jean Thomas (Angry Homeless Man), Lorraine Toussaint (Flo Ayres), Annette Valley (Annette), Ilia Volok (Harry Barnoff), Charlie Weirauch (Atheist), Jacqueline Sue West (Jackie)

Robert Downey Jr., Jamie Foxx © DreamWorks/Paramount

Journalist Steve Lopez tries to help as disturbed, Juilliard-trained violinist who is living on the streets regain his life.

OBSESSED

(SCREEN GEMS) Producer, Will Packer; Executive Producers, Glenn S. Gainor, Mathew Knowles, Beyoncé Knowles, Earvin "Magic" Johnson, David Loughery, Damon Lee, Jeff Graup; Co-Producer, Nicholas Stern; Director, Steve Shill; Screenplay, David Loughery; Photography, Ken Seng; Designer, Jon Gary Steele; Costumes, Maya Lieberman; Music, Jim Dooley; Editor, Paul Seydor; Casting, Valorie Massalas, Ron Digman; a Rainforest Films production; Dolby; Deluxe color; Rated PG-13; 108 minutes; Release date: April 24, 2009

Ali Larter

CAST

Derek	**Idris Elba**
Sharon	**Beyoncé Knowles**
Lisa	**Ali Larter**
Ben	**Jerry O'Connell**
Marge	**Bonnie Perlman**
Reese	**Christine Lahti**
Kyle	**Nathan Myers, Nicolas Myers**
Patrick	**Matthew Humphreys**
Samantha	**Scout Taylor-Compton**
Hank	**Richard Ruccolo**
Security Man	**Bryan Ross**
Doctor	**Nelson Mashita**
Joe Gage	**Bruce McGill**
Roger	**Ron Roggé**
Hotel Clerk	**George Ketsios**

Meredith Roberts (Connie), Catherine Georges (Cocktail Waitress), Dana Cuomo (Rachel), Jon Rowland (John), Janora McDuffie (Nurse), Monica Ford (Sally Sloan)

An office temp sets out to make her married boss's life a living hell after he rejects her sexual advances.

Jerry O'Connell

Idris Elba, Ali Larter

Beyoncé Knowles, Idris Elba © Screen Gems

Kim Basinger, Billy Bob Thornton © Senator Distribution

THE INFORMERS

(SENATOR ENTERTAINMENT) Producer, Marco Weber; Executive Producers, Bret Easton Ellis, Vanessa Coifman, Brian Young, Jere Hausfater, Nicholas Jarecki; Director, Gregor Jordan; Screenplay, Bret Easton Ellis, Nicholas Jarecki; Based on the novel by Bret Easton Ellis; Photography, Petra Korner; Designer, Cecelia Montiel; Costumes, Sophie De Rakoff; Music, Christopher Young; Music Supervisor, Justin Meldal-Johnsen; Editor, Robert Brakey; Casting, John Papsidera; a Marco Weber production; Dolby; Super 35 Widescreen; Color; Rated R; 98 minutes; Release date: April 24, 2009

CAST

William Sloan	**Billy Bob Thornton**
Laura Sloan	**Kim Basinger**
Peter	**Mickey Rourke**
Cheryl Laine	**Winona Ryder**
Graham Sloan	**Jon Foster**
Christie	**Amber Heard**
Roger	**Rhys Ifans**
Les Price	**Chris Isaak**
Martin	**Austin Nichols**
Tim Price	**Lou Taylor Pucci**

Mel Raido (Bryan Metro), Brad Renfro (Jack), Theo Rossi (Spaz), Milena Arango (Miss Nebraska), Suzanne Ford (Bruce's Mom), Aaron Himelstein (Raymond), Simone Kessell (Nina Metro), Diego Klattenhoff (Dirk), Noli McCool (Joe), Katy Mixon (Patty), Daniel Rosenberg (Rocko), Angela Sarafyan (Mary), Peter Scanavino (Leon), Jessica Stroup (Rachel), Fernando Consagra (Bruce), Germán Tripel (Bryan's Guitarist), Cameron Goodman (Susan Sloan), Diego Leske (Gary Gray), Stefanie Neukirch (Darlene), Brady Matthews (Maitre D'), Diego Klattenhoff (Dirk)

A glimpse into the unhappy lives of some superficial Los Angelenos circa 1983, including a Hollywood executive and his pill-popping wife; a kidnapper; and a self-destructive rock star.

TYSON

(SONY CLASSICS) Producers, James Toback, Damon Bingham; Executive Producers, Mike Tyson, Harlan Werner, Nicholas Jarecki, Henry Jarecki, Bob Yari, Carmelo Anthony, David Haines; Co-Producers, Warren Farnes, Bill Newcomb Salaam Remi; Director, James Toback; Photography, Larry McConkey; Music, Salaam Remi; Editor, Aaron Yanes; a Fyodor Productions and Wild Bunch presentation; DR Group Color; HD; Rated R; 90 minutes; Release date: April 24, 2009

WITH
Monica Turner, Mike Tyson

A documentary on the turbulent life and career of former heavyweight champion Mike Tyson.

Mike Tyson © Sony Pictures Classics

X-MEN ORIGINS: WOLVERINE

(20TH CENTURY FOX) Producers, Lauren Shuler Donner, Ralph Winter, Hugh Jackman, John Palermo; Executive Producers, Richard Donner, Stan Lee; Co-Producer, Louis G. Freidman; Director, Gavin Hood; Screenplay, David Benioff, Skip Woods; Photography, Donald M. McAlpine; Designer, Barry Robinson; Costumes, Louise Mingenbach; Music, Harry Gregson-Williams; Editors, Nicolas De Toth, Megan Gill; Visual Effects Supervisor, Patrick McClung; Visual Effects, Hydraulx, Soho VFX, Luma Pictures, Method Studios, Rising Sun Pictures; Special Makeup Effects, Alec Gillis, Tom Woodruff Jr.; Stunts, Glenn Boswell, Dean Choe, Michael Mitchell; a Donners' Co., Seed production, presented in association with Marvel Entertainment; Dolby; Panavision; Deluxe color; Rated PG-13; 107 minutes; Release date: May 1, 2009

CAST
Logan/Wolverine	**Hugh Jackman**
Victor Creed/Sabretooth	**Liev Schreiber**
Gen. William Stryker	**Danny Huston**
John Wraith	**Will.i.am**
Kayla Silverfox	**Lynn Collins**
Fred Dukes/Blob	**Kevin Durand**

Dominic Monaghan (Chris Bradley/Bolt), Taylor Kitsch (Remy LeBeau/Gambit), Daniel Henney (David North/Agent Zero), Ryan Reynolds (Wade Wilson), Scott Adkins (Weapon XI), Tim Pocock (Scott Summers), Julia Blake (Heather Hudson), Max Cullen (Travis Hudson), Troye Sivan (Young James Howlett), Michael-James Olsen (Young Victor Creed), Peter O'Brien (John Howlett), Aaron Jeffrey (Thomas Logan), Alice Parkinson (Elizabeth Howlett), Phil Patterson (Firing Squad Leader), Anthony Gee (Carnival Guy), Adelaide Clemens (Carnival Girl), Karl Beattie (School Child), Tom O'Sullivan (Logging Supervisor), Myles Pollard (Phelan), Stephen Anderton (Marcuse), Chris Sadrinna (Van Mier), Septimus Caton (Bartender), Matthew Dale (Surgeon), Nathin Butler, Peter Barry (Male Nurses), David Ritchie (Dr. Abraham Cornelius), Asher Keddie (Dr. Carol Frost), Socratis Otto (Lead Technician – Alkali Lake), Stephen Leeder (Gen. Munson), James D. Dever (Platoon Leader), Martin Obuga (Muttering Man), Rita Affua Connell (Nervous African Woman), John Shrimpton (Stryker Aide), Henry Browne (Curtis), Tahyna Tozzi (Emma Frost), Daniel Negreanu (Poker Player #1), Alex Davies (Woman of the Night), Don Battee (Huge Doorman), Evan Sturrock (Drunken Man in Alley), Rob Flanagan (Driver #1), Hakeem Kae-Kazim (African Businessman), Alison Araya (Teacher), Eric Breker (Special Forces Commander), Eileen Bui (Vietnamese Child #1), Adrian Hughes, Byron Chief-Moon (Hunters), Mike Dopud (Vietnam Army Officer #1), Beatrice Ilg, Kanako Takegishi (Waitresses), Panou (Tank Soldier), Johnson Phan (Vietnamese Man), Elizabeth Thai (Vietnamese Woman), Jade Tang, Joelle Tang (Mutant Twins), Patrick Stewart (Prof. Charles Xavier)

Logan, a mutant whose knuckles are equipped with retractable blades, reluctantly consents to Gen. Stryker's top-secret experiment that will render him with super human strength, and allow him to do battle with his deadly brother, Victor, who was responsible for the death of Logan's girlfriend.

Ryan Reynolds

Hugh Jackman, Liev Schreiber

Tahyna Tozzi, Lynn Collins

Taylor Kitsch © Twentieth Century Fox

Tom Bastounes, Guy Van Swearingen

Kelly Macdonald

Michael Keaton, Kelly Macdonald © Samuel Goldwyn Co.

THE MERRY GENTLEMAN

(SAMUEL GOLDWYN CO.) Producers, Paul J. Duggan, Tom Bastounes, Steven A. Jones; Co-Producer, Christina Varotsis; Director, Michael Keaton; Screenplay, Ron Lazzeretti; Photography, Chris Seager; Designer, Jennifer Dehghan; Costumes, Susan Kaufmann; Music, Edward Shearmur; Editors, Howard E. Smith, Grant Myers; Casting, Rachel Tenner, Mickie Paskal, Jennifer S. Rudnicke; a Southwater Pictures production; Dolby; Panavision; Color; Rated R; 99 minutes; Release date: May 1, 2009

CAST
Frank Logan	**Michael Keaton**
Kate Frazier	**Kelly Macdonald**
Dave Murcheson	**Tom Bastounes**
Diane	**Darlene Hunt**
Billy Goldman	**Guy Van Swearingen**
Mr. Weiss	**William Dick**
Michael	**Bobby Cannavale**

Mike Bradecich (Jerry), Debbi Burns (Office Worker at Christmas Party), Maritza Cabrera, Gerald O. Heller, Toni-Marie Spera, John Thurner (Restaurant Patrons), Jay Disney (Drunken Businessman), Mike Falevits (Guy at Party #1), Sean Fortunato (Ted), Shaun Gayle (Doctor), Lori Ann Gerdisch, Lisa Wolf (Co-Workers), Steven H. Hansen (MOB Businessman), Randall Jones (Customer), Bob Kolbey (Office Party Guest), Joseph Mazurk (Lawyer), Doug McDade (Sleeping Man), Greg Mills (Steve), Aleh Neliubin (Yoga Guru), Larry Neumann Jr. (Lester), Henry Sandifer (Business Professional), David Dino Wells Jr. (Passerby)

An office worker who has recently left her abusive husband finds herself drawn to an ailing hitman, to whose recent job she had been a witness.

Bobby Cannavale

GHOSTS OF GIRLFRIENDS PAST

(NEW LINE CINEMA) Producers, Jon Shestack, Brad Epstein; Executive Producers, Toby Emmerich, Cale Boyter, Samuel. J. Brown, Mark Waters, Jessica Tuckinsky, Marcus Viscidi; Co-Producer, Ginny Brewer; Director, Mark Waters; Screenplay, Jon Lucas, Scott Moore; Photography, Daryn Okada; Designer, Cary White; Costumes, Denise Wingate; Music, Rolfe Kent; Editor, Bruce Green; Casting, Marci Liroff; a Jon Shestack/Panther production; Distributed by Warner Brothers; Dolby; Panavision; Deluxe color; Rated PG-13; 100 minutes; Release date: May 1, 2009

Lacey Chabert, Matthew McConaughey

CAST

Connor Mead	**Matthew McConaughey**
Jenny Perotti	**Jennifer Garner**
Uncle Wayne	**Michael Douglas**
Paul Mead	**Breckin Meyer**
Sandra	**Lacey Chabert**
Sgt. Volkom	**Robert Forster**
Vondra Volkom	**Anne Archer**
Allison Vandermeersh	**Emma Stone**
Melanie	**Noureen DeWulf**
Brad	**Daniel Sunjata**

Rachel Boston (Deena the Bridesmaid), Camille Guaty (Donna the Bridesmaid), Amanda Walsh (Denice the Bridesmaid), Emily Foxler (Nadja), Catherine Haena Kim (Charlece), Noa Tishby (Kiki), Logan Miller (Teenage Connor), Christa B. Allen (Teenage Jenny), Olga Maliouk (Ghost of Girlfriends Future), Rachelle Wood (Brunette Lingerie Model), Erin Wyatt (Blonde Lingerie Model), Stephanie Oum (Kako), Micah Sherman, Albert J. Chan, Michael Anastasia (Groomsmen), Paul Cassell (Wedding Guest Jeff), Dan Whelton (Foyer Bartender), Devin Brochu (Young Connor), Kasey Russell (Young Jenny), Scott Powers (Connor's Dad), Heather Wilde (Connor's Mom), Michael R. Pouliott (Parents' Funeral Priest), Chad Mountain (D.J.), Samantha Goober (Jenny's Friend Marissa), Alyssa McCourt (Jenny's Friend Clarissa), Sam Byrne (Pete Hastings), Gina Gesamondo (Ice Cold Blonde), Toni Saladna (Slapping Brunette), Abigail Kuklis (Blonde Club Model), Paula Merritt (Brunette Club Model), Kortney Adams (Jenny's Colleague), Cindy Lentol (Amy the Stewardess), Kimberly Carvalho, Ashley Carvalho (Bar Twins), Travis Clough (Bar Man "Shawna"), Jasmine Tang (Chinese Bar Woman), Genevieve Glenn ("Two Days" Bar Woman), Farah Casis ("For an Hour" Bar Woman), Lauren Tangard ("48 Seconds" Bar Woman), Layla Hosseini ("In Your Car" Bar Woman), Quiana Grant ("On Your Car" Bar Woman), Taylar Eliza Bunts ("Washed Your Car" Bar Woman), Munjeet Geyer ("Never Called Again" Bar Woman), Erin McParland (Pageant Queen Bar Woman), Allyssa Maurice ("Jenny" Bar Woman), Alicia Barrett (French Bar Woman), Natalie Alain Loisou (Dominatrix Bar Woman), Tom Kemp (Wedding Minister), Stephen L. Russell (Connor Funeral Minister), Tyler Christopher (Snow Shoveling Kid), Lexi Lawson (Wedding Band Singer), Artie Sgaraglio, J. Levine, Michael Hannigan, Robert Ellis (Wedding Band)

Michael Douglas, Matthew McConaughey © New Line Cinema

A marriage-phobic womanizer is visited by three ghosts of girlfriends past, present, and future to show him the error of his ways.

Matthew McConaughey, Daniel Sunjata, Jennifer Garner

Emma Stone, Matthew McConaughey

Hiam Abbass, Gael García Bernal © Focus Features

Tilda Swinton, Isaach De Bankolé

THE LIMITS OF CONTROL

(FOCUS FEATURES) Producers, Stacey Smith, Gretchen McGowan; Executive Producer, Jon Kilik; Director/Screenplay, Jim Jarmusch; Photography, Christopher Doyle; Designer, Eugenio Caballero; Costumes, Bina Daigeler; Music, Boris; Editor, Jay Rabinowitz; Casting, Ellen Lewis; a PointBlank production, presented in association with Entertainment Farm; Dolby; Deluxe color; Rated R; 116 minutes; Release date: May 1, 2009

CAST

Lone Man	Isaach De Bankolé
Creole	Alex Descas
French	Jean-François Stévenin
Violin	Luis Tosar
Nude	Paz de la Huerta
Blonde	Tilda Swinton
Molecules	Youki Kudoh
Guitar	John Hurt
Mexican	Gael Garcia Bernal

Óscar Jaenada (Waiter), Hiam Abbass (Driver), Bill Murray (American), Héctor Colomé (Second American), Marísa Isasi (Flamenco Club Waitress), Norma Yessenia Paladines (Flight Attendant), Alexander Muñoz Biggie, Cristina Sierra Sánchez, Pablo Lucas Ortega (Street Kids), La Truco (Flamenco Dancer), Talegón de Córdoba (Flamenco Singer), Jorge Rodriguez Padilla (Flamenco Guitarist)

A stoic hit man arrives in Spain to complete his latest assignment.

NEXT DAY AIR

(SUMMIT) Producers, Scott Aronson, Inny Clemons; Executive Producers, Bryan Turner, Shaun Livingston, Steve Markoff, Bruce McNall, Steve Belser; Co-Producers, Donald Faison, Melina Kevorkian, Gerald Rawles; Director, Benny Boom; Screenplay, Blair Cobbs; Photography, David Armstrong; Designer, Bruton Jones; Costumes, Rita McGhee; Music, The Elements; Music Supervisor, Paul Stewart; Editor, David Checel; Stunts, Julius LeFlore; Casting, Robi Reed; a Melee Entertainment production in association with A-Mark Entertainment, Rock Capital Films, Secret Society Films; Dolby; Color; Rated R; 84 minutes; Release date: May 8, 2009

CAST

Leo	Donald Faison
Brody	Mike Epps
Guch	Wood Harris
Shavoo	Omari Hardwick
Bodega	Emilio Rivera
Buddy	Darius McCrary
Jesus	Cisco Reyes

Yasmin Deliz (Chita), Lobo Sebastian (Rhino), Malik Barnhardt (Hassie), Mos Def (Eric), Debbie Allen (Ms. Jackson), Lauren London (Ivy), Jo D. Jonz (Wade), Shawn Michael Howard (Derrick), Peedi Crakk (Hector), Lombardo Boyar (Carlos), Barry "Cassidy" Reese (Cass), Inny Clemons (Deuce), Alexandra Merejo (Shavoo's Girl), Sundy Carter (On Scene News Reporter), Trinidad Mann, Ravyn Douglas (Fine Women), Madison Shockley, Kevin Benton (Old Men), Brizona Gayles (Security Guard), Gerald Rawles (Bank Manager), Clarence B. Douglas (The Elevator Guy), Shannen "Lacey" Franklin (Kera), Christina Ly (Kera's Friend)

A stoned courier accidentally delivers a stash of cocaine to a pair of inept bank robbers, causing the intended recipient, a dangerous drug dealer, to seek revenge.

Darius McCrary, Omari Hardwick © Summit Entertainment

STAR TREK

(PARAMOUNT) Producers, J.J. Abrams, Damon Lindelof; Executive Producers, Bryan Burk, Jeffrey Chernov, Roberto Orci, Alex Kurtzman; Director, J.J. Abrams; Screenplay, Roberto Orci, Alex Kurtzman; Based on *Star Trek* created by Gene Roddenberry; Photography, Dan Mindel; Designer, Scott Chambliss; Costumes, Michael Kaplan; Music, Michael Giacchino; Editors, Maryann Brandon, Mary Jo Markey; Visual Effects & Animation, Industrial Light & Magic; a Spyglass Entertainment presentation of a Bad Robot production; Dolby; Panavision; Rated PG-13; 126 minutes; Release date: May 8, 2009

CAST

James T. Kirk	**Chris Pine**
Spock	**Zachary Quinto**
Spock Prime	**Leonard Nimoy**
Nero	**Eric Bana**
Captain Christopher Pike	**Bruce Greenwood**
Dr. Leonard "Bones" McCoy	**Karl Urban**
Nyota Uhura	**Zoë Saldana**
Montgomery "Scotty" Scott	**Simon Pegg**
Hikaru Sulu	**John Cho**
Pavel Chekov	**Anton Yelchin**
Sarek	**Ben Cross**
Amanda Grayson	**Winona Ryder**
George Kirk	**Chris Hemsworth**
Winona Kirk	**Jennifer Morrison**
Gaila	**Rachel Nichols**
Captain Robau	**Faran Tahir**
Ayel	**Clifton Collins Jr.**
Officer Pitts	**Antonio Elias**
Tactical Officer	**Sean Gerace**
Young Kirk	**Jimmy Bennett**
Young Spock	**Jacob Kogan**
Admiral Richard Barnett	**Tyler Perry**
Admiral James Komack	**Ben Binswagner**

Randy Pausch, Tavarus Conley, Jeff Castle (Kelvin Crew Members), Tim Griffin (Kelvin Engineer), Freda Foh Shen (Kelvin Helmsman), Katarzyna Kowalczyk (Kelvin Alien), Jason Brooks (Romulan Helmsman), Sonita Henry (Kelvin Doctor), Kelvin Yu, Marta Martin (Medical Technicians), Billy Brown (Med Evac Pilot), Greg Grunberg (Voice of Stepdad), Spencer Daniels (Johnny), Jeremy Fitzgerald (Iowa Cop), Zoe Chernov, Max Chernov (Vulcan Students), James Henrie, Colby Paul, Cody Klop (Vulcan Bullies), Akiva Goldsman, Anna Katarina (Vulcan Council Members), Douglas Tait (Long Face Bar Alien), Tony Guma (Lew the Bartender), Gerald W. Abrams, James McGrath Jr. (Barflies), Jason Matthew Smith, Marcus Young (Burly Cadets), Bob Clendenin (Shipyard Worker), Darlena Tejeiro (Flight Officer), Reggie Lee, Jeffrey Byron (Test Administrators), Jonathan Dixon (Simulator Tactical Officer), Margot Farley (College Council Stenographer), Paul McGillion, Lisa Vidal (Barracks Officers), Alex Nevil (Shuttle Officer), Kimberly Arland, Sufe M. Bradshaw, Jeff Chase (Cadet Aliens), Charlie Haugk, Nana Hill, Michael Saglimbeni, John Blackman, Jack Millard, Shaela Luter, Sabrina Morris, Michelle Parylak (Enterprise Crew Members), Oz Perkins (Enterprise Communications Officer), Amanda Foreman (Hannity), Michael Berry Jr. (Romulan Tactical Officer), Lucia Rijker (Romulan Communications Officer), Pasha Lychnikoff (Romulan Commander), Matthew Beisner, Neville Page, Jesper Inglis (Romulan Crew Members), Greg Ellis (Chief Engineer Olson), Marlene Forte (Transport Chief), Leonard O. Turner, Mark Bramhall, Ronald F. Hoiseck, Irene Roseen, Jeff O'Haco (Vulcan Elders), Scottie Thompson (Nero's Wife), Deep Roy (Keensar), Majel Barrett Roddenberry (Starflett Computer Voice)

The story of how rebellious James T. Kirk and half-Vulcan Spock became captain and first officer of the *U.S.S. Enterprise*, while battling a Romulan bent on destruction. Prequel to the 1966-69 NBC series and the several Paramount theatrical features featuring the original television cast that were produced between 1979 and 1991. Leonard Nimoy, from that series and those films, repeats his role as Spock.

2009 Academy Award Winner for Best Makeup.

This film received additional Oscar nominations for visual effects, sound mixing, sound effects editing.

Zachary Quinto

Simon Pegg

Chris Pine

Chris Pine

Anton Yelchin, Chris Pine, Simon Pegg, Karl Urban, John Cho, Zoë Saldana

Chris Pine, John Cho © Paramount Pictures

Zachary Quino, Chris Pine

Eric Bana

Bruce Greenwood

Anton Yelchin

Tom Hanks, Ayelet Zurer, Thure Lindhardt, Ewan McGregor

Armin Mueller-Stahl, Ewan McGregor © Columbia Pictures

Tom Hanks, Ayelet Zurer

Tom Hanks, Ayelet Zurer

ANGELS & DEMONS

(COLUMBIA) Producers, Brian Grazer, Ron Howard, John Calley; Executive Producers, Todd Hallowell, Dan Brown; Director, Ron Howard; Screenplay, David Koepp, Akiva Goldsman; Based on the novel by Dan Brown; Photography, Salvatore Totino; Designer, Allan Cameron; Costumes, Daniel Orlandi; Music, Hans Zimmer; Editors, Dan Hanley, Mike Hill; Visual Effects Supervisor, Angus Bickerton; Casting, Jane Jenkins, Janet Hirshenson, Michelle Lewitt, Beatrice Kurger, Debbie McWilliams; an Imagine Entertainment presentation of a Brian Grazer/John Calley production; Dolby; Super 35 Widescreen; Deluxe color; Rated PG-13; 138 minutes; Release date: May 15, 2009

CAST

Robert Langdon	**Tom Hanks**
Camerlengo Patrick McKenna	**Ewan McGregor**
Vittoria Vetra	**Ayelet Zurer**
Commander Richter	**Stellan Skarsgård**
Inspector Olivetti	**Pierfrancesco Favino**
Assassin	**Nikolaj Lie Kaas**
Cardinal Strauss	**Armin Mueller-Stahl**
Chartrand	**Thure Lindhardt**
Claudio Vincenzi	**David Pasquesi**
Father Simeon	**Cosimo Fusco**
Lt. Valentini	**Victor Alfieri**
Cardinal Lamasse	**Franklin Amobi**
Cardinal Ebner	**Curt Lowens**
Cardinal Guidera	**Bob Yerkes**
Cardinal Baggia	**Marco Fiorini**

Carmen Argenziano (Silvano Bentivoglio), Howard Mungo (Cardinal Yoruba), Rance Howard (Cardinal Beck), Steve Franken (Cardinal Colbert), Gino Conforti (Cardinal Pugini), Elya Baskin (Cardinal Petrov), Richard Rosetti (Conclave Cardinal), Silvano Marchetto (Conclave Cardinal), Thomas Morris (Urs Weber), Jonas Fisch (Adrian Bachman), August Fredrik, Ben Bela Böhm, Paul Schmitz (Swiss Guardsmen), Jeff Boehm (Swiss Guard Blue), Xavier J. Nathan (Philippe), Steve Kehela (American Reporter), Urusal Brooks, Rashmi (British Reporters), Yan Cui (Chinese Reporter), Fritz Michel (French Reporter), Maria Cristina Heller, Pascal Petardi (Italian Reporters), Yesenia Adame (Mexican Reporter), Kristof Konrad (Polish Reporter), Masasa Moyo (South African Reporter), Ed F. Martin (South American Reporter), Cheryl Howard, Endre Hules, Norbert Weisser (CERN Scientists), Shelby Zemanek (Little Girl in Square), Vanna Salviati, Raffi Di Blasio (Protesters), Todd Schneider, Roberto Donati, Rocco Passafaro, Emanuele Secci (Carabinieris), Anna Katarina (Docent), James Ritz, Felipe Torres (Tourists)

Symbologist Robert Langdon is called upon to help track down the Illuminati, a secret society who have kidnapped three cardinals, with the intention of killing one every hour before destroying the Vatican. Sequel to the 2006 film *The Da Vinci Code* with Tom Hanks repeating his role.

MANAGEMENT

(SAMUEL GOLDWYN) Producers, Sidney Kimmel, Wyck Godfrey, Marty Bowen; Executive Producers, William Horberg, Bruce Toll, Jim Tauber, Nan Morales, Jennifer Aniston; Director/Screenplay, Stephen Belber; Photography, Eric Edwards; Designer, Judy Becker; Costumes, Christopher Lawrence; Music, Mychael Danna, Rob Simonsen; Editor, Kate Sanford; an Imagine Entertainment and Sidney Kimmel Entertainment presentation of a Temple Hill production; Dolby; Deluxe color; Rated R; 93 minutes; Release date: May 15, 2009

CAST

Sue Claussen	**Jennifer Aniston**
Mike	**Steve Zahn**
Trish	**Margo Martindale**
Jerry	**Fred Ward**
Al	**James Hiroyuki Liao**
Jango	**Woody Harrelson**
Corporate Bliss Receptionist	**Katie O'Grady**
Marissa	**Yolanda Suarez**
Jed	**Kevin Heffernan**
Businessman	**Don Stewart Burns**
Colleague	**Kimberly Howard**
Wally	**Collin Crowley**
Priest	**Gilberto Martin del Campo**
Jack	**Mark Boone Junior**
Bus Driver	**Garfield Wedderburn**
Barry	**Josh Lucas** (billed as "Easy Dent")

Dominic Fumusa (Stan Ball), Tzi Ma (Truc Quoc), Joan Riordan (Mary), Robert Projansky, Jerry Foster (Homeless Men), Yugin Wang (Betty)

A lonely motel clerk falls in love with a sales rep stopping at his establishment, going so far as to track her down at her place of business when she returns home.

Jennifer Aniston, Steve Zahn

Jennifer Aniston, Steve Zahn

Woody Harrelson

Jennifer Aniston, Steve Zahn © Samuel Goldwyn Co.

THE BROTHERS BLOOM

(SUMMIT) Producers, Ram Bergman, James D. Stern; Executive Producers, Wendy Japhet, Douglas E. Hansen; Co-Producer, Tom Karnowski; Director/Screenplay, Rian Johnson; Photography, Steve Yedlin; Designer, Jim Clay; Costumes, Beatrix Aruna Pasztor; Music, Nathan Johnson; Music Supervisor, Brian Reitzell; Editor, Gabriel Wrye; Casting, Shannon Makhanian, Mary Vernieu; a Ram Bergman production, presented with Endgame Entertainment; Dolby; Panavision; FotoKem color; Rated PG-13; 109 minutes; Release date: May 15, 2009

CAST

Penelope Stamp	**Rachel Weisz**
Bloom	**Adrien Brody**
Stephen	**Mark Ruffalo**
Bang Bang	**Rinko Kikuchi**
Diamond Dog	**Maximilian Schell**
The Curator	**Robbie Coltrane**
Narrator	**Ricky Jay**
Young Bloom	**Zachary Gordon**
Young Stephen	**Max Records**
Charleston	**Andy Nyman**
The Duke	**Noah Segan**
Rose	**Nora Zehetner**
Himself	**Ram Bergman**
Apple Cart Vendor	**Craig Johnson**
Albino	**Dubravko Jovanovic**

Esme Tyler (Young Girl), Jovan Vitas (Young Boy), Ana Sofrenovic (Charleston's Wife), Vladimir Kulhavy (Chief of Police), Alek Rodic (Snack Car Attendant), Josif Tatic (Oafish Foster Father), Slobodan Custic (Foster Dad), Branka Pujic (Foster Mom), George Bocchetti, Elis Derham (Excited Boys), Joseph Gordon-Levitt, Lukas Haas (Bar Patrons)

Eager to leave his life of swindling behind, Bloom agrees to participate in one last con with his brother Stephen, targeting eccentric heiress Penlope Stamp.

Adrien Brody, Mark Ruffalo

Adrien Brody, Rachel Weisz © Summit Entertainment

Adrien Brody, Rachel Weisz, Mark Ruffalo

Rinko Kikuchi, Mark Ruffalo, Robbie Coltrane

Bryce Dallas Howard, Christian Bale, Moon Bloodgood

Christian Bale

TERMINATOR SALVATION

(WARNER BROTHERS) Producers, Moritz Borman, Jeffrey Silver, Victor Kubicek, Derek Anderson; Executive Producers, Mario F. Kassar, Andrew G. Vajna, Peter D. Graves, Dan Lin, Jeanne Allgood, Joel B. Michaels; Co-Producer, Chantal Feghali; Director, McG; Screenplay, John Brancato, Michael Ferris; Photography, Shane Hurlburt; Designer, Martin Laing; Costumes, Michael Wilkinson; Music, Danny Elfman; Editor, Conrad Buff; Visual Effects Supervisor, Charles Gibson; Visual Effects Coordinator, Bill Sturgeon; Visual Effects, Industrial Light & Magic, Asylum, Rising Sun Pictures, Pacific Title and Art Studio, Matte World Digital; Stunts, Tom Struthers; Casting, Justine Baddeley, Kim Davis Wagner; a Halcyon Co. presentation of a Mortiz Borman production, in association with Wonderland Sound and Vision; Dolby; Super 35 Widescreen; Technicolor; Rated PG-13; 116 minutes; Release date: May 21, 2009

CAST

John Connor	**Christian Bale**
Marcus Wright	**Sam Worthington**
Blair Williams	**Moon Bloodgood**
Dr. Serena Kogan	**Helena Bonham Carter**
Kyle Reese	**Anton Yelchin**
Star	**Jadagrace Berry**
Kate Connor	**Bryce Dallas Howard**
Barnes	**Common (Lonnie Rashid Lynn)**
Virginia	**Jane Alexander**
General Ashdown	**Michael Ironside**
General Losenko	**Ivan G'Vera**
Morrison	**Chris Browning**
David	**Dorian Nkono**
Lisa	**Beth Bailey**
Mark	**Victor Ho**

Buster Reeves (Tunney), Kevin Wiggins (Gen. Olsen), Greg Serano (Hideki), Po Chan (Naima), Babak Tafti (Malik), Bruce McIntosh (Priest), Treva Etienne (Len), Dylan Kenin (Turnbull), Michael Papajohn (Carnahan), Chris Ashworth (Richter), David Midthunder, Emerson Brooks, Diego Lopez (Soldiers), Greg Plitt (Hybrid Male), Omar Paz Trujillo (Guard #2), Terry Crews (Capt. Jericho), Zach McGowan (Soldier on Osprey), Isaac Kappy (Barbarosa), Boots Southerland (Warden), Rafael Herrera (Mexican Husband), Maria Bethke (Mexican Wife), Marc Maurin (French Fighter), Anjul Nigam (Rahul), Lorenzo Callender (Comms Officer), David Douglas (Technician), Joe Basile (Radar Operator), Esodie Geiger-Mavestrand (Transmitter Technician), Roland Kickinger (T-800), Linda Hamilton (Voice of Sarah Connor)

To ensure that humanity has a future, John Connor and his team of rebels fight to stop Skynet from wiping out the human race and replacing the world with cyborgs. Previous entries: *The Terminator* (Orion, 1984), *Terminator 2: Judgment Day* (TriStar, 1991), and *Terminator 3: Rise of the Machines* (WB, 2003).

Christian Bale, Sam Worthington © Warner Bros.

Jane Alexander, Jadagrace Berry, Anton Yelchin

DANCE FLICK

(PARAMOUNT) Producers, Keenen Ivory Wayans, Shawn Wayans, Marlon Wayans, Rick Alvarez; Executive Producers, Richard Vane, Craig Wayans, Damien Dante Wayans; Director, Damien Dante Wayans; Screenplay, Keenen Ivory Wayans, Shawn Wayans, Marlon Wayans, Craig Wayans, Damien Dante Wayans; Photography, Mark Irwin; Designer, Aaron Osborne; Costumes, Judy Ruskin Howell; Music, Erik Willias, Dwayne Wayans; Music Supervisor, Lisa Brown; Editor, Scott Hill; Choreographer, Dave Scott; Visual Effects Supervisor, Kevin Elam; Casting, Lisa Beach, Sarah Katzman; Dolby; Deluxe color; Rated PG-13; 83 minutes; Release date: May 22, 2009

CAST
Megan	**Shoshana Bush**
Thomas	**Damon Wayans Jr.**
Charity	**Essence Atkins**
Sugar Bear	**David Alan Grier**
Ms. Cameltoe	**Amy Sedaris**
Jack	**Brennan Hillard**
A-Con	**Affion Crockett**

Luis Dalmasy (Dancer #9), Chris Elliott (Ron), George Gore II (Ray), Chelsea Makela (Tracy Transfat), Christina Murphy (Nora), Ross Thomas (Tyler), Kim Wayans (Ms. Dontwannabebothered), Marlon Wayans (Mr. Moody), Shawn Wayans (Baby Daddy), Lauren Bowles (Glynn), Sufe Bradshaw (Keloid), Yves Lola St. Vil (Uglisha), Kevin Knotts (Patrol Man), Ellia English (Lady on Train), Craig Wayans (Truck), Keenen Ivory Wayans (Mr. Stache), Terry Rhoads (Audition Judge), Chaunte Wayans (Free Gas Pedestrian), Brien Perry (Officer Dillon), Corey Holcomb (Sugar Bear Henchman), Michael Wayans (Confessing Crew Member), Casey Lee (Undercover Cop), Tichina Arnold (Ray's Mamma), Dan Kelpine (Slave Master), Howard Alonzo (Will), Phil Beauman (Officer), Shane Miller, Vincent Oshana (Students), Kylee Dodson (Megan's Sister), Elimu Nelson (Prison Guard), Louisa Abernathy (Thomas' Grandma), Andrew McFarlane (D), Cara Mia Wayans (Club Girl), Page Kennedy (Security Guard), Heather McDonald (Girl's Gym Teacher), Gregory Wayans Benson Jr. (Mr. Moody's Favorite Student), Lochlyn Munro (Coach Effron), Chynna Dulac, Brandy Olgesby, Hannah Douglass, Garland Spencer, Katie Orr, Lucas Raynaud, Jason Geoffrey, Zhara Hamani, Richard Vazquez (Dancers)

An aspiring dancer falls in love with a gang member who agrees to enter a dance-off in order to pay back a drug debt in this spoof of recent dance-theme moved.

Damon Wayans Jr., Shoshana Bush © Paramount Pictures

Shoshana Bush, Essence Atkins, Affion Crockett, Damon Wayans Jr.

Sasha Grey © Magnolia Pictures

THE GIRLFRIEND EXPERIENCE

(MAGNOLIA) Producer, Gregory Jacobs; Executive Producers, Todd Wagner, Mark Cuban; Director, Steven Soderbergh; Screenplay, Brian Koppelman, David Levien; Photography, Peter Andrews; Art Director, Carlos Moore; Costumes, Christopher Peterson; Music, Ross Godfrey; Editor, Mary Ann Bernard; Casting, Carmen Cuba; an Extension 765 production, presented in association with 2929 Entertainment; Dolby; Color; HD; Rated R; 77 minutes; Release date: May 22, 2009

CAST
Chelsea	**Sasha Grey**
Chris	**Chris Santos**
Wealthy Client	**Peter Zizzo**

Philip Eytan (Phillip), T. Colby Trane (Waiter), Vincent Dellacera (Chelsea's Driver), Jim Kempner (Art Gallery Owner), David Levien (David), Mark Jacobson (Interviewer), Alan Milstein (Pete), Sukhdev Singh (Super), Ted Jessup (Chatty "John") , Dennis Shields (Dennis), Glenny Kenny (The Erotic Connoisseur)

Five days in the lives of a high price call girl and her gym trainer boyfriend.

Hank Azaria

Christopher Guest, Jon Bernthal, Alain Chabat

Ben Stiller © Twentieth Century Fox

NIGHT AT THE MUSEUM:
BATTLE OF THE SMITHSONIAN

(20TH CENTURY FOX) Producers, Shawn Levy, Chris Columbus, Michael Barnathan; Executive Producers, Thomas M. Hammel, Josh McLagen, Mark Radcliffe; Director, Shawn Levy; Screenplay, Robert Ben Garant, Thomas Lennon; Photography, John Schwartzman; Designer, Claude Pare; Costumes, Marlene Stewart; Music, Alan Silvestri; Editors, Don Zimmerman, Dean Zimmerman; Special Effects Supervisor, Dan Deleeuw; Visual Effects, Rhythm & Hues; Stunts, JJ Makaro, Garrett Warren; Casting, Donna Isaacson; a 21 Laps and 1492 Pictures production; Dolby; Technicolor; Rated PG; 104 minutes; Release date: May 22, 2009

CAST

Larry Daley	**Ben Stiller**
Amelia Earhart	**Amy Adams**
Jedediah Smith	**Owen Wilson**
Kahmunrah/Voice of the Thinker/	
Voice of Abraham Lincoln	**Hank Azaria**
Teddy Roosevelt	**Robin Williams**
Ivan the Terrible	**Christopher Guest**
Napoleon Bonaparte	**Alain Chabat**
Octavius	**Steve Coogan**
Dr. McPhee	**Ricky Gervais**
General George Custer	**Bill Hader**
Al Capone	**Jon Bernthal**
Attila the Hun	**Patrick Gallagher**
Nicky Daley	**Jake Cherry**

Rami Malek (Ahkmenrah), Mizuo Peck (Sacajawea), Kerry van der Griend, Matthew Harrison, Rick Dobran (Neanderthals), Randy Lee, Darryl Quon, Gerald Wong, Paul Chih-Ping Cheng (Huns), Jay Baruchel (Sailor Joey Motorola), Mindy Kaling (Docent), Keith Powell, Craig Robinson (Tuskegee Airmen), Samuel Chu, Augustus Oicle, Kai James (Teenage Boys), Thomas Morley (Darth Vader), Clint Howard, Matty Finochio (Air and Space Mission Control Techs), George Foreman (Himself), Josh Byer (Capone Gangster #1), Sophie Levy, Tess Levy (Young Girls), Alberta Mayne (Kissing Nurse), Christina Schild, Robert Thurston (American Gothic), Clifton Murray (Kissing Sailor), Caroll Spinney (Voice of Oscar the Grouch), Dan Joffre (Town Car Driver), Dave Hospes (Astronaut), Regina Taufen (New York Reporter), Shawn Levy (Infomercial Father), Kevin Jonas, Joe Jonas, Nick Jones (Voice of Cherubs), Brad Garrett (Voice of Easter Island Head), Eugene Levy (Voice of Albert Einstein), Robert Ben Garant (Orville Wright), Thomas Lennon (Wilbur Wright), Jonah Hill (Brundon the Security Guard)

Former security guard Larry Daley hopes to help the living exhibits at the Smithsonian do battle with the reawakened 3,000 year old Egyptian Ruler Kahmunrah, who plans to conquer the world. Sequel to the 2006 Fox film, with several principals repeating their roles.

Robert B. Sherman, Richard M. Sherman © Disney Enterprises

Robert B. Sherman, Richard M. Sherman, Walt Disney

THE BOYS: THE SHERMAN BROTHERS' STORY

(WALT DISNEY STUDIOS) Producers, Jeffrey C. Sherman, Gregory V. Sherman; Executive Producers, Stephen Buchsbaum, David Permut, Ben Stiller, Stuart Cornfeld; Co-Producers, Patrick J. O'Grady, Jeff Kurtti, Bruce Gordon, Steve Longi; Directors, Jeffrey C. Sherman, Gregory V. Sherman; Photography, Richard Numeroff; Music, Robert B. Sherman, Richard M. Sherman; Editor, Rich Evirs; a Crescendo/Traveling Light production; Dolby; Color; Rated PG; 101 minutes; Release date: May 22, 2009

WITH
Robert B. Sherman, Richard M. Sherman, Julie Andrews, Roy E. Disney, Samuel Goldwyn Jr., John Landis, Angela Lansbury, John Lasseter, Kenny Loggins, Leonard Maltin, Alan Menken, Hayley Mills, Randy Newman, Robert Osborne, Debbie Reynolds, Stephen Schwartz, Ben Stiller, Dick Van Dyke, Tony Walton, Lesley Ann Warren, Johnny Whittaker, John Williams

Documentary on the sibling songwriting team of Robert B. and Richard M. Sherman, their successful professional collaboration contrasted with their mostly strained personal relationship.

Robert B. Sherman, Richard M. Sherman

Richard M. Sherman, Julie Andrews, Dick Van Dyke, Robert B. Sherman

DRAG ME TO HELL

(UNIVERSAL) Producers, Rob Tapert, Grant Curtis; Executive Producers, Joe Drake, Nathan Kahane; Co-Producers, Cristen Carr Strubbe, Ivan Raimi; Director, Sam Raimi; Screenplay, Sam Raimi, Ivan Raimi; Photography, Peter Deming; Designer, Steve Saklad; Costumes, Isis Mussenden; Music, Christopher Young; Editor, Bob Murawski; Visual Effects Supervisor, Bruce Jones; Special Makeup Effects, Gregory Nicotero, Howard Berger; Stunts, Randy Beckman; Casting, John Papsidera; a Ghost House Pictures presentation; Dolby; Panavision; Color; Rated PG-13; 99 minutes; Release date: May 29, 2009

CAST

Christine Brown	**Alison Lohman**
Clay Dalton	**Justin Long**
Sylvia Ganush	**Lorna Raver**
Rham Jas	**Dileep Rao**
Jim Jacks	**David Paymer**
Shaun San Dena	**Adriana Barraza**
Leonard Dalton	**Chelcie Ross**
Stu Rubin	**Reggie Lee**
Trudy Dalton	**Molly Cheek**
Ilenka Ganush	**Bojana Novakvic**
Milos	**Kevin Foster**

Alexis Cruz (Farm Worker), Ruth Livier (Farm Worker's Wife), Shiloh Selassie (Farm Worker's Son), Flor de Maria Chahua (Young Shaun San Dena), Christopher Young (Pedestrian with Cupcake), Ricardo Molina, Fernanda Romero (Mortgage Customers), Joanne Baron (Mr. Jacks's Secretary), Ted Raimi (Doctor), Ali Dean (Pawnbroker), Octavia Spencer, Mia Rai (Bank Co-Workers), Bill E. Rogers (Security Guard), Cherie Franklin (Cackling Woman at Death Feast), Olga Babtchinskaia (Violinist at Death Feast), Alex Veadov (Man with Ponytail at Death Feast), Bonnie Aarons (Mother at Death Feast), Emma Raimi (Daughter at Death Feast), Michael Peter Bolus, Peter Popp, Scott Spiegel (Mourners at Death Feast), Bridget Hoffman (Ghost at Séance), Tom Carey (Old Man in Headlights), Lia Johnson (Waitress), Jay Gordon, Henry Raimi, Lorne Raimi (Family at Diner), Chloe Dykstra, Nick Vlassopoulos (Young Couple at Diner), John Paxton, Irene Roseen (Old Couple at Diner), Aimee Miles (Salesman), Art Kimbro (Voice of Lamia)

Hoping her decision will land her a coveted assistant manager job, bank employee Christine Brown chooses to ignore the pleas of an old lady for an extension on her mortgage and ends up with an evil curse placed upon her.

Dileep Rao, Adriana Barraza, Alison Lohman

Alison Lohman, Justin Long

Lorna Raver, Alison Lohman © Rogue/Universal

Alison Lohman

AWAY WE GO

(FOCUS) Producers, Edward Saxon, Marc Turtletaub, Peter Saraf; Executive Producers, Mari Jo Winkler-Ioffreda, Pippa Harris; Director, Sam Mendes; Screenplay, Dave Eggers, Vendela Vida; Photography, Ellen Kuras; Designer, Jess Gonchor; Costumes, John Dunn; Music, Alexi Murdoch; Music Supervisor, Randall Poster; Editor, Sarah Flack; Casting, Ellen Lewis, Debra Zane; an Edward Saxon/Big Beach production in association with Neal Street Productions; Dolby; Panavision; Color; Rated R; 97 minutes; Release date: June 5, 2009

CAST

Burt Farlander	**John Krasinski**
Verona De Tessant	**Maya Rudolph**
Gloria Farlander	**Catherine O'Hara**
Jerry Farlander	**Jeff Daniels**
Grace De Tessant	**Carmen Ejogo**
Lily	**Allison Janney**
Lowell	**Jim Gaffigan**
LN Fisher-Herrin	**Maggie Gyllenhaal**
Roderick Herrin	**Josh Hamilton**
Tom Garnett	**Chris Messina**
Munch Garnett	**Melanie Lynskey**
Courtney Farlander	**Paul Schneider**
Ashley	**Samantha Pryor**
Taylor	**Conor Carroll**
Wolfie	**Bailey Harkins**
Baby Neptune	**Brendan Spitz, Jaden Spitz**
James	**Colton Parsons**
Katya	**Katherine Vaskevich**
Ibrahim	**Jerome Walter Stephens**
Cammie	**Brianna Eunmi Kim**
Annabelle	**Isabelle Moon Alexander**
Professor Ruby	**Finnerty Steeves**
Performance Mom	**Stephanie Kurtzuba**
Beckett	**Pete Wiggins**
Gwen	**Audrey Amey**
Dana	**Shirley Roeca**
Carrie	**Troy Wood**

Michael Breckley, Steve Lai, Randy Lee, Duane Sequira, Vivien Eng, Leah O'Donnell (Dancers), Hector Flores (Valet), Alexandra Henderson (Star-Spangled Danner Singer)

Expecting their first child and uncertain of their future, Burt and Verona find themselves flying off to various locations to revisit old friends, in hopes of finding the right place in which to settle down.

Allison Janney, John Krasinski, Jim Gaffigan, Maya Rudolph

Bailey Harkins, Maya Rudolph, Maggie Gyllenhaal, John Krasinski, Josh Hamilton

Maggie Gyllenhaal

Catherine O'Hara, Jeff Daniels

Carmen Ejogo, Maya Rudolph

John Krasinski, Maya Rudolph

John Krasinski, Maya Rudolph © Focus Features

John Krasinski, Maya Rudolph

Maya Rudolph, John Krasinski

Ed Helms, Heather Graham

Ed Helms © Warner Bros.

Mike Tyson

THE HANGOVER

(WARNER BROTHERS) Producers, Todd Phillips, Dan Goldberg; Executive Producers, Thomas Tull, Jon Jashni, William Fay, Scott Budnick, Chris Bender, J.C. Spink; Co-Producers, David A. Siegel, Jeffrey Wetzel; Director, Todd Phillips; Screenplay, Jon Lucas, Scott Moore; Photography, Lawrence Sher; Designer, Bill Brzeski; Costumes, Louise Mingenbach; Music, Christophe Beck; Music Supervisors, George Drakoulias, Randall Poster; Editor, Debra Neil-Fisher; Casting, Juel Bestrop, Seth Yanlewitz; a Green Hat Films production, presented in association with Legendary Pictures; Dolby; Technicolor; Rated R; 99 minutes; Release date: June 5, 2009

CAST

Phil Wenneck	**Bradley Cooper**
Stu Price	**Ed Helms**
Alan Garner	**Zach Galifianakis**
Doug Billings	**Justin Bartha**
Jade	**Heather Graham**
Tracy Garner	**Sasha Barrese**
Sid Garner	**Jeffrey Tambor**
Mr. Chow	**Ken Jeong**
Melissa	**Rachael Harris**
Himself	**Mike Tyson**
Black Doug	**Mike Epps**
Leonard	**Jernard Burks**

Rob Riggle (Officer Franklin), Cleo King (Officer Garden), Bryan Callen (Eddie Palermo), Matt Walsh (Dr. Valsh), Ian Anthony Dale, Michael Li (Chow's Men), Sondra Currie (Linda Garner), Gillian Vigman (Stephanie), Nathalie Fay (Lisa), Chuck Pacheco (Hotel Guest at Valet), Jesse Erwin (Hotel Valet), Dan Finnerty (Wedding Singer), Keith Lyle (Casino Dealer), Brody Stevens (Officer Foltz), Todd Phillips (Mr. Creepy), Mike Vallely (Neeco), James Martin Kelly (Police Clerk), Murray Gershenz (Felix), Andrew Astor (Eli Wenneck), Casey Margolis (Budnick), Joe Alexander (Pit Boss), Ken Flaherty (Old Timer at Gas Station), Constance Broge (Woman in Elevator), Sue Pierce (Mini-Mart Cashier), Floyd Levine (Tailor), Robert A. Ringler (Minister), Britt Barrett, Chauntae Davies, Alisa Allapach (Bridesmaids), Nicholas Furu (Stun Gun Boy), Angelica Flameno (Stun Gun Girl), Lily Winn (Screaming Girl), Katerina Moutsatsou (Eddie's Assistant), Faleolo Alailima (Tyson's Bodguard)

After a night of extreme partying that none of them can remember, three groomsmen search Las Vegas in hopes of finding their missing friend in time for his upcoming wedding.

Zach Galifianakis, Ed Helms, Justin Bartha, Bradley Cooper

LAND OF THE LOST

(UNIVERSAL) Producers, Jimmy Miller, Sid Krofft, Marty Krofft; Executive Producers, Daniel Lupi, Julie Wixson Darmody, Adam McKay, Brad Silberling, Ryan Kavanaugh; Co-Producers, John Swallow, Josh Church; Director, Brad Silberling; Screenplay, Chris Henchy, Dennis McNicholas; Based on the TV series by Sid & Marty Krofft; Photography, Dion Beebe; Designer, Bo Welch; Costumes, Mark Bridges; Music, Michael Giacchino; Editor, Peter Teschner; Visual Effects Supervisor, Bill Westenhofer; Creature Designer, Crash McCreery; Creature and Makeup Effects, Mike Elizalde; Casting, Avy Kaufman; a Sid & Marty Krofft/Mosaic production, presented in association with Relativity Media; Dolby; Panavision; Color; Rated PG-13; 101 minutes; Release date: June 5, 2009

CAST

Dr. Rick Marshall	**Will Ferrell**
Holly Cantrell	**Anna Friel**
Will Stanton	**Danny McBride**
Cha-Ka	**Jorma Taccone**
Enik	**John Boylan**
Himself	**Matt Lauer**

Bobb'e J. Thompson, Sierra McCormick, Shannon Lemke, Steven Wash Jr. (Tar Pits Kids), Brian Huskey (Teacher), Kevin Buitrago, Noah Crawford, Jon Kent Ethridge, Logan Manus (Teenagers), Ben Best (Ernie), Scott Dorel, Sean Michael Guess (Elder Pakunis), Dennis McNicholas (Ice Cream Man), Chris Henchy (Stage Manager), Kurt Carley, Travis Samuel Clark, Daniel George, Todd Christian Hunter, Marti Matulis, Tim Soergel, Douglas Tait, Patrick Wedge, Andreas Anderson, Seth Bauer, Trevor Brunsink, David Craig, Ben Hansen, Shane Huseman, Danko Iordanov, Kenny Jackson, Matt Kavanaugh, Darren Kendrick, Frederick Keeve, Terence Leclere, Nathan Luginbill, Christian Pogorzelski, Tommy Ruddell, David Szabo, Nathan Udall, Kyle Weishaar, Joey Zadwarny (Sleestaks), Ana Alexander, Moran Atias, Jesse Golden, Eve Mauro, Pollyanna McIntosh, Ania Spiering (Pakuni Women), Paul Adelstein (Astronaut Voice), Adam Behr, Daamen J. Krall (Library Skulls), Leonard Nimoy (The Zarn)

Quantum paleontologist Rick Marshall and his party are sucked into a vortex into a primeval world.

Anna Friel, Will Ferrell

Will Ferrell, Anna Friel, Danny McBride, Jorma Taccone

Will Ferrell © Universal Studios

Sleestaks

Herbert Vogel, Dorothy Vogel © Arthouse Films

HERB AND DOROTHY

(ARTHOUSE FILMS) Producer/Director, Megumi Sasaki; Executive Producers, Karl Katz, Catherine Price; Photography, Rafael dela Uz, Axel Baumann, Morgan Fallon, Ian Saladyga, Erik Shirai, Vladimir Subotic; Music, David Majzlin; Editor, Bernadine Colish; Color; Not rated; 89 minutes; Release date: June 5, 2009

WITH
Herbert Vogel, Dorothy Vogel, Lucio Pozzi, Pat Steir, Richard Tuttle, Will Barnet, Lynda Benglis, Robert Barry, Christo and Jeanne-Claude, Chuck Close, Robert Mangold, Sylvia Mangold, James Siena, Lawrence Weiner

Documentary on how postal clerk Herb Vogel and his wife, librarian Dorothy Vogel, managed to build up one of the world's major art collections.

TETRO

(AMERICAN ZOETROPE) Producer/Director/Screenplay, Francis Ford Coppola; Executive Producers, Anahid Nazarian, Fred Roos; Photography, Mihai Malaimare Jr.; Designer, Sebastian Orgambide; Costumes, Cecilia Monti; Music, Osvaldo Golijov; Editor, Walter Murch; Casting, Walter Rippel; American-Argentinian-Spanish-Italian; Dolby; HDCAM Widescreen; Black and white/color; Not rated; 127 minutes; Release date: June 10, 2009

CAST
Tetro	**Vincent Gallo**
Bennie	**Alden Ehrenreich**
Miranda	**Maribel Verdu**
Carlo	**Klaus Maria Brandauer**
Alone	**Carmen Maura**

Rodrigo De La Serna (Jose), Leticia Brédice (Josefina), Mike Amigorena (Abelardo), Sofia Castiglione (Maria Luisa), Francesca De Sapio (Amalia), Adriana Mastrángelo (Angela), Silvia Pérez (Silvana), Erica Rivas (Ana)

Teenage Bennie arrives in Buenos Aires to track down his older brother, who had reneged on his promise to return to him years ago.

Vincent Gallo, Alden Ehrenreich © American Zoetrope

Vincent Gallo, Alden Ehrenreich

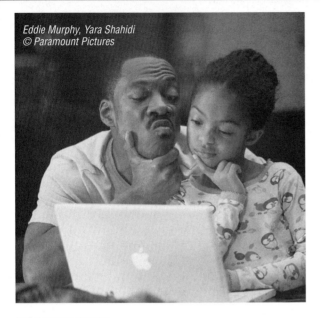

Eddie Murphy, Yara Shahidi
© Paramount Pictures

IMAGINE THAT

(PARAMOUNT) Producers, Lorenzo di Bonaventura, Ed Solomon; Executive Producer, Ric Kidney; Director, Karey Kirkpatrick; Screenplay, Ed Solomon, Chris Matheson; Photography, John Lindley; Designer, William Arnold; Costumes, Ruth E. Carter; Music, Mark Mancina; Editor, David Moritz; Special Effects Coordinator, John Perry; Casting, Jeanne McCarthy; a di Bonaventura Pictures production, presented with Nickelodeon Movies; Dolby; Super 35 Widescreen; Deluxe color; Rated PG; 107 minutes; Release date: June 12, 2009

CAST
Evan Danielson	**Eddie Murphy**
Johnny Whitefeather	**Thomas Haden Church**
Olivia Danielson	**Yara Shahidi**
Tricia Danielson	**Nicole Ari Parker**
Tom Stevens	**Ronny Cox**
Noah Kulick	**Stephen Rannazzisi**
Dante D'Enzo	**Martin Sheen**

DeRay Davis (John Strother), Vanessa Williams (Lori Strother), Lauren Weedman (Rose), Timm Sharp (Tod), Daniel Polo (Indigo Whitefeather), Stephen Root (Fred Franklin), Richard Schiff (Carl Simons), Marin Hinkle (Ms. Davis), Bobb'e J. Thompson (Fo Fo Figgley's Kid), Blake Hightower (Will Strother), Michael McMillian (Brock Pressman), Catherine McGoohan (Mrs. Pressman), James Patrick Stuart (Mr. Pratt), Tonita Castro (Graciella), Charlie Koznick (Rick), Talen Riley (Ella Strother), Jonathan Mangum (Franklin's Associate), Mike Vorhaus (Franklin's Trustee), Bob Rumnock (Whip Bryson), Allen Iverson, Carmelo Anthony, George Karl (Themselves), Heidi Marnhout (Cheryl Whitefeather), John Nance (Rowe's Accountant), Jeff Kosloski (Evan's Neighbor), Allen Ross (Old Red Bear), Rachael Bard (Wealthy Dowager), Bernard Cottonwood (Proud Hawk), Blanche Zembower (Old Red Bear's Wife), Robert Seay (Mike), Tom Wiens (High Net Worth Man), Kellie Sprague (Nurse), Piper Ngubo (Julia), Allison Weintraub (Party Coordinator), Erik R. Norris (Bob), Joe Sikorra (Jim), Diane Goldberg (Steven's Secretary), Luke McEndarfer (Choir Director), Mel Harris (Maggie Johnson)

A neglectful dad discovers that his daughter's invisible playmates can provide him with the investment advice needed to push him ahead at his firm.

FOOD, INC.

(MAGNOLIA) Producers, Robert Kenner, Elise Pearlstein; Executive Producers, William Pohlad, Jeff Skoll, Robin Schorr, Diane Weyermann; Co-Producers, Eric Schlosser, Richard Pearce, Melissa Robledo; Director, Robert Kenner; Screenplay, Robert Kenner, Elise Pearlstein, Kim Roberts; Photography, Richard Pearce; Music, Mark Adler; Editor, Kim Roberts; a Participant Media & River Road Entertainment presentation; Dolby; Color; Rated PG; 93 minutes; Release date: June 12, 2009

WITH
Eric Schlosser, Richard Lobb, Vince Edwards, Carole Morison, Michael Pollan, Troy Roush, Larry Johnson, Allen Trenkle, Patricia Buck, Barbara Kowalyck, Diana DeGette, Phil English, Eldon Roth, The Orozco Family, Rosa Soto and Healthy Teens on the Move, Joel Salatin, Eduardo Peña, Gary Hirshberg, Moe Parr, David Runyon, Stephen R. Pennell, William P. Kealey

Documentary on the hidden side of the American food industry that has been sanctioned by the government's regulatory agencies.

This film received an Oscar nomination for documentary feature.

Troy Roush © Magnolia Pictures

Joel Salatin

THE TAKING OF PELHAM 123

(COLUMBIA/MGM) Producers, Todd Black, Tony Scott, Jason Blumenthal, Steve Tisch; Executive Producers, Barry Waldman, Michael Costigan, Ryan Kavanaugh; Co-Executive Producers, Linda Favila, Anson Downes; Director, Tony Scott; Screenplay, Brian Helgeland; Based on the novel by John Godey; Photography, Tobias Schliessler; Designer, Chris Seagers; Costumes, Renée Ehrlich Kalfus; Music, Harry Gregson-Williams; Editor, Chris Lebenzon; Senior Visual Effects Supervisor, Nathan McGuinness; Casting, Denise Chamian; a Scott Free/Escape Artists production, presented in association with Relativity Media; Dolby; Panavision; Deluxe color; Rated R; 106 minutes; Release date: June 12, 2009

John Travolta, Robert Vataj

CAST

Walter Garber	**Denzel Washington**
Ryder	**John Travolta**
Phil Ramos	**Luis Guzman**
Bashkim	**Victor Gojcaj**
Camonetti	**John Turturro**
Mayor	**James Gandolfini**
John Johnson	**Michael Rispoli**
Delgado	**Ramon Rodriguez**
Dispatcher One	**Saidah Arrika Ekulona**
Deputy Mayor LaSalle	**John Benjamin Hickey**
George	**Alex Kaluzhsky**
Wallace	**Gbenga Akinnagbe**
Mom	**Katherine Sigismund**
8-Year-Old Boy	**Jake Siciliano**
Jerry Pollard, Motorman	**Gary Basaraba**
Undercover Cop	**Sean Meehan**
Therese Garber	**Aunjanue Ellis**
Regina, Conductor	**Tonye Patano**
"Q" Train Motorman	**Anthony Annarumma**
Mr. Thomas	**Jason Butler Harner**
Emri	**Robert Vataj**
Supervisor	**Todd Susman**

Denzel Washington, John Turturro

Glen Tortorella, Bobby Bojorklund (Maintenance Workers), Jasmin Tavarez (Puerto Rican Girl), J. Bernard Calloway (Officer Moran), Chip Brookes (Zealous Aide), Zach Poole (LaSalle's Aide), Reuben Jackson (Reporter at MTA), Sean Nelson (ESU One), Deak Evgenikos (ESU Two), Ty Jones (Sniper), Lee Shepherd (Dr. Weiss), Mike Houston (Money Car Driver), René Ifrah (Money Car Shotgun), Frank Wood (Police Commissioner Sterman), Brian Haley (Police Captain Hill, MTA), Maria Bartiromo (Financial Reporter), John Lavelle (Team Member, NYPD), Chance Kelly (ESU Captain), Peter Buccosi (SUV Driver), Steve Routman (Heckler), Laurie Cole (Reporter at 42nd Street & Vanderbilt), Nick Loren (Tunnel Commander), Daniel Stewart Sherman (ESU Lieutenant Staley), John Keiser, Patrick J. Dalton (MTA Workers), Adrian Martinez (Cabbie), Jordan Gelber (Commuter), Rose DelCastillo (Reporter), Joe Forbrich, Jason Cerbone, Billy Devlin (ESU Guys), Jonathan Rau (Federal Reserve Supervisor), Mike Mihm (ESU Desk Officer), Alice Kremelberg (George's Girlfriend), Sammy Miraglia, Kenneth Natal, Robert Perry (Motormen)

Ryder and his team hijack a subway car and put New York City officials at their mercy when they demand $10 million to prevent them from executing the hostages onboard. Remake of the 1974 United Artists film that starred Walter Matthau and Robert Shaw.

Denzel Washington, James Gandolfini

Denzel Washington

John Travolta

Denzel Washington

Luis Guzman © Columbia Pictures

Gary Basaraba, John Travolta, Luis Guzman

James Gandolfini

YEAR ONE

(COLUMBIA) Producers, Harold Ramis, Judd Apatow, Clayton Townsend; Executive Producer, Rodney Rothman; Co-Producer, Laurel Ward; Director/ Story, Harold Ramis; Screenplay, Harold Ramis, Gene Stupnitsky, Lee Eisenberg; Photography, Alar Kivilo; Designer, Jefferson Sage; Costumes, Debra McGuire; Music, Theodore Shapiro; Editors, Craig P. Herring, Steve Welch; Visual Effects Supervisor, Jamie Dixon; Casting, Jeanne McCarthy; an Ocean Pictures/Apatow Co. production; Dolby; Deluxe color; Rated PG-13; 97 minutes; Release date: June 19, 2009

Jack Black, Michael Cera, Christopher Mintz-Plasse, Hank Azaria
© Columbia Pictures

CAST

Zed	**Jack Black**
Oh	**Michael Cera**
High Priest	**Oliver Platt**
Cain	**David Cross**
Issac	**Christopher Mintz-Plasse**
Sargon	**Vinnie Jones**
Abraham	**Hank Azaria**
Eema	**Juno Temple**
Princess Inanna	**Olivia Wilde**
Maya	**June Diane Raphael**
King	**Xander Berkeley**
Queen	**Gia Carides**

Horatio Sanz (Enmebaragesi), David Pasquesi (Prime Minister), Matthew J. Willig (Marlak), Harold Ramis (Adam), Rhoda Griffis (Eve), Gabriel Sunday (Seth), Eden Riegel (Lilith), Kyle Gass (Zaftig the Eunuch), Bill Hader (Shaman), Marshall Manesh (Slave Trader), Rion Hunter (Bedouin Sheik), Gene Stupnitsky (First Guard), Lee Eisenberg (Sodom Sentry), Eric Gipson (Sodom Vendor), Lacie Manshack (Banana Girl), Matt Besser (Guy in Crowd), Drue Franklin (Squanto), Weston Hollenshead (Kid Stoner), Paul Scheer (Bricklayer), Joaquin Townsend (Slave Child), Bryan Massey (New Guard), Keet Davis (Desert Soldier), Tim Hilton (Pedestrian Villager), Ashley Nicole Caldwell (Gold Statue), Mark Cotone (Angry Baker), Jack Walker (Village Child), Jamal Sims, Paul Benshoof, Kelly Connolly, Leslie Geldbach, Katherine Miller, Michael Morris, Sarah Christine Smith (Dancers), Paul Rudd (Abel)

Jack Black, June Diane Raphael

After being banished from their Neanderthal tribe a pair of misfits make their way to Sodom in hopes of finding their destiny.

Paul Rudd, Jack Black, David Cross

Jack Black, Juno Temple, Michael Cera

Sandra Bullock © Touchstone Pictures, Inc.

Ryan Reynolds, Sandra Bullock

Betty White, Mary Steenburgen, Ryan Reynolds, Craig T. Nelson

THE PROPOSAL

(TOUCHSTONE) Producers, David Hoberman, Todd Lieberman; Executive Producers, Alex Kurtzman, Roberto Orci, Mary McLaglen, Sandra Bullock; Director, Anne Fletcher; Screenplay, Peter Chiarelli; Photography, Oliver Staplton; Designer, Nelson Coates; Costumes, Catherine Marie Thomas; Music, Aaron Zigman; Editor, Priscilla Nedd Friendly; Casting, Amanda Mackey, Cathy Sandrich; a Walt Disney Studios Motion Pictures release of a Touchstone presentation of a Mandeville Films production; Dolby; Technicolor; Rated PG-13; 107 minutes; Release date: June 19, 2009

CAST

Margaret Tate	**Sandra Bullock**
Andrew Paxton	**Ryan Reynolds**
Grace Paxton	**Mary Steenburgen**
Joe Paxton	**Craig T. Nelson**
Grandma Annie	**Betty White**
Mr. Gilberston	**Denis O'Hare**
Gertrude	**Malin Akerman**
Ramone	**Oscar Nunez**
Bob Spaulding	**Aasif Mandvi**
Chairman Bergen	**Michael Nouri**
Chuck	**Michael Mosley**
Jim McKittrick	**Dale Place**
Coffee Barista	**Alicia Hunt**
Immigration Clerk	**Alexis R. Garcia**

Kortney Adams (Colden Books Receptionist), Chris Whitney (Medivac Pilot), Jerell Lee Wesley (Jordan), Gregg Edelman (Lead Counsel Malloy), Phyllis Kay (Mrs. McKittrick), Kate Lacey (Party Guest), Gene Fleming (Store Owner), Mary Linda Rapelye (Executive Secretary), Anne Fletcher (Jill), B. Johnson (Guy in Office)

Told she will be deported, tyrannical book editor Margaret Tate blackmails Andrew, her put-upon assistant, into marrying her so that she can stay in the country and he can hold on to his job.

Betty White, Sandra Bullock

Evan Rachel Wood, Henry Cavill

Larry David, Michael McKean, Conleth Hill

Larry David, John Gallagher Jr., Evan Rachel Wood

WHATEVER WORKS

(SONY CLASSICS) Producers, Letty Aronson, Stephen Tenenbaum; Executive Producers, Vincent Maraval, Brahim Chioua; Co-Producer, Helen Robin; Co-Executive Producers, Jack Rollins, Charles H. Joffe; Director/Screenplay, Woody Allen; Photography, Harris Savides; Designer, Santo Loquasto; Costumes, Suzy Benzinger; Editor, Alisa Lepselter; a Wild Bunch/Gravier Productions presentation of a Perdido production; American-French; Dolby; Technicolor; Rated PG-13; 92 minutes; Release date: June 19, 2009

CAST

Boris Yellnikoff	**Larry David**
Melody St. Ann Celestine	**Evan Rachel Wood**
Marietta	**Patricia Clarkson**
John	**Ed Begley Jr.**
Joe	**Michael McKean**
Randy James	**Henry Cavill**
Perry	**John Gallagher Jr.**
Helena	**Jessica Hecht**
Jessica	**Carolyn McCormick**
Howard	**Christopher Evan Welch**
Leo Brockman	**Conleth Hill**
Boris' Friends	**Adam Brooks, Lyle Kanouse**
Boy on Street	**Clifford Lee Dickson**
Boy's Mother	**Yolonda Ross**
Chess Mother	**Samantha Bee**

Marcia DeBonis (Lady at Chinese Restaurant), Willa Cuthrell-Tuttleman (Chess Girl), Nicole Patrick (Perry's Friend), Olek Krupa (Morgenstern), Lindsay Michelle Nader, Armand Schultz (Television Voices)

An endlessly kvetching misanthrope finds himself unexpectedly drawn to a simple girl he has found sleeping on the streets of Manhattan.

Patricia Clarkson © Sony Pictures Classics

TRANSFORMERS: REVENGE OF THE FALLEN

(DREAMWORKS/PARAMOUNT) Producers, Don Murphy, Tom DeSanto, Lorenzo di Bonaventura, Ian Bryce; Executive Producers, Steven Spielberg, Michael Bay, Brian Goldner, Mark Vahradian; Co-Producer, Allegra Clegg; Director, Michael Bay; Screenplay, Ehren Kruger, Roberto Orci, Alex Kurtzman; Based on Hasbro's Transformers action figures; Photography, Ben Seresin; Designer, Nigel Phelps; Costumes, Deborah L. Scott; Music, Steve Jablonsky; Editors, Roger Barton, Thomas Muldoon, Joel Negron, Paul Rubell; Visual Effects Supervisor, Richard Kidd; Visual Effects, Industrial Light & Magic, Asylum, Digital Domain; Stunts, Kenny Bates, Bob Brown; a di Bonaventura Pictures and Tom DeSanto/Don Murphy production, presented in association with Hasbro; Distributed by Paramount; Dolby; Super 35 Widescreen; Deluxe color; Rated PG-13; 149 minutes; Release date: June 24, 2009

CAST

Sam Witwicky	**Shia LaBeouf**
Mikaela Banes	**Megan Fox**
Major Lennox	**Josh Duhamel**
USAF Tech Sgt. Epps	**Tyrese Gibson**
Agent Simmons	**John Turturro**
Leo Spitz	**Ramon Rodriguez**

Kevin Dunn (Ron Witwicky), Julie White (Judy Witwicky), Isabel Lucas (Alice), John Benjamin Hickey (Galloway), Matthew Marsden (Graham), Andrew Howard (Special Air Services Forces), Michael Papajohn (Cal), Glenn Morshower (Gen. Morshower), John Eric Bentley (Aide), Erin Naas (Arcee Rider), Rainn Wilson (Prof. Colan), Katie Lowes (April the Resident Asst.), Jonathon Trent (Fassbinder), Walker Howard (Sharsky), America Olivo (Frisbee Girl), Aaron Hill, Jareb Dauplaise (Frat Guys), John Sandeford, Christopher Curry (Pundits), Cas Anvar, Michael Benyaer (Egyptian Interpol Officers), Deep Roy (Egyptian Guard), Ruben Martinez (Bedouin with Donkey), Spencer Garrett (Air Force Chief of Staff), Ralph Meyering Jr. (NORAD General), Aaron Norvell (Air Force Military Police), Eric Pierpoint (NSA Officer), Annie Korzen (Simmons' Mom), Sean T. Krishnan (Yakov), David Bowe, Kamal Jones (Smithsonian Guards), Aaron Lustig, Jim Holmes, Kristen Welker (Reporters), Cornell Womack (FBI Director), David Luengas (Ticket Agent), Derek Alvarado, Alex Fernandez, Casey Nelson, Jason Roehm (Join Ops Staff), John Nielsen (Capt. Wilder), Rick Cramer, Arnold Chun, Marvin Jordan (Diego Garcia Soldiers), Marc Evan Jackson (Commander, US Central Command), Jayson Floyd, Aaron Garrido, Josh Kelly, Joel Lambert, David Olsen, Geoffrey M. Reeves (Strike Force Team) **VOICE CAST:** Peter Cullen (Optimus Prime), Mark Ryan (Jetfire), Reno Wilson (Mudflap), Jess Harnell (Ironhide), Robert Foxworth (Ratchet), André Sogliuzzo (Sideswipe), Grey DeLisle (Arcee), Hugo Weaving (Megatron), Tony Todd (The Fallen), Charlie Adler (Starscream), Frank Welker (Soundwave/Devastator/Reedman/Grindor/Ravage), Tom Kenny (Wheelie/Skids), Calvin Wimmer (Wheelbot), John Di Crosta (Doctor), Michael York, Robin Atkin Downes (Primes), Kevin Michael Richardson (Rampage)

The Decepticons hope to free their leader and gain possession of the remaining pieces of a powerful cube that can control the world. Sequel to the 2007 DreamWorks/ Paramount film *Transformers*.

Megan Fox

Shia LaBeouf, John Turturro

Optimus Prime

MY SISTER'S KEEPER

(NEW LINE CINEMA) Producers, Mark Johnson, Chuck Pacheco, Scott L. Goldman; Executive Producers, Toby Emmerich, Merideth Finn, Mark Kaufman, Diana Pokorny, Stephen Furst, Mendel Tropper; Co-Producers, Hillary Sherman, Steven Posen; Director, Nick Cassavetes; Screenplay, Jeremy Leven, Nick Cassavetes; Based on the novel by Jodi Picoult; Photography, Caleb Deschanel; Designer, Jon Hutman; Costumes, Shay Cunliffe; Music, Aaron Zigman; Editors, Alan Heim, Jim Flynn; Casting, Matthew Barry, Nancy Green-Keyes; a Mark Johnson/Curmudgeon/Scott L. Goldman production; Distributed by Warner Brothers; Dolby; Panavision; Deluxe color; Rated PG-13; 108 minutes; Release date: June 29, 2009

CAST

Sara Fitzgeald	**Cameron Diaz**
Anna Fitzgerald	**Abigail Breslin**
Campbell Alexander	**Alec Baldwin**
Brian Fitzgerald	**Jason Patric**
Kate Fitzgerald	**Sofia Vassileva**
Aunt Kelly	**Heather Wahlquist**
Judge De Salvo	**Joan Cusack**
Taylor Ambrose	**Thomas Dekker**
Jesse Fitzgerald	**Evan Ellingson**
Dr. Chance	**David Thornton**

Walter Raney (Pawn Shop Proprietor), Nicole Lenz (Gloria), Brennan Bailey (Jesse Fitzgerald – age 10), Olivia Hancock (Kate, age 2), Jeffrey Markle (Dr. Wayne), Emily Deschanel (Dr. Farquad), John DeRosa, Marcos De La Cruz (EMTs), Noni Tulk-Perna (Ellen), Matt Barry (Uncle Tommy), Annie Wood (Uncle Tommy's Wife), Mark M. Johnson (Uncle Pervis), Chris Kinkade (Dr. Nguyen), E.G. Daily (Nurse Susan), Rico Simonini (Process Server), Frank Cassavetes (Gus), David Bortolucci (Harry), Olivia Jade Fine (Anna, age 6), Andrew Schiff (Nurse Stephen), Paul Christopher Butler (Jesse, age 3), Andrew Shack (Lawyer for Previous Cae), Angel Garcia (Gangbanger's Mom), Frank Peluso (Bailiff #2), Daniel Guzman (Gangbanger's Lawyer), Paul Anthony Olguin (Gangbanger), Big Al (Bailiff Bert), Mimi Fletcher (De Salvo's Secretary), Lin Shaye (Nurse Adele), Eric Cueto, Lex Ryan (Street Hustlers), Nina Barry (Miss Swearingen), Ellia English (Nurse Alice), Mary Jo Deschanel (Saleswoman), Jonah Johnson (Lead Prom Singer), Rob Giles (Prom Guitarist), Kaiulani Kimbrell (Backup Prom Singer), Dylan Showalter (Prom Bass Player), Jarred Tibbetts (Prom Dummer), Precious Hanley (Mandy), Michael Chow (Dr. Chow), Jon Moonves (Percy Smith, Esquire)

Discension disrupts the Fitzgerald family when their 11-year-old daughter Anna announces her descision to sue for "medical emancipation" to ensure that she will not be obliged to donate a kidney to save the life of her older sister Kate, who is suffering from leukemia.

Abigail Breslin, Alec Baldwin

Evan Ellingson, Abigail Breslin

Jason Patric, Cameron Diaz, Sofia Vassilieva © New Line Cinema

Thomas Dekker, Sofia Vassilieva

James Caviezel, Shohreh Aghdashloo

David Diaan, Ali Pourtash, Parviz Sayyad

Mozhan Marnó

THE STONING OF SORAYA M.

(ROADSIDE) Producers, Steve McEveety, John Shepherd; Executive Producers, Thomas J. Papa, Lisa Maria Falcone, Diane Hendricks; Co-Producers, Deborah Aquila, Todd Burns; Co-Executive Producers, David Segel, Tina Segel, Ken Ferguson; Director, Cyrus Nowrasteh; Screenplay, Cyrus Nowrasteh, Betsy Griffin Nowrasteh; Based on the book by Freidoune Sahebjam; Photography, Joel Ransom; Designer, Judy Rhee; Costumes, Jane Anderson; Music, John Debney; Editors, Geoffrey Rowland, David Handman; Makeup Effects, Christien Tinsley's Tinsley Transfers; Special Effects Supervisor, Jason Hamer; Casting, Deborah Aquila, Tricia Wood, Jennifer Smith; a Mpower Pictures presentation; Dolby; Widescreen; Deluxe color; Rated R; 114 minutes; Release date: June 29, 2009

CAST
Zahra	**Shohreh Aghdashloo**
Soraya M.	**Mozhan Marnò**
Freidoune	**James Caviezel**
Ali	**Navid Negahban**
Mullah	**Ali Pourtash**

David Diaan (Ebrahim), Parviz Sayyad (Hashem), Vida Ghahremani (Bita), Vachik Mangassarian (Soraya's Father), Maggie Parto (Vo), Prasanna Puwanarajah (Revolutionary Guard), Bita Sheibani (Leila), Yousef Shweihat (Ringmaster)

Zahra tells a French-Iranian journalist the disturbing story of how her niece Soraya was falsely accused of adultery by her husband to ensure that he could put an end to their arranged marriage.

Mozhan Marnó, Shohreh Aghdashloo © Roadside Attractions

PUBLIC ENEMIES

(UNIVERSAL) Producers, Kevin Misher, Michael Mann; Executive Producers, G. Mac Brown; Co-Producers, Bryan H. Carroll, Gusmano Cesaretti, Kevin de la Noy; Director, Michael Mann; Screenplay, Ronan Bennett, Michael Mann, Ann Biderman; Based on the book *Public Enemies: America's Greatest Crime Wave and the Birth of the FBI, 1933-34* by Bryan Burrough; Photography, Dante Spinotti; Designer, Nathan Crowley; Costumes, Colleen Atwood; Music, Elliot Goldenthal; Music Supervisors, Bob Badami, Kathy Nelson; Special Visual Effects, Illusion Arts, VFX Collective, Hammerhead, Invisible Effects, Wildfire Visual Effects, Pixel Playground, Lowry Digital; Visual Effects Supervisor, Robert Stadd; Stunts, Darrin Prescott; Casting, Avy Kaufman, Bonnie Timmermann; a Forward Pass/Misher Films production in association with Tribeca Productions and Appian Way, presented in association with Relativity Media; Dolby; Super 35 Widescreen; Color; HD; Rated R; 140 minutes; Release date: July 1, 2009

CAST

John Dillinger	**Johnny Depp**
Melvin Purvis	**Christian Bale**
Billie Frechette	**Marion Cotillard**
John "Red" Hamilton	**Jason Clarke**
Agent Carter Baum	**Rory Cochrane**
J. Edgar Hoover	**Billy Crudup**
Homer Van Meter	**Stephen Dorff**
Charles Winstead	**Stephen Lang**
Phil D'Andrea	**John Oritz**
Alvin Karpis	**Giovanni Ribisi**
Harry "Pete" Pierpont	**David Wenham**
Martin Zarkovich	**John Michael Bolger**
Frank Nitti	**Bill Camp**
Gerry Campbell	**Matt Craven**
Clarence Hunt	**Don Frye**
Baby Face Nelson	**Stephen Graham**
Louis Piquett	**Peter Gerety**
Agent John Madala	**Shawn Hatosy**
Tommy Carroll	**Spencer Garrett**
Agent Hugh Clegg	**John Hoogenakker**
Anna Sage	**Branka Katic**
Gilbert Catena	**Domenick Lombardozzi**
Senator Kenneth D. McKellar	**Ed Bruce**
Walter Dietrich	**James Russo**
Charles Makley	**Christian Stolte**
Pretty Boy Floyd	**Channing Tatum**
Carol Slayman	**Carey Mulligan**
Sheriff Lillian Holley	**Lili Taylor**
Polly Hamilton	**Leelee Sobieski**

John Judd (Turnkey), Michael Vieau (Ed Shouse), John Kishline (Guard Dainard), Wesley Walker (Jim Leslie), John Scherp (Earl Adams), Elena Kenney (Viola Norris), William Nero Jr. (Farm Boy), Madison Dirks (Agent Warren Barton), Len Bajenski (Police Chief Fultz), Adam Clark (Sport), Andrew Krokowski (Oscar Lieboldt), Casey Siemaszko (Harry Berman), Peter Defaria (Grover Weyland), Jonathan Macchi (Teller), Jeff Shannon (Angry Cop), Michael Sassone (Farmer), Emilie de Ravin (Barbara Patzke), Brian Connelly (Officer Chester Boyard), Geoffrey Cantor (Harry Suydam), Chandler Williams (Clyde Tolson), Robert B. Hollingsworth Jr., David Paul Innes, Joe Carlson, Ben Mac Brown (Hoover Reporters), Diana Krall (Torch Singer), Duane A. Sharp (Doorman at the Gold Coast), Richard Short (Agent Sam Cowley), Randy Ryan (Agent Julius Rice), Kurt Naebig (Agent William Rorer), Adam Mucci (Agent Harold Reinecke), Rebecca Spence (Doris Rogers), Danni Simon (May Minczeles), Don Harvey (Customer at Steuben Club), Shanyn Belle Leigh (Helen Gillis), Laurence Mason (Porter at Union Station), Randy Steinmeyer (Cop Eyman), Kris Wolff (Deputy), Donald G. Asher, Andrew Steele, Philip M. Potempa, Craig A. Spidle (Reporters), Brian McConkey (Photographer), Alan Wilder (Robert Estill), David Warshofsky (Warden Baker), Michael Bentt (Herbert Youngblood), John Lister (Judge Murray), Jimmy Carrane (Sam Cahoon), Joseph Mazurk (Guard Bryant), John Fenner Mays (Deputy Blunk), Rick Uecker (Edward Saager), Jason T. Arnold, Andrew Blair (Other Jr. G-Men), Mark Vallarta (Harry Berg), Dan Maldonado (Jacob Solomon), Sean Rosales (Joe Pawlowski), Stephen Spencer (Emil Wanatka), Patrick Zielinski (Doctor), Gareth Saxe (Agent Ray Suran), Guy Van Swearingen (Agent Ralph Brown), Jeff Still (James Probasco), Lance Baker (Freddie Barker), Steve Key (Doc Barker), David Carde (Capt. O'Neill), Gerald Goff, Aaron Weiner (Special Agents), Keith Kupferer (Agent Sopsic), Turk Muller, Tim Grimm (Other East Chicago Cops), Martie Sanders (Irene the Ticket Taker), Robyn Scott (Ella Natasky)

FBI director J. Edgar Hoover enlists Melvin Purvis to put an end to the crime wave sweeping the mid-West, with a special priority to bring down notorious bank robber John Dillinger.

Johnny Depp

Christian Bale, Billy Crudup © Universal Studios

Scratte, Scrat © Twentieth Century Fox

Crash, Ellie, Eddie

Crash, Eddie, Buck

ICE AGE: DAWN OF THE DINOSAURS

(20TH CENTURY FOX) Producers, Lori Forte, John C. Donkin; Executive Producer, Chris Wedge; Director, Carlos Saldanha; Co-Director, Michael Thurmeier; Screenplay, Michael Berg, Peter Ackerman, Mike Reiss, Yoni Brenner; Story, Jason Carter Eaton; Music, John Powell; Editor, Harry Hitner; Character Designer, Peter De Seve; Art Director, Michael Knapp; CG Supervisors, Bryan Useo, Michael Eringis; Supervising Animator, Galen Tan Chu; Casting, Christian Kaplan; Dolby; Deluxe color; 3-D; Rated PG; 93 minutes; Release date: July 1, 2009

VOICE CAST

Manny	**Ray Romano**
Sid	**John Leguizamo**
Diego	**Denis Leary**
Buck	**Simon Pegg**
Ellie	**Queen Latifah**

Seann William Scott (Crash), Josh Peck (Eddie), Bill Hader (Gazelle), Kristen Wiig (Pudgy Beaver Mom), Chris Wedge (Scrat), Eunice Cho (Diatryma Girl), Karen Disher (Scratte), Harrison Fahn (Glypto Boy), Maile Flanagan (Aardvark Mom), Jason Fricchione (Adult Molehog), Kelly Keaton (Molehog Mom/Shovelmouth Mom), Joey King (Beaver Girl), Allegra Leguizamo (Aardvark girl), Lucas Leguizamo (Aardvark Boy/Beaver Kid #2), Clea Lewis (Start Mom), Jane Lynch (Diatryma Mom), Christian Pikes (Little Johnny), Avery Christopher Plum (Beaver Kid #1), Joe Romano (Ronald), Carlos Saldanha (Dinosaur Babies/Flightless Bird), Manoela Scarpa Saldanha, Sofia Scarpa Saldanha (Molehog Girls), Cindy Slattery (Bird)

Manny and his friends go in search of Sid the Sloth, who has been dragged underground by an angry dinosaur after he has taken it upon himself to raise her three offspring.

Buck

BRÜNO

(ÜNIVERSAL) Producers, Sacha Baron Cohen, Jay Roach, Dan Mazer, Monica Levinson; Executive Producer, Anthony Hines; Co-Producers, Jon Poll, Todd Schulman; Director, Larry Charles; Screenplay, Sacha Baron Cohen, Anthony Hines, Dan Mazer, Jeff Schaffer; Story, Sacha Baron Cohen, Peter Baynham, Anthony Hines, Dan Mazer; based on characters created by Sacha Baron Cohen; Photography, Anthony Hardwick, Wolfgang Held; Art Directors, Denise Hudson, David Saenz de Maturana; Costumes, Jason Alper; Music, Erran Baron Cohen; Editors, James Thomas, Scott M. Davids; Makeup and Hair, Thomas Kolarek; Casting, Allison Jones; a Media Rights Capital presentation of a Four by Two Films and Everyman Pictures production; Dolby; Deluxe color; HD; Rated R; 81 minutes; Release date: July 10, 2009

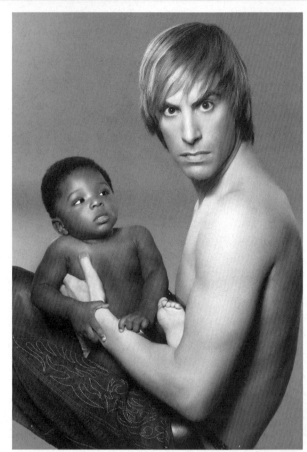

CAST

Brüno	**Sacha Baron Cohen**
Lutz	**Gustaf Hammarsten**
Diesel	**Clifford Bañagale**
O.J.	**Chibundu Orukwowu, Chigozie Orukwowu**
Kookus	**Josh Meyers**
Mexican Gardeners	**Toby Hoguin, Robert Huerta, Gilbert Rosales, Thomas Rogales Jr., Marco Xavier**
"Dove of Peace" Singers	**Bono, Chris Martin, Elton John, Slash, Snoop Dogg, Sting**
Themselves	**Paula Abdul, Richard Bey, Harrison Ford, Brittny Gastineau, Ron Paul, Miguel Sandoval**

Dominziano Arcangeli (Fashion Show Director in Milan), John Grant Gordon (German Model), David Hill (Reporter), Hugh B. Holub (Focus Group Curmudgeon), Michelle McLaren (Dominatrix), Stephen Sepher (Photographer), Alexander von Roon (German Reporter)

Following his expulsion from German television, self-involved Brüno journeys around the globe in hopes of becoming an international celebrity, make no apologies for his outrageously gay behavior.

Chibundu/Chigozie Orukwowu, Sacha Baron Cohen

Sacha Baron Cohen

Sacha Baron Cohen © Üniversal Studios

Alycia Delmore © Magnolia Pictures

Mark Duplass, Joshua Leonard

HUMPDAY

(MAGNOLIA) Producer/Director/Screenplay, Lynn Shelton; Executive Producer, Dave Makayama; Co-Producers, Jennifer Maas, Steven Schardt; Photography, Benjamin Kasulke; Designer, Jasminka Vukcevic; Music, Vinny Smith; Editor, Nat Sanders; a Seashell Pictures presentation; Dolby; Color; Rated R; 94 minutes; Release date: July 10, 2009

CAST
Ben	**Mark Duplass**
Anna	**Alycia Delmore**
Andrew	**Joshua Leonard**
Monica	**Lynn Shelton**
Lily	**Trina Willard**
Boy on Bike	**Stellan Matheisen**
Disgruntled Driver	**Steven Schardt**

David Bundgren, J. Martin Dunn, Patrick Evans-Winfield, Joy Brooke Fairfield, Monica Fisk, Lori Goldston, Jane Hall, Tinka Jonakova, Tania Kupczak, Julia Martlew, John Naito, Clyde Peterson, Eric Richards, Jessie Smith ("Dionysus" Extras)

Two heterosexual best friends decide to enter a contest to make the best amateur porn, figuring there would be something unique about seeing two straight men having sex.

YOO-HOO, MRS. GOLDBERG

(INTERNATIONAL FILM CIRCUIT) Producer/Director/Screenplay, Aviva Kempner; Photography, Tom Kaufman, Dennis Boni, Tom Hurwitz, Barry Kirk, Learan Kahanov, David Waldman; Music, Fred Karns; Editor, Judith E. Herbert; a Ciesla Foundation production; Dolby; Color/black and white; Not rated; 92 minutes; Release date: July 10, 2009

WITH

Ruth Bader Ginsburg, Ed Asner, Norman Lear, Madeline Guilford, Larry Robinson, Arlene McQuade, Viola Harris, Anne Schwartz, David Schwartz, Glen D. Smith Jr., Susan Stamberg, Judith Abrams, Margaret Nagle, Joyce Antler, Adam Berg, Anna Berger, Chris Milanos Downey, Gary David Goldberg, Henry Schwartz, Andrea Roane Skehan, Menashe Shulnick, Robert Thompson, Jack Urbont, Mindy Weisel

Documentary on radio and television actress-writer-producer Gertrude Berg and her long-running series *The Goldbergs*.

Gertrude Berg © Intl. Film Circuit

Arlene McQuade, Philip Loeb, Gertrude Berg, Larry Robinson

Jim Broadbent, Robbie Coltrane, Daniel Radcliffe

Alan Rickman, Emma Watson, Rupert Grint, Daniel Radcliffe, Maggie Smith

Evanna Lynch

Frank Dillane

Dave Legeno, Helena Bonham Carter

Hero Fiennes-Tiffin, Amelda Brown, Michael Gambon

Alan Rickman, Jim Broadbent, Jessie Cave, Daniel Radcliffe

Rupert Grint

Tom Felton

Michael Gambon, Daniel Radcliffe © Warner Bros.

HARRY POTTER AND THE HALF-BLOOD PRINCE

(WARNER BROTHERS) Producers, David Heyman, David Barron; Executive Producer, Lionel Wigram; Director, David Yates; Screenplay, Steve Kloves; Based on the novel by J.K. Rowling; Photography, Bruno Delbonnel; Designer, Stuart Craig; Costumes, Jany Temime; Music, Nicholas Hooper; Editor, Mark Day; Visual Effects Supervisor, Tim Burke; Visual Effects and Animation, Industrial Light & Magic; Casting, Fiona Weir; a Heyday Films production; Dolby; Panavision; Technicolor; Rated PG; 153 minutes; Release date: July 15, 2009

CAST

Harry Potter	**Daniel Radcliffe**
Ron Weasley	**Rupert Grint**
Hermione Granger	**Emma Watson**
Bellatrix Lestrange	**Helena Bonham Carter**
Prof. Horace Slughorn	**Jim Broadbent**
Rubeus Hagrid	**Robbie Coltrane**
Prof. Albus Dumbledore	**Michael Gambon**
Prof. Severus Snape	**Alan Rickman**
Prof. Minerva McGonagall	**Maggie Smith**
Wormtail	**Timothy Spall**
Remus Lupin	**David Thewlis**
Argus Filch	**David Bradley**
Prof. Filius Flitwick	**Warwick Davis**
Draco Malfoy	**Tom Felton**
Ginny Weasley	**Bonnie Wright**
Luna Lovegood	**Evanna Lynch**
Fenrir Greyback	**Dave Legeno**
Narcissa Malfoy	**Helen McCrory**
Molly Weasley	**Julie Walters**
Arthur Weasley	**Mark Williams**
Madam Pomfrey	**Gemma Jones**
Neville Longbottom	**Matthew Lewis**
Tom Riddle – age 11	**Hero Fiennes-Tiffin**
Tom Riddle – age 16	**Frank Dillane**
Waitress	**Elarica Gallacher**
George Weasley	**Oliver Phelps**
Fred Weasley	**James Phelps**
Lily Potter	**Geraldine Somerville**
Lavender Brown	**Jessie Cave**
Nymphadora Tonks	**Natalia Tena**
Cormac McLaggen	**Freddie Stroma**

Johnpaul Castrianni (Yaxley), Alfie Enoch (Dean Thomas), Robert Knox (Marcus Belby), Amber Evans, Ruby Evans (Twins), Louis Cordice (Blaise Zabini), Scarlett Byrne (Pansy Parkinson), Jamie Waylett (Vincent Crabbe), Josh Herdman (Gregory Goyle), William Melling (Nigel), Anna Shaffer (Romilda Vane), Devon Murray (Seamus Finnigan), Georgina Leonidas (Katie Bell), Isabella Laughland (Leanne), Afshan Azad (Padma Patil), Shefali Chowdhury (Parvati Patil), Amelda Brown (Mrs. Cole), Jack Pryor (Skinny Kid), Mark Lockyer (Waiter), Paul Ritter (Eldred Worple), Joerg Stadler, Caroline Wildie (Inferis), Ralph Ineson (Amycus Carrow), Suzanne Toase (Alecto Carrow), Rod Hunt (Thorfinn Rowle)

As the Dark Lord's plan of destruction gains power, Professor Dumbledore persuades Horace Slughorn to return to Hogwarts in hopes of him revealing pertinent information about Voldemort from when he had been a student at the school. Sixth entry in the Warner Brothers series.

(500) DAYS OF SUMMER

(FOX SEARCHLIGHT) Producers, Jessica Tuchinsky, Mark Waters, Mason Novick, Steven J. Wolfe; Co-Producer, Scott G. Hyman; Director, Marc Webb; Screenplay, Scott Neustadter, Michael H. Weber; Photography, Eric Steelberg; Designer, Laura Fox; Costumes, Hope Hanafin; Music, Mychael Danna, Rob Simonsen; Editor, Alan Edward Bell; Casting, Eyde Belasco; a Watermark production; Dolby; Panavision; Deluxe color; Rated PG-13; 95 minutes; Release date: July 17, 2009

CAST

Tom Hansen	**Joseph Gordon-Levitt**
Summer Finn	**Zooey Deschanel**
McKenzie	**Geoffrey Arend**
Rachel Hansen	**Chloe Moretz**
Paul	**Matthew Gray Gubler**
Vance	**Clark Gregg**
Millie	**Patricia Belcher**
Alison	**Rachel Boston**
Girl at Interview (Autumn)	**Minka Kelly**
Douche	**Ian Reed Kesler**
Bus Driver	**Darryl Alan Reed**

Valente Rodriguez (Employee #1), Yvette Nicole Brown (New Secretary), Nicole Vicius, Natalie Boren (Partygoers), Maile Flanagan (Rhoda), Darryl Sivad (Usher), Gregory A. Thompson (Minister), Michael Bodie (Man), John Mackey (Mime), Jacob Stroop (Cupid), Kevin Michael (Wedding Singer), Sid Wilner (Grossman), Richard McConagle (Narrator); Jean-Paul Vignon (French Narrator), Olivia Howard Bagg (Summer – age 12), Jennifer Hetrick (Sarah), Kenneth Hughes, Nathan Prevost (Dancers), Kevin Leung (Chinese Father), Eileen Reardon (Lookalike), Jason Robinson (The Puma), Charles Walker (Millie's New Husband), Adam Emery (Tom – age 12)

The tremulous, up-and-down relationship between Tom and Summer is recounted over a 500 day period.

Joseph Gordon-Levitt, Zooey Deschanel

Joseph Gordon-Levitt, Zooey Deschanel © Fox Searchlight

Joseph Gordon-Levitt, Zooey Deschanel

Zooey Deschanel, Joseph Gordon-Levitt

Zach Galifianakis, Kelli Garner © Disney Enterprises/Jerry Bruckheimer

G-FORCE

(WALT DISNEY STUDIOS) Producer, Jerry Bruckheimer; Executive Producers, Duncan Henderson, David P.I. James, Chad Oman, Mike Stenson; Co-Producer, Todd Arnow; Director, Hoyt H. Yeatman Jr.; Screenplay, The Wibberleys; Story, Hoyt H. Yeatman Jr., David P.I. James; Photography, Bojan Bazelli; Designer, Deborah Evans; Costumes, Ellen Mirojnick; Music, Trevor Rabin; Editors, Mark Goldblatt, Jason Hellmann; Music Supervisor, Kathy Nelson; Visual Effects Supervisor, Scott Stokydk; Digital Effects, Seth Maury; Animation Supervisor, Troy Salba; Casting, Ronna Kress; Presented with Jerry Bruckheimer Films; Dolby; 3-D; Technicolor; Rated PG; 87 minutes; Release date: July 24, 2009

CAST
Leonard Saber	**Bill Nighy**
Darwin (voice)	**Sam Rockwell**
Kip Killian	**Will Arnett**
Hurley (voice)	**Jon Favreau**
Ben	**Zach Galifianakis**
Speckles (voice)	**Nicolas Cage**
Marcie	**Kelli Garner**
Juarez (voice)	**Penélope Cruz**
Connor	**Tyler Patrick Jones**
Bucky (voice)	**Steve Buscemi**
Penny	**Piper Mackenzie Harris**
Blaster (voice)	**Tracy Morgan**
Agent Trigstad	**Gabriel Casseus**
Agent Carter	**Jack Conley**
Rosalita	**Niecy Nash**

Justin Mentell (Terrell), Loudon Wainwright III (Grandpa Goodman), Chris Ellis (FBI Director), Travis Davis, James Huang, Corey Eubanks, Steve Kelso, Eddie Yansick, Troy Robinson (Agents), Mini Anden (Christa, Saber's Assistant), Cameron Engels (Skateboarder #1), Algerita Wynn Lewis (Traffic Cop), Bob Sherer (Golf Course Exterminator), Jennifer England (Falling Waitress), Jason Hellmann (Fireworks Tech), Nicholas L. Teta (SWAT Leader), Hoyt Yeatman, Max Favreau (Mice Voices), Dee Bradley Baker (Mooch Voice), Vincent De Paul (Mr. Bates), Helen Tucker (Mrs. Bates), Paul Joyner (NSA Agent), Michael Papajohn (FBI Techie)

A group of specially trained animal operatives tries to stop shifty coffee manufacturer Leonard Saber from wiping out civilization by way of a computer virus.

ORPHAN

(WARNER BROTHERS) Producers, Joel Silver, Susan Downey, Jennifer Davisson Killoran, Leonardo DiCaprio; Executive Producers, Steve Richards, Don Carmody, Michael Ireland; Co-Producers, Richard Mirisch, David Barrett, Erik Olsen; Director, Jaume Collet-Serra; Screenplay, David Leslie Johnson; Story, Alex Mace; Photography, Jeff Cutter; Designer, Tom Meyer; Costumes, Antoinette Messam; Music, John Ottman; Editor, Tim Alverson; Visual Effects Supervisor, Richard Yuricich; Casting, Ronnie Yeskel; an Appian Way production, presented in association with Dark Castle Entertainment; Dolby; Technicolor; Rated R; 123 minutes; Release date: July 24, 2009

CAST
Kate Coleman	**Vera Farmiga**
John Coleman	**Peter Sarsgaard**
Esther	**Isabelle Fuhrman**
Sister Abigail	**CCH Pounder**
Daniel Coleman	**Jimmy Bennett**
Dr. Browning	**Margo Martindale**

Karel Roden (Dr. Värava), Aryana Engineer (Max Coleman), Rosemary Dunsmore (Grandma Barbara), Jamie Young (Brenda), Lorry Ayers (Joyce), Brendan Wall (Detective), Genelle Williams (Sister Judith), Mustafa Abdelkarim, Landon Norris (Daniel's Friends), Julien Elia (Hospital Receptionist), Leni Parker (Delivery Room Nurse), Gemma James Smith (Teacher), Pia Ajango (Saarne Institute Receptionist), Matthew Raudsepp (Saarne Institute Orderly), Sugith Varughese (ICU Doctor), Luis Olivia (ICU Nurse), Ferelith Young (Waiting Room Nurse), Andrew Shaver (Injection Doctor)

Kate and John Coleman, hoping to compensate for the tragic loss of one of their children, adopt a little girl who very soon begins showing signs of imbalance and murderous rage.

Aryana Engineer, Jimmy Bennett, Peter Sarsgaard, Isabelle Fuhrman, Vera Farmiga © Warner Bros.

Kevin Spacey © Roadside Attractions

SHRINK

(ROADSIDE ATTRACTIONS) Producers, Michael Burns, Braxton Pope, Dana Brunetti; Co-Producers, John Saviano, Pell James; Director, Jonas Pate; Screenplay, Thomas Moffett; based on a story by Henry Rearden; Photography, Lukas Ettlin; Designer, Mark Hutman; Costumes, Johanna Argan; Music, Brian Reitzell, Ken Andrews; Editor, Luis Carballar; Casting, Sheila Jaffe; a Trigger Street Productions, Ithaka Entertainment and Ignite Productions presentation; Dolby; Color; Rated R; 110 minutes; 104 minutes; Release date: July 24, 2009

CAST

Henry Carter	**Kevin Spacey**
Robert Carter	**Robert Loggia**
Daisy	**Pell James**
Jemma	**Keke Palmer**
Kate Amberson	**Saffron Burrows**
Shamus	**Jack Huston**
Patrick	**Dallas Roberts**

Gore Vidal (George Charles), Laura Ramsey (Keira), Mark Webber (Jeremy), Jesse Plemons (Jesus), Robin Williams (Holden), Derek Alvarado (Ramirez), Damian Cecere (Intern Supervisor), Kendall Clement (Uncle Jim), Robert Farrior (Bryce), Sierra Aylina McClain (Carina), Mei Melançon (Miyu), Troy Metcalf (O.T.), Joe Nieves (Lil King), Mina Olivera (Make-up Artist), Brian Palmero (Mitch), Philip Pavel (Neil), Clayton Rohner (Dr. McBurney), Andrew Sibner (Richie), Pleasant Wayne (Jemma's Mother), Ken Weiler (Jason), Jillian Armenante (Studio Executive), Joseph A. Nuñez (Recording Supervisor), Ada Luz Pla (Teacher), Joel Gretsch (Evan), Aimee Garcia (Checkout Girl), Tiernan Burns (Tiernan), Mystro Clark (Dr. Morton), Justin Alston (Rio), Michelle Columbia (Geisha Hostess), Ashley Michele Greene (Missy), Branden Morgan (Eric), Brian Huskey (Film Executive), Jennifer Rade (Fan), Thomas Moffett (Director), Bobby Arnot (Intern) Griffin Dunne

A wearied, pot smoking Los Angeles psychiatrist must cope with his own demons while dealing with the various lost souls who make up his patients.

THE UGLY TRUTH

(COLUMBIA) Producers, Steven Reuther, Kimberly di Bonaventura, Deborah Jelin Newmyer, Tom Rosenberg, Gary Lucchesi; Executive Producers, Andre Lamal, Eric Reid, Katherine Heigl, Nancy Heigl, Karen McCullah Lutz, Kirsten Smith, Ryan Kavanaugh; Director, Robert Luketic; Screenplay, Nicole Eastman, Karen McCullah Lutz, Kirsten Smith; Story, Nicole Eastman; Photography, Russell Carpenter; Designer, Missy Stewart; Costumes, Betsy Heimann; Music, Aaron Zigman; Editor, Lisa Zeno Churgin; Casting, Tricia Wood, Deborah Aquila; a Lakeshore Entertainment/Steven Reuther production, presented in association with Relativity Media; Dolby; Panavision; Deluxe color; Rated R; 95 minutes; Release date: July 24, 2009

CAST

Abby Richter	**Katherine Heigl**
Mike Chadway	**Gerard Butler**
Colin	**Eric Winter**
Cliff	**Jesse D. Goins**
Georgia	**Cheryl Hines**
Larry	**John Michael Higgins**

Bree Turner (Joy), Eric Winter (Colin), Noah Matthews (Jonah), Bonnie Somerville (Elizabeth), John Sloman (Bob), Yvette Nicole Brown (Dori), Nate Corddry (Josh), Allen Maldonado (Duane), Steve Little (Steve), Dan Callahn (Rick), Tess Parker (Bambi), Arielle Vandenberg (Candi), Kevin Connolly (Jim), Rocco DiSpirito (Guest Chef), Valente Rodriguez (Javier), Jamison Yang, Blake Robbins (KPQU Big Wigs), Austin Winsberg (KPQU Joe), Tom Virtue (Balloon Pilot), Adam Harrington (Jack Magnum), J. Claude Deering (Drunk Guy), Alexis Krause (Cute Brunette), Craig Ferguson (Himself), Caleb De Oliveira (Kid), Jade Marx (Hostess), Lenny Schmidt, Nathan Potter (Waiters), Mimi Michaels (Fan), Donnie Smith (Boyfriend), Kate Mulligan (Waitress), Earl Carroll (Security Guard), Marc D. Wilson (Bell Man), Jeff Newburg (KPQU Production Assistant), Ryan Surratt (Bartender), Vicki Lewis (Saleswoman), David Lowe (Cameraman), Yolanda Pecoraro (Sexy Woman), Brooke Stone (Karen), Stephanie Mace (TV Production Assistant), Bob Morrisey (Harold), Holly Weber (Chef Megan)

In order to help her station's floundering ratings, producer Abby Richter reluctantly accepts the hiring of shock jock Mike Chadway, who enjoys pushing women's buttons with his outspoken, chauvinistic views on female behavior.

Gerard Butler, Katherine Heigl © Columbia Pictures

Rose Byrne, Peter Gallagher, Amy Irving

Rose Byrne, Hugh Dancy

Rose Byrne, Hugh Dancy

Rose Byrne, Hugh Dancy © Fox Searchlight

ADAM

(FOX SEARCHLIGHT) Producers, Leslie Urdang, Miranda de Pencier, Dean Vanech; Executive Producers, Dan Revers, Christina Weiss Lurie; Co-Producers, Gary Giudice, Geoff Linville; Director/Screenplay, Max Mayer; Photography, Seamus Tierney; Designer, Tamar Gadish; Costumes, Alysia Raycraft; Music, Christopher Lennertz; Music Supervisor, Robin Urdang; Editor, Grant Myers; Casting, Sig de Miguel, Stephen Vincent; an Olympus Pictures production, in association with Serenade Films, Deer Path Productions, Vox3 Films; Dolby; Arri-Widescreen; Color; Rated PG-13; 97 minutes; Release date: July 29, 2009

CAST

Adam Raki	**Hugh Dancy**
Beth Buchwald	**Rose Byrne**
Marty Buchwald	**Peter Gallagher**
Rebecca Buchwald	**Amy Irving**
Harlan	**Frankie Faison**
Sam Klieber	**Mark Linn-Baker**
Lyra	**Haviland Morris**
Mr. Wardlow	**Adam LeFevre**
Judge	**Mike Hodge**
Williams	**Peter O'Hara**
Beranbaum	**John Rothman**
Michael	**Terry Walters**
Jen	**Susan Porro**
Robin	**Maddie Corman**

Jeff Hiller (Rom), Karina Arroyave (Teacher Assistant), Steffany Huckaby (Carol), Mark Doherty, Tom Levanti (Cops), Ursula Abbott (Kelli), Luka Kain (Bruce), Brooke Johnston (Stephanie), Lonnie McCullough (Expert Witness), Tyler Poelle (Bryan), Andrew Patrick Ralston (Mr. Garland, Tour Leader), Torsten N. Hillhouse (Guest #1), Bill Dawes (Scottie), Hunter Reid (Child)

Beth Buchwald finds herself falling in love with her neighbor, Adam Raki, a lonely young man who suffers from asperger's syndrome.

FUNNY PEOPLE

(UNIVERSAL/COLUMBIA) Producers, Judd Apatow, Clayton Townsend, Barry Mendel; Executive Producers, Seth Rogen, Evan Goldberg, Jack Giarraputo; Co-Producers, Andrew J. Cohen, Brendan O'Brien; Director/Screenplay, Judd Apatow; Photography, Janusz Kaminski; Designer, Jefferson Sage; Costumes, Nancy Steiner, Betsy Heimann; Music, Jason Schwartzman, Michael Andrews; Editors, Brent White, Craig Alpert; Casting, Allison Jones; an Apatow and Madison 23 production, presented in association with Relativity Media; Dolby; Technicolor; Rated R; 146 minutes; Release date; July 31, 2009

Adam Sandler, Eric Bana, Seth Rogen

CAST

George Simmons	**Adam Sandler**
Ira Wright	**Seth Rogen**
Laura	**Leslie Mann**
Clarke	**Eric Bana**
Leo Koenig	**Jonah Hill**
Mark Taylor Jackson	**Jason Schwartzman**
Daisy Danby	**Aubrey Plaza**
Chuck	**RZA**
Ingrid	**Iris Apatow**
Mable	**Maude Apatow**
Dr. Lars	**Torsten Voges**
Dr. Stevens	**Allan Wasserman**
Comedy & Magic Manager	**Wayne Federman**
MySpace Escort	**Mike O'Connell**
Dawn	**Nicole Parker**
Mandy	**Nydia McFadden**
Lisa, George's Sister	**Nicol Paone**
George's Dad	**George Coe**
George's Agent	**Bryan Batt**
Rachel	**Maggie Siff**

Rod Man, James Taylor, Andy Dick, Charles Fleischer, Budd Friedman, Monty Hoffman, Carol Leifer, Paul Reiser, Mark Schiff, George Wallace, Norm MacDonald, Dave Attell, Sarah Silverman, Eminem, Ray Romano, Tom Anderson, Orny Adams, Al Lubel, Jerry Minor (Themselves), Aziz Ansari (Randy), Jon Brion, Sebastian Steinberg, James Gadson (Jam Musicians), Arshad Aslam, Bo Burnham, M. Michelle Nishikawa, Kenny Copeland Jr., Calvin Sykes, Ca'Shawn Sims, Mandi Kreisher, Phillip Andre Botello (*Yo Teach …!* Cast Members), Carla Gallo (Miss Pruitt on *Yo Teach …!*), Ernest Thomas (*Yo Teach … !* Principal), Tonita Castro (Bonita), Carlos Andrade (Gardener), Steve Bannos (Deli Manger), Justin Long (*Re-Do* Guy), Lucas Dick, Tyler Spindel (College Guys with Cameras), Deamor Yi (Eight-Year-Old Fan), Elaine Kao (Mom with Camera), King Kedar, Andre Butler Jr., Tanya Acker (Family with Camera), Jarrett Grode (Magician), Qiana Chase (Chuck's Wife), John Hartmann (Private Jet Pilot), Dave Rath (San Franciscio Theatre Manager), Dan Harmon, Brandon Cournoyer, Kyle Kinane (Paparazzi at Medical Center), Mark Cohen (Emcee at Improv), Denise Meyerson, Joanie Marx (Deli Customers), Da'Vone McDonald (Hot Dog-Eating Co-Star), Adam J. Bernstein (Hot Dog-Eating Champion's Son), Eleanor Zee (George's Mom), Ben Meyerson (George's Brother-in-Law), Sammy Jack (George's Young Nephew), Kim Taylor, Andrea Zonn, Kate Markowitz, Arnold McCuller, Larry Goldings, Luis Conte, Russ Kunkel, Jimmy Johnson (James Taylor's Musicians), Brad Grunberg, Brian Lally (Comedy & Magic Club Audience Members)

Seth Rogen, Aubrey Plaza

Aspiring comedian Ira Wright thinks he has fallen into a dream job when he ends up working as a personal assistant to successful stand-up comic-turned-movie star George Simmons, a short-tempered egotist facing a potential health crisis.

Adam Sandler, Leslie Mann

Jonah Hill, Seth Rogen, Jason Schwartzman

Jonah Hill, Jason Schwartzman, Adam Sandler © Universal Studios

Seth Rogen, Adam Sandler

Jason Schwartzman, Seth Rogen, Jonah Hill

Seth Rogen

RZA, Seth Rogen

COLD SOULS

(SAMUEL GOLDWYN CO.) Producers, Dan Carey, Elizabeth Giamatti, Paul Mezey, Andrij Parekh, Jeremy Kipp Walker; Executive producers, John Hynansky, D.J. Martin, James Shifren; Co-Producer, Alexandre Mallet-Guy; Director/Screenplay, Sophie Barthes; Photography, Andrij Parekh; Designer, Elizabeth Mickle; Costumes, Erin Benach; Music, Dickon Hinchcliffe; Music Supervisor, Tracy McKnight; Editor, Andrew Mondshein; Casting, Daniel Swee; a Two Lane Pictures and Winner Arts presentation of a Journeyman Pictures/Touchy Feely Films production, in association with Memento Films Production and Arte France Cinema; American-French; Dolby; Color; Rated PG-13; 101 minutes; Release date: August 7, 2009

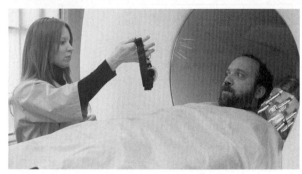

Lauren Ambrose, Paul Giamatti © Samuel Goldwyn Films

CAST

Paul Giamatti	**Paul Giamatti**
Nina	**Dina Korzun**
Claire	**Emily Watson**
Dr. Flintstein	**David Strathairn**
Sveta	**Katheryn Winnick**
Stephanie	**Lauren Ambrose**

Boris Kievsky (Oleg), Oksana Lada (Sasha), Natalia Zvereva (Anastasia), Rebecca Brooksher (Yelena), Yevgeniy Dekhtyar (Hotel Receptionist), Fabrizia Dal Farra, Alexandra Donhoeffner (Ballerinas), Michael Aronov (Maifoso), Marie-Pierre Beausejour (Sonya), Erin Cronican (Assistant to Director), Ted Koch (INS Officer), Gregory Korostishevsky (Yuri), Armand Schultz (Astrov), Stella Stark (Paul's Mother), Wendy Rich Stetson (Soul Storage Mother), Michael Tucker (Frank the Theatre Director), Laura Heisler (Client in Promo), Brienin Bryant (Young Woman in Cold Storage), Gregory Korostishevsky (Igor), Seth Austin (Androgynous Person), Jeanette Gould (Marya), Stella Stark (Paul's Mother), Michael Stuhlbarg (Hedge Fund Consultant),

Finding himself burdened by the heavy role he is playing a production of *Uncle Vanya*, actor Paul Giamatti enlists the services of a high-tech company promising to alleviate suffering by deep freezing his soul.

David Strathairn, Paul Giamatti

Katheryn Winnick

Byung-hun Lee © Paramount Pictures

Channing Tatum

Byung-hun Lee, Sienna Miller

G.I. JOE: THE RISE OF COBRA

(PARAMOUNT) Producers, Lorenzo di Bonaventura, Brian Goldner, Bob Ducsay; Executive Producers, David Womark, Stephen Sommers, Gary Barber, Roger Birnbaum, Erik Howsam; Co-Producer, JoAnn Perritano; Director, Stephen Sommers; Screenplay, Stuart Beattie, David Elliot, Paul Lovett; Story, Michael B. Gordon, Stuart Beattie, Stephen Sommers; based on Hasbro's G.I. Joe characters; Photography, Mitchell Amundsen; Designer, Ed Verreaux; Costumes, Ellen Mirojnick; Music, Alan Silvestri; Editor, Bob Ducsay; Visual Effects Supervisor, Boyd Shermis; Visual Effects, Digital Domain, The Moving Picture Co., CIS Group, Prime Focus; Stunts, R.A. Rondell; Fight Choreographer, Marcus Young; Casting, Ronna Kress; a Di Bonaventura Pictures production, presented with Spyglass Entertainment, in association with Hasbro; Dolby; Panavision; Deluxe color; Rated PG-13; 118 minutes; Release date: August 7, 2009

CAST

Heavy Duty	**Adewale Akinnuoye-Agbaje**
James McMullen/Destro	**Christopher Eccelston**
The Doctor/Rex Lewis	**Joseph Gordon-Levitt**
Storm Shadow	**Byung-hun Lee**
Ana/Baroness	**Sienna Miller**
Shan "Scarlett" O'Hara	**Rachel Nichols**
Snake Eyes	**Ray Park**
U.S. President	**Jonathan Pryce**
General Abernathy/Hawk	**Dennis Quaid**
Breaker	**Saïd Taghmaoui**
Captain Duke Hauser	**Channing Tatum**
Ripcord	**Marlon Wayans**

Grégory Fitoussi (Baron de Cobray), Leo Howard (Young Snake Eyes), Karolina Kurkova (Courtney A. Kreiger/Cover Girl), David Murray (James McCullen - 1641), Kevin J. O'Connor (Dr. Mindbender), Gerald Okamura (Hard Master), Brandon Soo Hoo (Young Storm Shadow), Arnold Vosloo (Zartan), Chris Akers, Wayne Lopez (G.I. Joe Security Techs), Fabrice Baral (CNN Reporter), Michael Benyaer (Fligth Control Technician), Peter Breitmayer (Dr. Hundtkinder), Michael Broderick (Screaming Man), Elena Evangelo, Mark Hames (White House Staff), Jacques Frantz (Bastille Prison Warden), Kellie Matteson (G.I. Joe Control Room Tech), Burton Perez (Bravo Soldier), Bob Rumnock (M.A.R.S. Lab Worker), Robert Russell (Bastille Prison Priest), Ashley Sommers (Little Girl), Michael Sommers (Neo Viper Secret Service), Gunner Wright (Secret Service Agent), Duncan Bravo, Charles Howerton, Robert Almodovar, David Jean Thomas (Foreign Generals), Ken Thomas, Frederic Doss (Apache Navigators), Buzz Covington, Ron Thompson (Apache Helicopter Pilots), Brendan Fraser (Sgt. Stone)

James McCullen plots to steal back a pair of nanotechnology-based warheads that are in the possession of the G.I. Joe's, an elite military unit of special operatives who hoped to keep the madman from carrying out his plan of using the weapons to destroy an entire city.

Rachel Nichols, Marlon Wayans

JULIE & JULIA

(COLUMBIA) Producers, Amy Robinson, Eric Steel, Laurence Mark, Nora Ephron; Executive Producers, Scott Rudin, Donald J. Lee Jr., Dana Stevens; Director/Screenplay, Nora Ephron; Based on the books *Julie & Julia* by Julie Powell and *My Life in France* by Julia Child, with Alex Prud'homme; Photography, Stephen Goldblatt; Designer, Mark Ricker; Costumes, Ann Roth; Music, Alexandre Desplat; Editor, Richard Marks; Casting, Francine Maisler, Kathy Driscoll-Mohler; an Easy There Tiger/Amy Robinson production, a Laurence Mark production; Dolby; Deluxe color; Rated PG-13; 122 minutes; Release date: August 7, 2009

Amy Adams, Chris Messina

CAST

Julia Child	**Meryl Streep**
Julie Powell	**Amy Adams**
Paul Child	**Stanley Tucci**
Eric Powell	**Chris Messina**
Simone Beck	**Linda Emond**
Louisette Bertholle	**Helen Carey**
Sarah	**Mary Lynn Rajskub**
Dorothy McWilliams	**Jane Lynch**
Madame Brassart	**Joan Juliet Buck**
Ernestine	**Crystal Noelle**
Chef Max Bugnard	**George Bartenieff**
Cassie	**Vanessa Ferlito**
Regina	**Casey Wilson**
Annabelle	**Jillian Bach**
John O'Brien	**Andrew Garman**
Ivan Cousins	**Michael Brian Dunn**
John McWilliams	**Remak Ramsay**
Phila McWilliams	**Diane Kagan**
Instructor at Le Cordon Bleu	**Pamela Holden Stewart**
Minister	**Jeff Brooks**
Irma Rombauer	**Frances Sternhagen**
Mr. Misher	**Brooks Ashmanskas**
Tim	**Eric Sheffer Stevens**
Garth	**Brian Avers**
Woman at the Party	**Megan Byrne**
Avis De Voto	**Deborah Rush**
Dorothy De Santillana	**Helen Coxe**

Amy Adams

Kacie Sheik (Annette), Amanda Hesser (Herself), Maryann Urbano, Simon Jutras, Felicity Jones (Dinner Guests), Meg Kettell (Simca's Concierge), Stephen Bogardus (Scott McLeod), Byron Jennings, Kelly AuCoin, Richard Bekins (Houghton Mifflin Executives), Luc Palun (The Chestnut Vendor), Rémy Roubakha (Oyster Man), Marceline Hugot (Madame Bernheim), Erin Dilly (Judith Jones), Robert Emmet Lunney (Bill Koshland), Guiesseppe Jones (Mailman), Jeff Talbot, Johnny Sparks (Interrogators), Simon Feil, Paul Borghese, Mark Gindick, D.L. Shroder, Darin De Paul (GI's), Tom Galantich (American Ambassador), Allyn Burrows (Waiter in Paris Café), Natalie Cenovia Cummins, Maxim Moston, Shmuel Katz, Paul Ognissanti, Eric G. Halvorson (Musicians at the Wedding), Julia Prud'homme (Bridge Teacher), Dimitri Radochevitch (Fish Monger), Emmanuel Suarez (Baker), Christelle Cornil (Baker's Wife), Françoise Lebrun (Baker's Mother), Teddy Bergman (Cobb Salad Waiter), Jean-Pierre Becker (Fruit Store Owner), Mark Wilkins (Butcher), Jamie D. Hall (Cheese Guy), Francesco David (Butcher), Denise M. Whalen, Luis Villabon, Valentine Aprile, Alexander Brady (Dancers), Roy William Gardner (Exhibit Guest), Dianne Dreyer (American Housewife), Evalyn B. Taucher (Hat-Making Teacher), Mary Kay Place (Voice of Julie's Mom)

Amy Adams

The true story of how Julia Child became one of the foremost cooking experts; contrasted with how Julie Powell found some purpose in life by making it her mission to make every recipe in Child's groundbreaking book, *Mastering the Art of French Cooking*, and blogging about it.

This film received an Oscar nomination for actress (Meryl Streep).

Stanley Tucci

Meryl Streep

Jane Lynch, Meryl Streep, Stanley Tucci

Rémy Roubakha, Meryl Streep

Amy Adams

Meryl Streep

Michael Cera, Charlyne Yi © Overture Films

PAPER HEART

(OVERTURE) Producers, Elise Salomon, Sandra Murillo; Executive Producers, Nicholas Jasenovec, Charlyne Yi; Director, Nicholas Jasenovec; Screenplay, Nicholas Jasenovec, Charlyne Yi; Photography, Jay Hunter; Music, Michael Cera, Charlyne Yi; Editor, Ryan Brown; Puppet Designers, Charlyne Yi, Luciano Yi; Casting, Eileen Kennedy; an Anchor Bay Entertainment presentation of a Paper Heart production; Dolby; Color; HD; Rated PG-13; 88 minutes; Release date: August 7, 2009

CAST
Charlyne	**Charlyne Yi**
Michael	**Michael Cera**
Nicholas Jasenovec	**Jake M. Johnson**

Sarah Baker, Matthew Bass, Matthew Craig, Don Emerson, Sally Emerson, Gabrielle Felder, Sidney Hardy, Kirsti Manna, Demetri Martin, Brendan Paul, John Pivovarnick, Seth Rogen, Paul Rust, David Sartor, Faith Shannon, Given Sharp, Martin Starr, Bob Sullivan, Lois Sullivan, Gill Summers, Bill Warner, Derek Waters, Morgan Williams, Luciano Yi, Lydia Yi, Mike Modrak, Bill Hase (Themselves)

While making a documentary about the quest for love, stand-up comic Charlyne Yi finds herself becoming involved with actor Michael Cera.

A PERFECT GETAWAY

(ROGUE PICTURES) Producers, Ryan Kavanaugh, Mark Canton, Tucker Tooley, Robbie Brenner; Executive Producer, Robert Bernacchi; Co-Producer, Kenneth Halsband; Director/Screenplay, David Twohy; Photography, Mark Plummer; Designer, Joseph Nemec III; Costumes, Laura Goldsmith; Music, Boris Elkis; Music Supervisor, Gina Amador; Editor, Tracy Adams; Casting, Anne McCarthy, Jay Scully, Freddy Luis; a Relativity Media production in association with QED Intl.; Dolby; Super 35 Widescreen; Technicolor; Rated R; 97 minutes; Release date: August 7, 2009

CAST
Cliff	**Steve Zahn**
Nick	**Timothy Olyphant**
Cydney	**Milla Jovovich**
Gina	**Kiele Sanchez**
Cleo	**Marley Shelton**
Kale	**Chris Hemsworth**

Anthony Ruivivar (Chronic), Dale Dickey (Earth Momma), Peter Navy Tuiasosopo (Supply Guy), Wendy Braun (Debbie Mason), Jim Cruz (Helicopter Pilot), Angela Sun (Counter Girl), Leandra Gillis (TV Anchor), Amit Yogev (Waiter), Carlos Alberto Lopez (Camera Samaritan), Katie Chonacas, Natalie Garza, Lindsay Halladay (KC Girls), Mercedes Leggett (Katie Nakamura), Leif Riddell (Perimeter Cop), Matt Birman (Trekker), Tory Kittles (Sherman, Kayaker), Brandon Olive (Rick, Kayaker), Holt McCallany (Police Lieutenant), Isaac Santiago (Police Shooter), Gugun Deep Singh (Woody), Ryan Gesell (Groom), Evelyn Lopez (Bride), John T. Cogan (Best Man), Michael Traynor, Spencer Hill, Mike Begovich (Groosmen), Elizabeth Maxwell, Lindsey Huang (Bridesmaids), Katelin Chesna Henke (Cydney's Sister), Andy Hoff (Clueless Husband), Travis Willingham (Tommy), Webster Williams (Father of Groom), Cristina Soler (Mother of Groom), Grigsby Poland (Cheap Man), Grace Connelly (Cheap Man's Wife)

While on their honeymoon in Hawaii, Cliff and Cydney link up with another couple, leading to various tensions and suspicions when word gets out about a pair of unidentified murderers at large.

Milla Jovovich © Rogue/Universal

A Perfect Getaway, Milla Jovovich, Steve Zahn

Ron Livingston

Rachel McAdams, Eric Bana

Rachel McAdams, Eric Bana © New Line Cinema

Rachel McAdams

THE TIME TRAVELER'S WIFE

(NEW LINE CINEMA) Producers, Nick Wechsler, Dede Gardner; Executive Producers, Brad Pitt, Richard Brener, Michele Weiss, Justis Greene; Director, Robert Schwentke; Screenplay, Bruce Joel Rubin; Based on the novel by Audrey Niffenegger; Photography, Florian Ballhaus; Designer, Jon Hutman; Costumes, Julie Weiss; Music, Mychael Danna; Music Supervisor, Bob Bowen; Editor, Thom Noble; Visual Effects Supervisor, David M.V. Jones; Stunts, John Stoneham Jr.; Casting, Deborah Aquila, Tricia Wood; a Plan B/Nick Wechsler production; Distributed by Warner Brothers; Dolby; Super 35 Widescreen; Deluxe color; Rated PG-13; 107 minutes; Release date: August 14, 2009

CAST

Clare Abshire	**Rachel McAdams**
Henry DeTamble	**Eric Bana**
Richard DeTamble	**Arliss Howard**
Gomez	**Ron Livingston**
Dr. David Kendrick	**Stephen Tobolowsky**
Annette DeTable	**Michelle Nolden**
Charisse	**Jane McLean**
Alba at Nine and Ten	**Hailey McCann**
Alab at Four and Five	**Tatum McCann**
Clare at Six and Eight	**Brooklynn Proulx**
Henry at Six	**Alex Ferris**

Katherine Trowell (Hospital Receptionist), Bart Bedford (Library Researcher), Esther Jun (Waitress), Matt Birman, Craig Snoyer (Chicago Police), Carly Street (Librarian), Romyen Tangsubutra (Thai Waiter), Brian Bisson (Mark Abshire), Maggie Castle (Alicia Abshire), Fiona Reid (Lucille Abshire), Philip Craig (Philip Abshire), Mario Tufino (Barber), Shawn Storer (Moving Man), David Talbot (Pastor), James Lafazanos (Jeremy, Gallery Owner), Dan Duran (Lottery Announcer), Kenner Ames (TV Sales Person), Alison MacLeod (Realtor), Donald Carrier (Dr. Osman), Jan Caruana (Dr. Osman's Nurse), Jean Yoon (Dr. Montague), Duane Murray (Resident Doctor), Paul Francis (Hunting Buddy), Jon Bruno (Chicago Radio Show Host), Kevin Drew (Band Singer), Brendan Canning, Andrew Whiteman, Justin Peroff (Broken Social Scene - The Band)

Clare and Henry's attempt to build a solid relationship is hindered by the fact that he is fated to continually jump through time at the most unexpected, random moments.

THE GOODS: LIVE HARD, SELL HARD

(PARAMOUNT VANTAGE) Producers, Adam McKay, Will Ferrell, Kevin Messick, Chris Henchy; Executive Producer, Louise Rosner; Director, Neal Brennan; Screenplay, Andy Stock, Rick Stempson; Photography, Daryn Okada; Designer, Stefania Cella; Costumes, Mary Jane Fort; Music, Lyle Workman; Music Supervisors, Dave Jordan, Jojo Villanueva; Editors, Michael Jablow, Kevin Tent; Casting, Allison Jones, Jennifer Euston; a Gary Sanchez Productions production; Dolby; Panavision; Deluxe color; Rated R; 89 minutes; Release date: August 14, 2009

CAST

Don Ready	**Jeremy Piven**
Jibby Newsome	**Ving Rhames**
Ben Selleck	**James Brolin**
Brent Gage	**David Koechner**
Babs Merrick	**Kathryn Hahn**
Paxton Harding	**Ed Helms**

Jordana Spiro (Ivy Selleck), Tony Hale (Wade Zooha), Ken Jeong (Teddy Dang), Rob Riggle (Peter Selleck), Alan Thicke (Stu Harding), Charles Napier (Dick Lewiston), Jonathan Sadowski (Blake), Noureen DeWulf (Heather), Wendie Malick (Tammy Selleck), Craig Robinson (DeeJay), Bryan Callen (Jason Big Ups!), Joey Kern (Ricky Big Ups!), Kristen Schaal (Stewardess Stacey), Christopher Gartin, Jessica St. Clair (Selleck Customers Couple), Mary Castro (Stripper), Gary Sanchez (Passenger Mariachi), Matt Walsh (Capt. Ortiz), Samantha Albert (Selleck Auto Trader Customer), Ian Roberts (Gary, a Selleck Customer), Jean Villepique (Mother, a Selleck Customer), Brooke Lenzi (Karaoke Pretty Girl), Morgan Murphy (Karaoke Bartender), Gwen Stewart, Courtney Bradshaw (McDermott Angels), T.J. Miller (Cessna Jim), Molly Erdman (Selleck Customer of Zooha), Paul Lieberstein (Selleck Last Customer), Erica Vittina Phillips (Selleck Customer, Teddy), Sabrina Maahs (Don's Stripper), Brianne Van Cuyck (Brent's Stripper), Will Ferrell (McDermott), Gina Gershon

In a desperate attempt to save his rapidly failing used car dealership, Ben Selleck hires a crack team of "car mercenaries" to ramp up sales over one weekend. As he undertakes his newest mission, and quickly falls for the boss's daughter, he realizes he'll have to trust more than his cars and his crafty skills in deceit to succeed.

Jordana Spiro, Rob Riggle, James Brolin, Wendie Malick, Jeremy Piven, David Koechner © Paramount Vantage

Jack White, Jimmy Page, The Edge

Jack White © Sony Pictures Classics

IT MIGHT GET LOUD

(SONY CLASSICS) Producers, Davis Guggenheim, Peter Afterman, Thomas Tull, Lesley Chilicott; Executive Producers, Bert Ellis, Michael Mailis; Director, Davis Guggenheim; Photography, Erich Roland, Guillermo Navarro; Music Supervisor, Margaret Yen; Editor, Greg Finton; Associate Producers, Jimmy Page, Rebecca Hartzell, Alba Tull, Michael Birtel, Diana Derycz-Kessler, Erica Beaney; a Thomas Tull presentation; Dolby; Color; HD; Rated PG; 97 minutes; Release date: August 14, 2009

WITH
Jimmy Page, The Edge, Jack White

Documentary on the importance of the electric guitar, as endorsed by three rock legends, Jimmy Page, The Edge, and Jack White.

Tim Jo, Ryan Donowho, Charlie Saxton, Gaelan Connell

Tim Jo, Aly Michalka, Charlie Saxton © Summit Entertainment/Walden

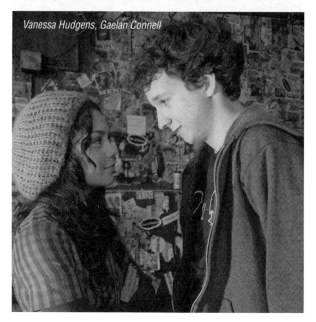

Vanessa Hudgens, Gaelan Connell

BANDSLAM

(SUMMIT) Producer, Elaine Goldsmith-Thomas; Executive Producers, Ron Schmidt, Marisa Yeres; Director, Todd Graff; Screenplay, Josh A. Cagan, Todd Graff; Story, Josh A. Cagan; Photography, Eric Steelberg; Designer, Jeff Knipp; Costumes, Ernesto Martinez; Music, Junkie XL; Music Supervisors, Lindsay Fellows, Linda Cohen; Editor, John Gilbert; Casting, Nancy Nayor Battino; a Walden Media presentation of a Goldsmith-Thomas production; Dolby; Panavision; Color; Rated PG; 111 minutes; Release date: August 14, 2009

CAST

Charlotte Banks	**Aly Michalka**
Sa5m	**Vanessa Hudgens**
Will Burton	**Gaelan Connell**
Ben Wheatley	**Scott Porter**
Basher	**Ryan Donowho**
Bug	**Charlie Saxton**
Karen Burton	**Lisa Kudrow**
Omar	**Tim Jo**
Irene (Cello)	**Elvy Yost**
Kim Lee (Keyboards)	**Lisa Chung**
Dylan Dyer (Glory Dogs Guitar)	**J.W. Wright II**

Blair Bomar (Megan), Casey Williams (Ms. Wittenberg), Maggie Maye (Kyra 17-1), Jennifer Blair (Kyra's Friend), Zach Thatcher (Kid Talking About Miles), Derek Cox Berg, Matt Hensarling (Rapping Boys), Cassidy Johnson (Slapping Girl), Landon Henninger (Rory), Michael Cuomo (Mr. Berry), Nathan McCray (Glue Boy), Kai Roach (Glory Dogs Bass), Christopher Copeland (Glory Dogs Drummer), James Hairston (Glory Dogs Saxophone), Chance Morgan, Matt Moody (Burning Hotels Guitar/Vocals), Marley Whistler (Burning Hotels Bass/Vocals), Wyatt Woodruff Adams (Burning Hotels Drummer), Farah White (Sa5m's Mom), Nikka Graff Lanzarone (New Art Teacher), Bobby Bones (Bandslam MC), Jonathan Rice (Stage Manager), Ryan Ciardo (Bully at Bus Stop), Will Johnson (Scott Donnelly), Bryan Chafin, Rebecca Petro (Kids), David Bowie (Himself), Valin Zamarron (Hip-Hop Group "Zeale"), Candice Jackson (Hip-hop Group "Candice"), Manjeri Krishna (Hip-Hop Group "DJ"), Ben Kessler (ICGO Saxophone), Andy Rector (ICGO Trombone), Juan Lopez (ICGO Trumpet), Evan Buts (The Daze Guitar/Vocals), Chris Ritchie (The Daze Bass), Aaron Lemke (The Daze Drummer), Krystal Morton (Art Class Girl), Todd Graff (Screaming Teacher), Julian Riano (Dewey Kid), Joey Olivares (Rock-n-Roller), Joshua Montoya (Screaming Fan), Nadia Sahari (Charlotte's Aunt)

Will Burton, the new kid in school, takes over the management of a struggling garage band to whip them into shape so that they can participate in the annual Bandslam competitions.

Aly Michalka, Gaelan Connell, Scott Porter

INGLOURIOUS BASTERDS

(WEINSTEIN COMPANY/UNIVERSAL) Producer, Lawrence Bender; Executive Producers, Erica Steinberg, Lloyd Phillips, Bob Weinstein, Harvey Weinstein; Co-Producers, Henning Molfenter, Carl L. Woebcken, Cristoph Fisser; Director/Screenplay, Quentin Tarantino; Photography, Robert Richardson; Designer, David Wasco; Costumes, Anna B. Sheppard; Music Supervisor, Mary Ramos; Editor, Sally Menke; Visual Effects Designer, John Dykstra; Casting, Johanna Ray, Jenny Jue, Simone Bar, Olivier Carbone; a Band Apart (U.S.)/Zehnte Babelsberg (Germany) production; American-German; Dolby; Panavision; Deluxe color; Rated R; 152 minutes; Release date: August 21, 2009

CAST

Lt. Aldo Raine	**Brad Pitt**
Shosanna Dreyfus	**Mélanie Laurent**
Col. Hans Landa	**Christoph Waltz**
Sgt. Donny Donowitz	**Eli Roth**
Lt. Archie Hicox	**Michael Fassbender**
Bridget von Hammersmark	**Diane Kruger**
Pvt. Fredrick Zoller	**Daniel Brühl**
Sgt. Hugo Stiglitz	**Til Schweiger**
Cpl. Wilhelm Wicki	**Gedeon Burkhard**
Marcel	**Jacky Ido**
Pfc. Smithson Utivich	**B.J. Novak**
Pfc. Omar Ulmer	**Omar Doom**
Maj. Dieter Hellstrom	**August Diehl**
Perrier LaPadite	**Denis Menochet**
Joseph Goebbels	**Sylvester Groth**
Adolf Hitler	**Martin Wuttke**
Gen. Ed Fenech	**Mike Myers**
Francesca Mondino	**Julie Dreyfus**
Sgt. Werner Rachtman	**Richard Sammel**
Master Sgt. Wilhelm/Pola Negri	**Alexander Fehling**
Winston Churchill	**Rod Taylor**
Pvt. Butz/Walter Frazer	**Sönke Möhring**
Pfc. Gerold Hirschberg	**Samm Levine**
Pfc. Andy Kagan	**Paul Rust**
Pfc. Michael Zimmerman	**Michael Bacall**
Winnetou/German Soldier	**Arndt Schwering-Sohnrey**
Beethoven/German Soldier	**Petra Hartung**
German Soldier/Edgar Wallace	**Zack Volker Michalowski**
German Soldier/Mata Hari	**Ken Duken**
Proprietor Eric	**Christian Berkel**
Mathilda	**Anne-Sophie Franck**
Charlotte LaPadite	**Léa Seydoux**
Julie LaPadite	**Tina Rodriguez**
Suzanne LaPadite	**Lena Friedrich**
Cpt. Wolfgang	**Ludger Pistor**

Jana Pallaske (Babette), Wolfgang Lindner (Herrman #1), Michael Kranz (Herrman #3), Rainer Bock (Gen. Schonherr), André Penvern (Old French Veterinarian), Sebastian Hülk (Hellstrom's Driver/Nazi Usher #1), Buddy Joe Hooker (Gaspar), Carlos Fidel (Pfc. Simon Sakowitz), Christian Brückner (Voice of Kleist), Hilmar Eichhorn (Emil Jannings), Patrick Elias (Jakob Dreyfus), Eva Löbau (Miriam Dreyfus), Salvadore Brandt (Bob Dreyfus), Jasper Linnewedel (Amos Dreyfus), Wilfried Hoccholdinger (German Company Sgt.), Olivier Girard (Maxim's Waiter), Michael Scheel (Gen. Frank), Leo Plank, Andreas Tietz (Motorcycle Riders), Bo Svenson (American Colonel), Enzo G. Castellari (Himself), Anastasia Schifler (Marie), Samuel L. Jackson (Narrator), Harvey Keitel (Voice of OSS Commander)

In World War II France, a young Jewish woman whose family was murdered by the Nazis sees her chance for revenge when the cinema she owns is chosen for the premiere of a propaganda film, to be attended by top German leaders, including Adolf Hitler.

2009 Academy Award Winner for Best Actor in a Supporting Role (Christoph Waltz).

This film received additional Oscar nominations for picture, director, original screenplay, cinematography, film editing, sound mixing, and sound editing.

Brad Pitt

Christoph Waltz

Mélanie Laurent

Eli Roth, Brad Pitt

Eli Roth © TheWeinstein Co.

Diane Kruger

Til Schweiger

Christoph Waltz, Martin Wuttke

Brad Pitt

Chris Noth, Renée Zellweger © Freestyle Releasing

Kevin Bacon

Nick Stahl

MY ONE AND ONLY

(FREESTYLE) Producers, Aaron Ryder, Norton Herrick; Executive Producers, George Hamilton, Elayne Herrick, Michael Herrick; Co-Producer, Vicki Dee Rock; Co-Executive Producers, Ronnie Ward, Robert Pritchard, Robert Kosberg; Director, Richard Loncraine; Screenplay, Charlie Peters; Photography, Marco Pontecorvo; Designer, Brian Morris; Costumes, Doug Hall; Music, Mark Isham; Music Supervisor, Steve Lindsey; Visual Effects Supervisor, Richard Higham; Editor, Humphrey Dixon; Casting, Mary Gail Artz, Shani Ginsberg; a Herrick Entertainment presentation of a Raygun production, in association with Merv Griffin Entertainment and George Hamilton Entertainment; Dolby; Widescreen; Color; Rated PG-13; 107 minutes; Release date: August 21, 2009

CAST

Anne Devereaux	**Renée Zellweger**
George Devereaux	**Logan Lerman**
Dan Devereaux	**Kevin Bacon**
Becker	**Troy Garity**
Bill Massey	**David Koechner**
Tom	**J.C. MacKenzie**
Charlie	**Eric McCormack**
Dr. Harlan Williams	**Chris Noth**

Molly C. Quinn (Paula), Mark Rendall (Robbie), Nick Stahl (Bud), Phoebe Strole (Wendy), Steven Weber (Wallace McAllister), Robin Weigert (Hope), Dan John Miller (Mickey), Joe Tunney (Car Salesman), Thomas C. Hessenauer (Henry the Doorman), Gwendolyn Briley-Strand (Bernice), Holly Palmer (Tanya, Blonde Singer), Rachel Specter (Sherry), Jerry Whiddon (NYC School Principal), John Badila (Banker), David DeBoy (Sales Manager), Kyle Prue (Boston Waiter), Aidan Hughes (Boston Maitre D'), Rosemary Knower (Old Woman), Matthew Bowerman (Drama Teacher), Russ Widdall (Oliver Pierson), David Press (Pawnbroker), Veronica Taylor (Nancy), Michael Mack (Butler), Ed Matz (West Penn Doorman), Jon Jolles (Carl), Cleo Reginald Pizana (Nate), Clay Steakley (Stage Manager), Anthony Addabbo (Frank), Steve Gonzalez (Police Officer), Tara Garwood (Diner Woman), Michael Gell (Diner Child), Bobby J. Brown (Diner Man), Indra Ové (Diner Waitress), Lauren Klein (Mrs. Donahue), Stephen Schmidt (Joe Conner), Chris Kies (Painter Ted), Maury Ginsberg (Mr. Dillon), Laurien Clay (Oedipus Chorus Girl), Michael Traeger (St. Louis Principal), Susan Rome (Marla Massey), Mark Brutsche (Greeb), Michael Gabel (Mr. Pelker), John B. Crye (Assistant Director), Paul L. Nolan (Martin Kamen), Rachel Weber (Judy), R. Scott Williams (Radford Teacher #2), Tony Abatemarco (Director), Jennifer Christopher (Candy/Mary Beth), Lyndsay Rini (Teen Girl), William Lawrence Allen (Medic), Sandy Racher (Cook), Vivienne Shub (Woman with Dog), Karen Carbone (Band Woman #1), Geoff Rock (Bellboy)

Leaving behind her philandering bandleader husband, Ann Devereaux takes off on the road with her two sons, in hopes of finding herself a wealthy new spouse to relieve her of any financial pressures.

Mark Rendall, Renée Zellweger, Logan Lerman

PASSING STRANGE

(SUNDANCE SELECTS) Producers, Spike Lee, Steve Klein; Executive Producers, Ken Greif, Larry Horn, Steve Klein, Will Kohane; Director, Spike Lee; Book and Lyrics, Stew; Songs, Stew, Heidi Rodewald; Photography, Matthew Libatique; Editor, Barry Brown; an Apple Core Holdings presentation of a Forty Acres and a Mule production; Color; HD; Not rated; 136 minutes; Release date: August 21, 2009

CAST

Narrator	Stew
Youth	Daniel Breaker
Edwina/Mariannae/Sudabey	De'Adre Aziza
Mother	Eisa Davis
Mr. Franklin/Joop/Mr.Venus	Colman Domingo
Rev. Jones/Terry/	
Christophe/Hugo	Chad Goodridge
Sherry/Renata/Desi	Rebecca Naomi Jones
Drums	Christian Cassan
Guitar/Keyboard/	
Backing Vocals	Christian Gibbs
Bass/Vocals	Heidi Rodewald

A Los Angeles youth journeys to Amsterdam sexually liberated scene and Berlin's radical art-politik fringe in hopes of discovering "the real" and hopefully find his own identity. Filming of the 2008 Broadway musical.

Colman Domingo, Daniel Breaker, Chad Goodridge

Daniel Breaker, Stew, Eisa Davis

Eisa Davis, De'Adre Aziza © Passing Strange Productions

Chad Goodridge, Daniel Breaker, Colman Domingo, Stew, Rebecca Naomi Jones

WORLD'S GREATEST DAD

(MAGNOLIA) Producers, Tim Perell, Howard Gertler, Sean McKittrick, Richard Kelly; Executive Producers, Edward H. Hamm Jr., Jennifer Roth; Co-Producer/Costumes, Sarah de Sa Rego; Director/Screenplay, Bobcat Goldthwait; Photography, Horacio Marquinez; Designer, John Paino; Music, Gerald Brunskill; Editor, Jason Stewart; Casting, Ruth Lambert, Robert McGee; a Darko Entertainment presentation of a Process production in association with Jerkschool Productions; Dolby; Color; Rated R; 102 minutes; Release date: August 21, 2009

Alexie Gilmore, Robin Williams, Zach Sanchez

CAST
Lance Clayton	**Robin Williams**
Kyle Clayton	**Daryl Sabara**
Murphy	**Morgan Murphy**
Ginger	**Naomi Glick**
Dan	**Dan Spencer**
Principal Anderson	**Geoff Pierson**
Mike Lane	**Henry Simmons**
Peter	**Zach Sanchez**
Claire	**Alexie Gilmore**
Andrew	**Evan Martin**
Jennifer	**Ellie Jameson**
Chris	**Michael Thomas Moore**
Jason	**Jermaine Williams**
Bonnie	**Mitzi McCall**

Alles Mist (Metal Kid), Lorraine Nicholson (Heather), Rebecca Erwin Spencer, Cheri Minns, Zazu (Nosy Neighbors), Tony V. (Dr. Pentola), Krist Novoselic (Newsstand Vendor), Zoe (The Fighting Pug), Tom Kenny (Jerry Klein), Jill Talley (Make-Up Woman), Toby Huss (Bert Green), Deborah Horne (Dr. Dana), Bruce Hornsby (Himself), Bobcat Goldthwait (Chauffeur)

When Lance Clayton's foul-mouthed, anti-social teenage son accidentally kills himself under embarrassing circumstances his grieving father tries to revamp the boy's image as the model son.

Evan Martin

Henry Simmons © Magnolia Pictures

Daryl Sabara

Jake Short, Trevor Gagnon, Jimmy Bennett, Kat Dennings, William H. Macy

Jimmy Bennett

SHORTS

(WARNER BROTHERS) Producers, Robert Rodriguez, Elizabeth Avellán; Executive Producers, Dan Lin, Hunt Lowry, Mohammed Khalaf, Edward Borgerding; Director/ Screenplay/Photography/Visual Effects Supervisor, Robert Rodriguez; Designer, Steve Joyner; Costumes, Nina Proctor; Music, Robert Rodriguez, Carl Thiel, George Oldziey; Editors, Robert Rodriguez, Ethan Maniquis; Special Makeup Effects, Greg Nicotero, Howard Berger, KNB EFX Group; Casting, Mary Vernieu, JC Cantu; a Troublemaker Studios production, presented in association with Imagenation Abu Dhabi and Media Rights Capital; Dolby; Technicolor; Rated PG; 89 minutes; Release date: August 21, 2009

CAST

Toe Thompson	**Jimmy Bennett**
Nose Noseworthy	**Jake Short**
Stacey Thompson	**Kat Dennings**
Loogie	**Trevor Gagnon**
Laser	**Leo Howard**
Helvetica Black	**Jolie Vanier**
Lug	**Rebel Rodriguez**
Dad Thompson	**Jon Cryer**
Dr. Noseworthy	**William H. Macy**
Mom Thompson	**Leslie Mann**
Mr. Black	**James Spader**
Cole Black	**Devon Gearhart**
Teacher	**Angela Lanza**
John, Boyfriend	**Alejandro Rose-Garcia**
Blinkers	**Cambell Westmoreland, Zoe Webb**
Goofy Host	**Chris Orf**

Tina Rodriguez, Jack Hurst (Employees), Jonathan Breck (Security Guard), Racer Rodriguez, Rocket Rodriguez (Bullies), Elizabeth Avellán (Voice of the Baby), Bianca Rodriguez (The Baby)

Havoc erupts in the small suburban town of Black Hills, when a neglected kid discovers a magic rock capable of granting wishes.

Jimmy Bennett, Leslie Mann, Jon Cryer © Warner Bros.

Jolie Vanier, Jimmy Bennett

TAKING WOODSTOCK

(FOCUS) Producers, James Schamus, Ang Lee, Celia Costas; Executive Producer, Michael Hausman; Director, Ang Lee; Screenplay, James Schamus; Based on the book *Taking Woodstock: A True Story of a Riot, a Concert, and a Life* by Elliot Tiber, with Tom Monte; Photography, Eric Gautier; Designer, David Gropman; Costumes, Joseph G. Aulisi; Music, Danny Elfman; Editor, Tim Squyres; Visual Effects Supervisor, Brendan Taylor; Casting, Avy Kaufman; Dolby; Super 35 Widescreen; Deluxe color; Rated R; 121 minutes; Release date: August 26, 2009

Demetri Martin

CAST

Elliot Teichberg	**Demetri Martin**
Devon	**Dan Fogler**
Jake Teichberg	**Henry Goodman**
Michael Lang	**Jonathan Groff**
Max Yasgur	**Eugene Levy**
Dan	**Jeffrey Dean Morgan**
Sonia Teichberg	**Imelda Staunton**
VW Guy	**Paul Dano**
VW Girl	**Kelli Garner**
Tisha	**Mamie Gummer**
Billy	**Emile Hirsch**
Vilma	**Liev Schreiber**
John Roberts	**Skylar Astin**
Jackson Spiers	**Kevin Chamberlin**
Joel Rosenman	**Daniel Eric Gold**
Mel Lawrence	**Steven Kunken**
Artie Kornfield	**Adam Pally**
Bob	**Andy Prosky**
Stan	**Kevin Sussman**
Reverend Don	**Richard Thomas**
British Gentleman	**Edward Hibbert**
Frank	**Clark Middleton**
Annie	**Bette Henritze**
Margaret	**Sondra James**
Carol	**Christina Kirk**

Emile Hirsch © Focus Features

Gail Martino (Town Clerk), Takeo Lee Wong (George the Doorman), Adam LeFevre (Dave), Carmel Amit, Zachary Booth, Jennifer Merrill, Ivan Sandomire, Matthew Shear, Darcy Bledsoe, Halley Cianfarini, Jesse Kile, Ashley Middlebrook, Bec Stupak (Earthlight Players), Gabriel Sunday (Steven), Pippa Pearthree (Miriam), Leonard Berdick, Sharon J. Giroux, William B. Ward Jr. (Angry Diner Patrons), Louisa Krause (Hippie Girl), Spadaque Volcimus (Hippie Guy), Bill Coelius, Nick Taylor (Inspectors), Michael Izquierdo (John Morris), Katherine Waterston (Penny), Will Janowitz (Chip Monck), Jeremy Shamos (Steve Cohen), Malachy Cleary (Wes Pomery), Sebastian Beacon, Kelly Klein (Assistants), Garett Ross (Woodstock Ventures PA), Darren Pettie (Paul), Andrew Katz (Hippie in Line), Patrick Cupo (Charlie), Boris McGiver (Doug), Caitlin Fitzgerald (Young Woman), Michael J. Burg, Taunia Hottman-Hubbard, David Lavine (Journalists), Stefano Da Fre (Young Man), Michael Zegen (Bernie), Andrew Zox (Sam), Angus Hamilton, Christopher Meier, Richard Phelan McGreal, Casson Rugen, Joseph Ulmer (Hairy Pretzel), Harry Zittel (Young Guy at Phone), Alyssa May Gold (Young Girl at Phone), Gaston Jean-Baptiste (Bongo Player), Michael McGinnis (Flautist), Dan Knobler (Guitar Player), Jon Seale (Congo Player), David Wilson Barnes (News Reporter), James Hanlon (State Trooper AJ Hamilton), Don Puglisi (Dealer), Kirsten Bach, Rachel Morrall (Bra Burners), Anthoula Katsimatides (Esther), Marjorie Austrian (St. Paul Lady), Kyle Plante (Interviewer), Lew Zucker (Worker)

Elliot Teichberg seizes the chance to bring some needed business to his parents' fading Catskills resort when the Woodstock music festival is stuck without a venue and comes looking for a last minute replacement.

Kelli Garner, Demetri Martin, Paul Dano

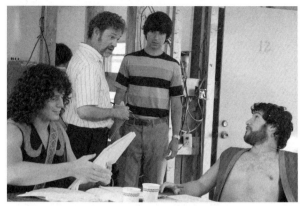

Jonathan Groff, Richard Thomas, Demetri Martin, Adam Pally

Mamie Gummer, Jonathan Groff, Demetri Martin

Eugene Levy, Demetri Martin

Demetri Martin, Eugene Levy

Demetri Martin, Liev Schreiber

Henry Goodman, Demetri Martin, Imelda Staunton

BIG FAN

(FIRST INDEPENDENT) Producers, Jean Kouremetis, Elan Bogarin; Executive Producer, Jen Cohn; Co-Producer, Joshua Trank; Director/Screenplay/Casting, Robert Siegel; Photography, Michael Simmonds; Designer, Sharoz Makarechi; Costumes, Vera Chow; Music, Philip Watts; Editor, Joshua Trank; an Economy Pictures presentation; Dolby; Color; DV; Rated R; 86 minutes; Release date: August 28, 2009

CAST

Paul Aufiero	**Patton Oswalt**
Sal	**Kevin Corrigan**
Philadelphia Phil	**Michael Rapaport**
Paul's Mom	**Marcia Jean Kurtz**
Jeff	**Gino Cafarelli**
Detective Velarde	**Matt Servitto**
Quantrell Bishop	**Jonathan Hamm**

Patton Oswalt, Kevin Corrigan

Serafina Fiore (Gina).Polly Humphreys (Christine), Joe Garden (Dennis), Sidné Anderson (Dr. Parker), Julian Lane (Birthday Boy), Caroline Gallo (Gina and Jeff's Daughter), Maya Louise Dispenza (Christine and Dennis' Daughter), Cookie Bradshaw (Law-Office Ad Woman), Malik Bradshaw (Shady House Guy), Jason Hardee, Ronnie Amadi, Angel Estrada, Billy Parker, Farouk Adelekan (Quantrell Buddies), Mifit Hodzic (Strip Club Valet),Michael Mederrick (Doorman), Nicole Mcgee (Bartender), Latawnya Haynes (Waitress), Dr. Dan Dineberg, Sebastian Elliott (Bouncers), Christiane Figueiredo (Paul and Sal's Stripper), Nick Stevens (Play-by-Play Announcer), Wilson Hall (Color Commentator), Alan Cross (Zone Reporter Ed Rosen), Nick Gallo (Radio Caller), Ginny Sisti, Jordan Cohn, Debbie Sutin (Parking Garage Drivers), Paul Sisti, Daniella Tineo-Cohn (Passengers), Robert Siegel, Yori Tondrowski (Front-Lawn Reporters), Cabbie (Wrong Phil), Joshua Tank (Wrong Phil's Buddy)

An obsessive New York Giants fan finds his dream becoming a nightmare when a chance encounter with his favorite player takes a disastrous turn.

Patton Oswalt

Patton Oswalt © First Independent Films

Patton Oswalt, Marcia Jean Kurtz

Grace Coddington, Anna Wintour © Roadside Attractions

André Leon Talley, Anna Wintour

THE SEPTEMBER ISSUE

(ROADSIDE ATTRACTIONS) Producers, R.J. Cutler, Eliza Hindmarch, Sadia Shepard; Executive Producers, Molly Thompson, Robert DiBitetto, Robert Sharenow, R.J. Cutler; Co-Producer, Mary Lisio; Director, R.J. Cutler; Photography, Bob Richman; Music, Craig Richey; Music Supervisor, Margaret Yen; Editor, Azin Samari; an A&E IndieFilms presentation in association with Actual Reality Pictures; Dolby; Color; Rated PG-13; 89 minutes; Release date: August 28, 2009

WITH
Anna Wintour, André Leon Talley, Grace Coddington, Mario Testino, Patrick DeMarchelier, Oscar de la Renta, Vera Wang, Jean-Paul Gaultier, John Galliano, Candy Pratt, Hilary Rhoda, Coca Rocha, Caroline Trentini, Daria Werbowy

Documentary on how the all-important September issue of *Vogue* magazine is created under the iron rule of Editor-in-chief Anna Wintour.

THE FINAL DESTINATION

(NEW LINE CINEMA) Producers, Craig Perry, Warren Zide; Executive Producers, Richard Brener, Walter Hamada, Sheila Hanahan Taylor; Co-Producer, Art Schaefer; Director, David R. Ellis; Screenplay, Eric Bress; Based on characters created by Jeffrey Reddick; Photography, Glen MacPherson; Designer, Jaymes Hinkle; Costumes, Claire Breaux; Music, Brian Tyler; Editor, Mark Stevens; Visual Effects Supervisor, Erik Henry; Casting, David H. Rappaport, Lindsey Hayes Kroeger; a Warner Brothers release of a Practical Pictures/Parallel Zide production; Dolby; Widescreen; Deluxe color; 3-D; Rated R; 82 minutes; Release date: August 28, 2009

CAST

Nick O'Bannon	**Bobby Campo**
Lori Milligan	**Shantel VanSanten**
Hunt Wynorski	**Nick Zano**
Janet Cunningham	**Haley Webb**
George Lanter	**Mykelti Williamson**
MILF/Samantha	**Krista Allen**

Andrew Fiscella (Mechanic), Justin Welborn (Racist), Stephanie Honore (Mechanic's Girlfriend), Lara Grice (Racist's Wife), Jackson Walker (Cowboy, Jonathan Groves), Phil Austin (Samantha's Husband), William Aguillard, Brendan Aguillard (Kids), Juan Kincaid (Newscaster), Monique Detraz (Anchorwoman), Chris Fry (Greensman), Tina Parker (Cheyenne), Cecile Monteyne (Dee Dee), Stacey Dizon (Pedicurist), Dane Rhodes (Grandstate Manager), Gabrielle Chapin (Girl on Top), Harold X. Evans (Homeless Man), Camille E. Bourgeois III (Water Gun Brat), Curtis E. Akin (Golfer), Eric Paulsen (Anchorman), Belford Carver (Mr. Suby), Dennis Nguyen (Chinese Orderly), Jedda Jones (Nurse), Joseph T. Ridolfo (Toy Helicopter Operator), Chris Langlois (Toy Car Operator), Trey Burvant (Theatre Manager), Larry E. Lundy Jr. (Usher). Courtney James (Scaffolder)

Although Nick and his friends are spared death at a NASCAR event, his premonitions that the grim reaper will catch up with them all becomes reality. Fourth entry in the series following *Final Destination* (2000), *Final Destination 2* (2003), and *Final Destination 3* (2006).

Haley Webb, Nick Zano © Warner Bros.

Dustin Milligan

Jason Bateman, Mila Kunis

EXTRACT

(MIRAMAX) Producers, Michael Rotenberg, John Altschuler; Executive Producers, Dave Krinsky, Tom Lassally, Glenn Lucas; Co-Executive Producer, Michael Flynn; Director/Screenplay, Mike Judge; Photography, Tim Suhrstedt; Designer, Maher Ahmad; Costumes, Alix Friedberg; Music, George S. Clinton; Editor, Julia Wong; Casting, Mary Vernieu, Venus Kanani; a Ternion Entertainment production in association with F+A Productions and 3 Arts Entertainment; Dolby; Deluxe color; Rated R; 91 minutes; Release date: September 4, 2009

CAST

Joel Reynolds	**Jason Bateman**
Cindy	**Mila Kunis**
Suzie Reynolds	**Kristen Wiig**
Dean	**Ben Affleck**
Brian	**J.K. Simmons**
Step	**Clifton Collins Jr.**
Brad	**Dustin Milligan**
Nathan	**David Koechner**
Mary	**Beth Grant**
Rory	**T.J. Miller**
Hector	**Javier Gutiérrez**
Gabriella	**Lidia Porto**
Joe Adler	**Gene Simmons**
Willie	**Matt Schulze**
Victor	**Lamberto Guiterrez**
Phil	**Brent Briscoe**

Hal Sparks, Nick Thune (Guitar Salesmen), Tom Virtue (Guitar Customer), Christopher Ryan Rocha (Pawn Shop Guy), Jenny O'Hara (Joel's Secretary), Matthew Williams (Band Member), Mike Judge (Jim), Gary Cole (Bar Patron)

Frustrated with the lack of sex he's getting at home, extract factory manager Joel Reynolds finds himself attracted to a new employee, unaware that the woman is plotting to scam some money out of his company.

Jason Bateman, Kristen Wiig © Miramax Films

Ben Affleck, Jason Bateman

GAMER

(LIONSGATE) Producers, Tom Rosenberg, Gary Lucchesi, Skip Williamson, Richard Wright; Executive Producers, Mark Neveldine, Brian Taylor, Eric Reid, David Scott Rubin, Michael Paseornek, James McQuaide; Co-Producer, Robert Bennum; Directors/Screenplay, Mark Neveldine, Brian Taylor; Photography, Ekkehart Pollack; Designer, Jerry Fleming; Costumes, Alix Friedberg; Music, Robert Williamson, Geoff Zanelli; Editors, Peter Amundson, Fernando Villena; Visual Effects Supervisors, James McQuaide, Gabriel Sanchez, Thomas Duval, Payam Shohadai, Vincent Cirelli, Justin Daneman; Stunts, Darrin Prescott; a Lakeshore/Lionsgate production; Dolby; Color; Rated R; 95 minutes; Release date: September 4, 2009

CAST

Kable	**Gerard Butler**
Ken Castle	**Michael C. Hall**
Angie	**Amber Valletta**
Gina Parker Smith	**Kyra Sedgwick**
Simon Silverton	**Logan Lerman**
Trace	**Alison Lohman**
Hackman	**Terry Crews**

Ramsey Moore (Gorge), Chris "Ludacris" Bridges (Humanz Brother), Aaron Yoo (Humanz Dude), Jonathan Chase (Geek Leader), Dan Callahan (Backup Geek), Brighid Fleming (Delia), Johnny Whitworth (Scotch), Keith Jardine (Mean Slayer), Michael Weston (Producer), Joe Reitman (Board OP), John de Lancie (Chief of Staff), Milo Ventimiglia (Rick Rape), Zoe Bell (Sandra), John Leguizamo (Freek), Noel Gugliemi (Upgrade Guard), Jarvis George, Jai Stefan (Brown Soldiers), Richard Machowicz (Blue Soldier #1), Ken Smith (Lifer), Henry Hayashi (Razorblade), Dylan Kenin (Train Guard), Keith David (Agent Keith), Maggie Lawson, James Roday, Antoinette Antonio, Donnie Smith (News Hosts), Sam Witwer (Caseworker), Rebekah Tarin (Dale), Kate Mulligan (Sorority Chick), Med Abrous (Pig Nose), Ashley Rickards (2Katchapredator), Nikita Ramsey, Jade Ramsey (Kumdumpstas), Mimi Michaels (Stikkimuffin), Sadie Alexandru (Society Victim), Ariana Scott (Sissypuss Shelley), Cynthia Robertson (Porn Girl), Lloyd Kaufman (Genericon), Stephanie Mace (Geek Girl), Adam Loeb (Ben Richard), Efren Ramirez (DJ), David Scott Rubin (Lab Tech), Fred Loeb (Society Concierge)

Forced to fight for billionaire virtual reality mastermind Ken Castle, Kable tries to persuade the teen operating his every move to shut down the game and allow him to destroy his opponents by his own means.

Gerard Butler, Logan Lerman © Lionsgate

Sandra Bullock, Bradley Cooper © Twentieth Century Fox

ALL ABOUT STEVE

(20TH CENTURY FOX) Producers, Sandra Bullock, Mary McLaglen; Executive Producers, Ted Field, Nick Osborne, Trevor Engelson; Director, Phil Traill; Screenplay, Kim Barker; Photography, Tim Suhrstedt; Designer, Maher Ahmad; Costumes, Gary Jones; Music, Christophe Beck; Music Supervisor, John Houlihan; Casting, Juel Bestrop, Seth Yanklewitz; a Fox 2000 Pictures presentation in association with Radar Pictures of a Fortis Films production; Dolby; Panavision; Deluxe color; Rated PG-13; 98 minutes; Release date: September 4, 2009

CAST

Mary Horowitz	**Sandra Bullock**
Hartman Hughes	**Thomas Haden Church**
Steve	**Bradley Cooper**
Angus	**Ken Jeong**
Howard	**DJ Qualls**
Corbitt	**Keith David**

Howard Hesseman (Mr. Horowitz), Beth Grant (Mrs. Horowitz), Katy Mixon (Elizabeth), M.C. Gainey (Norm the Truck Driver), Holmes Osborne (Soloman), Delaney Hamilton (Little Deaf Girl), Jason Jones (Vasquez), Carlos Gómez (Rescue Supervisor), George Sharperson (Rescuer), Luenell Campbell (Protestor Lydia), Christina Carlisi (Teacher), Joe D'Angerio (ABC News Producer), Shanda Laurent (Bus Driver), Kerri Kenney-Silver (Miss Hancock), Stephanie Venditto (KNYT Reporter), P.J. Marino (KNYT Sound Tech), Wayne Grace (Retired Mine Supervisor), Mickey Giacomazzi (Skinny Fireman), Noah Munch (Large Kid), Bridget Shergalis (Mini Mary), James Martin Kelly (Mine Safety Expert), Andrew Caldwell (Young Rescuer), Bryan Moore (Assistant), Rachel Sterling (Botanist), Jackie Johnson (CCN Meteorologist), Regino Montes (Maintenance Guy), Elliott Cho (Daniel), Justin Grafman (Deaf Boy), Joy Darash (Hipster Girl), Jordan Green (Kid), Geraldo Rivera (Himself), Beverly Polcyn (Old Lady), Misha Dibono (Paula), Dori Kancher (Payroll Clerk), Bone Hampton (Security Guard), Hari Kondabolu (Crossword Businessman), Jordan Morris (Protestor Winston), Dorie Barton, Patrick Brown, Alvera DeLeon (Horowitz House Reporters), Gillian Vigman (Misc. News Reporter), Michael Joseph Carr (BBC Reporter), Larry Dorf (MSNBC Reporter), Darcy Fowers (Guest Expert), Charlyne Yi (Young Protester), Tyrone Giordano (Dad), Hollie Stenson, Kurt Ela (Reporters), Paul Beller III (Firefighter), Kelli Kirkland Powers (Receptionist), Lucy Davis (Patient)

A socially inept crossword puzzle constructor is so smitten by the cameraman she meets on a blind date that she makes it her goal to land him, despite his complete disinterest in her.

9

(FOCUS) Producers, Jim Lemley, Tim Burton, Timur Bekmambetov, Dana Ginsburg; Co-Producers, Jinko Gotoh, Marci Levine; Director/Story, Shane Acker; Screenplay, Pamela Pettler; Designers, Robert J. St. Pierre, Fred Warter; Music, Danny Elfman, Deborah Lurie; Editor, Nick Kenway; Character Designer, James Feeley; Visual Effects Supervisor, Jeff Bell; Visual Effects, Starz Animation; Casting, Mindy Marin; a Jim Lemley/Tim Burton/Timur Bekhambetov production, presented in association with Relativity Media; Dolby; Deluxe Color; Rated PG-13; 79 minutes; Release date: September 9, 2009

VOICE CAST

#9	Elijah Wood
#1	Christopher Plummer
#2	Martin Landau
#5	John C. Reilly
#6	Crispin Glover
#7	Jennifer Connelly
#8/Radio Announcer	Fred Tatasciore
The Scientist	Alan Oppenheimer
Dictator	Tom Kane
Newscaster	Helen Wilson

#2

In the aftermath of a devastating war that has left the Earth a wasteland, a group of tiny humanoids are given the task of perpetuating life on the planet. Expanded from the short film of the same name that was nominated for an Oscar in 2006.

Cat Beast, #9

© Focus Features

#7, #9

#6, #5, #8, #9

Michael Douglas © Anchor Bay/After Dark

BEYOND A REASONABLE DOUBT

(ANCHOR BAY) Producers, Mark Damon, Ted Hartley, Limor Diamant; Director/Screenplay/Photography, Peter Hyams; Based on the screenplay by Douglas Morrow; Designer, Jim Gelarden; Costumes, Susanna Puisto; Music, David Shire; Editor, Jeff Gullo; Stunts, Gary Hymes; Casting, Ryan Glorioso; an Autonomous Films, Foresight Unlimited and RKO Pictures presentation of a Signature Entertainment production; Dolby; Color; Rated PG-13; 105 minutes; Release date: September 11, 2009

CAST
C.J. Nicholas	**Jesse Metcalfe**
Ella Crystal	**Amber Tamblyn**
Mark Hunter	**Michael Douglas**
Corey Finley	**Joel David Moore**
Ben Nickerson	**Orlando Jones**
Lt. Merchant	**Lawrence Beron**

Sewell Whitney (Martin Weldon), David Jensen (Gary Spota), Sharon London (Judge Sheppard), Krystal Kofie (Taiesha), Randel Reeder (Survivalist Man), Ryan Glorioso (Animal Shelter Attendant), Jon McCarthy (Det. Rawley), Grant James (Aaron Wakefield), Eric Gipson (Allen), Gerry May (Anchorman), Carl Savering (Bailiff), Kelvin Payton (Cameraman), Michele Williams (Danielle), Arlando Smith (Dell), Dan Harville (Deputy), Fred Ellis (Forensics Expert), Wallace Merck (Gilbert Romans), Michelle White Lafitte (Kelly Gertner), Robert Larriviere (Kevin Tarlow), Juli Erickerson (Madlyn Urlanger), Edrick Browne (Manager), Carri Slaughter (Marsha), Ron Flagg (Property Clerk), David Born (Property Sergeant), Michael Flannigan, Jeff Ferrell, Darcel Moreno, Derek Johnson (Reporters), Megan Brown (Roberta), Tony Bently (Roger Milner), Andrei Constantinescu (Bruce Stern), John McConnell (Vernon Green), Meade Patton (Det. Reddick), Sarah Kearney (Anchorwoman), Robin McGee (Soundman), Sigal Diamant (Maralyn), Illana Shoshan (Mrs. Hunter)

Certain that high profile lawyer Mark Hunter tampers with evidence in order to win his cases, reporter C.J. Nicholas pretends to be guilty of a crime so that he can prove his suspicions are correct.

SORORITY ROW

(SUMMIT) Producers, Mark Karz, Darrin Holdender; Executive Producers, Mark Rosman, Jay Boberg, Josie Rosen; Co-Producer, Bill Bannerman; Director, Stewart Hendler; Screenplay, Josh Stolberg, Peter Goldfinger; Based on the original screenplay *Seven Sisters* by Mark Rosman; Photography, Ken Seng; Designer, Phil Toolin; Costumes, Marian Toy; Music, Lucian Piane; Editor, Elliot Greenberg; a Karz Entertainment production; Dolby; Widescreen; Color; Rated R; 101 minutes; Release date: September 11, 2009

CAST
Cassidy	**Briana Evigan**
Jessica	**Leah Pipes**
Ellie	**Rumer Willis**
Claire	**Jamie Chung**
Megan	**Audrina Patridge**
Andy	**Julian Morris**
Chugs	**Margo Harshman**
Kyle	**Matt Lanter**
Mrs. Crenshaw	**Carrie Fisher**
Garrett	**Matt O'Leary**

Teri Andrzejewski (Bra-Clad Sister), Adam Berry (Danny), Megan Elizabeth Wolfley (Trampoline Sister), Robert Belushi (Amazed Senior Guy), Marie Blanchard (Over-It Sister), Zack Garrett (Thwarted Guy), Debra Gordon (Mrs. Tappan), Matthew Cannon (Nerdy Underclassman), Caroline D'Amore (Maggie), Maxx Hennard (Mickey), Ken Bolden (Dr. Rosenberg), Ashtin Petrella (Already Drunk Sister), Rick Applegate (Senator), Deja Kreutzberg (Riley), Nicole Moore (Joanna), Melissa Lukon (Slutty Sister), Chris Conroy (Hot Guy), Justin Wachsberger (Katie), Joe Forgione (Sea Pig), Kelly Dessoye, Katie Woolridge (Naïve Girls), Jeff Krajci (Stoned Dude), Natalia Dove (Bucky), Justin Tully (Wasted Guy), Marlee Fritz (Becky Reed), Anna McGhee (Cora), Marie Blanchard (Over-It Sister)

After a prank lead to murder, a group of sorority sisters who hide the dead body are dismayed by mysterious threats that indicate that someone is aware of their crime. Remake of the 1983 film *The House on Sorority Row.*

Audrina Partridge, Leah Pipes, Jamie Chung, Briana Evigan, Rumer Willis, Margo Harshman © Summit Entertainment

Mary J. Blige

Gladys Knight, Marvin Winans, Taraji P. Henson

Tyler Perry's I CAN DO BAD ALL BY MYSELF

(LIONSGATE) Producers, Tyler Perry, Reuben Cannon; Executive Producer, Michael Paseornek; Co-Producers, Roger M. Bobb, Jerry P. Jacobs; Director/Screenplay, Tyler Perry; Photography, Alexander Gruszynski; Designer, Ina Mayhew; Costumes, Keith G. Lewis; Music, Aaron Zigman; Music Supervisor, Joel C. High; Editor, Maysie Hoy; Casting, Robi Reed, Alpha Tyler; a TPS presentation of a Reuben Cannon/Lionsgate production; Dolby; Color; Rated PG-13; 113 minutes; Release date: September 11, 2009

CAST
Madea/Uncle Jo	**Tyler Perry**
April	**Taraji P. Henson**
Sandino	**Adam Rodriguez**
Randy	**Brian White**
Jennifer	**Hope Olaide Wilson**
Manny	**Kwesi Boakye**
Byron	**Frederick Siglar**
Wilma	**Gladys Knight**
Tanya	**Mary J. Blige**
Pastor Brian	**Marvin Winans**
Man #1	**Eric Mendenhall**
Miller	**David Paulus**
Mr. Bradley	**Randall Taylor**
Ms. Sullivan	**Tess Malis Kincaid**

Joe E. Taylor Jr. (Announcer), Cheryl B. Pratt (911 Dispatcher), Judith Franklin, Jameaka Tubbs, Thomasina Walker, Jamilah Windham (Rock Steady Background Singers), Greta Glenn (Mama Rose), Tanya R. Rodriguez (Waitress), Toni Redd (Background Singer)

An affair with a handsome Mexican immigrant causes hard-drinking nightclub singer April to patch up her troubled relationship with her three kids.

Tyler Perry

Frederick Siglar, Hope Olaide Wilson, Kwesi Boakye, Taraji P. Henson © Lionsgate

THE OTHER MAN

(IMAGE ENTERTAINMENT) Producers, Frank Doelger, Tracey Scoffield, Michael Dreyer; Executive Producers, Richard Eyre, Jan Mojito, Mary Beth O'Connor, David Richenthal; Director, Richard Eyre; Screenplay, Richard Eyre, Charles Wood; Based on the story by Bernhard Schlink; Photography, Haris Zambarloukos; Designer, Gemma Jackson; Costumes, Phoebe de Gaye; Music, Stephen Warbeck; Editor, Tariq Anwar; Casting, Nina Gold; a Rainmark Films presentation in association with Gotham Productions; American-British; Dolby; Deluxe color; Rated R; 89 minutes; Release date: September 11, 2010

CAST
Peter	**Liam Neeson**
Ralph	**Antonio Banderas**
Lisa	**Laura Linney**
Abigail	**Romola Garai**
George	**Craig Parkinson**

Abigail Canton (Designer), Pam Ferris (Vera), Paterson Joseph (Ralph), Lola Peploe (Eleanor), Sophie Wu (Shop Assistant), Richard Graham (Eric), Lisa McDonald (Receptionist), Emma Fielding (Gail), Paul Ritter (Guy), Amanda Drew (Joy), Guido Adorni (Waiter), Romolo Bruni (Owner), Stefano Chiodaroli (Taxi Driver), Joseph Long (Maitre d'), Priyanga Burford (Dr. Emma Hurd)

Peter is certain that his wife is having an affair, and makes it his mission to track the man down and find out just who he is.

Antonio Banderas, Liam Neeson © Image Entertainment

Laura Linney, Antonio Banderas

Aaron Eckhart, Jennifer Aniston © Universal Studios

LOVE HAPPENS

(UNIVERSAL) Producers, Scott Stuber, Mike Thompson; Executive Producers, J. Miles Dale, Rick Solomon, Ryan Kavanaugh; Director, Brandon Camp; Screenplay, Brandon Camp, Mike Thompson; Photography, Eric Edwards; Designer, Sharon Seymour; Costumes, Trish Keating; Music, Christopher Young; Music Supervisor, Kathy Nelson; Editor, Dana E. Glauberman; Casting, Deborah Aquila, Tricia Wood, Jennifer Smith; a Stuber production in association with Camp/Thompson Pictures, presented in association with Relativity Media; Dolby; Technicolor; Rated PG-13; 109 minutes; Release date: September 18, 2009

CAST
Burke	**Aaron Eckhart**
Eloise	**Jennifer Aniston**
Lane	**Dan Fogler**
Walter	**John Carroll Lynch**
Burke's Father-in-Law	**Martin Sheen**
Marty	**Judy Greer**
Eloise's Mom	**Frances Conroy**

Joe Anderson (Tyler), Sasha Alexander (Jessica), Clyde Kusatsu (Cab Driver), Anne Marie DeLuise, Tyler McClendon, Panou (Unicom Executives), Michael Kopsa (Unicom CEO), Michelle Harrison (Cynthia), Darla Vandenbossche (Beehive), Tom Pickett (Don), Patricia Harras (Lorraine), Aurelio Dinunzio (Moustache), Danielle Dunn-Morris (Book Fan), Maxine Miller (Barbara), Tim Henry (Welling Eyes), Ellie Harvie (Martha), Randall Newsmoe (Waiter), Carol Hodge (Becky), Craig Anderson (Ian), Brandon Jay McLaren (Mohawk), Rekha Sharma (Nose-Ring), Alessandro Juliaini (Tattoos), Ellen Ewusie (Hookah Waitress), Angie Scandale (Hookah Bartender), Deirdre Blades (Burke's Mother-in-Law), Dee Jay Jackson (Hotel Bartender), Monica Marko (Old Lady), Shaine Jones (Valet), Angus Adair, Zaccheus Jackson, Kevan Cameron (Slam Poets), Michael Bean (Concierge), Michael P. Northey (Bathroom Man), Rylee Stiles (Lollipop Kid), Domonique Danielle (Cashier), William "Big Sleeps" Stewart (Cabbie), Alexa Devine, Larry Romero, Madeline Elder, Elfina Luk, Glynis Davies (Workshoppers), Zach Rogue, Dominic Julian East, William Cameron Jasper, Graham Edward Lebron, Patrick Benton Spurgeon (Rogue Wave)

A widower, who has turned his emotional grief into a career as a self-help guru, finds himself falling in love with a flower-shop owner.

THE INFORMANT!

(WARNER BROTHERS) Producers, Michael Jaffe, Howard Braunstein, Kurt Eichenwald, Gregory Jacobs, Jennifer Fox; Executive Producers, George Clooney, Jeff Skoll, Michael London; Co-Producer, Michael Polaire; Director, Steven Soderbergh; Screenplay, Scott Z. Burns; Based on the book *The Informant: A True Story* by Kurt Eichenwald; Photography, Peter Andrews; Designer, Doug Meerdink; Costumes, Shoshana Rubin; Music, Marvin Hamlisch; Editor, Stephen Mirrione; Casting, Carmen Cuba; a Section Eight-Jaffe/Braunstein Enterprise production, presented in association with Participant Media and Groundswell Productions; Dolby; Technicolor; HD; Rated R; 108 minutes; Release date: September 18, 2009

Matt Damon, Melanie Lynskey

CAST

Mark Whitacre	**Matt Damon**
FBI Special Agent Brian Shepard	**Scott Bakula**
FBI Special Agent Bob Herndon	**Joel McHale**
Ginger Whitacre	**Melanie Lynskey**
Terry Wilson	**Rick Overton**
Mick Andreas	**Tom Papa**
Mark Cheviron	**Tom Wilson**
Aubrey Daniel	**Clancy Brown**
James Epstein	**Tony Hale**
Robin Mann	**Ann Cusack**
FBI Special Agent Dean Paisley	**Allan Havey**
Liz Taylor	**Rusty Schwimmer**
Dwayne Andreas	**Tom Smothers**
Judge Harold Baker	**Dick Smothers**

Matt Damon, Tom Papa, Rick Overton, Tom Smothers, Bob Zany, Clancy Brown © Warner Bros.

Lucas Carroll (Alexander Whitacre), Eddie Jemison (Kirk Schmidt), Craig Ricci Shaynak (Discouraged Foreman), Scott Adsit (Sid Hulse), Ann Dowd (FBI Special Agent Kate Medford), Howie Johnson (Rusty Williams), Nick Craig, Cody Puckett (Kids at Pool), Andrew Daly (Marty Allison), David Campbell (Budweiser Client Representative), Carolyn R. Feltner (Budweiser Receptionist), Jean-Pierre Gillain (Zurich Bank Security Officer), Elena Eustache (Zurich Bank Receptionist), Hans Tester (Peter Dreyer), Ludger Pistor (Reinhard Richter), Rome Kanda (Hirokazu Ikeda), Yoshio Be (Kazutoshi Yamada), Raymond Ma (Kanji Mimoto), Hervé Deschamps (Philippe Rollier), Pascal Ifri (Alain Crouy), Dann Seki (Joon Mo Suh), Jayden Lund (James Mutchnik), Chic Daniel (FBI Agent at Raid), Joe Chrest (Visiting Client), J.D. Mathein (Phone Agent), William Marsh (FBI Special Agent Ken Temples), Bob Zany (John Dowd), Richard Horvitz (Bob Zaideman), Tara Barrett, Tim Cain, Ken Frye, Huey Freeman (Reporters), Brian Gallivan (Ron Henkoff), Daniel Hagen (Scott Roberts), Patton Oswalt (Ed Herbst), Samantha Albert (Mary Spearing), Jimmy Brogan (Dr. Derek Miller), Paul F. Tompkins (FBI Special Agent Anthony D'Angelo), Adam Paul (FBI Special Agent Michael Bassett), Wayne Pére (Sheldon Zenner), Scott England (Local News Anchor), Joshua Funk (FBI Special Agent Robert Grant), Candy Clark (Mark's Mother), Frank Welker (Mark's Father), Larry Clarke (Whiteacre's Second Attorney), Steve Seagren (Correctional Officer)

The true story of how a high-ranking executive at the agribusiness firm of Archer Daniels Midland agreed to cooperate with the FBI in order to expose the price fixing schemes prevalent in his company.

Matt Damon

Megan Fox © Twentieth Century Fox

JENNIFER'S BODY

(20TH CENTURY FOX) Producers, Mason Novick, Daniel Dubiecki, Jason Reitman; Executive Producer, Diablo Cody; Co-Producer, Brad Van Arragon; Director, Karyn Kusama; Screenplay, Diablo Cody; Photography, M. David Mullen; Designer, Arv Greywal; Costumes, Katio Stano; Music, Theodore Shapiro, Stephen Barton; Music Supervisor, Randall Poster; Editor, Plummy Tucker; Visual Effects Supervisor, Erik Nordby; Stunts, Scott Ateah, Ed Anders; Casting, Mindy Marin; a Fox Atomic presentation of a Dubiecki/Novick/Reitman production, in association with Dune Entertainment; Dolby; Panavision; Deluxe color; Rated R; 101 minutes; Release date: September 18, 2009

CAST
Jennifer Check	**Megan Fox**
Needy Lesnicky	**Amanda Seyfried**
Chip	**Johnny Simmons**
Nikolai Wolf	**Adam Brody**
Mr. Wroblewski	**J.K. Simmons**
Needy's Mom	**Amy Sedaris**
Colin Gray	**Kyle Gallner**
Roman Duda	**Chris Pratt**
Chip's Mom	**Cynthia Stevenson**
Chastity	**Valerie Tian**
Chas	**Sal Cortez**
Mick	**Ryan Levine**
Dirk	**Juan Riedinger**

Colin Askey (Keyboardist), Juno Ruddell (Officer Warzak), Josh Emerson (Jonas Kozelle), Nicole Leduc (Camille), Aman Johal (Ahmet from India), Dan Joffre (Raymundo), Candus Churchill (Nutritionist), Carrie Genzel (Jennifer's Mom), Emma Gallello (Little Jennifer), Megan Charpentier (Little Needy), Jeremy Schuetze (Craig), Emily Tennant (Gossiping Girl), Karissa C. Tynes (Other Girl), Eve Harlow, Michael Brock, Genevieve Buechner (Goths), Adrian Hough (Colin's Dad), Gabrielle Rose (Colin's Mom), Michael Bean (Priest), Bill Fagerbakke (Jonas' Dad), Marilyn Norry (Jonas' Mom), Cut Chemist (DJ at Dance), Zoe Laliberté, Chelsey Smith, Whitney Chow, Michael Orstad (Candlelight Vigil Singers), Robby Robinson, Ed Anders (Orderlies), Roxanne Wong, Diana Dutra (Patients), Maya Toews (The Creepy Hand), Lance Henriksen (Motorist)

Needy is horrified to discover that after a traumatic encounter with an evil rock band, the most desirable girl in her high school is literally feasting on the males who desire her.

Amanda Seyfried

Johnny Simmons, Megan Fox

Megan Fox, Amanda Seyfried

Baby Brent

Mayor Shelbourne

Earl Deveraux, Cal Deveraux

Flint Lockwood

Sam Sparks

© Columbia Pictures

Sam Sparks, Flint Lockwood

Steve, Tim Lockwood

CLOUDY WITH A CHANCE OF MEATBALLS

(COLUMBIA) Producer, Pam Marsden; Executive Producer, Yair Landau; Co-Producers, Lydia Bottegoni, Chris Juen; Directors/Screenplay, Phil Lord, Christopher Miller; Based on the book written by Judi Barrett and illustrated by Ron Barrett; Editor, Robert Fisher; Music, Mark Mothersbaugh; Designer, Justin K. Thompson; Art Director, Michael Kurinsky; Visual Effects Supervisor, Rob Bredow; Character Designer, Carey Yostl; Senior Animation Supervisor, Peter Nash; Head of Layout, David Morehead; Casting, Mary Hidalgo; a Sony Pictures Animation production; Dolby; Widescreen; 3D; Color; Rated PG; 90 minutes; Release date: September 18, 2009

VOICE CAST

Flint Lockwood	**Bill Hader**
Sam Sparks	**Anna Faris**
Tim Lockwood	**James Caan**
"Baby" Brent	**Andy Samberg**
Mayor Shelbourne	**Bruce Campbell**
Earl Devereaux	**Mr. T**
Cal Devereaux	**Bobb'e J. Thompson**
Manny	**Benjamin Bratt**
Steve	**Neil Patrick Harris**
Patrick Patrickson	**Al Roker**
Fran Lockwood	**Lauren Graham**
Joe Towne	**Will Forte**
Young Flint	**Max Neuwirth**
Rufus	**Peter Siragusa**
Regina Devereaux	**Angela Shelton**

Neil Flynn (Weather News Network Producer), Liz Cackowski (Flint's Teacher), Isabella Acres, Lori Alan, Shane Baumel, Bob Bergen, Cody Cameron, Marsha Clark, John Cygan, Ann Dominic, Paul Eiding, Jess Harnell, Gary A. Hecker, Phil Lord, Sherry Lynn, Danny Mann, Mona Marshall, Mickie McGowan, Chris Miller, Laraine Newman, Jan Rabson, Grace Rolek, Jeremy Shada, Will Shadley, Melissa Sturm, Ariel Winter (Additional Voices)

In an effort to help his economically depressed town, Flint Lockwood invents a gadget that transforms water into a variety of foods, turning Swallow Falls into a booming tourist attraction.

Flint Lockwood, Tim Lockwood

CAPITALISM: A LOVE STORY

(OVERTURE) Producers, Michael Moore, Anne Moore; Executive Producers, Kathleen Glynn, Bob Weinstein, Harvey Weinstein; Co-Producers, Rod Birleson, John Hardesty; Director/Screenplay, Michael Moore; Photography, Dan Marracino, Jayme Roy; Music, Jeff Gibbs; Editors, John Walter, Conor O'Neill; a Paramount Vantage, Overture Films presentation in association with the Weinstein Co. of a Dog Eat Dog production; Dolby; Color; HD; Rated R; 127 minutes; Release date: September 23, 2009

WITH
Michael Moore, Frank Moore, Thora Birch, William Black, Elijah Cummings, Baron Hill, Marcy Kaptur, Wallace Shawn, Elizabeth Warren

A documentary on the bank industry's part in the recent economic crisis.

Michael Moore

Michael Moore

Michael Moore

Michael Moore

Michael Moore © Overture Films

Anna Maria Perez de Tagle, Paul McGill, Paul Iacono, Kay Panabaker

FAME

(MGM) Producers, Tom Rosenberg, Gary Lucchesi, Richard Wright, Mark Canton; Executive Producers, Eric Reid, David Kern, Beth DePatie, Harley Tannenbaum; Co-Producer, Brian McNelis; Director, Kevin Tancharoen; Screenplay, Allison Burnett; Based on the motion picture written by Christopher Gore; Photography, Scott Kevan; Designer, Paul Eads; Costumes, Dayna Pink; Music, Mark Isham; Editor, Myron Kerstein; Performance Sequences Editor, Fernando Villena; Choreographer, Marguerite Chapman; Casting, Deborah Aquila, Tricia Wood; a Lakeshore Entertainment and United Artists presentation; Dolby; Panavision; Deluxe color; Rated PG; 107 minutes; Release date: September 25, 2009

CAST

Marco	**Asher Book**
Rosie Martinez	**Kristy Flores**
Neil Baczynsky	**Paul Iacono**
Kevin Barrett	**Paul McGill**
Denise Dupree	**Naturi Naughton**
Jenny Garrison	**Kay Panabaker**
Alice Ellerton	**Kherington Payne**
Malik Washburn	**Collins Pennié**
Victor Tarvares	**Walter Perez**
Joy	**Anna Maria Perez de Tagle**

Debbie Allen (Principal Angela Simms), Charles S. Dutton (James Dowd), Kelsey Grammer (Martin Cranston), Megan Mullally (Fran Rowan), Bebe Neuwirth (Lynn Kraft), Cody Longo (Andy Matthews), Julius Tennon (Denise's Dad), April Grace (Denise's Mom), Michael Hyatt (Malik's Mom), Laura Johnson (Alice's Mom), James Read (Alice's Dad), Ryan Surratt (Eddie), Howard Gutman (Neil's Dad), Dale Godboldo (Music Executive), J.T. Horenstein (Dance Teacher), Stephanie Mace (Mr. Cranston's Assistant), Patrick Censoplano (Brooklyn Boy), Donnie "Burger" Winston (Hype Man), Marcus Hopson (Senior Rapper), Krystle "Ak'sent" Johnson (Rapper), Tynisha Keli (Singer), Kate Mulligan (Karaoke Singer), Donnie Smith (Film Set PA), Earl Carroll (Camera Shop Clerk), Oren Waters (Singing Homeless Man), Tim Jo (Korean Boy), Mikey Reid (Red Haired Boy), Leslie Ishii (Administrator), Gavin Turek (Ethnic Girl), Paulina Gretzky (Gorgeous Blonde Senior), Alex Liddy (Friend of Brooklyn Boy), Bre Morgan (Intense Girl), Anastasia Boissier (Little 10-Year-Old Girl), Kasha Kropinski (Ballerina), Jessie Sherman (Drama Helper), Jeremy Hudson, Mallauri Esquibel (Dancers), Annika Daniel, Sophia Daniels (Marco's Little Sister), Tiffany Espensen (Joy's Sister), Scott Wood (Teacher), Eli Myers (Cafeteria Jam Piano Student), Seth Daly (Cafeteria Jam Violin Student), Miss Lola Rose (Butcher Shop Customer), Nisha Bedi, Nick Grimes, Angela Alexander, Eva Ramirez, Whitney Barncord, Brittany Magill, Smyth Campbell, Gino Barletta, Philomena Bankston (Drama Students), Ronald Kartoon Antwine (Nightclub Bouncer), Sharon Pierre-Louis (Broadway Girl), Hailey Villaire (Opera Girl), Deanna Knott, Krys Ivory (Club Jam Vocals), Betty Griffin-Keller (Orchestra Conductor)

A look into the lives of several aspiring show business wannabes as they attend New York's High School of Performing Arts. Remake of the 1980 MGM film of the same name.

Naturi Naughton © Metro-Goldwyn-Mayer

Asher Book, Kay Panabaker

Bruce Willis, Radha Mitchell

SURROGATES

(TOUCHSTONE) Producers, David Hoberman, Todd Lieberman, Max Handelman; Executive Producers, David Nicksay, Elizabeth Banks; Director, Jonathan Mostow; Screenplay, John Brancato, Michael Ferris; Based on the graphic novel by Robert Venditti, Brett Weldele; Photography, Oliver Wood; Designer, Jeff Mann; Costumes, April Ferry; Music, Richard Marvin; Editor, Kevin Stitt; Visual Effects Supervisor, Mark Stetson; Visual Effects, Sandbox FX, MPC, Synthespian Studios, Brickyard Filmworks; Makeup Effects, Gregory Nicotero, Howard Berger; Stunts, Jery Hewitt; Casting, Jane Jenkins, Janet Hirshenson, Michelle Lewitt; a Mandeville Films/Top Shelf production; Distributed by Walt Disney Studios Motion Pictures; Dolby; Panavision; Technicolor; Rated PG-13; 88 minutes; Release date: September 25, 2009

Rosamund Pike, Boris Kodjoe

CAST

Tom Greer	**Bruce Willis**
Jennifer Peters	**Radha Mitchell**
Maggie Greer	**Rosamund Pike**
Andrew Stone	**Boris Kodjoe**
Young Canter	**James Francis Ginty**
Dr. Lionel Canter	**James Cromwell**
The Prophet	**Ving Rhames**
Strickland	**Jack Noseworthy**
Bobby	**Devin Ratray**
Col. Brendon	**Michael Cudlitz**
Armando	**Jeffrey De Serrano**
JJ the Blonde	**Helena Mattsson**

Michael Phillip (Uniformed Cop), Danny Smith (Victim), Brian Parrish (Hard Hat), Jennifer Alden (Landlady), Shane Dzicek (Jarid Canter), Andrew Haserlat, Justin Goodrich (Undergrads), Lisa Hernandez, Kirk Hawkins (Newscasters), Rachel Sterling (Assistant), Meta Golding (Counsel), Taylor Cole (Lawyer), Jordan Belfi (Victor Welch), J.L. Highsmith (Steinberg), Nicholas Purcell (Pulaski/Commando), Max Murphy (Captain), Victor Webster (Lopez), David Klefeker (Cop), Dorothy Brodesser (Dread), Valeria Azlynn (Bridget), Michael O'Toole (Hirosuke), Chad Williams (Salesman), Mike Randy (Hunk), Tyson Eberly (40% Off), Michael DeMello (Gate Guard), Ron Murphy (Pedestrian), Genevieve Johnson (Older Woman), David Conley (Miller), Bruce-Robert Serafin (Bud), Cody Christian (Boy Canter), Ian Novick (Andre), Todd Cahoon (Brian), Ella Thomas (Lisa), Gabriel Olds, Eamon Brooks (Agents), Rodney Weber (FBI Guard), De'Lon Grant, Matthew Souris (Commandos), Trevor Donovan (Surrie/Greer), Brock Gloor (Riot Agent), Rick Malambri (Clerk), Paul Shafer (Human Sniper), Christine Mascott (Big Woman), Ari Mostow, Nathan Mostow (Kids), Eliza Bunts (Receptionist), Edward McCabe (Controller/Commando), Anya Monzikova (Beautiful Woman)

Ving Rhames © Touchstone Pictures

In a world where people live life virtually by having robot duplicates go through their daily routine, an FBI agent is enlisted to find out why two humans died when their surrogates were "killed."

Bruce Willis (right)

BRIEF INTERVIEWS WITH HIDEOUS MEN

(IFC FILMS) Producers, Eva Kolodner, Yael Melamede, James Suskin, John Krasinski; Executive Producer, Kevin Connors; Associate Producers, Chris Hayes, Mike Schur, Dori Oskowitz, Thomas Fatone; Line Producer, George Paaswell; Director/Screenplay, John Krasinski; Based on the book by David Foster Wallace; Photography, John Bailey; Designer, Stephen Beatrice; Costumes, Vicki Farrell; Music Supervisor, Linda Cohen; Additional Music, Billy Mohler, Nate Wood; Casting, Billy Hopkins, Suzanne Smith, Kerry Barden; Dolby; Color; Not rated; 80 minutes; Release date: September 25, 2009

CAST
Sara Quinn	Julianne Nicholson
Subject #14	Ben Shenkman
Prof. Adams, Subject #30	Timothy Hutton
Subject #15	Michael Cerveris
Subject #51	Corey Stoll
Subject #19	Chris Messina
Kevin, Subject #28	Max Minghella
Evan, Subject #28	Lou Taylor Pucci
Subject #11	Will Arnett

John Krasinski (Ryan, Subject #20), Will Forte (Subject #72), Joey Slotnick (Tad, Subject #59), Clarke Peters (Subject #31), Dominic Cooper (Daniel, Subject #46), Ben Gibbard (Harry, Subject #20), Bobby Cannavale (Subject #40), Christopher Meloni (R, Subject #3), Denis O'Hare (A, Subject #3), Josh Charles (Subject #2), Frankie Faison (Subject #42), Malcolm Goodwin (Father of Subject #42), Rashida Jones (Hannah), Marin Ireland (Samantha), Lorri Bagley (Airport Girl)

As part of her graduate studies, Sara Quinn interviews several men about their relationships and their feelings towards women.

Lou Taylor Pucci, Max Minghella

Julianne Nicholson, Timothy Hutton © IFC Films

Katie Featherston, Micah Sloat © Paramount Pictures

PARANORMAL ACTIVITY

(PARAMOUNT) Producers, Oren Peli, Jason Blum; Executive Producer, Steven Schneider; Associate Producer, Amir Zbeda; Director/Screenplay/ Photography/ Casting/Editor, Oren Peli; a Blumhouse Productions and Solana Films production; Color; HD; Rated R; 85 minutes; Release date: September 25, 2009

CAST
Micah	Micah Sloat
Katie	Katie Featherston
The Pyschic	Mark Fredrichs

Amber Armstrong (Amber), Randy McDowell (Lt. Randy Hudson), Ashley Palmer (Diane – Girl on Internet), James Piper (Richard), Crystal Cartwright (Exorcism Nanny)

A San Diego couple must confront a terrifying, unseen supernatural force that has invaded their home.

THE INVENTION OF LYING

(WARNER BROTHERS) Producers, Lynda Obst, Oly Obst, Ricky Gervais, Dan Lin; Executive Producers, Sue Baden-Powell, Ted Field, Paris Kasidokostas Latsis, Terry Douglas; Directors/Screenplay, Ricky Gervais, Matthew Robinson; Photography, Tim Suhrstedt; Designer, Alexander Hammond; Costumes, Susie DeSanto; Music, Tim Atack; Music Supervisor, Dana DuFine; Editor, Chris Gill; Casting, Francine Maisler, Lynn Kressel; a Lynda Obst production, presented in association with Radar Pictures and Media Rights Capital; Dolby; Technicolor; Rated PG-13; 99 minutes; Release date: October 2, 2009

Fionnula Flanagan, Ricky Gervais, Jason Bateman

CAST
Mark Bellison	**Ricky Gervais**
Anna McDoogles	**Jennifer Garner**
Frank	**Jonah Hill**
Greg	**Louis C.K.**
Anthony	**Jeffrey Tambor**
Martha Bellison	**Fionnula Flanagan**
Brad Kessler	**Rob Lowe**
Shelley	**Tina Fey**
Nathan Goldfrappe	**Christopher Guest**

Donna Sorbello (Anna's Mother), Stephanie March (Blonde), Ruben Santiago-Hudson (Landlord), John Hodgman (Wedding Overseer), Nathan Corddry (News Reporter), Jimmi Simpson (Bob), Martin Starr (Waiter #1), Jason Bateman (Doctor), Philip Seymour Hoffman (Jim the Bartender), Edward Norton (Cop), Alton Fitzgerald White (Angelo Badsmith), Roz Ryan, Nada Despotovich (Nurses), Michael Patrick Gough (Homeless Man), Arnie Burton (Waiter at Fancy Restaurant), Ashlie Atkinson (Bank Teller), Bobby Moynihan (Assistant), Shaun Williamson (Richard Bellison), Stephen Merchant (Man at the Door), Cole Jensen (Short Fat Brian), Conner Rayburn (Son), Lisa Paige Robinson, Matt Stadelmann (Arguing Couple), Jared Voss, Jessica Baade, Elena Wohl., Matthew Robinson (People), Donald Foley (Yelling Man), Lance Norris, Joe Wong, Colin Knight, Eric André, Gene Amoroso, Armen Garo, Patrick Shea, Joe Stapleton (Men), Dennis Lemoine (Young Man), Brigid O'Connor, Christine Mascott, Ellen Colton, Layla Hosseini, Erica Newhall, Nydia Calon, Hope Farley (Women), Dreama Walker (Receptionist), Paul Donlon, Mauriel Gould, Mary Klug (Elderly), Rachel Harker (Woman in Business Suit), Brett Cramp (Crying Man), Toni Saldana (Cocktail Waitress), Guy Strauss (Pit Man), Nick Towne (Roulette Dealer), Tate Ellington (Waiter #2), Luz Alexandra Ramos (Chip Woman), Ken Cheeseman (Shouting Man), David Pittu (Tour Guide), Danielle Perry (Hostess in LaBonisera), Joseph Badalucco Jr. (Blue Collar Guy), Douglass Bowen Flynn (Tourist #1), Celeste Oliva (Secretary), Jake Watkins (Bully Kid), Valerie Hager, Alison Quinn, Mitchell Roche (Talking Heads)

Rob Lowe, Tina Fey

Mark Bellison suddenly becomes the only person capable of lying in a world where everyone tells the truth.

Ricky Gervais, Jennifer Garner, Louis C.K. © Warner Bros.

Jeffrey Tambor, Ricky Gervais

Jesse Eisenberg, Amber Heard

Jesse Eisenberg

Jesse Eisenberg, Emma Stone, Abigail Breslin, Woody Harrelson
© Columbia Pictures

ZOMBIELAND

(COLUMBIA) Producer, Gavin Polone; Executive Producers, Ezra Swerdlow, Paul Wernick, Rhett Reese, Ryan Kavanaugh; Director, Ruben Fleischer; Screenplay, Rhett Reese, Paul Wernick; Photography, Michael Bonvillain; Designer, Maher Ahmad; Costumes, Magali Guidasci; Music, David Sardy; Editors, Peter Amundson, Alan Baumgarten; Visual Effects Supervisor, Paul Linden; Makeup Effects Prostethics Designer, Tony Gardner; Stunts, G.A. Augilar, Jeffrey Lee Gibson; Casting, John Papsidera; a Pariah production, presented in association with Relativity Media; Dolby; Panavision; Deluxe color; Rated R; 87 minutes; Release date: October 2, 2009

CAST

Tallahassee	**Woody Harrelson**
Columbus	**Jesse Eisenberg**
Wichita	**Emma Stone**
Little Rock	**Abigail Breslin**
406	**Amber Heard**
Himself	**Bill Murray**
Clown Zombie	**Derek Graf**
Gas Station Attendant	**Mike White**

Jacob G. Atkins, Elle Alexander, Michael August, Chris Burns, Ernest Dancy, Travis Grant, Robert Hatch, Amir Khan, Shaun Lynch, Justin Price, Steve Prouty, Michelle Sebek, Brian Stretch, Sonya Thompson, Steve Warren, Travis Young (Zombies)

A group of surviours join together in hopes of keeping one step ahead of the danger as the world is overrun by flesh eating zombies.

Woody Harrelson, Travis Young

A SERIOUS MAN

(FOCUS) Producers/Directors/Screenplay, Joel Coen, Ethan Coen; Executive Producers, Tim Bevan, Eric Fellner, Robert Graf; Photography, Roger Deakins; Designer, Jess Gonchor; Costumes, Mary Zophres; Music, Carter Burwell; Editor, Roderick Jaynes; Casting, Ellen Chenoweth, Rachel Tenner; a Working Title production, presented in association with StudioCanal and Relativity Media; Dolby; Deluxe color; Rated R; 104 minutes; Release date: October 2, 2009

CAST

Larry Gopnik	**Michael Stuhlbarg**
Uncle Arthur	**Richard Kind**
Sy Ableman	**Fred Melamed**
Judith Gopnik	**Sari Lennick**
Danny Gopnik	**Aaron Wolff**
Sarah Gopnik	**Jessica McManus**
Mr. Brandt	**Peter Breitmayer**
Mitch Brandt	**Brent Brunaschweig**
Clive Park	**David Kang**
Solomon Schultz	**Michael Lerner**
Danny's Reefer Buddy	**Benjamin Portnoe**
Boy on Bus	**Jack Swiler**
Cursing Boy on Bus	**Andrew S. Lentz**
Mike Fagle	**Jon Kaminski Jr.**
Arlen Finkle	**Ari Hoptman**
Rabbi Marshak	**Alan Mandell**
Mrs. Samsky	**Amy Landecker**
Rabbi Nachtner	**George Wyner**
Dr. Sussman	**Michael Tezla**
Friend at the Picnic	**Katherine Borowitz**
Clive's Father	**Stephen Park**
Velvel, Shtetl Husband	**Allen Lewis Rickman**
Dora, Shtetl Wife	**Yelena Shmulenson**
Treitle Groshkover Dybuuk?	**Fyvush Finkel**
Hebrew School Teacher	**Ronald Schultz**
Dr. Shapiro	**Raye Birk**
Larry's Secretary	**Jane Hammill**

Claudia Wilkens (Marshak's Secretary), Simon Helberg (Rabbi Scott), Adam Arkin (Divorce Lawyer), Jim Cada (Cop #1), Charles Brin (Hebrew School Principal), Michael Engel (Torah Blesser), Tyson Bidner (Magbiah), Phyllis Harris (Hebrew School Tea Lady), Sigel Bruse (D'vorah Piper), Hannah Nemer (Sarah's Friend), Rita Vassallo (Law Firm Secretary), Warren David Keith (Dick Dutton), Neil Newman (Cantor), Tim Russell, Jim Lichtscheidl (Detectives), Wayne Evenson (Russell Krauss), Scott Baker (Sci-Fi Movie Hero)

A physics professor finds his Midwest suburban life unraveling from the pressures he's experiencing, including the abrupt departure of his wife for another man.

This film received Oscar nominations for picture and original screenplay.

Richard Kind, Aaron Wolff

Sari Lennick, Jessica McManus

Fred Melamed, Sari Lennick

Richard Kind

Michael Stuhlbarg, Adam Arkin © Focus Features

Peter Breitmayer, Michael Stuhlbarg

Aaron Wolff, Michael Stuhlbarg

Amy Landecker, Michael Stuhlbarg

Drew Barrymore, Ellen Page, Kristen Wiig

Jennifer Lewis, Ellen Page

Ellen Page, Alia Shawkat

WHIP IT

(FOX SEARCHLIGHT) Producers, Barry Mendel, Drew Barrymore; Executive Producers, Peter Douglas, Nancy Juvonen, Kirsten Smith, Nathan Kahane, Joe Drake, Chris Miller; Co-Producers, Nicole Brown, Kelli Konop, Jason Lust, Karyn McCarthy; Director, Drew Barrymore; Screenplay, Shauna Cross, based on her novel *Derby Girl*; Photography, Robert Yeoman; Designer, Kevin Kavanaugh; Costumes, Catherine Marie Thomas; Music, The Section Quartet; Music Supervisor, Randall Poster; Casting, Justine Baddeley, Kim Davis-Wagner; a Vincent Pictures/Flower Films/Rye Road production, presented in association with Mandate Pictures; Dolby; Panavision; Deluxe Color; Rated PG-13; 111 minutes; Release date: October 2, 2009

CAST

Bliss Cavendar ("Babe Ruthless")	**Ellen Page**
Brooke Cavendar	**Marcia Gay Harden**
Maggie Mayhem	**Kristen Wiig**
Smashley Simpson	**Drew Barrymore**
Iron Maven	**Juliette Lewis**
Earl Cavendar	**Daniel Stern**
Oliver	**Landon Pigg**
Pash Amini	**Alia Shawkat**
Coach Razor	**Andrew Wilson**
"Hot Tub" Johnny Rocket	**Jimmy Fallon**
Bloody Holly	**Zoe Bell**
Rosa Sparks	**Eve**
Eva Destruction	**Ari Graynor**
Shania Cavendar	**Eulala Scheel**

Sarah Habel (Corbi), Shannon Eagen (Amber), Edward Austin Austin (Pageant Coordinator), Mary Callaghan Lynch (Val), Barbara Coven (Pageant Mother), Nina Kircher (Trudy), Mark Boyd (Ronny), Carlo Alban (Birdman), Doug Minckiewicz (Colby), Michael Petrillo (Poindexter), Sean O'Reilly, Sam Zikakis (Colby's Friends), Kent Cummins, Sarah Yaeger (Atomic City Clerks), Chloe Trueheart, Kyle Kentala, Genevieve Harrison (Atomic City Girls), John Eatherly, Jonas Stein, Max Van Peebles (Turbo Fruits), Rusty Mewha (Holy Rollers Coach), Will Brick (Referee), Madge Levinson (Helen), Alexis O'Neill (Pocket Rocket), Eli Bleiler (Jaba the Slut), Kristen Adolfi, Rachel Piplica (Manson Sisters), LaTasha Pippen (Juana Beat'n), Sydney Bennett (Kami Kaze), Danny Mooney (Smashley's Fiance), Brent Kyle (Savage), Har Mar Superstar (Flight Attendants' Coach), Claudia Rodgers (Mrs. Weaver), Wallace Bridges, John Lepard (Cops), Patrick Moug (Terrifying Cop), Austin Bickel (Riley)

Unhappy with the formal life her parents have planned for her, teenager Bliss Cavendar secretly joins a women's roller derby team.

Ellen Page, Landon Pigg © Fox Searchlight

COUPLES RETREAT

(UNIVERSAL) Producers, Vince Vaughn, Scott Stuber; Executive Producers, Victoria Vaughn, Guy Riedel; Co-Producer, John Isbell; Director, Peter Billingsley; Screenplay, Jon Favreau, Vince Vaughn, Dana Fox; Photography, Eric Edwards; Designer, Shepherd Frankel; Costumes, Susan Matheson; Music, A.R. Rahman; Editor, Dan Lebenthal; Casting, Sarah Halley Finn; a Wild West Picture Show/Stuber Pictures production, presented in association with Relativity Media; Dolby; Color; Rated PG-13; 113 minutes; Release date: October 9, 2009

CAST
Dave	**Vince Vaughn**
Jason	**Jason Bateman**
Joey	**Jon Favreau**
Shane	**Faizon Love**
Lucy	**Kristin Davis**
Ronnie	**Malin Akerman**
Cynthia	**Kristen Bell**
Briggs	**Temuera Morrison**
Marcel	**Jean Reno**
Trudy	**Kali Hawk**
Jennifer	**Tasha Smith**
Salvadore	**Carlos Ponce**
Sctanley	**Peter Serafinowicz**

Jonna Walsh (Lacey), Gattlin Griffith (Robert), Colin Baiocchi (Kevin), Vernon Vaughn (Granpa Jim Jim), Jersey Jim (Magician), Paul Boese (Motorcycle Salesman), Daniel Theodore, Phillip Jordan (Tile Store Salesmen), John Michael Higgins, Ken Jeong, Charlotte Cornwell, Amy Hill (Therapists), Karen David (Spa Attendant), Alyssa Smith, Alexis Knapp (San Diego Dance Academy), Joy Bisco (Maitre d'), Janna Fassaert (Masseuse), Xavier Tournaud (Masseur), Dana Fox (Waitress), Justin Deeley, Scott Burn (Trainers), Micah Mason (Waiter), Christophe Santoro, Yann Marequa, Sacha Perreault (Bellmen), Zofia Moreno (Greeter), Brendan Wayne (Drunk Guy), David Merheb (Guitar Hero Bellman), Billy Loa, Chu Vang (Cooks), Jeremy Olson (Eden East Buff Guy), Bronx Style Bob (Eden East DJ), J-Ray Hochfield, Hanna Brophy, Lyndsay Magellan, Marketa Janska (Eden East Girls), Chantelle Barry (Eden East Shot Girl), James Ferris, Jordann Kimley, Jon Fleming (White Swallow DJ)

Hoping to repair their faltering marriage, Jason and Cynthia sign up for a tropical vacation, convincing their friends to join them for two weeks of "therapy."

Malin Akerman, Kristen Bell, Jason Bateman, Jean Reno

Jason Bateman, Carlos Ponce, Vince Vaughn, Malin Akerman

Jason Bateman, Kristen Bell, Jon Favreau, Kristin Davis, Vince Vaughn, Faizon Love, Malin Akerman, Kali Hawk © Universal Studios

Jason Bateman, Vince Vaughn

Carol, Max Records

Max Records

Max Records, KW © Warner Bros.

Max Records, Carol

Max Records, Alexander

Max Records, Ira, Judith

Max Records

WHERE THE WILD THINGS ARE

(WARNER BROTHERS) Producers, Tom Hanks, Gary Goetzman, John Carls, Maurice Sendak, Vincent Landay; Executive Producers, Thomas Tull, Jon Jashni, Scott Mednick, Bruce Berman; Director, Spike Jonze; Screenplay, Spike Jonze, Dave Eggers; Based on the book by Maurice Sendak; Photography, Lance Acord; Designer, K.K. Barrett; Costumes, Casey Storm; Creature Costumes, Jim Henson's Creature Shop; Music, Karen Orzolek, Carter Burwell; Music Supervisor, Ren Klyce; Editors, Eric Zumbrunnen, James Haygood; Animation and Visual Effects Supervisor, Daniel Jeannette; Animation and Visual Effects, Framestore; Casting, Justine Baddeley, Kimberly Davis-Wagner; a Playtone/Wild Things production, presented in association with Legendary Pictures and Village Roadshow Pictures and KGL Film Invest; Dolby; Panavision; Technicolor; Rated PG; 100 minutes; Release date: October 16, 2009

CAST

Max	**Max Records**
Mom	**Catherine Keener**
Boyfriend	**Mark Ruffalo**
Claire	**Pepita Emmerichs**
Teacher	**Steve Kouzakis**
Claire's Friends	**Max Pfeifer, Madeleine Greaves, Joshua Jay, Ryan Corr**

VOICE CAST

Carol	**James Gandolfini**
KW	**Lauren Ambrose**
Douglas	**Chris Cooper**
Judith	**Catherine O'Hara**
Ira	**Forest Whitaker**
Alexander	**Paul Dano**
The Bull	**Michael Berry Jr.**

An overly rambunctious 9-year-old boy, feeling neglected and misunderstood by his mom, escapes to a world where he is declared ruler by a pack of wild creatures.

The Bull, Douglas, Alexander, Judith, Max Records, Ira, Carol

Max Records, Catherine Keener

Carol, Max Records

NEW YORK, I LOVE YOU

(VIVENDI) Producers, Emmanuel Benbihy, Marina Grasic; Executive Producers, Michael Benaroya, Glenn Stewart, Marianne Maddalena, Taylor Kephart, Bradford W. Smith, Claus Clausen, Jan Korbelin, Steffen Aumueller, Pamela Hirsch, Celine Rattray, Susanne Bohnet, Rose Ganguzza; Co-Producer, Parker Bennett; Concept, Emmanuel Benbihy; Based on a premise by Tristan Carné; Main Editor, Affonso Gonçalves ; Music Supervisor, Ed Gerrard; Costumes, Victoria Farrell; Designer, Teresa Mastropierro; Casting, Kerry Barden, Paul Schnee; an Emmanuel Benbihy and Marina Grasic production, in association with Sherezade Films, Benaroya Pictures, Grosvenor Park Media, Ever So Close, Visitor Pictures, 2008NY5 and Grand Army Entertainment; Dolby; Color; HD-to-35mm; Rated R; 103 minutes; Release date: October 16, 2009

SEGMENT 1 – Director, Jiang Wen; Screenplay, Hu Hong, Meng Yao; Adaptation, Israel Horovitz; Photography, Mark Lee Ping Bing; Editor, Affonso Gonçalves ; Music, Tonino Baliardo. **CAST: Hayden Christensen** (Ben), **Andy Garcia** (Garry), **Rachel Bilson** (Molly), **Sinsu Co** (Mystery Bar Girl), **Jeff Chena** (Bartender)
SEGMENT 2 – Director, Mira Nair; Screenplay, Suketu Mehta; Photography, Declan Quinn; Editor, Allyson C. Johnson; Music, Mychael Danna. **CAST: Natalie Portman** (Rifka), **Irrfan Khan** (Mansuhkhbai), **Eliezer Meyer** (Grand Rabbi Elli), **Eddie D'vir** (Rabbi), **Aron Charach** (Young Hasid), **Brad Naprixas** (Hassid in Wedding)
SEGMENT 3 – Director/Screenplay/Editor, Shunji Iwai; Adaptation, Israel Horovitz; Photography, Michael McDonough; Music, Shoji Mitsui. **CAST: Orlando Bloom** (David), **Christina Ricci** (Camille)
SEGMENT 4 – Director, Yvan Attal; Screenplay, Olivier Lécot, Yvan Attal; Photography, Benoît Debie; Editor, Jennifer Auge. **CAST: Ethan Hawke** (Writer), **Maggie Q** (Call Girl), **Robin Wright Penn** (Anna), **Chris Cooper** (Alex)
SEGMENT 5 – Director, Brett Ratner; Screenplay, Jeff Nathanson; Photography, Pawel Edelman; Editor, Mark Helfrich; Music, Mark Mothersbaugh. **CAST: Anton Yelchin** (Boy in the Park), **James Caan** (Mr. Riccoli), **Olivia Thirlby** (Actress), **Blake Lively** (Girlfriend), **Ashley Klein, Jordann Beal** (Prom Girls), **Adam Moreno** (DJ Blue)
SEGMENT 6 – Director, Allen Hughes; Screenplay, Xan Cassavetes, Stephen Winter; Photography, Michael McDonough; Editor, Cindy Mollo; Music, Atticus Ross, Leopold Ross, Claudia Sarne. **CAST: Drea de Matteo** (Lydia), **Bradley Cooper** (Gus)
SEGMENT 7 – Director, Shekhar Kapur; Screenplay, Anthony Minghella; Photography, Benoit Debie; Editor, Jacob Craycroft; Music, Paul Cantelon. **Cast: Julie Christie** (Isabelle), **Shia LaBeouf** (Jacob), **John Hurt** (Waiter)
SEGMENT 8 – Director/Screenplay, Natalie Portman; Photography, Jean-Louis Bompointl Editor, Tricia Cooke; Music, Nicholas Britell. **CAST: Taylor Geare** (Teya), **Cesar De León** (Dominican), **Carlos Acosta** (Dante), **Amy Raudenbush** (Mom #1), **Jacinda Barrett** (Maggie)
SEGMENT 9 – Director/Screenplay, Faith Akin; Photography, Mauricio Rubinstein; Editor, Melody London; Music, Ilhan Ersahin. **CAST: Ugur Yücel** (Painter), **Shu Qi** (Woman), **Burt Young** (Landlord)
SEGMENT 10 – Director/Screenplay, Joshua Marston; Photography, Andrij Parekh; Editor, Affonso Gonçalves ; Music, Marcelo Zarvos. **CAST: Eli Wallach** (Abe), **Cloris Leachman** (Mitzie), **Gary Cherkassky** (Skater Punk)
TRANSITIONS – Director, Randy Balsmeyer; Screenplay, Hall Powell, Israel Horovitz; Photography, Michael McDonough; Editor, Affonso Gonçalves . **CAST: Eva Amurri** (Sarah), **Justin Bartha** (Sarah's Boyfriend), **Emilie Ohana** (Zoe), **Richard Chang** (Mr. Su), **Gurdeep Singh** (Badal), **Juri Henley-Cohn** (Ali), **Vedant Gokhale** (Cab Driver), **Loukas Papas** (Pizza Patron), **Robert d Scott** (Du-Rag), Andy Karl (Evan), **Simon Dasher** (Guitarist), **Duane Nakia Cooper** (Haitian Cab Driver), **Adam S. Phillips** (Jogger), **Himad Beg** (Indian Man)

A collection of eleven short films by eleven different filmmakers telling brief tales taking place in New York that tie into the common theme of finding love. This film is the second episode of the *Cities of Love* franchise created by Emmanuel Benbihy.

Justin Bartha, Eva Amurri

Rachel Portman

Julie Christie, Shia LaBeouf

Christina Ricci, Orlando Bloom

Ethan Hawke, Maggie Q

Anton Yelchin, James Caan

Rachel Bilson, Andy Garcia,
Hayden Christensen

Drea de Matteo, Bradley Cooper

Olivia Thirlby, Anton Yelchin © Vivendi Entertainment

Cloris Leachman, Eli Wallach

LAW ABIDING CITIZEN

(OVERTURE) Producers, Lucas Foster, Gerard Butler, Alan Siegel, Mark Gill, Kurt Wimmer, Robert Katz; Executive Producers, Neil Sacker, Michael Goguen; Co-Producers, Jeff Waxman, Ian Watermeier; Director, F. Gary Gray; Screenplay, Kurt Wimmer; Photography, Jonathan Sela; Designer, Alex Hajou; Costumes, Jeffrey Kurland; Music, Brian Tyler; Music Supervisor, Jim Black; Visual Effects, Image Engine, Entity FX, Rethink VFX; Stunts, Artie Malesci; Editor, Tariq Anwar; Casting, Joseph Middleton, Deanna Brigidi Stewart; a Warp Films production in association with Evil Twins; presented with The Film Department; Dolby; Super 35 Widescreen; Technicolor; Rated R; 108 minutes; Release date: October 16, 2009

CAST
Nick Rice	**Jamie Foxx**
Clyde Shelton	**Gerard Butler**
Jonas Cantrell	**Bruce McGill**
Det. Dunnigan	**Colm Meaney**
Sarah Lowell	**Leslie Bibb**
Kelly Rice	**Regina Hall**
Det. Garza	**Michael Irby**
Warden Iger	**Gregory Itzin**
Denise Rice	**Emerald-Angel Young**
Clarence Darby	**Christian Stolte**

Annie Corley (Judge Laura Burch), Richard Portnow (Bill Reynolds), Viola Davis (Mayor), Michael Kelly (Bray), Josh Stewart (Rupert Ames), Roger Bart (Brian Bringham), Dan Bittner (Sereno), Evan Hart (Collins), Reno Laquintano (Dwight Dixon), Jason Babinsky (Del Frisco Waiter), Rich Barlow (Older Cop), Greg Young (SWAT Captain), Jim Gushue (SWAT Troop #1), Charlie Edward Alston (Inmate), Anthony Lawton (Trunk Cop), Julian Marzal (Sheriff at Shed), David Villalobos (Print Reporter), Ksenia Hulayev (Clyde's Daughter), Brooke Mills (Clyde's Wife), Todd Lewis (Cop), Bijean Ngo (Marvelle), Cecelia Ann Birt (Nick's Assistant), Lamont Clayton (FBI Agent), Lynn Boianelli (Princess on Air Mattress), Dave Huddleston (Newscaster at Execution), Gabra Zackman (Another Reporter), Brian Anthony Wilson (Homeland Security Supervisor), Stephanie Humphrey, Tracy Toth (Local Newscasters), Patrick F. McDade (Charlie – City Hall Security), Jim Fitzpatrick (Messenger), Lawrence Laravela, Barbara Lambert (Bailiffs), Timothy Whiteside (Prison Guard), Nakia Dillard (City hall Sheriff), Robert Bizik (Deputy Police Chief), Ruben Fischman (Prison Administrator), Keith Hammer (Recital Spectator), Joe Pawlenko (Hero Guard), Andy Sinatra (Police Commissioner Asst.)

Devastated when one of the men who murdered his family is permitted to go free, Clyde Shelton decides to strike out with his own form of vengeance on the legal system.

Jamie Foxx, Michael Irby © Overture Films

Bruce McGill, Leslie Bibb, Jamie Foxx

Colm Meaney, Gerard Butler, Jamie Foxx

Viola Davis

Dylan Walsh

Dylan Walsh, Penn Badgley © Screen Geams

THE STEPFATHER

(SCREEN GEMS) Producers, Mark Morgan, Greg Mooradian; Executive Producers, Robert Green, Julie Meldal-Johnsen, Meredith Zamsky, J.S. Cardone, Guy Oseary; Director, Nelson McCormick; Screenplay, J.S. Cardone; Story, Carolyn Starin, Brian Garfield, Donald E. Westlake; Based on a screenplay by Donald E. Westlake; Photography, Patrick Cady; Designer, Steven Jordan; Costumes, Lyn Elizabeth Paolo; Music, Charlie Clouser; Music Supervisor, Michael Friedman; Editor, Eric L. Beason; Casting, Lisa London, Catherine Stroud; a Maverick/Imprint Entertainment/Granada production; Dolby; Deluxe color; Rated PG-13; 101 minutes; Release date: October 16, 2009

CAST
David Harris	**Dylan Walsh**
Susan Harding	**Sela Ward**
Michael Harding	**Penn Badgley**
Kelly Porter	**Amber Heard**
Leah	**Sherry Stringfield**
Jackie Kerns	**Paige Turco**
Jay	**Jon Tenney**

Nancy Linehan Charles (Mrs. Cutter), Marcuis Harris (Detective Shay), Braeden Lemasters (Sean Harding), Deirdre Lovejoy (Det. Tylar), Skyler Samuels (Beth Harding), Blue Deckert (Capt. Mackie), Jason Wiles (Dylan Bennet), Kara Briola (Real Estate Assistant), Jessalyn Gilsig (Julie King), Cathy Schenkelberg (Waitress), David Guzzone, Amandah Reyne (Buyers), Carmen Mormino (Taxi Driver), Todd Cosgrove (Mailman), Tracey Costello (Mrs. Rivers), Cheryl Anderson (Older Woman), Pride Grinn (Car Salesman), Sean Moran (Gus, Hardware Clerk), Jack Chang (Cell Phone Clerk), Savannah Levin (Lisa Bennett)

Returning home from military school, Michael Harding is shocked to discover his mother has remarried, little realizing that her new husband is escaping from his criminal past. Remake of the 1987 New Century Vista film of the same name that starred Terry O'Quinn, Jill Schoelen, and Shelley Hack.

BLACK DYNAMITE

(APPARITION) Producers, Jon Steingart, Jenny Wiener Steingart; Executive Producers, Deanna Bekeley, James Berkeley; Co-Producers, Jillian Apfelbaum, Alison Engel, Steven Funk, Seth Harrison, Matt Richards, Jenna Segal, Paul Segal; Director, Scott Sanders; Screenplay, Scott Sanders, Michael Jai White, Byron Minns; Story, Michael Jai White, Byron Minns; Photography, Shawn Maurer; Designer, Denise Pizzini; Costumes, Ruth E. Carter; Music/Editor, Adrian Younge; Music Supervisor, David Hollander; Fight Coordinator, Roger Yuan; Stunts, Ron Yuan; Casting, Rick Montgomery; an Ars Nova production, in association with Harbor Entertainment; Dolby; Color; Super 16-to-35mm; Rated R; 84 minutes; Release date: October 16, 2009

CAST
Black Dynamite	**Michael Jai White**
Honey Bee	**Kym Whitley**
Cream Corn	**Tommy Davidson**
O'Leary	**Kevin Chapman**
Bullhorn	**Byron Minns**
Gloria	**Salli Richardson-Whitfield**
Chocolate Giddy-Up	**Cedric Yarbrough**
Chicago Wind	**Mykelti Williamson**

Arsenio Hall (Tasty Freeze), Richard Edson (Dino), Chris Spencer, Darrel Heath, Jesse Lewis IV (Militants), Buddy Lewis (Gunsmoke), Pete Antico (Abraham Lincoln), Sorana Black (Diguised Waitress #1), Juka Cesay (Valet Girl), Sean Christopher (Nipsy), Dionne Gipson (Afroditey), Jason Edwards (Soul Brother), Jon Kent Ethridge, Neil Lewis (Young Black Dynamite), Cory Gluck (Young Jimmy), Andray Johnson (Karate Instructor), John Kerry (Mafia Chief), Lauren Mary Kim (Hoe), Brian McKnight (Sweetmeat), James McManus (Richard Nixon), Jessica Moreno (Dumb Blonde), Phil Morris (Saheed), Miguel A. Núñez Jr. (Mo), John Salley (Kotex), Tucker Smallwood (Congressman James), Mike Starr (Rafelli), Larnell Stovall (Pool Hall Thug), Nicole Sullivan (Patricia Nixon), Nakia Syvonne (Euphoria), Al Vicente (Capo), Ashlie R. Jackson (Black Girl), Jimmy Walker Jr. (Roscoe), Bokeem Woodbine (Black Hand Jack), Roger Yuan (Fiendish Dr. Wu) Phyllis Applegate (Aunt Billy), Obba Babatundé (Osiris), Cheryl Carter (Black Dynamite's Mother), Loren Oden (Leon St. James), Nicole Ari Parker (Mahogany Black), Cancade Rice (Shawanda), Paul Taylor (Pretty Terry), Baron Vaughn (Jimmy), Billy "Sly" Williams (Willy Sly), Andre Younge (Reggie),

Black Dynamite seeks revenge on the drug dealers responsible for the murder of his brother in this spoof of '70s blaxploitation flicks.

Nicole Sullivan, Michael Jai White, Salli Richardson © Apparition

AMELIA

(FOX SEARCHLIGHT) Producers, Ted Waitt, Kevin Hyman, Lydia Dean Pilcher; Executive Producers, Ron Bass, Hilary Swank; Co-Producer, Don Carmody; Director, Mira Nair; Screenplay, Ron Bass, Anna Hamilton Phelan, based on the books *East to the Dawn* by Susan Butler and *The Sound of Wings* by Mary S. Lovell; Photography, Stuart Dryburgh; Designer, Stephanie Carroll; Costumes, Kasia Walicka Maimone; Music, Gabriel Yared; Music Supervisor, Linda Cohen; Editors, Allyson C. Johnson, Lee Percy; Visual Effects, Mr. X, Inc.; Stunts, Steve Lucescu; Casting, Avy Kaufman; an Avalon Pictures presentation; Dolby; Panavision; Deluxe color; Rated PG; 111 minutes; Release date: October 23, 2009

Richard Gere, Hilary Swank

CAST

Amelia Earhart	**Hilary Swank**
George Putnam	**Richard Gere**
Gene Vidal	**Ewan McGregor**
Fred Noonan	**Christopher Eccleston**
Bill	**Joe Anderson**
Eleanor Roosevelt	**Cherry Jones**
Elinor Smith	**Mia Wasikowska**
Slim Gordon	**Aaron Abrams**
Leo Bellarts	**Dylan Roberts**
William Dalten	**Scott Yaphe**
Balfour	**Tom Fairfoot**
Young Amelia	**Ryann Shane**
Gore Vidal	**William Cuddy**

Elizabeth Shepherd (Frances Putnam), Richard Donat (Gallagher), Scott Anderson (Parade Reporter), Sarah Kitz (George's Secretary), Keelin Jack (Student), Jeremy Akerman (Sheriff), Derek Keurvorst (Minister), Thomas Hauff, Sarah Dood, Danielle Bourgon (Patrons at Opera House), Hamish McEwan (Paul), Michael Daly (Frank Cipriani), Jeffrey Knight (Cmdr. Thompson), Paul Johnston (Thomas O'Hare), Michael Richard, Daniel Janks, Ron Smerczak (Reporters), Kerin McCue (Movie Tone Announcer), Richard Lothian (Coast Guard), Divine Brown (Torch Singer), Elizabeth Saunders (Louise Thaden), Precious Chong (Gladys O'Donnell), Kathryn Haggis (Powder Puff Aviator), Joe Renzi, Geoff Gillespie (Welsh Singers), Andrea Ciacci, Julia Juhas, Alexandra MacLean, Kristen Munro, Eva Redpath, Jamie Holmes, Brittany Gray, Karissa Strain, Katie Strain, Valeria Saija, Nina Strazzulla (Commodification Montage Dancers)

Hilary Swank © Fox Searchlight

The true story of how Amelia Earhart broke gender barriers and became the most famous female flier of the Depression era, climaxing with her mysterious disappearance during a flight over the Pacific in 1937.

Hilary Swank, Ewan McGregor

Joe Anderson, Hilary Swank

Patrick Fugit, Chris Massoglia, Jessica Carlson

John C. Reilly, Salma Hayek

CIRQUE DU FREAK: THE VAMPIRE'S ASSISTANT

(UNIVERSAL) Producers, Lauren Shuler Donner, Paul Weitz, Ewan Leslie, Andrew Miano; Executive Producers, Courtney Pledger, Sarah Radclyffe, Dan Kolsrud, Kerry Kohansky; Co-Producer, John Swallow; Director, Paul Weitz; Screenplay, Paul Weitz, Brian Helgeland; Based on the *Cirque du Freak* series of books by Darren Shan; Photography, James Muro; Designer, William Arnold; Costumes, Judianna Makovsky; Music, Stephen Trask; Music Supervisor, Kathy Nelson; Editor, Leslie Jones; Special Effects Supervisor, Jefferson "Zuma Jay" Wagner; Visual Effects Supervisor, Todd Shifflett; Creature and Makeup Effects Designers, Alec Gillis, Tom Woodruff Jr.; Casting, Joseph Middleton; a Donners Co/Depth of Field production in association with Relativity Media; Dolby; Super 35 Widescreen; Technicolor; Rated PG-13; 108 minutes; Release date: October 23, 2009

CAST
Larten Crepsley	**John C. Reilly**
Mr. Tall	**Ken Watanabe**
Steve	**Josh Hutcherson**
Darren Shan	**Chris Massoglia**
Rebecca	**Jessica Carlson**
Mr. Tiny	**Michael Cerveris**
Murlaugh	**Ray Stevenson**
Evra the Snake Boy	**Patrick Fugit**
Gavner Purl	**Willem Dafoe**
Madame Truska	**Salma Hayek**

Daniel Newman (Pete), Morgan Saylor (Annie), Don McManus (Mr. Shan), Colleen Camp (Mrs. Shan), Orlando Jones (Alexander Ribbs), Frankie Faison (Rhamus Twobellies), Kristen Schaal (Gertha Teeth), Patrick Breen (Mr. Kersey), Tom Woodruff Jr. (Wolfman), Jane Krakowski (Corma Limbs), Drew Rin Varick (Loaf Head), John D. Crawford (Audience Member), Ritchie Montgomery (Pastor), Ted Manson (Policeman), Ann Mckenzie (Woman from Town), Monica Monica (Teacher), Adella Gauthier (Nurse), Beau Holden (Trucker), Patrick Fulton (Kid Passing By), Tyler Chetta (Kid in Hallway), Shaun Grant (Vampaneze), Trey Burvant (Singing Dad), Beth Burvant (Singing Mother), Evelyn Burvant, Anna Irene Dawson (Singing Kids), Jonathan Nosan (Hans Hands), Madeline Gaudet (Shreiking Student), Erika Jensen (Rain Girl), Armal J. Perkins (Mr. Pipps), Ron Fagan (The Crying Man), Shawn Knowles (Mr. Kersey), Sam Medina (Madame Truska's Man)

A teenager is invited to join a traveling freak show where he becomes a half-vampire and assists Larten Crepsley in battling a more deadly group of blood suckers called the Vampaneze.

John C. Reilly, Chris Massoglia

Josh Hutcherson, Willem Dafoe, John C. Reilly © Universal Studios

Toby, Dr. Tenma © Summit Entertainment

Toby, Orrin

ASTRO BOY

(SUMMIT) Producer, Maryann Garger; Executive Producers, Francis Kao, Cecil Kramer, Ken Tsumura, Paul Wang; Director/Story, David Bowers; Screenplay, Timothy Hyde Harris, David Bowers; Based on the manga by Tezuka Osamu; Photography, Pepe Valencia; Head of Animation, Ti Cheung; Animation Directors, Jakob Hjort Jensen, Kim Ooi; Visual Effects Supervisor, Yan Chen; Music Supervisor, Todd Homme; Editor, Robert Anich Cole; a Summit Entertainment (U.S.)/Imagi Studios (Hong Kong) presentation in association with Endgame Entertainment; Dolby; Color; Rated PG; 94 minutes; Release date: October 23, 2009

VOICE CAST

Toby/Astro	**Freddie Highmore**
Cora	**Kristen Bell**
Hamegg	**Nathan Lane**
Orrin	**Eugene Levy**
Sparx	**Matt Lucas**
Dr. Elefun/Robotsky	**Bill Nighy**
President Stone	**Donald Sutherland**

Charlize Theron ("Our Friends" Narrator), Samuel L. Jackson (Zog), Nicolas Cage (Dr. Tenma), Moises Arias (Zane), Ryan Stiles (Mr. Moustachio), Madeline Carroll (Widget/Grace), Sterling Beaumon (Sludge), Victor Bonavida (Sam), Tony Matthews (Cora's Dad), Alan Tudyk (Mr. Squeegee/Scrapheap Head/Stinger Two), Elle Fanning (Grace), Dee Bradley Baker (Trashcan), David Alan Grier (Mr. Squirt/Math Cowboy/Boxer Robot), David Bowers (Mike the Fridge), Newell Alexander (Gen. Heckler), Bob Logan (Stinger One),

Following an accident, a grieving scientist "recreates" his late son as an android replica with an ability to fly.

(UNTITLED)

(SAMUEL GOLDWYN CO.) Producers, Catherine di Napoli, Jonathan Parker, Andreas Olavarria; Executive Producers, Adam Goldberg, Matt Luber; Director, Jonathan Parker; Screenplay, Jonathan Parker, Catherine di Napoli; Photography, Svetlana Cvetko; Designer, David Snyder; Costumes, Deirdre Wegner; Music, David Lang; Editor, Keiko Deguchi; Original Artwork, Kyle Ng, Sam Parker, Frank Holliday; Casting, Deanna Brigidi-Stewart; a Parker Film Co. production; Widescreen; Dolby; Color; DV; Rated R; 96 minutes; Release date: October 23, 2009

CAST

Adrian Jacobs	**Adam Goldberg**
Madeleine Gray	**Marley Shelton**
Josh Jacobs	**Eion Bailey**
The Clarinet	**Lucy Punch**
Ray Barko	**Vinnie Jones**
Porter Canby	**Zak Orth**

Ptolemy Slocum (Monroe), Michael Panes (Grant), Svetlana Efremova (Russian Singer), Marceline Hugot (Corporate Art Buyer), Janet Carroll (Helen Finkelstein), Ben Hammer (Morton Cabot), David Beach (Critic at Morton Cabot's Concert), David Cale, Dean Wareham (Critics at Adrian's Concert), Kelly Deadmon, Marla Sucharetza (Socialites at Art Dinner), Carole Schweid (Mother), Stan Carp (Father), Ray DeMattis (Restaurant Manager), Michael Hauschild (Adrian's Fan), Frank Holliday (Security Guard), Lawson White (Seth)

Self-important composer Adrian Jacobs finds it hard to justify his lack of attention while his brother Josh's more commercial art work brings him tremendous success.

Adam Goldberg, Marley Shelton

Vinnie Jones © Samuel Goldwyn Films

Michael Jackson

Michael Jackson © Columbia Pictures

Michael Jackson

Michael Jackson's THIS IS IT

(COLUMBIA) Producers, Randy Phillips, Kenny Ortega, Paul Gongaware; Executive Producers, John Branca, John McClain; Co-Producers, Chantal Feghali, Frank Dileo; Director, Kenny Ortega; Photography, Tim Patterson, Sandrine Orabona; Original Score, Michael Bearden; Original Concert Production Creators, Michael Jackson, Kenny Ortega; Designer/Title Design, Michael Cotton; Lighting Designer, Patrick Woodroffe; Editors, Don Brochu, Brandon Key, Tim Patterson, Kevin Stitt; Presented in association with The Michael Jackson Company and AEG Live; Dolby; Deluxe color; Rated PG; 111 minutes; Release date: October 28, 2009

WITH
Michael Jackson, Kenny Ortega, Stacy Walker; Michael Bearden (Music Supervision/Keyboards), **Bashiri Johnson** (Percussion), **Jonathan Moffett** (Drums), **Orianthi Panagaris, Tommy Organ** (Guitars), **Alex Al** (Electric and Synth Bass), **Mo Pleasure** (Keyboards/Trumpet); **Darryl Phinnessee, Ken Stacey, Judith Hill** (Vocalists); **Nick Bass, Daniel Celebre, Mekia Cox, Misha Gabriel, Chris Grant, Shannon Holtzapffel, Devin Andrew Jamieson, Charles Klapow, Dres Reid, Tyne Stecklein, Timor Steffens** (Dancers)

A compilation of interviews, rehearsals and backstage footage of Michael Jackson as he prepared for his for his planned 2009 London concert. Michael Jackson died June 25, 2009.

THE HOUSE OF THE DEVIL

(MAGNET) Producers, Josh Braun, Roger Kass, Larry Fessenden, Peter Phok; Executive Producer, Greg Newman; Co-Producer, Derek Curl; Director/Screenplay/Editor, Ti West; Photography, Eliot Rockett; Designer, Jade Healy; Costumes, Robin Fitzgerald; Music, Jeff Grace; Special Makeup Effects, Christian Fitzgerald; Visual Effects Supervisor, John Loughlin; Stunts, Tony Vincent; Casting, Lisa Fields; an MPI Media Group presentation, in association with Constructovision/Ring the Jing Entertainment, of a Glass Eye Pix production; Dolby; Color; Rated R; 93 minutes; Release date: October 30, 2009

CAST
Samantha	**Jocelin Donahue**
Megan	**Greta Gerwig**
Mrs. Ulman	**Mary Woronov**
Mr. Ulman	**Tom Noonan**
Victor Ulman	**AJ Bowen**
Mother	**Danielle Noe**
Landlady	**Dee Wallace**

Heather Robb (Heather), Darryl Nau (Random Guy), Brenda Cooney (Nurse), Mary B. McCann (Elaine Cross), John Speredakos (Ted Stephen), Lena Dunham (911 Operator), Christina Sciongay (Student), Kamen Velkovsky (Demon), William M. Bradley (Blue Demon), Graham Reznick (Local DJ), Ti West (Favorite Teacher)

College student Samantha makes the mistake of accepting a job to watch Mr. & Mrs. Ulman's eccentric mother in their sinister-looking Victorian mansion.

Jocelin Donahue

Tom Noonan © Magnet Releasinga

James Marsden © Warner Bros.

Frank Langella, Cameron Diaz

THE BOX

(WARNER BROTHERS) Producers, Sean McKittrick, Richard Kelly, Dan Lin; Executive Producers, Sue Baden-Powell, Edward H. Hamm Jr., Ted Field, Paris Kasidokostas Latsis, Terry Douglas; Director/Screenplay, Richard Kelly; Based on the short story *Button, Button* by Richard Matheson; Photography, Steven Poster; Designer, Alexander Hammond; Costumes, April Ferry; Music, Win Butler, Régine Chassagne, Owen Pallett; Editor, Sam Bauer; Visual Effects Supervisor, Thomas Tannenberger; Special Effects Supervisor, Justin Bell; Casting, Mary Vernieu, Venus Kanani; a Radar Pictures and Media Rights Capital presentation of a Darko Entertainment production; Dolby; Panavision; Technicolor; Rated PG-13; 113 minutes; Release date: November 6, 2009

CAST
Norma Lewis	**Cameron Diaz**
Arthur Lewis	**James Marsden**
Arlington Steward	**Frank Langella**
Norm Cahill	**James Rebhorn**
Dick Burns	**Holmes Osborne**

Sam Oz Stone (Walter Lewis), Gillian Jacobs (Dana), Celia Weston (Lana Burns), Deborah Rush (Clymene Steward), Lisa K. Wyatt (Rhonda Martin), Mark Cartier (Martin Teague), Kevin Robertson (Wendel Matheson), Michele Durett (Rebecca Matheson), Ian Kahn (Vick Brenner), John Magaro (Charles), Ryan Woodle (Jeffrey Carnes), Basil Hoffman (Don Poates), Robert Harvey (NASA Executive #1), Gentry Lee (Chief Engineer), Andrew Levitas (Black Op), Gabriel Field (Waiter), Frank Ridley (Det. Starrs), Daniel Stewart Sherman, Matthew C. Flynn, Patrick Canty (Police Officers), Sam Blumenfeld (Timothy), Kevin DeCoste (Malcolm), Mary Klug (Neighbor), Allyssa Maurice (Suzanne Weller), Danny DeMiller (Estelle), Michael Zegen (Garcin), Rachael Hunt (Inez), Cheryl McMahon (911 Operator), Evelina Oboza (Deborah Burns), Bill Buell (Dr. Earl Stupe), Sal Lizard (Santa Claus), Donald Warnock (Doctor Y), W. Kirk Avery (Doctor Z), Don Hewitt, Floyd Richardson, Dave McDonough (Employees), Rick L'Heureux, Nicholas Cairis, Robert Denton, Paul Locke, Danielle Heaton (Chase Employees)

A couple is offered one million dollars if they will agree to push a button on a mysterious box that will, in turn, kill a total stranger.

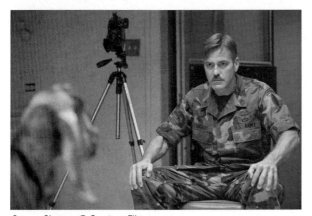

Jeff Bridges, George Clooney

George Clooney © Overture Films

George Clooney, Ewan McGregor

THE MEN WHO STARE AT GOATS

(OVERTURE) Producers, Paul Lister, George Clooney, Grant Heslov; Executive Producers, Barbara A. Hall, James Holt, Alison Owen, David M. Thompson; Director, Grant Heslov; Screenplay, Peter Straughan; Inspired by the book by Jon Ronson; Photography, Robert Elswit; Designer, Sharon Seymour; Costumes, Louise Frogley; Music, Rolfe Kent; Music Supervisor, Linda Cohen; Editor, Tatian S. Riegel; Visual Effects Supervisor, Thomas J. Smith; Casting, Cathy Sandrich Gelfond, Amanda Mackey; a Smokehouse/Paul Lister production, presented in association with Winchester and BBC Films; American-British; Dolby; Panavision: Deluxe color; Rated R; 93 minutes; Release date: November 6, 2009

CAST
Lyn Cassady	**George Clooney**
Bob Wilton	**Ewan McGregor**
Bill Django	**Jeff Bridges**
Larry Hooper	**Kevin Spacey**
Brigadier General Dean Hopgood	**Stephen Lang**
Todd Nixon	**Robert Patrick**
Mahmud Daash	**Waleed Zuaiter**
Gus Lacey	**Stephen Root**
Major Holtz	**Glenn Morshower**
Scotty Mercer	**Nick Offerman**
Tim Kootz	**Tim Griffin**

Rebecca Mader (Debora Wilton), Jacob Browne (Lt. Boone), Todd La Tourrette (Dave), Brad Grunberg (Ron), Elsa Villafane (Gus' Mother), Fawad Masood Siddiqui (Kuwait Waiter), Samuel Gates, McCaleb Burnett (Journalists), Sean Phillips (Vietnam Soldier), Matt Newton (Vietnam Private Chris), Minh Tu Van (VC Woman), Robert Curtis Brown (Gen. Brown), Hrach Titizian, Shafik N. Bahou (Kidnappers), Christopher Maher (Iraqi Driver), Drew Seltzer (Technician), Donn Lamkin (Lyn's Father), Sean Curley (Lyn, 12 years old), Merik Tadros (Irate Insurgent), Michael-David Aragon (Insurgent), Morse Bicknell (Ben Echmeyer), Terry Serpico (Krom – Phil Driver), Wiley M. Pickett (Krom – Texan), Diego Serrano (Krom – Chilean), Reginald Huc (Krom – 3rd Security Man), Kevin Geer (CIA Agent), Kevin Wiggins (Maj. Gen. Jack Gillian), JJ Raschel (Clifford Hickox), Arron Shiver (Norm Pendleton), Jaime Margarida (Maj. Gen. Pendleton), Steve Witting, Hunter Bell (PSIC Workers), Edward Holley (Army Soldier), Christopher Robinson (Stryker Soldier), William Sterchi (Bob's Editor), Robert Anthony Brass (Sgt. Bishop), Paul J. Porter (Capt. Wogolman)

Journalist Bob Wilton investigates the bizarre story behind a team of top-secret "psychic spies" trained to use their powers during wartime.

Kevin Spacey

PRECIOUS: Based on the novel
Push by Sapphire

(LIONSGATE) Producers, Lee Daniels, Sarah Siegel-Magness, Gary Magness; Executive Producers, Lisa Cortés, Tom Heller, Oprah Winfrey, Tyler Perry; Co-Producer, Mark G. Mathis; Director, Lee Daniels; Screenplay, Geoffrey Fletcher, based on the novel *Push* by Sapphire; Photography, Andrew Dunn; Designer, Roshelle Berliner; Costumes, Marina Draghici; Music, Mario Grigorov; Music Supervisor, Lynn Fainchtein; Editor, Joe Klotz; Casting, Billy Hopkins, Jessica Kelly; an Oprah Winfrey and Tyler Perry presentation of a Lee Daniels Entertainment/Smokewood Entertainment Group production; Dolby; Technicolor; Rated R; 109 minutes; Release date: November 6, 2009

Mariah Carey, Gabourey Sidibe

CAST

Claireece Precious Jones	**Gabourey Sidibe**
Mary	**Mo'Nique**
Ms. Rain	**Paula Patton**
Nurse John	**Lenny Kravitz**
Ms. Weiss	**Mariah Carey**
Cornrows	**Sherri Shepherd**
Rita	**Stephanie Andujar**
Rhonda	**Chyna Layne**
Jermaine	**Amina Robinson**
Joann	**Xosha Roquemore**
Consuelo	**Angelic Zambrana**
Tootsie	**Aunt Dot**
Mrs. Lichtenstein	**Nealla Gordon**
Social Worker	**Grace Hightower**
Tom Cruise	**Barret Isaiah Mindell**
Katherine	**Kimberly Russell**
Mr. Wicher	**Bill Sage**
Fairy Godmother	**Susan Taylor**
Abdul, New Born	**Kendall Toombs, Alexander Toombs**
Abdul, 9 Months	**Cory Davis**
AIDS Clerk	**Rochelle McNaughton**
Boy #1	**Roy Anthony Tarell Harvey**
Bunny	**Abigail Savage**
Carl	**Rodney "Bear" Jackson**
Day Care Woman	**Sapphire**
Clerk	**Linda Watson**
Girls	**Emani Reid, DaShawn Robinson**
Girl with Jermaine	**Ashley Livingston**
Italian Language Instructor	**Maurizio Arseni**
KFC Cashier	**Mugga**
Men Exiting Elevator	**Chazz Menendez, Roy T. Anderson**
Mongo	**Quishay Peanan**
Nurse	**Vivien Eng**
Pretty Blonde Girl	**Sije Vallevik**
Reggie	**Matt Bralow**
Ruby	**Shayla Stewart**
Sheila	**Erica Faye Watson**

Ephraim Benton, Shortee Red, Timothy Allen (Skinny Boys), Nigel Joaquin, Esley Tate (Unruly Boys)

An illiterate, overweight African American teenager, pregnant for the second time by her father, hopes to better her hellish life by enrolling in an alternative school.

2009 Academy Award Winner for Best Supporting Actress (Mo'Nique) and Best Adapted Screenplay.

This film received additional Oscar nominations for picture, director, actress (Gabourey Sidibe), and film editing.

Chyna Layne, Angelic Zambrana, Gabourey Sidibe, Stephanie Andujar
© Lionsgate

Mo'Nique

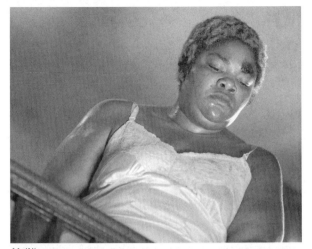

Mo'Nique

Paula Patton

Gabourey Sidibe

Gabourey Sidibe, Mo'Nique, Quishay Peanan

Gabourey Sidibe

Gabourey Sidibe, Paula Patton

Belle, Ebenezer Scrooge, The Ghost of Christmas Past, Young Ebenezer

The Ghost of Christmas Present, Ebenezer Scrooge

Bob Cratchit, Tiny Tim © Walt Disney Studios

Fred, Ebenezer Scrooge

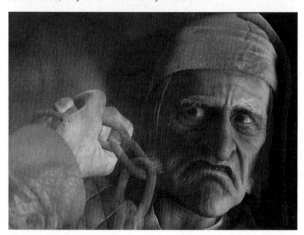

Ebenezer Scrooge

Ebenezer Scrooge, Tiny Tim

Mr. Fezziwig

Ebenezer Scrooge

Disney's A CHRISTMAS CAROL

(WALT DISNEY PICTURES) Producers, Steve Starkey, Robert Zemeckis, Jack Rapke; Co-Producer, Steven Boyd; Director/Screenplay, Robert Zemeckis; Based on the novella by Charles Dickens; Photography, Robert Presley; Designer, Doug Chiang; Music, Alan Silvestri; Editor, Jeremiah O'Driscoll; Visual Effects Supervisor, George Murphy; Animation Supervisor, Jenn Emberly; Casting, Nina Gold; a Walt Disney Pictures and ImageMovers Digital presentation; Dolby; 70mm Widescreen; Deluxe color; 3D; Rated PG; 95 minutes; Release date: November 6, 2009

CAST

Ebenezer Scrooge/Ghosts of Christmas Past, Present, & Yet to Come	**Jim Carrey**
Bob Crachit/Marley/Tiny Tim	**Gary Oldman**
Fred	**Colin Firth**
Mr. Fezziwig/Old Joe	**Bob Hoskins**
Fan/Belle	**Robin Wright Penn**
Portly Gentleman #1/Dick Wilkins/ Mad Fiddler/Guest #2/Business Man #1	**Cary Elwes**
Mrs Dilber	**Fionnula Flanagan**
Funerary Undertaker/Topper	**Steve Valentine**
Undertaker's Apprentice/Tattered Caroler/Beggar Boy/Peter Cratchit/ Well-Dressed Caroler	**Daryl Sabara**
Tattered Caroler	**Sage Ryan**
Tattered Carolers/Well-Dressed Carolers	**Amber Gainey Meade, Bobbie Page, Ron Bottitta**
Tattered Caroler/Beggar Boy/ Young Cratchit Boy/Ignorance Boy/ Young Boy with Sleigh/ Tiny Tim	**Ryan Ochoa**
Fat Cook/Portly Gentleman #2/Business Man #3	**Julian Holloway**
Mrs. Fezziwig/Fred's Sister-in-Law/ Well-Dressed Caroler	**Jacquie Barnbrook**
Mrs. Cratchit	**Leslie Manville**
Belinda Cratchit	**Molly C. Quinn**
Martha Cratchit/Guest #1/ Caroline	**Fay Masterson**
Fred's Wife	**Leslie Zemeckis**
Guest # 3/Business Man #2	**Paul Blackthorne**
Guest #4	**Michael Hyland**
Adult Ignorance	**Kerry Hoyt**
Adult Want	**Julene Renee**
Caroline's Child	**Raymond Ochoa**
Caroline's Husband	**Callum Blue**
Poulterer	**Matthew Henerson**
Well-Dressed Caroler	**Aaron Rapke**
Well-Dressed Caroler/Fred's Housemaid	**Sonje Fortag**

Miserly Ebenezer Scrooge is visited by three ghosts who hope to show him the error of his selfish and unkind ways. Previous film versions include those made in 1992 (*The Muppet Christmas Carol*), 1970 (*Scrooge*), 1951 and 1938.

THE FOURTH KIND

(UNIVERSAL) Producers, Paul Brooks, Joe Carnahan, Terry Lee Robbins; Executive Producers, Scott Niemeyer, Norm Waitt, Ioana A. Miller; Co-Producers, Guy A. Danella, Jeff Levine, Michele Greco; Co-Executive Producers, David Pupkewitz, Jon Bjarni Gudmundsson, Vinca Liane Jarrett; Director/Screenplay, Olatunde Osunsanmi; Story, Olatunde Osunsanmi, Terry Lee Robbins; Photography, Lorenzo Senatore; Designer, Carlos Da Silva; Costumes, Johnetta Boone; Music, Atli Örvarsson; Editor, Paul J. Covington; Visual Effects Supervisors, Mark Freund, Andrew Somers; Stunts, Ben Bray, Frank Torres; Casting, Sue Jones; a Chambara Pictures, Dead Crow Pictures production presented with Gold Circle Films; Dolby; Super 35 Widescreen; Color; Rated PG-13; 98 minutes; Release date: November 6, 2009

CAST

Dr. Abigail Emily Tyler	**Milla Jovovich**
Sheriff August	**Will Patton**
Dr. Abel Campos	**Elias Koteas**
Tommy Fisher	**Corey Johnson**
Scott Stracinsky	**Enzo Cilenti**
Dr. Awolowa Odusami	**Hakeem Kae-Kazim**

Alisha Seaton (Cindy Stracinsky), Daphne Alexander (Theresa), Mia McKenna-Bruce (Ashley), Olatunde Osunsanmi (Himself), Eric Loren (Deputy Ryan), Raphaël Coleman (Ronnie Tyler), Tyne Rafaeli (Sarah Fisher), Pavel Stefanov (Timothy Fisher), Kiera McMaster (Joe Fisher), Sarah Houghton (Jessica), Julian Vergov (Will Tyler), Yoan Karamfilov (Ralph)

Dr. Abigail Emily Tyler seeks the help of a psychiatrist in hopes of determining whether or not her husband and child were abducted by aliens.

Elias Koteas

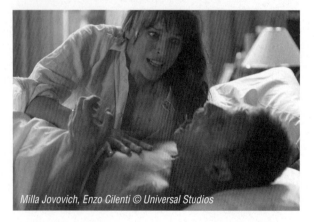

Milla Jovovich, Enzo Cilenti © Universal Studios

Carrie Preston, Mia Wasikowska, Hal Holbrook
© Freestyle Releasing

Ray McKinnon

THAT EVENING SUN

(FREESTYLE) Producers, Laura Smith, Terence Berry, Raymond McKinnon, Walton Goggins; Executive Producers, Adrian Jay, Larsen Jay, Raul L. Celaya; Co-Producer, Jeanine Rohn; Director/Screenplay, Scott Teems; Based on the story *I Hate to See That Evening Sun Go Down* by William Gay; Photography, Rodney Taylor; Designer, Mara Lepere-Schloop; Costumes, Alexis Scott; Music, Michael Penn; Music Supervisor, Linda Cohen; Casting, Emily Schweber; a Dogwood Entertainment production, in association with Ginny Mule Pictures; Dolby; Widescreen; Deluxe color; Rated PG-13; 109 minutes; Release date: November 6, 2009

CAST

Abner Meecham	**Hal Holbrook**
Lonzo Choat	**Ray McKinnon**
Paul Meecham	**Walton Goggins**
Pamela Choat	**Mia Wasikowska**
Ludie Choat	**Carrie Preston**
Thurl Chessor	**Barry Corbin**
Ellen Meecham	**Dixie Carter**

Barlow Jacobs (J.D. the Cabbie), Anthony Reynolds (Hollis the Phone Worker), Brian Keith (Deputy Keith), Bruce McKinnon (Sheriff Roller), William J. Mode (Deputy Davies), Jacob Parkhurst (Steve Goodwin Jr.)

An 80-year-old Tennessee farmer skips out of the nursing home where he has been dumped by his son with the intention of returning to his farm only to find out that it has been leased to someone else.

Kristofferson, Ash

Kylie, Rat, Beaver, Mr. Fox, Badger, Rabbit, Mole

Mr. Fox © Fox Searchlight

FANTASTIC MR. FOX

(FOX SEARCHLIGHT) Producers, Allison Abbate, Scott Rudin, Wes Anderson, Jeremy Dawson; Executive Producers, Steven Rales, Arnon Milchan; Co-Producer, Molly Cooper; Director, Wes Anderson; Screenplay, Wes Anderson, Noah Baumbach; Based on the book by Roald Dahl; Photography, Tristan Oliver; Designer, Nelson Lowry; Music, Alexandre Desplat; Editor, Andrew Weisblum; Visual Effects Supervisor, Tim Ledbury; Animation Director, Mark Gustafson; Animation Supervisor, Mark Waring; Puppets Fabricator, MacKinnon and Saunders; an American Empirical Picture presented in association with Indian Paintbrush and Regency Enterprises; Dolby; Deluxe color; Rated PG; 88 minutes; Release date: November 13, 2009

VOICE CAST

Mr. Fox	**George Clooney**
Mrs. Fox	**Meryl Streep**
Ash	**Jason Schwartzman**
Badger	**Bill Murray**
Kylie	**Wally Wolodarsky**
Kristofferson	**Eric Anderson**
Franklin Bean	**Michael Gambon**
Rat	**Willem Dafoe**
Coach Skip	**Owen Wilson**
Petey	**Jarvis Cocker**
Weasel	**Wes Anderson**
Linda Otter	**Karen Duffy**
Walter Boggis	**Robin Hurlstone**
Nathan Bunce	**Hugo Guinness**
Mrs. Bean	**Helen McCrory**
Squirrel Contractor	**Roman Coppola**
Agnes	**Juman Malouf**
Beaver's Son	**Jeremy Dawson**
Bean's Son	**Garth Jennings**
Action 12 Reporter	**Brian Cox**

Tristan Oliver (Explosives Man), James Hamilton (Mole), Steven Rales (Beaver), Rob Hersov (Pilot), Jennifer Furches (Dr. Badger), Allison Abbate (Rabbit's Ex-Girlfriend), Molly Cooper, Mario Batali (Rabbits), Adrien Brody (Field Mouse), Martin Ballard (Fire Chief)

Mr. Fox causes war between himself and three angered farmers when he decides to return to his old ways of poaching.

This film received Oscar nominations for animated feature and music.

Mr. Fox, Mrs. Fox

2012

(COLUMBIA) Producers, Harald Kloser, Mark Gordon, Larry Franco; Executive Producers, Roland Emmerich, Ute Emmerich, Michael Wimer; Co-Producers, Wolker Engel, Marc Weigert; Director, Roland Emmerich; Screenplay, Harald Kloser, Roland Emmerich; Photography, Dean Semler; Designer, Barry Chusid; Costumes, Shay Cunliffe; Music, Harald Kloser, Thomas Wander; Editors, David Brenner, Peter S. Elliot; Visual Effects Supervisors, Volker Engel, Marc Weigert; Visual Effects and Digital Environments, Uncharted Territory; Visual Effects, Scanline VFX, Double Negative, Pixomondo, Hydraulx; Special Visual Effects and Animation, Sony Pictures Imageworks, Digital Domain; Stunts, John Stoneham Jr.; 2nd Unit Director, Aaron Boyd; Casting, April Webster; a Centropolis production; Dolby; Panavision; Deluxe color; Rated PG-13; 158 minutes; Release date: November 13, 2009

CAST

Jackson Curtis	**John Cusack**
Kate Curtis	**Amanda Peet**
Adrian Helmsley	**Chiwetel Ejiofor**
Laura Wilson	**Thandie Newton**
Carl Anheuser	**Oliver Platt**
Gordon Silberman	**Tom McCarthy**
Charlie Frost	**Woody Harrelson**
President Thomas Wilson	**Danny Glover**
Noah Curtis	**Liam James**
Lilly Curtis	**Morgan Lily**
Yuri Karpov	**Zlatko Buric**
Tamara	**Beatrice Rosen**
Alec Karpov	**Alexandre Haussmann**
Oleg Karpov	**Philippe Haussmann**
Sasha	**Johann Urb**
Professor West	**John Billingsley**
Nima	**Osric Chau**
Grandfather Sonam	**Chang Tseng**
Grandmother Sonam	**Lisa Lu**
Harry Helmsley	**Blu Mankuma**
Tony Delgatto	**George Segal**
Captain Michaels	**Stephen McHattie**
Roland Picard	**Patrick Bauchau**
Dr. Satnam Tsurutani	**Jimi Mistry**
Scotty	**Ryan McDonald**

Chin Han (Tenzin), Merrilyn Gann (German Chancellor), Henry O (Lama Rinpoche), Patrick Gilmore, Dean Marshall (Ark Communications Officers), Ron Selmour, Viv Leacock, Chris Boyd (Ark Boarding Officers), Donna Yamamoto, Doron Bell Jr. (AF1 Science Officers), David Orth (AF1 Lieutenant), Lyndall Grant (Governor), Jason Diablo (Ark Tech Officer), Ty Olsson (AF1 Officer), Zinaid Memisevic (Pres. Sergey Makarenko), Vincent Cheng (Chinese Colonel), Igor Morozov (Russian Interpreter), BJ Harrison (Woman Comforting Child), Dominic Zamprogna (Paramedic), Karin Konoval (Sally, President's Secretary), Mary Gillis (Jackson's Neighbor), Rick Tae (Megaphone Officer), Parm Soor (Saudi Prince), Gerard Plunkett (Isaacs – M16 Officer), Paul Tryl (Zultan), Andrei Kovski (Zultan's Trainer), Val Cole (News Reporter – Tikal), Eve Harlow (Cashier), Sean Tyson (Interrogating Officer), Leonard Tenisci (Italian Prime Minister), Michael Buffer (Boxing Announcer), Daren A. Herbert (Ship Waiter), Craig Stanghetta (Vegas Rescue Worker), Mateen Devji (Ajit – age 5), Qayam Devji (Ajit – age 9), Jody Thompson (CNN Anchor), Tanya Champoux (Mrs. Birnbaum), Frank C. Turner (Preacher), Kinua McWatt (Yoko Delgatto), Laara Sadiq (British Newscaster), Gillian Barber, Candus Churchill, Beverley Elliott (Cruise Ship Ladies), Agam Darshi (Aparna), Raj Lal (Gurdeep), Pesi Daruwalla (Dr. Lokesh), Jacob Blair, Jay Williams (AF1 Stewards), Scott Miller (Ark Naval Officer), Anna Mae Routledge (Officer Tay), John Stewart (Pilot), Ryan Cook, Brandon Haas, Eddie Hassell (Surfers), Betty Phillips, Georgina Hegedos (Elderly Drivers), Luis Javier

(Vegas Tow Truck Driver), Dean Redman (Vegas Fireman), Gordon Lai (Security Commander), Mark Docherty (Field Reporter – Tikal), Mark Oliver (Fundraiser Security), Andrew Moxham (Policeman), Alexandra Castillo (Paris Reporter), Farouk A. Afify (Saudi Senior Security), Shaun Wilson (US Army Worker), Leo Chiang (Chinese Soldier), Elizabeth Richard (Queen Elizabeth), Kyle Riefsnyder (Cho Ming Platform Officer), John Mee (Angry Billionaire), George Trochta (American Ark Steward), Geoff Gustafson, Jase Anthony Griffith, Jill Morrison, Thomas Parkinson, Leona Naidoo, Quentin Guyon, Nicole Rudell, Chad Riley, Simon Leung, Kevin Haaland (Ark Bridge Crew), Leigh Burrows (U.S. Army Worker), Alex Zahara (Mr. Anton), Eddie L. Fauria (Sgt. Lourke), Ayana Haviv (Voice of Singer), Marco Khan (Preacher), William Myers (DoomSayer), Michael Karl Richards (Wil Delgado), David Ricmond-Peck (Political Aide), Jerome Young (Tony)

Realizing that global annihilation is imminent, several world citizens race against time to prepare for the inevitable end and the possibility of a safe escape.

Lisa Lu, Amanda Peet

John Cusack, Woody Harrelson

Amanda Peet, John Cusack

Lily Morgan, Thandie Newton, Chiwetel Ejiofor

Thandie Newton, Chiwetel Ejiofor © Columbia Pictures

John Cusack

Thandie Newton, Danny Glover

Oliver Platt

DARE

(IMAGE ENTERTAINMENT) Producers, Mary Jane Skalski, Jason Orans; Co-Producer/Screenplay, David Brind; Director, Adam Salky; Photography, Michael Fimognari; Art Director, Michael David Crenshaw; Music, Duncan Sheik, David Poe; Music Supervisor, Dave Golden; Editor, John F. Lyons; Casting, Kerry Barden, Paul Schnee; a Next Wednesday/Gigantic Pictures production; Dolby; Color; Rated R; 90 minutes; Release date: November 13, 2009

CAST
Alexa Walker	**Emmy Rossum**
Johnny Drake	**Zach Gilford**
Ben Berger	**Ashley Springer**
Ruth Berger	**Ana Gasteyer**
Courtney	**Rooney Mara**
Dr. Serena Mohr	**Sandra Bernhard**
Grant Matson	**Alan Cumming**
Dr. Kolton	**Cady Huffman**

Brianne Berkson (Gabby), Chris Riggi (Josh), Brea Bee (Mel Drake), Lucy McMichael (Ms. Davis), Suzanne Savoy (Deirdre Walker), Wayne Pyle (Alan Berger), Adam Fleming (Detention Teacher), Annie Hibbs (Donna), Michael Braun (Actor), Emily McNamara (Grant's Actress Friend), Matthew Garrick (Headmaster), Ellis Lane, Jake Lane (Coffee Shop Twins), Susan Triggiani (School Secretary), Nathan Unsworth (Josh's Jock Buddy), David Brind (Nick)

An aspiring actress and her socially awkward gay friend become unexpectedly entangled in a complicated relationship with the school's brooding bad boy.

Ashley Springer, Emmy Rossum, Zach Gilford © Image Entertainment

Lynn Collins, Joseph Gordon-Levitt

Joseph Gordon-Levitt, Lynn Collins © IFC Films

UNCERTAINTY

(IFC FILMS) Producers/Directors/Screenplay, Scott McGehee, David Siegel; Photography, Rain Li; Designer, Debbie De Villa; Costumes, Stacey Battat; Music, Peter Nashel; Editor, Paul Zucker; Casting, Billy Hopkins, Suzanne Crowley, Kerry Barden, Paul Schnee; a KinoCorp picture; Widescreen; Color; Not rated; 104 minutes; Release date: November 13, 2009

CAST
Bobby Thompson	**Joseph Gordon-Levitt**
Kate Montero	**Lynn Collins**
Sylvia Montero	**Assumpta Serna**
Sophie Montero	**Olivia Thirlby**
Felix	**Nelson Landrieu**
Greg	**Manoel Felciano**
Emily	**Jenn Colella**

Giana Luca (Annabelle), Sofia Luca (Adelaide), Sara Chase (Alex), Marin Gazzaniga (Nurse), Michaela M. Hill (Jackie), Ana Cruz Kayne (Beth), Robert C. Kirk (Duty Officer), Madeline Lee (Elderly Woman), Chris Meyer (Curtis), Doua Moua (Internet Café Clerk), Ted Oyama (Asian Assassin), Al Roffe (Bodega Customer), Joe Starr (Mechanic)

A young couple flips a coin to decide how they will spend Independence Day, and both possibilities unfold: one as they choose to attend a family barbecue in Brooklyn, the other finding them running for their lives after finding a cell phone in a Manhattan taxi cab.

Woody Harrelson, Ben Foster

Samantha Morton © Oscilloscope Pictures

THE MESSENGER

(OSCILLOSCOPE) Producers, Mark Gordon, Lawrence Inglee, Zach Miller; Executive Producers, Ben Goldhirsh, Christopher Mapp, Matthew Street, David Whealy, Glenn M. Stewart, Steffen Aumueller, Claus Clausen, Bryan Zuriff, Shaun Redick; Director, Oren Moverman; Screenplay, Oren Moverman, Alessandro Camon; Photography, Bobby Bukowski; Designer, Stephen Beatrice; Costumes, Catherine George; Music, Nathan Larson; Editor, Alex Hall; Casting, Laura Rosenthal, Ali Farrell; an Omnilab Media Group presentation in association with Sherezade Film Development Co. and BZ Entertainment of a Mark Gordon Co./ Good Worldwide production; Dolby; Super 35 Widescreen; Color; Rated R; 112 minutes; Release date: November 13, 2009

CAST

Staff Sgt. Will Montgomery	**Ben Foster**
Captain Tony Stone	**Woody Harrelson**
Olivia Pitterson	**Samantha Morton**
Kelly	**Jena Malone**
Dale Martin	**Steve Buscemi**
Col. Stuart Dorsett	**Eamonn Walker**
Monica Washington	**Yaya DaCosta**
Mrs. Burrell	**Portia**
Emily	**Lisa Joyce**
Dr. Grosso	**Peter Francis James**
Motorcycle Cop	**Paul Diomede**
Matt Pitterson	**Jahmir Duran-Abreau**
Recruiter Brown	**Gaius Charles**
Recruiter Olson	**Brendan Sexton III**

Brian Adam DeJesus, T.J. Allen (Teenagers), Halley Feiffer (Marla Cohen), Peter Friedman (Mr. Cohen), Jeremy Strong (Returning Soldier), Fiona Dourif (Returning Soldier's Wife), Lindsay Michelle Nader (Claire), Merritt Wever (Lara), Carl Anthony Payne II (Pitterson's Father), Francis A. Adams (Firing Party Team Leader), J. Salome Martinez Jr. (Capt. Garcia), Angel Caban (Mr. Vasquez), Kevin Hagan (Mr. Flanigan), Marceline Hugot (Mrs. Flanigan), Michael Chernus (Alan), Stevie Ray Dallimore (Kelly's Father), Dale Soules (Cashier), Karen Summerton (Flirty Girl)

After being wounded in Iraq, Will Montgomery chooses to finish out his time by working for the Casualty Notification Office, which proves to be just as challenging an assignment.

This film received Oscar nominations for supporting actor (Woody Harrelson) and original screenplay.

Ben Foster, Woody Harrelson

Sandra Bullock, Phillip Fulmer, Ray McKinnon, Quinton Aaron
© Warner Bros.

Quinton Aaron, Sandra Bullock

Quinton Aaron, Jae Head, Sandra Bullock, Lily Collins

Kathy Bates, Quinton Aaron

Jae Head, Quinton Aaron

Jae Head, Quinton Aaron, Sandra Bullock

Nick Saban, Tim McGraw, Lily Collins, Sandra Bullock

Tim McGraw, Lily Collins, Jae Head, Quinton Aaron, Sandra Bullock

THE BLIND SIDE

(WARNER BROTHERS) Producers, Gil Netter, Andrew A. Kosove, Broderick Johnson; Executive Producers, Molly Smith, Timothy M. Bourne, Erwin Stoff; Co-Producers, Yolanda T. Cochran, Steven P. Wegner; Director/Screenplay, John Lee Hancock; Based on the book *The Blind Side: Evolution of a Game* by Michael Lewis; Photography, Alar Kivilo; Designer, Michael Corenblith; Costumes, Daniel Orlandi; Music, Carter Burwell; Music Supervisor, Julie Michaels; Editor, Mark Livolsi; Football Coordinator, Michael Fisher; Casting, Ronna Kress; an Alcon Entertainment presentation of a Gil Netter production; Dolby; Technicolor; Rated PG-13; 128 minutes; Release date: November 20, 2009

CAST

Leigh Anne Tuohy	**Sandra Bullock**
Sean Tuohy	**Tim McGraw**
Michael Oher	**Quinton Aaron**
SJ Tuohy	**Jae Head**
Collins Tuohy	**Lily Collins**
Coach Burt Cotton	**Ray McKinnon**
Mrs. Boswell	**Kim Dickens**
Denise Oher	**Adriane Lenox**
Miss Sue	**Kathy Bates**
Mrs. Smith	**Catherine Dyer**
Principal Sandstrom	**Andy Stahl**
Literature Teacher	**Tom Nowicki**
Sarcastic Teacher	**Libby Whittemore**
Jay Collins	**Brian Hollan**
History Teacher	**Melody Weintraub**
Investigator Granger	**Sharon Morris**
"Big Tony" Hamilton	**Omar Dorsey**
Steve Hamilton	**Paul Amadi**
David	**Hampton Fluker**
Beth	**Rhoda Griffis**
Elaine	**Eaddy Mays**
Sherry	**Ashley LeConte Campbell**
DMV Employee	**Stacey Turner**
CPS Caseworker	**Afemo Omilami**

IronE Singleton (Alton), Elizabeth Omilami (Jenny Defacs), Maria Howell (CPS Welfare Worker), Patrick G. Keenan (Man in CPS Line), Eric Benson (Milford #66), David Dwyer (Milford Dad), Catherine Combs, Kelly Johns (Collins's Friends), Robert Pralgo (Lemming's Associate), Whitney Branan, Brian Sutherin (Lemming's Secretaries), Rachel St. Gelais (Little Girl on Playground), Brandon Rivers (Michael, age 7), Jody Thompson (Paramedic), James Donadio (Photographer), L. Warren Young (Big and Tall Salesman), Brett Rice (Cousin Bobby), Kevin Nichols (Memphis Policeman), Preston Brant (Marcus), Matthew Atkinson (Valet Parker), Trey Best (Michael's Brother, age 12), Omid Soltani (Rug Salesman), Destiny Long (Alton's Girlfriend), April Rich (Teacher in Lounge), Jaye Tyroff (Milford Player #35), Ben Keen (Wingate Quarterback), John Newberg (Official), John Henry Hancock (Rabid Ole Miss Fan), Joe Chrest (Clemson Coach), Michael Fisher (Georgia Assistant Coach), Lamont Koonce (Tennessee Assistant Coach), Philip Fulmer, Lou Holtz, Tom Lemming, Houston Nutt, Ed Orgeron, Franklin "Pepper" Rodgers, Nick Saban, Tommy Tuberville (Themselves)

The true story of how a well-to-do Memphis woman and her family took in a homeless, barely educated young black man who went on to play professional football.

2009 Academy Award Winner for Best Actress in a Leading Role (Sandra Bullock).

This film received an additional Oscar nomination for picture.

Sandra Bullock, Patrick G. Keenan, Maria Howell

NEW MOON

(SUMMIT) Producers, Wyck Godfrey, Karen Rosenfelt; Executive Producers, Marty Bowen, Greg Mooradian, Mark Morgan, Guy Oseary; Co-Producer, Bill Bannerman; Director, Chris Weitz; Screenplay, Melissa Rosenberg; Based on the novel by Stephenie Meyer; Photography, Javier Aguirresarobe; Designer, David Brisbin; Costumes, Tish Monaghan; Music, Alexandre Desplat; Editor, Peter Lambert; Visual Effects Supervisors, Phil Tippett, Matt Jacobs; Fight Choreographer, Mike Desabrais; Casting, Joseph Middleton; a Temple Hill production in association with Maverick/Imprint and Sunswept Entertainment; Dolby; Super 35 Widescreen; Rated PG-13, 130 minutes; Release date: November 20, 2009

CAST

Bella Swan	**Kristin Stewart**
Edward Cullen	**Robert Pattinson**
Jacob Black	**Taylor Lautner**
Alice Cullen	**Ashley Greene**
Victoria	**Rachelle Lefevre**
Charlie Swan	**Billy Burke**
Dr. Carlisle Cullen	**Peter Facinelli**
Rosalie Hale	**Nikki Reed**
Emmett Cullen	**Kellan Lutz**
Jasper Hale	**Jackson Rathbone**
Jessica	**Anna Kendrick**
Aro Volturi	**Michael Sheen**
Jane	**Dakota Fanning**
Mike	**Michael Welch**
Eric	**Justin Chon**
Angela	**Christian Serratos**
Gran/Bella	**Christina Jastrzembska**
Mr. Berty	**Russell Roberts**

Jamie Campbell Bower (Caius), **Graham Greene** (Harry Clearwater), **Christopher Heyerdahl** (Marcus), Curtis Caravaggio (Rogue Vampire), Daniel Cudmore (Felix), Charlie Bewley (Demetri), Elizabeth Reaser (Esme Cullen), Chaske Spencer (Sam Uley), Gil Birmingham (Billy Black), Adrien Dorval (Bob Marks, Neighbor), Michael Adamthwaite (Chet), Alexander Mendeluk, Hunter Jackson, Gavin Bristol, Sean McGrath (Frat Boys), Kiowa Gordon (Embry Call), Tyson Houseman (Quil Ateara), Alex Meraz (Paul), Bronson Pelletier (Jared), Edi Gathegi (Laurent), Tinsel Korey (Emily), Corinna Russo (Italian Child), Maria Grazia Pompei (Italian Mother), Roberto Marchetti (Italian Father), Alessandro Federico (Police Officer), Justin Wachsberger (Gianna), Cameron Bright (Alec), Noot Seear (Heidi), Tom Townsend (Grath)

After her vampire lover Edward Cullen abruptly departs, a devastated Bella Swan finds comfort in her friend Jacob who holds a supernatural secret of his own. Second in the *Twilight* (following the 2008 film *Twilight*) series with most of the principals repeating their roles.

Robert Pattinson, Dakota Fanning

Charlie Bewley, Daniel Cudmore © Summit Entertainment

Justin Chon, Michael Welch, Anna Kendrick, Christian Serratos

Ashley Greene

Kellan Lutz, Nikki Reed, Jackson Rathbone, Elizabeth Reaser, Peter Facinelli

Robert Pattinson, Kristen Stewart

Michael Sheen, Jamie Campbell Bower, Cameron Bright

Alex Meraz, Kiowa Gordon, Chaske Spencer

Kristen Stewart, Edi Gathegi

Kristen Stewart, Taylor Lautner

PLANET 51

(TRISTAR) Producers, Ignacio Perez Dolset, Guy Collins; Executive Producers, Juan Antonio Perez Ramirez, Peter Graves, Michael Ryan, Jose A. Rodriguez Diaz, Albie Hecht; Director, Jorge Blanco; Co-Directors, Javier Abad, Marcos Martinez; Screenplay, Joe Stillman; Original Idea, Javier Abad, Jorge Blanco, Marcos Martinez, Ignacio Perez Dolset; Designer, Julian Romero; Music, James Brett; Editor, Alex Rodriguez; Characters Supervisor, Juan Solis; Characters Designer, Ignacio Guejes; Casting, Ruth Lambert, Robert McGee; U.K. European Casting, Karen Lindsay-Stewart; an Ilion Animation Studios (Spain) production in association with Handmade Films Intl. (U.K.); American-Spanish-British; Dolby; Color; Rated PG; 91 minutes; Release date: November 20, 2009

VOICE CAST

Capt. Charles "Chuck" Baxter	**Dwayne Johnson**
Neera	**Jessica Biel**
Lem	**Justin Long**
General Grawl	**Gary Oldman**
Skiff	**Seann William Scott**
Professor Kipple	**John Cleese**

Freddie Benedict (Eckle), Alan Marriott (Glar), Mathew Horne (Soldier Vesklin), James Corden (Soldier Vernkot), Lewis Macleod, Rupert Degas, Rebecca Font, Vincent Marzello, Emma Tate, Pete Atkin, Laurence Bouvard, Brian Bowles (Additional Voices)

An astronaut lands on what he believes to be an uninhabited planet only to discover that it is populated by alien beings living a lifestyle not unlike that of '50s America.

Lem, Capt. Charles Baxter

Neera, Skiff, Lem, Rover © TriStar Pictures

Val Kilmer, Nicolas Cage

THE BAD LIEUTENANT: PORT OF CALL – NEW ORLEANS

(FIRST LOOK) Producers, Edward R. Pressman, Randall Emmett, Alan Polsky, Stephen Belafonte, John Thompson, Gabe Polsky; Executive Producers, Avi Lerner, Danny Dimbort, Trevor Short, Boaz Davidson, Elliot Lewis Rosenblatt, Alessandro Camon; Director, Werner Herzog; Screenplay, William Finkelstein; Photography, Peter Zeitlinger; Designer, Toby Corbett; Costumes, Jill Newell; Music, Mark Isham; Editor, Joe Bini; Casting, Johanna Ray; A Millennium Films/Polsky Films presentation of an Edward R. Pressman production, a Saturn Films production in association with Osiris Productions; Dolby; FotoKem Color; Rated R; 122 minutes; Release date: November 20, 2009

CAST

Lt. Terence McDonagh	**Nicolas Cage**
Stevie Pruit	**Val Kilmer**
Frankie Donnenfield	**Eva Mendes**
Genevieve	**Jennifer Coolidge**
Heidi	**Fairuza Balk**
Ned Schoenholtz	**Brad Dourif**
Mundt	**Michael Shannon**
Armand Benoit	**Shawn Hatosy**
Big Fate	**Alvin "Xzibit" Joiner**

Denzel Whitaker (Daryl), Katie Chonacas (Tina), Shea Whigham (Justin), Irma P. Hall (Binnie Rogers), Brandi Coleman (Yvonne), Tom Bower (Pat McDonagh), Vondie Curtis-Hall (James Brasser), Lance E. Nichols (Jerimiah Goodhusband), Lauren Pennington (Young Woman), Jillian Batherson (D.A.'s Assistant), Marco St. John (Eugene Gratz), Deneen Tyler (Pharmacist), J.D. Evermore (Rick Fitzsimon), Deena Beasley (Miamouna), Lucius Baston (Deshaun "Midget" Hackett), Kyle Russell Clements (Lawrence), Sam Medina (Andy), Tim Bellow (Gary "G" Jenkins), Armando Leduc (Jeff), Tony Bentley (Hurley), Sean Boyd (Lt. Stoyer), Noel Arthur (Renaldo Hayes), Nick Gomez (Evaristo Chavez), J. Omar Castro (Narcotics Detective), Douglas M. Griffin (Sergeant), Roger Timber (Security Guard), David Joseph Martinez (Juan Michel), Jaime San Andres (Officer Lasseigne), Joe Nemmers (Officer Larry Moy), Joel Davis (Voice of TV Play-by-Play Announcer), Robert Pavlovich (Dr. Milburn), Jeremy Aaron Johnson (Det. Yasco), Trey Burvant (Dealer), Joshua Gillum (Host), Matt Borel (Bernie), Michael Zimbrich (Waiter), Lauren Swinney (Antoinette Fahringer), William Finkelstein (Dave Jacobs),

A drug addicted New Orleans police officer searches through the city's underworld to find the drug dealer responsible for killing five illegal Senegalese immigrants.

Kodi Smit-McPhee, Viggo Mortensen

Michael Kenneth Williams

Viggo Mortensen, Kodi Smit-McPhee

THE ROAD

(DIMENSION) Producers, Nick Wechsler, Paula Mae Schwartz, Steve Schwartz; Executive Producers, Todd Wagner, Mark Cuban, Marc Butan, Rudd Simmons; Director, John Hillcoat; Screenplay, Joe Penhall; Based on the novel by Cormac McCarthy; Photography, Javier Aguirresarobe; Designer, Chris Kennedy; Costumes, Margot Wilson; Music, Nick Cave, Warren Ellis; Editor, Jon Gregory; Casting, Francine Maisler; a Nick Wechsler and Chockstone Pictures production, presented with 2929 Productions; Dolby; Super 35 Widescreen; Technicolor; Rated R; 110 minutes; Release date: November 25, 2009

CAST

Man	**Viggo Mortensen**
Boy	**Kodi Smit-McPhee**
Woman	**Charlize Theron**
Old Man	**Robert Duvall**
The Veteran	**Guy Pearce**
Motherly Woman	**Molly Parker**
The Thief	**Michael Kenneth Williams**
Gang Member	**Garret Dillahunt**
Bearded Men	**Bob Jennings, Jack Erdie**
Bearded Face	**Kirk Brown**
Archer's Woman	**Agnes Herrmann**
Archer	**Buddy Sosthand**

David August Lindauer (Man on Mattress), Gina Preciado, Mary Rawson (Well Fed Women), Jeremy Ambler, Chaz Moneypenny (Men in Cellar), Kacey Byrne-Houser (Woman in Cellar), Brenna Roth (Road Gang Member), Jarrod DiGiorgi (Well Fed Man), Mark Tierno (Baby Eater)

In a ravaged, post-apocalyptic world, a man and his young son survive as best they can as they search for food and some sign of hope.

Charlize Theron

"Big Daddy" LaBouff, Eudora, Charlotte LaBouff © Disney Enterprises

JuJu, Mama Odie

Dr. Faciller, Lawrence, Prince Naveen

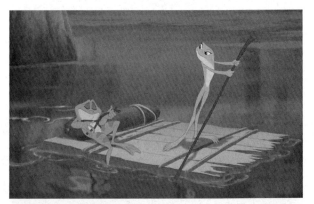

Frog Naveen, Frog Tiana

Frog Tiana, Frog Naveen, Louis

Frog Naveen, Princess Tiana

Princess Tiana, Prince Naveen

Ray

Eudora, Young Tiana, James

THE PRINCESS AND THE FROG

(WALT DISNEY PICTURES) Producer, Peter Del Vecho; Executive Producer, John Lasseter; Directors, John Musker, Ron Clements; Screenplay, Ron Clements, John Musker, Rob Edwards; Story, Ron Clements, John Musker, Greb Erb, Jason Oremland; Story inspired in part by "The Frog Princess" by E.D. Baker; Associate Producer, Craig Sost; Original Songs and Score/Conductor, Randy Newman; Additional song "Never Knew I Needed" written and performed by Ne-Yo; Editor, Jeff Draheim; Art Director, Ian Gooding; Visual Effects Supervisor, Kyle Odermatt; Artistic Supervisors: Story, Don Hall; Layout, Rasoul Azadani; Backgrounds, Sunny Apinchapong; Clean-up Animation, Vera Pacheco; Effects Animation, Marlon West; Color Styling and Compositing, Maria Dolores Gonzalez; Technical and Artistic Support, Gina Bradley; Dolby; Deluxe color; Rated G; 99 minutes; Release date: November 25, 2009

VOICE CAST

Tiana	**Anika Noni Rose**
Prince Naveen	**Bruno Campos**
Dr. Facilier, The Shadow Man	**Keith David**
Louis	**Michael-Leon Wooley**
Charlotte La Bouff	**Jennifer Cody**
Ray	**Jim Cummings**
Lawrence	**Peter Bartlett**
Mama Odie	**Jenifer Lewis**
Eudora	**Oprah Winfrey**
James	**Terrence Howard**
"Big Daddy" La Bouff	**John Goodman**
Young Tiana	**Elizabeth M. Dampier**
Young Charlotte	**Breanna Brooks**
Reggie	**Ritchie Montgomery**
Darnell	**Don Hall**
Two Fingers	**Paul Briggs**
Mr. Henry Fenner	**Jerry Kernion**
Mr. Harvey Fenner	**Corey Burton**
Buford	**Michael Colyar**
Marlon the Gator	**Emeril Lagasse**
Ian the Gator	**Kevin Michael Richardson**
Cousin Randy	**Randy Newman**
Louis' Trumpet Playing	**Terence Blanchard**
Georgia	**Danielle Moné Truitt**

Believing she will help a cursed prince who has been turned into a frog return to human form, Tiana instead ends up a frog herself.

This film received Oscar nominations for animated feature and two songs ("Almost There" and "Down in New Orleans").

Tiana

OLD DOGS

(WALT DISNEY STUDIOS) Producers, Andrew Panay, Robert L. Levy, Peter Abrams; Executive Producer, Garrett Grant; Director, Walt Becker; Screenplay, David Diamond, David Weissman; Photography, Jeffrey L. Kimball; Designer, David Gropman; Costumes, Joseph G. Aulisi; Music, John Debney; Music Supervisor, Dave Jordan; Editors, Tom Lewis, Ryan Folsey; Casting, Anne McCarthy, Jay Scully, Kathleen Chopin; a Tapestry Films production; Dolby; Color; Rated PG; 88 minutes; Release date: November 25, 2009

CAST

Charlie	**John Travolta**
Dan	**Robin Williams**
Vicki	**Kelly Preston**
Zach	**Conner Rayburn**
Emily	**Ella Bleu Travolta**
Amanda	**Lori Loughlin**
Craig	**Seth Green**

Bernie Mac (Jimmy Lunchbox), Matt Dillon (Barry), Ann-Margret (Martha), Rita Wilson (Jenna), Amy Sedaris (Condo Woman), Residente (Tattoo Artist), Saburo Shimono (Yoshiro Nishamura), Kevin W. Yamada (Riku), Kevin Dean-Hackett (Tijuana Priest), Laura Allen (Kelly), Sam Travolta, Nick Loren, Panama Redd(Singing Waiters), Margaret Travolta (Singing Hostess), Kenneth Maharaj (Indian Guy), Nova Mejia, Alexa Havins, Alison Pelletier (Hot Waitresses), Margaret Goodman (Grandma), Jerome Weinstein (Grandpa), Allie Woods Jr. (Old Guy), Keenan Shimizu, Akira Takayama, Shirô Oishi, Yoshio Mita, Seiji Kakizaki, Keisuke Jim Nagahama (Japanese Executives), Dominick Riccardi (Driver), Costas Panay (Little Kid), Kate Lacey (Rayburn & Reed Employee), Denise Violante (Spanish Lady), Tonia-Marie Gallo (Lazy Pooch Employee), Jin Hwa Hwang (Japanese Flight Attendant), Marcel Becker (Waiter), Dylan Sprayberry, Joey Pordan (Cute Soccer Kids), Jason Davies, Alicia Mazepa, Marielys Molina, Charlene Smith, Tera Lee Pollin, Brendan King, Jason Dougherty, Kevin Aubin (Dancers), Christine Anderson, Crystal Anderson, Erynn Dickerson (Back-Up Singers), Edward Noel, MacNeal John Kennedy, Matt Vogel, Josh Cohen, R. Bruce Connelly, Joe Kovacs (Muppets), Harry L. Seddon (Businessman, Escalator), Michael Enright (Mike the Waiter), Luis Guzman (Nick, Child Proofer), Dax Shepard (Gary, Child Proofer), Justin Long (Troop Leader Adam)

A divorcé and his womanizing best friend find their lives as single men disrupted when they are forced to take care of the twins the former never even realized he had with his second wife.

Seth Green, John Travolta, Robin Williams © Disney Enterprises

Shô Kosugi, Joon Lee © Warner Bros.

NINJA ASSASSIN

(WARNER BROTHERS) Producers, Joel Silver, Andy Wachowski, Larry Wachowski, Grant Hill; Executive Producers, Thomas Tull, Jon Jashni, Steve Richards; Director, James McTeigue; Screenplay, Matthew Sand, J. Michael Straczynski; Story, Matthew Sand; Photography, Karl Walter Lindenlaub; Designer, Graham "Grace" Walker; Costumes, Carlo Poggioli; Music, Ilan Eshkeri; Editors, Gian Ganziano, Joseph Jett Sally; Special Effects Supervisor, Uli Nefzer; Stunts, Chad Stahelski, Noon Orsatti; Fight Choreographers, Jon Valera, Peng Zhang; Casting, Lucinda Syson; a Silver Pictures production, in association with Anarchos Productions; American-German; Dolby; Super 35 Widescreen; Color; Rated R; 99 minutes; Release date: November 25, 2009

CAST

Raizo	**Rain**
Mika Coretti	**Naomie Harris**
Ryan Maslow	**Ben Miles**
Takeshi	**Rick Yune**
Lord Ozuno	**Shô Kosugi**

Guido Förweißer (Europol Agent), Stephen Marcus (Kingpin), Wladimir Tarasjanz (Aleksei Sabatin), Randall Duk Kim (Tattoo Master), Sung Kang (Hollywood), Jonathan Chan-Pensley (Yakuza Henchman), Yuki Iwamoto (Yakuza Couch), Ill-Young Kim (Yakuza Mohawk), Linh Dan Pham (Pretty Ninja), Fang Yu (Laundromat Manager), Adriana Altaras (Landlady), Shô Kosugi (Ozunu), Kylie Liya Goldstein (Young Kiriko), Yoon Sungwoong (Young Raizo), Eleonore Weisgerber (Mrs. Sabatin), Wladimir Tarasjanz (Aleksei Sabatin), Joon Lee (Teenage Raizo), Kai Fung Rieck (Teenage Takeshi), Anna Sawai (Teenage Kiriko), Thorston Manderlay (Zabranski), Richard van Weyden (Battuta), Mina Ghousi (Kid with Envelope), Hans Hohlbein (Mika's Neighbor), Nhi Ngoc Nguyen-Hermann (Girl on Roof), Tim Williams (Europol Cell Guard), David Leitch (Europol Door Guard), Wolfgang Stegemann (Europol Pointman), Steffen Groth, Jens Neuhaus (Europol Guards), Patrick Pinheiro (Maslow's Aide), Matthias Schendel (Task Force Agent), Johannes Ahn (Medic)

Trained as a ninja by an underground organization called the Ozunu, Raizo sees his chance to avenge their murder of his sweetheart when the Ozunu set their aim on destroying a Europol agent who has uncovered the group's connection to a series of recent political assassinations.

Robin Wright Penn, Keanu Reeves © Screen Media Films

Keanu Reeves, Robin Wright Penn

Alan Arkin, Blake Lively

THE PRIVATE LIVES OF PIPPA LEE

(SCREEN MEDIA) Producers, Lemore Syvan, Dede Gardner; Executive Producers, Jean Luc De Fanti, Jeff Sagansky, Jeremy Kleiner, Jill Footlick, Warren T. Goz, Stewart McMichael; Director/Screenplay, Rebecca Miller; Photography, Declan Quinn; Designer, Michael Shaw; Costumes, Jennifer von Mayrhauser; Music, Michael Rohatyn; Editor, Sabine Hoffman; An IM Global/Winchester Capital Management presentation of a Plan B/Inspired Actions production produced in association with 2008PLG, LLC and Grand Army Entertainment, LLC; Dolby; Color; DV-to-35mm; Rated R; 98 minutes; Release date: November 27, 2009

CAST

Pippa Lee	**Robin Wright Penn**
Chris Nadeau	**Keanu Reeves**
Kat	**Julianne Moore**
Herb Lee	**Alan Arkin**
Sandra Dulles	**Winona Ryder**
Sully Sarkissian	**Maria Bello**
Gigi Lee	**Monica Bellucci**
Grace Lee	**Zoe Kazan**
Ben Lee	**Ryan McDonald**
Young Pippa	**Blake Lively**
Trish Sarkissian	**Robin Weigert**
Sam Shapiro	**Mike Binder**
Des Sarkissian	**Tim Guinee**
Dot Nadeau	**Shirley Knight**

Cornel West (Don Sexton), Arnie Burton (Doctor), Drew Beasley (Chester Sarkissian, age 6), Madeline McNulty (Young Pippa, age 7), Beckett Melville (Chester Sarkissian, age 13), Billy Wheelan (Waiter), Joan Copeland (Piano Player), J.R. Horne (Jonnie Nadeau), Adam Shonkwiler (Chester Sarkissian, age 22), Richard DeDomenico (Elderly Man), Christin Sawyer Davis (Shelly), Zero (Craig Simms), Adam Grupper (Max Kessler), Sean-Michael Bowles (Jed), Audrey Lynn Weston (Terry), Angela Trento (Woman), Teresa Yenque (Alphonsa), Lola Pashalinski (Mrs. Mankievitz), Myra Lucretia Taylor (Night Nurse), Annie Purcell (Nurse), Sean Casey (Calvin)

After moving to a retirement community to accommodate her much older husband, Pippa Lee starts to wonder if it isn't time to tend to her own needs and find her own identity in the world.

Julianne Moore

UP IN THE AIR

(PARAMOUNT) Producers, Daniel Dubiecki, Jeffrey Clifford, Ivan Reitman, Jason Reitman; Executive Producers, Ted Griffin, Michael Beugg, Tom Pollock, Joe Medjuck; Director, Jason Reitman; Screenplay, Jason Reitman, Sheldon Turner; Based on the novel by Walter Kirn; Photography, Eric Steelberg; Designer, Steve Saklad; Costumes, Danny Glicker; Music, Rolfe Kent; Editor, Dana E. Glauberman; Associate Producers, Ali Bell, Jason Blumenfeld, Helen Estabrook; Casting, Mindy Marin; a Montecito Pictures Co. production, in association with Rickshaw Pictures, in association with Right of Way Films, presented in association with Cold Spring Pictures and DW Studios; Dolby; Deluxe color; Rated R; 109 minutes; Release date: December 4, 2009

George Clooney, Vera Farmiga

CAST

Ryan Bingham	**George Clooney**
Alex Goran	**Vera Farmiga**
Natalie Keener	**Anna Kendrick**
Craig Gregory	**Jason Bateman**
Kara Bingham	**Amy Morton**
Julie Bingham	**Melanie Lynskey**
Bob	**J.K. Simmons**
Maynard Finch	**Sam Elliott**
Jim Miller	**Danny McBride**
Steve	**Zach Galifianakis**
Kevin	**Chris Lowell**
Samuels	**Steve Eastin**
Himself	**Young MC (Marvin Young)**
Conference DJ	**Cut Chemist (Lucas McFadden)**
Tammy	**Adrienne Lamping**
Flight Attendant	**Meagan Flynn**
Ned	**Dustin Miles**
Club Hostess	**Tamara Tungate**
Check-In Lady	**Laura Ackermann**
Business Woman	**Meghan Maguire**
Airport Clerk	**Courtney Kling**
Voice of Alex's Husband	**Matt O'Toole**
Hilton Clerk	**Alan David**
Dianne	**Erin McGrane**
Purser	**Cari Mohr**

George Clooney

Jerry Vogel (San Francisco Manager), Adhir Kalyan (Irate IT), Jeff Witzke (Goalquest Host), Dave Engfer (Software Dude), Paul Goetz (Rental Car Assistant), Michelle Reitman (Conference Worker), Jennifer Nitzband (Wedding Cousin), Bill Yancey (Wedding Pastor), John Mebruer (Band Leader), Ellen Gutierrez (Wedding Coordinator), Kevin Pila, Kelly Bertha, Cozy Bailey, Lamorris Conner, Deborah L. Norman, Casey Bartels, Billy Phelan, Arthur Hill, Patricia Allison, David F. Rybicki, George Batten, Jo Michelle Favaro, Andy Glantzman, Marlene Gorkiewicz, Stephanie Janiunas, Scott Lapinski, K. Darnell Lewis, Thomas M. Martillotti, Grace Smith, Mark Sommers, Wilbur Weidlich, Erin Welsh-Krengel (Terminated Employees)

A man whose job it is to do the dirty work for corporations by firing employees finds himself drawn to his solitary life of flying from one place to another, using it as an excuse not to have human attachments or relationships of any kind.

This film received Oscar nominations for picture, director, actor (George Clooney), two for supporting actress (Vera Farmiga, Anna Kendrick), and adapted screenplay.

Melanie Lynskey, Amy Morton, George Clooney

Anna Kendrick, George Clooney

Vera Farmiga, George Clooney

Ann Kendrick, George Clooney

Danny McBride, Melanie Lynskey

George Clooney © Paramount Pictures

Amaury Nolasco

Milo Ventimiglia

ARMORED

(SCREEN GEMS) Producers, Joshua Donen, Dan Farah; Executive Producers, Debra James, Russell Hollander; Co-Executive Producers, Luis Guerrero, Chris Lemos; Director, Nimród Antal; Screenplay, James V. Simpson; Photography, Andrzej Sekula; Designer, Jon Gary Steele; Costumes, Maya Lieberman; Music, John Murphy; Editor, Armen Minasian; Stunts, Lance Gilbert; Casting, David H. Rapaport, Lindsey Hayes Kroeger; a Stars Road Entertainment production, in association with Farah Films; Dolby; Panavision; Deluxe color; Rated PG-13; 88 minutes; Release date: December 4, 2009

CAST

Mike Cochrane	**Matt Dillon**
Quinn	**Jean Reno**
Baines	**Laurence Fishburne**
Palmer	**Amaury Nolasco**
Duncan Ashcroft	**Fred Ward**
Eckehart	**Milo Ventimiglia**
Dobbs	**Skeet Ulrich**
Ty Hackett	**Columbus Short**
Jimmy Hackett	**Andre Jamal Kinney**
Dispatcher #1	**Andrew Fiscella**
Homeless Man	**Nick Jameson**
Joe the Cook	**Glenn Taranto**
Child Welfare Agent	**Lorna Rave**r
Federal Guards	**Garry Guerrier, Shawn Devorse**
Bank Guard	**Robert Harvey**

Desperate for cash, armored guard Ty Hackett reluctantly agrees to join his cohorts in a robbery, with disastrous results.

Columbus Short, Laurence Fishburne, Matt Dillon © Screen Gems

Jean Reno

BROTHERS

(LIONSGATE) Producers, Ryan Kavanaugh, Sigurjon Sighvatsson, Michael De Luca; Executive Producers, Tucker Tooley, Zach Schiff-Abrams; Co-Producers, Mark Fischer, Matt Battaglia; Co-Executive Producer, Jeremiah Samuels; Director, Jim Sheridan; Screenplay, David Benioff; Based on the motion picture *Brødre* (*Brothers*) by Susanne Bier, Anders Thomas Jensen; Photography, Frederick Elmes; Designer, Tony Fanning; Costumes, Durinda Wood; Music, Thomas Newman; Music Supervisor, Gina Amador; Editor, Jay Cassidy; Visual Effects Supervisor, Jonah Loop; Casting, Avy Kaufman; a Sighvatsson Films, Relativity Media, Michael De Luca Productions, Inc. production, presented in association with Relativity Media; Dolby; Super 35 Widescreen; Technicolor; Rated R; 104 minutes; Release date: December 4, 2009

Bailee Madison, Natalie Portman, Taylor Geare

CAST

Capt. Sam Cahill	**Tobey Maguire**
Tommy Cahill	**Jake Gyllenhaal**
Grace Cahill	**Natalie Portman**
Hank Cahill	**Sam Shepard**
Elsie Cahill	**Mare Winningham**
Isabelle Cahill	**Bailee Madison**
Maggie Cahill	**Taylor Geare**
Pvt. Joe Willis	**Patrick Flueger**
Major Cavazos	**Clifton Collins Jr.**
Cassie Willis	**Carey Mulligan**
Tina	**Jenny Wade**
Yusuf	**Omid Abtahi**
Murad	**Navid Negahban**

Ethan Suplee (Sweeney), Arron Shiver (A.J.), Ray Prewitt (Owen), Rebekah Wiggins, Carrie Fleming (Marine Wives), Sheila Ivy Traister (Pilot), Chad Brummett (Co-Pilot), Jason Hill (Lt. Sanderson), Kevin Wiggins (Navy Chaplain), Yousuf Azami (Taliban Leader), James Dever (Sgt. Major Dever), Kevin Adkins (Flag Detail Commander), Johnnie Hector, Jeremiah Bitsui, William L. Allen, Benjamin D. Baldwin (Cops), Michael-David Aragon (Terrorist), Richard Wade (Crew Chief), Luce Rains (The Nose), Enayat Delaway (Ahmed), Rick La Monda (Elvis), Paul Ramos (Sentry), Shawn Bryan (Marine Cadence), Oscar Mejia (Uniform in Helicopter), David Bachelor (U.S. Navy Chaplain), Zachary Grand (Afghanistan Boy), Iris Dunbar (Burka Woman), Justin Marmion (Marine Hostage), Robert Mitchell, Collin D. Barry (Marine Rescuers), Janet Sanford, Casey Sanford (Mourners at Church), Colleen Frye (Woman in Church), James Duffy (Man in Church), David Manzanares (Bartender Dave), Michael Castellano (Afghan Fighter), Carol A. Salazar (Woman on Bridge), Wendell Sweet (Orderly)

Jake Gyllenhaal, Tobey Maguire © Lionsgate

Believing her husband Sam to have been killed during duty in Afghanistan, Grace Cahill finds herself turning to Sam's brother for solace.

Tobey Maguire, Jake Gyllenhaal

Jake Gyllenhaal, Sam Shepard, Mare Winningham

EVERYBODY'S FINE

(MIRAMAX) Producers, Gianni Nunnari, Ted Field, Vittorio Cecchi Gori, Glynis Murray; Executive Producers, Craig J. Flores, Meir Teper, Mike Weber, Joe Rosenberg, Callum Greene; Co-Producer, Nathalie Peter-Contesse; Director/Screenplay, Kirk Jones; Based on the screenplay *Stanno tutti bene* directed by Giuseppe Tornatore, with screenplay by Giuseppe Tornatore, Tonino Guerra, Massimo de Rita; Photography, Henry Braham; Designer, Andrew Jackness; Costumes, Aude Bronson-Howard; Music, Dario Marianelli; Editor, Andrew Mondshein; Casting, Kerry Barden, Paul Schnee; a Hollywood Gang production, presented in association with Radar Pictures; Dolby; Color; Rated PG-13; 99 minutes; Release date: December 4, 2009

Sam Rockwell, Robert De Niro © Miramax Films

CAST

Frank Goode	**Robert De Niro**
Rosie	**Drew Barrymore**
Amy	**Kate Beckinsale**
Robert	**Sam Rockwell**
Jack	**Lucian Maisel**
Jeff	**Damian Young**
Tom	**James Frain**
Colleen	**Melissa Leo**
Jilly	**Katherine Moennig**
Mugger	**Brendan Sexton III**
Dr. Ed	**James Murtaugh**
David	**Austin Lysy**

Chandler Frantz (Young David), Lily Sheen (Young Amy), Seamus Davey-Fitzpatrick (Young Robert), Mackenzie Milone (Young Rosie), Kene Holliday (Butcher), E.J. Carroll (Wine Man), Lou Carbonneau (BBQ Salesman), Mandell Butler (Delivery Man), Caroline Clay (Amtrak Ticket Agent), Katy Grenfell (Young Woman on 1st Train), Lynn Cohen (Old Woman on 1st Train), Jayne Houdyshell (Alice), William J. Slinsky Jr. (Man on Platform), Kelly McAndrew (Hooker), Jason Harris, Julián Rebolledo (Cab Riders), Ben Liff (Young Man in Diner, 94 yrs.), Harvey Liff (Young Man in Diner, 86 yrs.), Lynn Blades (Anchorwoman), Kevin Collins (Anchorman), Patricia Phillips (NY Woman on Street), Kevin Martin (Man on Bus), Ben Schwartz (Writer), Debargo Sanyal (Art Director), Jackie Cronin (Booking Office Lady), Erika Boseski (Orchestra Member), Allie Woods Jr. (Greyhound Station Attendant), Sonja Stuart (Jean Goode), Mimi Lieber (Jean Goode's Voice), Ethan Munsch, Harrison Munsch (Baby Max), Kira Visser (Flight Attendant), Mattie Hawkinson (Art Gallery Girl)

When each of his children cancels their planned visit, widower Frank Goode decides to drop in on each one of them as a surprise, hoping to connect in ways that he's never felt capable of.

Kate Beckinsale, Robert De Niro

Robert De Niro, Drew Barrymore

Leleti Khumalo, Adjoa Andoh, Morgan Freeman, Danny Keogh

Matt Damon (center)

Morgan Freeman, Matt Damon © Warner Bros.

INVICTUS

(WARNER BROTHERS) Producers, Clint Eastwood, Lori McCreary, Robert Lorenz, Mace Neufeld; Executive Producers, Morgan Freeman, Tim Moore, Gary Barberm, Roger Birnbaum; Director, Clint Eastwood; Screenplay, Anthony Peckham; Based on the book *Playing the Enemy* by John Carlin; Photography, Tom Stern; Designer, James J. Murakami; Costumes, Deborah Hopper; Music, Kyle Eastwood, Michael Stevens; Editors, Joel Cox, Gary D. Roach; Visual Effects Supervisor, Michael Owens; Casting, Fiona Weir; a Revelations Entertainment/Mace Neufeld and Malpaso production, presented in association with Spyglass Entertainment; Dolby; Panavision; Technicolor; Rated PG-13; 134 minutes; Release date: December 11, 2009

CAST

Nelson Mandela	**Morgan Freeman**
Francois Pienaar	**Matt Damon**
Jason Tshabalala	**Tony Kgoroge**
Linga Moonsamy	**Patrick Mofokeng**
Hendrick Booyens	**Matt Stern**
Etienne Feyder	**Julian Lewis Jones**
Brenda Mazibuko	**Adjoa Andoh**
Nerine	**Marguerite Wheatley**
Mary	**Leleti Khumalo**
Mr. Pienaar	**Patrick Lyster**
Mrs Pienaar	**Penny Downie**

Sibongile Nojila (Eunice), Bonnie Henna (Zindzi), Shakes Myeko (Minister of Sport), Louis Minaar (Springbok Coahc), Danny Keogh (Rugby President), Dan Robbertse (Boer), Robin Smith (Johan De Villiers), David Dukas (Captain of 747), Grant Swanby (Co-Captain of 747), Josias Moleele (Face Painter), Langley Kirkwood, Robert Hobbs, Melusi Yeni, Vuyo Dabula, Daniel Hadebe (Presidential Guards), Jodi Botha (High School Boy), Hennie Bosman (High School Coach), Refiloe Mpakanyane (Jessie), Jakkie Groenewald, Murray Todd (Johannesburg Cops), Japan Mthembu (Local Cop), Albert Maritz (Springbok Manager), Sello Motloung (Mandela's Doctor), Meren Reddy (Minister of the Environment), Lida Botha (Mrs. Brits), Susan Danford (Mrs. Cole), Sylvia Mngxekeza (Mrs. Dlamini), James Lithgow (New Zealand PM), Malusi Skenjana (NSC Firebrand), Bart Fouche (Prison Guard), Johnny Cicco, Wayne Harrison (Staff Members), Ashley Taylor, Gift Lotlela (Team Crew), Kgosi Mongake (Sipho), Given Stuurman, Vuyolwethu Stevens, Ayabulela Steven (Township Kids), Nambitha Mpumlwana (Trophy Wife), Andre Jacobs (Television Announcer), McNeil Hendricks (Chester Williams), Scott Eastwood, Grant Roberts, Mark Bown-Davies, Dale Stephen Dunn, Andries Le Grange, Clive Richard Samuel, Richard Abrahamse, Sean Pypers, Riaan Wolmarans, Ryan Scott, Daniel Deon Wessels, Vaughn Thompson, Charl Engelbrecht, Rolf Ernst Fitschen, Andrew Nel, Rudi Zandberg, Abraham Vlok, Graham Lindemann, Thomas Boyd, Herman Botha, Louis Pieterse, Richard Morris, Ryan Oliver, Warren Edwards, Renzo Puccini, Geoff Brown(South African Springboks), Zak Feaunati (Jonah Lomu)

The true story of how South African President Nelson Mandela encouraged his country's rugby team, the Springboks, to win the World Cup in hopes that their victory would unite the nation's black and white population.

This film received Oscar nominations for actor (Morgan Freeman) and supporting actor (Matt Damon).

Saoirse Ronan, Reece Ritchie

Mark Wahlberg, Stanley Tucci

Susan Sarandon

THE LOVELY BONES

(DREAMWORKS/PARAMOUNT) Producers, Carolynne Cunningham, Fran Walsh, Peter Jackson, Aimee Peyronnet; Executive Producers, Tessa Ross, Steven Spielberg, Ken Kamins, James Wilson; Co-Producers, Philippa Boyens, Anne Bruning, Marc Ashton; Director, Peter Jackson; Screenplay, Fran Walsh, Philippa Boyens, Peter Jackson; Based on the novel by Alice Sebold; Photography, Andrew Lesnie; Designer, Naomi Shohan; Costumes, Nancy Steiner; Music, Brian Eno; Editor, Jabez Olssen; Senior Visual Effects Supervisor, Joe Letteri; Visual Effects Supervisor, Christian Rivers; Digital Visual Effects, Weta Digital; Casting, Victoria Burrows, Scot R. Boland, Jina Jay, Liz Mullane; a DreamWorks presentation in association with Film 4 of a Wingnut Films production; American-British; Dolby; Widescreen; Deluxe color; DV; Rated PG-13; 136 minutes; Release date: December 11, 2009

CAST

Jack Salmon	**Mark Wahlberg**
Abigail Salmon	**Rachel Weisz**
Grandma Lynn	**Susan Sarandon**
George Harvey	**Stanley Tucci**
Len Fenerman	**Michael Imperioli**
Susie Salmon	**Saoirse Ronan**
Lindsey Salmon	**Rose McIver**
Buckley Salmon	**Christian Thomas Ashdale**
Ray Singh	**Reece Ritchie**

A.J. Michalka (Clarissa), Jake Abel (Brian Nelson), Tom McCarthy (Principal Caden), Nikki SooHoo (Holly), Andrew James Allen (Samuel Heckler), Carolyn Dando (Ruth Connors), Anna George (Mrs. Singh), Charlie Saxton (Ronald Drake), Robyn Malcolm (Foreman's Wife), Stink Fisher (Mr. Connors), Flora Hernandez (Stefania Owen), Bravo (Holiday the Dog), Steven Moreti (Diner Customer), Tina Graham (Sophie Cichetti), Seth F. Miller (Soccer Coach), Evelyn Lennon (Susie, age 3), Ashley Brimfield (Teenage Girl in Parking Lot), John Jezior (Mr. O'Dwyer), Kirit Kapadia (Mr. Singh), Richard Lambeth, William Zielenski, Glen Drake (Deputies), Dan Kern, Greg Wood (Hospital Doctors), Freya Milner (Jackie Meyer), Katie Jackson (Leah Fox), Roby Hudson (Lana Johnson), Tina Graham (Sophie Cichetti), Phoebe Gittins, Anna Dawson, Lili Bayliss (Harvey Victims), Bruce Phillips (Grandfather), Veronica Horn (Grace Tarking), Jack Hoffman (Fashion Show MC), David C. Roehm Sr. (Mr. Coleman), Seth F. Miller (Soccer Coach), Lee Miller, Michael A. Salvato, William Hummel, James Vassanelli, Scott Evans (Townspeople), Billy Jackson (Mall Shopper), Grace Carden-Horton, Gabby Greig (Police Station Girls), Peter Jackson (Man at Pharmacy)

Following her gruesome murder, 14-year-old Susie Salmon keeps an eye on her grieving family and the neighbor who has gotten away with the crime. This film received an Oscar nomination for supporting actor (Stanley Tucci).

Rachel Weisz, Christian Thomas Ashdale © DreamWorks/Paramount

A SINGLE MAN

(WEINSTEIN COMPANY) Producers, Tom Ford, Chris Weitz, Andrew Miano, Robert Salerno; Co-Producer, Jason Alisharan; Director, Tom Ford; Screenplay, Tom Ford, David Scearce; Based on the novel by Christopher Isherwood; Photography, Eduard Grau; Designer, Dan Bishop; Costumes, Arianne Phillips; Music, Abel Korzeniowski; Additional Music, Shigeru Umebayashi; Music Supervisor, Julia Michels; Editor, Joan Sobel; Casting, Joseph Middleton; a Fade to Black presentation, in association with Depth of Field; Dolby; Widescreen; Deluxe color; Rated R; 102 minutes; Release date: December 11, 2009

Colin Firth, Julianne Moore

CAST
George Falconer	**Colin Firth**
Charley	**Julianne Moore**
Kenny Potter	**Nicholas Hoult**
Jim	**Matthew Goode**
Carlos	**Jon Kortajarena**
Alva	**Paulette Lamori**
Jennifer Strunk	**Ryan Simpkins**
Mrs. Strunk	**Ginnifer Goodwin**
Mr. Strunk	**Teddy Sears**
Christopher Strunk	**Paul Butler**
Tom Strunk	**Aaron Sanders**
Grant	**Lee Pace**
Myron	**Adam Shapiro**
Maria	**Marlene Martinez**

Ridge Canipe (Young Boy), Elisabeth Harnois (Young Woman), Erin Daniels (Bank Teller), Nicole Steinwedell (Doris), Tricia Munford (Cashier), Jon Hamm (Voice of Hank Ackerley), Keri Lynn Pratt, Jenna Gavigan, Alicia Carr (Secretaries), Don Bachardy (Man in Office)

Unable to cope with the unexpected death of his lover, a grieving college professor contemplates ending his own life.

This film received an Oscar nomination for actor (Colin Firth).

Colin Firth

Matthew Goode, Colin Firth

Nicholas Hoult © Weinstein Co.

CRAZY HEART

(FOX SEARCHLIGHT) Producers, Robert Duvall, Rob Carliner, Judy Cairo, T Bone Burnett; Executive Producers, Jeff Bridges, Michael A. Simpson, Eric Brenner, Leslie Belzberg; Director/ Screenplay, Scott Cooper; Based on the novel by Thomas Cobb; Photography, Barry Markowitz; Designer, Waldemar Kalinowski; Costumes, Doug Hall; Music, Stephen Bruton, T Bone Burnett; Editor, John Axelrad; Casting, Mary Vernieu, Lindsay Graham, Jo Edna Boldin; an Informant Media/Butcher's Run Films production; Dolby; Panavision; FotoKem color; Rated R; 112 minutes; Release date: December 16, 2009

CAST
Bad Blake	**Jeff Bridges**
Jean Craddock	**Maggie Gyllenhaal**
Wayne	**Robert Duvall**
Bill Wilson	**Tom Bower**
Tommy Sweet	**Colin Farrell**
Manager	**James Keane**
Doctor	**William Marquez**
Tony	**Ryan Bingham**
Jack Greene	**Paul Herman**
Wesley Barnes	**Rick Dial**
Buddy	**Jack Nation**

Anna Felix (Barmaid), Beth Grant (Jo Ann), Debrianna Mansini (Ann), Jerry Hardy (Cowboy), Ryil Adamson (Ralphie), J. Michael "Yak" Oliva (Bear), David Manzanares (Nick), Chad Brummett (Young Guy), José Marquez (Older Hispanic Man), LeAnne Lynch (Nurse), Richard Gallegos (Jesus/Juan), Brian Gleason (Steven Reynolds), Harry Zinn (Bartender), Josh Berry (Security Guard), William Sterchi (Pat)

A down-on-his-luck, alcoholic country singer, reduced to performing in small-town bowling alleys to eke out a living, finds himself unexpectedly falling in love with the young woman who has been assigned to write a story about him.

2009 Academy Award Winner for Best Actor in a Leading Role (Jeff Bridges) and Best Original Song, ""The Weary Kind" (Theme from *Crazy Heart*) Music and Lyric by Ryan Bingham and T Bone Burnett.

This film received an additional Oscar nomination for supporting actress (Maggie Gyllenhaal).

Jeff Bridges, Maggie Gyllenhaal

Jeff Bridges, Robert Duvall

Jeff Bridges

Jeff Bridges © Fox Searchlight

Rupert Friend, Emily Blunt

Jim Broadbent

Mark Strong, Miranda Richardson, Emily Blunt © Apparition

THE YOUNG VICTORIA

(APPARITION) Producers, Graham King, Martin Scorsese, Tim Headington, Sarah Ferguson; Executive Producer, Colin Vaines; Co-Producers, Denis O'Sullivan, Anita Overland; Director, Jean-Marc Vallée; Screenplay, Julian Fellowes; Photography, Hagen Bogdanski; Designer, Patrice Vermette; Costumes, Sandy Powell; Music, Ilan Eshkeri; Editors, Jill Bilcock, Matt Garner; Makeup and Hair Designer, Jenny Shircore; Visual Effects Supervisor, Marc Cote; Casting, Susie Figgis; a GK Films presentation; American-British; Dolby; Super 35 Widescreen; Color; Rated PG; 104 minutes; American release date: December 18, 2009

CAST
Queen Victoria	**Emily Blunt**
Prince Albert	**Rupert Friend**
Lord Melbourne	**Paul Bettany**
Duchess of Kent	**Miranda Richardson**
King William	**Jim Broadbent**
King Leopold of Belgium	**Thomas Kretschmann**
Sir John Conroy	**Mark Strong**
Baron Stockmar	**Jesper Christensen**
Queen Adelaide	**Harriet Walter**
Baroness Lehzen	**Jeanette Hain**

Julian Glover (Duke of Wellington), Michael Maloney (Sir Robert Peel), Michiel Huisman (Ernest), Genevieve O'Reilly (Lady Flora Hastings), Rachael Stirling (Duchess of Sutherland), Morven Christie (Watson), Josef Altin (Edward Oxford), Tom Brooke (Man on Soap Box), Michaela Brooks (Victoria, age 11), Grace Smith (Victoria, age 5), Sophie Roberts (Lady Portman), Charlie Clarke (The Newsboy), Robert Cambrinus (Kammerrher Turner), Tom Fisher (Lord Chamberlain), Shaun Dingwall (The Footman), Alice Glover (Duchess of Montrose), David Horovitch (Sir James Clark), Jo Hartley (Landlady), Bernard Lloyd (Archbishop of Canterbury), Johnnie Lyne-Pirkis (Earl of Derby), Iain Mitchell (Speaker), David Robb (Whig Member), Malcolm Sinclair (Charles Kemble), Julia St. John (Marchioness of Hastings), Thomas Michael Voss (Dance Master), Julie McDonnell (Lady in Waiting), Liam Scott (Duke of Sussex), Mark Beesley, Richard Quine (Opera Singers), Nick Chopping (Footman), Kelly Dent (Cupid), Mark Henson (Falling Bishop), Dominic Preece (Officer of Escort), Peter White (Apprehending Pedestrian)

Believing her 18-year-old daughter Victoria ill-prepared to take the throne of England, the Duchess of Kent and her ambitious advisor plot to shift the balance of power over to themselves.

2009 Academy Award for Best Costume Design.

This film received an additional Oscar nomination for art direction.

Emily Blunt

NINE

(WEINSTEIN COMPANY) Producers, Marc Platt, Harvey Weinstein, John DeLuca, Rob Marshall; Executive Producers, Ryan Kavanaugh, Tucker Tooley, Bob Weinstein, Kelly Carmichael, Michael Dreyer; Co-Executive Producers, Arthur L. Kopit, Maury Yeston; Director, Rob Marshall; Screenplay, Michael Tolkin, Anthony Minghella; Based on the 1982 Tony Award-winning musical with book by Arthur L. Kopit, music and lyrics by Maury Yeston, adapted from the screenplay for 8 ½ by Mario Fratti; Photography, Dion Beebe; Designer, John Myhre; Costumes, Colleen Atwood; Music and Lyrics, Maury Yeston; Original Score Music, Andrea Guerra; Executive Music Producer, Matthew Rush Sullivan; Music Supervisor/Conductor, Paul Bogaev; Orchestrations, Doug Besterman; Editors, Claire Simpson, Wyatt Smith; Choreographers, Rob Marshall, John DeLuca; Hair and Makeup Designer, Pete King; Casting, Francine Maisler; a Weinstein Brothers/Marc Platt/Lucamar production, a Relativity Media production, presented with Relativity Media; Dolby; Panavision; Technicolor/Black and white; Rated PG-13; 118 minutes; Release date: December 18, 2009

CAST

Guido Contini	**Daniel Day-Lewis**
Luisa Contini	**Marion Cotillard**
Carla	**Penélope Cruz**
Claudia	**Nicole Kidman**
Lilli	**Judi Dench**
Stephanie	**Kate Hudson**
Mamma	**Sophia Loren**
Saraghina	**Fergie**
Dante	**Ricky Tognazzi**
Fausto	**Giuseppe Cederna**
Pierpaolo	**Elio Germano**
Benito	**Andrea Di Stefano**
Jaconelli	**Roberto Nobile**
Roberta	**Roberta Mastromichele**
Radio Reporter	**Francesco De Vito**
Dinardo	**Francesca Fanti**
Leopardi	**Enzo Cilenti**
De Rossi	**Valerio Mastandrea**
Bellman	**Damiano Bisozzi**
Doctor	**Marcello Magni**
Nurse	**Anna Maria Everett**
Cardinal	**Remo Remotti**
Don Mario	**Michele Alhaique**
Donatella	**Martina Stella**
'Folies' Pianist	**Mark Bousie**
Young Guido	**Giuseppe Spitaleri**
Principal	**Mario Vernazza**
Band Singer	**Marco Liotti**
Pensione Matron	**Monica Scattini**
Doctor Rondi	**Roberto Citran**
Matron's Daughter	**Georgina Leonidas**
Luigi	**Vincent Riotta**

Romina Carancini, Alessandro Denipotti, Alessandro Fiore, Erica Gohdes, Gianluca Frezzato, Paola Zaccari (Production Assistants), Enzo Squillino Jr., Michael Peluso, Jonathan Del Vecchio, Jake Canuso, Eliot Giuralarocca, Tommaso Colognese, Jennifer Iacono, Vicky Lambert, Lavinia Savignoni (Reporters), Pietro Lais, Samuele Minotti, Francesco Manuel Pappalardo, Pietro Revelli, Gianluigi Tosti Di Valminuta (Boys on the Beach), Massimiliano Belsito, Roberto Sbraccia (Priests on the Beach), Shannon Belcastro, Jean Martin, Joey Pizzi, Kerry Warn (Film Crew), Eleonora Scopelliti, Ilaria Cavola (Screen Test Actresses), Alessia Piovan (Alessia), Giovanni Luca Izzo (Man with Luisa), Simone Cappotto (Simone), Giacomo Valdameri (Actor), Anna Safroncik (Actress)

Unable to come up with a script for his new film, renowned Italian filmmaker Guido Contini thinks of the many women who have played an important part in his often chaotic and inconsiderate life.

This film received Oscar nominations for supporting actress (Penelope Cruz), art direction, costume design, and original song ("Take it All").

Kate Hudson (second from right)

Kate Hudson, Daniel Day-Lewis

Daniel Day-Lewis, Sophia Loren

Daniel Day-Lewis, Marion Cotillard © Weinstein Co.

Fergie (center)

Judi Dench

Nicole Kidman, Daniel Day-Lewis

Penélope Cruz

Giovanni Ribisi, Sigourney Weaver

Michelle Rodriguez

Sam Worthington

Stephen Lang © Twentieth Century Fox

Sam Worthington, Zoë Saldana

Thanator, Na'vi Warrior

Stephen Lang

AVATAR

(20TH CENTURY FOX) Producers, James Cameron, Jon Landau; Executive Producers, Colin Wilson, Laeta Kalogridis; Co-Producers, Brooke Breton, Josh McLaglen; Director/Screenplay, James Cameron; Photography, Mauro Fiore; Designers, Rick Carter, Robert Stromberg; Costumes, Mayes C. Rubeo, Deborah L. Scott; Music, James Horner; Editors, Stephen Rivkin, John Refoua, James Cameron; Senior Visual Effects Supervisor, Joe Letteri; Weta Visual Effects Supervisors, Stephen Rosenbau, Eric Saindon, Dan Lemmon, Guy Williams; ILM Visual Effects Supervisor, John Knoll; Visual Effects and Animation, Weta Digital, Industrial Light & Magic, Prime Focux; Animation Supervisors, Richard Baneham, Andrew R. Jones; Performance Capture Technology and Production Services, Giant Studios; Stan Winston Character Design Supervisor, John Rosengrant; Stunts, Garrett Warren (U.S.), Stu Thorpe, Allan Poppleton (New Zealand); Lead Creature Designer, Neville Page; Na'vi Language Creator, Paul Frommer; Casting, Margery Simkin; Presented in association with Dune Entertainment and Ingenious Film Partners; Dolby; Widescreen; Deluxe color; HD; 3D; Rated PG-13; 163 minutes; Release date: December 18, 2009

CAST

Jake Sully	**Sam Worthington**
Neytiri	**Zoe Saldana**
Dr. Grace Augustine	**Sigourney Weaver**
Col. Miles Quaritch	**Stephen Lang**
Trudy Chacon	**Michelle Rodriguez**
Parker Selfridge	**Giovanni Ribisi**
Norm Spellman	**Joel David Moore**
Moat	**CCH Pounder**
Eytukan	**Wes Studi**
Tsu'tey	**Laz Alonso**
Dr. Max Patel	**Dileep Rao**
Cpl. Lyle Wainfleet	**Matt Gerald**
Pvt. Fike	**Sean Anthony Moran**
Cryo Vault Med Tech	**Jason Whyte**
Venture Star Crew Chief	**Scott Lawrence**
Lock Up Trooper	**Kelly Kilgour**
Shuttle Pilot	**James Pitt**
Shuttle Co-Pilot	**Sean Patrick Murphy**
Shuttle Crew Chief	**Peter Dillon**
Tractor Operator	**Kevin Dorman**
Dragon Gunship Pilot	**Kelson Henderson**
Dragon Gunship Gunner	**David Van Horn**
Dragon Gunship Navigator	**Jacob Tomuri**
Suits	**Michael Blain-Rozgay, Jon Curry**
Ambient Room Techs	**Julene Renee, Luke Hawker, Woody Schultz**
Horse Clan Leader	**Peter Mensah**
Link Room Tech	**Sonia Yee**
Basketball Avatar	**Ilram Choi**
Na'vi Child	**Kyla Warren**

Sam Worthington, Michelle Rodriguez, Sigourney Weaver, Joel David Moore

A wheelchair bound marine becomes an Avatar, combining his human DNA with that of a species called the Na'vi, so that he can live among those people on Pandora in hopes of making them understand that the United States needs to mine a precious mineral exclusive to their planet and essential to prevent ecological disaster.

2009 Academy Award Winner for Best Art Direction, Best Cinematography, and Best Visual Effects.

This film received additional Oscar nominations for picture, director, music, film editing, sound mixing, and sound editing.

Sam Worthington

DID YOU HEAR ABOUT THE MORGANS?

(COLUMBIA) Producers, Martin Shafer, Liz Glotzer; Executive Producers, Anthony Katagas, Ryan Kavanaugh; Co-Producer, Melissa Wells; Director/ Screenplay, Marc Lawrence; Photography, Florian Ballhaus; Designer, Kevin Thompson; Costumes, Christopher Peterson; Music, Theodore Shapiro; Music Supervisor, Robert Schaper; Editor, Susan E. Morse; Special Effects Coordinator, Drew Jiritano; Stunts, Manny Siverio; Casting, Ilene Starger; a Castle Rock Entertainment/Banter Films production, presented in association with Relativity Media; Dolby; Deluxe color; Rated PG-13; 103 minutes; Release date: December 18, 2009

CAST
Paul Morgan	**Hugh Grant**
Meryl Morgan	**Sarah Jessica Parker**
Clay Wheeler	**Sam Elliott**
Emma Wheeler	**Mary Steenburgen**
Jackie Drake	**Elisabeth Moss**
Vincent	**Michael Kelly**
Earl Granger	**Wilford Brimley**

Jesse Liebman (Adam Feller), David Call (Doc Simmons), Kim Shaw (Nurse Kelly), Natalia Klimas (Monique Rabelais),Vincenzo Amato (Girard Rabelais), Seth Gilliam (U.S. Marshal Lasky), Sandor Tecsy (Anton Forenski), Kevin Brown (U.S. Marshal Henderson), Steven Boyer (U.S. Marshal Ferber), Sharon Wilkins (U.S. Marshal King), Dana Ivey (Trish Pinger), Gracie Bea Lawrence (Lucy Granger), Beth Fowler (Ma Simmons), Christopher Atwood (U.S. Marshal at Rodeo), Bobbie Bates, Carol J. Connors, Brad Dulin, Laura Fremont, Michael Higgins, Brent Keast, Anthony Marciona, Sarah Mitchell, Mandy Jo Moore, Chris Moss, Nikole Smith, Carey Ysais (Dancers)

A Manhattan couple on the verge of divorce find themselves being placed together in the Witness Relocation Program and shipped off to the wilds of Wyoming after witnessing a murder.

Sarah Jessica Parker, Hugh Grant © Columbia Pictures

Jeanette, Brittany, Eleanor © Twentieth Century Fox/ Regency Enterprises

ALVIN AND THE CHIPMUNKS: THE SQUEAKQUEL

(20TH CENTURY FOX) Producers, Janice Karman, Ross Bagdasarian; Executive Producers, Karen Rosenfelt, Arnon Milchan, Michele Imperato, Steve Waterman; Director, Betty Thomas; Screenplay, Jon Vitti, Jonathan Aibel, Glenn Berger; Based on the characters Alvin and the Chipmunks created by Ross Bagdasarian and the Chipettes created by Janice Karman; Photography, Anthony B. Richmond; Designer, Marcia Hinds; Costumes, Alexandra Welker; Music, David Newman; Music Supervisor, Julianne Jordan; Editor, Matthew Friedman; Animation Supervisor, Rhythm & Hues; Choreographer, Rosero McCoy; Casting, Juel Bestrop, Seth Yanklewitz; a Fox 2000 Pictures and Regency Enterprises presentation, a Bagdasarian Company production; Dolby; Deluxe color; Rated PG; 88 minutes; Release date: December 23, 2009

CAST
Toby	**Zachary Levi**
Ian	**David Cross**
Dave	**Jason Lee**
Voice of Alvin	**Justin Long**
Voice of Simon	**Matthew Gray Gubler**
Voice of Theodore	**Jesse McCartney**

Amy Poehler (Voice of Eleanor), Anna Faris (Voice of Jeanette), Christina Applegate (Voice of Brittany); and Wendie Malick (Dr. Rubin), Anjelah Johnson (Julie), Kathryn Joosten (Aunt Jackie), Kevin G. Schmidt (Ryan), Chris Warren Jr. (Xander), Bridgit Mendler (Becca), Aimee Carrero (Emily), Alexandra Shipp (Valentina), Gregg Binkley (Emcee), Charice Pempengco (Herself), Bernard White (Doctor), Adele Jacques (Nurse), Joy Osmanski (Airline Rep), Archie Hahn (Agent), Lanny Joon (Paramedic), Brando Eaton (Jeremy), Michael Bruno, Andrew Lee, Alexander Noyes, Jason Rosen (Honor Society), Ali Mikles (Screaming Fan), Eric Bauza (Voice of Digger), Sean Astin (Meerkat Manor Narrator), Marty Dew, Richard Jackson, Mihran Kirakosian (Chipmunk Dancers), Janelle Ginestra, Thomasina E. Gross, Rachele Smith (Chipette Dancers), Daniel Ryan Conferido, Ryan Feng, Brian Hirano, Victor Kim, Hokuto Konishi, Dominic Sandoval, Steven Terada (Li'l Rosero Dancers)

Alvin and the Chipmunks hope to save their school's music program by winning the $25,000 prize in a battle of the bands where their chief competition is a female group of singing chipmunks, The Chippettes.

Robert Downey Jr., Jude Law © Warner Bros.

Robert Downey Jr., Rachel McAdams

Kelly Reilly, Jude Law

Mark Strong, James Fox

SHERLOCK HOLMES

(WARNER BROTHERS) Producers, Joel Silver, Lionel Wigram, Susan Downey, Dan Lin; Executive Producers, Michael Tadross, Bruce Berman; Co-Producer, Steve Clark-Hall; Director, Guy Ritchie; Screenplay, Michael Robert Johnson, Anthony Peckham, Simon Kinberg; Screen Story, Lionel Wigram, Michael Robert Johnson; Based on the characters created by Arthur Conan Doyle; Photography, Philippe Rousselot; Designer, Sarah Greenwood; Costumes, Jenny Beavan; Music, Hans Zimmer; Editor, James Herbert; Visual Effects Supervisor, Chas Jarrett; Visual Effects, Double Negative, Framestore, Prologue Films; Stunts, Franklin Henson, Frank Ferrera; Fight Coordinator, Richard R. Ryan; Associate Producers, Lauren Meek, Peter Eskelsen; Casting, Reg Poerscout-Edgerton; a Silver Pictures and Wigram production, presented in association with Village Roadshow Pictures; Dolby; Technicolor; Rated PG-13; 128 minutes; Release date: December 25, 2009

CAST

Sherlock Holmes	**Robert Downey Jr.**
Dr. John Watson	**Jude Law**
Irene Adler	**Rachel McAdams**
Lord Blackwood	**Mark Strong**
Inspector Lestrade	**Eddie Marsan**
Dredger	**Robert Maillet**
Mrs. Hudson	**Geraldine James**
Mary Morstan	**Kelly Reilly**
Constable Clark	**William Houston**
Lord Coward	**Hans Matheson**
Sir Thomas Rotheram	**James Fox**

William Hope (Ambassador Standish), Clive Russell (Captain Tanner), Oran Gurel (Reordan), David Garrick (McMurdo), Kylie Hutchinson (Maid), Andrew Brooke (Guard Captain), Tom Watt, John Kearney (Carriage Drivers), Sebastian Abineri (Coach Driver), Jonathan Gabriel Robbins (Guard), James A. Stephens (Captain Philips), Terry Taplin (Groundskeeper), Bronagh Gallagher (Palm Reader), Ed Tolputt (Anonymous Man), Joe Egan (Big Man), Jefferson Hall (Young Guard), Miles Jupp (Waiter), Marn Davies (Police Officer), Andrew Greenough (Prison Guard), Ned Dennehy (Man with Roses), Martin Ewens (Removable Man), Amanda Grace Johnson (Young Woman Sacrifice), James Greene (Governor), David Emmings, Ben Cartwright, Chris Sunley (Grave Policemen), Michael Jenn (Preacher), Timothy O'Hara (Porter/Smith), Guy Williams (Golden Dawn Envoy), Peter Miles (Thug)

Intrepid sleuth Sherlock Holmes and his faithful aide, Dr. Watson, investigate the inexplicable return from the grave of occultist and serial killer Lord Blackwood.

This film received Oscar nominations for art direction and music.

IT'S COMPLICATED

(UNIVERSAL) Producers, Nancy Meyers, Scott Rudin; Executive Producers, Ilona Herzberg, Suzanne Farwell; Director/Screenplay, Nancy Meyers; Photography, John Toll; Designer, Jon Hutman; Costumes, Sonia Grande; Music, Hans Zimmer, Heitor Pereira; Editors, Joe Hutshing, David Moritz; Casting, Ellen Chenoweth; a Waverly Films/Scott Rudin production, presented in association with Relativity Media; Dolby; Color; Rated R; 120 minutes; Release date: December 25, 2009

CAST

Jane Adler	**Meryl Streep**
Adam	**Steve Martin**
Jake Adler	**Alec Baldwin**
Harley	**John Krasinski**
Agness	**Lake Bell**
Joanne	**Mary Kay Place**
Trisha	**Rita Wilson**
Diane	**Alexandra Wentworth**
Luke	**Hunter Parrish**
Gabby	**Zoe Kazan**
Lauren	**Caitlin Fitzgerald**

Emjay Anthony (Pedro), Nora Dunn (Sally), Bruce Altman (Ted), Robert Curtis Brown (Peter), James Patrick Stuart (Dr. Moss), Peter Mackenzie (Dr. Allen), Pat Finn (Hotel Doctor), Heitor Pereira, Ramin Djawadi, Ryeland Allison (Party Musicians), Sean Hamrin (Oliver), Valente Rodriguez (Reynaldo), Emily Kinney (Waitress), Amelia Rasche (Bakery Manager), Zack Robidas (Hotel Reception Clerk), Lisa Lynn Masters (Woman in Elevator), Scott Geyer (Man in Elevator), Andrew Stewart-Jones (Restaurant Host), Jon Frazier, Ryan Silverman (Bartenders), Jennifer Restivo, Dana Power (Women at Bar), Michael Kopp (Self-Help Narrator), Michael Rivera (Eddie), Jennifer Eatz, Blanchard Ryan, Geneva Carr (Women at Fertility Clinic), Eric Rath, Philip Coccioletti (Men at Fertility Clinic), Deidre Goodwin (Fertility Nurse), Rosalie Ward (Biltmore Reception Clerk), Jessica St. Clair (Wedding Specialist), Marina Squerciati (Melanie), Ricardo Chacon, Michael Yavnieli (Police Officers), Robert Adamson, Patrick King (College Kids at Party)

Divorcee Jane Adler suddenly finds herself carrying on a passionate affair with her ex-husband, thereby complicating her relationship with an architect who has taken a romantic interest in her.

Meryl Streep, Steve Martin

Meryl Streep, Steve Martin, Alec Baldwin, Lake Bell

Alec Baldwin, Meryl Streep

Alec Baldwin, Caitlin Fitzgerald, John Krasinski, Zoe Kazan, Meryl Streep

Zoe Kazan, Hunter Parrish, Caitlin Fitzgerald

Meryl Streep, Alec Baldwin © Universal Studios

Meryl Streep, Alec Baldwin

Steve Martin

Rita Wilson

Meryl Streep, John Krasinski, Caitlin Fitzgerald

Bryce Dallas Howard

Bryce Dallas Howard

THE LOSS OF A TEARDROP DIAMOND

(PALADIN) Producer, Brad Michael Gilbert; Executive Producers, Ron Gilbert, Catherine Kellner; Director, Jodie Markell; Screenplay, Tennessee Williams; Photography, Giles Nuttgens; Designer, Richard Hoover; Costumes, Chris Karvonides; Music, Mark Orton; Editor, Susan E. Morse; a Constellation Entertainment production; Dolby; Technicolor; Rated PG-13; 102 minutes; Release date: December 30, 2010

CAST

Fisher Willow	**Bryce Dallas Howard**
Jimmy Dobyne	**Chris Evans**
Miss Addie	**Ellen Burstyn**
Julie	**Mamie Gummer**
Cornelia	**Ann-Margret**
Mr. Dobyne	**Will Patton**
Vinnie	**Jessica Collins**
Mr. Van Hooven	**Peter Gerety**
Esmeralda	**Marin Ireland**
Mathilde	**Zoe Perry**
Mrs. Dobyne	**Barbara Garrick**
Mr. Fenstermaker	**Zach Grenier**
Mrs. Fenstermaker	**Laila Robins**
Addie's Nurse	**Susan Blommaert**
Susie	**Carol Sutton**
Secretary	**Rhoda Griffis**
William	**Harold Evans**
Nurse	**Geraldine Singer**
Mr. Willow	**Marco St. John**
Caroline	**Jennifer Sipes**
Relative	**Melissa Odom**
Fats	**Terrance Taplin**
Dottie	**Alan McNair**
Bathroom Man	**Douglas Griffin**

Charles Pineda (Hank), Derrick Denicola (Tommy), John Willard, Hevin Hampton (Drunk Boys), Trent Dee (Happy), Natalya Payne (Gypsy)

In 1920s Mississippi, the fiercely independent Fisher Willow engages an employee on her father's plantation to take her to an important social event, where she loses a valuable earring.

Chris Evans, Bryce Dallas Howard
© Paladin

YONKERS JOE (Magnolia) Producer, Trent Othick; Executive Producers, John Gaughan, Matt Othick, Phil Ivey, Chazz Palminteri; Line Producer, Richard DiPatri; Co-Executive Producers, Jim Click, Vince Schettler, Bill Wortman, J. Todd Harris; Co-Producers, Fred David, Robert H. Moretti, Illya Trincher; Director/Screenplay, Robert Celestino; Photography, Michael Fimognari; Designer, Jonathan Carlson; Costumes, Luellyn Harper; Music, Chris Hajian; Editors, Jim Makiej, Gary A. Friedman; Casting, Billy Hopkins, Kerry Barden, Suzanne Crowley; a GO Productions presentation of a Trent Othick production; Color; Rated R; 102 minutes; Release date: January 9, 2009. **CAST:** Chazz Palminteri (Yonkers Joe), Christine Lahti (Janice), Thomas Guiry (Joe Jr.), Michael Lerner (Stanley), Linus Roache (Teddy), Michael Rispoli (Mickey), Roma Maffia (Santini), Frank John Hughes (Tom Vincent), Patrick Hughes (Polo Shirt), Thomas DiGiacomo (AC Dealer), Lauri Johnson (Hammer), John "Fast Jack" Farrell (Fitz), Donny Souder, Michael Rizza (Poker Players), Anthony Tarantola, Chuck Meola (Heavies), Rusty Meyers (Committee Man), Saverio Guerra (Bam), Arthur Nascarella (Dino), Tyler Baze (Jockey), Kirsten Love (Attendant), Tom Cassell (Stickman), Charlie DiPinto (Boxman), William Allison (Pit Boss), Allen Fawcett, Nate Bynum (Technicians), Don Mirault (Guard), Dean Marrazzo (Casino Manager), Chad McKnight (Simon)

Thomas Guiry, Chazz Palminteri, Christine Lahti in Yonkers Joe © *Magnolia*

MOCK UP ON MU (Other Cinema) Producer/Director/Screenplay, Craig Baldwin; Photography, Bill Daniel, James T. Hong; Designer, Lars Auvinen; Editors, Sylvia Schedelbauer, Bill Daniel; an Other Cinema production; Color/Black and white; 16-to-DigiBeta; Not rated; 114 minutes; Release date: January 14, 2009. **CAST:** Stoney Burke (Lockheed Martin), Damon Packard (L. Ron Hubbard), Michelle Silva (Agent C, Marjorie Cameron), Kalman Spelletich (Jack Parsons)

THE SUBLET (No Logik Films) Producer/Director/Editor, Georgiana Nestor; Executive Producers, Cori Sullins, Shane Sills, Luiza Petre, Shravan Kambam; Photography, Kamil Plocki; Music, Corneliu Esanu; Color; HD; Not rated; 78 minutes; Release date: January 16, 2009. **CAST:** Roger Hendricks Simon (Walter), Tiffany Lee (Maggie), Ross Pivec (Hit Man), Doris Dunigan (Maggie's Mother), Daniel Simon (Maggie's Friend), Anthony Carpinelli (Target), Amanda Lippert (Goth Girl), Motoki Kobayashi (Japanese Guest), Michael Jared Thomas, Peter Schmitz (Gay Men), Joiee Thorpe (Porn Star), Christopher Calliope (Frist Byron), Clay Drinko, Matthew Krause, Matthew W. Downay (Punk Rockers), Jeff Essex (Lawyer), Brie Walker (Little Girl), E. Talley II, Will Brown (Gangsters), Seth Livingston (Deaf Visitor), Edgar Felix (Gothic Man)

Roger Hendricks Simon, Tiffany Lee in The Sublet © *No Logik Films*

THE VILLAGE BARBERSHOP (Monterey Media) Producers, Chris Ford, Jason Newmark; Executive Producer, Scott Gragson; Director/Screenplay, Chris Ford; Photography, Cliff Traiman; Designer, Natalie Sanfilippo; Costumes, Jihyun Kim; Music, Michael Tremante; Editor, Ian Montgomery; a Hot Shave production; Color; Widescreen; HD; Not rated; 99 minutes; Release date: January 16, 2009. **CAST:** John Ratzenberger (Art Leroldi), Shelly Cole (Gloria MacIntyre), Cindy Pickett (Josie), George McRae (George), Daron Jennings (Colin), Josh Hutchinson (Rickert), Cory DuVal (Richie), Liz Anderson (Wendy), Courtney Black (Jenny), Kevin Blackton (Judge), Chandler Bolt (Kimmel), Todd Brotze (Sprow), Elwood Carlisle (Elmer), Bettina Devin (Dolly), Mackenzie Firgens (Amy), Amos Glick (John Jacobi), Cindy Goldfield (Lanie), Luke Hoffman (King), Ed Holmes (Johnny), Peter Judd (Warhol), Michael Kasin (Redneck), Eli Nelson (Mullet), Robert Anthony Peters, Jeffrey Rios (Cross Dressers), Bob Saenz (Wilson), Michael X. Sommers (Tony), Daniel Souza (Jim), Samantha Weaver (Rochelle), Laurelle Westaway (Gladys), Chris Yule (Stan)

Cindy Pickett, John Ratzenberger in The Village Barbershop © *Monterey Media*

THE LODGER (Samuel Goldwyn Films) Producers, Michael Mailer, David Ondaatje; Executive Producer, Scott Putnam; Director/Screenplay, David Ondaatje; Based on the novel by Marie Belloc Lowndes; Photography, David A. Armstrong; Designer/Costumes, Franco-Giacomo Carbone; Music, John Frizzell; Editor, William Flicker; a Michael Mailer/Merchant Pacific production; Dolby; Color; Rated R; 96 minutes; Release date: January 23, 2009. **CAST:** Alfred Molina (Chandler Manning), Hope Davis (Ellen), Shane West (Street), Simon Baker (Malcolm), Rachael Leigh Cook (Amanda), Donal Logue (Bunting), Philip Baker Hall (Capt. Smith), Rebecca Pidgeon (Dr. Jessica Westmin), Mel Harris (Margaret) Michael Albala (Forensic Expert), Daphne Ashbrook (Attractive Woman), Krista Ayne, Tarajia Morrell (Slender Women), Donnell C. Barret (Street Pimp), Tia Barr (Annie Chapman), François Chau (Sam), Virgina Williams (Rachel Madison), Bert Rosario (Juan Dantierro), J.P. Foster Jr. (Timmy), Kirk Fox (Officer 3000), Ernie Grunwald (Gregor), Jamison Jones (Officer Bittner), Jasmine Lobe (Wife), Mocean Melvin (Young Detective), Michael O'Hagan (Bruce Lester), Gary Poux (Bill), Lancer Dean Shull (Internal Affairs Agent), Stephen Steelman (Matt), David Storrs (Warehouse Worker), Juting Tsang (Mary Ann Lee), Jennifer Webb (2nd Victim), Roy Werner (Dr. Stevens)

CRIPS AND BLOODS: MADE IN AMERICA (Verso Entertainment/Balance Vector) Producers, Baron Davis, Dan Halsted, Stacy Peralta, Shaun Murphy, Gus Roxburgh, Cash Warren; Executive Producers, Steve Luczo, Quincy "QD3" Jones; Director, Stacy Peralta; Screenplay, Stacy Peralta, Sam George; Photography, Tony Hardmon; Music, Kamasi Washington; Music, Matter; Editor, T.J. Mahar; Narrator, Forest Whitaker; a Form Production; Dolby; Black and white/color; Not rated; 93 minutes; Release date: January 23, 2009. Documentary on South Los Angeles' notorious African-American gangs, the Crips and the Bloods.

Baron Davis in Crips and Bloods © *Verso/Balance Vector*

OUTLANDER (Third Rail Releasing) Producers, Chris Roberts, John Schimmel; Executive Producers, Don Carmody, Andy Grosch, Marcus Schoefer, Barrie Osborne, Vincent Maraval, Philip Elway, Dirk Blackman, Karen Loop, Kia Jam, Christopher Eberts; Director, Howard McCain; Screenplay, Dirk Blackman, Howard McCain; Photography, Pierre Gill; Designer, David Hackl; Costumes, Debra Hanson; Music, Geoff Zanelli; Editor, David Dodson; Special Effects Supervisor, David Kuklish; a Weinstein Co., Virtual Films presentation of an Ascendant Pictures (U.S.)/VIP Medienfonds 4 (Germany) production; American-German; Dolby; Panavision; Color; Rated R; 115 minutes; Release date: January 23, 2009. **CAST:** Jim Caviezel (Kanian), Sophia Myles (Freya), Jack Huston (Wulfric), Cliff Saunders (Boromir), Ron Perlman (Gunanr), John Hurt (Rothgar), Patrick Stevenson (Unferth), Bailey Maughan (Erick), Aidan Devine (Einar), John E. Nelles (Donal), James Rogers (Bjorn), Scott Owen (Aethril), Petra Prazak (Mara), Owen Pattison (Galen), Matt Cooke (Captain), Katie Bergin (Sonja),

Todd Godin (Lars), Mauralea Austin (Jona), Matthew Amyotte (Arn), John Beale (Edmund), Ted Ludzik (Olaf), James Binkley (Leader), Liam McNamara (Finn), Brian Renfro (Grey-Haired Warrior), Jon Loverin (Sheepherder), Andrew Albert (Drunken Reveler #1), Brian Heighton (Trader), Danny Lima (Slave), Glen Wadman (Wailing Man), Simon Northwood, Todd William Schroeder (Warriors), Martha Irving (Weeping Woman), Tess McCain (Viking Girl)

KILLSHOT (Weinstein Co.) Producers, Lawrence Bender, Richard Gladstein; Director, John Madden; Screenplay, Hossein Amini; Based on the novel by Elmore Leonard; Photography, Caleb Deschanel; Designer, Andrew Jackness; Costumes, Beth Pasternak; Music, Klaus Badelt; Editors, Mick Audsley, Lisa Gunning; a Lawrence Bender production; Dolby; Super 35 Widescreen; Color; Rated R; 84 minutes; Release date: January 23, 2009. **CAST:** Diane Lane (Carmen Colson), Mickey Rourke (Armand "The Blackbird" Degas), Thomas Jane (Wayne Colson), Rosario Dawson (Donna), Joseph Gordon-Levitt (Richie Nix), Don McManus (Nelson Davies), Lois Smith (Lenore), Hal Holbrook (Papa), Brandon McGibbon (Blackbird's Kid Brother), Peter Kelly Gaudreault (Blackbird's Brother), Michelle Arzivu (Nurse), Richard Zeppieri (Son-in-Law), Robert Gow, Catherine Hayos (Prospective Buyers), Craig Blair (Construction Site Foreman), Lynne Deragon (Mrs. Palino), Hazel Desjarlais (Old Woman, Walpole Island), Aldred Wesley Montoya (Lionel), Tim Campbell, Tim Eddis (Michigan Officers), Beatriz Yuste (Checkout Girl), Tom McCamus (Paul Scallen), Michael Joseph Bernier (Mechanic), Jim Cordington, Karen Robinson, Steve Cumyn (FBI Agents), James Anthony (Drydock Foreman), Christine Brubaker (Dockworker's Wife), Alexis Butler (Girl in Hotel Room)

Diane Lane, Thomas Jane in Killshot © *Weinstein Co.*

BLESSED IS THE MATCH: THE LIFE AND DEATH OF HANNAH SENESH (Balcony) Producer, Lisa Thomas; Executive Producer, Marta Kauffman; Director, Roberta Grossman; Screenplay, Sophie Sartain; Photography, Dyanna Taylor; Designer, Frank Gampel; Costumes, Rona Doron; Music, Todd Boekelheid; Editor, Blake West; Narrator, Joan Allen; a Katahdin Foundation production; Color/Black and white; HD-to-35mm; Super 8-to-35mm; Not rated; 86 minutes; Release date: January 28, 2009. Documentary on Hannah Senesh who left Palestine to help in a doomed effort to rescue Jews from Hungary during World War II. **CAST** (reenactment scenes): Meri Roth (Hannah Senesh), Marcela Nokynkova (Catherine Senesh), Zdenek Kozakovic (Giora Senesh), Zdenek Astr (Captain Simon), Jindrich Hinke (Interrogator Rozsa), Monika Malacov (Elizabeth Marton), Anredj Poka (Tissandier), Akiva Zasman (Kallos), Pavla Beretova, Zuzana Stavna (Teenage Girls)

Hannah Senesh in Blessed is the Match © *Balcony Releasing*

BETWEEN LOVE & GOODBYE (Embrem Entertainment) Producers, Casper Andreas, Markus Goetze; Executive Producers, Michael Curry, Don T. Kojima, Mich Lyon, Ken Margala, George Taninatz; Director/Screenplay, Casper Andreas; Photography, Jon Fordham; Designer, Jana Mattioli; Costumes, Martina Melendez; Music, Scott Starrett; Editor, Christina Kelly; a Goodbye Love production; Color; HD; Not rated; 97 minutes; Release date: January 30, 2009. **CAST:** Simon Miller (Kyle), Rob Harmon (April/Cole), Ryan Turner (Tommy), Austin Head (Gutter Punk), Jane Elliott (Sarah), Justin Tensen (Marcel), Caroline Delran (Catherine), Aaron Michael Davies (Danny), Kenny Wade Marshall (Judge), Jared Gertner (Ben), Mich Lyon (Jilted John), Mackenzie Shivers (Waitress), Sabrina Samone (Gina), Carol Carter (Immigration Receptionist), Peter Chien Jr. (Immigration Lawyer), Deirdre Brennan (Immigration Interviewer), Filippa Edberg (Jenny), Maurice Neuhaus (Doctor), Michelle Akeley (Lea), Matthew Ludwinski (Rob), Paul Borghese (Officer Borgatti), Paul Rackley (Marcel's Lawyer), Dennis Williams, Elizabeth Burke (Immigration Officers)

Justin Tensen, Simon Miller in Between Love & Goodbye © *Embrem Entertainment*

MEDICINE FOR MELANCHOLY (IFC Films) Producer, Justin Barber; Co-producer, Cherie Saulter; Director/Screenplay, Barry Jenkins; Photography, James Laxton; Music, Nat Sanders; Music Supervisor, Greg O'Bryant; a Strike Anywhere presentation of a Baldry Film production; Color; HD; Not rated; 88 minutes; Release date: January 30, 2009. **CAST:** Wyatt Cenac (Micah), Tracey Heggins (Joanne), Melissa Bisgani (Cassandra Jay), Elizabeth Acker, Powell DeGrange, Chida Emeka, John Friedberg, Dana Julius, Phoebe Chi Ching Kwok, Tommi Avicolli Mecca, Adam Moskowitz, Jennifer Sanchez, Kenyatta Sheppard (Housing Rights Committee Members), Emily Taplin (Receptionist), Brent Weinbach (Waiter)

Wyatt Cenac in Medicine for Melancholy © *IFC Films*

OUR CITY DREAMS (First Run Features) Producers, Chiara Clemente, Tanya Selvaratnam, Bettina Sulser; Director, Chiara Clemente; Photography, Theo Stanley; Music, Thomas M. Lauderdale; Editor, Martin Levenstein; a Di San Luca Films production; Color/Black and white; DV; HD; Not rated; 87 minutes; Release date: February 4, 2009. Documentary on five women artists in Manhattan. **WITH:** Swoon, Ghada Amer, Kiki Smith, Marina Abramovic, Nancy Spero

Nancy Spero in Our City Dreams © *First Run Features*

MEMORIAL DAY (Independent) Producers, Hunter Gray, Paul Mezey, Laura Wagner; Executive Producers, Tyler Brodie, Jim McKay, Michael Stipe; Director/Screenplay/Photography/Editor, Josh Fox; Designer, Nicolas Locke; an Artists Public Domain, Intl. WOW Company presentation, in association with Bay Bridge Productions, C-Hundred Film Corp., Journeyman Pictures; Dolby; Color; DV; Not rated; 94 minutes; Release date: February 4, 2009. **CAST:** Harold Kennedy German, Robert Humphreys, Neil Knox, Nick Konow, Maria McConville, Tess Mix, Sarah Nedwek, Giovanni Rich, Pedro Rafael Rodriguez, Robert Saietta, David Skeist

INCENDIARY (Capitol Films) Producers, Andy Paterson, Anand Tucker, Adrienne Maguire; Executive Producers, Simon Fawcett, Tessa Ross, Philip Erdoes, Daria Jovici; Director/Screenplay, Sharon Maguire; Based on the novel by Chris Cleave; Photography, Ben Davis; Designer, Kave Quinn; Costumes, Stephanie Collie; Music, Shigeru Umebayashi; Editor, Valerio Bonelli; a Film 4 presentation, in association with Aramid Entertainment, of an Archer Street, Sneak Preview production; British; Color; Not rated; 96 minutes; American release date: February 6, 2009. **CAST:** Michelle Williams (Young Mother), Ewan McGregor (Jasper), Matthew Macfadyen (Terrence), Sidney Johnston (The Boy), Nicholas

Greaves (Lenny), Usman Khokhar (The Bomber's Son), Sasha Behar (The Bomber's Wife), Alibe Parsons (Pearl), Stewart Wright (Charlie), Al Hunter Ashton (Survivor), Benjamin Wilkin (Young Policeman), Robin Berry (Dazed Supporter), Mercy Ojelade (Nurse Mena), Joe Marshall (Gary, VT Man), Nicholas Courtney (Archbishop of Canterbury), Jonathan Andrews (Police Officer at Station), Monty Fromant (Sedurity Guard), Victoria Alcock (Stropy Woman), Emil Elhaji (Sonny Ghorbani), Alan Parry (Match Commentator), Jeremy Thompson, Kay Burley (Sky Presenters), Toby Hales (Baby)

Ewan McGregor in Incendiary © *Aramid Entertainment*

LIFE. SUPPORT. MUSIC. (Merigold Moving Pictures) Producer/Director/Photography/Editor, Eric Daniel Metzgar; Music, Eric Liebman; Color; DV; Not rated; 79 minutes; Release date: February 6, 2009. Documentary on guitarist Jason Crigler's recovery from a massive cerebral hemorrhage. **WITH:** Jason Crigler, Monica Crigler, Marjorie Crigler, Carol Crigler, Lynn Crigler, Norah Jones, Teddy Thompson, Marshall Crenshaw

Jason Crigler, Ellie Crigler in Life. Support. Music.
© *Merigold Moving Pictures*

THE CALLER (Arts Alliance/Olive Press) formerly *On the Hook*; Producers, Rene Bastian, Linda Moran, Richard Ledes; Co-Producer, Ged Dickersin; Director, Richard Ledes; Screenplay, Alain Didier-Weill, Richard Ledes; Photography, Stephen Kazmierski; Designer, Kelly McGehee; Costumes, Tere Duncan; Music, Robert Miller; Music Supervisor, Beth Amy Rosenblatt; Editor, Madeleine Gavin; Casting, Todd Thaler; a Chapeau Films presentation of a Belladonna production; Color; Rated PG-13; 95 minutes; Release date: February 13, 2009. **CAST:** Frank Langella (Jimmy Stevens), Elliott Gould (Frank Turlotte), Laura Harring (Eileen), Anabel Sosa (Lila), Chandler Williams (Sammy), Axel Feldmann (Young Jimmy),

Grégory Ellis (Lulu), Corey Johnson (Paul Wainsail), Robert Bagnell (Jeff), Edoardo Ballerini (Teddy), David Ballog (Peter), Jean Brassard (Young Jimmy's Father), Julia Carothers Hughes (Attractive Girl), Maria-Jose Davo (Waitress), Kyle Emelander (Restaurant Doorman), Laura Holloway (Secretary), Edward James Hyland (John), Julie Jones Ivey (Religious Young Woman), Devin Luke (Limo Driver), Charles Nordeen (Waiter), Marion Servole (Young Jimmy's Mother)

Frank Langella, Elliott Gould in The Caller © *Arts Alliance*

FIRED UP! (Screen Gems) Producers, Matthew Gross, Peter Jaysen, Charles Weinstock; Executive Producers, Will Gluck, Paddy Cullen, Marcy Gross, Ann Weston; Director, Will Gluck; Screenplay, Freedom Jones; Photography, Thomas Ackerman; Designer, Marcia Hindes; Costumes, Mynka Draper; Music, Richard Gibbs; Choreographer, Zachary Woodlee; Casting, Lisa Miller Katz; a Moving Pictures AMG/Gross Entertainment/Charles Weinstock production; Dolby; Panavision; Deluxe color; Rated PG-13; 89 minutes; Release date: February 20, 2009. **CAST:** Nicholas D'Agosto (Shawn Colfax), Eric Christian Olsen (Nick Brady), Sarah Roemer (Carly), Molly Sims (Diora), Danneel Harris (Bianca), David Walton (Dr. Rick), Adhir Kalyan (Brewster), AnnaLynne McCord (Gwyneth), Juliette Goglia (Poppy), Philip Baker Hall (Coach Byrnes), John Michael Higgins (Coach Keith), Smith Cho (Beth), Margo Harshman (Sylvia), Hayley Marie Norman (Angela), Jake Sandvig (Downey), Nicole Tubiola (Marcy), Collins Pennie (Adam), Edie McClurg (Ms. Klingerhoff), Michael Blaiklock (Mookie), James Earl (Turk), Keeshan Giles (Kyle), Alan Ritchson (Bruce), Shoshana Bush (Girl), Casey Graf (Guy), Kelen Coleman (Maddy), Kate Lang Johnson (Jennifer), Jill Latiano (Haley), Amber Stevens (Sara), Dan Fine (Kreg), Steven West (Bill), Francia Raisa (Marly), Madison Riley (Lily), Joy Osmanski (Curious Cheerleader), Jessica Szohr (Kara), Tanya Chisholm (Denise), Krista Kalmus (Anna), Kate French (Cute Captain), Julianna Guill (Agy), Lindsay Schoenweis (Yet Another Girl), Heather Morris (Fiona), Kayla Ewell (Margot Jane Lindsworth-Calligan), Sandra Sanchez, Brian Unger (Commentators), Masi Oka (Eagle), Libby Mintz (Janine), Lucy Griffin (Charlie), Karlee Eldridge (Matty), Nicholas James (Chester), Lance Kerfuffle (Miles Monahan), Andrew Fleming (Klete Vanderjack), Rebekah Giles (Tiger Cheerleader), Taisha Clark, Amber Estrada, Amber Exum, Janelle Ginestra, Erin Yvonne Hernandez, Glenda Morales, Katrina Katie Norman, Rachele Brooke Smith (Tiger Dancers), Janel Parrish (Lana)

Nicholas D'Agosto, Sarah Roemer in Fired Up! © *Screen Gems*

ELEVEN MINUTES (Regent) Producers/Directors, Michael Selditch, Rob Tate; Executive Producers, Lydia Tenaglia, Christopher Collins; Photography, Alex Wolfe, Michael Selditch, Rob Tate; Music Supervisor, John Sands; Editor, Rob Tate; a Zero Point Zero production, in association with Maximum Vacuum; Color; Rated R; 108 minutes; Release date: February 20, 2009. Documentary that follows *Project Runway* winner Jay McCarroll as he enters the real world of fashion. **WITH:** Jay McCarroll, Nancy Kane, Kelly Cutrone, Malan Breton, Lee Deekle, Jason Low, Omahrya, Eve Salvail, Carson Kressley, Thomas Onorato, Michael Rucker, George Whipple III, Max Wixom

MUST READ AFTER MY DEATH (Gigantic) Producer/Director/Screenplay/Editor, Morgan Dews; Executive Producer, Alison Palmer Bourke; Co-Producer, Cristina Girones; Photography, Allis; Music, Paul Damian Hogan; a Morgan Dews production, in co-production with Frame Zero; Stereo; Color; Not rated; 73 minutes; Release date: February 20, 2009. Documentary in which filmmaker Morgan Dews' uncovered video and audio footage from his later grandmother unearthed certain family secrets.

Must Read After My Death © *Gigantic*

ECHELON CONSPIRACY (After Dark Films) Producers, Steve Richards, Alexander Leyviman, Roee Sharon Reed; Executive Producers, Jonathan Tzachor, Navid McIlhargey, Charles V. Bender; Co-Producer/Story, Michael Nitsberg; Director, Greg Marcks; Screenplay, Michael Nitsberg, Kevin Elders; Photography, Lorenzo Senatore; Designer, Antonello Rubino; Music, Bobby Tahouri; Editor, James Herbert; a Mobicom Entertainment production; Color; Rated PG-13; 105 minutes; Release date: February 27, 2009. **CAST:** Shane West (Max Peterson), Edward Burns (John Reed), Ving Rhames (Agent Dave Grant), Jonathan Pryce (Mueller), Tamara Feldman (Kamila), Sergey Gubanov (Yuri Malanin), Martin Sheen (Raymond Burke), Yuriy Kutsenko (Russian General), Steven Elder (Charles), Ilan Goodman (Dennis), Trevor White (Paul Spencer), Sandra De Sousa, Greg Donaldson (Casino Techs), Andrea Enright (NSA Tech #2), Todd Jensen (Agent Fletcher), Danko Jordanov (Max's Attacker), Marianne Stanicheva (Pentagon Woman), Mike Straub (NSA Operator #3), Vee Vimolmal (Receptionist)

Shane West in Echelon Conspiracy © *After Dark Films*

THE TROUBLE WITH ROMANCE (Girls Club Entertainment) Producers, Emily Liu, Gene Rhee, Jennifer Siebel Newsom; Executive Producer, Mark G. Mathis; Director, Gene Rhee; Screenplay, Gene Rhee, Sharri Hefner, Mike Su; Photography, Nathan Wilson; Designer, Nicolas Plotquin; Costumes, Cynthia Obsenares; Music, Daniel Cage; Music Supervisor, Amy Driscoll; Editor, Jacqueline Cambas; Casting, D. Taylor Loeb; Presented in association with Sweet Violet Films; Color; HD; Not rated; 88 minutes; Release date: February 27, 2009. **CAST:** Jennifer Siebel (Jill), Kip Pardue (Jack), Coby Ryan McLaughlin (Steve), David Eigenberg (Paul), Josie Davis (Karen), Portia Dawson (Rachel), Emily Liu (Stephanie), Roger Fan (Jimmy), Sheetal Sheth (Nicole), Jordan Belfi (Charlie), John Churchill (Mark), Valeria Hernandez (Rosa), Mitch Malem (Ed), Judith Montgomery (Dolores), Garikayi Mutambirwa (Zhi)

PLAY THE GAME (Slowhand Releasing) Producer/Director/Screenplay, Marc Feinberg; Photography, Gavin Kelly; Designer, Chris Anthony Miller; Costumes, Laura Brody; Music, Jim Latham; Editor, Kimberley Generous White; a Story Films production; Color; Rated PG-13; 105 minutes; Release date: February 27, 2009. **CAST:** Paul Campbell (David Mitchell), Andy Griffith (Grandpa Joe), Doris Roberts (Rose Sherman), Marla Sokoloff (Julie Larabee), Liz Sheridan (Edna Gordon), Clint Howard (Dick), Rance Howard (Mervin), Geoffrey Owens (Rob), Juliette Jeffers (Carrie), Omar Adam (James), Lisa Benedict (Jennifer), Michael Bretten (Trendy Player in Bar), Marie Caldare (Rebecca), Andrea Chung (Miss Linebacker), Hannah Cowley (Girl with Football), Thomas Crawford (Paul), Sergio Enrique (Bartender), Monica Garcia (Ann), Rhett Giles (Jeff), Brenda Goodbread (Car Buyer), Christopher Goodman (Customer), Andres Saenz-Hudson (Mechanic), Robert A. Johnson (Referee), Donald Sage Mackay (Director), Rafael J. Noble (Doorman), Michelle Pierce (Susan), Leigh Rose (Iris), Dulce Maria Solis (Taxi Driver), Frantz Turner (Husband), Les Williams (Doug), Travis Winfrey (Trainer)

Paul Campbell, Andy Griffith in Play the Game © *Slowhand Releasing*

AN AMERICAN AFFAIR (Screen Media) Producers, Kevin Leydon, William Sten Olsson; Executive Producer, John Daly; Co-Producer/Screenplay, Alex Metcalf; Director, William Sten Olsson; Photography, David Insley; Designer, Vincent Peranio; Costumes, Rolande Glicenstein; Music, Dustin O'Halloran; Music Supervisors, Karyn Rachtman, Bobby Lavelle; Casting, Johanna Ray; an Astrakan Films presentation, in association with Films and Music Entertainment; Dolby; Color; Rated R; 92 minutes; Release date: February 27, 2009. **CAST:** Gretchen Mol (Catherine Caswell), James Rebhorn (Lucian Carver), Cameron Bright (Adam Stafford), Mark Pellegrino (Graham Caswell), Perrey Reeves (Adrienne Stafford), Noah Wyle (Mike Stafford), J.P. Aaron (White House Sentry), Kris Arnold (Charlie), Laurel Astri (Faith), Jimmy Bellinger (Jimmy), Jermaine Crawford (Andre), Lisa-Lisbeth Finney (Sister Mary Eunice), Jerry Hart (Carl), Sarah Hart (Patricia), Courtney Miller (Carol), Gerry Paradiso (Del Valle), Monika Samtani (Sita), Jerry Whiddon (Jacques), Hannah Williams (Magda), Sam Navarro (JFK)

Cameron Bright in An American Affair © *Screen Media*

ROBERT BLECKER WANTS ME DEAD (Atlas Media) Producer, Bruce David Klein; Executive Producers, Bruce David Klein, Richard Abramowitz, Kaki Kirby; Director, Ted Schillinger; Photography, Matt Howe; Music, Dan Dolan; Editors, Kendrick Simmons, Ted Schillinger; Color; HD; Not rated; 95 minutes; Release date: February 27, 2009. Documentary on pro-death penalty crusader Robert Blecker. **WITH:** Robert Blecker, Daryl Holton

HORSEMEN (Lionsgate) Producers, Michael Bay, Brad Fuller, Andrew Form; Executive Producers, Ted Field, Joe Drake, Nathan Kahane, Joe Rosenberg; Co-Producers, Nicole Brown, Kelli Konop, Jeremiah Samuels, Michael Weber; Director, Jonas Akerlund; Screenplay, David Callaham; Photography, Eric Broms; Designer, Sandy Cochrane; Costumes, B.; Music, Jan A.P. Kaczmarek; Editors, Jim May, Todd E. Miller; Casting, Lindsey Hayes Kroeger, David Rappaport; a Mandate Films, Michael Bay presentation of a Platinum Dunes, Radar Pictures production; Dolby; Color; Rated R; 88 minutes; Release date: March 6, 2009. **CAST:** Dennis Quaid (Aidan Breslin), Ziyi Zhang (Kristen), Lou Taylor Pucci (Alex Breslin), Clifton Collins Jr. (Stingray), Barry Shabaka Henley (Tuck), Patrick Fugit (Corey), Eric Balfour (Taylor), Paul Dooley (Father Whiteleather), Thomas Mitchell (Thug), Liam James (Sean Breslin), Chelcie Ross (Police Chief Krupa), Manfred Maretzki (Bob), Arne MacPherson (Navratil), David Dastmalchian (Terrence), Peter Stormare (David Spitz), Darren Felbel (Control Room Guy), Mel Stocking (Old Man with Dog), Aaron Hughes (Young Officer), Stephen Eric McIntyre (Banksy), Joanne Rodriguez (Metal Face), Carly Marentette (Teresa Spitz), Natasha Kuzyk (Angie Spitz), John Callander (Officer), Darren Wall (Random Officer), Omar Khan (Officer Booker), Kevin Power (Gregor), Brenda Gorlick (Lee Shoemaker), Onalee Ames (Mary Anne Spitz), Deborah Odell (Ms. Bradshaw), Carey Smith (Uniformed Officer)

Ziyi Zhang, Dennis Quaid in Horsemen © *Lionsgate*

SHERMAN'S WAY (Intl. Film Circuit) Producers, Craig Saavedra, Michael Shulman, Tom Nance; Director, Craig Saavedra; Screenplay, Tom Nance; Photography, Joaquin Sedillo; Designer, Laurent Turlure; Music, David Michael Frank; Editor, Christopher Gay; a Starry Night Entertainment production; Fujicolor; 16mm-to-HD; Not rated; 98 minutes; Release date: March 6, 2009. **CAST:** James LeGros (Palmer), Enrico Colantoni (D.J.), Michael Shulman (Sherman Black), Lacey Chabert (Marcy), Donna Murphy (Evelyn Black), Brooke Nevin (Addy), M. Emmet Walsh (Hoyt), Thomas Ian Nicholas (Tom), Tad Hilgenbrink (Taylor), Thomas R. Nance (Doug), Ryan Hansen (Kevin), Bob Bancroft (Prof. Ardevaas), Cory DuVal (Repoman), Margaret Beach (Travel Agent), Olivia Leigh (Waitress), Linda Ignazi (Coffee Shop Server), Al Roffe (Homeless Man), Chuck Lewis (Jeweler), David Brawley (Patrick), Johnny Rowles (Antique Store Clerk), Michael J. Ardevaas (Short Fat Airline Patron), Kelley Mckee (Streaker), Keyla Wood (College Streaker)

Michael Shulman, James LeGros in Sherman's Way © *Intl. Film Circuit*

SHUTTLE (Magnet) Producers, Mark Williams, Todd Lemley, Allan Jones, Michael Pierce, Mark Donadio; Director/Screenplay, Edward Anderson;Photography, Michael Fimognari; Designer, Roger Danchik; Costumes, Virginia B. Johnson; Music, Henning Lohner; Editor, William Yeh; a Pierce/Williams Entertainment production in association with Moody Street Pictures, Future Films, and Fourth Wall Productions; Color; HDCam; Rated R; 106 minutes; Release date: March 6, 2009. **CAST:** Peyton List (Mel), Cameron Goodman (Jules), Tony Curran (Driver), Cullen Douglas (Andy), Dave Power (Matt), James Snyder (Seth), Tom Kemp (Serene Man), Kaylan Tracey (Deaf Girl), Jen Alison Lewis (Mother of Deaf Girl), James Ryan (Young Doctor), Jackie Davis (Cashier), Roy Souza (Forklift Operator)

Peyton List in Shuttle © *Magnet*

NEW YORK CITY SERENADE (Archer Entertainment) Producer, Rachel Peters; Executive Producer, Rick Whealen; Director/Screenplay, Frank Whaley; Photography, Ryan Samul; Designer, Dara Wishingrad; Costumes, Virginia Cook; Music, Ed Harcourt; Editor, Miran Miosic; Dolby; Color; Rated R; 104 minutes; Release date: March 6, 2009. **CAST:** Freddie Prinze Jr. (Owen), Chris Klein (Ray), Jamie-Lynn Sigler (Lynn), Ben Schwartz (Russ), Christopher DeBlasio (Ben), Todd Barry (Smark), Kate Bayley (Condiments Girl), Emma Bell (Melinda), George Bryant II (Limo Driver), Heather Bucha (Mary), Alexnader Chaplin (Terry), Joanna Chilcoat, Missy O'Reilly (Girls), Chase Coleman (Jock #1), Raymond De Felitta (Chuck McGrady), Nada Despotovich (Miss Lormph), James Gale (Clerk), Diana Gettinger (Rachel), Nancy Jundi (Voice of Clerk), Paul Lazar (Festival Chairman), Elizabeth Lundberg (Katy), Johnnie Mae (Lois), Emma Nettleton (Karen), Sophie Nyweide (Francie), Kat Pogo (Waitress), Melissa Rocco (Frat Party Girl), Sebastian Roché (Noam Broder), Wallace Shawn (Himself), Jeff Skowron (Matt), Jarret Sumers (Gate Attendant), Marty Weisse (Bertrand), John Wernke (Four Seasons Waiter), Stefanie Zadravec (Stewardess)

REUNION (Talking Pictures Company) Producers, Petina Cole, Jonathan Gray, Matt Tauber; Director/Screenplay, Alan Hruska; Photography, Learan Kahanov; Music, Eric V. Hachikian; Editor, Peter C. Frank; Casting, Mary Gail Artz, Shani Ginsberg; Reunion Productions; Color; Not rated; 90 minutes; Release date: March 6, 2009. **CAST:** Derek Cecil (Stanley), Sam Coppola (Max), Brett Cullen (Jake), Alice Evans (Minerva), Jessica Hecht (Beth), Anna Khaja (Anna), Christopher McDonald (Eamon), Zoe McLellan (Averil), Josh Pais (Saul), Amy Pietz (Sadie), J. Santiago (Maintenance Man in Conference Room), Jamey Sheridan (Barnaby), Felix Solis (Pete), Cynthia Stevenson (Emily), David Thornton (Lloyd), Keyla Wood (Waitress), Damian Young (Farley)

PHOEBE IN WONDERLAND (ThinkFilm) Producers, Lynette Howell, Ben Barnz; Executive Producers, Doug Dey, Chris Finazzo; Director/Screenplay, Daniel Barnz; Photography, Bobby Bukowski; Designer, Therese DePrez; Costumes, Kurt & Bart; Music, Christophe Beck; Editor, Robert Hoffman; a Silverwood Films presentation, in association with Salty Features of a Silverwood Films/Lifetime Pictures production; Dolby; Widescreen; Color; Rated PG-13; 98 minutes; Release date: March 6, 2009. **CAST:** Felicity Huffman (Hillary Lichten), Elle Fanning (Phoebe Lichten), Patricia Clarkson (Miss Dodger), Bill Pullman (Peter Lichten), Campbell Scott (Principal Davis), Ian Colletti (Jamie), Mackenzie Milone (Sally), Austin Williams (Tommy), Tessa Albertson (Alice), Max Baker (2nd Teacher/King of Hearts), Maya N. Blake (Debby), Conor Carroll (Jeremy), Maddie Corman (1st Teacher/White Rabbit), Connor Douglas (Richie), Teala Dunn (Jenny), Peter Gerety (Dr. Miles/Humpty Dumpty), Tyler Hanes (Prince), Madhur Jaffrey (Miss Reiter), Cindy Joo (Sara), Danielle Kotch (2- and 3-year-old Phoebe), Gracie Lawrence (Julie), Bailee Madison (Olivia Lichten), Alicia Nakhjavan (Ellen/White Rabbit), April Yvette Thompson, Michael Nostrand (Colleagues), Marquis Rodriguez (Martin), Mirana Wilkins (Janet)

Elle Fanning in Phoebe in Wonderland *© ThinkFilm*

SEVERED WAYS: THE NORSE DISCOVERY OF AMERICA (Magnet) Producer/Director/Screenplay/Editor, Tony Stone; Executive Producers, Amy Hobby, David Raymond; Photography, Nathan Corbin, Damien Paris; Designers, Tony Stone, Bob Braine, Bill Stone; Costumes, Clare Amory, Ketuta Meshkavali, Peggy Waldman; Special Effects, Mark Bero; a Heathen Films presentation; Color; Widescreen; HD; Rated Not rated; 109 minutes; Release date: March 13, 2009. **CAST:** Fiore Tedesco (Volnard), Tony Stone (Orn), David Perry, Sean Dooley (Monks), Gaby Hoffmann (Orn's Wife), Noelle Bailey (Abenaki Woman), James Fuentes (Abenaki Man), Clare Amory (Volnard's Sister), Nathan Corbin (Viking Thrall)

Tony Stone in Severed Ways *© Magnet*

MISS MARCH (Fox Searchlight) Producers, Tom Jacobson, Steve J. Wolfe, Tobie Haggerty, Vincent Cirrincione; Executive Producers, Richard Rosenzweig, Jason Burns; Co-Producers, Monnie Wills, Scott G. Hyman; Directors/Screenplay, Zach Cregger, Trevor Moore; Story, Dennis Haggerty, Ryan Homchick, Thomas Mimms; Photography, Anthony B. Richmond; Designer, Cabot McMullen; Costumes, Sarah De Sa Rego, Alexis Scott; Music, Jeff Cardoni; Editor, Tim Mirkovich; Casting, Sheila Jaffe; a Fox Atomic presentation of a Jacobson Co./Alta Loma Entertainment production; Dolby; Deluxe color; Rated R; 89 minutes; Release date: March 13, 2009. **CAST:** Zach Cregger (Eugene Bell), Trevor Moore (Tucker Cleigh), Craig Robinson (Phil, Horsedick), Raquel Alessi (Cindi Whitehall), Molly Stanton (Candace), Cedric Yarbrough (Doctor), Hugh M. Hefner (Himself), Carla Jimenez (Nurse Juanita), Geoff Meed (Fireman Rick), Slade Austin Pearce (Young Eugene), Remy Thorne (Young Tucker), Tanjareen Martin (Crystal), Eve Mauro (Vonka), Alexis Raben (Katja), Windell Middlebrooks (Bouncer #1), Lindsay Schoneweis (Sheila), David Wells (Principal), Britten Kelley (Chevonne), Barry Sigismondi (Mr. Whitehall), Alex Donnelly (Mrs. Whitehall), Josh Fadem (Flava Flav Kid), Paul Rogan (Mr. Biederman), Kate Luyben (Mrs. Biederman), Seth Moss (Boss), Michael Busch (Employee), Ryan Kitley (Waiter), Anthony Jeselnik (Director), Niki J. Crawford (Janine), Deanie Ballard (Posse Member #1), Tory Gasaway [aka 40 Glocc] (Posse Member #2), Bonita Friedericy (Diner Waitress), Carrie Keagan, Shark Firestone, Sarah Jean Underwood, Quinton "Rampage" Jackson (Themselves), Jessica Vilchis, Lyndsay Haldorson (Sex Girls), Betsy Rue (Strawberrius), Madison Riley (Socialite), Da'Vone McDonald, Doc Newman (Guards), Brittany Buckner (Lorraine), Garrett Warren, Chris Durand, Chris Gann, Gary Wayton, Mike Massa, Brett A. Jones, Landon Ashworth, Bob Garrigus (Firemen), Corina Boettger (Gertrude), Melissa Ordway (Gorgeous)

Trevor Moore, Hugh M. Hefner, Zach Gregger in Miss March
© Fox Searchlight

CARMEN AND GEOFFREY (First Run Features) Producers/Directors/ Photography/Editors, Nick Doob, Linda Atkinson; a Three Wheel Productions presentation and production; Color; DigiBeta; Not rated; 79 minutes; Release date: March 13, 2009. Documentary on long-married dancers Carmen de Lavallade and Geoffrey Holder. **WITH:** Carmen de Lavallade, Geoffrey Holder, Boscoe Holder, Leo Holder, Gus Solomons Jr., Dudley Williams, Judith Jamison, Jennifer Dunning, Alvin Ailey

Carmen de Lavallade, Geoffrey Holder in Carmen and Geoffrey
© First Run Features

THE OBJECTIVE (IFC Films) Producers, Jeremy Wall, Zev Guber; Director, Daniel Myrick; Screenplay, Daniel Myrick, Mark A. Patton, Wesley Clark Jr.; Story, Daniel Myrick, Mark A. Patton; Photography, Stephanie Martin; Designer, Frank Bollinger; Costumes, Glenn Gregory Krah; Music, Kays Al-Atrakchi; Editors, Robert Florio, Michael J. Duthie; Casting, John Jackson; a Darclight Films presentation of a JAZ Films, Gearhead Pictures production; Color; Not

rated; 90 minutes; Release date: March 13, 2009. **CAST:** Jonas Ball (Benjamin Keynes), Matthew R. Anderson (Chief Warrant Officer Wally Hamer), Jon Huertas (Sgt. Vincent Degetau), Michael C. Williams (Sgt. Trinoski), Sam Hunter (Sgt. Tim Cole), Jeff Prewett (Sgt. Pete Sadler), Kenny Taylor (MSgt. Tanner), Chems-Eddine Zinoune (Abdul), Ozaibar Allal (Village Chief), Hammou Abaou (Abdul's Mother), Rikia Chkaroll (Village Woman in Burka), Ibtihal Iataren (Girl with the Woman), El Hayrani Lekbir (Hermit), P. David Miller (Maj. Matt McCarthy), Vanessa Johansson (Stacy Keynes), Jacqueline Harris (Matilde Seymour – BBC Reporter)

Jonas Ball in The Objective © IFC Films

THROW DOWN YOUR HEART (Argot) Producers, Bela Fleck, Sascha Paladino; Director, Sascha Paladino; Photography, Kirsten Johnson; Editors, Scott A. Burgess, Bela Fleck, Sascha Paladino; a FleckPaladino Films production; Color; HD; Not rated; 97 minutes; Release date: March 13, 2009. Documentary follows banjo player Bela Fleck as he journeys through four African countries. **WITH:** Bela Fleck, Oumou Sangare, Bassekou Kouyate

Bela Fleck in Throw Down Your Heart © Argot Pictures

BOB FUNK (Cinema Epoch) Producers, Keith Kjarval, Kurt Rauer, Tim Montijo; Executive Producer, Ben Ruffman; Director/Screenplay, Craig Carlisle; Photography, Lisa Wiegand; Designer, April Glover; Costumes, Vanessa King; Music, Tim Montijo; Editor, Josh Beal; Casting, Kathleen Black; a Unified Pictures presentation; Dolby; Widescreen; Deluxe color; Rated R; 108 minutes; Release date: March 20, 2009. **CAST:** Michael Leydon Campbell (Bob Funk),

Rachael Leigh Cook (Ms. Thorne), Grace Zabriskie (Mrs. Funk), Amy Ryan (Ms. Wright), Eddie Jemison (Ron Funk), Stephen Root (Steve), Alex Désert (Sonny), Ron Canada (Smiley), Lucy Davis (Janet), Nadia Dajani (Jean), Terri Mann (Dr. Day), Robert John Brewer (Brewer), Jules Bruff (Ms. Agnew), Christina Elizabeth Cavallero (Gretel), Patty Cornell (Ms. Long), Shelly Desai (Sanjay), Tyne Firmin (Mr. Got-Rocks), Nancy Guerriero (Steve's Mom), Tania Gunadi (Connie), Tommy Hinkley (Over-Eaters Anonymous Guy), Shaun Majumder (Raymundo), Dan Martin (Mark), Anne-Marie Pritchett (Ms. Berman), Sonya Rokes (Laura), Romy Rosemont (Ruthie), Jack Story (Knight #1), Khleo Thomas (Cupcake), Tommy Wilson-O'Brien (Mr. Mann)

PERESTROIKA (REF Productions) Producers, Nina V. Kerova, Slava Tsukerman; Executive Producer, Robert Field; Director/Screenplay, Slava Tsukerman; Photography, Mikhail Iskandarov; Designer, Mikhail Rubtsov; Costumes, Mimi Maxman, Tatiana Vdovina; Music, Alexander Zhurbin; Editor, Arnold Schlisser; Color; Not rated; 116 minutes; Release date: March 20, 2009. **CAST:** F. Murray Abraham (Prof. Gross), Maria Andreeva (Elena), Sam Robards (Sasha), Jicky Schnee (Jill), Ally Sheedy (Helen), Oksana Stashenko (Natasha)

SKILLS LIKE THIS (Shadow Distribution) Producers, Donna Dewey, Tim Gray, Brian D. Phelan, Paul Aaron, Rock Obenchain; Executive Producer, Greg Camalier; Director, Monty Miranda; Screenplay, Spencer Berger; Story, Spencer Berger, Gabriel Tigerman; Photography, Robert F. Smith; Designer, Pamela Chavez; Costumes, Mimi Kaupe; Music, Andy Monley; Music Supervisor, Shawn Smos; Editor, Rock Obenchain; Casting, Corbin Bronson, Annie Hamilton; a Dewey-Obenchain Films production in association with Suntaur Entertainment; Dolby; Color; Super 16-to-HD-to-35mm; Not rated; 86 minutes; Release date: March 20, 2009. **CAST:** Spencer Berger (Max), Brian D. Phelan (Tommy), Gabriel Tigerman (Dave), Kerry Knuppe (Lucy), Jennifer Batter (Lauren), Ned Bellamy (Uncle Morris), Marta Martin (Rosa), Zach Cumer (Cousin Jeramiah), Paige Black (Girl on Bridge), Tupper Cullum (Englehard), Donna Dewey (TV Reporter), Amy Rose Drucker (Nurse), Patty Figel (Max's Grandma Uta), Quintin Gamer (Hall Pass Kid), Chris Grundy (Man with Nice Suit), Travis Kellog (Clerk in 24-Hour Store), Rev. Leon Kelly (Leon), Jeremy Make (Rusty), David Mijares (Kid in 24-Hour Store), John Nance (Mr. Levar), Ry Feder Pruett (Late Kid), Paul Rohrer (Grandiose Actor), Marian Rothschild (Max's Mom), Matthew D. Sheahan (Sheingold), Harry Sterling (Grandpa Abe), Daniell Taff (Gonzalo), Roslyn D. Washington (God-fearing Woman in Bank), Marcus Waterman (Mr. Nam)

SUPER CAPERS (Roadside Attractions) Producers, Ray Griggs, Reuben Lim; Executive Producer, Michael Kim Binder; Director/Screenplay, Ray Griggs; Photography, Martin Rosenberg; Designer, Scott Enge; Costumes, Francine Lecoultre; Music, Nathan Lanier; Editor, Stacy Katzman; Casting, Joe Lorenzo; an RG Entertainment, Ltd. presentation; Dolby; Color; Rated PG; 98 minutes; Release date: March 20, 2009. **CAST:** Justin Whalin (Ed Gruberman), Michael Rooker (The Dark Winged Vesper), Ryan McPartlin (Will Powers), Sam Lloyd (Herman Brainard), Danielle Harris (Felicia Freeze), Ray Griggs (Puffer Boy), Christine Lakin (Red), Jon Polito (Captain Sludge), Adam West (Cab Driver), June Lockhart (Mother), Doug Jones (Agent Smith #1), Clint Howard (Mugger), Tom Sizemore (Roger Cheatem), Steve Braun (Agent Guard), Paul Terrell Clayton (Police Officer #1), Pat Crawford Brown (Gertrude), Bobby "Slim" Jones (Cretan), Tommy "Tiny" Lister (Sarge), Beverly Long (Marge), Pancho Moler (Robo), Oliver Muirhead (Herbert Q), Taylor Negron (Chauffer), Chris Owen (Igniter Boy), Eva Pigford (News Reporter), Isaac C. Singleton Jr. (Agent Smith #2), Aaron Skinner (Police Officer in Alley), Camille Solari (Lady in Distress), George Stults (Police Officer #2)

Clint Howard in Super Capers © *Roadside Attractions*

WE PEDAL UPHILL (Cinevolve Studios) Producer, Darren Chilton; Executive Producer, John R. Tilley; Director/Screenplay/Music, Roland Tec; Photography, Boris Grygor, Kathleen Mann; Editor, Agnes Challe-Grandits; a Pinkplot presentation, in association with Rosie Little Pictures, of a Spade-a-Spade production; Color; HD; Not rated; 111 minutes; Release date: March 20, 2009. **CAST:** Polly Adams (Nancy), Jenny Bacon (Phyl), Judith Barcroft (Constance), Stephen Bienskie (Steph), Ian Blackman (Lewis), Kate Blumberg (Daryl), Tom Bozell (Jimmy), Peter Bubriski (Smith), Marylouise Burke (Linda), Cori Lynn Campbell (Deanna), Sandi Carroll (Angie), Ellen Colton (Esther), Nat DeWolf (Ben), David Drake (Andy), Marissa Danielle Duricko (Monica), Alvin Epstein (Mortimer), Bruce Faulk (Mark), Maureen Keiller (Rita), John Magaro (Kyle), Peggy Ann O'Neal (Bored Tourist), Paul Outlaw (Whitman), Carl Palmer (Al), Rick Park (Kelly), Charles Parnell (Horton), Nicholas Pelczar (Derek), Merle Perkins (Sonya), Molly Powell (Sandi), Molly Purves (Lucy), Robert Saoud (Jones), Cherlyn Schaefer (Santa Fe Tourist), J. Tucker Smith (Mather), Roland Tec (Joel), Stephen Barker Turner (Oliver), Matt Walton (Anthony), Kate Weiman (June)

THE NEW TWENTY (Argot Pictures) Producers, Aina Abiodun, Chris Mason Johnson; Executive Producers, Laura Heberton, Colin Stewart; Director, Chris Mason Johnson; Screenplay, Ishmael Chawla, Chris Mason Johnson; Photography, David Tumblety; Designer, Gregory Kenney; Costumes, Anne Kenney; Music, Jeff Toyne; Editors, Todd Holmes, Adam Raponi; Casting, Stephen Vincent, Sig De Miguel; a Serious Productions presentation; DuArt Color; Not rated; 91 minutes; Release date: March 20, 2009. **CAST:** Bill Sage (Robert Cameron), Terry Serpico (Louie Kennick), Nicole Bilderback (Julie Kim), Colin Fickes (Ben Barr), Andrew Wei Lin (Tony Kim), Ryan Locke (Andrew Hatch), Thomas Sadoski (Felix Canavan), Cordelia Reynolds (Lucy), Karen Olivo (Bethany), Heather Litteer (Nadia), Larisa Polonsky (Vera), Bridget Moloney (Samantha), Michael Sirow (Matt), Ryan Templeton (Drunk Girl), Jessalyn Wanlim (Amy), Matt Kerr (Cheesy Guy), Scott DuQuette (Running Boy), Jenna Laurenzo (Runnig Girl), Larry Pine (Old Cowboy), Nikki E. Walker (Paramedic), Matt Wilkus (Cruisy Guy)

Andrew Wei Lin, Bill Sage in The New Twenty © *Argot Pictures*

STEAM (Tavix/Fencesitter) Producers, Lisa Basson, Kenneth Martin, Kyle Schickner, Sam Jones; Director/Screenplay, Kyle Schickner; Photography, David Takashi Oye; Designer, Beth Mickle; Costumes, Charlotte Kruse; Music, Damian Montano; Editors, Thom Obarski, Christopher Gosch; Color; HD; Not rated; 118 minutes; Release date: March 20, 2009. **CAST:** Ruby Dee (Doris), Ally Sheedy (Laurie), Kate Siegel (Elizabeth), Reshma Shetty (Niala), Dick Anthony Williams (August), Alan Ritchson (Roy), Zach Mills (TJ), Maxine Bahns (Susan), Charles Robinson (Rev. Patterson), Lane Davies (Frank), Joanne Baron (Diane), Chelsea Handler (Jacky), Alain Van Beaux (Drunken Undercover Cop), Alex Boling (Reba), Camila Borrero (Gena), Ron Bottitta (Tom), Cylk Cozart (William), Jordan Eubanks (Football Husband), Laurence Gates (Parishioner), Jason Hastings (Jason), Hazz Noble, Jose Hernandez Jr. (Customers), Ernestine Jackson (Alice), Sandrine Marlier (Debbie), Lynne Matthew (Brenda), Nicole Montano (Sexually Harassed Woman), Richard Tanner (Professor #1), Andrea Walker (Abused Woman), Angela Watson (Singer), DeWanda Wise (Lynn), Carol Woods (Ella)

SPINNING INTO BUTTER (Screen Media Films) Producers, Ryan Howe, Norman Twina, Lou Pitt; Executive Producers, Mark Davis, Roger Howe, Tom Wilson, Nicolas Stiliadis; Director, Mark Brokaw; Screenplay, Rebecca Gilman, Doug Atchison; based on the play by Rebecca Gilman; Photography, John Thomas; Designer, Michael Shaw; Costumes, Laura Cunningham; Music, David Van Tieghem; Editor, Suzy Elmiger; Casting, Daniel Swee; a Whitsett Hill Films presentation of a Norman Twain/Lou Pitt production; Dolby; Color; Rated R; 86 minutes; Release date: March 27, 2009. **CAST:** Sarah Jessica Parker (Sarah Daniels), Mykelti Williamson (Aaron Carmichael), Beau Bridges (Burton Strauss), Miranda Richardson (Catherine Kenney), James Rebhorn (Winston Garvey), Victor Rasuk (Patrick Chibas), Paul James (Simon Brick), Michelle Beck (Sasha), Betsy Beutler (Lee), Sophia Chang (Misako), Jimonn Cole (Tyler Hogan), Genevieve Elam (Rita Chambers), Peter Friedman (Jay Salter), Christopher Michael Gerrard (Matthew), Enver Gjokaj (Greg), Daniel Eric Gold (Nathan Glazer), Rusty Gray (Prof. Shawn), Joel Johnstone (Eric Aller), Amelia Kallman (Jana), Emma Myles (Anika), Linda Powell (Ellen Jenkins), Jennifer Rapp (Lori), Richard Riehle (Campus Security Guard), Derek Simmons (Bumper), Jake M. Smith (Jason Thorn), Zach Wegner (Deadhead), DeWanda Wise (Claudia Thompson), Philip Adkins (College Student Being Interviewed), Margaret Baker (Anika's Friend), Joseph DeBona (Photographer), Kevin Momenee (Jock), Maggie Moore (Bartender), Josh Roseberry (Hooded Thug)

Sarah Jessica Parker in Spinning into Butter *© Screen Media*

AMERICAN SWING (Magnolia) Producers, Mathew Kaufman, Jon Hart, Gretchen McGowan, Christian Hoagland; Directors/Screenplay, Mathew Kaufman, Jon Hart; Based on an article by Jon Hart; Photography, Christian Hoagland; Music, Jim Coleman; Editor, Keith Reamer; an HDNet presentation of a Zip Dog production; Color; HD; Not rated; 81 minutes; Release date: March 27, 2009. Documentary on Plato's Retreat, the Manhattan-based sex club of the late 1970s/ early '80s. **WITH:** Helen Gurley Brown, Professor Irwin Corey, Betty Dodson, Dan Dorman, Donna Ferrato, Jamie Gillis, Al Goldstein, Dian Hanson, Buck Henry, Ron Jeremy, Ed Koch, John Leo, Fred J. Lincoln, Melvin Van Peebles, Howard Smith, Annie Sprinkle

American Swing *© Magnolia Pictures*

12 ROUNDS (20th Century Fox) Producers, Mark Gordon, Josh McLaughlin, Michael Lake; Executive Producer, Becki Cross Trujillo; Director, Renny Harlin; Screenplay, Daniel Kunka; Photography, David Boyd; Designer, Nicholas Lundy; Costumes, Jill Newell; Music, Trevor Rabin; Editor, Brian Berdan; Visual Effects Supervisor, Raymond McIntyre Jr.; Stunts, Steven Ritzi; Casting, John Papsidera; a Fox Atomic presentation, in association with WWE Studios of a Mark Gordon Co. production; Dolby; Panavision; Color; Rated PG-13; 108 minutes; Release date: March 27, 2009. **CAST:** John Cena (Danny Fisher), Aidan Gillen (Miles Jackson), Ashley Scott (Molly Porter), Steve Harris (George Aiken), Brian White (Hank Carver), Gonzalo Menendez (Ray Santiago), Taylor Cole (Erica Kessen), Kyle Clements (Dave Fisher), Peter Navy Tuiasosopo (Willie Dumaine), Travis Davis (Anthony Deluso), Nick Gomez (Samuel), Brian Stanton (FBI Agent Gator), Rosalind Rubin (FBI Agent Sheila), Billy Slaughter (Technician), Kim Collins (Phil the Plumber), Lara Grice (Cell Store Owner), Wayne Ferrara (Battallion Commander), Douglas M. Griffin (Peter Gerard), Vincent Flood (Det. Chuck Jansen), Robert Pralgo (Camoflague Agent), Wally Crowder (Streetcar Conductor), Luke Albright (Johnny "Tube Sock" Jenkins), Bryan Johnson (Sleeping Streetcar Passenger), Lukas Harlin (Streetcar Kid), John Wilmot (Elderly Man), Louis Herthum (BEP Employee), David Frye (Officer Phelps), Bill Martin Williams (Ferry Patrolman), J. Omar Castro (FBI Agent), Brandi Coleman (Pedestrian), Roy Huang (Sharpshooter), Mikki Val (Nurse), Jada K. Cox (Jesse Lou Mackie), Pauline Boudreaux (Medic), Hunter Burke (Hot Tub Man), Danie Coleman (Hot Tub Woman)

John Cena in 12 Rounds *© Twentieth Century Fox*

THE PERFECT SLEEP (Cinema Epoch) Producers, Jeremy Alter, Keith Kjarval, Anton Pardoe; Executive Producer, Jay Sedrish; Director, Jeremy Alter; Screenplay, Anton Pardue; Photography, Charles Papert; Designer, Clayton Hartley; Costumes, Kristen Anacker; Music, Dave Vanian; Editor, Martin Hunter; a United Pictures production; Color; Rated R; 105 minutes; Release date: March 27, 2009. **CAST:** Anton Pardoe (The Narrator), Roselyn Sanchez (Porphyria), Patrick Bauchau (Nikolai), Peter J. Lucas (Ivan), Tony Amendola (Dr. Sebastian), Sam Thakur (The Rajah), Dominique Vandenberg (Keller), Cameron Daddo (Rogozhin), Michael Paré (Officer Pavlovich), Isaac C. Singleton Jr. (Gregor), John Fleck (Van Heflin), Dmitri S. Boudrine (Kolya), Anthony Dee (Walter), Keith Allan (The Doctor), Pasha Lynchnikoff (Vassily), Daniel Goddard (Sergei), Scarlett Chorvat (Tatiana), Frank Bruynbroek (Young Nikolai), Stefan Pardoe (Ganya), Scout Alter (Young Narrator), Denyse Tontz (Young Porphyria), Amanda Gallo (Femme Fatale), Tristan Thomas (Young Ivan), Franc Ross (Generator Repairman), Amy Jo Traicoff (Dr. Sylvia), Jeremy Batiste (Guard), Damion Poitier (Ganyov)

GUEST OF CINDY SHERMAN (Trela Media) Producers, Paul H-O, Tom Donahue, Anura Idupaganti; Co-Producer, Christopher Trela; Directors, Paul H-O, Tom Donahue; Photography, Dane Lawing; Music, Leigh Roberts; Editor, Tom Donahue; a Filmlike presentation in association with Sundance Channel; Color; Mini-DV; Hi-8 Video, DV; Not rated; 88 minutes; Release date: March 27, 2009. Documentary on how Paul H-O, a host of a cable access show, hooked up with influential 1980s artist Cindy Sherman. **WITH:** Paul H-O, Cindy Sherman, Eric Bogosian, Eli Broad, Bronwyn Carlton, Danny DeVito, Eric Fischl, David Furnish, Gaby Hoffmann, Kelly Jones, Carol Kane, Robert Longo, Molly Ringwald, Ingrid Sischy, Roberta Smith, Christopher Trela, Christine Vachon, John Waters

Paul H-O, Cindy Sherman in Guest of Cindy Sherman © Trela Media

THE CROSS (Gener8xion Entertainment) Producers, Matthew Crouch, Laurie Crouch, Richard J. Cook, Stephan Blinn; Executive Producer, Jack Hunter; Director, Matthew Crouch; Screenplay/Editor, Stephan Blinn; Photography, Caylan Crouch, Cody Crouch, Stephan Blinn, Truett Hancock, Pete Sanchez; Music, Matthew R. Long; Color/Black and white; Widescreen; Rated PG; 92 minutes; Release date: March 27, 2009. Documentary on Arthur Blessitt's 40-year trek throughout the world, carrying a cross and dispensing prayers. **WITH:** Arthur Blesitt

ENLIGHTEN UP! (Balcony) Producer/Director, Kate Churchill; Executive Producers, Jeanne Hagerty, Tom Hagerty; Screenplay, Kate Churchill, Jonathon Hexner; Story, Kate Churchill, Jonathon Hexner, Khari Streeter; Music, Krishna Vankatesh; Editors, Khari Streeter, Jonathan Sahula; a Tuka Productions/Nama Productions production; Color; Not rated; 82 minutes; Release date: April 1, 2009. Documentary on journalist Nick Rosen's conversion from skeptic to yoga enthusiast. **WITH:** Nick Rosen, B.K.S. Iyengar, Pattabhi Jois, Norman Allen, Sharon Gannon, David Life, Dharma Mittra, Diamond Dallas Page, Sharath Rangaswamy, Madan Kataria, Rodney Yee, Cindi Lee, Gurmukh Kaur Khalsa, Alan Finger, Baron Baptiste, Beryl Bender Birch, Natasha Rizopoulos

Nick Rosen in Enlighten Up! © Balcony Releasing

C ME DANCE (Wins Distribution) Producers, Greg Robbins, Laura Romeo; Executive Producers, Georgann Miller, Roy Miller; Director/Screenplay, Greg Robbins; Photography, Robert J. Sommer; Designers, Bolle Movmon, Babs Himelfarb; Music, Stephen Tammearu; Choreographer, Tara Drew; an Uplifting Entertainment production; Color; Rated PG; 89 minutes; Release date: April 3, 2009. **CAST:** Christina DeMarco (Sheri), Greg Robbins (Vince), Laura Romeo (Dr. Beth Crowl), Hugh McLean (Pastor Jeff), Lesley Bowen (Miss Tucker), Peter Kent (The Devil), Samantha Sham (Ally), Lauren Bayer (Claire), Joe Pawlenko (Jacob), Randy Oliva (Ally's Dad), Scott Kerschbaumer (Pastor Tony), Katrina Miller (Rebecca), Arnold Zegarelli (Client), Eddie Mekka (Lowell), Kelly Sham (Nora), Tracy Paris (Jacob's Mom), Nelson Scott Simpson (Biker), Aline McAdams (Sheri's Mom), Gary Crain (Ralph), Richard Keith, Michael Brenner (TV Executives), Betty Rainier (TV Receptionist), B.J. Tench, Travis Trotter (Bullies), David Kosor (Director), Emilio Cornacchione (Hair Person), Terri Bercelli (Film Person), Kim Hosilyk (Stage Hand), Ryan Davis Locke (Young Vince), Jordan Kocott (Young Sheri), Carol Ertel (Transient), Tamyka Artist (News Reporter), Shauna Robbins (Stage Manager)

LIFELINES (Kanbar Entertainment) formerly *Wherever You Are*; Producer/Director/Screenplay, Rob Margolies; Executive Producers, Robert Fagenson, Andrew Margolies; Photography, David Sperling; Designer, Leah MacLeod; Music, Robert Miller; Editor, Jason Stewart; a Different Duck Films production; Color; HD; Not rated; 95 minutes; Release date: April 3, 2009. **CAST:** Jane Adams (Nancy Bernstein), Josh Pais (Ira Bernstein), Joe Morton (Dr. Livingston), Robbie Sublett (Michael Bernstein), Dreama Walker (Meghan Bernstein), Jacob Kogan (Spencer Bernstein), Ben Levin (Chris), Susan Molloy (Jenn, Waitress), Edloe Blackwell (Debra Livingston), Andre Ward (Arthur Livingston), Keith Herron (Pat Hennessey), Sandra Elizabeth Rodriguez (Corrine), Robin Madel (Mother in Restaurant), Fallon Mulerman (Hostess in Restaurant), Alyse Mandel (Manager in Restaurant), Damian Baldet (Waiter in Restaurant), Elizabeth Laime, Ryan Elizabeth Walsh (Waitresses in Restaurant), Alex Roberts (Little Boy in Restaurant), Felipe Santos, William Ramirez (Gardeners)

IN A DREAM (IndiePix/Intl. Film Circuit) Producer, Jeremy Yaches; Executive Producers, Ross Kauffman, Geralyn White Dreyfuss, Pamela Tanner Boll; Director, Jeremiah Zagar; Photography, Erik Messerschmidt; Designers/Animators, Cassidy Gearhart, Yussef Cole; Music, Kelli Scarr; Editors, Keiko Deguchi, Jeremiah Zagar; a Herzliya Films presentation in association with Red Light Films; Color; HD; Not rated; 78 minutes; Release date: April 10, 2009. Documentary on eccentric Philadelphia artist Isaiah Zagar. **WITH:** Isaiah Zagar, Julia Zagar, Ezekiel Zagar, Jeremiah Zagar

Isaiah Zagar in In a Dream © *IndiePix*

ROYAL KILL (21ˢᵗ Century Film Production) Director/Screenplay, Babar Ahmed; Photography, Jonathan Belinski; Designer, Brian Rzepka; Music, Kenneth Lampl; Editor, J.D. Beales; Color; Rated PG-13; 90 minutes; Release date: April 10, 2009. **CAST:** Pat Morita (Exhibition Manager), Eric Roberts (Dad), Lalaine (Jan), Alexander Wraith (Adam Arthavan), Gail Kim (Assassin), Jeannie Crist (Royal Maid), Nicole Brown (Andrea), Darren Kendrick (Neighbor), Jimmy Yang, J. Douglas (Cops), Nafees Ahmed (Mehreen Abassi)

AN UNLIKELY WEAPON (Morgan Cooper Productions) Producer/Director, Susan Morgan Cooper; Co-Producer, Cindy Lou Adkins; Photography, Isaac Hagy; Music, Kyle Eastwood, Michael Stevens; Editors, Isaac Hagy, James Mitchell; Narrator, Kiefer Sutherland; Dolby; Color/Black and white; Not rated; 85 minutes; Release date: April 10, 2009. Documentary on photographer Eddie Adams, the man responsible for the iconic picture of a Vietcong prisoner being shot through the head. **WITH:** Eddie Adams, Marc Anthony, Peter Arnett, Tom Brokaw, Bill Clinton, Bill Eppridge, Peter Jennings, Kerry Kennedy, David Hume Kennedy, Gordon Parks, Thi Kim Phuc Phan, Morley Safer, Tracey Ullman

THE GOLDEN BOYS (Roadside Attractions) Producer, Michael Mailer; Director/Screenplay, Daniel Adams; Based on the novel *Cap'n Eri* by Joseph C. Lincoln; Photography, Phillip D. Schwartz; Designer, David Allen; Costumes, Deborah Newhall; Music, Jonathan Edwards; Editors, Stan Cole, Susan Graef; Casting, Carolyn Pickman; Dolby; Color; Rated PG; 97 minutes; Release date: April 17, 2009. **CAST:** David Carradine (Capt. Zebulon Hedge), Rip Torn (Capt. Jeremiah Burgess), Bruce Dern (Capt. Perez Ryder), Mariel Hemingway (Martha Snow), Charles Durning (John Bartlett), John Savage (Web Saunders), Angelica Torn (Melissa Busteed), Christy Scott Cashman (Elizabeth Preston), Jason Alan Smith (Ralph Hazeltine), Julie Harris (Melodeon Player), Stephen Mailer (Squealer Wixon), Lila Dupree (Pasha Norris), Jonathan Edwards (Rev. Perly), Donald Foley (Bluey Batchelder), Peter Jordan (Ezekial), Stephen Russell (Luther Norris), Roger Dillingham Jr., Lauri Kriva (Townspeople)

Rip Torn, Bruce Dern, David Carradine in The Golden Boys
© *Roadside Attractions*

CRANK: HIGH VOLTAGE (Lionsgate) Producers, Tom Rosenberg, Gary Lucchesi, Richard Wright, Skip Williamson; Executive Producers, Mark Neveldine, Brian Taylor, David Scott Rubin, Eric Reid, Michael Paseornek, Peter Block, Michael Davis, James McQuaide; Directors/Screenplay, Mark Neveldine, Brian Taylor; Photography, Brandon Trost; Designer, Jerry Fleming; Costumes, Dayna Pink; Music, Mike Patton; Music Supervisors, Brian McNelis, Eric Craig; Editor, Fernando Villena; Stunts, Jason Rodriguez; Casting, Kelly Martin Wagner; a Lakeshore Entertainment presentation and production, in association with Radical Media; Dolby; Deluxe color; HD-to-35mm; Rated R; 96 minutes; Release date: April 17, 2009. **CAST:** Jason Statham (Chev Chelios), Amy Smart (Eve), Dwight Yoakam (Doc Miles), Efren Ramirez (Venus), Julanne Chidi Hill (Dark Chocolate), Reno Wilson (Orlando), Keone Young (Don Kim), Art Hsu (Johnny Vang), Joseph Julian Soria (Chico), Bai Ling (Ria), Clifton Collins Jr. (El Huron),David Carradine (Poon Dong), Corey Haim (Randy), Geri Halliwell (Karen Chelois), Billy Unger (Young Chev), Jamie Harris (Talk Show Host), John de Lancie (Fish Halman), Ho-Kwan Tse, Galen Yuen (Chinese Doctors), Shu Lan Tuan (Asian Nurse), Setu Taase (Shot Gun Triad), Henry Hayashi (Long Beach Nose Punch Triad), Najja Meeks (Sierra), Annie Girard (Nevada), Yeva-Genevieve Lavlinski (Pepper), David Rolas (Low Rider #1), Moses Romero (Latino Teen), Dewey Kim (Young Asian Dude), Portis Hershey (Cypress Triad Hood #1), Atticus Todd (Cypress Fat Chinese Guy), Peter Mark (Los Vatos Punk), Chad Damiani (Strip Please Cop #1), Jai Stefan, Tom Roach (Donut Cops), Maynard James Keenan, Danny Lohner (Dog Walkers), Chester Bennington (Hollywood Park Guy), Danna Hansen (Glenda Lansing), Ted Garcia (Ted), Cherinda Kincherlow (La Precious), Billy Gillespie (Inglewood Cop), Samuel Hubinette (Ambulance Driver), Michael Weston, Dan Callahan (Paramedics), Lloyd Kaufman (Maintenance Guy #1), Joe Reitman (Detective), Lexington Steel (Striking Actor), Monique Alexander, Nick Manning, Jennifer Corrales, Kate Mulligan, Ron Jeremy Hyatt, Ed Powers, Larry David Eudene (Porn Stars), Reid Harper (Classmate), David Scott Rubin (Teacher), Mandy Amano (The Yoga Girl), Jay Xcala (Alex Verona)

Jason Statham, Corey Haim in Crank: High Voltage © *Lionsgate*

SLEEP DEALER (Maya Entertainment) Producer, Anthony Bregman; Executive Producers, Guy Naggar, Peter Klimt; Director/Editor, Alex Rivera; Screenplay, Alex Rivera, David Riker; Photography, Lisa Rinzler; Designer, Miguel Angel Alvarez; Costumes, Adela Cortazar; Music, tomandandy (Tom Hajdu and Andy Milburn); Music Supervisor, Lynn Fainchtein; Visual Effects Supervisor, Mark Russell; a Starlight Film Financing presentation of a Likely Story production; Dolby; Color; HD; Rated PG-13; 89 minutes; Release date: April 17, 2009. **CAST:** Leonor Varela (Luz Martinez), Jacob Vargas (Rudy), Luis Fernando Peña (Memo), Emilio Guerrero (Ricky), Marius Biegai (Camera Man), Jake Koenig (Foreman), Ursula Tania (Prostitute)

Luis Fernando Peña, Leonor Varela in Sleep Dealer © Maya Entertainment

The Garden © Oscilloscope

TREELESS MOUNTAIN (Oscilloscope) Producers, Bradley Rust Gray, Ben Howe, Lars Knudsen, Jay Van Hoy, So Yong Kim; Executive Producers, Ian McGloin, Jamie Mai, Charlie Ledley; Director/Screenplay, So Yong Kim; Photography, Anne Misawa; Designer, See Hee Kim; Music, Asobi Seksu; Editors, So Yong Kim, Bradley Rust Gray; a Soandbrad/Parts and Labor production, in association with Strange Loop; American-South Korean; Dolby; Technicolor; Super 16-to-35mm; Not rated; 89 minutes; Release date: April 22, 2009. **CAST:** Hee Yeon Kim (Jin), Song Hee Kim (Bin), Soo Ah Lee (Mom), Mi Hyang Kim (Big Aunt), Boon Tak Park (Grandma)

NURSERY UNIVERSITY (Argyle Productions) Producers, Marc H. Simon, Matthew Makar; Director/Screenplay, Marc H. Simon; Co-Director, Matthew Makar; Photography, Samuel Henriques, Bob Richman; Music, Chris Hajian; Music Supervisor, Jim Black; Editors, Miki Watanabe Milmore, Tom Patterson; Presented in association with Elementary Films; Color; HD; Not rated; 90 minutes; Release date: April 24, 2009. Documentary on the competitive desire of some rich Manhattanites to get their children into the best pre-schools. **WITH:** Wyatt Kapadia, Sneha Kapadia, Layla Kapadia, Roderick Moon, Heidi Moon, Jackson Moon, Aleta St. James, Tony Pratofiorito, Cynthia Pratofiorito, Juliana Pratofiorito, Kim Ashton, Kris Ragoonath, Gabriella Rowe

JAZZ IN THE DIAMOND DISTRICT (Truly Indie) Producers, Erica Chamblee, Lindsey Christian; Executive Producers, Alphonso A. Christian, Michaele Chamblee Christian, Peggy Cooper Cafritz; Director, Lindsey Christian; Screenplay, Lindsey Christian, Sia Tiambi Barnes; Story, Eric Chamblee; Photography, Christopher T.J. McGuire; Designer, Hiroshi Matsuko; Costumes, Olani Jones; Music, Carl "Chucky" Thompson; Music Supervisor, Bryan Walsh; Choreographer, Neil Whitehead; Editors, Terry Dawson, Daniel Rezende; a Soblu production; Color; HD; Rated R; 79 minutes; Release date: April 24, 2009. **CAST:** Monique Cameron (Jasmine "Jazz" Morgan), Wood Harris (Gabriel Marx), Erica Chamblee (Leah Morgan), Andre Strong (Flight), Olani Jones (Sara Brooks), Clifton Powell (Blair Morgan), Ruth Chamblee-Lee (Willow Morgan), Michael Bailey (Mike), Elisha Efua Bartels (Donna Jones), Eric Brooks (Patron), Kenny Burns (Bo), William Chambers (Bartender), Cameron Chamblee-Lee (Young Jazz), Marcus Clark (DLB Percussion Player), Molyneau DuBelle (Nightclub Dancer), Mikal Evans (Nurse), Keanna Faircloth (Girl in the Brown Dress), Carl Gray (Mr. Reed), Charles Hairston (Mr. Otis), Robert Lee Hardy (Malik), Marcus Heath (DLB Keyboard Player), Kirk Jennings (Malik's Friend), Shantice Jones, Stephanie Norwood (Dancers), Kawan Karadaghi (Club Patron), Eric Mann (Easy), Terrence Mann (Friend at Cookout), Joshua Moody (Easy's Friend), Roger Payano (Coke), Perrin Radley, Laurel Radley (Selection Committee Members), Jennifer Ray (Shayla), Edward Robinson (Man on the Street), Robert Stevens (Victim's Friend), Antonio Woods (Jack), Amber Yates (Anoterh Girl), Rashad Young (DLB Bass Player)

Hee Yeon Kim, Song Hee Kim in Treeless Mountain © Oscilloscope

THE GARDEN (Oscilloscope) Producer/Director/Photography, Scott Hamilton Kennedy; Executive Producers, Julie Bergman Sender, Stuart Sender; Music, Gabriel Tenorio, Doug DeAngelis; Editors, Alex Blatt, Tyson Fitzgerald, Scott Hamilton Kennedy; a Black Valley Films production in association with Katahdin Productions; Stereo; Color; DV; Not rated; 79 minutes; Release date: April 24, 2009. Documentary on the conflicts that have arisen over South Central Los Angeles' Community Garden at 41st Street and Alameda. **WITH:** Rufina Juarez, Tezozomoc, Josefina Medina, "Don" Eddie Luvianos Rumbos, Deacon Alexander, Miguel Perez, Jan Perry, Juanita Tate, Dan Stormer, Ron Kaye, Larry Frank, Doris Bloch, Antonio Villaraigosa, Daryl Hannah, John Quigley, Joan Baez, Dennis Kucinich, Maxine Waters, Zak de la Rocha, Danny Glover

BABY ON BOARD (Angry Monkey Entertainment) Producers, Russell Scalise, Emilio Ferrari; Director, Brian Herzlinger; Screenplay, Russell Scalise, Michael Hamilton-Wright; Photography, Denis Maloney; Designer, Lisa Wolff; Costumes, Emma Potter; Music, Teddy Castellucci; Editor, Ross Albert; Casting, Louis DiGiaimo; an A Plus Entertainment, Big Shot Productions presentation; Color; Rated R; 95 minutes; Release date: April 24, 2009. **CAST:** Heather Graham (Angela), Jerry O'Connell (Curtis), John Corbett (Danny), Lara Flynn Boyle (Mary), Katie Finneran (Sylvia), Brian Sills (Ralphy), Anthony Starke (Dr. Robert Taylor), Heather

Prete (Mrs. Jenkins), John Turk (Chauffeur), Jessica Zorn (Meghan), Jaiden Hidalgo (Ryan), Kirk Anderson (Mr. Rhohe), Peggy Roeder (Ella), Bob Weagant (Morris Jenkins), Keith Uchima (Mr. Namashuto), Sherry Shaoling (Candy), Pam Levin (Ms. Black), Cindy Chang (Madame Kang), Alana Arenas (Nurse), Joe Yau (Japanese Businessman), Jeff Sassinsky (Curtis' Assistant), Wendye Clarendon (Lamaze Teacher), Thomas Gaitsch (TV Anchorman), Nevena Milicevic (Hot Girl), Matt DeCaro (Judge), Kevin Gudahl (Opposing Lawyer), Carla Abruzzo (Stripper), Caroline Boneham (Clerk), John T. Zinn (Elevator Man), Jay Black (Tunnel Man), Ithamar Enriquez (Stranger), Magdalena Schpider (Russian Girl), Jessica Stramer (Five-year-old Girl), Noah Grey (Baby)

THE SKEPTIC (IFC Films) Producers, Tennyson Bardwell, Isen Robbins, Aimee Schoff, Mary-Beth Taylor; Director/Screenplay, Tennyson Bardwell; Photography, Claudio Rocha; Designer, Susan Block; Costumes, Sarah Beers; Music, Brett Rosenberg; Editor, Ann Marie Lizzi; Casting, Christine Sheaks; Color; Not rated; 89 minutes; Release date: May 1, 2009. **CAST:** Timothy Daly (Bryan Becket), Tom Arnold (Sully), Zoe Saldana (Cassie), Andrea Roth (Robin Becket), Edward Herrmann (Shepard), Robert Prosky (Father Wymond), Bruce Altman (Koven), Christina Rouner (Nurse), Lea Coco (Deputy), Sarah Weaver (Helena Becket), James DiSalvatore (Law Adversary), Charles Fletcher (Lawyer), Chris Silipigno (Raz), L.J. Foley (Young Becket), Paul Tietjen (Michael), J.J. Buchner (Matt), Cassidy Catanzaro (Dillion), Alex Demers (Derek), Cailey Bardwell, Molly Bardwell (Goblins), Tennyson Taylor Bardwell (Halloween Ghost), Wayland Taylor Bardwell (Devil), Alex Beer (Scarecrow), Gabriel Beer (Mummy), Max Beer (Joker), Lee Bieler (Pub Bartender), Steve Chick (Attorney in Hall), Jessica DeLong, Kayla Murphy, Allayla Silipigno (Witches), Ann Marie Lizzi (Teacher), Shannon Rafferty, Nicole Signore (Paralegals), Julia Ricciardi (Lizzi Borden), Meg Savage (Krista), Ciara Silipigno (Princess), Judy Spevack (Dead Mrs. Deaver), Catherine Wyler (Carol)

Timothy Daly, Robert Prosky in The Skeptic *© IFC Films*

BATTLE FOR TERA (Lionsgate/Roadside) a.k.a. *Terra*; Producers, Keith Calder, Jessica Wu, Dane Allan Smith, Ryan Colucci; Director, Aristomenis Tsirbas; Screenplay, Evan Spiliotopoulos; Music, Abel Korzeniowski; Editor, J. Kathleen Gibson; Senior CG Sequence Supervisor, Will Wira; Visual Effects Supervisor, Dimitri Longinowski; a Snoot Entertainment presentation in association with MeniThings Entertainment; Dolby; FotoKem color; Rated PG; 85 minutes; Release date: May 1, 2009. VOICE **CAST:** Evan Rachel Wood (Mala), Brian Cox (General Hemmer), Luke Wilson (Jim Stanton), James Garner (Doron), Chris Evans (Stewart Stanton), Dennis Quaid (Roven), Chad Allen (Terrian Scientist), Rosanna Arquette (Professor Lina), Timi Prulhiere, Bill Birch (Terrians), Brooke Bloom (Technician Quinn), Tom Connolly (Technician Williams), David Cross (Giddy), Beverly D'Angelo (Interrogator Wright), Jim Devoti (Col. Wheeler), Danny Glover

(President Chen), Mark Hamill (Elder Orin), Alec Holden (Tulo), Masam Holden (Tumi), Vanessa Johansson (Sora), Brian Johnson (Lt. Johnson), David Krumholtz (Terrian Commander), Phil LaMarr (Fabric Merchant), Justin Long (Senn), Worm Miller (Tuki), Laraine Newman (Toy Merchant), Amanda Peet (Maria Montez), Ron Perlman (Elder Vorin), Michael Scovotti (Lt. Evans), Zoe Sidel (Kima), Danny Trejo (Elder Barum)

Giddy, Mala, Jim Stanton in Battle for Tera *© Lionsgate/Roadside*

A WINK AND A SMILE (First Run Features) Producers, Jack Timmons, Deirdre Allen Timmons; Director, Deirdre Allen Timmons; Photography, Peter Waweru, Marie Joëlle Rizk; Editors, Deirdre Allen Timmons, Peter Waweru; a Golden Echo Films production;; Color; HD; Not rated; 90 minutes; Release date: May 1, 2009. Documentary on the art of stripping. **WITH:** Miss Indigo Blue, The Shanghai Pearl, Tamara the Trapeze Lady, The Swedish Housewife, Waxie Moon, Vienna la Rouge, Lily Verlaine, Kitten LaRue, Inga Ingenue, Ernie Von Schmaltz, Ultra, Casey Ellison, Janie Hanson, Megan Keller, Amy Klar, Vicky R. Moczi, Christi Jo Petrucelli, Sara Robinson, Rachel Shimp, Tami Veralund, Babette La Fave

Miss Indigo Blue in A Wink and a Smile *© First Run Features*

ICE PEOPLE (Milestone) Producers, Benoit Gryspeerdt, Anne Aghion; Director, Anne Aghion; Photography, Sylvestre Guidi; Music, Laurent Petitgand; Editor, Nadia Ben Rachid; American-French; Color; HD; Not rated; 77 minutes; Release date: May 1, 2009. Documentary on scientists who work in minus-60 degrees temperatures in Antarctica. **WITH:** Allan A. Ashworth, Adam R. Lewis, Andre Podoll, Kelly Gorz

HOME (Monterey Media) Producers, Mary Haverstick, Michele Mercure, Chad Taylor; Executive Producers, Paul Ware, Judy Ware; Co-Producers, Pete Catalano, Darla Catalano; Director/Screenplay/Editor, Mary Haverstick; Photography, Richard Rutkowski; Art Director, Judy Carson; Costumes, Nina Schelich; Music, Michele Mercure; Casting, Eva Battaglia; a Haverstick Films presentation; Rated PG-13; 84 minutes; Release date: May 1, 2009. **CAST:** Marcia Gay Harden (Inga), Marian Seldes (Peggy), Michael Gaston (Herman), Eulala Scheel (Indigo), Candy Buckley (Mother), Reathal Bean (Father), Pamela Jane Henning (Young Inga), Paul L. Nolan (Doctor), Thomas Roy (Pastor)

Marcia Gay Harden, Eulala Scheel in Home © *Monterey Media*

CODY: THE FIRST STEP (Christopher Productions) Producer/Director, Chris Schueler; Photography, Randy McComas, Bob Willis, Dean Butler, Chris Schueler, Patrick O'Donnell, Ed Smith; Music, Jeff Jolly; Narrator, Glenn Close; Color; Not rated; 66 minutes; Release date: May 1, 2009. Documentary on how being stricken with transverse myelitis made Cody Unser determined to bring awareness to the disease. **WITH:** Cody Unser

LOVE N' DANCING (Screen Media Films) Producers, Robert Royston, Sylvia Caminer, Tom Malloy; Director, Robert Iscove; Screenplay, Tom Malloy; Photography, Frank Byers; Designer, Ben Woolverton; Costumes, Rob Saduski; Music, Matt Seigel; Editor, Casey O. Rohrs; Choreographer, Robert Royston; Color; Rated PG-13; 93 minutes; Release date: May 8, 2009. **CAST:** Amy Smart (Jessica Donovan), Tom Malloy (Jake Mitchell), Billy Zane (Kent Krandel), Nicola Royston (Corinne Kennedy), Caroline Rhea (Bonnie), Leila Arcieri (Danielle), Rachel Dratch (Kalle), Betty White (Irene), Purva Bedi (Ritu), Frank Bond (Bob Licando), Elise Eberle (Brianna), Jordan Frisbee (Matt), Gregory Harrison (Uncle Carl), David House (Principal Bees), Ross Kelly (Terry), Gloria Martin (Joy), Maulik Pancholy (Gunmay), Kenny Resch (J.T.), Tom Romero (Frank the Bartender), Benji Schwimmer (Keith Miller), Kieran Sequoia (Miranda), Kisha Sierra (Tina), Catherine Mary Stewart (Aunt Katie), Dan Strakal (Dance Event Host), Brandi Tobias (Dance Aficionado)

Amy Smart, Tom Malloy in Love n' Dancing © *Screen Media*

BROTHERS AT WAR (Samuel Goldwyn Co.) Producers, Norman S. Powell, Jake Rademacher; Executive Producers, Gary Sinise, David Schatling; Director/Screenplay, Jake Rademacher; Photography, Marc Miller, Stan Eng; Music, Lee Holdridge; Editor, Robert DeMaio; a Metanoia Films production; Dolby; Color; HD-to-35mm; Rated R; 110 minutes; Release date: May 8, 2009. Documentary in which filmmaker Jake Rademacher follows his brother Isaac during his third Iraq deployment. **WITH:** Mahmoud Hamid Ali, Edward Allier, Ryan Baker, Zack Corke, Danelle Fields, Ben Fisher, Jason Grundy, Patrick Irvine, Kevin Keniston, Frank McCann, Brandon "Mongo" Phillips, Claus Rademacher, Isaac Rademacher, Jake Rademacher, Jenny Rademacher, Joe Rademacher, Robert Smallwood

Brothers at War © *Samuel Goldwyn Co.*

AUDIENCE OF ONE (Indiepix) Producers, Michael Jacobs, Zach Sanders, Matt Woods; Executive Producers, Gary Jacobs, Randy Woods; Director, Michael Jacobs; Photography, Michael Jacobs; Art Director, Alex Lyman; Music, Jeff Forrest; Editor, Kyle Henry; a Revolve production; Color; DV; Not rated; 88 minutes; Release date: May 8, 2009. Documentary on how a San Francisco minister made the independent sci-fi Biblical epic, *Gravity: The Shadow of Joseph*, after insisting he'd received a vision from God. **WITH:** Richard Gazowsky

OBJECTIFIED (Swiss Dots Productions) Producer/Director, Gary Hustwit; Photography, Luke Geissbuhler; Designer, Brian Bracken; Music, Kristian Dunn; Editor, Joe Beshenkovsky; Color; HD; Not rated; 75 minutes; Release date: May 8, 2009. Documentary on the relationship between several noted designers and their products. **WITH:** Paola Antonelli, Marc Newsom, Dieter Rams, Alice Rawasthorn, Jonathan Ive, Karim Rashid, Andrew Blauvet, Naoto Fukasawa, Chris Bangle, Dan Formosa, Erwan Bouroullec, Ronan Bouroullec, Hella Jongerius, Fiona Raby, Amber Shonts

Objectified © *Swiss Dots Prods.*

POWDER BLUE (Speakeasy Releasing) Producers, Timothy Linh Bui, Forest Whitaker, Tracee Stanley, Ross M. Dinerstein; Director/Screenplay, Timothy Linh Bui; Story, Timothy Linh Bui, Stephane Gauger; Photography, Jonathan Sela; Designer, Keith Neely; Costumes, Magali Guidasci; Music, Didier Lean Rachou; Editor, Leo Trombetta; Casting, Ronnie Yeskel, Michelle Levy; Dolby; Color; Rated R; 108 minutes; Release date: May 8, 2009. **CAST:** Jessica Biel (Rose Johnny), Eddie Redmayne (Qwery Doolittle), Forest Whitaker (Charlie), Ray Liotta (Jack Doheny), Lisa Kudrow (Sally), Patrick Swayze (Velvet Larry), Kris Kristofferson (Randall), Alejandro Romero (Lexus), Sanaa Lathan (Diana), Chandler Canterbury (Billy), Jeffery Adam Baker (Slim), Navid Negahban (Dr. Brooks), Ravi Patel (Sanjay), Billy Wirth (David), Don Swayze (Bouncer), Ben Bray (Security), Joe Holt (ER Doctor), L. Scott Caldwell (Nurse Gomez), Mandy June Turpin (Jenkins), Armando Cosio (Jose), Riki Lindhome (Nicole), Jesse Henecke (Loan Manager), Ana Berry (Host), Leyna Nguyen (Newscast Reporter), Chad Christopher (Undercover Security), Soledad Campos (Catholic Nun), Clent Bowers (Bus Driver), Danvy Pham (Lotus), Luoc Lee (Drag Queen)

OUTRAGE (Magnolia) Producer, Amy Ziering; Executive Producers, Tom Quinn, Jason Janego, Ted Sarandos, Chad Griffin, Kimball Stroud, Bruce Brothers, Tectonic Theater Project; Director, Kirby Dick; Photography, Thaddeus Wadleigh; Music, Peter Golub; Editor, Doug Blush, Matt Clarke; a Camera Pictures/Magnolia Pictures presentation; Color; HD; Not rated; 90 minutes; Release date: May 8, 2009. Documentary on closeted gay politicians who have voted against gay rights issues. **WITH:** Michael Rogers, Tammy Baldwin, Wayne Barrett, Jim McGreevey, Barney Frank, Andrew Sullivan, Tony Kushner, Larry Kramer, Larry Gross

Jim McGreevey in Outrage © *Magnolia Pictures*

THE BIG SHOT-CALLER (Stella Films) Producer/Editor, Christine Giorgio; Co-Producer, Erika Yeomans; Director/Screenplay, Marlene Rhein; Photography, Paolo Cascio; Art Director, Mel Puerto; Music, Justin Asher; Color; DigiBeta; Widescreen; Not rated; 92 minutes; Release date: May 15, 2009. **CAST:** David Rhein (Jamie), Marlene Rhein (Lianne), Laneya Wiles (Elissa), Robert Costanzo (Rudy), Leslie Eva Glaser (Rebecca), Rodney Lopez, Mariana Parma (Dance Instructors), Natasha A. Williams (Carol), Maria Soccer (Veronica Colucci), Paul Borghese (Victor), Stephanie Bush (Sandy), Phil La Rocco (Big Mike), Johnny Solo (Gino), John Marean (Weasel), Aliya Yasmeen (Giselle), Bob Adrian (Upper Management Man), Helen Proimos (Dance School Receptionist), Ron Gordon (Cop), Leslie C. Nemet, Ellen DiStasi, Fabian Quintero (Dance Students), Edwin Perez (Lead Vocalist), La Excelencia (Salsa Band), Dante Nero (Bouncer), Christopher Negrin, Sean Mik'ael (Salsa Dancers), Michael Ciesla, Julie Ariella Marcus (Real Estate Brokers), J. Hanna (Bartender)

Laneya Wiles, David Rhein in The Big Shot-Caller © *Stella Films*

ANAGLYPH TOM (TOM WITH PUFFY CHEEKS) (Independent) Director/Editor, Ken Jacobs; 1905 Photography, Bill Bitzer; 3-Dimension; Not rated; 118 minutes; Release date: May 15, 2009. A re-imagining of the 1905 Biography short, *Tom, Tom, the Piper's Son.*

MILTON GLASER: TO INFORM AND DELIGHT (Arthouse Films) Producer/Director, Wendy Keys; Executive Producer, Edgar B. Howard; Photography, David W. Leitner; Music, Hayes Greenfield; Editor, Tom Piper; Color; HD; Not rated; 73 minutes; Release date: May 22, 2009. Documentary on influential designer Milton Glaser. **WITH:** Milton Glaser, Ralph Caplan, Katrina vanden Heuvel, Steve Heller, Walter Bernard, Wendy Keys, Jivan Tabibian, Deborah Adler, Walter Bernard, George Lang

Milton Glaser in To Inform and Delight © *Arthouse Films*

GHOSTS OF THE HEARTLAND (ABL Communications) Producer/Director/ Screenplay, Allen Blumberg; Photography, Antoine Vivas Denisov; Designer, Roshelle Bernliner; Costumes, Michael Bevins; Music, Tom Hiel; Editor, Emily Paine; Black and white; Not rated; 80 minutes; Release date: May 22, 2009. **CAST:** Phil Moon (Roland Lu), Michael Santoro (Frank Dugan), David Midthunder (Ray), Marcus Ho (Phil), Rosanne Ma (Liz), William Kozy (Freddy), Bill Cain (Radio Roy), James Saito (John Lu), Karen Tsen Lee (Dorothy), Michelle Peters (Carol), James McAllister (Rick), Aysha Quinn (Sarah), Georgina Lightning (Tani), Kelly AuCoin (Wellman), Jeff Jerome (Barney), Dan Guggenheim (Dr. Stafford), Fiona Lee, Jennifer Herzog (Prostitutes), Gregor Trieste, Roger Poole (Masked Men)

Rosanne Ma in Ghosts of the Heartland © *ABL Communications*

NEW WORLD ORDER (IFC Films) Producer, Tom Davis; Executive Producers, Julie Goldman, Krysanne Katsoolis, Caroline Stevens, Debbie DeMontreaux, Christine Lubrano, Evan Shapiro; Directors/Photography, Luke Meyer, Andrew Neel; Music, John Ollsin, Jonah Rapino; Editor, Nathan Caswell; a SeeThink production in association with Cactus Three Films; Color; HD; Not rated; 86 minutes; Release date: May 22, 2009. Documentary on conspiracy theorists. **WITH:** Alex Jones, Luke Rudowski, Jack McLamb, Jim Tucker, Timucin Leflef, Geraldo Rivera, Bill Clinton, Paul Dorneanu, Jan Dotson, Marty Dotson, Aaron Dykes, Mike Edgarton, Seth Jackson, Rob Jacobson, Jim Marrs

PRESSURE COOKER (Participant Media) Producer, Jennifer Grausman; Executive Producers, Jeff Skoll, Diana Weyermann; Directors, Jennifer Grausman, Mark Becker; Photography, Justin Schein, Leigh Iacobucci; Music, Prince Paul, Donald Newkirk; Editor, Mark Becker; a Non Sequitor production; Color; DV; Not rated; 99 minutes; Release date: May 27, 2009. Documentary about a group of culinary arts students learning their craft at Philadelphia's Frankford High School. **WITH:** Wilma Stephenson, Erica Gaither, Fatoumata Dembele, Tyree Dudley

Pressure Cooker © Participant Media

WHAT GOES UP (Three Kings) Producers, RD Robb, Jonathan Glatzer; Executive Producers, Kirk Shaw, Joseph Nasser, Jack Nasser, Steve Coogan, Thomas N. Greenauer, James Hoke, Anthony Miranda, Joseph Nahas; Co-Producer, Robert Lawson; Director, Jonathan Glatzer; Screenplay, Jonathan Glatzer, Robert Lawson; Photography, Antonio Calvache; Designer, Tony Devenyi; Costumes, Andrea Des Roches; Music, Roddy Bottum; Editors, Jonathan Glatzer, Jennifer Godin; a Nasser Entertainment Group and Insight Film Studios presentation of a Station 3 production; Dolby; Color; Rated R; 107 minutes; Release date: May 29, 2009. **CAST:** Steve Coogan (Campbell Babbitt), Hilary Duff (Lucy Diamond), Olivia Thirlby (Tess Sullivan), Josh Peck (Jim Lement), Molly Shannon (Penelope Little), Molly Price (Donna Arbetter), Max Hoffman (Fenster Itski), Sarah Lind (Peggy Popoladopolous), Laura Konechny (Lute Lement), Ingrid Nilson (Ann), Andrea Brooks (Sue), Andrew Wheeler (Principal Dick Person), Gabrielle Rose (Mrs. Bridgian), Colleen Rennison (Sylvia), Aubrey Mozino (Blythe), Aaron Brooks (Ezra), Barry Greene (Sam Calallucci), David Sochet (Voice of Sam), Katie Messina (Gina), Alana Husband (Angela), Kendra Sue Waldman (Dusty Drake), Barbara Greenbaum (Librarian), Brenna O'Brien (Diminutive Girl), Aiden Lane Robson (Gustave Person), David Allan Pearson (Grease Monkey), Jilena Cori (Mrs. Svetlana Person), Patricia Drake (Mrs. Itski), Brett Kelly, Ashley Whillans, Calum Worthy, Advah Soudack, Robin Eder-Warren (Blastoff! Chorus)

Steve Coogan in What Goes Up © *Three Kings*

AUTISM: MADE IN THE U.S.A. (Gary Null & Associates) Producers/Directors, Gary Null, Manette Loudon; Photography, Robert Kehoe; Music, Hal Cragin; Editor, Julie Chabot; Color; Not rated; 101 minutes; Release date: June 3, 2009. Documentary in which its makers blame the rise in autism on vaccines. **WITH:** Lawrence Palevsky, Stan Kutz, Cindy Schneider, Gary Null, Beth Clay

MY LIFE IN RUINS (Fox Searchlight) Producers, Michelle Chydzik Sowa, Nathalie Marciano; Executive Producers, Tom Hanks, Gary Goetzman, Rita Wilson, Peter Safran, Jeff Abberley, Julia Blackman; Co-Producers, Denise O'Dell, Mark Albela; Director, Donald Petrie; Screenplay, Mike Reiss; Photography, Jose Luis Alcaine; Designer, David Chapman; Costumes, Lala Huete, Lena Mossum; Music, David Newman; Editor, Patrick J. Don Vito; Casting, Sheila Jaffe; a 26 Films production, in association with Kanzaman Productions; Dolby; Color; Rated PG-13; 95 minutes; Release date: June 5, 2009. **CAST:** Nia Vardalos (Georgia), Richard Dreyfuss (Irv), Alexis Georgoulis (Poupi Kakas), Alistair McGowan (Nico), Caroline Goodall (Dr. Tullen), Ian Ogilvy (Mr. Tullen), Sophie Stuckey (Caitlin), María Adánez (Lena), Sheila Bernette (Dorcas), Maria Botto (Lala), Rachel Dratch (Kim), Ralph Nossek (Barnaby), Bernice Stegers (Maria), Harland Williams (Big Al), Brian Palermo (Marc), Jareb Dauplaise (Gator), Simon Gleeson (Ken), Natalie O'Donnell (Sue), Rita Wilson (Elinor), Takis Papamattheou (Souvenir Shop Owner), Serenella Magriny (Svetlana), Marta Schwizer (Olga), Maria Ripalda

(Lenka), Nacho Pérez (Doudi), Nadaf Malamud, Roland Sanden (Greek Men), Vasilis Psichogiopoulos (Souvlaki guy), José Sacristán (Jewelry Shop Owner), Alberto Santiago (Bar Owner), Alejandro Sanchez Spijksma (Bartender), María José Goyanes (Dour Nurse), Jennifer Rope (Pretty Nurse), Melina Kyriakopoulou (Angry Canadian), Denise Moreno (Kathy), Abdeltif Louzar, Oreste Papadopol, Valentin Stoica (Greek Band)

Nia Vardalos, Richard Dreyfuss in My Life in Ruins © Fox Searchlight

THE ART OF BEING STRAIGHT (Regent) Producers, Amy Wasserman, Ursula Camack; Executive Producer, Laurence Ducceschi; Director/Screenplay, Jesse Rosen; Photography, Aaron Torres; Designer, Karuna Karmarkar; Editor, Rob Schulbaum; a Malvern Productions, Great Graffiti Films production, in association with Squarenone Cinema; Color; HD-to-DigiBeta; Not rated; 77 minutes; Release date: June 5, 2009. **CAST:** Jesse Rosen (John), Rachel Castillo (Maddy), Jared Grey (Andy), Johnny Ray (Paul), Jesse Janzen (Brian), Tyler Jenich (Cole), Alan LaPolice (Rand), Bryan McGowan (Matt), Peter Scherer (Aaron), Anne Reeder (Simone), Emilia Richeson (Anna), Jim Dineen (Young Office Assistant), Dana May Salah (Renee), Jen Zaborowski (Bela)

Jesse Rosen (center) in The Art of Being Straight © Regent Releasing

KASSIM THE DREAM (IFC Films) Producers, Kief Davidson, Liz Silver; Executive Producers, Luke Thornton, Forest Whitaker, Keisha Whitaker, Joshua Green; Director, Kief Davidson; Photography, Tony Molina Jr.; Music, Leo Heiblum, Jacobo Liberman, Andres Solis; Editors, Tony Breuer, Kief Davidson; a Believe Media/Urban Landscapes production; Color; HD; Not rated; 87 minutes; Release date: June 5, 2009. Documentary on boxing champ Kassim "The Dream" Ouma. **WITH:** Kassim Ouma, Tom Moran, Russell Peltz, Jermain Taylor

Kassim "The Dream" Ouma in Kassim the Dream © IFC Films

CAYMAN WENT (41 Inc.) Executive Producers, Jim Ritterhoff, Bob Eick, Sara Feldmann Sheehan, Kim Ketchell, Tony Kobylinski; Producer, Gil Wadsworth; Director, Bobby Sheehan; Screenplay, Bobby Sheehan, Jim Ritterhoff; Photography, Russell Swanson; Music Producer, Randy Lee; Color; Rated PG; 89 minutes; Release date: June 5, 2009. **CAST:** Michael Lombardi (Josh Anders), Susan Misner (Darby Thomas), Jeffrey DeMunn (Rodgers Bowman), Franklin Ojeda-Smith (Aniston Turnkey), Peter Maloney (Seaver Weston), John Mainieri (Hans Kopechne), Tuffy Questell (Lawson Peakes), Lisa Barnes (Max's Mom), Rita Estevanovich (Bartender), Laura Ford (Policewoman), Ellie Kemper (Woman from L.A.), Tenson Scott (Himself), John Speredakos (Miles Baskin), Robin Weigert (Rachel), Peter Wiggins (Max)

DOWNLOADING NANCY (Strand) Producers, David Moore, Igor Kovacevich, Jason Essex, Cole Payne; Executive Producers, Blizzard Fils, Julie Aaron, Adam Bataz, Philip H. Clinkscales III, Maddox Pace Clinkscales, Chris Hanley, Sean McVity, Mark Mueller, Stephen Onda, Daniel Sachs; Director, Johan Renck; Screenplay, Pamela Cumings, Lee H. Ross; Photography, Christopher Doyle; Designer, Lauri Faggioni; Costumes, Denis Ostholm; Music, Krister Linder; Editor, Johan Sodernberg; Casting, Mary Vernieu, Venus Kanani; a Tule River Films production from World Premiere Entertainment in association with P.H. Clinkscales Sr. Enterprises; Dolby; FotoKem color; Not rated; 102 minutes; Release date: June 5, 2009. **CAST:** Maria Bello (Nancy Stockwell), Jason Patric (Louis Farley), Rufus Sewell (Albert Stockwell), Amy Brenneman (Carol), Michael Nyqvist (Stan), David Brown (Billy Ringel), Matthew Harrison (Golf Pro), Sunny Doench (News Anchor), Justin Scot (Golf Guru), Josh Strait (Medic)

Maria Bello, Rufus Sewell in Downloading Nancy © Strand

TENNESSEE (Vivendi) Producer, Lee Daniels; Executive Producers, Sarah Siegel-Magness, Gary Magness, Lisa Cortes, Dave Robinson, Damon Dash, Jane Kosek, Tom Heller; Director, Aaron Woodley; Screenplay, Russell Schaumburg; Photography, David Greene; Designer, Aidan Leroux; Costumes, Deborah Everton; Music, Mario Grigorov; Editor, Steve Edwards; Casting, Billy Hopkins, Suzanne Crowley; a Lee Daniels Entertainment production in association with Smokewood Entertainment; Dolby; Widescreen; Color; Rated R; 99 minutes; Release date: June 5, 2009. **CAST:** Adam Rothenberg (Carter), Ethan Peck (Ellis), Mariah Carey (Krystal), Lance Reddick (Frank), Ryan Lynn (Carter at 18), Michele Harris (Karen), Bill Sage (Roy), Melissa Benoist (Laurel), Michele Ammon (Voice of Police Dispatcher), Christopher Andrews (Jackson), Jerry Biggs (Manager), Ellie Braverman (Woman in Line), Donna Brazier (Nurse), Forrest Broadley (Groundskeeper), Chris Browning (Bouncer), Lawrence Bull Jr., Chris Ranney, Lee Vervoort (Bar Patrons), Harp Corrigan (The Stranger), Aunt Dot (Cook), Mary Evans (Jackson's Mom), John Hardman (Arkansas Clerk), David House (Eugene), Dylan Kenin (Boyfriend), Mary Layne (Skinny Woman), Camryn Magness (Patron), Alex Manette (Dr. McCullough), Debrianna Mansini (Nurse Meyers), Nasser Metcalf (Dr. Maxwell), Tony Nudo (Security Guard), Luce Rains (Oklahoma Motel Clerk), Robyn Reede (Darlene), Russell Schaumberg (Host), Boots Southerland (Pawnshop Owner), Joshua Strother, Noah Lee Trudell (Young Carter), Sheila Ivy Traister (Girlfriend), Charles Tucker (Voice of Clerk)

Ethan Peck, Mariah Carey, Adam Rothenberg in Tennessee © *Vivendi*

BLAST! (Paul Devlin Productions) Producers, Paul Devlin, Claire Missanelli; Executive Producer, Nick Fraser; Director/Photography/Editor, Paul Devlin; Music, Richard Martinez; a Devlin production, in association with BBB Storyville/Discovery Channel Canada/SVT Sweden/YLE/FST Finland/ARTE France; American-Canadian-Swedish-Finnish-French; Color; DV; Not rated; 78 minutes; Release date: June 12, 2009. Documentary on the launch of a multi-million dollar telescope from a high altitude balloon. **WITH:** Mark Devlin, Barth Netterfield, Victor Davison, Jeff Klein, Marie Rex, Gaelen Marsden, Enzo Pascale, Christopher Semisch, Matthew Truch, Danny Ball, Ed Chapin, Jennifer Devlin, Kevin Evetalegak, Ross Hays, David Hughes, Erich Klein, Nick Thomas, Marco Viero, Don Wiebe, Werner Herzog

THE LAST INTERNATIONAL PLAYBOY (Black Note Films/CPlus) a.k.a. *Frost*; Producers, Mike Landry, Carlos Velazquez, Steve Clark, Terry Leonard; Executive Producers, Sean Campbell, Ian B. Wile; Director, Steve Clark; Screenplay, Steve Clark, Thomas Moffett; Photography, Brian Burgoyne; Designer/Costumes, Amanda Ford; Music, Peter Bradley Adams; Editor, Connor Kalista; Casting, Eve Battaglia; a Black Note Films, CPlus presentation; Color; HD; Not rated; 95 minutes; Release date: June 12, 2009. **CAST:** Jason Behr (Jack Frost), Monet

Blast! © *Paul Devlin Prods.*

Mazur (Carolina), Krysten Ritter (Ozzy), Lucy Gordon (Kate Hardwick), Mike Landry (Scotch Evans), India Ennenga (Sophie), Polina Frantsena (Serafina), Jessica Gomes (Cinnamon), Maria Jurado (Adriana), Lydia Hearst (Stella), Nicole Trunfio (Sappho), Leticia Cline (Herself), Amber Noelle Ehresmann (Parsley), Leah Cary (Natty), Shanna Click (Cayenne), Ruza Madarevic (Verushka), Gavin Bellour (Young Jack), Rob Bogue (Russell), Lauren Burns (Stephie), Lauren DeJulio (Anna), Charles Everett (Reggie the Bartender), Ashley Greenfield (Amy), Ira Lopez (Chauffeur), Meghan Marx (Victoria), Thomas Moffett (Henry), Kathy Searle (Receptionist), James A. Stephens (Cubby Hardwick), Carlos Velazquez (Investment Banker)

SEX POSITIVE (Regent) Producers, Daryl Wein, David Oliver Cohen; Director/Editor, Daryl Wein; Photography, Alex Bergman; Music, Michael Tremante; a Might and Main Film production; Color; HD-to-DigiBeta; Not rated; 78 minutes; Release date: June 12, 2009. Documentary on hustler-turned-safe sex advocate Richard Berkowitz. **WITH:** Richard Berkowitz, Dr. Joseph Sonnabend, Don Adler, Susan Brown, Demetre Daskalakis, Richard Dworkin, William Haseltine, Larry Kramer, Ardele Lister, Michael Lucas, Francisco Roque, Gabriel Rotello, Bill Stackhouse, Krishna Stone, Sean Strub, Edmund White

Richard Berkowitz in Sex Positive *© Regent Releasing*

WAR EAGLE, ARKANSAS (Empire) Producers, Vincent Insalaco, Marco Henry; Director, Robert Milazzo; Screenplay, Graham Gordy; Story, Vincent Insalaco, Graham Gordy; Photography, Masanobu Takayanagi; Designer, Sarah Frank; Costumes, Eden Miller; Music, Will Churchill; Editor, Ron Len; an Eric Parkinson, Dean Hamilton and Fred Shefte in association with Empire Film Group/Downstream People presentation; Dolby; Panavision; Color; Rated PG-13; 93 minutes; Release date: June 12, 2009. **CAST:** Luke Grimes (Enoch), Dan McCabe (Wheels), Misti Traya (Abby), Brian Dennehy (Pop), Mary Kay Place (Jessie), Mare Winningham (Belle), James McDaniel (Jack), Lynnsee Provence (Nardler), Paige Reynolds (June Hutchens), Michael Williamson (Shutty), Lila Collins (Hottie), Chris Crane (Caverns Manager), Christopher Crane (Ron), Mary Claire DePriest (Abby's Friend), Michael Witham, Vaughn Kent, James Frodyma (Nardler's Buddies), Dillon Hupp (Eagles Catcher), Michael Oaks (Austin), Arnold John Popa III (Real Estate Agent), Allen Quattlebaum (West Coach), Tim Sparks, Keith Sanders (Umpires), Suzanne Shaye (Caverns Clerk), Van Stewman Jr. (Highlanders Coach), Gordon Swaim (Coach Harville)

Luke Grimes, Dan McCabe in War Eagle, Arkansas *© Empire*

YOUSSOU NDOUR: I BRING WHAT I LOVE (Shadow) Producer/Director, Elizabeth Chai Vasarhelyi; Executive Producers, Edward Tyler Nahem, Patrick Morris, Jennifer Millstone, Jack Turner, Kathryn Tucker, Miklos C. Vasarhelyi; Photography, Nick Doob, JoJo Pennebaker, Scott Duncan, Hugo Berkeley; Music, James Newton Howard, Martin Davich; Editors, Jonathan Oppenheimer, Fernando Villena; a Groovy Griot presentation, in association with 57th & Irving Productions; Color; HD; Rated PG; 102 minutes; Release date: June 12, 2009. Documentary on Muslim pop star Youssou Ndour. **WITH:** Youssou Ndour, Kabou Gueye, Moustapha Mbaye, Peter Gabriel, Fathy Salama

Youssou Ndour in I Bring What I Love *© Shadow*

THE WINDMILL MOVIE (The Film Desk) Producer, Susan Meiselas; Co-Producer, David Grubin; Director/Screenplay/Editor, Alexander Olch; Photography, Richard P. Rogers; Music, Robert Humphreville; Black and white/color; DV; Not rated; 82 minutes; Release date: June 17, 2009. Documentary in which filmmaker Richard P. Rogers' examines his own dissatisfied upper class existence, as completed by filmmaker Alexander Olch. **WITH:** Richard P. Rogers, Susan Meiselas, Wallace Shawn, Bob Balaban

Richard P. Rogers in The Windmill Movie *© The Film Desk*

UNDER OUR SKIN (Shadow) Producer/Director/Screenplay/Photography, Andy Abrahams Wilson; Executive Producer, The Swartz Foundation; Music, Justin Melland; Editor, Eva Ilona Brzeski; an Open Eye Pictures production; Color; Not rated; 104 minutes; Release date: June 19, 2009. Documentary on Lyme disease. **WITH:** Mandy Hughes, Sean Cobb, Dana Walsh, Jordan Fisher-Smith, Marlena Connors, Elise Brady-Moe, Ben Petrick, Dr. Alan MacDonald, Kris Newby, Dr. Joseph Jemsek, Dr. Charles Ray Jones, Dr. Gary Wormser, Dr. Eugene Shapiro

Under Our Skin © *Shadow Releasing*

THE NARROWS (Cinedigm) Producers, Leslie Urdang, Ami Armstrong, Tatiana Blackington; Executive Producers, Michael Nozik, Todd James, Dean Vanech, Daniel Revers, Nicolas Velle, Michael Hoffman; Director, Francois A. Velle; Screenplay, Tatiana Blackington; Based on the novel *The Heart of the Old Country* by Tim McLoughlin; Photography, Seamus Tierney; Designer, Aleta Shaffer; Music, Richard Marvin; Editor, Patrick Gallagher; a Serenade Films production, in association with Mr. Nice and Olympus Pictures; Color; HD; Rated R; 106 minutes; Release date: June 19, 2009. **CAST:** Kevin Zegers (Mike Manadoro), Vincent D'Onofrio (Vinny Manadoro), Sophia Bush (Kathy Popovich), Eddie Cahill (Nicky Shades), Monica Keena (Gina), Roger Rees (Prof. Reyerson), Michael Kelly (Danny), Titus Welliver (Tony), Tony Cucci (Big Lou), Anthony Fazio (Little Joey), Louis Mustillo (Fat Sal), Esau Pritchett (Todd), Radu Spinghel (Edward), Melina Lizette (Luz), Jeff Skowron (Financial Aid Advisor), Kate Rogal (Xander), Josh Segarra (White Gangsta), Scott DuQuette (Jared), Jerome Preston Bates (Chuckie), Drucie McDaniel (Bedraggled Woman), Kate Nowlin (Waitress), Priscilla Shanks (Sociology Professor), Saul Stein (Phil Zaccaro), Teresa Woods (Mike's Mother), Lucille Patton (Mrs. Gattei), Michael De Nola (Tall Hasid), Michael Sirow (Big Guy), Colleen Hawks (Eileen Zaccaro), Eunice Anderson (Frail Old Lady), Kelly Abbondanzo, Scott Abbondanzo (Tenement Kids), Michael Ciesla (Photography Student), Christian Eriksen, Matthew Seife (Young Mike), Bryan Fitzgerald (Young Nicky), Richard Frallicciardi (Waiter), Jeff Grossman (Russian Mobster), Tony Kost (Restaurant Patron), Evan Lewis (Street Punk), Jessica Mazo (Student), Sal Mistretta (Marco), Diana Shneider (Prostitute), Ken Sladyk (Street Bum), Joe Wissler (Russian Mobster)

IRENE IN TIME (Rainbow) Producer, Rosemary Marks; Director/Screenplay/Editor, Henry Jaglom; Photography, Hanania Baer; Designer, Barbara Drake; Costumes, Cynthia Obsenares; Music, Harriet Schock; Color; Rated PG-13; 95 minutes; Release date: June 19, 2009. **CAST:** Tanna Frederick (Irene), Victoria Tennant (Eleanor), Lanre Idewu (Jakub), Andrea Marcovicci (Helen), Karen Black (Sheila), Jack Maxwell (Mikey), David Proval (Norm Forentino), Zack Norman (Larry), Kelly De Sarla (JoJo), Adam Davidson (Gordon), Claudia Brown (Gaby), Robert Amico (Rick), Dato Bakhtadze (Max), Seymour Cassel (Rupert), James E. dePriest (Hacohen), Barbara Flood (Phyllis), David Frederick (Movies), Nancy Frederick (Paulette), Leila Goldoni (Isis), Kristne Horner (Cider), Sabrina Jaglom (Gigi), Simon Orson Jaglom (Ollie), Alicia Lara (Lara), Andrew Leeds (Warren), Wendy Luker (Ronnie), Joe Manganiello (Charlie), Michael Marchand (Jason),

Joel Marshall (Binky), Rob Mathes (Spence), Ruby McCollister (Young Irene), Julius Noflin (Bill), Carmen Perez (Gloria), Peter Perkins (Irene's Father), Frank Potter (Gigi's Father), Vanessa Robertson (Roberta), Reni Santoni (Sam), Harriet Schock (Sandie Fuse), Alison Simpson (Alison), Louis Stratten (Hostess), Richard Tanner (Manny)

Andrew Leeds, Tanna Frederick in Irene in Time © *Rainbow*

LOCAL COLOR (Monterey Media) Producers, David Permut, Mark Sennet, Julie Lott Gallo, James W. Evangelatos; Director/Screenplay, George Gallo; Photography, Michael Negrin; Designer, Robert Ziembicki; Costumes, Emily Draper; Music, Chris Boardman; Editor, Malcolm Campbell; Casting, Lynn Kressel; an Alla Prima Productions, Permut Presentations presentation of a James V. Evangelatos, Julie Lott Gallo production; Dolby; Panavision; Color; Rated R; 107 minutes; Release date: June 29, 2009. **CAST:** Armin Mueller-Stahl (Nicoli Seroff), Trevor Morgan (John Talia Jr.), Ray Liotta (John Talia Sr.), Charles Durning (Yammi), Samantha Mathis (Carla), Ron Perlman (Curtis Sunday), Diana Scarwid (Edith Talia), Julie Lott (Sandra Sunday), Tom Adams (Grey Artist), Nancy Casemore (Mrs. Huntington-Quail), Taso Papadakis (Mechanized Artist), David Sheftell (Girl-Voiced Kid), David Sosna (Mr. Ross), Tim Velasquez (No-Good Teenager)

LIFE IS HOT IN CRACKTOWN (Lightning Media) Producers, William D. Fisch, Larry Rattner; Executive Producers, Braxton Pope, Melissa Wilfley; Director/Screenplay, Buddy Giovinazzo, based on his book; Photography, Kat Westergaard; Designer, Russell M. Jager; Costumes, Lynn Brannelly; Music, Matter Music; Editor, Shilpa Sahi; a Lodestar Entertainment presentation; Technicolor; Rated R; 99 minutes; Release date: June 29, 2009. **CAST:** Kerry Washington (Marybeth), Victor Rasuk (Manny), Evan Ross (Romeo), Desmond Harrington (Benny), Shannyn Sossamon (Concetta), Edoardo Ballerini (Chas), Melissa Wilfley (Fay), Vondie Curtis-Hall (Dixon), Brandon Routh (Sizemore), Robert Fitzgerald Diggs [aka RZA] (Sammy), Thomas Ian Nichols (Chad Wesley), Tony Plana (Lou), Carmine Giovinazzo (Junkie), Richard Portnow (Guy from 4K), Jeremy West (Mr. Rutherford), Ridge Canipe (Willy), Ariel Winter (Suzie), Illeana Douglas (Mommy), Lara Flynn Boyle (Betty McBain), Stephanie Lugo (Debbie), Maurice Blake (Brazil), Omar Regan (Cremont), Jeffrey Lorenzo (Soby), Ten Travis (Ceasar), Gavin M. Enriquez, Noah G. Enriquez (Ramon), Amber Elena Franklin (Melody), Marci Canipe (Melody's Mom), Quddus Philippe (Terrance), Shawn McGill (Tiny Pinta), Zooka Jonathan Silva (Kenny Carter), Mark Webber (Ridley), Pierson Blaetz (Customer), Hope Olaide Wilson (Girl in Closet), Sara Pickett (Joy), Adriano Aragon (Cop #1), Paul Mabon (Marybeth's Father), Jamie Rae (Woman at Party), Carly Pope (Stacy), Katija Pevec (Becky), Bryan Becker (Pepperton), Luke LaFontaine (The Beret), Joseph Rye (Dr. Clark), James Saxenmeyer (Robber)

Brandon Routh, Ridge Canipe in Life is Hot in Cracktown
© *Lightning Media*

SURVEILLANCE (Magnolia) Producers, Kent Harper, David Michaels, Marco Mehlitz; Executive Producer, David Lynch; Co-Executive Producers, Gary Hamilton, Jeff Geoffray, Walter Josten; Co-Producer, Stephen Onda; Director, Jennifer Chambers Lynch; Screenplay, Jennifer Chambers Lynch, Kent Harper; Photography, Peter Wunstorf; Designer, Sara McCudden; Costumes, Cathy McComb, Sonja Clifton Remple; Music, Todd Bryanton; Editor, Daryl K. Davis; an Arclight Films, Blue Rider Pictures presentation of a Lago Film production, in association with Film Star Pictures; American-German; Dolby; Widescreen; Color; Video-to-35mm; Rated R; 97 minutes; Release date: June 29, 2009. **CAST:** Julia Ormond (Elizabeth Anderson), Bill Pullman (Sam Hallaway), Pell James (Bobbi Prescott), Ryan Simpkins (Stephanie), French Stewart (Jim Conrad), Kent Harper (Jack Bennett), Caroline Aaron (Janet), Kyle Briere (Curtis), Hugh Dillon (Dad), Gill Gayle (Degrasso), Daryl Haney (Drug Dealer), Michael Ironside (Capt. Billings), Shannon Jardine (Elaine Meyer), Mac Miller (Johnny), Charlie Newmark (Officer Wright), Cheri Oteri (Mom), Anita Smith (Tina), Josh Strait (Keith), Kent Wolkowski (Davied), David Gane (Grocery Man), Angela Lamarish (Maid), Gerald Lenton-Young (Coroner)

Ryan Simpkins, French Stewart in Surveillance © *Magnolia Pictures*

I HATE VALENTINE'S DAY (IFC Films) Producers, William Sherak, Madeleine Sherak, Jason Shuman; Executive Producers, Dominic Ianno, Michael Gallant; Director/Screenplay, Nia Vardalos; Story, Nia Vardalos, Stephen David, Ben Zook; Photography, Brian Przypek; Designer, Dara Wishingrad; Costumes, Jenny Gering; Music, Keith Power; Editors, Steve Edwards, Tony Lombardo; Casting, Todd Thaler; a Blue Star Entertainment and My Bench Productions production; Dolby; Color; Rated PG-13; 98 minutes; Release date: July 3, 2009. **CAST:** Nia Vardalos (Genevieve Gernier), John Corbett (Greg Gatlin), Stephen Guarino

(Bill), Amir Arison (Bob), Zoe Kazan (Tammy Greenwood), Gary Wilmes (Cal), Mike Starr (John), Jason Mantzoukas (Brian Blowdell), Judah Friedlander (Dan O'Finn), Rachel Dratch (Kathy Jeemy), Jay O. Sanders (Tim the Delivery Guy), Lynda Gravátt (Rose), Olive (Rose's Dog), Suzanne Shepherd (Edie), Dan Finnerty (Grouchy Guy), Ward Horton (Grouchy Guy), Ward Horton (Mark), Isiah Whitlock Jr. (Drummer), Salvador "Wally" Corona (Bus Boy), Howard Feller (Homeless Guy), Autumn Ready Potter (Barbie), Rose Abdoo (Attractive Woman), Ian Gomez (KJ Ken), Ben Schwartz (Tammy's Date), Tracy Thorpe (Giddy Woman), Kapil Bawa (Nerdy Man), Wali Collins (Desperate Customer), Miriam Tolan (Artsy Woman), Rachel Hamilton (Woman in Gallery), David Beach (Husband in Gallery), Gaetano Iacono (Big Worker), John Tormey (Moe)

Nia Vardalos, John Corbett in I Hate Valentine's Day © *IFC Films*

I LOVE YOU, BETH COOPER (20th Century Fox) Producers, Chris Columbus, Mark Radcliffe, Michael Barnathan; Executive Producers, Larry Doyle, Jenny Blum, Michael Flynn; Director, Chris Columbus; Screenplay, Larry Doyle, based on his novel; Photography, Phil Abraham; Designer, Howard Cummings; Costumes, Karen Matthews; Music, Christophe Beck; Music Supervisor, Patrick Houlihan; Editor, Peter Honess; a Fox Atomic presentation of 1492 Pictures production; Dolby; Panavision; Deulxe color; Rated PG-13; 102 minutes; Release date: July 10, 2009. **CAST:** Hayden Panettiere (Beth Cooper), Paul Rust (Denis Cooverman), Jack T. Carpenter (Rich), Lauren London (Cammy), Lauren Storm (Treece), Shawn Roberts (Kevin), Jared Keeso (Dustin), Brendan Penny (Sean), Marie Avgeropoulos (Valli Wooley), Josh Emerson (Greg Saloga), Alan Ruck (Mr. Cooverman), Cynthia Stevenson (Mrs. Cooverman), Pat Finn (Coach Raupp), Andrea Savage (Dr. Gleeson), Violet Columbus (Angelica, Sullen Girl), Anna Mae Routledge (Patty Keck), Anja Savcic (Victoria Smeltezer), William C. Vaughan (Paul Bergie), Dairen Provost (Young Rich), Samm Levine (Convenience Store Clerk), Ellie Harvie (Cop at High School), Dalias Blake (Cop at Lake), Emily Tennant, Maggie Ma (Raupp's Sophomores), Natalie von Rotsburg (Librarian), Dharrol Alves, Karyn Michelle Baltzer, Lucy Lu (Laughing Teens), Brandon Barton, John J. Gulayets (Party Boys), Dante Alridge, Ifeanyi Obany (Young Bullies)

Paul Rust, Lauren Storm, Hayden Panettiere, Jack T. Carpenter,
Lauren London in I Love You Beth Cooper © *Twentieth Century Fox*

SOUL POWER (Sony Classics) Producers, Jeffrey Levy-Hinte, David Sonenberg, Leon Gast; Director, Jeffrey Levy-Hinte; Photography, Paul Goldsmith, Kevin Keating, Albert Maysles, Roderick Young; Editor, David Smith; a DAS Films presentation of an Antidote Films production; Dolby; Color; 16mm-toHD; Rated PG-13; 92 minutes; Release date: July 10, 2009. An unreleased three-day concert that preceded Muhammad Ali and George Foreman's famous "Rumble in the Jungle" fight in 1974. **WITH:** Muhammad Ali, James Brown, Stokely Carmichael, the Crusaders, Celia Cruz and the Fania All-Stars, Don King, Stewart Levine, Miriam Makeba, Hugh Masakela, George Plimpton, the Spinners, Bill Withers

WEATHER GIRL (Secret Identity) Producers, Tricia O'Kelley, Steakhaus Productions; Executive Producer, Brandon Barrera; Director/Screenplay, Blayne Weaver; Photography, Brandon Trost; Designer, Michael Fitzgerald; Costumes, Sarah Trost; Music, Andrew Hollander; Editor, Abe Levy; Casting, Lauren Bass; a Secret Identity Productions production, in association with Steakhaus Productions, T&A Pictures and H2R Productions; Color; Rated R; 93 minutes; Release date: July 10, 2009. **CAST:** Tricia O'Kelley (Sylvia), Patrick J. Adams (Byron), Ryan Devlin (Walt), Mark Harmon (Dale), Kaitlin Olson (Sherry), Alex Kapp Horner (Emily), Marin Hinkle (Jane), Jon Cryer (Charles), Jane Lynch (J.D.), Blair Underwood (Fitz), Brandon Barrera (Ernest), Enrico Colantoni (George), Amie Donegan (Mary), Timothy Dvorak (Jack), Lucas Fleischer (Arthur), David Giuntoli (James), Rob Helms (Choking Man), Bubba Lewis (Irving), Omar Leyva (Juan), J.P. Manoux (Raymond), J.D. Nielsen (Paramedic), Kit Pongetti (Harper), Meredith Roberts (Charlotte), Adam Krill (Josh), Jamie Rosenblatt (Handsome), Hal Tryon (Waiter), Blayne Weaver (William)

THE WAY WE GET BY (International Film Circuit) Producer, Gita Pullapilly; Executive Producer, Warren Cook; Director/Screenplay/Editor, Aron Gaudet; Photography, Aron Gaudet, Dan Ferrigan; Music, Zack Martin; NTSC Color; DV-to35mm; Not rated; 84 minutes; Release date: July 17, 2009. Documentary on three Bangor, Maine residents who devote their lives to engaging with the troops en route to or from Iraq and Afghanistan. **WITH:** Joan Gaudet, Bill Knight, Jerry Mundy

The Way We Get By © Intl. Film Circuit

HEART OF STONE (Goodfootage) formerly *Hard to Be an Indian*; Producer, Beth Toni Kruvant; Executive Producers, Paul Bartick, Anand Kamalakar; Director, Beth Toni Kruvant; Photography, David Harges, Scott Schelley; Music, Ben Decter; Editor, Anand Kamalakar; Color; DV; Not rated; 84 minutes; Release date: July 17, 2009. Documentary on Principal Ron Stone's efforts to boost morale and grades at Newark's Weequahic High School. **WITH:** Ron Stone, Ray von Libson, Sharif Patterson, Hal Braff, Richie Roberts, Bashir Akinyele, Philip Roth, Al Attles, Cory Booker

OFF JACKSON AVENUE (Goltzius Productions) Producer, Michiel Pilgram; Executive Producer, Gill Holland; Director/Screenplay, John-Luke Montias; Photography, George Gibson; Designer, Tamar Gadish; Costumes, Sandra Alexandre; Music, Ed Tomney; Editor, Michiel Pilgram; a Goltzius production, in association with Group Entertainment; Color; Super 16-to-HD; Not rated; 80 minutes; Release date: July 17, 2009. **CAST:** Jessica Pimentel (Olivia), Stivi Paskoski (Milot), Jun Suenaga (Tomo), John-Luke Montias (Joey), Aya Cash (Olga), Gene Ruffini (Uncle Jack), Daniel Oreskes (Ivan), Judith Hawking (Donna), Michael Gnat (Wall Street Jimmy), Antonio Mastrantonio (Tommy), Richard Petrocelli (Dino), Jackson Loo (Wu), Grant Chang (Li), Sonia De Los Santos (Semka), Alona Tarniak (Dascha), Denise Ogaz (Corina), Jim Tooey (Russ), Chris Hanson (Benny), Aki Ando (Tomo's Mother), Norman Middleton (Archie), José Ramón Rosario (Luis), Shing Ka (Kwok), Ryo Okamura (Tong), Anthony Caso (Gabe), Clem Cheung (Eddie Chang), David Chan (Ho), Alexander Norton (Robbie)

THE WONDER OF IT ALL (Indican Pictures) Director, Jeffrey Roth; Screenplay, Jeffrey Roth, Stephen Beck; Photography, Paul Basta; Music, Scott Starrett; Editor, Andy Zall; Color; HD; Not rated; 82 minutes; Release date: July 17, 2009. Documentary on the men behind the Apollo space missions. **WITH:** Buzz Aldrin, Alan Bean, Eugene Cernan, Charlie Duke, Edgar D. Mitchell, Harrison Schmitt, John Young

HOMECOMING (Paper Street Films/Animus Films) Producers, Jim Young, Austin Stark, Bill Papariella, Bingo Gubelmann; Executive Producers, Benji Kohn, Chris Papavasiliou, Richard Bard, Nuala Barton; Director, Morgan J. Freeman; Screenplay, Katie Fetting, Jake Goldberger, Frank Hannah; Based on an idea by Tim O'Hair, Jim Young; Photography, Stephen Kazmierski; Designer, Mark White; Costumes, Teresa Duncan; Music, Jack Livesey; Editor, Keith Reamer; Casting, Scout Masterson; Dolby; Color; Not rated; 90 minutes; Release date: July 17, 2009. **CAST:** Mischa Barton (Shelby), Matt Long (Mike), Jessica Stroup (Elizabeth Mitchum), Michael Landes (Billy Fletcher), Allen Williamson (Adams), Joshua Elijah Reese (Billick), Nick Pasqual (Davis), Joe Forgione (Elfman), Alex Hooper (Joblanski), Byrdie Bell (Lisa), Amanda Jane Cooper (Aleisha), Denise Dal Vera (Mrs. Donaldson), Emily Martin, Olivia Duball (Posse Girls), Mary Griffin (Taylor), Benjamin Eran McGinn (Jock), Logan C. Sayre (Gym Boy), Danielle Simone (Jackie)

Jessica Stroup in Homecoming © *Paper Street/Animus*

DEATH IN LOVE (Screen Media) Producers, Boaz Yakin, Joseph N. Zolfo; Co-Producer, Alma Har'el; Director/Screenplay, Boaz Yakin; Photography, Frederik Jacobi; Designer, Dara Wishingrad; Costumes, Sue Gandy; Music, Lesley Barber; Editor, John Lyons; a Boaz Yakin production; Widescreen; Color; Rated R; 97 minutes; Release date: July 17, 2009. **CAST:** Josh Lucas (Eldest Son), Jacqueline Bisset (Mother), Lukas Haas (Youngest Son), Vanessa Kai (Asian Woman), Emma Bell (Young Girl), Adam Brody (Talent Agent), Fabrizia Dal Farra (Concentration Camp Woman), Francis Dumaurier (Old Lawyer), Seth Fisher (Hotel Receptionist), Kelli Giddish (Young Mother), Laura Holloway, Grace Massar (Women), Jamie Hurley (Woman Tending Child), Jacqueline Margolis (The Widow), Elizabeth Newman (The Waitress), Rich Odell (Agent), Stu Richel (Father), Nicholas Sireci (Young Brother), Matt Walton (Young Father)

Lukas Haas in Death in Love *© Screen Media*

CALIFORNIA COMPANY TOWN (Lee Anne Schmitt) Producer/Director/Screenplay/Photography/Editor, Lee Anne Schmitt; Color/black and white; 16mm; Not rated; 77 minutes; Release date: July 24, 2009. Documentary on the demise of several of California's towns because the industries that built them abandoned them.

THE ANSWER MAN (Magnolia) formerly *Arlen Faber*; Producers, Kevin Messick, Jana Edelbaum; Executive Producers, Rachel Cohen, Stephen Hays, Peter Graham, Michael Lesser; Director/Screenplay, John Hindman; Photography, Oliver Bokelberg; Designer, Alex DiGerlando; Costumes, Rebecca Bentjen; Music, Teddy Castellucci; Editor, Jerry Greenberg; an iDeal Partners Film Fund presentation, in association with 120 db Films, of a Kevin Messick production; Dolby; Technicolor; Rated R; 96 minutes; Release date: July 24, 2009. **CAST:** Jeff Daniels (Arlen Faber), Lauren Graham (Elizabeth), Lou Taylor Pucci (Kris Lucas), Olivia Thirlby (Anne), Kat Dennings (Dahlia), Nora Dunn (Terry Fraser), Tony Hale (Mailman), Annie Corley (Mrs. Gold), Max Antisell (Alex), Thomas Roy (Riley Lucas), Peter Patrikios (Ross), Greg Wood (Businessman #1), Richard G. Lyntoon (Journalist), Richard Barlow (Paul), Sally Mercer, David Mulholland (Customers), Lauren Emily Jacobs (Young Girl), Charles J. Corrado Jr. (Roy), Bev Appleton (Patient), Sylvia Kauders (Old Woman), Sandra Landers (Singing Wife), Ginny Graham (Singing Grandmother), Conor O'Brien (Singing Son), Morgan Turner (Singing Daughter)

Lou Taylor Pucci, Jeff Daniels in The Answer Man *© Magnolia Pictures*

LOREN CASS (Kino) Producers, Frank Craft, Chris Fuller, Kayla Tabish; Executive Producer, Owen Arcata; Director/Screenplay/Editor, Chris Fuller; Photography, William Garcia; Music, Jimmy Morey; Special Makeup Effects, Marcus Koch; a Jonesing Pictures production; Color; Not rated; 83 minutes; Release date: July 24, 2009. **CAST:** Kayla Tabish (Nicole), Travis Maynard (Jason), Lewis Brogan (Cale), Jacob Reynolds (The Suicide Kid), Mike Glausier (The Punk Kid), Din Thomas (The Fight Kid), Blag Dahlia, Keith Morris, Omali Yeshitela (Narrators), Matthew Bistok (The Fit Kid), John Holmstrom (Jason's Father), Rob Shepard (Nicole's Father), Donna Gilbert (Nicole's Mother), Peter Wallace (Assistant Principal), Jeff Hatch, Morgan Leiby (Bedroom Kids), Zay A. Rios-Dicamara (The Diner Kid), Adam Gnade (The Silent Kid), Medhat Gorgy (The Cop), Chris Barrows (Towtruck Operator), Chris Lima, Aaron Riley, Justin Thrift (Fight Kid's Friends), Arthur Corley (Bus Driver), Winky Wright, Fred Wahlscrom, German (Voices), Alec Baillie, Scott Sturgeon, Ezra Kire, Brandon Chevalier-Kolling (Band Members)

Kayla Tabish, Travis Maynard in Loren Cass *© Kino Intl.*

PARAISO TRAVEL (Peace Arch) Producers, Santiago Diaz, Juan Rendon, Alex Pereira, Isaac Lee; Director, Simon Brand; Screenplay, Juan Rendon, Jorge Franco; Based on the novel by Jorge Franco; Photography, Rafa Lluch; Designer, Miguel Angel Alvarez; Costumes, Sandra Camacho; Music, Angelo Milli; Editor, Alberto de Toro; a Paraiso Pictures (U.S./Colombia)/Grand Illusions Entertainment production; American-Colombian; Dolby; Color; Rated R; 116 minutes; American release date: July 24, 2009. **CAST:** Angelica Blandon (Reina), Pedro Capo (Giovanny), Raul Castillo (Carlos), Aldemar Correa (Marlon), Margarita Rosa de Francisco (Raquel), Ana de la Reguera (Milagros), Germán Jaramillo (Don Hernan), John Leguizamo (Roger Pena), Chiko Mendez (Los Simpaticos Guitarrist), Edward Steven Mesa (Rehab Patient), Luis Fernando Munera (Don Pastor), Jesús Ochoa (Mexicote Driver), Panama Redd (Menacing Man in Car), Eddie Rosado (Los Simpaticos Conga Player), Vicky Rueda (La Calena), Ana Maria Sánchez (Patricia), Indhira Serrano (Madame Taylor), Bob Weston (Cop)

DEADGIRL (Dark Sky Films) Producers/Directors, Marcel Sarmiento, Gadi Harel; Executive Producers, Chris Webster, Rob Hickman; Screenplay, Trent Haaga; Photography, Harris Charalambous; Designer, Diana Zeng; Costumes, Lynh Haaga; Music Supervisor, Kim Randall; Editor, Phillip Blackford; a Hollywoodmade production, in association with Sartistic; Widescreen; HD; Color; Rated R; 101 minutes; Release date: July 24, 2009. **CAST:** Shiloh Fernandez (Rickie), Noah Segan (J.T.), Michael Bowen (Clint), Candice Accola (JoAnn), Andrew DiPalma (Johnny), Eric Podnar (Wheeler), Nolan Gerard Funk (Dwyer), Christina Blevins (Amanda), Kelle Cantwell (Britt), Shushig DerStepanian (Elizabeth), David Alan Graf (Mr. Harrison), Dustin Hess (Walter), Susan Marie Keller (Nikki), Christina Masterson (Rosie), Casey Morgan (Riley), Timothy Muskatell (Wes), Jenny Spain (The Deadgirl), Dawson van Pelt (Kurt Lars), Luke Van Pelt (Chris Lars), Jessica Wilson (Student), Crystal Young (Kris)

ALIENS IN THE ATTIC (20th Century Fox) Producer, Barry Josephson; Executive Producers, Arnon Milchan, Marc S. Fischer; Director, John Schultz; Screenplay, Mark Burton, Adam F. Goldberg; Story, Mark Burton; Photography, Don Burgess; Designer, Barry Chusid; Costumes, Mona May; Music, John Debney; Editor, John Pace; Visual Effects Supervisor, Douglas Hans Smith; Visual Effects & Animation, Rhythm & Hues; a Josephson Entertainment production, presented in association with Regency Enterprises; Dolby; Color; Rated PG; 86 minutes; Release date: July 31, 2009. **CAST:** Carter Jenkins (Tom Pearson), Austin Butler (Jake Pearson), Ashley Tisdale (Bethany Pearson), Ashley Boetticher (Hannah Pearson), Henri Young (Art Pearson), Regan Young (Lee Pearson), Doris Roberts (Nana Rose Pearson), Robert Hoffman (Ricky Dillman), Kevin Nealon (Stuart Pearson), Gillian Vigman (Nina Pearson), Andy Richter (Uncle Nathan Pearson), Tim Meadows (Sheriff Doug Armstrong), Malese Jow (Julie), Megan Parker (Brooke), Maggie VandenBerghe (Annie Filkins), Doug MacMillan (Police Radio Dispatch), Warren Paeff (Radio Announcer), Thomas Haden Church (Voice of Tazer), Josh Peck (Voice of Sparks), J.K. Simmons (Voice of Skip), Kari Wahlgren (Voice of Razor)

Skip, Robert Hoffman in
Aliens in the Attic
© Twentieth Century Fox/
Regency Enterprises

FRAGMENTS (Peace Arch) formerly *Winged Creatures*; Producer, Robert Salerno; Executive Producers, Naomi Despres, Gilbert Alloul, John Flock, Lewin Webb, Devesh Chetty, Robyn Gardiner; Director, Rowan Woods; Screenplay, Roy Freirich, based on his novel; Photography, Eric Edwards; Designer, Max Biscoe; Costumes, Mary Claire Hannan; Music, Marcelo Zarvos; Music Supervisor, Matt Aberle; Editor, Meg Reticker; an Artina Films production, presented in association with RGM Entertainment; Dolby; FotoKem Color; Rated R; 95 minutes; Release date: July 31, 2009. **CAST:** Kate Beckinsale (Carla Davenport), Dakota Fanning (Anne Hagen), Guy Pearce (Dr. Bruce Laraby), Forest Whitaker (Charlie Archenault), Embeth Davidtz (Joan Laraby), Troy Garity (Ron Abler), Jackie Earle Haley (Bob Jasperson), Jennifer Hudson (Kathy Hammet), Josh Hutcherson (Jimmy Jasperson), Jeanne Tripplehorn (Doris Hagen), James LeGros (Dr. Dan Howard), Jaimz Woolvett (Swedish Cook), Marshall Allman (Dan the Bellhop), James Babson (Bike Shop Owner), Jacquie Barnbrook (Lori's Mom), Ankur Bhatt (Cubicle Neighbor), Kevin Cooney (Travis Carlson), Cohl Klop, Michael Drummond (Prayer Group Kids), Kevin Durand (Bagman), Andrew Fiscella (Numbers Man), Soren Fulton (Howard), Gina Gallego (Waitress), Ted Garcia (Funeral Reporter), Walton Goggins (Zack), Beth Grant (Carl's Mom), Tim Guinee (Aaron Hagen), Gwen Holloway (Social Worker), Elanie Loh (Losing Gambler), Brooke Mackenzie (Traci), Hayley McFarland (Lori Carline), Jamie McShane (Stickman), Debrah Neal (Casino Lounge Singer), Lu Parker (TV Reporter), Randall Park (Resident), Lara Phillips (Woman), Tarina Pouncy (ICU Nurse), Jeff Rector (Sheriff), Santos Reyes (Eddie), Al Ruscio (Angelo), Kent Shocknek (TV Reporter), Robin Weigert (Lydia Jasperson), Whittni Wright (Hannah)

THE COLLECTOR (Freestyle) formerly *The Midnight Man*; Producers, Brett Forbes, Julia Richardson, Patrick Rizzotti; Executive Producers, Jennifer Hilton, Mickey Liddell; Director, Marcus Dunstan; Screenplay, Marcus Dunstan, Patrick Melton; Photography, Brandon Cox; Designer, Ermanno Di Febo-Orsini; Costumes, Ashlyn Angel; Music, Jerome Dillon; Editors, Alex Luna, James Mastracco, Howard Smith; Special Effects Coordinator, Frank Ceglia; Stunts, Hiro Koda; Casting, Monika Mikkelsen; a Liddell Entertainment presentation of a Fortress Features production; Dolby; Technicolor; Rated R; 88 minutes; Release date: July 31, 2009. **CAST:** Josh Stewart (Arkin), Michael Reilly Burke (Michael Chase), Andrea Roth (Victoria Chase), Karley Scott Collins (Hannah Chase), Madeline Zima (Jill Chase), Juan Fernandez (The Collector), Robert Wisdom (Roy), Gregory Alan Williams (Sheriff), Haley Alexis Pullos (Cindy), Diane Ayala Goldner (Gena Wharton), Krystal Mayo (Dancer), Alex Feldman (Chad), Michael Showers (Deputy Sheriff), Jabari Thomas, Hiro Koda (Medics), Brett Forbes (Officer Hoss Wiggins), John Snell (Yard Worker), Daniella Alonso (Lisa), William Prael (Larry Wharton)

Josh Stewart in The Collector © Freestyle Releasing

GOTTA DANCE (N.B.A. Entertainment) Producer, Dori Berinstein; Executive Producers, Linda Goldstein Knowlton, Adam Miller, Alan Fisher, Glen Siegel; Co-Producer, Leo Lawrence; Director, Dori Berinstein; Screenplay, Dori Berinstein, Adam Zucker; Photography, Leo Lawrence; Music, Craig Sharmat; Editor, Adam Zucker; a Dramatic Forces production; Color; Not rated; 93 minutes; Release date: July 31, 2009. Documentary about a group of 12 women and one man, seniors ranging in age from 60 to 83, who became the New Jersey Nets' half-time attraction, a hip-hop dance team called the NETSationals. **WITH:** the 2007 NETSational Dance Team, Jaclyn Sabol, Marla Collins, Kiberlee Garris, Petra Pope

Gotta Dance © N.B.A. Entertainment

IF I DIE TONIGHT (Indican Pictures) Producers, Seyi Sonuga, Evelyn Palmer; Director/Screenplay/Music, Seyi Sonuga; Editors, Nola Schiff, Doug Forbes; Dolby; Color; Not rated; 92 minutes; Release date: July 31, 2009. Documentary about the aftermath of the shooting of Amadou Diallo. **WITH:** Greg Baglia, Elijah Cummings, De Lacy Davis, Saikou Diallo, Francois Joseph, Abner Louima, Brendan Miles, Madeline Neumann, Al Sharpton

Tilly Hatcher in Beeswax © Cinema Guild

BEESWAX (Cinema Guild) Producers, Ethan Vogt, Dia Sokol; Executive Producers, Houston King, Garry Stewart; Director/Screenplay/Editor, Andrew Bujalski; Photography, Matthias Grunsky; a Sisters Project production; Color; Super 16-to-35mm; Not rated; 100 minutes; Release date: August 5, 2009. **CAST:** Tilly Hatcher (Jeannie), Maggie Hatcher (Lauren), Alex Karpovsky (Merrill), Katy O'Connor (Corinne), David Zellner (Scott), Kyle Henry (Michael), S.J. Anderson (Teddy, Customer), Anne Dodge (Amanda), Betty Blackwell (Lila), Bryan Poyser (Jason, Study Buddy), Rebecca McInroy (Holly), Nathan Zellner (Lee), Atietie Tonwe (Emeka), Nina Sokol (Naomi), Jillian Glantz (Wynonna), Christy Moore (Paula's, Girls' Mom), Janet Pierson (Sally), D.J. Taitelbaum (A.C.), Becca Cohen (Annemarie), Moss Gillespie (Tony, Young Boy), Chad Nichols (Evan), Jimmy Gonzales (Yann), Dia Sokol (Maryann), Bob Byington (Tom), Smiley Moreno (Ralph), Peggy Chen (Jin)

OCEAN OF PEARLS (Lightpost Pictures) Producers, Sarab S. Neelam, Jaspal Kaur Neelam; Director, Sarab S. Neelam; Screenplay, V. Prasad; Story, Sarab S. Neelam, V. Prasad; Photography, Lon Stratton; Music, Pinar Toprak; Editor, Jason Stewart; Color; Rated PG-13; 97 minutes; Release date: August 7, 2009. **CAST:** Omid Abtahi (Amrit Singh), Heather McComb (Susan Clark), Ron Canada (Dr. William Ballard), Navi Rawat (Smita Sethi), Ajay Mehta (Ravinder Singh), Todd Babcock (Ryan Bristol), Dennis Haskins (Dr. Shultz), KT Thangavelu (Amrit's Mother), Rena Owen (Anna), Brenda Strong (Mary Stewart), Frank Zieger (TSA Officer), Loren Bass (Moderator), Zach Begle (David Stewart), Teri Clark (Nurse Receptionist), Don Cochran (Doctor), Shawntay Dalon, William C. Fox, Ayanna Fullilove (Travelers), Cameron Hall, Atif Hashwi (Young Boys in Airport), Jim Lewis (Security Guard #3), Lisa Maxine Melinn (Mother in Airport), Aphrodite Nikolovski (Anna's Daughter), Leisa Pulido (Social Worker)

SOUNDTRACK FOR A REVOLUTION (Louverture Films) Producers, Joslyn Barnes, Jim Czarnecki, Bill Guttentag, Dan Sturman, Dylan Nelson; Executive Producers, Danny Glover, Gina Harrell, Mark Downie, Marc Henry Johnson; Directors/Screenplay, Bill Guttentag, Dan Sturman; Photography, Buddy Squires, Jonathan Else, Stephen Kazmierski; Music, Philip Marshall; Editor, Jeffrey Doe; a Freedom Songs production, in association with Goldcrest Films Intl/Wild Bunch; American-French-British; Dolby; Color/Black and white; HD; Not rated; 82 minutes; Release date: August 7, 2009. Documentary on music's role in the civil rights movement. **WITH:** The Roots, John Legend, Wyclef Jean, Joss Stone, Richie Havens, Anthony Hamilton, The Blind Boys of Alabama, Angie Stone, Mary Mary, T.V. on the Radio, Harry Belafonte, Lula Joe Williams, Andrew Young, Lunda Lowery, Julian Bond, Rev. C.T. Vivian, John Seigenthaler, Dorothy Cotton, Candie Carawan, Guy Carawan, Joanne Bland, Mamie Brown-Mason, Robert Cohen, Farrell J. Duncombe, Jamila Jones, Rev. Edwin King, Samuel Kyles, Dorie Ladner, Dr. Bernard LaFayette Jr., James M. Lawson Jr., Charles McDew, Rev. Harold Middlebrook, Charles Neblett, Hank Thomas, Mary Williams, Robert Zellner

I SELL THE DEAD (IFC Films) Producers, Larry Fessenden, Peter Phok; Director/Screenplay/Editor, Glenn McQuaid; Photography, Richard Lopez; Designer, David Bell; Music, Jeff Grace; a Glass Eye Pix presentation; Color; Not rated; 85 minutes; Release date: August 7, 2009. **CAST:** Dominic Monaghan (Arthur Blake), Ron Perlman (Father Duffy), Larry Fessenden (Willie Grimes), Angus Scrimm (Dr. Vernon Quint), John Speredakos (Cornelius Murphy), Eileen Colgan (Maisey O'Connell), Brenda Cooney (Fanny Bryers), Daniel Manche (Young Arthur), Joel Garland (Ronnie), James Godwin (Mark 1), Alisdair Stewart (Bulger), Heather Robb (Myrtle Murphy), Aidan Redmond (Jack Flood), Heather Bullock (Valentine Kelly), Patrick Bucklew (Creature #2), Jackie Arnold (Young Cornelius), Jim Noonan (Bram Thatcher), Chris Shaw (Executioner), Charlie Simpson (Jippo Kelly), Haidyn Harvey (Dancing Girl), Conor Simpson (Modger Kelly), Jennifer Stackpole (Prostitute #1), Ken Robertson (Tommy Burke), Martin Pfefferkorn (Howling Man), Meagan Hooper (Town Girl), Todd Ryan Jones (Villager), Jonathan M. Parisen, Tom Loggins, Eddie Lentol, Amber Baldinelli (Town Folks)

Larry Fessenden, Brenda Cooney, Dominic Monaghan in
I Sell the Dead © *IFC Films*

SPREAD (Anchor Bay) Producers, Ashton Kutcher, Jason Goldberg, Peter Morgan; Executive Producers, Paul Kolsby, John Limotte, Myles Nestel, Anthony Callie; Director, David Mackenzie; Screenplay, Jason Dean Hall; Story, Jason Dean Hall, Paul Kolsby; Photography, Steven Poster; Designer, Cabot McMullen; Costumes, Ruth E. Carter; Music, John Swihart; Music Supervisor, Elizabeth Miller; Editor, Nicholas Erasmus; Casting, David Rubin, Richard Hicks; a Barbarian Film and Oceana Media Finance presentation of a Katalyst Films production; Dolby; Panavision; Color; Rated R; 97 minutes; Release date: August 14, 2009. **CAST:** Ashton Kutcher (Nicki), Anne Heche (Samantha), Margarita Levieva (Heather), Sebastian Star (Harry), Ashley Johnson (Eve), Eric Balfour (Sean), Sonia Rockwell (Christina), Rachel Blanchard (Emily), Maria Conchita Alonso (Ingrid), Hart Bochner (Will), Thomas Kijas (Jason, Head Waiter), Landon Ashworth (Prince Stelio's Guard), Shane Brolly (Prince Stelio), Sarah Buxton (Helen), Derek Carter (Delivery Guy), Peter Marc Jacobson (Plastic Surgeon), Dani Levine (Nadia), Vince Allen, Lanre Idewu, Marc Gruninger, Siso Kamburov (Sexy Pool Guys), Anya Assante (Clubgoer), Madison Bauer (Nicki's Mother), Candice A. Buenrostro, Christie Burson, Adrienne McQueen (Sexy Pool Girls), Jennifer Cambra, Lejla Hadzimuratovic, Jiffy Reed (Dancers), Rene Darmiento (Kissing Girl), Kris Edwards, Michael Sidisin Jr. (Bartenders), Iglesias Estefania (Bella), Lourdes Faberes (Prince Stelio's Gang Member), John Ierardi (Instigator), Lauri Johnson (Meter Maid), Jessica Rizo (Beautiful Latina Love Interest), Brianna Nicole Schlanger (Bikini Girl)

Anne Heche, Ashton Kutcher in Spread © *Anchor Bay*

EARTH DAYS (Zeitgeist) Producer/Director/Screenplay, Robert Stone; Executive Producer, Mark Samels; Photography, Howard Shack; Music, Michael Giacchino; Editor, Don Kleszy; an American Experience Films presentation; Color/Black and white; Not rated; 102 minutes; Release date: August 14, 2009. Documentary on America's efforts to improve the environment. **WITH:** Stewart Udall, Denis Hayes, Stewart Brand, Rusty Schweickart, Hunter Lovins, Dennis Meadows, Stephanie Mills, Pete McCloskey, Paul Ehrlich

Rusty Schweickart in Earth Days © *Zeitgeist Films*

GRACE (Anchor Bay) Producers, Kevin DeWalt, Cory Neal, Adam Green, Ingo Volkhammer; Executive Producers, Scott Einbinder, Simon Edery; Director/Screenplay, Paul Solet; Photography, Zoran Popovic; Designer, Martina Buckley; Costumes, Brenda Shenher; Music, Austin Wintory; Editors, John Coniglio, Darrin Navarro; Special Effects Coordinator, Wade Maurer; Casting, Kelly Martin Wagner, Carmen Kotyk; an Indigomotion presentation of an ArieScope Pictures production in association with Dark Eye Entertainment; Dolby; Color; Rated R; 85 minutes; Release date: August 14, 2009. **CAST:** Jordan Ladd (Madeline Matheson), Samantha Ferris (Patricia Lang), Gabrielle Rose (Vivian Matheson), Serge Houde (Henry Matheson), Stephen Park (Michael Matheson), Kate Herriot (Shelly), Troy Skog (ER Doctor), Malcolm Stewart (Dr. Richard Sohn), Jamie Stephenson (Skinny Clerk), Chris Cunningham (Lab Technician), Karen von Staden (Dr. Sohn's Secretary), Mark Claxton (Veterinarian), Tyler Kari Bzdel (Grace at 5 months)

POST GRAD (Fox Searchlight) Producers, Ivan Reitman, Joe Medjuck, Jeffrey Clifford; Executive Producer, Tom Pollock; Director, Vicky Jenson; Screenplay, Kelly Fremon; Photography, Charles Minsky; Art Director, Michael Rizzo; Costumes, Alexandra Welker; Music, Christophe Beck; Music Supervisor, Patrick Houlihan; Editor, Dana Congdon; Casting, Joanna Colbert, Richard Mento; a Montecito Picture Co. production in association with Cold Springs Pictures/Dune Entertainment; Dolby; Panavision; Deluxe color; Rated PG-13; 88 minutes; Release date: August 21, 2009. **CAST:** Alexis Bledel (Ryden Malby), Zach Gilford (Adam Davies), Michael Keaton (Walter Malby), Jane Lynch (Carmella Malby), Bobby Coleman (Hunter Malby), Carol Burnett (Grandma Maureen), Rodrigo Santoro (David Santiago), Catherine Reitman (Jessica Bard), Mary Anne McGarry (Barbara Snaff), J.K. Simmons (Roy Davies), Robert Arce (Chancellor), Jeanie Hackett (Woman at Graduation), Oscar "Big O'" Dillon (Security Officer), Vanessa Branch (Receptionist), Shirley Jordan (Interviewer), Craig Robinson (Funeral Director), Michael Grant Terry (College Grad), Melissa Tang, Brandon Phillips, Parisa Fitz-Henley (College Friends), Robert M. Koch (Gary the Buckle Man), Fred Armisen (Guacanator Pitchman), Donnie D. Stroud (Manager at the Mint), Alexandra Holden (Cute Funky Girl), Angel Oquendo (Police Officer), Desean Terry (Young Cop), Andrew Daly (Lloyd Hastings), Kirk Fox (Buckle-O-Bill), Anna Khaja (Juanita), Gino Woulard, Reid Harper, Samantha Epstein (Box Car Racers), Patrick O'Connor (Landlord), Dempsey Pappion (Basketball Player)

Michael Keaton, Carol Burnett, Bobby Coleman, Jane Lynch, Alexis Bledel, Zach Gilford in Post Grad © *Fox Searchlight*

X GAMES 3D: THE MOVIE (Walt Disney Motion Pictures) Producer, Phil Orlins; Executive Producers, Keith Clinkscales, Jed Drake, Ron Semiao, John Skipper, Norby Williamson; Director, Steve Lawrence; Screenplay, Steve Lawrence, Greg Jennings; Photography, Matt Goodman; Director of Stereoscopy, Pierre-Hughes Routhier; Music, Tobias Enhus; Music Supervisor, Kevin Wilson; Editor, Todd Crites; Graphic Designer, David Sparrgrove; Narrator, Emile Hirsch; an ESPN Films production; Dolby; Color; 3-D; Rated PG; 92 minutes; Release date: August 21, 2009. Documentary on Los Angeles' 2008 extreme sports X Games competitions. **WITH:** Shaun White, Danny Way, Bob Burnquist, Ricky Carmichael, Travis Pastrana, Kyle Loza, Jake Brown, Brian Deegan, Bucky Lasek, Sal Masekela, Dave Mirra, Paul Page

ART & COPY (Seventh Art) Producers, Jimmy Greenway, Michael Nadeau; Executive Producers, David Baldwin, Mary Warlick, Gregory Beauchamp, Kirk Souder; Director, Doug Pray; Photography, Peter Nelson; Editor, Philip Owens; The One Club, Art&Industry/Granite Pass production; Color; Not rated; 89 minutes; Release date: August 21, 2009. Documentary on the people behind some of the most influential ad campaigns of recent times. **WITH:** Lee Clow, Dan Wieden, David Kennedy, Phyllis K. Robinson, Hal Riney, George Lois, Rich Silverstein, Jeff Goodby, Mary Wells, Cliff Freeman, Jim Durfee, Charlie Moss, Ed Rollins

Art & Copy © *Seventh Art*

CONFESSIONSOFA EX-DOOFUS-ITCHYFOOTED MUTHA (Innocent Bystander) Producer/Director/Screenplay/Editor, Melvin Van Peebles; Photography, John Threat; Music Supervisor, William "Spaceman" Patterson; Black and white/color; HD; Not rated; 99 minutes; Release date: August 21, 2009. **CAST:** Melvin Van Peebles (Edwin/Doofus/Ex-Doofus), Stephanie Weeks (Rita), Glen Turner (Commandant), Teddy Hayes (Jones), Alfred Preisser (Fernando), Louis Johnson (The Saviour), Tamiko White (Landlady), U-Savior Washington (Sergeant), Mario Van Peebles (Pirate Captain)

THE MARC PEASE EXPERIENCE (Paramount Vantage) Producers, David Rubin, Michael London, Bruna Papandera; Executive Producer, Nan Moarles; Director, Todd Louiso; Screenplay, Jacob Kosoff, Todd Louiso; Photography, Tim Suhrstedt; Designer, Maher Ahmad; Costumes, Daniel Orlandi; Music, Christophe Beck; Editors, Julie Monroe, Peter Teschner; Casting, Richard Hicks; a Groundswell Productions presentation of a Firefly Pictures production; Dolby; Color; Rated PG-13; 84 minutes; Release date: August 21, 2009. **CAST:** Jason Schwartzman (Marc Pease), Ben Stiller (Jon Gribble), Anna Kendrick (Meg Brickman), Ebon Moss-Bacharach (Gavin), Gabrielle Dennis (Tracey), Jay Paulson (Gerry), Zachary Booth (Craig), Carissa Capobianco (Jen), Kelen Coleman (Stephanie), Cullen Moss (Young Father), Amber Wallace (Ilona), Patrick Stogner (Patrick, Stagehand), Kassie Hight, Laurie Kimsey (The Wiz Poppies), Jenny Gulley (The Good Witch), Twyla Banks (Auntie Em), Dikran Tulaine (Mr. Zeller), Taylow Kowalski (Rodney), Lucy Spain (Addaperle), Duncan M. Hill (Uncle Henry), Brittney McNamara (Dorothy), Patt Moday (Himself), Dylan Hubbard (Tin Man), Matt Cornwell (Rick Berger), Bridget Gethins (Craig's Mother), Austin Herring (Mr. Edwards), Ed Wagenseller (Science Teacher), Jared Grimes (Wiz/Thomas Pickney), Millard Darden (Pascal), Brooke Jaye Taylor (Young Mother), Tyler O'Neal Easter (Lion), Kameron King (Doran), Damien C. Haas (Techie), Justin R. Kennedy (Justin), Chaz McNeil (The Scarecrow)

WE LIVE IN PUBLIC (Abramorama) Producers, Keirda Bahruth, Ondi Timoner; Executive Producers, Sean McKeough, Vladamir Radovanov, John Battsek, Andrew Ruhemann; Director/Screenplay/Photography, Ondi Timoner; Music, Ben Decter, Marco D'Ambrosio; Editors, Josh Altman, Ondi Timoner; an Interloper Films production, in association with Passion Pictures; Color; Not rated; 90 minutes; Release date: August 28, 2009. Documentary on compulsive videographer and Internet pioneer Josh Harris. **WITH:** David Amron, Alex Arcadia, Zero Boy, Brett Brewer, Owen Bush, Jason Calacanis, Cal Chamberlain, Tanya Corrin, Jeffrey Deitch, Chris DeWolfe, Abby Ellin, Feedbuck, Leo Fernekes, Donna Ferrato, Robert Galinsky, Missy Galore, Marc Geiger, Jeff Gompertz, Anthony Haden-Guest, Jon Harris, Josh Harris, Nico Haupt, Alana Heiss, Max Heller, David Hershkovits, Harold Kaufman, Leon Koenig, Hillary Koob-Sassen, Gabriella Latessa, Mangina, Andy Morris, Gabrielle Penabaz, Nacho Platas, Stephanie Platas, Michael Portnoy, Adeo Ressi, Douglas Rushkoff, Ashkan Sahihi, Nancy Smith, Gabriel Snyder, Nikolas Van Egten, Josh White, Fred Wilson, Jessica Zaino

We Live in Public © *Abramorama*

GOSPEL HILL (ArtMattan Productions) Producers, Giancarlo Esposito, Cerise Hallam-Larkin, Emerson Machtus, Freddy Braidy, Scott Rosenfelt, Billie Greif; Director, Giancarlo Esposito; Screenplay, Jeff Stacy, Jeffrey Pratt Gordon, Terrell Tannen; Photography, David Tumblety; Designer, William A. Cimino; Music, Scott Bomar; Editor, Tina Pacheco; a Future Film presentation in association with Full Glass Films; Dolby; Color/Black and white; 16mm; Not rated; 99 minutes; Release date: August 28, 2009. **CAST:** Angela Bassett (Sarah Malcolm), Danny Glover (John Malcolm), Samuel L. Jackson (Peter Malcolm), Giancarlo Esposito (Dr. Palmer), Julia Stiles (Rosie), Adam Baldwin (Carl Herrod), Tom Bower (Jack Herrod), Nia Long (Mrs. Palmer), Robert Fitzgerald Diggs [aka RZA] (Lonnie), Taylor Kitsch (Joel Herrod), Chloe Bailey (Anna), Casey Belville, Coletrane Williams (Teasing Boys), Chucky Bibby (Dr. Bob Owens), Darlene Black (Nurse), Phillip Bloch (George), Shirley Jones Bird (Grandmother), Jason Downs (Tommy Duncan), Chris Ellis (L Donn Murray), Lee Freeman (Miriam), Jesse Gore (Calvin), Ralph Greene (Luther), Julia Grigg (White Cashier), David Haines (Interviewer), Charles Jones (Rev. Charles), Felix Justice (Citizen), Atyan Kennedy, Walker (Waitress), Jason Klemm (Police Officer), Ted Manson (Ernest Hatch), Raquel Oliver (Cop), Michael Parness (Cromwell), Brian Robinson (Valley Corp. Exec), John Sexton (Manager)

HALLOWEEN II (Dimension) Producers, Malek Akkad, Andy Gould, Rob Zombie; Executive Producers, Bob Weinstein, Harvey Weinstein, Matthew Stein, Andy La Marca; Director/Screenplay/Music Supervisor, Rob Zombie; Photography, Brandon Trost; Designer, Garreth Stover; Costumes, Mary McLeod; Music, Tyler Bates; Editor, Glenn Garland; Special Makeup Effects, Wayne Toth; Casting, Monika Mikkelsen; a Malek Akkad production; Dolby; Color; Super 16-to-35mm; Rated R; 105 minutes; Release date: August 28, 2009. **CAST:** Malcolm McDowell (Dr. Samuel Loomis), Tyler Mane (Michael Myers), Sheri Moon Zombie (Deborah Myers), Brad Dourif (Sheriff Lee Brackett), Scout Taylor-Compton (Laurie Strode), Danielle Harris (Annie Brackett), Brea Grant (Mya Rockwell), Howard Hesseman (Uncle Meat), Mary Birdsong (Nancy McDonald), Chase Vanek (Young Michael), Margot Kidder (Barbar Collier), Al Yankovic ("Weird Al"), Caroline Williams (Dr. Maple), Dayton Callie (Coroner Hooks), Richard Brake (Gary Scott), Octavia Spencer (Nurse Daniels), Richard Riehle (Buddy the Night Watchman), Angela Trimbur (Harley David), Diana Ayala Goldner (Jane Salvador), Adam Boyer (Bruce Cabot), Duane Whitaker (Sherman Benny), Betsy Rue (Jazlean Benny), Mark Boone Junior (Floyd), Brian Rae (Earl of Pumpkin/Deputy #9), Michael Deak (King Jack/Deputy #10), Mike Kasieske (Lord Treat/Deputy #11), Jack McKinnon (Bishop Trick/Deputy #12), Nicky Whelan (Wendy Snow), Jeffrey Daniel Phillips (Howard), Daniel Roebuck (Big Lou), Catherine Dyer (Reporter), Sylvia Jefferies (Misty Dawn), Silas Weir Mitchell (Chett Johns), Robert Curtis Brown (Kyle Van Der Klok), Bill Fagerbaake (Deputy Webb), Greg Travis (Deputy Neale), Chris Hardwick (David Newman), Matthew Lintz (Mark), Graham Marema (Janet), Jesse Dayton (Capt. Clegg), Mark Lynch (Teenage Zombie), Matt Bush (Wolfiie), Renae Geerilngs (Deputy Gwynne), Mark Christopher Lawrence (Deputy Fred King), Sean Whalen (Becks)

Tyler Mane in Halloween II © Dimension Films

AT THE EDGE OF THE WORLD (WealthEffectMedia) Producers, Dan Stone, Craig Stone; Director, Dan Stone; Co-Director, Patrick Gambuti Jr.; Photography, Mathieu Mauvernay, Simeon Houtman, Rip Odebralski; Music, Jeff Gibbs, Tierro Lee; Editors, Patrick Gambuti Jr., Kurt Engfehr; an Endeavor Media presentation; Dolby; Color; HD; Not rated; 90 minutes; Release date: August 28, 2009. Documentary in which Paul Watson and his crew hope to save endangered Antarctic mammals. **WITH:** Paul Watson, Alex Cornelissen

At the Edge of the World © WealthEffectMedia

MYSTERY TEAM (Roadside Attractions) Producer, Meggie McFadden; Executive Producers/Story, Dominic Dierkes, Dan Eckman, Donald Glover, Meggie McFadden, D.C. Pierson; Director/Editor, Dan Eckman; Screenplay, Dominic Dierkes, Donald Glover, D.C. Pierson; Photography, Austin F. Schmidt; Designer, Lisa Myers; Music, Donald Glover; Casting, Jodi Collins; a Derrick Comedy presentation; Color; HD; Rated R; 106 minutes; Release date: August 28, 2009. **CAST:** Donald Glover (Jason). D.C. Pierson (Duncan), Dominic Dierkes (Charlie), Aubrey Plaza (Kelly), Matt Walsh (Jim), Kevin Brown (Bouncer), Gregory Burke (Football Player), Kay Cannon (Destiny), Neil Casey (Broken Man), Lillian Chandler (Mrs. Kimel), Daphne Ciccarelle (Brianna), Jon Daly (Greg), Dan Eckman (Bread Squeezer), George Eckman (Old Man McGinty), Cheryl Freeman (Mrs. Rogers), Will Hines (Mr. Stevens), Heidi May Johnson (Robert's Wife), Glenn Kalison (Robert), Ellie Kemper (Jamie), Anthony King (Office Worker), Kristopher Kling (Sam), John Kneeland (Officer Mills), John Lutz (Frank), Meggie McFadden (Cathy), Bobby Moynihan (Jordy), Nick Packard (Dougie), Ben Rodgers (Caleb), Peter Saati (Leroy), Xavier Salazar (Eric), Calvin Santiago (Sad Kid), Ben Schwartz (Dougie's Buddy), John Sefel (Murphy), Tom Shillue (Alan McGinty), Ron Simons (Mr. Rogers), Steve Stout (Tyler), Robbie Sublett (Ricky Appleman)

AMERICAN CASINO (Argot Pictures) Producers/Screenplay, Leslie Cockburn, Andrew Cockburn; Director, Leslie Cockburn; Photography, Phil Geyelin, Gregory Andracke, Bill Cassara, Bob Goldsborough, Sam Painter; a Table Rock Films production; Color; DV; Not rated; 89 minutes; Release date: September 2, 2009. Documentary on the corruption behind the American mortgage business. **WITH:** Ben Bernanke, Sheila Dixon, Phil Gramm, Henry Paulson, Henry Waxman.

Patricia McNair in
American Casino © Argot Pictures

TICKLING LEO (Barn Door Pictures) Producers, Jeremy Davidson, Mary Stuart Masterson, Peter Masterson, Steven Weisman, Paul Schnee; Co-Producer, Maria Elena Lopez-Frank; Director/Screenplay, Jeremy Davidson; Photography, Peter Masterson; Designer, David Stein; Costumes, Oliera Gajic; Music, Abe Korzeniowski; Editor, Kate Eales; Produced in association with Highbrow Entertainment; Color; HD; Not rated; 91 minutes; Release date: September 4, 2009. **CAST:** Eli Wallach (Emil Pikler), Annie Parisse (Delphina Adams), Lawrence Pressman (Warren Pikler), Ronald Guttman (Robert Pikler), Daniel Sauli (Zak Pikler), Victoria Clark (Madeleine Pikler), Bern Cohen (Yosef Gottleib), Evan Neumann (Young Emil), Michael Marinoff (Young Oscar), Gameela Wright (Nurse), Lara Apponyi (Rivkta Pikler)

CARRIERS (Paramount Vantage) Producer, Anthony Bregman, Ray Angelic; Directors/Screenplay, Alex Pastor, David Pastor; Photography, Benoit Debie; Designer, Clark Hunter; Costumes, Jill Newell; Music, Peter Nashel, Brick Garner; Editor, Craig McKay; Casting, Jeanne McCarthy; a Likely Story production in association with This and That; Dolby; Color; Rated PG-13; 84 minutes; Release date: September 4, 2009. **CAST:** Lou Taylor Pucci (Danny), Chris Pine (Brian), Piper Perabo (Bobby), Emily VanCamp (Kate), Christopher Meloni (Frank), Kiernan Shipka (Jodie), Ron McClary (Preacher), Mark Moses (Doctor), Josh Berry, Tim Janis, Dale Malley (Survivalists), Dylan Kenin (Tom), LeAnne Lynch (Rose), Jan Cunningham (Passenger), Mary Peterson (Laura Merkin)

Piper Perabo, Chris Pine, Lou Taylor Pucci, Emily VanCamp in Carriers © Paramount Vantage

HOUSE OF NUMBERS: Anatomy of an Epidemic (Independent) Producer/ Director, Brent Leung; Producers/Editors, Brent Leung, Ursula Rowan; Executive Producers, Martin Penny, Bob Frisco, Andy Van Roon; Photography, Pouria Montazeri; Music, Joel Diamond; Color; Not rated; 90 minutes; Release date: September 4, 2009. Documentary on the lack of progress being made in the fight against AIDS. **WITH:** Donald Abrams, David Baltimore, Françoise Barré-Sinoussi, James Chin, Kenneth Cole, Niel Constantine, James Curran, Martin Delaney, Peter Duesberg, Anthony S. Fauci, Christian Fiala, Jim Fouratt, Donald P. Francis, Robert C. Gallo, Hans R. Gelderblom, Michael Gottlieb, Harry Haverkos, Harold Jaffe, Claus Koehnlein, Claudia Kücherer, Daniel R. Kuritzkes, Reinhard Kurth, Luc Montagnier, John P. Moore, Kary Mullis, Nancy Padian, Eleni Papadopulos-Eleopulos, Valendar Turner, Peter Piot, Robert R. Redfield, Kim Bannon, Ken Bundy, Claudia Cherer, Whoopi Goldberg, Bruce Vilanch

CRUDE (First Run Features) Producers, Joe Berlinger, Michael Bonfiglio, J.R. DeLeon, Richard Stratton; Executive Producers, Liesl Copland, Ted Sardanos, Joe Berlinger, Robert Friedman, Frank Scherma, Justin Wilkes, Jon Kamen; Director, Joe Berlinger; Photography, Juan Diego Perez; Music, Wendy Blackstone; Editor,

Alyse Ardell Spiegel; a Red Envelope Entertainment presentation of an Entendre Films production; Color; HD; Not rated; 104 minutes; Release date: September 9, 2009. Documentary on the lawsuit by thousands of Ecuadorans against Chevron due to their role in the contamination of the Amazon. **WITH:** Pablo Fajardo, Luis Yanza, Steven Donziger, Joseph Kohn, Alejandro Ponce, Adolfo Callejas, Diego Larrea, German Yanez, Richard Cabrera, Ricardo Reis Veiga, Sara McMillan, Emergildo Criollo, Atossa Soltani, Maria Garofalo, Silvia Yanez, Rosa Moreno, Rafael Correa, Trudie Styler

Crude © First Run Features

MARINA OF THE ZABBALEEN (Torch Films) Director/Screenplay, Engi Wassef; Photography, Rob Hauer; Editor, Nicholas Martin; Color; Not rated; 70 minutes; Release date: September 9, 2009. Documentary looking at the lives of the Zabbaleen people of Egypt; specifically 7-year-old Marina.

WHITEOUT (Warner Bros.) Producers, Susan Downey, David Gambino, Joel Silver; Executive Producers, Don Carmody, Steve Richards, Greg Rucka; Co-Producers, Richard Mirisch, Adam Kuhn; Director, Dominic Sena; Screenplay, Jon Hoeber, Erich Hoeber, Chad Hayes, Carey W. Hayes; Based on the graphic novel by Greg Rucka, Steve Lieber; Photography, Chris Soos; Designer, Graham "Grace" Walker; Costumes, Wendy Partridge, Nicoletta Massone; Music, John Frizzell; Editor, Martin Hunter; Visual Effects Supervisor, Dennis Berardi; Casting, Mary Gail Artz, Shani Ginsberg; a Dark Castle Entertainment production; Dolby; Panavision; Technicolor; Rated R; 101 minutes; Release date: September 11, 2009. **CAST:** Kate Beckinsale (Carrie Stetko), Gabriel Macht (Robert Pryce), Tom Skerritt (Dr. John Fury), Columbus Short (Delfy), Alex O'Loughlin (Russell Haden), Shawn Doyle (Sam Murphy), Joel Keller (Jack), Jesse Todd (Rubin), Arthur Holden (McGuire), Erin Hickock (Rhonda), Bashar Rahal, Julian Cain (Russian Pilots), Dennis Keiffer, Andrei Runtso, Roman Varshavsky (Russian Guards), Steve Lucescu (Mooney), Paula Jean Hixson (Lab Tech), Craig Pinckes (Aircraft Tech), Sean Tucker (Operations Tech), Marc James Beauchamp (Weiss), Nick Villarin (Newbie), Louis Dionne (Man in Hall), Patrick Saongui (Miami Prisoner)

Kate Beckinsale in Whiteout © Warner Bros.

THE PAINTER SAM FRANCIS (Body & Soul Productions) Producer/Director, Jeffrey Perkins; Photography, Samantha Bertolotto, Jeffrey Perkins, Larry Janss; Music, Charles Curtis; Editor, Marc Vives; Color; Super 8; Hi-8; DV; Not rated; 85 minutes; Release date: September 11, 2009. Documentary on abstract artist Sam Francis. **WITH:** Sam Francis, Osamu Francis, George Francis, Alfred Leslie, Peter Selz, Muriel Goodwin, Al Held, Pontus Hulten, Walter Hopps, Paul Shimmel, Masato Naito, Arata Izozaki, Eberhard Kornfeld, Elaine Anderson, Shingo Francis, Paula Kirkeby, Dan Cytron, Ed Ruscha, Ed Moses, Bruce Conner, James Turrell, Laddie Dill, Nancy Mozur, George Page, Jacob Samuel, Tom Kirsch, Gordon Onslow-Ford, Krauth Brand, Kayo Francis, Margaret Francis, Betty Freeman

NO IMPACT MAN: THE DOCUMENTARY (Oscilloscope) Producers, Laura Gabbert, Eden Wurmfeld; Executive Producers, Julia Parker Benello, Diana Barrett, Dan Cogan, Abigail Disney, Barbara Dobkin, Kevin Gruneich, Donna Gruneich, David Menschel, Adriana Mncuhin, Susan Myers, Gib Myers, Sarah John Redlich, Juliette Timsit, Caroleen Feeney; Directors/Screenplay, Laura Gabbert, Justin Schein; an Impact Partners presentation of an Eden Wurmfeld/Shadowbox Films/Laura Gabbert Films production; Color; Not rated; 93 minutes; Release date: September 11, 2009. Documentary about Colin Beavan's decision to leave behind his Manhattan-based lifestyle and return to nature, reluctantly joined by his wife Michelle Conlin. **WITH:** Colin Beavan, Michelle Conlin

Colin Beavan in No Impact Man © *Oscilloscope*

WALT & EL GRUPO (Walt Disney) Producer, Kuniko Okubo; Executive Producer, Walter E.D. Miller; Director/Screenplay, Theodore Thomas; Photography, Shana Hagen; Music, James Wesley Stemple; Editor, Lisa Palattella; a Walt Disney Family Foundation Films production in association with Theodore Thomas Productions; Dolby; Color; Rated PG; 104 minutes; Release date: September 11, 2009. Documentary on Walt Disney's 1941 goodwill tour of South America. **WITH:** Juan Carlos Gonzalez, Mariuza Barroso Salomao, Marcelo Nino, Virgilio Roig, John Canemaker, Blaine Gibson, Diane Miller, Harriett Woltcott, J.B. Kaufman

GOGOL BORDELLO NON-STOP (Lorber) Producers, Margarita Jimeno, Darya Zhuk, Munir Maluf Raad; Executive Producer, Ramon Jimeno; Director/Editor/Photography, Margarita Jimeno; a Hoptza Films production; Color/black and white; Not rated; 93 minutes; Release date: September 11, 2009. Documentary on New York gypsy punk band Gogol Bordello. **WITH:** Eugene Hutz, Ori Kaplan, Sergei Ryabtsev, Yuri Lemeshev, Eliot Ferguson, Pamela Racine, Elizabeth Sun, Piroska Racz, Manu Chao, Susan Donaldson, Eliot Ferguson, Thomas Gobena, Katheryn Mcgaffigan, Rea Mochiach, DJ Scratchy, Yuri Yunakov

NOT FORGOTTEN (Skyline Pictures) Producers, Donald Zuckerman, Dror Soref; Executive Producers, Michelle Seward, Kirk D'Amico, Alan Landau, Jamie Beardsley, Walter Josten, Jeff Geoffray, Howard Behar; Director, Dror Soref; Screenplay, Tomas Romero, Dror Soref; Photography, Steven Bernstein; Designer, Craig Stearns; Costumes, Deborah Everton; Music, Mark Isham, Cynthia O'Connor; Editor, Martin Hunter; a Skyline Pictures/Z Entertainment/Myriad Pictures production; Dolby; Deluxe color; Rated R; 97 minutes; Release date: September 11, 2009. **CAST:** Simon Baker (Jack Bishop), Paz Vega (Amaya), Chloe Moretz (Toby Bishop), Claire Forlani (Katie), Michael DeLorenzo (Casper Navarro), Ken Davitian (Father Salinas), Melinda Page Hamilton (Deputy Mindy), Benito Martinez (Det. Sanchez), Julia Vera (Doña), Jim Meskimen (Redd), Zahn McClarnon (Calvo), Daniel Escobar (Hector), Virginia Pereira (Karen De La Rosa), Carmen Perez (Carolina), Mark Rolston (Agent Wilson), Greg Safel (Canta), Isaac Kappy (Stoner Dude), Greg Serano (Deputy Valdez), Trina E. Siopy (Lourdes), Veronica Falcón (Reina), Lorri Oliver (Mary Alice), Carmen Serrano (Irena), Tamra Meskimen (Bored Waitress), Arron Shiver (Deputy Pratt), Kisha Sierra (Lumi), Carlos A. Cabarcas (Deputy Gomez), Elena Lyons (Newscaster), Gedde Watanabe (Agent Nakamura), Tyler Cross (Jack look-alike Transvestite), Kevin Wiggins (Deputy Simpson), Amber Midthunder (Young Amaya), Lillian Hurst (Hotel Manager), Henry Jacobson (Roy)

Michael DeLorenzo in Not Forgotten © *Skyline Pictures*

SKIPTRACERS (Falling Rock Productions) Producers, Harris Mendheim, Andy Stuckey, D.L. Glickman; Director, Harris Mendheim; Screenplay, Harris Mendheim, Brian J. Saliba, Andy Stuckey; Photography, Ken Woo; Editor, Mary Reese; Dolby; Color; HD; Not rated; 96 minutes; Release date: September 11, 2009. **CAST:** Daniel Burnley (Big Donald Trawick), Michael H. Cole (Deputy Hardy), Cynthia Evans (Mrs. Owens), Eddie Galey (Nanny Trawick), Peter Gantenbein (Yoates), Angie Harrell (Beverly), Porter Harris (J.D. Trawick), Dustin Kerns (Tucker Trawick), Gary Klotzman (Rev. Ike Pinder), Montgomery Maguire (Clyde Owners Sr.), Harris Mendheim (Chunt), Rich Muscadin (Black Bart), Andy Stuckey (Rusty)

THE MOST DANGEROUS MAN IN AMERICA: DANIEL ELLSBERG AND THE PENTAGON PAPERS (First Run Features) Producers/Directors, Judith Ehrlich, Rick Goldsmith; Executive Producer, Jodie Evans; Screenplay, Lawrence Lerew, Rick Goldsmith, Judith Ehrlich; Based on the books *Secrets* and *Papers on the War* by Daniel Ellsberg; Photography, Vincente Franco; Music, Blake Leyh; Editors, Michael Chandler, Rick Goldsmith, Lawrence Lerew; Narrator, Daniel Ellsberg; a co-production of Judith Ehrlich and Rick Goldsmith and the Independent Television Service (ITVS); Color; Not rated; 93 minutes; Release date: September 16, 2009. Documentary on Pentagon official and Vietnam strategist Daniel Ellsberg. **WITH:** Daniel Ellsberg, Patricia Ellsberg, John Dean, Egil "Bud" Krogh, Hedrick Smith, Max Frankel, Tony Russo

Daniel Ellsberg in The Most Dangerous Man in America
© *Independent Television Service*

FATAL PROMISES (GreenKat Productions) Producers, Anneliese Rohrer, Kat Rohrer, Tom Greenman; Director/Editor, Kat Rohrer; Photography, Tom Marschall; Music, Joseph Fogarazzo; Color; Not rated; 80 minutes; Release date: September 16, 2009. Documentary on human trafficking. **WITH:** Katja, Anya, Gloria Steinem, Emma Thompson, Jeff Labovitz

HARMONY AND ME (Forlorn Penguin) Producer, Kristen Tucker; Director/Screenplay, Bob Byington; Photography, Jim Eastburn; Designer, Yvonne Boudreaux; Editors, Frank Ross, Jacob Vaughan; Color; HD; Not rated; 72 minutes; Release date: September 18, 2009. **CAST:** Justin Rice (Harmony), Kevin Corrigan (Carlos), Pat Healy (Matt), Kristen Tucker (Jessica), Allison Latta (Natasha), Alex Karpovsky (Mean Man Mike), Margie Beegle (Mom), Keith Poulson (Wes), Jeremy Pollet (Piano Teacher), Bob Byington (Jim), Bob Schneider (Wedding Singer), Nick Holden (Prince Valiant), Kevin Bewersdorf (Talkative Barista), Blair Bomar (Friend in Store), Chris Doubek (Chatty Co-Worker), John Gatins (Homeless Tom), Baseera Khan (Milius), Devin Moss (Good-Looking Doctor), Suzy Nakamura (Doctor), Nick Offerman (Meter Maid Man), Aundrus Poole (Store Clerk), Todd Sklar (John Counterman), Steve Uzzell (Gordon), Bill Wise (Meter Maid Subordinate)

Justin Rice in Harmony and Me © *Forlorn Penguin*

IF ONE THING MATTERS: A FILM ABOUT WOLFGANG TILLMANS (WhyMakeThings Productions) Producer/Director/Screenplay/Photography/Editor, Heiko Kalmbach; American-German; Color; Not rated; 72 minutes; Release date: September 18, 2009. Documentary on photographer Wolfgang Tillmans.

THE BURNING PLAIN (Magnolia) Producers, Walter F. Parkes, Laurie MacDonald; Executive Producers, Todd Wagner, Mark Cuban, Marc Butan, Charlize Theron, Alisa Tager, Ray Angelic; Director/Screenplay, Guillermo Arriaga; Photography, Robert Elswit; Designer, Dan Leigh; Costumes, Cindy Evans; Music, Omar Rodriguez-Lopez, Hans Zimmer; Editor, Craig Wood; Casting, Debra Zane; Dolby; Color; Rated R; 106 minutes; Release date: September 18, 2009. **CAST:** Charlize Theron (Sylvia), Kim Basinger (Gina), Jennifer Lawrence (Mariana), José Maria Yazpik (Carlos), Joaquim de Almeida (Nick), Tessa la (Maria), Diego J. Torres (Cristobal), J.D. Pardo (Young Santiago), Danny Pino (Santiago), John Corbett (John), Brett Cullen (Robert), Gray Eubank (Lawrence), Rafael Hernández (Dr. Armendariz), Toni Marie Lopez (The Woman), Sean McGrath (Scott), Cesar Miramontes (Plaza Street Vendor), Marty Papazian (Young Man), TJ Plunkett (Pat), Chris Ranney (Grocery Shopper), Aide Rodriguez (Operator), Fernanda Romero (Sophie), Kacie Thomas (Vivi), Robin Tunney (Laura), Malcolm Ullery (Priest's Helper), Stacy Marie Warden (Monnie), Taylor Warden (Bobby)

Kim Basinger in The Burning Plain © *Magnolia Pictures*

FUEL (Greenlight Theatrical) Producers, Greg Reitman, Dale Rosenbloom, Daniel Assael, Darius Fisher, Rebecca Harrell; Director, Josh Tickell; Screenplay, Johnny O'Hara; Photography, James Mulryan; Music, Ryan Demaree, Edgar Rothermich; Editors, Tina Imahara, Michael Horwitz; Color; Not rated; 111 minutes; Release date: September 18, 2009. Documentary on the oil industry's disastrous effect on the environment. **WITH:** Josh Tickell, Barbara Boxer, Richard Branson, Sheryl Crow, Larry David, Laurie David, Deborah Dupre, Jeremiah Dupre, Perry Freezse, Larry Hagman, Woody Harrelson, Jay Inslee, Robert Kennedy Jr., Frank Lautenberg, Willie Nelson, Scott Ritter, Julia Roberts, David M. Walker. Neil Young

Fuel © *Greenlight Theatrical*

THE BLUE TOOTH VIRGIN (Regent) Producers, Russell Brown, Roni Deitz; Director/Screenplay, Russell Brown; Photography, Marco Fargnoli; Editors, Curtiss Clayton, Christopher Munch; Casting, Michael Hothorn; Color; HD; Rated R; 79 minutes; Release date: September 25, 2009. **CAST:** Austin Peck (Sam), Bryce Johnson (David), Tom Gilroy (Louis), Lauren Stamile (Rebecca), Amber Benson (Jennifer), Karen Black (Zena), Roma Maffia (Dr. Christopher)

Bryce Johnson in The Blue Tooth Virgin © *Regent Releasing*

PANDORUM (Overture) Producers, Jeremy Bolt, Paul W.S. Anderson, Robert Kulzer; Executive Producers, Martin Moszkowicz, Dave Morrison, Travis Milloy; Director, Christian Alvart; Screenplay, Travis Milloy; Based on a story by Travis Milloy, Christian Alvart; Photography, Wedigo von Schultzendorff; Designer, Richard Bridgland; Costumes, Ivana Milos; Music, Michl Britsch; Editors, Philipp Stahl, Yvonne Valdez; Makeup Effects, Stan Winston Studio; Visual Effects Supervisor, Viktor Muller; Stunts, Francois Doge; Casting, Randi Hiller, Sarah Halley Finn, Ana Davilla; a Constantin Film, Impact Pictures production; presented in association with Constantin Film; Dolby; Widescreen; Color; Rated R; 108 minutes; Release date: September 25, 2009. **CAST:** Dennis Quaid (Payton), Ben Foster (Bower), Cam Gigandet (Gallo), Antje Traue (Nadia), Cung Le (Manh), Eddie Rouse (Leland), Norman Reedus (Shepard), André Hennicke (Hunter Leader), Friederike Kempter (Evalon), Niels-Bruno Schmidt (Insane Officer "Eden"), Jonah Mohmand (Childhunter), Delphine Chuillot (Young Bower's Mother), Wotan Wilke Möhring (Young Bower's Father), Julian Rappe (Young Bower), Domenico D'Ambrosio (Wounded Officer "Eden"), Jon Foster (Big Russian Passenger), Jeff Burrell (Trapped Officer "Eden"), Neelesha BaVora (Crew Officer), Yangzom Brauen (2nd Lieutenant, Team 4), Marco Albrecht (Hunter Weasel), Dawid Szatarski (Hunter Shape), Nico Marquardt (Hunter Brute)

Antje Traue, Ben Foster in Pandorum © *Overture Films*

The Providence Effect © *Slowhand Releasing*

I HOPE THEY SERVE BEER IN HELL (Freestyle) Producers, Richard Kelly, Sean McKittrick, Tucker Max, Nils Parker, Max Wong, Karen Firestone, Aaron Ray; Executive Producers, Edward Hamm Jr., Shaun Redick, Raymond Mansfield; Director, Bob Gosse; Screenplay, Tucker Max, Nils Parker; Based on the novel by Tucker Max; Photography, Suki Medencevic; Designer, Eve Cauley Turner; Costumes, Alison Parker; Music, James L. Venable; Editor, Jeff Kushner; Casting, Joseph Middleton; a Darko Entertainment, Radius Films production, in association with Pink Slip Pictures, the Collective; Dolby; Color; Rated R; 106 minutes; Release date: September 25, 2009. **CAST:** Matt Czuchry (Tucker Max), Jesse Bradford (Drew), Geoff Stults (Dan), Keri Lynn Pratt (Kristy), Marika Dominczyk (Lara), Susie Abromeit (Leslie), Nicole Muirbrook Wagner (Christina), Meagen Fay (Mrs. Jorgens), Ali Costello (Amy), Yvette Yates (Deaf Girl), Jessica Williams (Loretta), Melissa Fumero (Melissa), Brooke Long (Chloe), Edward Hibbert (Professor), Bill Dawes (Murphy), Amanda Phillips (Liz), Olivia Ari (Friend of Chubby), Elise Ivy (Mary), Randal Reeder (Bouncer), Karissa Staples (Target Girl), Lena Clark (Turtle Girl), Michael A. Worley (Young Tucker Max), Lyndsey Jolly (Maid of Honor), Tricia Munford (Tucker's Mom), Patshreba Williams (Ashley), Summer DeLin (Candy), Michael Byrnes (Cop), Craig Coyne (Logan), James B. McDaniel (Wedding Guest), Briston Meeney (Angry Guy), Michael Liu (Front Desk Clerk), Tammy Eaton (Woman at Grill), Cervantes Reck (Mexican Numero Uno), Derek Wayne Johnson (Friend #2), Brent Weisner (Store Salesman), Lindsay Soileau (Angry Guy's Girlfriend), Steven Miramontz (Drew P/D), Jabari Thomas (Bartender), Eric Kelly McFarland (Mad Driver), Roger Timber (Jail Clerk), Noah Podell (Jack), Patrick Kirton (Mr. Jorgens), Patrick Michael Carney (Officer), Thomas Wallace (Wedding Photographer)

Jesse Bradford, Matt Czuchry, Geoff Stults in
I Hope They Serve Beer in Hell © *Freestyle Releasing*

THE PROVIDENCE EFFECT (Slowhand Releasing) Producers, Tom Hurvis, Rollin Binzer; Executive Producer, Julie Esch Hurvis; Director, Rollin Binzer; Photography, Robert Tutuman; Music, Tom Dumont, Ted Matson; Editor, Richard La Porta; a Dinosaurs of the Future production; Dolby; Color; HD; Rated PG; 92 minutes; Release date: September 25, 2009. Documentary on Providence's St. Mel prep school's high success rate in college placement. **WITH:** Paul Adams III, Jeanette DiBella, John W. Fountain

BLIND DATE (Variance) Producers, Bruce Weiss, Gijs van de Westelaken; Executive Producer, Nick Stiliadis; Director, Stanley Tucci; Screenplay, Stanley Tucci, David Schechter; Based on the film by Theo van Gogh; Photography, Thomas Kist; Designer, Loren Weeks; Costumes, Victoria Farrell; Editor, Camilla Toniolo; Color; Not rated; 80 minutes; Release date: September 25, 2009.**CAST:** Stanley Tucci (Don), Patricia Clarkson (Janna), Thijs Römer (Waiter), Gerdy De Decker (Tango Dancer), Georgina Verbaan (Cute Woman), Robin Holzauer (Little Girl), Sarah Hyland (Voice of Child), Peer Mascini (Sole Drinker)

Patricia Clarkson, Stanley Tucci in Blind Date © *Variance*

THE HORSE BOY (Zeitgeist) Producer/Narrator, Rupert Isaacson; Director/Photography, Michel Orion Scott; Music, Kim Carroll, Lili Haydn; Editor, Rita K. Sanders; Color; Not rated; 93 minutes; Release date: September 30, 2009. Documentary on how writer and former horse trainer Rupert Isaacson and his wife psychology professor Kristin Neff journeyed to Mongolia in an effort to cure their son's autism. **WITH:** Simon Baron-Cohen, Temple Grandin, Roy Richard Grinker, Rowan Isaacson, Rupert Isaacson, Kristin Neff

Rowan Isaacson in The Horse Boy © *Zeitgeist Films*

AFTERSCHOOL (IFC Films) Producers, Josh Mond, Sean Durkin; Executive Producers, Andrew Renzi, Victor Aaron, Susan Shopmaker, Rose Ganguzza; Director/Screenplay/Editor, Antonio Campos; Photography, Jody Lee Lipes; Designer, Kris Moran; Costumes, Catherine Akana; Music, Rakotondrabe Gael; Casting, Randi Glass, Susan Shopmaker; a Borderline Films production, in association with Hidden St. Productions; Widescreen; Color; Not rated; 107 minutes; Release date: October 2, 2009. **CAST:** Ezra Miller (Robert), Jeremy White (Dave), Emory Cohen (Trevor), Michael Stuhlbarg (Mr. Burke), Addison Timlin (Amy), Rosemarie Dewitt (Teacher), Lee Wilkof (Mr. Wiseman), Paul Sparks (Detective), Bill Raymond (Mr. Williams), Gary Wilmes (Mr. Virgil), Christopher

McCann (Mr. Ullman), Danielle Baum, Anna Maliere (Fighting Girls), Byrdie Bell (Cherry Dee), Paul Lucenti, Daniel Trinh (Students), Dariusz M. Uczkowski (Peter)

Jeremy White, Ezra Miller in Afterschool © *IFC Films*

A BEAUTIFUL LIFE (New Films Intl.) Producers, Deborah Calla, Nesim Hason; Executive Producers, Bob Holof, Sezin Hason, Serap Acuner, Lusi Filiba, Izak Filiba; Director, Alejandro Chomski; Screenplay, Deborah Calla, Wendy Hammond; Based on a play by Wendy Hammond; Photography, Nancy Schreiber; Designer, Natalie Sanfilippo; Music, Ruy Folguera; Editor, Alex Blatt; a Calla Productions, New Film International and Bob Holof production; Color; DV; Not rated; 81 minutes; Release date: October 2, 2009. **CAST:** Debi Mazar (Susan) Bai Ling (Esther), Dana Delany (Anne), Walter Perez (Enrico), Jonathan LaPaglia (Vince), Jesse Garcia (David), Rena Owen (Sam), Angela Sarafyan (Maggie), Enrique Castillo (Don Miguel), Meltem Cumbul (Antanas), Ronnie Gene Blevins (Henry), Saadet Aksoy (Denise), Stefan Banica Jr. (Gangster), Ho-Jung (Korean Wife Store Owner), Andreea Banica (Romanian Lady), Bree Elise (Lady), Brandon Ficara (Homeless Man), Deidra Edwards (Call Center Receptionist), Dan Kelpine (Jim), Bill Lithgow (Hippie Vendor), Gloria Alexandra (Stripper), Royana Black (Cathy), Tim Moore (Building Security)

Ronnie Gene Blevins, Bai Ling in A Beautiful Life © *New Films Intl*

MORE THAN A GAME (Lionsgate) Producers, Harvey Mason, Kristopher Belman, Matthew Perniciaro, Kevin Mann; Executive Producers, Maverick Carter, LeBron James; Director/Photography, Kristopher Belman; Screenplay, Brad Hogan, Kristopher Belman; Music, Harvey Mason; Editor, V. Scott Balcerek; a Harvey Mason Media presentation, in association with Interscope Productions; Color; HD; Rated PG; 105 minutes; Release date: October 2, 2009. Documentary on Akron, Ohio's St. Vincent-St. Mary High School basketball team. **WITH:** LeBron James, Dru Joyce, Romeo Travis, Sian Cotton, Willie McGee

LeBron James in More Than a Game © *Lionsgate*

After the Storm © *Priddy Brothers*

AS SEEN THROUGH THESE EYES (Menemsha) Producers, Hilary Helstein, Michael Rosendale, Amy Janes; Director/Screenplay, Hilary Helstein; Executive Producers, Michael Jacobs, Jerry Offsay, Irv Weintraub; Music, Lawrence Brown; Editors, Sean Hubbert, Tanya Phipps; Narrator, Maya Angelou; a Parkchester Pictures presentation, produced in association with the Sundance Channel; Color; Not rated; minutes; Running time: 70 minutes; Release date: October 2, 2009. Documentary on artists who survived the Holocaust. **WITH:** Ela Weissberger, Yehuda Bacon, Willi Groag, Frederick Terna, Inge Kantor, Alfred Kantor, Judith Goldstein, Samuel Bak, Karl Stojka, Dina Gottliebova-Babbitt, Simon Wiesenthal, Henry Rosmarin, Trudie Strobel, Tony Kushner, Aaron Simon Gross

THE YES MEN FIX THE WORLD (Shadow) Producers, Andy Bichlbaum, Mike Bonnano, Doro Bachrach, Ruth Charny, Laura Nix; Executive Producers, Patrice Barrat, Alan Hayling, Jess Search, Juliette Timsit; Directors/Screenplay, The Yes Men (Andy Bichlbaum, Mike Bonanno); Co-Director, Kurt Engfehr; Photography, Sarah Price; Music, Neel Murgai; Editor, April Merl; Animation, Patrick Lichty, Noisola; a Common Decency, Article Z (U.S.)/Arte France (France) production, with the support of Renegade Pictures U.K., Charny-Bachrach Entertainment, the Channel 4 Britdoc Foundation; American-French-British; Color; HD; Not rated; 96 minutes; Release date: October 7, 2009. Documentary that follows the exploits of the Yes Men, pranksters who pretend to represent large, nefarious corporations in order to expose the questionable practices and policies of the real thing. **WITH:** Andy Bichlbaum, Mike Bonanno, Reggie Watts

As Seen Through These Eyes © *Menemsha*

Mike Bonanno, Andy Bichlbaum in The Yes Men Fix the World © *Shadow Distribution*

AFTER THE STORM (Priddy Brothers) Producers, Hilla Medalia, John Priddy, Ed Priddy; Executive Producer, James Lecesne; Director, Hilla Medalia; Screenplay, Bob Eisenhardt, Hilla Medalia; Photography, Ran Shetreet, William Sabourin O'Reilly, Guy Jackson; Music, Steven Flaherty; Editor, Bob Eisenhardt; a Priddy Brothers presentation in association with Know Producitons; Color; DV; Not rated; 89 minutes; Release date: October 5, 2009. Documentary on activist James Lecesne's efforts to stage a production of the musical *Once on This Island* in the aftermath of hurricane-ravaged New Orleans using local teenagers. **WITH:** James Lecesne, Randy Redd, Gerry McIntyre, Peg Culligan, Rayan Arnold, Annie Britton, Eric T. Calhoun, Griffin Collins III, Deshawn Dabney, Joel Callonia Dyson, Hannah Guillory, Grant Hunter, Taylor Mars, Ashley Rose Richard, Jasmin Simmons, Jon Stevenson, April Stewart

STARK RAVING BLACK (D&E Entertainment) Producers, Jack Gulick, Benjamin Brewer; Executive Producers, Lewis Black, Mark Lonow; Line Producer, Tom Case; Director, Adam Dubin; Editor, Christine Mitsogiogakis; Stark Raving Black Productions; Color; Not rated; 80 minutes; Release date: October 8, 2009. Comedian Lewis Black in performance.

GOOD HAIR (Roadside Attractions) Producers, Chris Rock, Kevin O'Donnell, Jenny Hunter; Executive Producer, Nelson George; Director, Jeff Stilson; Screenplay, Chris Rock, Jeff Stilson, Lance Crouther, Chuck Sklar; Photography,

Cliff Charles; Music, Marcus Miller; Music Supervisor, P.J. Bloom; Editors, Paul Marchard, Greg Nash; an HBO Films presentation of a Zahrlo production, an Urban Romance production; Dolby; Color; HD-to-25mm; Rated PG-13; 95 minutes; Release date: October 9, 2009. Documentary in which comedian Chris Rock explores the diversities of African American hair styles. **WITH:** Chris Rock, Maya Angelou, Vanessa Bell Calloway, Salt-N-Pepa, Eve, Melyssa Ford, Meagan Good, Andre Harrell, Ice-T, Sarah Jones, KRS-One, Nia Long, Paul Mooney, T-Pain, Raven-Symoné, Salli Richardson-Whitfield, Al Sharpton, Tracie Thoms, Kerry Washington, Tanya Crumel, Kevin Kirik, Jason Griggers

Chris Rock in Good Hair © *Roadside Attractions*

FREE STYLE (Goldwyn) Producers, Rob Cowan, Christian Arnold-Beutel, Jim O'Grady, David Reivers, Donald Paul Pemrick, Dean E. Fronk; Executive Producers, Tim McGrath, David Doerksen; Director, William Dear; Screenplay, Joshua Leibner, Jeffrey Nicholson; Photography, Karl Hermann; Designer, Tink; Costumes, Maria Livingstone; Music, Stephen Endelman; Stunts, Mike Carpenter, Kirk Jarrett, Jodi Stecyk; a Canal Street Films (U.S.)/Up North Entertainment (Canada) production, in association with Bleuman Entertainment of a Rob Cowan-John F.S. Lang production, presented with Rigel Entertainment; American-Canadian; Dolby; Color; Rated PG; 94 minutes; Release date: October 9, 2009. **CAST:** Corbin Bleu (Cale Bryant), Madison Pettis (Bailey Bryant), Sandra Echeverria (Alex Lopez), Jesse Moss (Justin Maynard), Matt Bellefleur (Derek Black), David Reivers (Dell), Penelope Ann Miller (Jeanette Bryant), Scott Patey (Trent), Tegan Moss (Crystal), Gustavo Febres (Angel Lopez), Mike Antonakos (Pizza Manager), Giacomo Paessato (Drunken Partier), Tosca Baggoo (Carmen Lopez), Gary Chalk (Home Track Announcer), Kim Clarke (Pizza Woman), Val Cole (News Reporter), Brandon Dabul-Sanchez (Edwardo Lopez), Stefan Dabul-Sanchez (Hector Lopez), Patricia Drake (Manager), Paul Jarrett (Frank), Woody Jeffreys (National Official), Hannah R. Lay (Lilian), Nels Lennarson (John Lamport), Wally Levy (Wally), Tyler McClendon (Don Ryan), Martin Rattigan (Coby), Michael Ryan (Herman Black), John Shaw (Sheriff Bud Williams), Chris Shields (Doctor), Clay St. Thomas (MX Commentator)

Sandra Echeverria, Corbin Bleu in Free Style © *Samuel Goldwyn Co.*

TRUCKER (Monterey Media) Producers, Celine Rattray, Galt Niederhoffer, Daniela Taplin Lundberg, Scott Hanson; Executive Producers, Pamela Hirsch, John Allen, Ed Hart, Bruce Lunsford, Reagan Silber, Michelle Monaghan, Frank Frattaroli, Robert Kessel; Directors/Screenplay, James Mottern; Photography, Lawrence Sher; Designer, Cabot McMullen; Music, Mychael Danna; Editor, Deirdre Slevin; a Plum Pictures presentation in association with Hart-Lunsford Pictures; Color; Rated R; 93 minutes; Release date: October 9, 2009. **CAST:** Michelle Monaghan (Diane Ford), Nathan Fillion (Runner), Benjamin Bratt (Leonard Bonner), Joey Lauren Adams (Jenny), Jimmy Bennett (Peter), Mika Boorem (Plum), Dennis Hayden (Trucker), Bryce Johnson (Rick), Franklin Dennis Jones (Jonnie), Johnny Simmons, Stephen Sowan (Teens), Brandon Hanson (Tom), Maya McLaughlin (Molly), Ricky Ellison (Robert), Matthew Lawrence (Scott)

Jimmy Bennett, Michelle Monaghan in Trucker © *Monterey Media*

ADVENTURES OF POWER (Variance) Producer, Andrea Sperling; Executive Producers, Gill Holland, Christopher Woodrow; Director/Screenplay, Ari Gold; Photography, Lisa Weigand; Designer, Walter Barnett; Costumes, Victoria Auth; Music, Ethan Gold; Editors, Dan Schalk, Geraud Brisson, David Blackburn; a Grack Films presentation, in association with Group Entertainment, SpaceTime Films, of an Andrea Sperling production; Dolby; Color; Super 16; Rated PG-136; 96 minutes; Release date: October 9, 2009. **CAST:** Ari Gold (Power), Michael McKean (Harlan), Jane Lynch (Joni), Shoshannah Stern (Annie), Chi Ling Chiu (Michael Fong), Adrian Grenier (Dallas Houston), Luis Accinelli (Jalisco), Jenny Barbosa, Jacki R. Chan, Samantha Maloney (Seattle Girls), Karen Berg (Dallas's Girl), John Bianco (Union Delgate), Markie Dunn (Samantha), Richard Fancy (Dick Houston), Annie Golden (Farrah), Garry Goodrow (Trenchcoat Man), Jeff Holman (Biff the Handler), Wai Chign Ho (Yolanda Fong), Albert Huerta (Raul), Tod Huntington (Bobby), Jimmy Jean-Louis (Aubelin), Reggie Jernigan (Funk Bank Member), Travis John (Brian "Brain Dog" Calucci), Helen Kelly (Stickless Air Drummer), Nick Kroll (Versatio Bakir), Neil Peart (Himself), Olivia Peterson (Young Annie), Tuffy Questell (Freddie), Kevin Rodriguez (Sid), Summer Rona (Linda), Kimberly Topper (News Anchor), Nicole Wagner, Tanya White (Music Video Girls), Eric Wareheim (Money), Steven Williams (Carlos)

Ari Gold, Adrian Grenier in Adventures of Power © *Variance*

PETER AND VANDY (Strand) Producers, Jay DiPietro, Peter Sterling, Austin Stark, Benji Koh, Bingo Gubelmann; Executive Producers, Amanda Gruss, Lawrence Levine; Director/Screenplay, Jay DiPietro; Photography, Frank G. DeMarco; Designer, Lucio Seixas; Costumes, David Withrow; Music, Jason Lifton; Editor, Geoffrey Richman; Casting, James Calleri; Dolby; Color; Not rated; 80 minutes; Release date: October 9, 2009. **CAST:** Jason Ritter (Peter), Jess Weixler (Vandy), Jesse L. Martin (Paul), Tracie Thoms (Marissa), Noah Bean (Andrew), Kristina Klebe (Michelle), Zak Orth (Keith), Bruce Altman (Dad), Dana Eskelson (Emma), Maryann Plunkett (Mom), Grant Varjas (Gary), Amanda Gruss (Bartender), Rose DiPietro (Delia), Lawrence Levine (Mike), John Becker Good (Not Keith), Chris Lopaa (Not Keith's Friend), Jamie Farrell (Bride), B. Reeves (The Groom), David Rasche (Alan), Grant Varjas (Gary)

Jess Weixler, Jason Ritter in Peter and Vandy © *Strand Releasing*

EATING OUT: ALL YOU CAN EAT (Ariztical Entertainment) Producers, Kirk Cruz, Michael Shoel; Director, Glenn Gaylord; Screenplay/Editor, Phillip J. Bartell; Based on characters created by Q. Allan Brocka; Photography, Tom Camarda; Designer, Justin Lieb; Music, Meiro Stamm; Color; HD; Not rated; 80 minutes; Release date: October 9, 2009. **CAST:** Rebekah Kochan (Tiffani), Daniel Skelton (Casey), Chris Salvatore (Zack), Michael E.R. Walker (Ryan), Julia Cho (Tandy), Mink Stole (Helen), Leslie Jordan (Harry), John Stallings (Lionel), Maximiliano Torandell (Ernesto), Sumalee Montano (Pam), Cristina Balmores (Candy), Rick D'Agostino (Shirtless Stud), Greg McKeon, Ryan Adames, Derick Bell (Hunks)

John Stallings, Daniel Skelton in Eating Out: All You Can Eat © *Ariztical Entertainment*

VISUAL ACOUSTICS (Arthouse Films) Producers, Eric Bricker, Babette Zilch; Executive Producers, Lisa Hughes, Michelle Oliver; Director, Eric Bricker; Screenplay, Eric Bricker, Phil Ethington, Jessica Hundley, Lisa Hughes; Photography, Aiken Weiss, Dante Spinotti; Music, Charlie Campagna; Editor, Charlton McMillan; Animation Design, Trollback & Co.; Narrator, Dustin Hoffman; a Visual Acoustics, Shulman Project Partners, Out of the Box production; Color/ Black and white; DV; Not rated; 83 minutes; Release date: October 9, 2009. Documentary on noted architecture photographer Julius Shulman. **WITH:** Julius Shulman, Frances Anderton, Tom Ford, Frank O. Gehry, Recardo Legorreta, Kelly Lynch, Leo Marmol, Judy McKee, Raymond Richard Neutra, Jergen Nogai, Ed Ruscha, Dante Spinotti, Angelika Taschen, Benedikt Taschen

Visual Acoustics © *Arthouse Films*

THE HERETICS (MoMA) Producers, Joan Braderman, Crescent Diamond; Executive Producer, Bob Reckman; Director/Screenplay, Joan Braderman; Photography, Lily Henderson, Liz Rubin; Music, June Millington, Lee Madeloni; Editor, Scott Hancock; a No More Nice Girls production; American-Italian-Spanish; NTSC Color; Not rated; 91 minutes; Release date: October 9, 2009. Documentary on the second wave of the Women's Movement. **WITH:** Emma Amos, Ida Applebroog, Patsy Beckert, Joan Braderman, Mary Beth Edelson, Su Friedrich, Janet Froelich, Harmony Hammong, Sue Heinemann, Elizabeth Hess, Joyce Kozloff, K8 Hardy, Arlene Ladden, Lucy Lippard, Mary Miss, Sabra Moore, Marty Pottenger, Miriam Schapiro, Carolee Schneemann, Amy Sillman, Joan Snyder, Elke Solomon, Pat Steir, May Stevens, Susana Torre, Cecilia Vicuña, Sally Webster, Nina Yankowitz

FROM MEXICO WITH LOVE (Roadside Attractions) Producers, Glen Hartford, Daniel Toll; Executive Producers, James Pascucci, Ken Herts; Director, Jimmy Nickerson; Screenplay, Glen Hartford, Nicholas Siapkaris; Photography, Rick Lamb, Ted Chu; Designer, Allee Harati; Music, John Frizzell; Editors, Paul Harb, Sean Albertson; a Cineamour Entertainment presentation of a Hartford/Toll production; Technicolor; Rated PG-13; 97 minutes; Release date: October 9, 2009. **CAST:** Kuno Becker (Hector), Steven Bauer (Tito), Stephen Lang (Big Al Stevens), Alex Nesic (Robert Stevens), Danay Garcia (Maria), Bruce McGill (Billy), Steve Bilich (Patrolman Pete), Carl Ciarfalio (Jake), Anthony Cristo (Hector's Sparring Partner), Eddy Donno (Ring Announcer), Tony Donno (Robert's Sparring Partner), Charlane Meyer (Hostess), Richard Dyer (Travis), Glen Hartford (Lefty), Lu Johnson (Ringside Orthopedic Doctor), Michael Klesic (The Accountant), Robert E. Martinez, J.E. Meris (Migrant Workers), Juan Gabriel Pareja (Chucho), Fred Parker Jr. (Jake's Lackey), Kourtney Pogue (Ring Girl), Monica Ramon (Hector's Friend), Amanda Rivas (Lupe), Lisa Suaez (Lupe), Brandon Turpin (Ollie), Araceli Vasquez (Migrant Woman), Ron Yuan (Joe Scar)

THE MINISTERS (Maya Entertainment) Producers, Franc. Reyes, Jill Footlick; Executive Producers, Glenn M. Stewart, Steffen Aumueller, Claus Clausen, Aaron Ray; Co-Producers, John Leguizamo, Matthew Myers; Director/Screenplay, Franc. Reyes; Photography, Frank Byers; Designer, Dara Wishingrad; Costumes, Rahimah A. Yoba, Michael Anazalone; Music, George Acogny; Editors, Philip Pucci, Tony Cicone; Casting, Sig de Miguel, Stephen Vincent; a Sherezade Film Development Company presentation of an Alumbra Films and Grow Pictures production; Color; Rated R; 90 minutes; Release date: October 16, 2009. **CAST:** John Leguizamo (Dante Mendoza/Perfecto Mendoza), Harvey Keitel (Joe Bruno), Florencia Lozano (Celeste Lozano), Diane Venora (Gina Santana), Wanda de Jesus (Capt. Diaz), Manny Perez (Det. Manso), Saul Stein (Det. DeMarco), Susan Porro (Karen Rossin), Luis Antonio Ramos (Carlos Rojas), Jamie Tirelli (Father Gorbia), Raquel Castro (Nereida), Tammy Trull (Liz), Raquel Jordan (Alma), Gabreilla Loren (Celeste, age 18), Tomorrow Baldwin Montgomery (Little Girl), Charlene Biton (Girlfriend), Ivan Cardona (Dante's Father/Photo Op), David Castro (Dante/Perfecto, age 10), Peter Conboy (Fire Marshal), Jaidig Cruz (Carlos' Girlfriend), Kristina Dargelyte (Girl at the Bar), Dashia (Hispanic Woman), Sally Simone Dealy (Newscaster), Stracy Diaz, Antonio Saillant, Tania Santiago (Detectives), Tibor Feldman (Phil Morgan), Jason Fiore-Ortiz (Luis, age 12), Julia Frisoli (Hostess), Andrew Ginsburg (Waiter), John Hillmer (Jeff Kane), Melina Lizette (Kathy), Alex Luria (Dante/Perfecto, age 23), Adrian Martinez (Mike), Allyssa Maurice (Bartender), Benny Nieves (Alberto Santana), Michael Angelo Ortiz (Chino's Drug Dealer), Henry Santos (Carlos Rojas' Soldier), Josh Segarra (Luis Mendoza, age 25), Rick Sepulveda (Jesse Montoya), Michael Sirow (Young Cop), Bill Sorice, Steven Weisz, Bob Weston (EMTs), Monica Steuer (Bartender)

THE JANKY PROMOTERS (Third Rail Releasing) Producers, Ice Cube, Matt Alvarez; Executive Producers, Bob Weinstein, Harvey Weinstein, Neil Machlis; Director, Marcus Raboy; Screenplay, Ice Cube; Photography, Tom Priestly; Designer, Bradley Thordarson; Costumes, Dana Campbell; Music, John Murphy; Music Supervisor, Spring Aspers; Editor, Robert Ivison; Casting, Kim Taylor-Coleman; a Dimension Pictures presentation of a Cube Vision production; Dolby; Technicolor; Rated R; 85 minutes; Release date: October 16, 2009. **CAST:** Ice Cube (Russell Redds), Mike Epps (Jellyroll), Young Jeezy (Himself), Darris Love (Mondo), Lahmard Tate (Percy), Julio Oscar Mechoso (John Glanville), Tamala Jones (Regina), Lil' JJ aka James Lewis (Yung Semore), Glenn Plummer (Officer Ronnie Stixx), Juanita Jennings (Momma), Aloma Wright (Ms. Ann), Jowharah Jones (Loli Tyson), Joey Greco (Kevin Maline), Vernon Hawthorne (T.C.)Leland White (KK), Reghan Alexander (Valerie), Paul Ambrus, Cisco Reyes (Security), Malik Barnhardt (CW), Proscha Coleman (Sandra), Mark Craig (Cop #1), Gabrielle Dennis (Fan), Lorenzo Eduardo (Entourage #1), Tiffany Haddish (Michelle), Mark Alexander Herz (FBI), Terricka Hudson (Clubgoer), Kerisse Hutchinson (Lisa), Page Kennedy (House DJ), J. Kristopher (Mondo's Crew), Helen McCardle (Head Maid), Danny Minnick (Rioter #1), Elvada Seleithia, Sandra Valladres (Concertgoers), Paul Webster (Chris)

CHELSEA ON THE ROCKS (Aliquot Films) Producers, Jen Gatien, David D. Wasserman; Executive Producers, Kris Haber, Ovidio E. Diaz; Director, Abel Ferrara; Screenplay, Christ Zois, David Linter, Abel Ferrara; Photography, David Hausen, Ken Kelsch; Music, Robert Burger; Editor, Langdon Page; a Deerjen production; Color; Panavision; Rated R; 88 minutes; Release date: October 17, 2009. Documentary on New York's fabled Chelsea Hotel. **WITH:** Vito Acconci, Donald Baechler, Stanley Bard, Sathima Bea Benjamin, Jamie Burke, Ira Cohen, Robert Crumb, Abel Ferrara, Milos Forman, Adam Goldberg, Ethan Hawke, Gaby Hoffman, Dennis Hopper, Aline Kominsky, Caitlin Mehner, Bijou Phillips, Elizabeth Pugh, Arthur Weinstein; and Sherry Cosovic (Peggy), Giancarlo Esposito (Tip), Grace Jones (Bev), Shanyn Leigh (Jan), Robert Oppel (Jack), Christy Scott Cashman (Vera)

SAW VI (Lionsgate) Producers, Greg Hoffman, Oren Koules, Mark Burg; Executive Producers, Daniel Jason Heffner, James Wan, Leigh Whannell, Stacey Testro, Peter Block, Jason Constantine; Co-Producer, Troy Begnaud; Director, Kevin Greutert; Screenplay, Patrick Melton, Marcus Dunstan; Photography, David A. Armstrong; Designer, Tony Ianni; Costumes, Alex Kavanaugh; Music, Charlie Clouser; Editor, Andrew Coutis; Special Effects Supervisor, Rob Sanderson; Prosthetics, Francois Dagenais; Stunts, Shelley Cook; Casting, Stephanie Gorin; a Twisted Pictures presentation of a Burg/Koules/Hoffman production; Dolby; Deluxe color; Rated R; 90 minutes; Release date: October 23, 2009. **CAST:** Tobin Bell (Jigsaw/John), Costas Mandylor (Mark Hoffman), Betsy Russell (Jill Tuck), Mark Rolston (Dan Erickson), Peter Outerbridge (William Easton), Shawnee Smith (Amanda Young), Athena Karkanis (Agent Lindsey Perez), Samantha Lemole (Pamela Jenkins), Caroline Cave (Debbie), George Newbern (Harold Abbott), Tanedra Howard (Simone), Marty Moreau (Eddie), Shawn Ahmed (Allen), Janelle Hutchison (Addy), Gerry Mendicino (Janitor), Shauna MacDonald (Tara), Devon Bostick (Brent), Darius McCrary (Dave), Shawn Mathieson (Josh), Melanie Scrofano (Gena), Karen Cliché (Shelby), James Gilbert (Aaron), Larissa Gomes (Emily), Dan Duran (Newscaster), James Van Patten (Coroner), Jon Mack, Francois Sagat (Addicts), Elle Downs (Nurse Elis), Tenika Davis (Irate Clinic Woman), Karl Campbell (Security Guard), Ginger Busch (Sachi), Jessie Rusu (Officer), Mpho Koaho (Tim)

Peter Outerbridge in
Saw VI © Lionsgate

EULOGY FOR A VAMPIRE (Willing Suspension Films) Producer/Director, Patrick McGuinn; Executive Producer, Peter Perrone; Screenplay, André Salas; Photography, Nickolas Dylan Rossi; Art Director, Susan Morningstar; Music, Christian Hawkins; Visual Effects, Jesse LeChok; Fujicolor; Not rated; 107 minutes; Release date: October 23, 2009. **CAST:** Wilson Hand (Father Anthony), David McWeeney (Father Lars), Damacio Ruiz (Rafael), Angelo Tursi (Sebastian), Ryan G. Metzger (Florian), Craig Philip Lumsden (Eric), Darin Guerrasio (Brother Matthew), Nate Steinwachs (Stefano), Shawn Hollenbach (McGee), Sal Bardo (Young Anthony)

Eulogy for a Vampire © Willing Suspension Films

STAN HELSING (Anchor Bay Entertainment) Producers, Scott Steindorff, Bo Zenga, Kirk Shaw; Executive Producers, Karen Lauder, Mark Jacobs, Christian Arnold-Beutel, Gregory R. Greenfield, Lionel S. Margolick, Scott M. Boggio, William G. Brown, Scott LaStaiti, Lindsay Macadam, Dylan Russell; Director/Screenplay, Bo Zenga; Photography, Robert New; Designer, Chris August; Costumes, Angelina Kekich; Music, Ryan Shore; Editors, Dennis M. Hill, Sterling Scott; Special Effects Coordinators, Brant McIllroy, Martin Testa; a Stone Village Picture and Boz Productions (U.S.) presentation of an Insight Film Studios (Canada) production; American-Canadian; Dolby; Color; Rated R; 90 minutes; Release date: October 23, 2009. **CAST:** Steve Howey (Stan Helsing), Diora Baird (Nadine), Kenan Thompson (Teddy), Desi Lydic (Mia), Leslie Nielsen (Kay), Kit Zenga (Orphan), Darren Moore (Crazy), Twan Holliday (Pleatherface), Ben Cotton (Fweddy), Travis MacDonald (Hitcher), Lee Tichon (Michael Criers), Ken Kirzinger (Mason), Charles Zuckermann (Needlehead), Jeff Gulka (Lucky), Chad Krowchuk (Sully), Nathan Dashwood (Busboy), Derek Watt (Timmy), Ray Thunderchild (Husband), Hilary Strang (Hippie Lady), Jeremy Crittenden (Altar Boy), Robin Nielsen, Lara Babalola (Employees), John Burnside (Security Guard), Zainab Musa (Blair Witch Spectator in Movie Store), Alain Chanoine (Guy #1), Denyc, Holly Eglington, Ildiko Ferenczi (Brides), Aaron Rota (Kid #1, Hockey Boy), Steven Garr (Vendor), Elysia Rotaru, Jessica Olfason (Hot Girls), Zorianna Kit (Herself), Bo Zenga (1st AD), Jenny Mitchell (Customer), John Wildman (Director), Kathryn Kirkpatrick (Bathroom Lady), James Ashcroft (Dead Body), John DeSantis (Frankenstein), Ryan Steele (Wolfman), Tara Wilson (Screaming Woman), Colin Foo (Choking Old Man), Gray Szakacs (Michael Jackson), Chris Shields (Barack Obama), Duane Dickinson (Fire Patron)

MOTHERHOOD (Freestyle) Producers, Jana Edelbaum, Rachel Cohen, Pamela Koffler, Christine Vachon; Executive Producer, John Wells, Stephen Hays, Peter Graham, Patricia Lambrecht; Director/Screenplay, Katherine Dieckmann; Photography, Nancy Schreiber; Designer, Debbie De Villa; Costumes, Susan Lyall; Music, Joe Henry; Editor, Michael R. Miller; Casting, Laura Rosenthal; an iDeal Partners Film Fund presentation of a Killer Films/John Wells production, in association with 120db Productions; Dolby; Technicolor; Rated PG-13; 90 minutes; Release date: October 23, 2009. **CAST:** Uma Thurman (Eliza Welch), Anthony Edwards (Avery Welch), David Schallipp (Lucas Welch), Matthew Schallipp (Lucas Welch), Daisy Tahan (Clara Welch), Alice Drummond (Edith), Stephanie Szostak (French Neighbor), Celina Vignaud (Her Daughter), Minnie Driver (Sheila), Dale Soules (Hester), James Lecesne (Annoyed Man), Marceline Hugot (Curious Tourist), Victor Colicchio (Roofer in Truck), Brian Tarantina (Opera Lover in Car), Kerry Bishé (Good Sharing Mom), Betsy Aidem (Jordan's Mom), Neal Huff (Stay-at-Home Dad), Orlagh Cassidy (Scarsdale Mom), Jodie Foster (Herself), Clea Lewis (Lily), Jose Constanino (Bodhi), Jake Smith (Snotty Production Assistant), Aunjanue Ellis (Sample Sale Friend), Ellen Crown (Sample Sale Eavesdropper), Maya Ri Sanchez (Mom in Party Store), Valentino Bonaccio (Jorge), Lois Robbins (Tense Woman in Party Store Line), Samantha Bee (Alison Hopper), Javier Picayo (Annoyed Guy in Party Store Line), Jenny Kirlin (Bakery Clerk), Shannon Burkett (Woman in Bakery Line), Arjun Gupta (Nikesh)

Uma Thurman, Minnie Driver in Motherhood *© Freestyle Releasing*

KILLING KASZTNER (Sky Island Films) Producers, Andrew Cohen, Gaylen Ross, Noam Shalev, Gus D. Samios, Anne Feinsilber; Executive Producer, Tony Tabatznik; Director, Gaylen Ross; Screenplay, Gaylen Ross, Andy Cohen; Photography, Gaylen Ross, Andrew Cohen; Music, Blake Leyh, Shlomit Aharon; Editors, Gaylen Ross, Andrew Ford, Laure Sullivan; a GR Films Inc. production in association with Highlight Films (Israel)/AC Films/Dogfactory (U.K.); American-Israeli-British; Color; Not rated; 114 minutes; Release date: October 23, 2009. Documentary on Rezso Kasztner, a Jew whose dealings with the Nazis allowed him to rescue 1,700 of his people yet provoked condemnation and controversy. **WITH:** Larry Pine (Voice of Kasztner), Ze'ev Eckstein, Zsuzsi Kasztner, Merav Michaeli, Michal Michaeli, Keren Michaeli, Uri Aveneri

Rezso Kasztner in Killing Kasztner *© Sky Island Films*

THE BOONDOCK SAINTS II: ALL SAINTS DAY (Apparition) Producers, Don Carmody, Chris Brinker; Executive Producers, Lloyd Segan, Rob Freid; Director/Screenplay, Troy Duffy; Story, Troy Duffy, Taylor Duffy; Photography, Miroslaw Baszak; Designer, Dan Yarhi; Costumes, Georgina Yarhi; Music, Jeff Danna; Music Supervisor, Ross Elliot; Editors, Bill Deronde, Paul Kumpata; Casting, Veronica Collins Rooney; a Stage 6 Films presentation of a Don Carmody/Chris Brinker production; Dolby; Super 35 Widescreen; Color; Rated R; 115 minutes; Release date: October 30, 2009. **CAST:** Sean Patrick Flanery (Connor MacManus), Norman Reedus (Murphy MacManus), Billy Connolly (Poppa M), Clifton Collins Jr. (Romeo), Julie Benz (Special Agent Eunice Bloom), Peter Fonda (The Roman), Paul Johansson (Rick), Judd Nelson (Concezio Yakavetta), David Della Rocco (Rocco), Bob Marley (Det. Greenly), Brian Mahoney (Det. Duffy), David Ferry (Det. Dolly), Gerard Parkes (Doc), Richard Fitzpatrick (The Chief), Daniel DeSanto (Crew Cut), Willem Dafoe (Paul Smecker), Matt Lemche (Noah), Robert Mauriell (Louie)

Sean Patrick Flanery, Billy Connolly, Norman Reedus, Clifton Collins Jr. in The Boondock Saints II *© Apparition*

GENTLEMEN BRONCOS (Fox Searchlight) Producers, Mike White, John J. Kelly; Executive Producers, Ben Leclair, Jerusha Hess, Jared Hess; Director, Jared Hess; Screenplay, Jared Hess, Jerusha Hess; Photography, Munn Powell; Designer, Richard A. Wright; Costumes, April Napier; Music, David Wingo; Editor, Yuka Ruell; Special Effects Supervisor, Jeferson "Zuma Jay" Wagner; Casting, Meredith Tucker; a Rip Cord production; Dolby; Color; Rated PG-13; 89 minutes; Release date: October 30, 2009. **CAST:** Michael Angarano (Benjamin Purvis), Jennifer Coolidge (Judith Purvis), Halley Feiffer (Tabatha), Héctor Jiménez (Lonnie Donaho), Sam Rockwell (Bronco/Brutus), Jemaine Clement (Ronald Chevalier), Mike White (Dusty), John Baker (Don Carlos), Robin D. Ballard (Assistant), Steve Berg (Obnoxious Fan), Kristin Brewer (Lady Shopper), Kristie Conway (Nerdy Girl), Rod Decker (Himself), Isaac Demke (Loyal Fan), Johnny Hoops (Kanaya/ Kenonka), Jizelle Jade Jurquina (Troll Girl), Daniel "Doc" Love (Camera Operator), Suzanne May (Vanaya/Venonka), Edgar Oliver (Duncan/Lord Daysius), Josh Pais (Todd Keefe), John Pleshette (Merve), Jeanette Puhich (Sherry), Clive Revill (Cletus), John D. Richards Jr. (Bank Teller), Isaac Russell (Skinny Boy), Jon Shere (Boom Operator), Brian Unger (Journalist), Edward Osborn (Gross Guy), Benji Hughes (Dad Photo)

Michael Angarano, Jemaine Clement in Gentlemen Broncos
© *Fox Searchlight*

LABOR DAY (Catalyst Media) Producers, Glenn Silber, Claudia Vianello; Director, Glenn Silber; Photography, John Saraf, Max Miller, Jon Ellison, Danny O'Shea, David Brown, Scott Winters, Kyle Gallagher; Music, Doug Hall; Editor, Phil Raymond; Color; DV; Not rated; 76 minutes; Release date: October 30, 2009. Documentary on how the Service Employees International Union impacted the presidential election.

HOW TO SEDUCE DIFFICULT WOMEN (Quadrant Entertainment) Producer/ Director/Screenplay, Richard Iemtchine; Executive Producer, Jason Young; Photography, Benjamin Chartier; Designer, Tommaso Ortino; Costumes, Sylvia Grieser; Music, Pedro da Silva; Editor, Michael Thomson; Casting, Sig de Miguel, Stephen Vincent; Color; Not rated; Running time: 90 minutes; Release date: October 30, 2009. **CAST:** Louis-Do de Lencquesaing (Philippe), Stephanie Szostak (Gigi), Jackie Hoffman (Book Publisher), Rachel Roberts (Sabrina), Opal Alladin (Betty), Pratima Anaé (Tequia), Brian Avers (Mitchell), Lorie Baker (Paula), David Wilson Barnes (Doug), Gregg Bello (Dan), Bill Dawes (Al), Natascia Diaz (Angelica), Alex Disdier (Curator Assistant), Celine du Tertre (Claire), Diana Gettinger (Julia), Anthony Guerino (Waiter), Jason Haitkin, Sal Longobordo (Construction Workers), Alexa Havins (Maureen), Jonathan Hova (Mo), Ann Hu (Mercedes), Dave Konig (Charlie Green), Paul Lazar (Sam), Adam LeFevre (Ira), Justin Morck (Restaurant Patron), Esau Pritchett (David), Nicole Roderick (Patrizia), David Lee Russek (Tom), Jeff Skowron (Ronnie), Robert Gordon Spencer (Eduardo), Lin Tucci (Sheila), Amy Williams (Woman in Bookstore), Teresa Woods (Diane Savior)

LOOKING FOR PALLADIN (Wildcat Releasing) Producer, Mahyad Tousi; Executive Producer, Majka Elczewska; Director/Screenplay, Andrzej Krakowski; Photography, Giovanni Fabietti, Alberto Chaktoura; Designers, Jorgi Rossi, Rene Bustamante; Costumes, Jennifer Miekle; Music, Alan Kushan; Music Supervisor, Giacomo Buonafina; Editor, Babak Rassi; Casting, Marsha Ellyn Long Marshall, Maria E. Nelson; a Pine Hill and Tousi production in association with Maya Cine Digital, Full Moon Angel Cine Independiente; Dolby; Color; Not rated; 115 minutes; Release date: October 30, 2009. **CAST:** Ben Gazzara (Jack Palladin), David Moscow (Joshua Ross), Talia Shire (Rosario), Pedro Armendáriz Jr. (Police Chief), Angélica Aragón (Helen), Roberto Diaz Gomar (Ed Giobbi), Sammy Morales, Jimmy Morales (Postmen), Vincent Pastore (Arnie), Luis Argueta (Paco the Cobbler), Jerry Carlson (Jerry), Arturo Castro (Nestor), Sofia Comparini (Waitress), Cecilia de Oribe (Mayor), "Chofo" Rodolfo Espinosa (Immigration Officer), Tuti Furlan (Ms. Sanders), Maria del Rosario Furlan (Mrs. Sanders), Carmen Godoy (Woman at Butcher's), Michelle Manterola (Mercedes), Joe Manuella (De Niro Impersonator), Kim Meisner (Clerk), Jairon Salguero (Butcher), Cecilia Santamarina (Mayor), Dick Smith (Hank), Joan Solo (Padre Lucio), Joan Antón Soló (Father Lucio), Bahman Soltani (Bahman), Josue Sotomayor (Old Fernandez), Robert Youngs (Mark)

YOU CANNOT START WITHOUT ME: Valery Gergiev, Maestro (Thirteen/ WNET) Producer/Director/Editor, Allan Miller; Executive Producers, R. Douglas Sheldon, Margaret Smilov; Photography, Don Lenzer; a production of White Nights Foundation of America; Color; Not rated; 86 minutes; Release date: November 2, 2009. Documentary on one year in the life of conductor Valery Gergiev. **WITH:** Valery Gergiev, Yefim Bronfman, Renée Fleming, Dmitri Hvorostovsky, Leonidas Kavakos, Uliana Lopatkina, Anna Netrebko

COLLAPSE (Vitagraph) Producer, Kate Noble; Director, Chris Smith; Photography, Max Malkin, Ed Lachman; Art Director, Andrew Reznik; Music, Didier Leplae; Editor, Barry Poltermann; a Bluemark presentation; Color; DV; Not rated; 80 minutes; Release date: November 6, 2009. Documentary in which Michael Ruppert points out why he believes the economy is about to collapse. **WITH:** Michael Ruppert

Michael Ruppert in Collapse © *Vitagraph*

SPLINTERHEADS (Paladin) Producers, Darren Goldberg, Christopher Marsh, Anisa Quershi; Executive Producers, Steven Voichik, Mike Bulger; Director/ Screenplay, Brant Sersen; Based on a story by Brant Sersen, McFeat Burke; Photography, Michael Simmonds; Designer, Chad Keith; Costumes, Cameron Folan; Music, John Swihart; Music Supervisor, Jim Black, Gabe Hilfer; Editor, Chris Lechler; Casting, Beth Bowling, Kim Miscia, Nadia Lubbe; an Atlantic

Pictures presentation in association with Offhollywood Pictures; Dolby; Color; HD-to-35mm; Not rated; 94 minutes; Release date: November 6, 2009. **CAST:** Thomas Middleditch (Justin Frost), Rachael Taylor (Galaxy), Christopher McDonald (Sgt. Bruce Mancuso), Lea Thompson (Susan Frost), Dean Winters (Reggie), Frankie Faison (Pope), Edmund Lyndeck (Albert), Pamela Shaw (Betty), Jason Rogel (Wayne), Brendan Burke (Thad), Jason Mantzoukas (The Amazing Steve), Lennon Parham (Wyoming), Shiro Aoki (Metal Dude), Michael Biscardi (Skinny Cameraman), Gary Buccola (Slim Jim), Nancy Buccola (Big Top), Schuylar Dane Croom (Might as Well Jump Guy), Rebecca Lynn Goldfarb (Girl at Carnival), Emmett Harty Jr. (Gas Station Attendant), Lauren Hunter (Hot Blonde Metal Chick), Jenny Jordan (Hot Brunette Metal Chick), Sam Kitchin (Man of the House), John Lutz (Guinness Man), Lucia Matioli (Voice of Janice), Paul Pontieri (Judge), Jenn Schatz (Splinterhead Girl), Noa Siegel (Little Girl)

Rachael Taylor, Thomas Middleditch in Splinterheads © Paladin

TURNING GREEN (New Films Intl.) Producers, Rob Malkani, Andrew Charas; Executive Producers, Anthony Moody, Jon Whelan; Directors/Screenplay, Michael Aimette, John G. Hofmann; Photography, Tim Fleming; Designer, Laurent Mellet; Costumes, Maeve Paterson; Music, Mitch Davis, Scott Brittingham; Editor, John G. Hofmann; Casting, Carmel O'Connor; a CurbSide Pictures presentation in association with Indalo Productions and NetReturn Entertainment; American-Irish, 2005; Dolby; Panavision; Technicolor; DV/16mm/DV-to-35mm; Not rated; 85 minutes; Release date: November 6, 2009. **CAST:** Timothy Hutton (Bill the Breaker), Alessandro Nivola (Bill the Bookie), Colm Meaney (Tom), Donal Gallery (James), Killian Morgan (Pete), Billie Traynor (Aunt Mary), Deirdre Monaghan (Aunt Maggie), Brid Ni Chionaola (Aunt Nora), Sinead C. Kavanagh (The Underwear Model), Katherine Kendall (The Muse), Gavin O'Connor (Post Office Clerk), Myles Purcell (Peadar), Jim Roche (Man in Bar), Killian Morgan (Pete)

Timothy Hutton, Alessandro Nivola, Donal Gallery in Turning Green © New Films Intl.

HUMBLE PIE (Monterey Media) formerly *American Fork*; Producers, Shannon B. Gardner, Derek Beumer, Jeremy Coon, Maya Browne; Executive Producer, Derek Ferguson; Director, Chris Bowman; Screenplay, Hubbel Palmer; Photography, Doug Chamberlain; Designer, Anne K. Black; Costumes, Mandi Line; Music, Bobby Johnston; Music Supervisor, Sheila Scott; Editor, Cary Gries; a Low Hanging Fruit and Bratt Pictures presentation of a Framework Pictures production; Deluxe color; Rated PG-13; 94 minutes; Release date: November 6, 2009. **CAST:** Hubbel Palmer (Tracy Orbison), William Baldwin (Truman Hope), Mary Lynn Rajskub (Peggy Orbison), Kathleen Quinlan (Agnes Orbison), Vincent Caso (Kendis Cooley), Nick Lashaway (Shawn Dunlop), Bruce McGill (Mr. Grigoratus), Rae Ritke (Helen), Scott Lincoln (Lyle), Micaela Nelligan (Laverne), Tarren McGray (Steve), Janet Varney (Joleen), Mike Eto (Hsao-Wei), Guangze Zhu (Mr. Wong), Bruce Abbott (Capt. Atticus), Simon Fusco (Lieutenant 7750), Brent Florence (Ensign Meehan), Tony Larimer (Old Man), Ron Frederickson (Mr. Waverly), Charles Halford (Curtis), Rob Steiner (Benji), Megan Ferguson (Young and Plain), Michael Todd Behrens (Police Officer), Robert Caso (Maitre D'), Lincoln Hoppe (Waiter), Dan Christensen (Ponytail Man), Bill Gillane (Award Presenter)

William Baldwin, Hubbel Palmer in Humble Pie © Monterey Media

THE GOOD SOLDIER (Artistic License) Producers/Directors, Lexy Lovell, Michael Uys; Co-Producer/Photography, Samuel Henriques; Music, JJ Grey; Editor, Sikay Tang; an Out of the Blue production; Color/Black and white; HD; Not rated; 79 minutes; Release date: November 11, 2009. Documentary in which five servicemen express their disdain for war. **WITH:** Pvt. Ed Wood, Staff Sgt. Will Williams, Chief Warrant Officer Perry Parks, Capt. Michael McPhearson, Staff Sgt. Jimmy Massey

Ed Wood in The Good Soldier © Artistic License

FOUR SEASONS LODGE (First Run Features) Producer, Matthew Lavine, Andrew Jacobs; Executive Producer, Kelly Sheehan; Director, Andrew Jacobs; Screenplay, Andrew Jacobs, Kim Connell; Photography, Albert Maysles, Andrew Federman, Avi Kastoriano, Justin Schein; Editors, Aaron Soffin, Kim Connell; Music, Eric Lewis; Co-Producers, Roger Bennett, Rhoda Herrick, Elyssa Hess; A Four Seasons Project production in association with Rainlake Productions; Color; Not rated; 97 minutes; Release date: November 13, 2009. Documentary on how in 1979 some 100 Jewish Holocaust survivors created a Catskills retreat called Four Seasons Lodge. **WITH:** Victor Lewis and Regina Lewis, Carl Potok, Esther Geizhals

Jamie Ambramowitz, Tasha Ambramowitz in Four Seasons Lodge
© *First Run Features*

WOMEN IN TROUBLE (Screen Media) Producer/Director/Screenplay, Sebastian Gutierrez; Photography, Cale Finot; Designer, Daniel Mailley; Costumes, Denise Wingate; Music, Robyn Hitchcock; Editors, Lisa Bromwell, Michelle Tesoro; a Gato Negro Films production; Dolby; Color; HD; Rated R; 95 minutes; Release date: November 13, 2009. **CAST:** Carla Gugino (Elektra Luxx), Connie Britton (Doris), Adrianne Palicki (Holly Rocket), Emmanuelle Chriqui (Bambi), Sarah Clarke (Maxine McPherson), Marley Shelton (Cora), Rya Kihlstedt (Rita), Cameron Richardson (Darby), Josh Brolin (Nick Chapel), Simon Baker (Travis McPherson), Joseph Gordon-Levitt (Bert Rodriguez), Isabella Gutierrez (Charlotte), Caitlin Keats (Addy Hunter), Garcelle Beauvais (Maggie), Paul Cassell (Jay), Elizabeth Berkley (Tracy), Antonio Grana (Jimbo), Lauren Katz (Tara), Xander Berkeley (Mr. Frost)

Marley Shelton, Garcelle Beauvais in Women in Trouble
© *Screen Media Films*

THE END OF POVERTY? (Cinema Libre) Producer, Beth Portello; Executive Producer, Clifford Cobb; Director/Screenplay/Photography, Philippe Diaz; Music, Cristian Bettler, Max Soussan; Editor, Tom Von Doom; Narrator, Martin Sheen; a Cinema Libre production, in association with the Robert Shalkenbach Foundation; Stereo; Color; Not rated; 104 minutes; Release date: November 13, 2009. Documentary that points the finger at Western corporations as the reason for the world's current state of poverty. **WITH:** John Christensen, William Eastlery, Susan George, Chalmers Johnson, Alvaro García Lineras, John Perkins, Amartya Sen, Joseph Stiglitz, Eric Toussaint

The End of Poverty? © *Cinema Libre*

WILLIAM KUNSTLER: DISTURBING THE UNIVERSE (Arthouse Films) Producers, Jesse Moss, Susan Korda, Emily Kunstler, Sarah Kunstler; Executive Producers, Vanessa Wanger, Sally Jo Fifer; Directors, Emily Kunstler, Sarah Kunstler; Screenplay, Sarah Kunstler; Photography, Brett Wiley, Martina Radwan; Music, Shahzad Ismaily; Editor/Narrator, Emily Kunstler; an Off Center Media production, in association with Chicken & Egg Pictures and ITVS; Color; HD; Not rated; 85 minutes; Release date: November 13, 2009. Documentary on radical lawyer William Kunstler. **WITH:** Herman Badillo, Harry Belafonte, Clyde Bellecourt, Daniel Berrigan, Julian Bond, Jimmy Breslin, Alan M. Dershowitz, Phil Donahue, Elizabeth M. Fink, Madonna Thunder Hawk, Tom Hayden, Bruce Jackson, Ron Kuby, Karin Kunstler Goldman, Nancy Kurshan, Gerald Lefcourt, C. Vernon Mason, Bill Means, Michael Ratner, M. Paul Redd, Yusef Salaam, Bobby Seale, Barry Slotnick, Michael Smith, Lynne Stewart, M. Wesley Swearingen, Leonard Weinglass

THE HAND OF FATIMA (Cultural Animal) Producer/Editor, Chris Arnold; Director, Augusta Palmer; Photography, Juan Carlos Borrero; Animator, Hongsun Yoon; Color; Not rated; 75 minutes; Release date: November 13, 2009. Documentary on music critic Bob Palmer's relationship with Sufi band Master Musician of Jajouka. **WITH:** Bachir Attar, Donovan Leitch, Genesis P-Orridge, John Giorno, Bill Laswell, Anthony DeCurtis, Master Musicians of Jajouka

Robert Palmer, Bachir Attar in The Hand of Fatima
© *Cultural Animal*

TEN9EIGHT: SHOOT FOR THE MOON (50 Eggs Films) Director/Screenplay, Mary Mazzio; Photography, Richard Klug; Music, Alex Lasarenko; Editor, Paul Gattuso; Color; Not rated; 84 minutes; Release date: November 13, 2009. Documentary about inner city kids competing in an annual business plan competition run by the Network for Teaching Entrepreneurship. **WITH:** Tatyana Blackwell, Jessica Cervantes, Gabriel Echoles, Rodney Walker, Macalee Harlis, Shan Shan Huang, Amanda Loyola, William Mack, Ja'Mal Willis, Robbie Martin, Anné Montague, Alexander Niles, Jasmine Lawrence, Howard Stubbs

William Mack, Ja'Mal Willis in Ten9Eight © *50 Eggs Films*

CREATING KARMA (Fantasy Creature Films) Producer/Director, Jill Wisoff; Screenplay, Carol Lee Sirugo, Jill Wisoff; Photography, Carter Bissell; Designer, Kathleen Muldoon; Costumes, Nina Simich; Music, Joel Diamond; Editors, Christine Giorgio, David Wright; Color; Not rated; 89 minutes; Release date: November 13, 2009. **CAST:** Carol Lee Sirugo (Karma), Jill Wisoff (Callie), Karen Lynn Gorney (Chanel "Lollipop Fields" Fontaine), Joe Grifasi (Prighorn), Roland Sands (Rajah), Peggy A. Kirkpatrick (Eleanor Martlin), Rahad Coulter-Stevenson (Vincent), Jeremy Ebenstein (Kevin Kingston), Jennifer Lee Mitchell (Barbara), Riana Hershenfeld (Trish), Leslie Levinson (Edith Rosenblatt), Moogy Klingman (Sidney Rosenblatt), David Wright (Young Rajah), Danielle Roth (Young Callie), Stephen Lemay (Neville), Norma Chu (Nurse), David Schecter (Rabbi), Harvey Kaufman (Lawyer), Pashu Pathi Ganeshan (Sabu), Mark Philip Patrick (Digsby Pembroke III), Brad Lee Wind (Freddie), Nick Raio (Morgana), Emily Mitchell (Minnie), Joe Cross (Sam), Robert Galinsky (Aldo), Cirilo Nunez (Ramon), Alexandre de Toulouse Lautrec (Francois), Dinarte (Dinner Party Intellectual), Jovis DePognon, Gray Stevenson, Stacie Bach, Marlene Villafane, Christian Pierrre, Tywan Williams (Therapy Patients)

THE WAR ON KIDS (Spectacle Films) Producers, Jeremy Carr, Dawn Fidrick, Cevin Soling; Director, Cevin Soling; Photography, Jeremy Carr; Music, Martin Trum; Color/Black and white; DV; Not rated; 95 minutes; Release date: November 18, 2009. Documentary on how high security has induced a state of paranoia and distrust in America's schools. **WITH:** Henry Giroux, Mike A. Males, John Gatto, Judith Browne, Dan Losen, Dr. Peter Breggin, John Whitehead, Laurie Couture, Morgan Emrich

The War on Kids © *Spectacle Films*

STATEN ISLAND (NEM) Producer, Sebastien Lemercier; Co-Producers, Luc Besson, Pierre-Ange Le Pogam; Director/Screenplay, James DeMonaco; Photography, Chris Norr; Designer, Stephen Beatrice; Costumes, Rebecca Hofherr; Music, Frédéric Verrières; Editors, Herve de Luze, Christel Dewynter; Casting, Beth Bowling, Kim Miscia; a Why Not U.S. (U.S.)/Europa Corp. (France) presentation of a Europa Corp., Why Not U.S. production, in association with Open City Films; American-French; Dolby; Super 35 Widescreen; Technicolor; Rated R; 95 minutes; Relese date: November 20, 2009. **CAST:** Ethan Hawke (Sully Halverson), Vincent D'Onofrio (Parmelo "Parmie" Tarzo), Seymour Cassel (Jasper), Julianne Nicholson (Mary Halverson), Jeremy Schwartz (Eddie), Ian Brennan (Hippie in Tree), Bill Cwikowski (Manny), J.D. Daniels (Vet), Rosemary De Angelis (Gianina), Mary Dimino (Train Passenger), Dominic Fumusa (Giammarino), Michael Hogan (Bill), Dominic Marcus (Chainsaw Man #2), Adrian Martinez (Officer Rodriguez), Larry Mitchell (Cop #1), Maggie Moore (Reporter), Frank Pando (Albie), Steven Randazzo (Franco), John Sharian (Tarquinio), David Vadim (The Tall Man), Lynn Cohen (Dr. Leikovic), Ken Marks (Land Owner), Sara Surrey (Marie Cacuoppo)

Ethan Hawke, Seymour Cassel in Staten Island © *NEM*

THE MISSING PERSON (Strand) Producers, Jesse Scolaro, Allen Bain, Lois Drabkin, Alex Estes; Executive Producers, Jason Orans, Amy Ryan; Director/Screenplay, Noah Buschel; Photography, Ryan Samul; Designer, Aleta Shaffer; Costumes, Eden Miller; Music Supervisor, Jim Black; Editor, Mollie Goldstein; Casting, Lois Drabkin; The 7th Floor and Apropos Films; Color; Not rated; 95 minutes; Release date: November 20, 2009. **CAST:** Michael Shannon (John Rosow), Amy Ryan (Miss Charley), Frank Wood (Harold Fullmer), Linda Emond (Megan Fullmer), Paul Sparks (Gus Papitos), Margaret Colin (Lana Cobb), John Ventimiglia (Hero Furillo), Yul Vazquez (Don Edgar), Merritt Wever (Mabel Page), Daniel Franzese (Agent Craig), Liza Weil (Agent Chambers), Paul Adelstein (Drexler Hewitt), Gary Wilmes (Officer Chehak), Halley Wegryn Gross (Chloe Cunningham), Betsy Hogg (Melody Hayward), Joe Lovano, Kenny Werner (Themselves), Kate Arrington (Jane Rosow), Lynne McCollough (Lynne McCartney), Rodrigo Lopresti (Carlos Clemente), Coati Mundi (Fernando Guerrero), Anthony Esposito (Javier Reyes), Steven Marcus (Sam Cotts), Marc J. Ventimiglia (Boo Boo Lefesti), Gray Madder (Blue Crassner), Ben Buschel (Quinn Duchamp), Jennie Epland (Kathryn Meany), Niesha Butler (Tanya Rogers), Michael Elian (Limo Driver), Charles Socarides (Homer Macauley), James A. Stephens (Old Doorman), Abbie Cobb (Leopard Girl), Eliza Swords (Desert Diner Waitress), Reiko Takahashi (L.A. Sushi Hostess)

Frank Wood, Michael Shannon, Amy Ryan in The Missing Person
© Strand Releasing

UNTIL THE LIGHT TAKES US (Variance Films) Producers/Directors, Aaron Aites, Audrey Ewell; Executive Producer, Gill Holland; Photography, Audrey Ewell, Odd Reinhardt Nicolaysen; Editor, Andrew Ford; a Field Pictures presentation, in association with Artists Public Domain and the Group Entertainment; Color; Not rated; 93 minutes; Release date: November 20, 2009. Documentary on Norway's black-metal scene. **WITH:** Gylve "Fenriz" Nagell, Varg "Count Grishnackh" Vikernes, Jan Axel "Hellhammer" Blomberg, Harmony Korine, Kjetil "Frost" Haraldstad, Bjarne Melgaard

Until the Light Takes Us © Variance Films

THE BROOKLYN HEIST (Image Entertainment) a.k.a. *Capers*; Producers, Brett Halsey, Joel Blanco, Michael Cecchi, Valerie Levitt, Danny Masterson, Dave Steck; Director, Julian M. Kheel; Screenplay, Julian M. Kheel, Brett Halsey; Photography, Carlo Scialla; Costumes, Alysia Raycraft; Music, David Poe; a Numeric Pictures, Capers Production; Color; Rated PG-13; 86 minutes; Release date: November 27, 2009. **CAST:** Danny Masterson (Fitz), Leon (Ronald), Aysan Celik (Lana), Michael Cecchi (Dino), Serena Reeder (Maya), Jonathan Hova (Slava), Blanchard Ryan (Samantha), Dominique Swain (Mercy), Phyllis Somerville (Connie), Craig muMs Grant [billed as "muMs da Schemer"] (Moose), Barney Cheng (Bo), John Henry Cox (Big Jim), Mackenzie Milone (Emily), Daniel Stewart Sherman (Douglas), Brett Halsey (Curtis), Noah Fleiss (Eric), Todd Barry (Isaac), Nick Kroll (Ruben), Steve Lemme (FBI Director), David Anzuelo (Hardware Store Clerk), E.J. Carroll (Tall Goon), Federico Castelluccio (R. Fadagucci), Berto Colon (Young FBI Agent), Ann Hu (Dr. Mehai Cheng), Ty Jones (Fireman), Leopold Lowe (Buck Fiddy), Joe Rosario (Goon)

SERIOUS MOONLIGHT (Magnolia) Producers, Andy Ostroy, Michael Roiff; Executive Producers, Cliff Chenfeld, David Graff, Dan Katcher, Todd King, Rick Milenthal, Dawn Porter, Isabel Rose, Todd Stein; Director, Cheryl Hines; Screenplay, Adrienne Shelly; Photography, Nancy Schreiber; Designer, Cecil Gentry; Costumes, Ariyela Wald-Cohain; Music, Andrew Hollander; Editor, Steven Rasch; Casting, Sunday Boling, Meg Morman; a Night & Day Pictures and All for A Films presentation; Dolby; Color; Rated R; 84 minutes; Release date: December 4, 2009. **CAST:** Meg Ryan (Louise), Timothy Hutton (Ian), Kristen Bell (Sara), Justin Long (Todd), Andy Ostroy (Police Officer), Nathan Dean (Detective), Kimberlee Peterson (Trashy Girl), Derek Carter, Bill Parks (Men)

Meg Ryan, Timothy Hutton in Serious Moonlight © Magnolia Pictures

TRANSYLMANIA (Full Circle) Producers/Directors, David Hillebrand, Scott Hillebrand; Executive Producers, Albert Miniaci, Brian Farber ; Screenplay, Patrick Casey, Worm Miller; Photography, Viorel Sergovici Jr.; Designer, Jack Cloud; Costumes, Ioana Corciova; Editor, Dave O'Brien; Casting, Aaron Griffith; a Hill & Brand Entertainment and Lifeworks Entertainment presentation; Color; Rated R; 92 minutes; Release date: December 4, 2009. **CAST:** Patrick Cavanaugh (Pete), Jennifer Lyons (Lynne), James DeBello (Cliff), Tony Denman (Newmar), Paul H. Kim (Wang), Oren Skoog (Rusty/Radu), David Steinberg (Dean Floca), Musetta Vander (Teodora van Sloan), Irena A. Hoffman (Draguta Floca), Natalie Garza (Lia), Nicole Garza (Danni), Ali Adawiya (Nightclub Owner), Ashley Barron (Pretty Girl), Adriana Butoi (Asha), Colin Campbell (Siegfried Fischbacher), Patrick Casey (Mike), Karin Young (Romanian Stripper), Carey Embry (Laverne), Jessica Gershen, Bonnie Morgan (Contortionists), Elena-Cristina Marchisano (Carrie), Worm Miller (Brady), Claudiu Trandafir (Van Sloan), Paul Zies (Bearded Guy)

Musetta Vander in Transylmania © Full Circle Releasing

BIG RIVER MAN (Revolver Entertainment) Producers, Maria Florio, Molly Lynch, John Maringouin, Kevin Ragsdale, Molly Hassell; Director/Photography, John Maringouin; Music, Rich Ragsdale; Editors, John Maringouin, Molly Lynch; Narrator, Borut Strel; a Self Pictures presentation in association with Earthworks Films; Stereo; Technicolor; HD; Not rated; 100 minutes; Release date: December 4, 2009. Documentary charting 52-year-old Martin Strel's attempts to swim the Amazon River. **WITH:** Martin Strel, Borut Strel, Matt Mohlke, Alfredo Chavez, Mattea de Leonni Stanonik

Martin Strel in Big River Man © Revolver Entertainment

LOOT (ADD Studios) Producer/Director/Screenplay/Editor, Darius Marder; Executive Producer, Dan Campbell; Photography, Darius Marder, Anson Call; Music, Max Avery Lichtenstein; Color; DigiBeta; Not rated; 88 minutes; Release date: December 4, 2009. Documentary on Lance Larson's obsession with finding a treasure of Asian currency from World War II, buried in the Philippines. **WITH:** Lance Larson, Andrew Seventy, Darrel Ross, Michael Larson, Otti Bruckbauer

Loot © ADD Studios

THE STRIP (Truly Indie) Producer/Director/Screenplay, Jameel Khan; Executive Producer, Jay Khan; Photography, Pete Biagi; Designer, Merje Veski; Costumes, Emma Potter; Music, John Swihart; Editor, Peck Prior; a Bata Films production; Color; Rated PG-13; 91 minutes; Release date: December 4, 2009. **CAST:** Dave Foley (Glenn), Rodney Scott (Kyle Davis), Billy Aaron Brown (Jeff), Federico Dordei (Avi), Jenny Wade (Melissa), Cory Christmas (Rick), Noureen DeWulf (Maliah), Chelcie Ross (Mr. Davis), Gail Rastorfer (Angela), Brittany Boardman (Lisa Rosenkrantz), Joe Canale, Maribeth Monroe (DVD Customers), Nicole DePue (Bar Patron), Alexandra Dinovi (Party Girl), Ryan Driscoll (Drunk Girl), Oksana Fedunyszyn (Mr. Schuesthberry), Kevin Fleming (Artex Customer), Ellen

Fox (Cheery Girl), Marc Goldberg (Cochise), Sam Jackel (Drive-Thru Guy), Anish Jethmalani (Amir), Thomas Kosik (Restaurant Patron), Holly Laurent (Cassie), Tenique Mathieu (Julie), Patrick Mene (Irate Customer), Susan Messing (Alarm Customer), David Musto (Vito the Book Store Loser), Kevin Oestenstad (Bill), Brian Posen (Cell Phone Customer), Al Samuels (Casting Director), Vivek Shah (Drunk Friend), Amy Stock-Poynton (Mrs. Davis), Rahul Thakkar (Drunk Indian Friend), Becky Wahlstrom (Becky), John Waller (Himself)

Dave Foley in The Strip © Truly Indie

ACROSS THE HALL (Dalton Pictures) Producers, Jeff Bowler, Stephen Fromkin, Marco Garibaldi, Ari Palitz, Bret Saxton; Executive Producers, Elton Brand, Evan Ferrante, Gary Gimelfarb; Director/Editor, Alex Merkin; Screenplay, Jesse Mittlestadt, Julian Schwab; Based on the short film by Alex Merkin; Photography, Andrew Carranza; Designer, Roy Rede; Costumes, Yasmine Mustaklim; Music, Bobby Tahouri; Casting, Barbara Fiorentino; a Milk & Media and Insomnia Media Group production in association with Godfather Entertainment and Cold Fusion Media Group; Dolby; Color; Rated R; 88 minutes; Release date: December 4, 2009. **CAST:** Mike Vogel (Julian), Danny Pino (Terry), Brittany Murphy (June), Brad Greenquist (The Porter), Arie Verveen (Lucas), Natalia Smyka (Anna), Guillermo Diaz (Cook), William Stanford Davis (Custodian), Mark Engelhardt, Chase Kim (Officers), Erika Seifred (Dominatrix)

LARGER THAN LIFE IN 3D (Cinedigm Entertainment) Producers, Wayne Miller, Jeffry Lewis, John Rubey; Executive Producers, Coran Capshaw, Patrick Jordan, Bruce Eskowitz, Bruce Flohr, John Rubey, Jeffry Lewis; Directors, Luke Harrison, Lawrence Jordan; Photography, Sean MacLeod Phillips; Editor, George Bellias; an Action 3D and AEG Network Live production; Color; HD; 3D; Rated PG; 88 minutes; Release date: December 11, 2009. The Dave Matthews Band in concert. **WITH:** Dave Matthews Band, Ben Harper & Relentless 7, Gogol Bordello

Ben Harper in Larger than Life © Cinedigm Entertainment

MY SON, MY SON, WHAT HAVE YE DONE (Absurda/Industrial) Producer, Eric Bassett; Executive Producers, Bingo Gubelmann, Benji Kohn, David Lynch, Stian Morck, Chris Papavasiliou, Jeff Rice, Ali Rougaghi, Austin Stark; Co-Executive Producers, Giulia Marletta, Ken Meyer; Co-Producer, Rick Spalla; Director, Werner Herzog; Screenplay, Herbert Golder, Werner Herzog; Photography, Peter Zeitlinger; Designers, Tyson Estes, Danny Caldwell; Costumes, Mikel Padilla; Music, Ernst

Reijseger; Editors, Joe Bini, Omar Daher; Casting, Jenny Jue, Johanna Ray; a David Lynch presentation of an Eric Bassett, Industrial Entertainment production in association with Absurda, Paper Street Films; American-German; Dolby; Widescreen; Color; HD; Not rated; 91 minutes; Release date: December 11, 2009. **CAST:** Willem Dafoe (Det. Hank Havenhurst), Brad Dourif (Uncle Ted), Michael Shannon (Brad McCullum), Chloë Sevigny (Ingrid), Michael Peña (Det. Vargas), Udo Kier (Lee Meyers), Grace Zabriskie (Mrs. McCullum), Irma P. Hall (Mrs. Roberts), Loretta Devine (Miss Roberts), Verne Troyer (Midget), Braden Lynch (Gary), Candice Coke (Officer Slocum), Noel Arthur (Naval Guard), James C. Burns (SWAT Cmdr. Brown), Jenn Liu (Receptionist), Julius Morck (Phil), Stefan Cap (Detective), James Lacey (Man in Theater).

Michael Shannon, Willem Dafoe in
My Son, My Son, What Have Ye Done © *Absurda/Industrial*

THE SLAMMIN' SALMON (Anchor Bay) Producer, Richard Perello; Executive Producers, Peter E. Lengyel, Julia Dray; Director, Kevin Heffernan; Screenplay, Jay Chandrasekhar, Kevin Heffernan, Steve Lemme, Paul Soter, Erik Stolhanske; Photography, Robert Barocci; Designer, Erich W. Schultz; Costumes, Tricia Gray; Music, Nathan Barr; Editor, Brad Katz; a Broken Lizard production in association with Arpad Productions and Cataland Films; Dolby; Color; Rated R; 98 minutes; Release date: December 11, 2009. **CAST:** Michael Clarke Duncan (Cleon "Slammin'" Salmon), Jay Chandrasekhar (Nuts), Kevin Heffernan (Rich), Steve Lemme (Connor), Paul Soter (Dave/Donnie), Erik Stolhanske (Guy), April Bowlby (Mia), Cobie Smulders (Tara), Lance Henriksen (Dick Lobo), Will Forte (Horace the Lone Diner), Vivica A. Fox (Nutella), Morgan Fairchild (Herself), Olivia Munn (Samara Dubois), Sendhil Ramamurthy (Marlon Spencer), Jeff Chase (Anthony), Carla Gallo (Stacy), Michael Yurchak (Jamie the Line Chef), Nat Faxon (Carl the Manager), Jolie Martin (Waitress), Carrie Clifford (Patty the Hostess), Rosalie Ward (Merlot Customer), Marc Evan Jackson (Dry Sac Customer), Dennis Gubbins (4lb. Lobster Dude), Jim Gaffigan (Stanley Bellin), Bobbi Sue Luther, Michael Merton, J.D. Walsh (Cod Customers), James Grace (Bachelor Party Guy), Alison Bower (Al the Lesbian), Koji Kataoka (Mr. Yamamuri), Smith Cho (Translator), Jim Rash (Disgusted Businessman), Elisabeth Noone, Melissa-Anne Davenport (Champagne Customers), Gillian Vigman (The Escort), Michael Weaver (The John), Sam Redford (British Guy), Peter Gaulke (Opera Customer), Rohit Sang (Frat Guy), Richard Perello (Fidel the Bartender), Avi Rothman (Steve Lemmaduche), Candace Smith (Mrs. Eva Salmon Parente), Philippe Brennikmeyer, Tara Brennikmeyer (King Crab Customers), Peter Navy Tuiasosopo (Miami Dophin #1)

Michael Clarke Duncan in The Slammin' Salmon © *Anchor Bay*

SINCERELY YOURS (Independent) Director/Producer, Rich Lee; Screenplay, Rich Lee, Shun Wen Hu; Photography, Ping-Bing Lee; Music, Rahayy Supanggah; Editor, Liao Ching-song; Taiwanese; Color; Not rated; 96 minutes; Release date: December 11, 2009. **CAST:** Lola Amaria (Setia), Banlop Lomnoi (Supayong), Li-Qi Wu (Wonpen), Keui-Mei Yang (Man-Guang Fei)

HANNAH FREE (Ripe Fruit) Producers, Tracy Baim, Sharon Zurek, Sharon Gless, Wendy Jo Carlton, Martie Marro, Paul Roesch; Director, Wendy Jo Carlton; Screenplay, Claudia Allen, based on her play; Photography, Gretchen Warthen; Designer, Rick Paul; Costumes, Iris Bainum-Houle; Music, Martie Marro; Editor, Sharon Zurek; Color; Not rated; 86 minutes; Release date: December 11, 2009. **CAST:** Sharon Gless (Older Hannah), Maureen Gallagher (Older Rachel), Kelli Strickland (Adult Hannah), Ann Hagemann (Adult Rachel), Taylor Miller (Marge), Jacqui Jackson (Greta), Adario Backus (Orderly Pushing Wheelchair), Marcy Baim (Waitress), Dolly Baruch (Resident in Park Playing Backgammon), Dana Bernadine (Park Nurse's Aide), Sharon Brown, Stephanie Palko, Ellen Peace (Nurse's Aides), Elaine Carlson (Day Nurse), Quinn Coleman (Infant Marge), Alice Cooperman (Resident in Garden), Meredith Drilling (Child Marge), Elita Ernsteen (Child Rachel), James S. Evans (Patient in Park), Hetor Flores, Lisa Junco (Nurses), Brad Harburgh (Male Nurse), Jorjet Harper (Wheelchair Old Lady), Leslie Hinderyckx (Old Man), Ayako Homma, Elizabeth A. Palmer (Visitors with Flowers), Wendy Hutton (Resident in Park), Pat Kane (Minister), Dan Kavanaugh (Man walking into Nursing Home), Sharon Kluge (Puzzle and Backgammon Resident), David Kravitz (Resident in Hall), Kate Mahoney (Jackie), Marty Mia, Kelsey Murphy Miles (Visitors in Hall), Shawn Murray (Activities Aide), Sarah Newport (Resident in Park and Yoga Resident), Bobbie O'Connor (WAC), Jon Philips (Puzzle Player), Daniel Rock-Hughes (Infant Roy), Mike Schmack (Nurse's Aide in Garden), Stephanie Serine (Woman in Park), Bev Spangler (Night Nurse), Dennis Stewart (Old Man in Hall), David Stzepek (Housecleaning Aide), Meg Thalken (Mail Lady), Casey Tutton (Child Hannah), Harry Walters (Resident by Organ and in Garden), Baron Whateley (Sleeping Resident), Fred Zucker (Yoga Resident)

Sharon Gless in Hannah Free © *Ripe Fruit*

THE VICIOUS KIND (72nd Street Productions) Producers, Tim Harms, Lindsay Lazillota, Lee Toland Krieger; Executive Producers, Neil LaBute, Chris Finerock, Ryan Horton, Andy Rudenstein, Jeff Gross; Director/Screenplay, Lee Toland Krieger; Photography, Bradley Stonesifer; Designer, Grady Cooley; Costumes, Lindy McMichael; Music, Jeff Cardoni; Editor, Regino Roy III; a Candleridge Entertainment production; Widescreen; Color; Rated R; 93 minutes; Release date: December 11, 2009. **CAST:** Adam Scott (Caleb Sinclaire), Brittany Snow (Emma Gainsborough), Alex Frost (Pete Sinclaire), J.K. Simmons (Donald Sinclaire), Vittorio Brahm (J.T.), Bill Buell (Rocky), Alysia Reiner (Samantha), Kate Krieger (Molly), Jordan Berkow (Hannah), Emily Oehler (Girl in Bar), Anne Gill (Waitress)

Adam Scott in The Vicious Kind © *72nd Street Prods.*

YESTERDAY WAS A LIE (Helicon Arts Cooperative) Producer, Chase Masterson; Executive Producer, James Kerwin; Director/Screenplay/Editor, James Kerwin; Photography, Jason Cochard; Designer, Jill Kerwin; Costumes, Sara Curran Ice; Music, Kristopher Carter; Casting, Victoria Anderson, Josh Waters; Dolby; Panavision; Black and white; HD; Rated PG; 88 minutes; Release date: December 11, 2009. **CAST:** Kipleigh Brown (Hoyle), Chase Masterson (Singer), John Newton (Dudas), Mik Scriba (Trench Coat Man), Nathan Mobley (Lab Assistant), Warren Davis (Psychiatrist), Megan Henning (Student), Jennifer Slimko (Nurse), Robert Siegel (Voice of Radio Interviewer), Peter Mayhew (Dead Man), Brian Carpenter (TV Shrink), Frank Payne (Coroner), John Ronald Dennis (Clerk), H.M. Wynant, Johanna McKay, Catherine O'Connor (Art Patrons), Bill Dempsey (Cabbie), Joe Leroy Reynolds Jr. (Bartender), Keri Holland (Waitress), Casey Alan Carver (Security Guard), Trevor Trout (Server), Howard Yeh (Newsie), Shadii, Amol Shah (Medics), Ed Cosico, Osbie Shepard (Other Trench Coat Men), Amara Cash (Other Student), Brock Branan, Claudia Croce (Couple in Therapy)

Chase Masterson, Kipleigh Brown in Yesterday Was a Lie © *Helicon Arts*

UNDER THE EIGHTBALL (Andalusian Dog) Producers, Timothy Grey, Breanne Russell, Patrick Paul, Eric Gustafson, D.C. Hayden, Steve Emling, Tj Luetz, Robert Bruce-Bushway, Philip Clyne, Ryan Tomie, Skyler Hobbs, Gabe Clark, Alyssa Russell; Directors/Screenplay/Editors, Timothy Grey, Breanne Russell; Photography, Breanne Russell, D.C. Hayden, Timothy Hall; a Movies for People presentation in association with Missing Lynx Pictures; Color/black and white; Not rated; 122 minutes; Release date: December 16, 2009. Documentary on how cases of Lyme disease have been misdiagnosed.

Polly Murray in Under the Eight Ball © *Andalusian Dog*

THE NEW DAUGHTER (Anchor Bay) Producer, Paul Brooks; Executive Producers, Scott Niemeyer, Norm Waitt; Director, Luis Alejandro Berdejo; Screenplay, John Travis; Based on a short story by John Connolly; Photography, Checco Varese; Designer, Chris Shriver; Costumes, Dana Campbell; Editors, Tom Elkins, Rob Sullivan; Special Effect Coordinator, David Beavis; Casting, Eyde Belasco; a Gold Circle Films production; Dolby; Color; Rated PG-13; 108 minutes; Release date: December 18, 2009. **CAST:** Kevin Costner (John James), Ivana Baquero (Luisa James), Gattlin Griffith (Sam James), Samantha Mathis (Cassandra), Noah Taylor (Prof. Evan White), Erik Palladino (Sheriff Ed Lowry), James Gammon (Roger Wayne), Sandra Ellis Lafferty (Ms. Amworth), Margaret Anne Florence (Alexis Danella), Christopher Harvey (Rick Ross), Brynn Massey (Sally), James Middleton (Scott), Guy Perry (Alpha Creature), Martin Thompson (Stewart Green), Nevaina Graves Rhodes (Pam), Bob Bonz (Adrian), Edmund Entin, Gary Entin (Creatures)

THE OTHER SIDE OF PARADISE (Striped Socks) Producers, Justin B. Hilliard, Arianne Martin, Ryan Hartsell; Director/Editor, Justin D. Hilliard; Screenplay, Justin D. Hilliard, Arianne Martin, Ryan Hartsell; Photography, Ryan Hartsell; Designer/Costumes, Randi Frances Hilliard; Casting, Justin D. Hilliard, Arianne Martin; Color; HD; Not rated; 114 minutes; Release date: December 18, 2009. **CAST:** Arianne Martin (Rose Hewitt), John Elliott (Alex Doran), Frank Mosley (Jamie Hewitt Jr.), Jodie Moore (James Hewitt Sr.), Susanna Gibb (Courtney Hewitt), Sandra Looney (Lola), Drew Waters (Jason), Melissa Odom (Michelle), Phil Harrington (Willie), Michael D. Price (Eli), Gordon Fox (Mr. Barrow), Robin Read (Heather), Jeff Fenter (George), Lindsey Holloway (Lori), Paul T. Taylor (Mr. Girard), Charlie S. Cruz (Dios De La Venta), Angela Gair (Senorita Dios De La Venta), Allison Nevins (Caucasian Mother), Bill Flynn (TV Harold), John Phelan (TV Virgil), Reece Rios (TV Luke), Brandi Price (TV Lucy), Edward A. Saenz (Bar

Hustler), Randi Frances Hilliard (Bitchy Cashier), Sean Bryant (Pobrecito Nut-Nut), Cara Hartoon (Diner Waitress), Wes Martin (The Lone Dancer)

Arianne Martin, Frank Mosley in The Other Side of Paradise
© *Striped Socks*

THE LIGHTKEEPERS (New Films Intl.) Producers, Harris Tulchin, Daniel Adams, Larry Frenzel, Penelope Foster; Executive Producers, Richard Dreyfuss, Nesim Hason, Sezin Hason, Straw Weisman, Serap Acuner, Judy James, Scott Fujita, Nick Stilladis; Director/Screenplay, Daniel Adams; Photography, Thomas Jewett; Designer, Marc Fisichella; Costumes, Mimi Maximen; Music, Pinar Toprak; Editor, Dean Goodhill; Casting, Sheila Jaffe; a Cape Cod Filmworks production in association with Dreyfuss/James Productions; Dolby; Technicolor; Not rated; 96 minutes; Release date: December 18, 2009. **CAST:** Richard Dreyfuss (Seth), Blythe Danner (Mrs. Bascom), Tom Wisdom (John Brown), Mamie Gummer (Ruth), Bruce Dern (Bennie), Julie Harris (Mrs. Deacon), Ben Dreyfuss (Boy), Jason Alan Smith (Ezra), Stephen Russell (Jedidiah Snow), Theodora Greece (Townsperson)

Richard Dreyfuss in The Lightkeepers © *New Films Intl.*

SITA SINGS THE BLUES (FilmKaravan) Producer/Director/Screenplay/Animation, Nina Paley; Based on the book *The Ramayana* by Valmiki; Music, Todd Michaelsen; a Nina Paley production; Dolby; Color; Not rated; 82 minutes; Release date: December 25, 2009. **VOICE CAST:** Reena Shah (Sita), Annette Hanshaw (Sita's Singing Voice), Sanjiv Jhaveri (Dave/Dasharatha/Ravana/Dhobi/Valmiki), Pooja Kumar (Surphanaka), Debargo Sanyal (Rama), Aladdin Ullah (Mareecha/Hanuman), Nitya Vidyasagar (Luv/Kush), Nina Paley (Nina), Deepti Gupta (Kaikeyi), Assem Chhabra, Bhavana Nagulapally, Manish Acharya (Narrators)

Sita Sings the Blues © *FilmKaravan*

FOREIGN FILMS A

2009 Releases / January 1–December 31

SILENT LIGHT

(PALISADES/TARTAN) a.k.a. *Stellet licht*; Producers, Jaime Romandia, Carlos Reygadas; Director/Screenplay, Carlos Reygadas; Photography, Alexis Zabé; Designer, Gerardo Tagle; Editor, Natalia Lopez; a Nodream Cinema & Mantarraya Production with the support of BAC Film (France), Arte France Cinema (France), Motel Films (Netherlands), IMCINE/Foprocine (Mexico), Estudios Churubusco (Mexico) and Ticoman (Mexico) with the support of World Cinema Fund (German), and Het Nederlands Fonds voor de Film (Netherlands); French-Mexican-German-Dutch; Dolby; Lomoscope; Color; Not rated; 136 minutes; American release date: January 7, 2009

CAST

Johan	**Cornelio Wall Fehr**
Esther	**Miriam Toews**
Marianne	**Maria Pankratz**
Father	**Peter Wall**
Mother	**Elizabeth Fehr**
Zacarias	**Jacobo Klassen**
Sara	**Irma Thiessen**
Alfredo	**Alfredo Thiessen**
Daniel	**Daniel Thiessen**
Autghe	**Autghe Loewen**
Jackob	**Jackob Loewen**

A married member of Mexico's Mennonite community risks breaking the laws of his faith when he falls in love with another woman.

Maria Pankratz, Cornelio Wall Fehr

Maria Pankratz © Palisades Tartan

Maria Dinulescu, Jamie Elman
© IFC Films

CALIFORNIA DREAMIN' (ENDLESS)

(IFC FILMS) a.k.a. *California Dreamin' (Nesfarsit)*; Producer, Andrei Boncea; Executive Producer, Iuliana Tarnovetchi; Director, Cristian Nemescu; Screenplay, Tudor Voican, Cristian Nemescu, Catherine Linstrum; Photography, Liviu Marghidan; Designer, Ioana Corciova; Costumes, Ana Ioneci; Editor, Catalin Cristutiu; Casting, Domnica Carciumaru; a MediaPro Pictures presentation, with the support of the Romanian National Film Center; Romanian, 2007; Dolby; Color; Super 35mm Widescreen; Not rated; 155 minutes; American release date: January 23, 2009

CAST

Capt. Doug Jones	**Armand Assante**
Sgt. David McLaren	**Jamie Elman**
Doiaru	**Razvan Vasilescu**
Monica	**Maria Dinulescu**
Andrei	**Alex Margineanu**
The Mayor	**Ion Sapdaru**
Rodriguez	**Alexandru Dragoi**
Soldier Marian	**Andi Vasluianu**
Despina	**Sabina Branduse**
Trade Union Chief	**Gabriel Spahiu**
Stelica	**Radu Gabriel**
Paul	**Constantin Dita**
Mitroi	**Eduard Dumitru**

Alexandru Georgescu (Cpl. Tanase), Cristi Olesher (Young Doiaru), Catalina Mustata (Ana), Cornel Bulai (Costel), Diana Dumbrava (Doiaru's Mother), Dan Astileanu (Doiaru's Father), Nicodim Ungureanu (Police Chief), Ionut Brancu (Minister of Transport), Tomi Cristin (Minister of Foreign Affairs), Teodor Corban (Secretary of State), Antonia Ionescu, Laura Voicu, Catalina Harabagiu, Ilinca Harnut, Crina Semciuc (Young Girls), Paul Ipate, Bogdan Marhodin (Romanian Soldiers), Nelu Craciun (Petre), Adrian Anghel (Fane), Bogdan Cotlet, Andrei Solomon (Nerds), Ileana Toma, Adela Mihai, Adriana Gheorghisor (Girls), Nicu Predica (SNCFR Director), Cristinel Botea (Engineer), Catalin Paraschiv (DJ), Aura Calarasu (Andrei's Mother), Elvis Romano (Niki Fortune), Ionut Chivu (Romanian Officer), Vitalie Urus (The Russian), Madalina Ghitescu (Luiza), Andreea Samson (Mayor's Secretary), Marcello Cobzarju (Foreman), Armand Utma, Andrei Pandele (Classmates), Constantin Draganescu (The Grandfather), Florin Penisoara (Archie), Christopher Troxler (Soldier), Marco Assante (Benny Harper), Bart Sidles (Bart Turner), Adrian Cazdaru (Controller), Florin Burcea (Child), Andrei Sever (Young Man)

A platoon of American marines on a mission in Romania, are sidetracked to a small village where they are forced into a standoff with the local railway station master who refuses to grant them free passage.

Jaclyn Jose

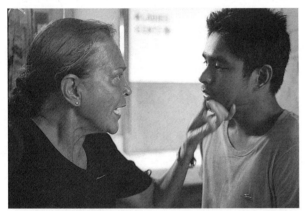

Gina Pareño, Coco Martin

SERBIS

(REGENT) a.k.a. *Service*; Producer, Ferdinand Lapuz; Executive Producer, Didier Costet; Director, Brillante Mendoza; Screenplay, Armando Lao; Photography, Odyssey Flores; Designers, Benjamin Padero, Carlo Tabije; Costumes, Hedji Calagui; Music, Gian Gianan; Editor, Claire Villa-Real; Casting, Ed Instrella; a Centerstage Prods. (The Philippines)/Swift Prods. (France) production, in association with Asian Cinema Fund, Pusan Intl. Film Festival, Hong Kong-Asia Film Financing Forum; Filipino-French-Hong Kong; Dolby; Color; Rated R; 91 minutes; American release date: January 27, 2009

CAST

Flor	**Gina Pareño**
Nayda	**Jaclyn Jose**
Lando	**Julio Diaz**
Alan	**Coco Martin**
Ronald	**Kristofer King**
Jerome	**Dan Alvaro**
Merly	**Mercedes Cabral**
Jewel	**Roxanne Jordan**

Dido dela Paz (Attorney Quintana), Buddy Salvador Caramat (Tonette), Bobby Jerome Go (Jonas), Jemmalyn Galicia (Susan), Julia Taylor, Clarence Ayuyao (Cross Dressers), Nico Taverna (Santy), Aaron Christian Rivera (Ricky), Billy Ray Gali (Student), Babylee Borromeo (Peter), Arnold Toledo, Aldrin Zubiri, Kevin Javier, J.B. Parker, Paul Espidido, Raymond Mendoza, Bryan Martin, Ricardo Valbuena III, Julius Habal, Orlando Abio, Alfie Baluyot, Jeff Batungbakal, Bong Santos, Herminio Batungbakal, J.R. Batungbakal, Diego Marx Dobles, Ryan Yanga (Serbis Boys), Benjie Filomeno (Thief), Arman Reyes (Old Gay from Manila), Armando Lao (Gay with Cell Phone), Rex Due, Rod Capua (Policemen), Ted Amo (Macho Gay), Blue Seal (Flower Vendor), Andy Picache (Edwin), Marites Nuñez (Carol), Emerson Salangsang, Ursula Tiotuico (Edwin Kids), Gina Villa (Distraught Mother), Ira Tuazon (Daughter), Erika de Jesus, Richard Rodriguez, Marvin Rea, Rey Yumang, Reymar Belano, Eddie Carlos, Amang de Guzman, Shiela Sanchez, Vic Baguio, Dario Leosa, Ronel Javier, Pancho Pantig, Joy Aronce, Angus Miranda (Gay Patrons)

The Pineda family struggles to stay afloat while running a rundown porn theater that caters principally to male hustlers.

Roxanne Jordan

Julio Diaz © Regent Releasing

TAKEN

(20TH CENTURY FOX) Producer, Luc Besson; Screenplay, Luc Besson, Robert Mark Kamen; Photography, Michel Abramowicz; Designer, Hugues Tissandier; Costumes, Olivier Beriot; Music, Nathaniel Mechaly; Editor, Frederic Thoraval; Visual Effects Supervisor, Roxane Fechner; Stunts, Philippe Guegan; Casting, Nathalie Cheron; a EuropaCorp, M6 Films, Grive Prods. production, with the participation of Canal Plus, M6, TPS Star; French; Dolby; Panavision; Color; Rated PG-13; 91 minutes; American release date: January 30, 2009

CAST

Bryan Mills	**Liam Neeson**
Kim	**Maggie Grace**
Lenore	**Famke Janssen**
Sam	**Leland Orser**
Casey	**Jon Gries**
Bernie	**David Warshofksy**
Sheerah	**Holly Valance**
Amanda	**Katie Cassidy**
Stuart	**Xander Berkeley**
Jean-Claude	**Olivier Rabourdin**
St-Clair	**Gérard Watkins**
Marko	**Arben Bajraktaraj**
Victor	**Nathan Rippy**
Isabelle	**Camille Japy**
Peter	**Nicolas Giraud**
Gregor	**Goran Kostic**
Anton	**Rasha Bukvic**

Mathieu Busson (Undercover Agent), Marc Amyot (Pharmacist), Rubens Hyka (Leka), Michel Flash (Gio), Fani Kolarova (Prostitute), Christophe Kourotchkine (Gilles), Valentin Kalaj (Vinz), Nabil Massad (Sheik Raman), Jalil Naciri (Ali), Edwin Kruger (Jean-Claude's Assistant), Anca Radici (Ingrid), Christy Reese (Paper Shop Clerk), Opender Singh (Singh), Helena Soubeyrand (Girl with the Jacket), Tommy Spahija (Nezir), Anatole Taubman (Dardan), Bertrand Treuil (Taxi Driver), George Hertzberg (Security at Stuart's Mansion), Ivette Gonzalez (Maid)

Former CIA agent-turned-bodyguard Bryan Mills takes action when his daughter Kim is kidnapped during a vacation in Paris.

Maggie Grace, Famke Janssen, Liam Neeson © Europacorp/M6 Films

Fani Kolarova, Liam Neeson

Olivier Rabourdin, Liam Neeson

Liam Neeson

GOMORRAH

(IFC FILMS) Producer, Domenico Procacci; Director, Matteo Garrone; Screenplay, Maurizio Braucci, Ugo Chiti, Gianni Di Gregorio, Matteo Garrone, Massimo Gaudioso, Roberto Saviano, Based on the book by Robert Saviano; Photography, Marco Onorato; Designer, Paolo Bonfini; Costumes, Alessandra Cardini; Music, Robert Del Naja, Neil Davidge, Euan Dickinson; Editor, Marco Spoletini; Casting, Teatri Uniti; a Fandango production in collaboration with Rai Cinema presented by Martin Scorsese; Italian; Dolby; Super 35 Widescreen; Color; Not rated; 136 minutes; American release date: February 13, 2009

CAST
Toto	**Salvatore Abruzzese**
Simone	**Simone Sacchettino**
Boxer	**Salvatore Ruocco**
Pitbull	**Vincenzo Fabricino**
Gaetano	**Vincenzo Altamura**
Italo	**Italo Renda**
Don Ciro	**Gianfelice Imparato**
Maria	**Maria Nazionale**
Scissionista	**Salvatore Striano**
Don Carlo	**Carlo Del Sorbo**
Bombolone	**Vincenzo Bombolo**
Franco	**Toni Servillo**
Roberto	**Carmine Paternoster**
Dante Serini	**Alfonso Santagata**
Imperenditore	**Massimo Emilio Gobbi**

Salvatore Caruso (Responsabile), Italo Celoro (Contadino), Salvatore Cantalupo (Pasquale), Gigio Morra (lavarone), Ronghua Zhang (Xian), Manuela Lo Sicco (Moglie di Pasquale), Marco Macor (Marco), Ciro Petrone (Ciro), Giovanni Venosa (Giovanni), Vittorio Russo (Pirata), Bernardino Terracciano (Zio Bernardino)

Several interwoven storylines show the destructive and violent grip on the population by the Camorra crime families of Naples.

Gianfelice Imparato (center) © IFC Films

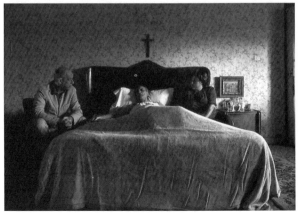

Ciro Petron, Marco Macor

Toni Servillo, Italo Celoro

Maja Ostaszewska, Artur Zmijewski © Koch Lorber

KATYN

(KOCH LORBER) Producer, Michal Kwiecinsky; Executive Producer, Katarzyna Fukacz-Cebula; Director/Screenplay, Andrzej Wajda; Co-Screeplay, Wladyslaw Pasikowski, Przemyslaw Nowakowski; Photography, Pawel Edelman; Designer, Kamil Przelecki; Costumes, Magdalena Bierddrzycka, Andrzej Szenajh; Music, Krzysztof Penderecki; Editor, Milenia Fielder; an Akson Studio, Telewizja Polska, Telekomunikacja Polska presentation, with the support of the Polish Film Institute; Polish, 2007; Dolby; Panavision; Color; Not rated; 121 minutes; American release date: February 18, 2009

CAST
Lt. Jerzy	**Andrzej Chyra**
Anna	**Maja Ostaszewska**
Andrzej	**Artur Zmijewski**
Róza	**Danuta Stenka**
General	**Jan Englert**
Agnieszka	**Magdalena Cielecka**
Irena	**Angieszka Glinska**
Lt. Piotr	**Pawel Malaszynski**

Maja Komorowska (Andrzej's Mother), Wladyslaw Kowalski (Professor Jan), Antoni Pawlicki (Tadeusz), Agnieszka Kawiorska (Ewa), Sergey Garmash (Maj. Popov), Joachim Assböck (Brunon Müller), Waldemar Barwinski (Polish Officer), Sebastian Bezzel (Propaganda Abteilung Officer), Jacek Braciak (Lt. Klin), Stanislaw Brudny (Old Man at Bridge), Stansilawa Celinska (Stasia), Leon Charewicz (UB Major), Alicja Dabrowska (Actress), Oleh Drach (Commisar), Aleksander Fabisiak (Teacher), Wiktoria Gasiewska (Weronika), Krzysztof Globisz (Professor of Chemistry), Krzysztof Kolberger, Leszek Piskorz (Priests), Zbigniew Kozlowski (Militia Officer), Olgierd Lukaszewicz (Priest), Josef Mika (German Translator), Andrzej Pieczynski (German Soldier), Waldemar Pokromski (Barber), Dariusz Poleszak (German Officer), Anna Radwan (Elzbieta), Jakub Przebindowski (Young Priest), Oleh Savkin (NKWD Officer), Tadeusz Wojtych (Photographer Wladyslaw), Wieslaw Wojcik (Postman), Krystyna Zachwatowicz (Mrs. Great), Ilia Zmiejew (Lt. Kozlow)

The true story of the 1940 massacre by the Soviets of 15,000 Polish Army officers in Katyn, Russia. This film received a 2007 Oscar nomination for Foreign Language Film.

12

(SONY CLASSICS) a.k.a. *12 Razgnevannyh Muzhchin*; Producers, Nikita Mikhalkov, Leonid Vereschagin; Director, Nikita Mikhalkov; Screenplay, Nikita Mikhalkov, Vladimir Moiseenko, Alexander Novototsky; Based on the screenplay *12 Angry Men* by Reginald Rose, from his television play; Photography, Vladislav Opeliants; Designer, Victor Petrov; Costumes, Natalia Dziubenko; Music, Edward Artemiev; Editors, Andrey Zaitsev, Enzo Meniconi; a Three T production; Russian, 2007; Widescreen; Color; Rated PG-13; 153 minutes; American release date: March 4, 2009

CAST
Juror #1	**Sergei Makovetsky**
Juror #2	**Sergey Garmash**
Juror #3	**Aleksei Petrenko**
Juror #4	**Yuriy Stoyanov**
Juror #5	**Sergey Gazarov**
Juror #6	**Nikita Mikhalkov**
Juror #7	**Mikhail Efremov**
Juror #8	**Valentin Gaft**
Juror #9	**Aleksey Gorbunov**
Juror #10	**Sergei Artsybashev**
Juror #11	**Viktor Verzhbitskiy**
Juror #12	**Roman Madyanov**

Aleksandr Adabashyan (Bailiff), Apti Magamayev (The Boy), Abdi Magamayev (Little Chechen), Natalya Surkova (Judge), Konstantin Glushkov (Defense Lawyer), Vladimir Nefyodov (Prosecutor), Vyacheslav Gilinov (Grandpa), Lyubov Rudneva (Eyewitness's Daughter), Olga Khohklova (Neighbor), Igor Vernik (Eyewitness in Golden Eyeglasses), Vladimir Komarov (Boy's Stepfather), Lasha Marykhuba (Guerilla), Ferit Myazitov (Gorbachev), Abdulbasur Gitinov (Little Boy), Mikael Bazorkin (Father), Mesedo Salimova (Mother), Soslan Sanakoyev, Alan Tsopanov (Dancers), Gennadi Ternvosky (Attack Group Commander), Andrei Sukharev (Cop)

Twelve jurors presiding over a murder case reveal their own personal stories and prejudices as they argue over the verdict. The original film version of *12 Angry Men* (UA, 1957) starred Henry Fonda and Lee J. Cobb.

Sergey Gazarov, Sergei Makovetsky, Yuriy Stoyanov, Valentin Gaft, Viktor Verzhbitskiy © Sony Pictures Classics

Jesper Christensen, Maria Heiskanen

Mikael Persbrandt, Maria Heiskanen

Mikael Persbrandt

Maria Heiskanen © IFC Films

EVERLASTING MOMENTS

(IFC FILMS) a.k.a. *Maria Larssons eviga ogonblick*; Producer, Thomas Stenderup; Co-Producers, Tero Kaukomaa, Christer Nilson, Christof Groos, Ute Schneider; Director, Jan Troell; Screenplay, Niklas Radstrom, Jan Troell, Agneta Ulfsater Troell; Based on a story by Ulsater Troell; Photography, Jan Troell, Mischa Gavrjusjov; Costumes, Karen Gram, Katja Watkins; Music, Matti Bye; Casting, Anja Schmidt; a Final Cut production, in association with Gotafilm, Motlys, Blind Spot Pictures, Schneider-Gross Film Produktion, Film 1 Skane, Filmpool Nord, Sveriges Television, Sandrew Metronome Intl.; Swedish-Danish-Norwegian-Finnish-German; Dolby; Color; Not rated; 131 minutes; American release date: March 6, 2009

CAST

Maria Larsson	**Maria Heiskanen**
Sigfrid Larsson	**Mikael Persbrandt**
Sebastian Pedersen	**Jesper Christensen**
Maja Larsson (age 15-22)	**Callin Öhrvall**
Maja Larsson (age 8 -10)	**Nellie Almgren**
Maja (narrator)/Aunt Tora	**Birte Heribertsson**
Miss Fagerdal	**Ghita Nørby**
Matilda	**Amanda Ooms**
Englund	**Emil Jensen**
Grandmother Karna	**Claire Wikholm**
Ida	**Ann Petrén**

Antti Reini (Finnish Sea Captain), Annika Lundgren (Miss Öst), Maria Lundqvist (Miss Petrén), Hans Henrik Clemensen (Mr. Fagerdal), Johanna Troell (Margareta), Rune Bergman (Maria's Father), Hans Alfredson (Prison Guard), Noah Stenberg (Sven Larsson, age 3-5), Max Eskilsson (Sven Larsson, age 14-17), Lydia Molin (Anna Larsson, age 5-6), Tova Dahan (Anna Larsson, age 8-9), Elena Alexandrova (Fru Pedersen), Pierre Lindstedt, Rolf Lydahl, Eddie Axberg, Linus Nilsson (Workers), Emil Dämhagen (Erik Larsson, age 5), Erika Ekman (Lilla Elsa), Martin Ersgård (Officer), Christian Fex (Police), Josefin Granqvist (Lodge Lass), Sune Hagström (Wagoner), Alexander Kathy (Anton Nilsson), Maria Kulle (Aunt Anna), Staffan Lahti (Drums-lodge party), Anna Larsson (Fiddle - beach), Boel Larsson (Kalle's Mother), Jan Lerning (Truck Driver), Karl Linnertorp (Gunnar Larsson, age 14-21), Mattias Lundgren (Accordion - beach), Berto Marklund (Berto), Jonathan Mårtensson (Kalle), Anneli Martini (Lodge Lady), Kenneth Milldoff (Pidder), Livia Millhagen (Ingeborg's Mother), Michael Odhag (Kvist), Sanna Persson (Månselotta), Inge Pettersson (Guitar - dance floor), Petra Quist (Violin - dance floor), Michael Segerström (Landlord), Asa Söderling (Lady Receiving Treatment), Richard Ulfsäter (Mr. Grevelius)

With her abusive husband made unemployed because of a dockworkers strike, Maria Larsson sets out to make money by selling her camera, only to realize she has a talent for photography.

THE EDGE OF LOVE

(CAPITOL) Producers, Rebekah Gilbertson, Sarah Radclyffe; Executive Producers, David Bergstein, Linda James, Hannah Leader, Joe Oppenheimer, Tim Smith, David M. Thompson, Paul Brett, Nick Hill; Director, John Maybury; Screenplay, Sharman Macdonald; Based on books by David N. Thomas and Esther Killick; Photography, Jonathan Freeman; Designer, Alan MacDonald; Costumes, April Ferry; Music, Angelo Badalamenti; Editor, Emma Hickox; Casting, Nina Gold; a Capitol Films, BBC Films presentation, in association with the Wales Creative IP Fund, Prescience Film Partners, of a Sarah Radclyffe, Rainy Day Films production; with the support of the U.K. Film Council Development Fund; British; Dolby; Technicolor; Rated R; 111 minutes; American release date: March 13, 2009

CAST

Vera Phillips	**Keira Knightley**
Caitlin MacNamara	**Sienna Miller**
Dylan Thomas	**Matthew Rhys**
William Killick	**Cillian Murphy**
Anita Shenkin	**Anne Lambton**
Nicolette	**Camilla Rutherford**
Anthony Devas	**Alastair Mackenzie**
The Crooner	**Suggs**

Simon Armstrong (Wilfred Hosgood), Ben Batt (Sergeant), Geoffrey Beevers (Registrar), Rachel Bell (Midwife), Paul Brooke (Mr. Justice Singleton), Huw Ceredig (John Patrick), Richard Clifford (Alistair Graham), Richard Dillane (Lt. Col. David Talbot Rice), Joel Dommett (Train Soldier), Rachel Essex (Mel), Craig Gallivan (Sailor beating Dylan), Callum Godfrey (Boy on Train), Simon Kassianides (Partisan), Ray Llewellyn (Dewi Ianthe), Neville Malcolm (Big Joe), Acacia Pattison Biggs/Bethany Towell (Rowatt, age 1 month), Jonny Phillips (John Eldridge), Kyle Redmond-Jones (Boy Soldier), Leo Robertson/Olivia Robertson (Rowatt, age 8 months), Jenny Runacre (Woman in Yellow Dress), , Lisa Stansfield (Ruth Williams), Diego Stephen, Lanark Stephens (Llewellyn), Nick Stringer (PC Williams)

During World War II, Dylan Thomas' former lover takes up residence with the poet and his wife while falling in love with a soldier, thereby causing tension in their relationships.

Keira Knightley, Sienna Miller

Sienna Miller, Keira Knightley

Matthew Rhys, Sienna Miller

Keira Knightley, Cillian Murphy © Capitol Films

Paulina Gaitan, Edgar Flores © Focus Features

Paulina Gaitan

Guillermo Villegas, Paulina Gaitan, Gerardo Taracena

SIN NOMBRE

(FOCUS FEATURES) Producer, Amy Kaufman; Executive Producers, Gerardo Barrera, Pablo Cruz, Diego Luna, Gael Garcia Bernal; Director/Screenplay, Cary Joji Fukunaga; Photography, Adriano Goldman; Designer, Claudio "Pache" Contreras; Costumes, Leticia Palacios; Music, Marcelo Zarvas; Music Supervisor, Lynn Fainchtein; Editors, Luis Carballar, Craig McKay; Casting, Carla Hool; a Primary Prods./Canana Films production; Mexican-American; Dolby; Super 35 Widescreen; Color; Rated R; 96 minutes; American release date: March 20, 2009

CAST
Sayra	**Paulina Gaitan**
Willy/El Casper	**Edgar Flores**
El Smiley	**Kristian Ferrer**
Lil' Mago	**Tenoch Huerta Mejia**
Martha Marlene	**Diana Garcia**
El Sol	**Luis Fernando Peña**
Leche/Wounded Man	**Hector Jimenez**

Marco Antonio Aguirre (Big Lips), Leonardo Alonso, Andrés Valdéz (Judical Police), Karla Cecilia Alvarado (Marera), Juan Pablo Arias Barrón, Rosalba Belén Barrón, Benny Manuel (Niños), Sixto Felipe Castro, Ignacio Gonzalez, Jesús Lira, Jose Miguel Moctezuma (Mareros), Rosalba Quintana Cruz (Tierra Blance Mujer), Marcela Feregrino (Kimberly), Giovanni Florido (El Sipe), Ariel Galvan (Migrante #1), Gabriela Garibaldi (Diana), Noé Hernández (Resistol), Lilibeth Flores (Yamila), Catalina López (Tia Toña), Hector Lortia (El Turbino), Fernando Manzano (Marera), May Paz Mata (Abuela Saira), Emire Meza (Peluquín), Emilio Miranda (Other Marero), Esperanza Molina (La Hermana), Iván Rafael (El Bomba), Gabino Rodríguez (El Scarface), David Serrano (El Smokey), Gerardo Taracena (Horacio), Harold Torres (El Picaro), Max Valencia Zúñiga (El Chino), Noé Velazquez (El Happy), Tulio Villavicencio (El Pájaro), Guillermo Villegas (Orlando)

A group of Central American migrants faces a myriad of problems as they journey through Mexico in an effort to cross into the United States.

Luis Fernando Peña

Julie Gayet, Michaël Cohen © Music Box Films

SHALL WE KISS?

(MUSIC BOX FILMS) a.k.a. *Un baiser s'il vous plaît*; Producer, Frederic Niedermayer; Director/Screenplay, Emmanuel Mouret; Photography, Laurent Desmet; Art Director, David Faivre; Editor, Martial Salomon; a Moby Dick Films production, in association with Arte France Cinema; French, 2007; Dolby; Color; Not rated; 102 minutes; American release date: March 27, 2009

CAST
Judith	**Virginie Ledoyen**
Nicolas	**Emmanuel Mouret**
Émilie	**Julie Gayet**
Gabriel	**Michaël Cohen**
Caline	**Frédérique Bel**
Claudio	**Stefano Accorsi**
Pénélope	**Mélanie Maudran**
Églantine	**Marie Madinier**
Louise	**Lucciana de Vogüe**
Waiter at Hotel Bar	**Jacques Lafoly**

Reluctant to kiss a new acquaintance goodnight, Emilie relates the story of how friends Judith and Nicolas risked their friendship when he asked her to help him overcome his problem of physical intimacy with women.

Virginie Ledoyen, Emmanuel Mouret

THE COUNTRY TEACHER

(FILM MOVEMENT) a.k.a. *Venkovský ucitel*; Producers, Pavel Strnad, Petr Oukropec, Karl Baumgartner, Thanassis Karathanos; Director/Screenplay, Bohdan Slama; Photography, Divis Marek; Designers, Vaclav Novak, Petr Pistek; Costumes, Zuzana Krejzkova; Music, Vladimir Godar; Editor, Jan Danhel; a Negativ (Czech Republic)/Pallas film (Germany)/Why Not Prods. (France) production, with the support of the State Fund for Czech Cinema, Czech TV, Mitteldeutsche Medienförderung, Eurimages; Czech-German-French, 2008; Dolby; Color; Not rated; 103 minutes; American release date: March 27, 2009

CAST
Petr	**Pavel Liska**
Marie	**Zuzana Bydzovská**
Lada	**Ladislav Sedivý**
Boyfriend	**Marek Daniel**
Beruska	**Tereza Vorísková**
Headmaster	**Cyril Drozda**
Headmaster's Wife	**Marie Ludviková**

Zuzana Kronerová (Mother), Miroslav Krobot (Father), Zdena Kucerová (Granny), Miloslav Vokatý (Jozin), Jaroslav Vicek (Jarda), Frantisek Prosek, Josef Prosek (Brothers), Anna Vladyková (Landlady), Pavel Vladyka (Innholder)

Following an unhappy relationship, a science teacher moves to the country where he becomes the object of attraction of a widowed farmer, while he himself falls in love with her teenage son.

Zuzana Bydzovská, Pavel Liska

Ladislav Sedivý, Pavel Liska © Film Movement

PARIS 36

(SONY CLASSICS) a.k.a. *Faubourg 36*; Producers, Jacques Perrin, Nicolas Mauvernay; Co-Producer, Romain Le Grand; Director/Screenplay, Christophe Barratier; Based on an original idea by Frank Thomas, Jean-Michel Derenne, Reinhardt Wagner; Photography, Tom Stern; Designer, Jean Rabasse; Costumes, Carine Sarfati; Music, Reinhardt Wagner; Editor, Yves Deschamps; Choreographer, Corinne Devaux; a Galatee Films, Pathé Pictures International, France 2, France 3 Cinema, Logline Studios, Novo Arturo Films (France)/Constantin Film (Germany)/Blue Screen Prods. (Czech Republic) production; French-German-Czech; Dolby; Panavision; Color; Rated PG-13; 120 minutes; American release date: April 3, 2009

CAST

Germain Pigoil	**Gérard Jugnot**
Milou	**Clovis Cornillac**
Jacky	**Kad Merad**
Douce	**Nora Arnezeder**
Moniseur TSF	**Pierre Richard**
Galapiat	**Bernard-Pierre Donnadieu**
Jojo	**Maxence Perrin**
Célestin	**François Morel**
Viviane	**Élisabeth Vitali**
Lebeaupin	**Christophe Kourotchkine**
Grevoul	**Eric Naggar**
Commissaire Tortil	**Eric Prat**
Mondain	**Julien Courbey**
Triquet	**Philippe Du Janerand**

Marc Citti (Inspector of Quai des Ofevres), Christian Bouillette (Dubrulle), Thierry Nenez (Crouzet), Frédéric Papalia (Clément), Stéphane Debac (Inspector of Social Services), Jean Lescot (Dorfeuil), Daniel Benoin (Borchard), Wilfred Benaïche (Jeannot), Reinhardt Wagner (Blaise), Manuela Gourary (Chanteuse Painter), Violette Barratier (Lebeaupin's Daughter), Gregoire Clamart, Thibaut Clamart (Thugs), Gérard Robert Gratadour (Theater Technician), Sophie Knittl (Madame Celestin)

With his personal life a shambles, Germain Pigoil becomes determined to reopen the shuttered Theater Chansonia and make it a success.

This film received an Oscar nomination for original song ("Loin de Paname")

Gérard Jugnot, Kad Merad, Clovis Cornillac, Nora Arnezeder

Bernard-Pierre Donnadieu

Maxence Perrin © Sony Pictures Classics

Kad Merad, Gérard Jugnot, Nora Arnezeder

THE ESCAPIST

(IFC FILMS) Producers, Adrian Stuges, Alan Moloney; Executive Producers, Brian Cox, Tristan Whalley; Co-Producer, Susan Mullen; Director, Rupert Wyatt; Screenplay, Rupert Wyatt, Daniel Hardy; Photography, Philipp Blaubach; Designer, Jim Furlong; Costumes, Maeve Paterson; Music, Benjamin Wallfisch; Editor, Joe Walker; Casting, Tamara Gillon; a U.K. Film Council presentation with the participation of the Irish Film Board of a Parallel Films/Picture Farm production; Irish-British, 2008; Dolby; Color; Not rated; 102 minutes; American release date: April 3, 2009

CAST
Frank Perry	**Brian Cox**
Lenny	**Joseph Fiennes**
Rizza Drake	**Damian Lewis**
Brodie	**Liam Cunningham**
Viv Batista	**Seu Jorge**
Lacey	**Dominic Cooper**
Tony	**Steven Mackintosh**

Ned Dennehy (Jumpy Con), Vincent McCabe (Sam), Jack Walsh (Sikes), Frank O'Sullivan (Hedges), Stephen Farrelly(Two Ton), Domhnall O'Donoghue (Mary), George Seremba (Stan), Eleanor McLynn (Frank's Daughter), Phelim Drew (Doctor), Bernadette McKenna (Frank's Wife), John Crean (Young Prison Guard), Pat Ainscough (Prison Guard), Alan Curran (Cockney Con), Tony Senior (Boxing Con), John Campion, Robert Prior (Screws), Marcel Vidal (Rizza's Lackey), Paul Vaughan (Prison Tannoy Voice)

A group of convicts looks back on the situations that brought them to the executing their big escape plan.

Domenic Cooper © IFC Films

Brian Cox, Damian Lewis

Tarik Kopty, Hiam Abbass © IFC Films

LEMON TREE

(IFC FILMS) a.k.a. *Etz limon*; Producers, Bettina Brokemper, Antoine de Clermont-Tonnerre, Michael Eckelt, Eran Riklis; Executive Producers, Moshe Edery, Leon Edery, David Silber; Co-Producer, Ira Riklis; Director, Eran Riklis; Screenplay, Suha Arraf, Eran Riklis; Photography, Rainer Klausmann; Designer, Miguel Merkin; Costumes, Rona Doron; Music, Habib Shehadeh Hanna; Editor, Tova Ascher; an Eran Riklis Prods. (Israel)/MACT Prods. (France)/Riva Filmproduktion, Heimatfilm (Germany) production; Israeli-French-German, 2008; Dolby; Fujicolor; Not rated; 106 minutes; American release date: April 17, 2009

CAST
Salma Zidane	**Hiam Abbass**
Defense Minister Israel Navon	**Doron Tavory**
Ziad Daud	**Ali Suliman**
Mira Navon	**Rona Lipaz-Michael**
Abu Hussam	**Tarik Kopty**
Commander Jacob	**Amos Lavie**
Leibowitz	**Amnon Wolf**
Tamar Gera	**Smadar Yaaron**
Private Itamar (Quickie)	**Danny Leshman**
Sigi Navon	**Hili Yalon**

Linon Banares (Gilad), Jamil Khoury (Son-in-Law), Makram J. Khoury (Abu Kamal), Yair Lapid, Einat Saruf (Themselves), Loai Nofi (Nasser Zidane), Ayelet Robinson (Shelly), Michael Warshaviak (Braverman, Attorney)

When the Israeli Defense Minister decides to build a new house for his family on the Israel-West Bank border, a Palestinian widower is shocked to find out that the lemon grove that butts up against the minister's property is deemed a "defense risk."

Michael Caine, Bill Milner © Optimum Releasing

Michael Caine

Bill Milner, Michael Caine

IS ANYBODY THERE?

(STORY ISLAND ENTERTAINMENT) Producers, David Heyman, Peter Saraf, Marc Turtletaub; Executive Producers, David M. Thompson, Christine Langan; Co-Producer, Rosie Alison; Director, John Crowley; Screenplay, Peter Harness; Photography, Rob Hardy; Designer, Kave Quinn; Costumes, Jane Petrie; Music, Joby Talbot; Editor, Trevor Waite; a Heyday Films (London)/Big Beach production, presented in association with BBC Films; British; Dolby; Super 35 Widescreen; Color; Rated PG-13; 92 minutes; American release date: April 17, 2009

CAST
Clarence	**Michael Caine**
Edward	**Bill Milner**
Mum	**Anne-Marie Duff**
Dad	**David Morrissey**
Elsie	**Rosemary Harris**
Reg	**Leslie Phillips**
Bob	**Peter Vaughan**
Prudence	**Elizabeth Spriggs**
Lilian	**Sylvia Syms**
Mavis	**Angie Inwards**
Ena	**Thelma Barlow**
Tanya	**Linzey Cocker**
Stuart	**Adam Drinkall**
Mr. Kelly	**Ralph Ineson**

Keith Hargreaves (Bus Driver), Miles Jupp (Vicar), Michael Keogh (Paramedic), Ralph Riach (Clive), David Rintoul (Harry Price), Edward Lees (Ben), Larry David (Fireman), Kevin Locke IV (Entertainer), Jennifer Hennessy (School Mother), Jamie Gilbert (Tanya's New Boyfriend), Garrick Hagon (Douglas), Peter Harness (Cashier), Sue Wallace (Mrs. Hitler), William Ilkley (Barry's Dad), Carly McCrystal, Andrew Turner (Undertakers)

An elderly, embittered magician reluctantly moves into a seaside retirement home where he bonds with the lonely son of the establishment's owners.

Bill Milner

EARTH

(WALT DISNEY PICTURES) Producers, Alix Tidmarsh, Sophokles Tasioulis; Executive Producers, Andre Sikojev, Nikolaus Weil, Stefan Beiten, Mike Phillips, Wayne Garvie, Martyn Freeman; Directors, Alastair Fothergill, Mark Linfield; Screenplay, Leslie Megahey, Alastair Fothergill, Mark Linfield; Photography, Andrew Anderson, Doug Anderson, Doug Allan, Paul Atkins, Barrie Birtton, Richard Burton, Simon Carroll, Rod Clarke, Martyn Colbeck, Justin Evans, Wade Fairley, Ted Giffords, Mike Holding, Michael Kelem, Simon King, Toshihiro Muta, Justin Maguire, Didier Noiret, Andrew Penniket, Rick Rosenthal, Adam Ravetch, Tim Shepherd, Andrew Shillabeer, Peter Shillabeer, Peter Scoones, Warwick Sloss, Paul Stewart, Gavin Thurston, Jeff Turner, John Waters; Music, George Fenton; Editor, Martin Elsbury; Narrator, James Earl Jones; a BBC Worldwide (U.K.)/Greenlight Media (Germany)/Discovery Channel presentation of a BBC Natural History Unit Film production; Distributed by Walt Disney Studios Motion Pictures; British-German, 2007; Dolby; Color; HD-to-35mm; Rated G; 90 minutes; American release date: April 22, 2009. Documentary capturing a full year's cycle of our planet, with special emphasis on the wildlife.

© BBC Worldwide

IL DIVO

(MUSIC BOX FILMS) Producers, Nicola Giuliano, Francesca Cima, Andrea Occhipinti, Maurizio Coppolecchia; Co-Producer, Fabio Conversi; Director/Screenplay, Paolo Sorrentino; Photography, Luca Bigazzi; Designer, Lino Fiorito; Costumes, Daniela Ciancio; Music, Teho Teardo; Editor, Cristiano Travaglioli; Makeup Effects, Vittorio Sodano; Casting, Annamaria Sambucco; an Indigo Film, Lucky Red, Parco Film (Italy)/Babe Films, Studio Canal, Arte France Cinema (France) production, in collaboration with Sky; Italian-French, 2008; Dolby; Color; Not rated; 117 minutes; American release date: April 24, 2009

CAST

Giulio Andreotti	**Toni Servillo**
Livia Danese Andreotti	**Anna Bonaiuto**
Eugenio Scalfari	**Giulio Bosetti**
Franco Evangelisti	**Flavio Bucci**
Paolo Cirino Pomincino	**Carlo Buccirosso**
Salvo Lima	**Giorgio Colangeli**
Signora Enea	**Piera Degli Esposti**
Aldo Moro	**Paolo Graziosi**
Don Mario	**Alberto Cracco**
Mino Pecorelli	**Lorenzo Gioielli**
Vincenzo Scotti	**Gianfelice Imparato**
Vittorio Sbardella	**Massimo Popolizio**
Giuseppe Ciarrapico	**Aldo Ralli**
Magistrato Scarpinato	**Giovanni Vettorazz**o
Caterina Stagno	**Cristina Serafini**
Fiorenzo Angelini	**Achille Brugnini**
French Ambassador	**Fanny Ardant**

The true story of the career of Italy's seven-time Prime Minister Giulio Andreotti, whose Christian Democrat party ruled the country for 44 years.

This film received an Oscar nomination for makeup.

Toni Servillo

Toni Servillo (Center) © Music Box Films

Toni Servillo

Toni Servillo

ELDORADO

(FILM MOVEMENT) Producer, Jacques-Henri Bronckart; Co-Producer, Jerome Vidal; Director/Screenplay, Bouli Lanners; Photography, Jean-Paul de Zaeytijd; Designer, Paul Rouschop; Costumes, Elisa Ancion; Music, Renaud Mayeur; Editor, Ewin Ryckaert; a Versus presentation of a Lazennec & Associés, RTBF production; Belgian-French, 2008; Dolby; Widescreen; Color; Not rated; 81 minutes; American release date: May 1, 2009

CAST

Yvan	**Bouli Lanners**
Elie	**Fabrice Adde**
The Collector	**Philippe Nahon**
The Nudist	**Didier Toupy**
Elie's Mom	**Françoise Chichéry**

Stefan Liberski, Baptiste Isaïa (The Mechanics), Jean-Jacques Rausin, Renaud Rutten (The Bikers), Jean-Luc Meekers (The Man from the Parking Lot)

A lonely car dealer ends up taking a road trip with the man who tried to rob him.

Bouli Lanners, Fabrice Adde

Bouli Lanners © Film Movement

Irina Potapenko

Johannes Krisch, Ursula Strauss
© Janus Films

REVANCHE

(JANUS) Producers, Mathias Forberg, Heinz Stussak, Götz Spielmann, Sandra Bohle; Director/Screenplay, Götz Spielmann; Photography, Martin Gschlacht; Designer, Maria Gruber; Costumes, Monika Buttinger; Editor, Karina Ressler; a Spielmannfilm, Prisma Film production; Austrian-Russian; Dolby; Color; Not rated; 121 minutes; American release date: May 1, 2009

CAST

Alex	**Johannes Krisch**
Susanne	**Ursula Strauss**
Robert	**Andreas Lust**
Tamara	**Irina Potapenko**
Grandfather Hausner	**Hannes Thanheiser**
Konecny	**Hanno Poeschl**

Magdalena Kropiunig (Prostitute in Hotel), Toni Slama (Tamara's Customer), Elisabetha Pejcinoska, Aniko Bärkanyi, Annamaria Haytö, Nicoletta Prokes (Cinderella Prostitutes), Rainer Gradischnig (Harry, Man Beating Tamara), Haris Bilajbegovic (Man stopping Harry), Aleksander Reljic-Bohigas (Owner of Cinderella), Michael-Joachim Heiss (Day Porter at Hotel), Günther Laha (Night Porter at Hotel), Max Schmiedl, Gerhard Liebmann Holzmann, Johannes Zeiler, Andreas Blauensteiner, Martin Aschauer, Sonja Lehninger (Police Officers), Peter Brunner (Trainer at Shooting Ranger), Thomas Radleff (Detective), Alexander Lhotzky (Bank Branch Manager), Doris Hindinger, Siegfried Auerböck, German Benedkit (Bank Employees), Renate Suppan, Johann Wessner (Bank Customer Service), Julia Schranz (Pregnant Wife), Jana McKinnon (Girl at Grill Party), Peter Josch (Robert's Father), Linde Prelog (Robert's Mother)

After robbing a bank, ex-con Alex takes refuge on his grandfather's farm.

Guillermo Francella, Diego Luna © Sony Pictures Classics

Gael Garcia Bernal

Diego Luna

RUDO Y CURSI

(SONY CLASSICS) Producers, Alfonso Cuarón, Alejandro González Iñárritu, Guillermo del Toro, Frida Torresblanco; Director/Screenplay: Carlos Cuarón; Photography, Adam Kimmel; Designer, Eugenio Caballero; Costumes, Annai Ramos, Ana Terrazas; Music, Felipe Pérez Santiago; Music Supervisor, Annette Fradera; Editor, Alex Rodríguez; Casting, Manuel Teil; a Cha Cha Chá in association with Focus Features International presentation; Mexican; Dolby; Deluxe color; Rated R; 103 minutes; American release date: May 8, 2009

CAST

Tato	**Gael García Bernal**
Beto	**Diego Luna**
Batuta	**Guillermo Francella**
Elvira	**Dolores Heredia**
Toña	**Adriana Paz**
Maya	**Jessica Mas**

Salvador Zerboni (Jorge W), Tania Esmeralda Aguilar (Nadia), Joaquin Cosio (Arnulfo), Alfredo Alfonso (Don Casimiro), Fermin Martinez (DT. Obduilo), Eduardo Von (DT. Bruno Lopez), Jorge Zárate (Voz Bruno Lopez), Axel Ricco (Mena), Gabino Rodriguez (Mafafo), Alexander Da Silva (Gringa Roldan), Armando Hernández (El Cienpiés), Alexandré Barceló (Fito), Jorge Mondragón (Porro), Enoc Leaño (Árbito), Jose Carlos Rodriguez (DT. Merodio), Martin Altomaro, Pablo Lach, David Faitelson, Antonio Rosique (TV Commentators), Claudia Becker (Quetis), Manuel Teil (Quico), René Campero, Sonia Guerrero, Jorge Guerrero, Andrés Alemida, Annette Fradera (Bookmakers), Olinka Velázquez (Mesera), Pedro De Tavira, Felipe de Lara, Jimena Cuarón (At Racetrack)

Stepbrothers Beto and Tato are plucked from their impoverished existence in rustic Mexico by a sports agent who turns them into soccer superstars.

Jessica Mas, Gael García Bernal

LITTLE ASHES

(REGENT) Producers, Carlo Dusi, Jonny Persey, Jaume Vilalta; Executive Producers, Stephen P. Jarchow, Paul Colichman, Debra Stasson, Luke Montagu; Co-Producers, Philippa Goslett, Stewart Le Marechal; Director, Paul Morrison; Screenplay, Philippa Goslett; Photography, Adam Suschitzsky; Designer, Pere Francesch; Costumes, Antonio Belart; Music, Miguel Mera; Editor, Rachel Tunnard; Casting, Merce Espelleta; a Factotum Barcelona (Spain)/Aria Films, Met Film (U.K.) production, in association with Apt Films/Regent Entertainment/Katapult Film Sales; Spanish-British; Dolby; Color; HD-to-35mm; Rated R; 111 minutes; American release date: May 8, 2009

Javier Beltrán, Robert Pattinson

CAST

Federico Garcia Lorca	**Javier Beltrán**
Salvador Dali	**Robert Pattinson**
Luis Buñuel	**Matthew McNulty**
Magdalena	**Marina Gatell**
Gala	**Arly Jover**
Fernando de Valle	**Simón Andreu**
Rafael	**Rubén Arroyo**
Police	**Adria Allue, Ferran Audí**
Titiritero	**Adrian Devant**
Professor	**Ramón Enrich Borrellas**
Señora	**Sue Flack**
Ana María	**Diana Gómez**
Señor Milagro	**Ferran Lahoz**
Adela	**Esther Nubiola**
Pepín Bello	**Bruno Oro**

Vicky Peña (Tia de Magdalena), Joan Pico (Young Official), Marc Pujol (Carlos), Christian Rodrigo (Young Reporter), Pep Sais (Professor de Arte), Xavi Siles (Man)

The true story of the tenuous, homosexual relationship that developed between poet Federico Garcia Lorca and artist Salvador Dali, starting from their days at a progressive arts school.

Marina Gatell, Javier Beltrán © Regent Releasing

Matthew McNulty, Javier Beltrán

Arly Jover

Tilda Swinton © Magnolia Pictures

JULIA

(MAGNOLIA) Producers, Francois Marquis, Bertrand Faivre; Director, Erick Zonca; Screenplay, Aude Py, Erick Zonca; Photography, Yorick Le Saux; Designer, François-Renaud Labarthe; Costumes, April Napier; Music, Darius Keeler, Pollard Berrier; Editor, Philippe Kotlarski; Casting, Lisa Essary, Heidi Levitt, Manuel Teil; a Bagheera, the Bureau production; French-American-Mexican-Belgian; Dolby; Color; Rated R; 144 minutes; American release date: May 8, 2009

CAST
Julia Harris	**Tilda Swinton**
Mitch	**Saul Rubinek**
Elena	**Kate del Castillo**
Tom	**Aidan Gould**
Nick	**Jude Ciccolella**
Diego	**Bruno Bichir**
Santos	**Horacio Garcia Rojas**

Kevin Kilner (Johnny), John Bellucci (Phillip), Ezra Buzzington (George), Roger Cudney (Frank), Eugene Byrd (Leon), Mauricio Moreno (José), Gastón Peterson (Miguel), Sandro Kopp (Marcus), MJ Karmi (AA Woman), Ken Davitian (Taxi Driver), Hiep Thi Le (Kitty), Jim Leske (Motel Clerk), Muriel Ricard (Journalist), Tania Verafield (Cleaning Lady), Atzinga (Carmen), Nadiedka (Carena), Mariana Elias (Raphaella)

Desperate for money after being fired from her job, self-destructive, alcoholic Julia Harris agrees to help her friend kidnap her son.

ADORATION

(SONY CLASSICS) Producers, Atom Egoyan, Simone Urdl, Jennifer Weiss; Executive Producers, Robert Lantos, Michele Halberstadt, Laurent Petin; Director/Screenplay, Atom Egoyan; Photography, Paul Sarossy; Designer, Phillip Barker; Costumes, Debra Hanson; Music, Mychael Danna; Editor, Susan Shipton; Visual Effects Supervisor, Robert Crowther; Casting, John Buchan, Jason Knight; a Serendipity Point Films (Canada)/ARP Selection (France) presentation of an Ego Film Arts (Canada) production, with the participation of Telefilm Canada, Super Ecran, Astral Media, Movie Central, Ontario Film & Television Tax Credit; Canadian-French; Dolby; Deluxe color; Rated R; 101 minutes; American release date: May 8, 2009

CAST
Tom	**Scott Speedman**
Rachel	**Rachel Blanchard**
Morris	**Kenneth Welsh**
Simon	**Devon Bostick**
Daniel	**Aaron Poole**
Cab Driver	**Dominic Cuzzocrea**
Hannah	**Katie Boland**
Sami	**Noam Jenkins**
Sabine	**Arsinée Khanjian**
Carole	**Geraldine O'Rawe**
Parking Security	**Duane Murray**
Jennifer	**Hailee Sisera**

Yuval Daniel (Security Agent), Jeremy Wright (Delivery Guy), Thomas Hauff (Nick), Martin Roach (Car Owner), Michael Barry (Skinhead), Louca Tassone (Young Simon), Tony Nardi (Principal Robert), Janice Stein (Janet), Vera Frenkel, Marc Glassman (Passengers), Ron Bell (Bus Driver), Paul Soles (Ira), Bathsheba Garnett (Holocaust Survivor), Soo Garay (Granddaughter), Maury Chaykin, Jack Blum, Shel Goldstein, Sharon Corder (Passengers), Ieva Lucas (Berating Woman), James Brinkley (Driver)

After Simon is encouraged by his teacher to present his paper about husband and wife terrorists as a documentation of his own life, the teen starts to question how his own parents died.

Rachel Blanchard, Noam Jenkins © Sony Pictures Classics

Jérémie Renier, Juliette Binoche, Charles Berling

Charles Berling, Max Ricat, Juliette Binoche, Isabelle Sadoyan, Alice de Lencquesaing, Dominique Reymond © IFC Films

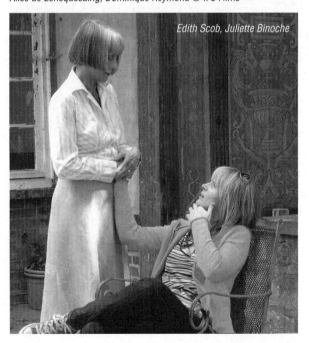

Edith Scob, Juliette Binoche

SUMMER HOURS

(IFC FILMS) a.k.a. *L'heure d'ete*; Producers, Marin Karmitz, Nathanael Karmitz, Charles Gilbert; Executive Producer, Claire Dornoy; Director/Screenplay, Olivier Assayas; Photography, Eric Gautier; Art Director, Francois-Renaud Labarthe; Costumes, Anais Romand, Jorgen Doering; Editor, Luc Barnier; Casting, Antoinette Boulat; an MK2 Prods. production, in association with France 3 Cinema, with the participation of Canal Plus, TPS Star, Musee d'Orsay; French, 2008; Dolby; Color; Not rated; 102 minutes; American release date: May 15, 2009

CAST

Adrienne	**Juliette Binoche**
Frédéric	**Charles Berling**
Jérémie	**Jérémie Renier**
Hélène	**Edith Scob**
Lisa	**Dominique Reymond**
Angela	**Valérie Bonneton**
Éloise	**Isabelle Sadoyan**
James	**Kyle Eastwood**
Sylvie	**Alice de Lencquesaing**
Pierre	**Emile Berling**
Michel Waldemar	**Jean-Baptiste Malartre**

Gilles Arbona (Maitre Lambert), Eric Elmosnino (Police Superintendent), Marc Voinchet (Radio Presenter), Sara Martins (Press Attachee), Christian Lucas (Éloise's Nephew), Philippe Paimblanc (Mayor of Valmondois), Luc Bricault (Tourist at the Musee d'Orsay), Arnaud Azoulay (Sylvie's Boyfriend), Marine Decroix, Lena Burger (Sylvie's Friends), Francois Marie Baier (President of the Date Commission), Philippe Thiebaut, Arnaud Brejon de la Lavergnee, Marc Plocki, Odile Michel (Members of the Commission), Michel Maket, Gerard Landrot, Michel Broomhead (Experts), Daisy Kechichiglonian, Pearl Kechichiglonian, Max Ricat, Lauda Pharaon, Alistair Forwood, Malo Gledhill (Children), Marie Belie Vaulet (Guide), Thierry Gausseron, Oliver Gabet (Curators), Matthieu Thenoz, Baptste Lavenne, Marie-France Cocheteux (Employees), Bruno Ecault (Restaurant Owner)

Three siblings must decide whether they will follow their late mother's wishes to have her extensive art collection preserved in a museum.

Dominique Reymond, Charles Berling

EASY VIRTUE

(SONY CLASSICS) Producers, Barnaby Thompson, Joe Abrams, James D. Stern; Executive Producers, James Spring, Douglas E. Hansen, Cindy Wilkinson Kirven, George McGhee, Ralph Kamp, Louise Goodsill, Paul Brett, Peter Nichols, Tim Smith; Co-Producer, Alexandra Ferguson; Director, Stephan Elliott; Screenplay, Stephan Elliott, Sheridan Jobbins; Based on the play by Noël Coward; Photography, Martin Kenzie; Designer, John Beard; Costumes, Charlotte Walter; Music, Marius de Vries; Music Supervisors, Tris Penna, Michelle de Vries; Editor, Sue Blainey; Casting, Celestia Fox, Deborah Aquila, Tricia Wood; an Ealing Studios presentation, in association with Endgame Entertainment, Odyssey Entertainment, BBC Films, of a Fragile Film, in association with Joe Abrams Prods. and Prescience Production Partnerships; British-American; Dolby; Color; Rated PG-13; 97 minutes; American release date: May 22, 2009

Jessica Biel, Ben Barnes

CAST

Larita Whittaker	**Jessica Biel**
John Whittaker	**Ben Barnes**
Mrs. Whittaker	**Kristin Scott Thomas**
Mr. Whittaker	**Colin Firth**
Hilda Whittaker	**Kimberely Nixon**
Marion Whittaker	**Katherine Parkinson**
Furber	**Kris Marshall**
Phillip Hurst	**Christian Brassington**
Sarah Hurst	**Charlotte Riley**
Jackson	**Jim McManus**
Lord Hurst	**Pip Torrens**
Davis	**Jeremy Hooton**
Cook	**Joanna Bacon**
Millie the Maid	**Maggie Hickey**

Georgie Glen (Mrs. Landrigin), David Longstaff (Reverend Burton), Michael Archer (Warwick Holborough), Rebel Penfold-Russell (Mrs. Winston), Stewart Clarke, Oliver Reid, Joe Reid (Young Men), Stephan Elliott, Sheridan Jobbins (Grumpy Party Guests), Fizz (Poppy).

John Whittaker's upper class British family barely hide their disdain for his new bride, an outspoken American automobile racer who refuses to cave in to their snobbery.

Kimberley Nixon, Kristin Scott Thomas, Charlotte Riley

Colin Firth, Jessica Biel

Kristin Scott Thomas © Sony Pictures Classics

O'HORTEN

(SONY CLASSICS) Producer/Director/Screenplay, Bent Hamer; Co-Producers, Jim Frazee, Mads Peter Ole Olsen, Christoph Friedl, Karl Baumgartner, Alexander Mallet-Guy; Photography, John Christian Rosenlund; Art Director, Kalli Juliusson; Music, John Erik Kaada; Editors, Pal Gengenbach, Silje Nortseth; a Bulbul Films (Norway)/Scanbox Entertainment (Norway)/Pandora Filmproduktion (Germany)/ ID Memento (France) production; Norwegian-German-French; Color; Rated PG-13; 89 minutes; American release date: May 22, 2009

Bård Owe, Per Jansen

CAST

Odd Horten	Bård Owe
Trygve Sissener	Espen Skjønberg
Fru Thøgersen	Ghita Nørby
Svea	Henny Moan
Flo	Bjørn Floberg
Steiner Sissener	Kai Remlov
Chariman	Per Jansen
Conductor	Bjarte Hjelmeland
Valkyrijen Walter	Bjorn Jenseg
Vera Horten	Kari Lolland
Connery	Lars Oyno
Opsahl	Trond-Viggo Torgersen
Nordahl	Peder Anders Lohne Hamer
Young Vera/Ski Jumper	Anette Sagen

Having reached the age of 67, Odd Horten is forced to step down from his job as a train engineer, leaving him to contemplate an uncertain future.

Bård Owe, Bjørn Floberg © Sony Pictures Classics

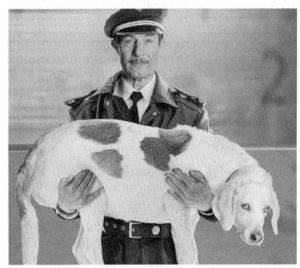

Bård Owe

Bård Owe, Espen Skjønberg

Masahiro Motoki, Takashi Sasano

Masahiro Motoki, Tsutomu Yamazaki

Kazuko Yoshiyuki, Ryoko Hirosue © Regent Releasing

DEPARTURES

(REGENT) a.k.a. *Okuribito*; Producers, Yasuhiro Mase, Toshiaki Nakasawa, Toshihisa Watai; Director, Yojiro Takita; Screenplay, Kundo Koyama; Photography, Takeshi Hamada; Designer, Fumio Ogawa; Costumes, Katsuhiko Kitamura; Music, Joe Hisaishi; Editor, Akimasa Kawashima; a Tokyo Broadcasting System, Sedic production; Japanese; Dolby; Color; Rated PG-13; 131 minutes; American release date: May 29, 2009

CAST

Daigo Kobayashi	**Masahiro Motoki**
Ikuei Sasaki	**Tsutomu Yamazaki**
Mika Kobayashi	**Ryoko Hirosue**
Tsuyako Yamashita	**Kazuko Yoshiyuki**
Yuriko Kamimura	**Kimiko Yo**
Shokichi Hirata	**Takashi Sasano**

After the orchestra to which he belonged disbands, a despondent Daigo Kobayashi returns to his hometown where he finds a job working in a mortuary.

2008 Academy Award winner for Best Foreign Language Film.

Masahiro Motoki

Yolande Moreau, Ulrich Tukur

Yolande Moreau

Yolande Moreau

SÉRAPHINE

(MUSIC BOX FILMS) Producers, Miléna Poylo, Gilles Sacuto; Director, Martin Provost; Screenplay, Martin Provost, Marc Abdelnour; Photography, Laurent Brunet; Designer, Thierry François; Music, Michael Galasso; Editor, Ludo Troch; Casting, Brigitte Moidon; a TS Productions production; French-Belgian; Dolby; Color; Not rated; 125 minutes; American release date: June 5, 2009

CAST
Séraphine Louis	**Yolande Moreau**
Wilhelm Uhde	**Ulrich Tukur**
Anne Marie Uhde	**Anne Bennett**
Madame Duphot	**Geneviève Mnich**
Helmut	**Nico Rogner**
Minouche	**Adélaïde Leroux**
Duval	**Serge Larivière**
Mother Superior	**Françoise Lebrun**

The true story of how German art collector Wilhelm Uhde realized that the simple maid working for him possessed an incredible talent for painting.

Yolande Moreau © Music Box Films

MOON

(SONY CLASSICS) Producers, Stuart Fenegan, Trudie Styler; Executive Producers, Michael Henry, Bill Zysblat, Trevor Beattie, Bil Bungay; Co-Producers, Nicky Moss, Alex Francis, Mark Folingo, Steve Milne; Director/Story, Duncan Jones; Screenplay, Nathan Parker; Photography, Gary Shaw; Designer, Tony Noble; Costumes, Jane Petrie; Conceptual Designer, Gavin Rothery; Music, Clint Mansell; Editor, Nicolas Gastor; Visual Effects and Character Animation, Cinesite; Casting, Jerry Zimmermann, Manuel Puro; a Stage 6 Films presentation of a Liberty Films production, in association with Xingu Films and Limelight; British-American; Dolby; Panavision; Color; Rated R; 97 minutes; American release date: June 12, 2009

Sam Rockwell

CAST

Sam Bell	**Sam Rockwell**
Voice of GERTY	**Kevin Spacey**
Tess Bell	**Dominique McElligott**
Overmeyers	**Matt Berry**
Sam Clone	**Robin Chalk**
Eve Bell	**Kaya Scodelario**
The Technician	**Malcolm Stewart**
Thompson	**Benedict Wong**
Little Eve	**Rosie Shaw**
Nanny	**Adrienne Shaw**

Sam Rockwell

After spending three years in solitude on a lunar mining base, Sam Bell is disturbed to find a clone of himself, claiming to be the real thing.

Dominique McElligott, Sam Rockwell

Sam Rockwell © Sony Pictures

$9.99

(REGENT) Producers, Emil Sherman, Amir Harel; Executive Producers, Mati Broudo, Hezi Bezalel; Director, Tatia Rosenthal; Screenplay, Tatia Rosenthal, Etgar Keret; Based on stories by Etgar Keret; Photography, Susan Stitt, James Lewis, Richard Bradshaw; Designer, Melinda Doring; Music, Christopher Bowen; Editor, Teena Economidis; Animators, Daniel Alderson, Yonatan Bereskin, Darren Burgess, Steve Cox, Anthony Elworthy, Jan-Erik Maas, Sharon Parker, Andy Spilsted, Norman Yeend; a Screen Australia (Australia)/Israel Film Fund (Israel) presentation of a Sherman Pictures (Australia)/Lama Films (Israel) production; Australian-Israeli; Dolby; Color; Rated R; 78 minutes; American release date: June 19, 2009

VOICE CAST

Angel	**Geoffrey Rush**
Jim Peck	**Anthony LaPaglia**
Dave Peck	**Samuel Johnson**
Michelle	**Claudia Karvan**
Ron	**Joel Edgerton**
Albert	**Barry Otto**

Leanna Walsman (Tanita), Ben Mendelsohn (Lenny Peck), Jamie Katsamatsas (Zack), Tom Budge (Bisley), Leon Ford (Stanton), Henry Nixon (Drazen/Beanbag/Radio Announcer)

A look at the lives of the residents of an urban Australian apartment building.

Albert, Angel

Dave © Regent Releasing

Lasse Valdal, Stig Frode Henriksen

Ørjan Gamst (left) © IFC Films

DEAD SNOW

(IFC FILMS) a.k.a. *Død snø*; Producers, Terje Stromstad, Tomas Evjen; Executive Producers, Kjetil Omberg, Magne Ek, Espen Horn, Harald Zwart; Director, Tommy Wirkola; Screenplay, Tommy Wirkola, Stig Frode Henriksen; Photography, Matthew Weston; Designer, Liv Ask; Music, Christian Wibe; Editor, Martin Stoltz; a Yellow Bastard Prods., News on Request, Euforia Film presentation of a Miho Film production; Norwegian; Color; Not rated; 88 minutes; American release date: June 19, 2009

CAST

Hanna	**Charlotte Frogner**
Herzog	**Ørjan Gamst**
Martin	**Vegar Hoel**
Roy	**Stig Frode Henriksen**
Erlend	**Jeppe Laursen**
Liv	**Evy Kasseth Røsten**
Chris	**Jenny Skavlan**
The Wanderer	**Bjørn Sundquist**
Sara	**Ane Dahl Torp**
Vegard	**Lasse Valdal**
Dying Zombie	**Tommy Wirkola**

A group of med students taking a vacation in the woods encounter zombie Nazis hungry for flesh.

Kathy Bates

Rupert Friend, Michelle Pfeiffer

Michelle Pfeiffer © Miramax Films

CHÉRI

(MIRAMAX) Producers, Bill Kenwright, Andras Hamori, Tracey Seaward, Thom Mount; Executive Producers, Francois Ivernel, Cameron McCracken, Christopher Hampton, Richard Temple, Simon Fawcett; Co-Producers, Ralf Schmitz, Bastie Griese, Raphael Benoliel; Director, Stephen Frears; Screenplay, Christopher Hampton; Based on the novels *Chéri* and *The Last of Chéri* by Colette; Photography, Darius Khondji; Designer, Alan Macdonald; Costumes, Consolata Boyle; Music, Alexandre Desplat; Editor, Lucia Zuchetti; Casting, Leo Davis, Victoria Thomas; a Bill Kenwright production, presented in association with Pathé UK Film Council, Aramid Entertainment with the participation of MMC Studios, Filmstiftung, NRW, DFF, Tiggy Films and Reliant Pictures Corporation; British-French-German; Dolby; Panavision; Deluxe color; Rated R; 92 minutes; American release date: June 29, 2009

CAST

Lea de Lonval	**Michelle Pfeiffer**
Madame Charlotte Peloux	**Kathy Bates**
"Chéri" Peloux	**Rupert Friend**
Edmee	**Felicity Jones**
Rose	**Frances Tomelty**
La Copine	**Anita Pallenberg**
La Loupiote	**Harriet Walter**
Marie Laure	**Iben Hjejle**
Baroness	**Bette Bourne**
Mme. Aldonza	**Nichola McAuliffe**
Lilli	**Gaye Brown**
Vicomte Desmond	**Tom Burke**
Mme. Roland	**Natasha Cashman**

Andras Hamori (Otto, the Silver-Haired Industrialist), Toby Kebbell (Patron), Joe Sheridan (Marcel), Hubert Tellegen (Ernest), Jack Walker (Monsieur Roland), Rollo Weeks (Guido), Stephen Frears (Narrator)

Madame Peloux encourages her friend, Lea de Lonval, an aging courtesan, to bed her spoiled son, only to have Lea fall hopelessly in love with the young man.

Michelle Pfeiffer, Rupert Friend

Agnès Varda (left)

Agnès Varda

Agnès Varda (center) © Cinema Guild

THE BEACHES OF AGNÈS

(CINEMA GUILD) a.k.a. *Les plages d'Agnes*; Producer/Director/Screenplay, Agnès Varda; Photography, Alain Sakot, Hélène Louvart, Arlene Nelson, Agnès Varda; Designer, Franckie Diago; Music, Joanna Bruzdowicz, Stéphane Vilar, Paule Cornet; Editors, Jean-Baptiste Morin, Baptiste Filloux; a Cine-Tamaris, ARTE France Cinema production, with the participation of Canal Plus and the support of the Region Ile-de-France, Region Languedoc-Rousillon, in partnership with the Centre National de la Cinematographie; French; Color; HD-to-DCP; Not rated; 114 minutes; American release date: July 1, 2009

WITH

Agnès Varda, Andé Lubrano, Blaise Fournier, Vincent Fournier, Andrée Vilar, Stéphane Vilar, Christophe Vilar, Rosalie Varda, Mathieu Demy, Christophe Vallaux, Mireille Henrio, Didier Rouget, Ann-Laure Manceau, Gerry Ayres, Jim McBride, Tracy McBride, Patricia Knop, Richard Scarry, Eguene Kotlyarenko, Zalman King

A documentary on the life of Agnes Varda, as made by the director herself.

Agnès Varda

Agnès Varda

THE GIRL FROM MONACO

(MAGNOLIA) a.k.a. *La fille de Monaco*; Producers, Bruno Pesery, Philippe Carcassonne; Director, Anne Fontaine; Screenplay, Anne Fontaine, Benoît Graffin, Jacques Fieschi; Photography, Patrick Blossier; Designer, Yves Fournier; Costumes, Catherine Leterrier; Music, Philippe Rombi; Editor, Maryline Monthieux; a Soudaine Compagnie, Ciné@ presentation; French; Dolby; Panavision; Color; Rated R; 95 minutes; American release date: July 3, 2009

Louise Bourgoin, Fabrice Luchini

CAST

Bertrand Beavois	**Fabrice Luchini**
Christophe Abadi	**Roschdy Zem**
Audrey Varella	**Louise Bourgoin**
Edith Lassalle	**Stéphane Audran**
Hélène	**Jeanne Balibar**
Louis Lassalle	**Gilles Cohen**
Alain	**Alexandre Steiger**
Inspector Taurand	**Philippe Duclos**
Carolina	**Hélène de Saint-Père**
Tony	**Christophe Vandevelde**
Boulie	**Pierre Bourgeon**
Girl from the Group	**Claire Joseph**
Denis	**Denis Dallan**
Hotel Guest	**Francisca Viudes**

While in Monaco to defend a noted criminal, neurotic attorney Bertrand Beauvois finds himself falling in love with a beautiful and uninhibited weather girl.

Roschdy Zem, Fabrice Luchini

Louise Bourgoin, Fabrice Luchini © Magnolia Pictures

Louise Bourgoin, Roschdy Zem

SOMERS TOWN

(FILM MOVEMENT) Producer, Barnaby Spurrier; Executive Producers, Greg Nugen, Nick Mercer, Robert Saville; Director, Shane Meadows; Screenplay, Paul Fraser; Photography, Natasha Braier; Designer, Lisa Marie Hall; Costumes, Jo Thompson; Music, Gavin Clarke; Editor, Richard Graham; a Tomboy Films, Mother Vision presentation of a Big Arty production; British; Dolby; Black and white/color; 16-to-35mm; Not rated; 75 minutes; American release date: July 17, 2009

CAST
Tomo	**Thomas Turgoose**
Jane	**Kate Dickie**
Marek	**Piotr Jagiello**
Mariusz	**Ireneusz Czop**
Graham	**Perry Benson**
Maria	**Elisa Lasowski**
Officer Workers	**Ben Porter, Jamie Belman**
Construction Workers	**Steve Hillman, Mark Monero**

Ryan Ford, Levi Hayes, Risade Campbell (Local Kid), Huggy Leaver (Café Owner), Trevor Cooper (Angry Resident), Eddy Hasson (French Man in Café), Wojciech Olczak, Wojtek Macierznski, Mariusz Gajewski, Tomasz Kamola, Nojaech Magenyuski, Sebastian Palka (Polish Friends), Anna Jenson (Polish Woman in Shop)

After being mugged upon his arrival in London, a 16-year-old orphan strikes up a friendship with a Polish lad who lives in the city's social housing area known as Somers Town.

Thomas Turgoose, Piotr Jagiello

Piotr Jagiello, Elisa Lasowski, Thomas Turgoose

Thomas Turgoose

Piotr Jagiello, Perry Benson, Thomas Turgoose © Film Movement

Juliane Köhler, Nina Hoss

A WOMAN IN BERLIN

(STRAND) a.k.a. *Anonyma: Eine Frau in Berlin*; Producers, Guenter Rohrbach; Executive Producer, Martin Moszkowicz; Director/Screenplay, Max Färberböck; Based on the diary *Anonyma: A Woman in Berlin*; Photography, Benedict Neuenfels; Designer, Uli Hanisch; Costumes, Lucia Faust; Music, Zbigniew Preisner; Editor, Ewa J. Lind; a Guenter Rohrbach, Constantin Film production, in association with ZDF, Tempus Film; German; Dolby; Widescreen; Color; Not rated; 131 minutes; American release date: July 17, 2009

CAST

Anonyma	**Nina Hoss**
Major Andrej Rybkin	**Yevgeni Sidikhin**
Widow	**Irm Hermann**
Eckhart	**Rüdiger Vogler**
Ilse Hoch	**Ulrike Krumbiegel**
Friedrich Hoch	**Rolf Kanies**
Bärbel Malthaus	**Jördis Triebel**
Anatol	**Roman Gribkov**
Elke	**Juliane Köhler**

Samvel Muzhikyan (Andropov), Viktor Zhalsanov (Mongol), Aleksandra Kulikova (Masha), Oleg Chernov (Soldier #1, Rapist), Anne Kanis (Refugee Girl), August Diehl (Gerd), Rosalie Thomass (Greta Maltaus), Sandra Hueller (Steffi), Erni Mangold (Eight-Year-Old Woman), Sebastian Urzendowsky (Young Soldier), Hermann Beyer (Dr. Wolf), Ralf Schermuly (Bookseller), Isabell Gerschke (Lisbeth), Alexander Samoylenko (Petka)

While hiding in a Berlin basement during the final days of World War II, a journalist seeks help from an understanding soldier to prevent her further assault at the hands of the Russian army.

Nina Hoss © Strand Releasing

Nina Hoss, August Diehl

Nina Hoss, Yevgeni Sidikhin

IN THE LOOP

(IFC FILMS) Producers, Kevin Loader, Adam Tandy; Executive Producers, Christine Langan, David M. Thompson, Paula Jalfon, Simon Fawcett; Director, Armando Ianucci; Screenplay, Jesse Armstrong, Simon Blackwell, Armando Ianucci, Tony Roche; Additional Dialogue, Ian Martin; Photography, Jamie Cairney; Designer, Cristina Casali; Costumes, Ros Little; Music, Adem Ilhan, Elysian Quartet; Editors, Billy Sneddon, Ant Boys; a BBC Films and U.K. Film Council production in association with Aramid Entertainment; British; Dolby; Color; HD; Not rated; 105 minutes; American release date: July 24, 2009

CAST

Malcolm Tucker	**Peter Capaldi**
Simon Foster	**Tom Hollander**
Judy Molloy	**Gina McKee**
Lt. Gen. George Miller	**James Gandolfini**
Toby Wright	**Chris Addison**
Liza Weld	**Anna Chlumsky**
Bob Adriano	**Enzo Cilenti**
Jamie MacDonald	**Paul Higgins**
Karen Clarke	**Mimi Kennedy**
Sir Jonathan Tutt	**Alex MacQueen**
A.J. Brown	**Johnny Pemberton**
Suzy	**Olivia Poulet**
Linton Barwick	**David Rasche**
Roz	**Joanna Scanlan**
Michael Rodgers	**James Smith**
Paul Michaelson	**Steve Coogan**
Mrs. Michaelson	**Rita May**
Chad	**Zach Woods**
Reporters	**Lucinda Raines, James Doherty**
Civil Servant	**Harry Hadden-Paton**
Malcolm's Secretary	**Samantha Harrington**
Annabelle Hsin	**Chipo Chung**
Mrs. McDiarmid	**Joanna Brookes**
New Minister	**Eve Matheson**
White House Tourist	**Del Pentecost**
New Adviser	**Will Smith**
Airport Security Official	**Reid Sasser**

After Simon Foster, Britain's Minister of International Development, makes fumbling comments during a radio interview, Malcolm Tucker, the Prime Minister's director of communications, jumps into overdrive in order to rectify the situation and downplay the decision to go to war.

This film received an Oscar nomination for original screenplay.

Steve Coogan, Joanna Scanlan

Peter Capaldi, James Gandolfini

Mimi Kennedy, James Gandolfini

Anna Chlumsky

Tom Hollander

Peter Capaldi, Chris Addison

Peter Capaldi © IFC Films

LORNA'S SILENCE

(SONY CLASSICS) a.k.a. *Le Silence de Lorna*; Producers, Jean-Pierre Dardenne, Luc Dardenne, Denis Freyd; Executive Producer, Olivier Bronckart; Director/ Screenplay, Jean-Pierre Dardenne, Luc Dardenne; Photography, Alain Marcoen; Designer, Igor Gabriel; Costumes, Monic Parelle; Editor, Marie-Helene Dozo; a Les Films du Feuve, Arte France Cinema (France)/Archipel 35, RTBF (Belgium)/ Lucky Red (Italy)/Arte/WDR (Germany) co-production; French-Belgian-Italian-German, 2008; Color; Rated R; 105 minutes; American release date: July 31, 2009

Arta Dobroshi, Jérémie Renier

CAST

Lorna	**Arta Dobroshi**
Claudy Moreau	**Jérémie Renier**
Fabio	**Fabrizio Rongione**
Sokol	**Alban Ukaj**
Spirou	**Morgan Marinne**
Inspector	**Olivier Gourmet**
Andrei	**Anton Yakovlev**
Kostia	**Grigori Manukov**
Monique Sobel	**Mireille Bailly**

Stéphanie Gob (Nurse), Laurent Caron (Commissaire), Baptiste Somin (Morgue Attendant), Alexandre Trocky, Cécile Boland (Doctors), Cédric Lenoir (Bank Attendant), Serge Larivière (Pharmacist), Philippe Jeusette (Locksmith), Sophie Leboutte (Claudy's Mother), François Sauveur (Claudy's Brother), Christian Lusshcentier (Male Nurse in Emergency Room), Stéphane Marsin (Dealer), Laurence Cordonnier (Bank Assistant), Anne Gerard (Woman at Funeral), Annette Closset (Cleaning Women's Boss), Isballe Dumont (Nurse at Gynecology), Patrizia Berti (Police Woman), Leon Michaux (Policeman in Plainclothes), Alao Kasongo (Receptionist at Emergency Room), Claudy Delfosse (Micky), Faruque Ahmed (Cashier at Telephone Shop), Marie-Ange Pougin (Colleague at Cleaning Company)

Fabrizio Rongione, Arta Dobroshi © Sony Pictures Classics

To secure Belgian citizenship, Albanian Lorna marries junkie Claudy with the intention of divorcing him soon afterwards.

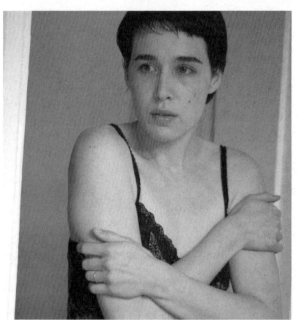

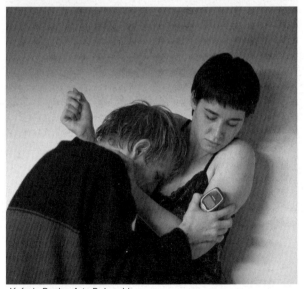

Jérémie Renier, Arta Dobroshi

Arta Dobroshi

Stine Stengade, Thure Lindhardt © IFC Films

FLAME & CITRON

(IFC FILMS) a.k.a. *Flammen & citronen*; Producer, Lars Bredo Rahbek; Co-Producers, Stefan Schubert, Ralph Schwingel, Charlie Weobcken; Director, Ole Christian Madsen; Screenplay, Lars K. Andersen, Ole Christian Madsen; Photography, Jorgen Johansson; Designers, Jette Lehmann, Friborg Nanna Due; Costumes, Manon Rasmussen; Music, Karsten Fundal; Editor, Soren B. Ebbe; Visual Effects Supervisors, Jonas Drehn, Dominik Trimborn; Casting, Rie Hedegaard; a Nimbus Film production in association with Danish Film Institute, TV2 Denmark, Sirena Film, MBB Berlin Brandenburg, Wuste Film, Filmforderung Hamburg, Deutsche Filmfordenfonds, Studio Babelsberg, Nordic Film & TV Funds, Eurimages; Danish-German, 2008; Dolby; Widescreen; Color; Not rated; 130 minutes; American release date: July 31, 2009

CAST

Flammen (Bent)	**Thure Lindhardt**
Citronen (Jorgen)	**Mads Mikkelsen**
Ketty Selmer	**Stine Stengade**
Aksel Winther	**Peter Mygind**
Bodil	**Mille Hoffmeyer Lehfeldt**
Spex	**Flemming Enevold**
Hoffmann	**Christian Berkel**
Gilbert	**Hanns Zischler**
Bananen	**Claus Riis Østergaard**
Frode Jacobsen (Ravnen)	**Lars Mikkelsen**
Flammens Far	**Jesper Christensen**

Lærke Winther Andersen (Cap), Peter Plaugborg (Lillebjørn), Martin Hestbæk (Storebjørn), Thomas Voss (Teddy), Martin Greis (Heinrich), Rene Benjamin Hansen (Carl), Jeppe Find (Bob), Jesper Kaplan (Skolelæreren), Rasmus Bjerg (Smalle), Jacque Lauritsen (Vinhandler), Charlotte Rathnov (Lis Bomhoff), Henrik Jandorf (Helmer Bomhoff), Rasmus Botoft (Liquor Store Owner), Mads Møllegaard Nielsen (Bodil's New Boyfriend), Malene Schwartz (Gilbert's Wife), Martin Hall (Østargaard Petersen), Karel Dobry (Seibold), Hans Henrik Clemensen (Redatør Gaust), Tina Robinson Simonsen (Fru Lorentzen), Jan Zuska (Hr. Lorentzen), Mai Holm Laureng (Anne), Marie Christensen-Dalsgaard (Nurse), Klaus Tange (Schalburg, Sergeant), Martin Vasquez (German Officer), Robert Reinhold, Roman Horn (Police Officers), Caspar Phillipson (Schalburg, Soldier with Glasses), Benjamin Boe Rasmussen (Ambulance Chief), Thomas Bendixen (Gestapo Chief), Oliver Hvidtfeldt (Injured Boy in Car), Tinus Løvento (Father of the Boy), Nikola Navrátil (Young Officer), Per Löwberg (Waiter), Per Löwberg (Tjener), Simona Vcalová (Liquor Store Owner's Wife)

The true story of Denmark's top resistance fighters, code-named Flame and Citron, who spent World War II tracking down and killing a large number of Nazis and Danish collaborators.

THIRST

(FOCUS) a.k.a. *Bakjwi*; Producers, Park Chan-wook, Ahn Suhyeon; Executive Producer, Miky Lee; Co-Executive Producer, Katharine Kim; Director, Park Chan-wook; Screenplay, Park Chan-wook, Jeong Seo-gyeong; Inspired by Emile Zola's novel *Therese Raquin*; Photography, Jeong Jeong-hun; Designer, Ryu Seong-hye; Costumes, Jo Sang-geyong; Music, Jo Yeong-wook; Editors, Kim Sang-beom, Kim Jae-beom; Special Effects Supervisor, Lee Jeon-hyeong; a CJ Entertainment (South Korea)/Focus Features Intl. (U.S.) presentation of a Moho Film production; South Korean-American; Dolby; Widescreen; Color; Rated R; 133 minutes; American Release date: July 31, 2009

CAST

Priest Sang-hyeon	**Song Kang-ho**
Tae-joo	**Kim Ok-vin**
Lady Ra	**Kim Hae-suk**
Kang-woo	**Shin Hay-kyun**
Priest Noh	**Park In-hwan**
Yeong-doo	**Oh Dal-su**
Seung-dae	**Song Yeong-chang**
Evelyn	**Mercedes Cabral**
Immanuel	**Eriq Ebouaney**

After contracting a deadly virus in his efforts to discover a vaccine, Sang-hyeon returns from the dead with a thrist for blood.

Kim Ok-vin, Shin Ha-kyun

Oh Dai-soo (on floor), Song Kang-ho, Kim Ok-vin © Focus Features

DISTRICT 9

(TRISTAR) Producers, Peter Jackson, Carolynne Cunningham; Executive Producers, Bill Block, Ken Kamins; Co-Producer, Philippa Boyens; Co-Executive Producers, Paul Hanson, Elliot Ferwerda; Director, Neill Blomkamp; Screenplay, Neill Blomkamp, Terri Tatchell; Photography, Trent Opaloch; Designer, Philip Ivey; Costumes, Diana Cilliers; Music, Clinton Shorter; Music Supervisor, Michelle Belcher; Editor, Julian Clarke; Visual Effects Supervisors, Dan Kaufman, Robert Habros, Matt Aitken, Trevor Adams, Patti Gannon; Weapons, Creatures and Makeup Effects, Weta Workshop; Stunts, Grant Hulley; Casting, Denton Douglas; a Peter Jackson presentation in association with TriStar Pictures and Block/Hanson of a WingNut Films production; New Zealand; Dolby; Color; HD-to-35mm; Rated R; 111 minutes; American release date: August 14, 2009

CAST

Wikus Van De Merwe	**Sharlto Copley**
Grey Bradnam, UKNR Chief Correspondent	**Jason Cope**
Sarah Livingstone	**Nathalie Boltt**
Dr. Katrina McKenzie	**Sylvaine Strike**
Les Feldman	**John Sumner**
Dirk Michaels	**William Allen Young**
Francois Moraneau	**Nick Blake**
Police Officer James Hope	**Jed Brophy**
Piet Smit	**Louis Minnaar**
Tania Van De Merwe	**Vanessa Haywood**
Sandra Van De Merwe	**Marian Hooman**
Michael Bloemstein, MNU Alien Civil Affairs	**Vittorio Leonardi**
Fundiswa Mhlanga	**Mandla Gaduka**
Nicolas Van De Merwe	**Johan van Schoor**
Phyllis Sinderson, MNU Alien Relations	**Stella Steenkamp**
Koobus Venter	**David James**
Thomas	**Kenneth Nkosi**
Clive Henderson, Entomologist	**Tim Gordon**
Reporter	**Mampho Brescia**
MNY Medic	**Morne Erasmus**
Paramedic	**Anthony Bishop**
Sangoma	**Hlengiwe Madlala**
Obesandjo's Lieutenant	**Siyabonga Radebe**
Antony Grobler	**Melt Sieberhagen**
Mike Van Kerland	**Andre Odendaal**
Craig Weldon	**Nick Boraine**
Ross Pienaar	**Robert Hobbs**

Elizabeth Mkandawie, Greg Melvill-Smith, Morena Busa Sesatsa, Themba Nkosi, Mzwandile Nqoba, Barry Strydom (Interviewees), David Clatworthy, Mike Huff, Jonathan Taylor (MNU Doctors), Anthony Fridjohn (MNU Executive), John Ellis, Louise Saint-Claire (MNU Medical Students), Nicolas Herbstein (MNU Biolab Technician), Sibulele Gcilitshana (Ü Günters Woman), Mahendra Raghunath (SABC Anchor Person), Phillip Mathebula (Meat Stall Seller), Claudine Bennent, Michelle Ayden, Antony Sarak, Billy Somagaca, Ryan Whittal, John Jacob, Yashik Maharaj, Fernando Saraiva, Sharon Waugh (MNU Office Workers), Brandon Auret, Jacques Gombault, Justin Strydom, Simo Magwaza, Theunis Nel, Sonni Chidiebere, Matt Stern, Danny Datnow, David Dukas (MNU Mercenaries), Daniel Hadebe, Wisani Mbokota, Craig Jackson, Justin Duplessis, Rodney Downey, Den Antonakis (MNU Guards), Bongo Mbutuma, Johnny Selema, Mashabela Galane, Mfazwe Sekobane, Nicholas Ratlou, Saint Gregory Nwokedi, Donalson Rabisi, Zephania Sibanda, Gideon Thodane, Mdu Mthabela, David Mikhethi, Jeffries Simelane, Shafique Allan (Nigerian Gangsters), Wendy Mbatha, Leigh Mashupye, Beauty Setai, Nkiyase Mondlana (Nigerian Hookers), Kuda Rusike, Morena Setatsa, Mpho Molao, Ntombi Nkuua, Absalom Dikane, Monthandazo Thomo, Norman Thabalala, Siphiwe Mbuko, Shiela Nene (Soweto Residents)

Years after an alien space ship has left its crew stranded in a makeshift slum in Johannesburg, authorities decide it is time to clear the inhabitants out and place them in relocation camps.

This film received Oscar nominations for picture, adapted screenplay, visual effects, and editing.

Sharlto Copley, Mandla Gaduka, Themba Nkosi

Sharlto Copley

Sharlto Copley

Sharlto Copley

Sharlto Copley

Sharlto Copley

Sharlto Copley

Sharlto Copley

© TriStar Pictures

Fujimoto, Ponyo

Gran Mamare

Lisa, Sosuke, Ponyo

Ponyo, Sosuke

PONYO

(WALT DISNEY PICTURES) a.k.a. *Gake no ue no Ponyo*; Producers, Frank Marshall, Kathleen Kennedy, Steve Alpert, Toshio Suzuki; Executive Producers, John Lasseter, Hayao Miyazaki, Koji Hoshino; Director/Screenplay, Hayao Miyazaki; Photography, Atsushi Okui; Art Director, Noboru Yoshida; Music, Joe Hisaishi; Editors, Hayao Miyazaki, Takeshi Seyama; Chief Animator, Matsuya Kondô; a Studio Ghibli Film; Japanese; Dolby; Color; Rated G; 101 minutes; American release date: August 14, 2009

VOICE CAST

Gran Mamare	**Cate Blanchett**
Ponyo	**Noah Cyrus**
Koichi	**Matt Damon**
Lisa	**Tina Fey**
Sosuke	**Frankie Jonas**
The Newscaster	**Kurt Knutsson**
Noriko	**Cloris Leachman**
Fujimoto	**Liam Neeson**
Kumiko	**Jennessa Rose**
Toki	**Lily Tomlin**
Yoshie	**Betty White**

A goldfish uses her father's magic to transform herself into a little girl who falls in love with the young son of a sailor.

Ponyo, Sosuke © Nibanki-GNDHDDT

CLOUD 9

(MUSIC BOX FILMS) a.k.a. *Wolke 9*; Producer, Peter Rommel; Director, Andreas Dresen; Screenplay, Andreas Dresen, Jörg Hauschild, Laila Stieler, Cooky Ziesche; Photography, Michael Hammon; Art Director, Susanne Hopf; Costumes, Sabine Greunig; Editor, Joerg Hauschild; a Rommel Film production, in association with Rundfunk Berlin-Brandenburg, Arte; German, 2008; Dolby; Color; Not rated; 97 minutes; American release date; August 14, 2009

CAST
Inge	**Ursula Wener**
Werner	**Horst Rehberg**
Karl	**Horst Westphal**
Petra	**Steffi Kühnert**

An elderly seamstress, married for over 30 years and bored with her husband's regimented life, has an affair with a client.

Horst Rehberg, Ursula Werner © Music Box Films

Ursula Werner, Horst Westphal

César Bordón, Maria Onetto © Strand Releasing

Maria Onetto

THE HEADLESS WOMAN

(STRAND) a.k.a. *La Mujer sin Cabeza*; Producers, Pedro Almodóvar, Agustin Almodóvar, Esther Garcia, Veronica Cura, Enrique Pineyro, Lucrecia Martel, Marianne Slot, Vieri Razzini, Cesare Petrillo, Tilde Corsi; Executive Producer, Veronica Cura; Director/Screenplay, Lucrecia Martel; Photography, Barbara Alvarez; Art Director, Maria Eugenia Sueiro; Costumes, Julio Suarez; Editor, Mugel Schverdfinger; an Aqua Films (Argentina)/El Deseo (Spain)/Slot Machine (France)/Teodora, R&C (Italy) production in association with Cine Argentino, Argeinta Cinema, ICAA, with the participation of Fonds Sud Cinema, Ministry of Culture and Communication (Agentina)/CNC, Ministry of Foreign and European Affairs (France); Argentine-Spanish-French-Italian, 2008; Dolby; Widescreen; Color; Not rated; 89 minutes; American release date: August 19, 2009

CAST
Veronica	**Maria Onetto**
Josefina	**Claudia Cantero**
Candita	**Inés Efron**
Juan Manuel	**Daniel Genoud**
Marcos	**César Bordón**
Marcelo	**Guillermo Arengo**
Tia Lala	**Maria Vaner**

A dentist who has hit a young boy with her car is haunted by her decision to not stop and offer help.

Moritz Bleibtreu, Johanna Wokalek

Moritz Bleibtreu

THE BAADER MEINHOF COMPLEX

(CONSTANTIN) a.k.a. *Der Baader Meinhof Komplex*; Producer, Bernd Eichinger; Executive Producer, Martin Moszkovicz; Co-Producers, Manuel Malle, Tomas Gabriss; Director, Uli Edel; Screenplay, Bernd Eichinger, Uli Edel; Based on the book by Stefan Aust; Photography, Rainer Klausmann; Designer, Bernd Lepel; Costumes, Birgit Missal; Music, Peter Hinderthür, Florian Tessloff; Editor, Alexander Berner; Casting, An Dorthe Braker; a Constantin Film/Bernd Eichinger presentation, in association with Nouvelles Editions de Films, G.T. Film Production, NDR, BR, WDR, Degeto; German, 2008; Dolby; Color; Not rated; 149 minutes; American release date: August 21, 2009

CAST

Ulrike Meinhof	**Martina Gedeck**
Andreas Baader	**Moritz Bleibtreu**
Gudrun Ensslin	**Johanna Wokalek**
Brigitte Mohnhaupt	**Nadja Uhl**
Peter Homann	**Jan Josef Liefers**
Holger Meins	**Stipe Erceg**
Jan Carl Raspe	**Niels-Bruno Schmidt**
Peter-Jürgen Boock	**Vinzez Kiefer**
Horst Mahler	**Simon Licht**
Petra Schelm	**Alexandra Maria Lara**

Hannah Herzsprung (Susanne Albrecht), Tom Schililng (Josef Bachmann), Daniel Lommatzsch (Christian Klar), Sebastian Blomberg (Rudi Dutschke), Eckhard Dilssner (Horst Bubeck), Heino Ferch (Horst Herold Assistant), Bruno Ganz (Horst Herold), Hans Werner Meyer (Klaus-Rainer Röhl), Katharina Wackernagel (Astrid), Anna Thalbach (Ingrid), Volker Bruch (Stefan Aust), Thomas Thieme (Richter Dr. Prinzing), Jasmin Tabatabai (Hanne), Susanne Bormann (Peggy), Gerald Alexander Held (Siegfried Buback), Michael Gwisdek (Gudrun's Father), Bernd Stegemann (Hanns Martin Schleyer), Hubert Mulzer (Jürgen Ponto), Annika Kuhl (Irmgard), Patrick von Blume (Herb), Sandra Borgmann (Ruth), Michael Schenk (Anwalt Hagemann), Hannes Wegener (Willy Peter Stoll), Johannes Suhm (Thorsten), Christian Schmidt (Paul), Stephan Möller-Titel (Thomas Lorenz), Jona Mues (Pranke), Elisabeth Schwarz (Gudrun's Mother), Britta Hemmelstein (Lisa), Christian Blümel (Siegfried Hausner), Jakob Diehl (Ulrich), Wolfgang Pregler (Stammheim), Christian Näthe (Kommunarde), Hassam Ghancy (Achmed), Marrtin Glade (Benno Ohnesorg), Nina Eichinger (Telefonistin), Sunnyi Melles (Fr. Buddenberg)

The true story of how a series of events gave birth to Germany's Red Army Faction in the late 1960's.

Nadja Uhl © Vitagraph Films

Stipe Erceg

FIVE MINUTES OF HEAVEN

(IFC FILMS) Producers, Eoin O'Callaghan, Stephen Wright; Executive Producers, Paul Trijbits, Francois Ivernel, Cameron McCracken, Ed Guiney, Andrew Lowe, Patrick Spence; Director, Oliver Hirschbiegel; Screenplay, Guy Hibbert; Photography, Ruairi O'Brien; Designer, Mark Lowry; Costumes, Maggie Donnelly; Music, David Holmes, Leo Abrahams; Editor, Hans Funch; Casting, Georgia Simpson; a Pathé Pictures, BBC and Northern Ireland Screen presentation with the participation of the Irish Film Board, of a Big Fish Films/Ruby Films production in association with Element Pictures; British-Irish; Color; Not rated; 89 minutes; American release date: August 21, 2009

CAST

Alistair Little	**Liam Neeson**
Joe Griffen	**James Nesbitt**
Vika	**Anamaria Marinca**
Michael	**Richard Dormer**
Young Alistair	**Mark Davison**
Young Joe	**Kevin O'Neill**

Juliet Crawford (Cathy), Niamh Cusack (Alistair's Mum), Gerry Doherty (Joe's Dad), Paul Garret (Alistair's Dad), Katy Gleadhill (Fiona), Jonathan Harden (David), Pauline Hutton (Sharon), Andrea Irvine (Sarah), Gerard Jordan (Jim), Paul Kennedy (Sound Recordist), Conor MacNeill (Dave), Mark Matthews (Martin, Cameraman), Matthew McElhinney (Stuart), Barry McEvoy (Joe's Chauffeur), Paula McFetridge (Joe's Mum), Diarmuid Noyes (Andy), Richard Orr (Alistair's Chauffeur), Lalor Roddy (Landlord)

33 years after his older brother was slain by a pro-England militant, Joe Griffen agrees to meet with the assassin in hopes of coming to an understanding.

Mark Davison

James Nesbitt, Liam Neeson © IFC Films

Jim Sturgess © Phase 4 Films

FIFTY DEAD MEN WALKING

(METRODOME GROUP) Producers, Peter La Terriere, Kari Skogland, Stephen Hegyes, Shawn Williamson; Executive Producers, Stephen Margolis, Guy Colilns, Michael Ryan, Nicole Carmen-Davis, Karyn Edwards, Kyle Lundberg, Cindy Cowan, Elsie Choi; Director/Screenplay, Kari Skogland; Based on the book by Nicholas Davies and Martin McGartland; Photography, Jonathan Freeman; Designer, Eve Stewart; Costumes, Stephanie Collie; Music, Ben Mink; Music Supervisor, Ian Neil; Editor, Jim Munro; Casting, John Hubbard; a Brightlight Pictures (Canada)/Future Films (U.K.) presentation; Canadian-British; Dolby; Color; Rated R; 118 minutes; American release date: August 21, 2009

CAST

Fergus	**Ben Kingsley**
Martin	**Jim Sturgess**
Sean	**Kevin Zegers**
Lara	**Natalie Press**
Grace	**Rose McGowan**
Mickey	**Tom Collins**
Ray	**William Houston**

Michael McElhatton (Robbie), Gerard Jordan (Kieran), David Pearse (Donovan), Joe Doyle (Quinn), Conor MacNeill (Frankie), Ewan & Oscar Harts (Little Patrick), Ciaran Nolan (Connie), Ali White (Lara's Mother), Frankie McCafferty (Paddy), Matt McArdle (Ambulance Attendant), Thomas O'Suilleabhain, Paul Kennedy (RUC Officers), Dessie Gallagher (Thomas, Head Officer), Kris Edlund (Mrs. Conlan), Sheila Kerr (Doris), Nick Dunning (Doctor), Pascal Friel (Jana), George McMahon (Johnny), Gavin O'Connor (Officer White), Gerry Doherty (Fred, CIO), Derek Halligan (McFarlane), James Doran (IRA Kidnapper), Michael Graham (Officer Clark), Anthony Brophy (Johnathan), Henry Deazley (Soldier), Nathan Hughes (Waiter), Karen Mason (Mother), Bridgid Erin Bates (Woman), Drew Thompson (Check Point Officer), Seamus Ball (Young Man's Father), Jonathan Harden (Young Man's Brother), Alexandra Ford (Nurse), Chris Patrick Simpson (Tortured Tout)

The true story of how Martin McGartland became an informant for the British in an effort to save men from being executed by the IRA.

STILL WALKING

(IFC FILMS) a.k.a. *Aruitemo aruitemo*; Producers, Yoshirio Kato, Hijiri Taguchi; Executive Producers, Kazumi Kawashiro, Yutaka Shigenobu, Takeo Hisamatsu, Bong-ou Lee; Director/Screenplay/Editor, Hirokazu Kore-eda; Photography, Yutaka Yamasaki; Designer, Toshihiro Isomi, Keiko Mitsumatsu; Costumes, Kazuko Kurosawa; Music, Gontiti; a Cine Qua Non production; Japanese, 2008; Color; Not rated; 114 minutes; American release date: August 28, 2009

CAST
Ryota Yokoyama	**Hiroshi Abe**
Yukari Yokoyama, Ryota's Wife	**Yui Natsukawa**
Chinami Kataoka	**You**
Nobuo Kataoka	**Kazuya Takahashi**
Atsushi Yokiyam, Ryota's son	**Shohei Tanaka**
Toshiko Yokoyama	**Kirin Kiki**
Kyohei Yokoyama	**Yoshio Harada**

Unsettled issues arise during the Yokoyama's annual gathering to commemorate the passing of their eldest son.

Kirin Kiki, Hiroshi Abe

Yui Natsukawa, Kirin Kiki, Shohei Tanaka, Hiroshi Abe © IFC Films

Michiel Huisman, Déborah François

Déborah François, Fernando Tielve © IFC Films

UNMADE BEDS

(IFC FILMS) Producers, Soledad Gatti-Pascual, Peter Ettedgui; Executive Producers, Peter Carlton, Lizzie Francke; Co-Producers, Al Clark, Rachel Robey, Alex O'Neal; Director/Screenplay, Alexis Dos Santos; Photography, Jackob Ihre; Designer, Kristian Milsted; Costumes, Kate Forbes; Music Supervisor, Valentina Brazzini; Editor, Olivier Bugge Coutte; Casting, Shaheen Baig; a Film4, U.K. Film Council, EM Media presentation, in association with Natixis Coficine, of a production from the Bureau; British; Dolby; Color; HD-to-35mm; Not rated; 96 minutes; American release date: September 2, 2009

CAST
Axl	**Fernando Tielve**
Vera	**Déborah François**
X Ray Man	**Michiel Huisman**
Mike	**Iddo Goldberg**
Anthony Hemmings	**Richard Lintern**
Hannah	**Katia Winter**
Lucas	**Leonardo Brzezicki**
Alejos	**Alexis Dos Santos**

Lucy Tillet (Lucy), Al Weaver (Kevin), Valentina Brazzini (Young Woman Wearing Underwear), Johnny Lambe (Young Man wearing Underwear), Tim Plester (Bookshop Customer), Anders Berg (Guitar Man in Broadway Market), Florencia Braier (Girl with Spectacles), Sinead Dosset (Alice), Rosie Edwards (Alice's Sister), Kate Forbes (Costume Girl), Kai Milsted (Alice's Friend), Mufadzi Nkomo (Alice's Friend's Mum), Sotiris Panopoulos (Guitar Player), Daniel Smith (Young Axl), Yannis Tsitsovits (Young Man in Pub), Heather Wright (Estate Agent), Sharon Young (Alice's Mum)

Young Axl treks from Spain to London in hopes of finding the British father he never knew.

BRIGHT STAR

(APPARITION) Producers, Jan Chapman, Caroline Hewitt; Executive Producers, Francois Ivernel, Cameron McCracken, Christine Langan, David M. Thompson; Director/ Screenplay, Jane Campion; From the biography *Keats* by Andrew Motion; Photography, Greig Fraser; Designer/Costumes, Janet Patterson; Music, Mark Bradsaw; Editor, Alexandre de Franceschi; Makeup/Hair, Konnie Daniel; Casting, Nina Gold; a Pathé Pictures, Screen Australia, BBC Films and the UK Film Council presentation in association with the New South Wales Film and Television Office and Hopscotch International of a Jan Chapman production in association with Caroline Hewitt; British-Australian; Dolby; Color; Rated PG; 119 minutes; American release date: September 16, 2009

Ben Whishaw, Abbie Cornish

CAST

Fanny Brawne	**Abbie Cornish**
John Keats	**Ben Whishaw**
Charles Armitage Brown	**Paul Schneider**
Mrs. Brawne	**Kerry Fox**
Joseph Severn	**Samuel Barnett**
Margaret "Toots" Brawne	**Edie Martin**
Samuel Brawne	**Thomas Sangster**
Maria Dilke	**Claudie Blakley**
Charles Dilke	**Gerard Monaco**
Abigail O'Donaghue Brown	**Antonia Campbell-Hughes**
Shop Keeper	**Roger Ashton-Griffiths**
John Reynolds	**Samuel Roukin**
Tom Keats	**Olly Alexander**
Mr. Haslam	**Sebastian Armesto**
Dilke Maid	**Joyia Fitch**
Charles Dilke Jr.	**Alfred Harmsworth**
Leigh Hunt	**Jonathan Aris**

Adrian Schiller (Mr. Taylor), Sam Gaukroger (Messenger Boy), Sally Reeve (Landlady), Will Garthwaite (Human Orchestra), Amanda Hale, Lucinda Raikes (Reynolds Sisters), Theresa Watson (Charlotte), Vincent Franklin (Dr. Bree), Eileen Davies (Mrs. Bentley), Lucas Motion (Suitor at Ball)

The true story of the final years of poet John Keats and his relationship with Fanny Brawne.

Abbie Cornish, Ben Whishaw

Ben Whishaw

Abbie Cornish © Apparition

35 SHOTS OF RUM

(CINEMA GUILD) a.k.a. *35 rhums*; Producer, Bruno Pesery; Co-Producers, Christophe Friedel, Claudia Steffen; Director, Claire Denis; Screenplay, Claire Denis, Jean-Pol Fargeau; Photography, Agnes Godard; Designer, Arnaud de Moleron; Costumes, Judy Shrewsbury; Music, Tindersticks; Editor, Guy Lecorne; Casting, Nicolas Ronchi; a Soudaine Compagnie (France)/Pandora Film (Germany)/ARTE France Cinema (France) production, in association with WDR/ARTE, Cofinova 4, Sofica Soficinema 4, with the participation of Canal Plus, TPS Star; French; Dolby; Color; Not rated; 102 minutes; American release date: September 16, 2009

CAST

Lionel	**Alex Descas**
Joséphine	**Mati Diop**
Noé	**Grégoire Colin**
Gabrielle	**Nicole Dogué**
Ruben	**Jean-Christophe Folly**
Martial	**Djédjé Apali**
Blanchard	**Eriq Ebouaney**

Ingrid Caven (German Aunt), Stéphane Pocrain (Professor), Julieth Mars Toussiant (René), Adele Ado (Bar Patron), Mary Pie (Lina), Cheikh Toure (Young Waiter), David Saada (Cowboy), Mario Canonge (Colleague)

The close relationship between metro conductor Lionel and his daughter Josephine reaches an impasse when the father finds himself drawn to another tenant in their building and the daughter starts spending time with a handsome neighbor.

Grégoire Colin, Mati Diop © Cinema Guild

Mati Diop, Alex Descas

Jessica Haines, John Malkovich

John Malkovich © Paladin

DISGRACE

(FORTISSIMO/PALADIN) Producers, Anna-Maria Monticelli, Emile Sherman, Steve Jacobs; Executive Producers, Julio DePietro, Wouter Barendrecht, Michael J. Werner; Co-Producers, Brigid Olen, Marlow De Mardt; Director, Steve Jacobs; Screenplay, Anna-Maria Monticelli; Based on the novel by J.M. Coetzee; Photography, Steve Arnold; Designers, Mike Berg, Annie Beauchamp; Music, Antony Partos, Graeme Koehne; Editor, Alexandre De Franceshi; a Fortissimo Films/Film Finance Corp. Australia presentation of a Wild Strawberries, Sherman Pictures, Disgrace production, in association with New South Wales Film and Television Office, the South Australia Film Corp, Do Prods.; Australian-South African; Dolby; Widescreen; Color; Not rated; 118 minutes; American release date: September 18, 2009

CAST

David Lurie	**John Malkovich**
Lucy	**Jessica Haines**
Petrus	**Eriq Ebouaney**
Melanie Isaacs	**Antoinette Engel**
Dr. Rasool	**Paula Arundell**
Ryan	**Charles Tertiens**

A poetry professor forced to resign from his university after an affair with a student, finds his world further shattered when he visits his daughter's Eastern Cape farm where the two of them are attacked by three local youths.

Juliette Binoche, Romain Duris

Juliette Binoche and children

Mélanie Laurent, Fabrice Luchini © IFC Films

PARIS

(IFC FILMS) Producer, Bruno Levy; Director/Screenplay, Cédric Klapisch; Photography, Christophe Beaucarne; Designer, Marie Cheminal; Costumes, Anne Schotte; Music, Loik Dury, Robert "Chicken" Burke; Editor, Francine Sandberg; a Ce Qui Me Meut, Studio Canal, Studio Canal Image, France 2 Cinema production, in association with Une Etoile 4, with the participation of Canal Plus France, TPS Star; French; Dolby; Panavision; Color; Not rated; 130 minutes; American release date: September 18, 2009

CAST
Elise	**Juliette Binoche**
Pierre	**Romain Duris**
Roland Verneuil	**Fabrice Luchini**
Jean	**Albert Dupontel**
Philippe Verneuil	**François Cluzet**
The Baker	**Karin Viard**
Franky	**Gilles Lellouche**
Laetitia	**Mélanie Laurent**
Mourad	**Zinedine Soualem**
Caroline	**Julie Ferrier**
Diane	**Olivia Bonamy**
The Psychiatrist	**Maurice Benichou**
Victoire	**Annelise Hesme**
Marjolaine	**Audrey Marnay**

Xavier Robic (TV Presenter), Farida Khelfa (Farida), Suzanne von Aichinger (Suzy "Miss Bidoche"), Marco Prince (Disco), Kingsley Kum Abang (Benoît), Judith El Zein (Mélanie Verneuil), Emmanuel Quatra (Grand Nanar), Nelly Antignac (Rachel), Joffrey Plaetl (Rémy), Renée Le Calm (Madame Renée), Sabrina Quaziani (Khadija)

A cabaret performer suffering from a fatal heart problem bonds with his sister and her children; a street vendor wonders about his future without his wife; and a professor longs for one last romance.

Romain Duris

George MacKay, Nicholas McAnulty, Clive Owen

George MacKay, Clive Owen, Nicholas McAnulty © Miramax Films

Nicholas McAnulty, Clive Owen

THE BOYS ARE BACK

(MIRAMAX) Producers, Greg Brenman, Tim White; Executive Producers, Peter Bennett-Jones, Clive Owen, David M. Thompson, Jane Wright; Co-Producer, Bella Wright; Director, Scott Hicks; Screenplay, Allan Cubitt; Based on the memoir *The Boys are Back in Town* by Simon Carr; Photography, Greig Fraser; Designer, Melinda Doring; Costumes, Emily Seresin; Music, Hal Lindes; Music Supervisors, Ian Neil, Chris Gough; Casting, Nikki Barrett, Nina Gold; a Tiger Aspect Pictures (U.K.) production, in association with Southern Light Films, presented in association with BBC Films (U.K.)/Screen Australia, South Australian Film Corp., Hopscotch Prods. (Australia); Australian-British; Dolby; Panavision; Color; Rated PG-13; 103 minutes; American release date: September 18, 2009

CAST

Joe Warr	**Clive Owen**
Laura	**Emma Booth**
Katy	**Laura Fraser**
Harry	**George MacKay**
Artie	**Nicholas McAnulty**
Barbara	**Julia Blake**
Tom	**Chris Haywood**
Digby	**Erik Thomson**
Flick	**Natasha Little**
Tim Walker	**Lewis Fitz-Gerald**
Lucy	**Nakia Pires**
Mia	**Emma Lung**

Steven Robertson (School Housemaster), Georgina Naidu (Paula), Daniel Carter, Adriana Conde, Chantal Dwarka, Connor Marinos, Elysia Markou, Briana Richards (Digby & Paula's Children), Donna Lean (Artie's Teacher), Johnny Frisina (Goldfish Boy), Cody Faucett (Kangaroo Boy), Nathan Page (Headbutter), Kate Roberts (School Secretary), Luke O'Loughlin (Bree), Susie Collins (Newspaper Office PA), Michael Allen, Andy Ciencela (Men on Beach), Eliza Lovell, Grace Sodeman (Eliza Lovell), Rainey Mayo, Alexandra Schepisi (Birthday Party Mothers), Anni Finsterer (Tennis Journalist), Susie Small (Smart Party Hostess), Sanjaya Patterson (Nurse), Lizzy Falkland, Susie Fraser, Ezra Juanta, Adam Morgan, Nick Pelomis, Terry Rogers (Editorial Meeting Journalists), Krystle Sansom (Beach Girl), Kassandra Clementi, William Cox, Tim Giessauf, Klayton Stainer (Beach Kids), Tommy Bastow, Rupert Simonian (Harry's Friends)

Following the tragic death of his wife, sports writer Joe Warr attempts to raise his two young sons with a minimum of restrictions.

Nicholas McAnulty, Clive Owen, Emma Booth

COCO BEFORE CHANEL

(SONY CLASSICS) Producers, Caroline Benjo, Carole Scotta, Philippe Carcassonne, Simon Arnal; Director, Anne Fontaine; Screenplay, Anne Fontaine, Camille Fontaine, Christopher Hampton, Jacques Fieschi; Based on the book *L'irreguliere, ou mon itineraire Chanel* by Edmonde Charles-Roux; Photography, Christophe Beaucarne; Designer, Olivier Radot; Costumes, Catherine Leterrier; Music, Alexandre Desplat; Editor, Luc Barnier; Casting, Brigitte Moidon; a Haut & Court, Cine@, Warners Bros. Entertainment France, France 2 Cinema production, in association with Films Distribution, Cofinova 5, Banque Populaire Images 9, Scope Pictures, with the participation of Canal Plus, CineCinema, France 2; French; Dolby; Panavision; Color; Rated PG-13; 105 minutes; Release date: September 25, 2009

Audrey Tautou, Marie Gillain

CAST

Gabrielle "Coco" Chanel	**Audrey Tautou**
Étienne Balsan	**Benoît Poelvoorde**
Arthur "Boy" Capel	**Alessandro Nivola**
Adrienne Chanel	**Marie Gillain**
Emilienne d'Alençon	**Emmanuelle Devos**
Alec, a Jockey	**Régis Royer**
Balsan Hotel Maitre d'	**Etienne Bartholomeus**
Maurice of Nexon	**Yan Duffas**
Boutique Patron	**Fabien Béhar**
Jean	**Roch Leibovici**
Cafe Director	**Jean-Yves Chatelais**
Theater Actor	**Pierre Diot**
Big Theater Man	**Vincent Nemeth**
Deauville Tailor	**Bruno Abraham-Kremer**
Gabrielle, 10 years old	**Lisa Cohen**
Adrienne, 10 years old	**Inès Bessalem**

Marie-Bénédicte Roy (Boutique Client), Emilie Gavois-Kahn (Replacement Couturière), Fanny Deblock (Balsan Prostitute), Claude Brécourt (Alcazar Director), Karina Marimon (Girl), Bruno Paviot, Franck Monsigny (Balsan Guests), Marie Parouty (Sophie, Emilenne's Friend), Jean-Chrétien Sibertin-Blanc (Raymond), Marie-Josée Hubert (Chef), Patrick Laviosa (Pianist), Kim Schwarck (Dressing Room Girl)

Emmanuelle Devos, Audrey Tautou

The true story of how Gabrielle "Coco" Chanel worked her way from provincial seamstress to the top of the Parisian fashion scene.

This film received an Oscar nomination for costume design.

Benoît Poelvoorde, Audrey Tautou © Sony Pictures Classics

Alessandro Nivola, Audrey Tautou

AN EDUCATION

(SONY CLASSICS) Producers, Finola Dwyer, Amanda Posey; Executive Producers, David M. Thompson, Jamie Laurenson, Nick Hornby, James D. Stern, Douglas E. Hansen, Wendy Japhet; Director, Lone Scherfig; Screenplay, Nick Hornby; Based on a memoir by Lynn Barber; Photography, John de Borman; Designer, Andrew McAlpine; Costumes, Odile Dicks-Mireaux; Music, Paul Englishby; Music Supervisor, Kle Savidge; Casting, Lucy Bevan; a BBC Films presentation of a Wildgaze Films/Finola Dwyer production in association with Endgame Entertainment; British; Dolby; Super 35 Widescreen; Deluxe color; Rated PG-13; 100 minutes; American release date: October 9, 2009

CAST

David Goldman	**Peter Sarsgaard**
Jenny Mellor	**Carey Mulligan**
Jack Mellor	**Alfred Molina**
Danny	**Dominic Cooper**
Helen	**Rosamund Pike**
Miss Stubbs	**Olivia Williams**
Headmistress	**Emma Thompson**
Marjorie Mellor	**Cara Seymour**
Graham	**Matthew Beard**
Sarah	**Sally Hawkins**
Hattie	**Amanda Fairbank-Hynes**
Tina	**Ellie Kendrick**
Small Boys	**William Melling, Connor Catchpole**
Auctioneer	**Nick Sampson**
Latin Teacher	**Kate Duchêne**
Small Girl	**Bel Parker**
Rachman	**Luis Soto**
Shakespeare Girls	**Olenka Wrzesniewski, Bryony Wadsworth**
Petrol Attendant	**Ashley Taylor-Rhys**
Student	**James Norton**
Nightclub Singer	**Beth Rowley**

Ben Castle, Mark Edwards, Tom Rees-Roberts, Arne Somogyi, Paul Wilkinson, Phil Wilkinson (Nightclub Band)

A cloistered teenage girl, longing to experience the pleasures of life, is befriended by a charming older man who provides her with just the kind of education she is looking for.

This film received Oscar nominations for picture, actress (Carey Mulligan), and adapted screenplay.

Carey Mulligan Peter Sarsgaard

Carey Mulligan © Sony Pictures Classics

Dominic Cooper, Peter Sarsgaard

Carey Mulligan, Peter Sarsgaard

Ellie Kendrick, Amanda Fairbank-Hynes, Carey Mulligan

Emma Thompson

Alfred Molina, Cara Seymour, Carey Mulligan, Peter Sarsgaard

Olivia Williams

Rosamund Pike, Dominic Cooper

Carey Mulligan

THE DAMNED UNITED

(SONY CLASSICS) Producer, Andy Harries; Executive Producers, Christine Langan, Hugo Heppell, Peter Morgan; Co-Producers, Grainne Marmion, Lee Morris; Director, Tom Hooper; Screenplay, Peter Morgan, based on the novel *The Damned Utd* by David Peace; Photography, Ben Smithard; Designer, Eve Stewart; Costumes, Mike O'Neill; Music, Rob Lane; Music Supervisor, Liz Gallacher; Editor, Melanie Oliver; Casting, Dan Hubbard; a Columbia Pictures, BBC Films presentation, in association with Screen Yorkshire of a Left Bank Pictures production; British; Dolby; Panavision; Color; Rated R; 97 minutes; American release date: October 9, 2009

CAST

Brian Clough	**Michael Sheen**
Peter Taylor	**Timothy Spall**
Don Revie	**Colm Meaney**
Manny Cussins	**Henry Goodman**
Jimmy Gordon	**Maurice Roëves**
Sam Longson	**Jim Broadbent**
Billy Bremner	**Stephen Graham**
Dave Mackay	**Brian McCardie**
Johnny Giles	**Peter McDonald**
Colin Todd	**Giles Alderson**
John O'Hare	**Martin Compston**

Joe Dempsie (Duncan McKenzie), Elizabeth Carling (Barbara Clough). Gillian Waugh (Lillian Taylor), David Roper (Sam Bolton), Jimmy Reddington (Keith Archer), Oliver Stokes (Nigel Clough), Mark Bazeley (Austin Mitchell), Mark Cameron (Norman Hunter), Frank Skillin (Young Nigel Clough), Dylan Van Hoof (Younger Simon Clough), Sydney Wade (Younger Elizabeth Clough), Mark Jameson (Groundsman), Liam Thomas (Les Cocker), Glyn Cunningham (Syd Owen), Tony Gubba, Sir Michael Parkinson, John Craven (Themselves), Stewart Robertson (Archie Gemmill), Laurie Rea (Terry Hennessey), Ralph Ineson (Journalist), Philip Childs (Commentator, Wembley), Terence Harvey (FA Committee Chairman), Gordon Hall (FA White Haired Elder), Isabella Eades-Jones (Elizabeth Clough), Paul Brown (Mike Bamber), Christopher Chilton (Floor Manager), Christophe Boulstridge (Colin Boulton), Bill Bradshaw (Terry Yorath), Damian Broadbent (Emlyn Hughes), Wayne Ewart (Tommy Smith), Stuart Gray (Eddie Gray), Alex Harker (Allan Clarke), Colin Harris (John McGovern), Nathan Head (Photographer), Carl Hicken (Alec Lindsay – Liverpool), Tomasz Kocinski (Roy McFarland), James MacColl (Luton Town Player), Lesley Maylett (Paul Reaney), Ben McFarlane (Kevin Keegan), Chris Moore (Paul Madeley), Stephen Nicholas (Alan Durban), Paul O'Brien (Phil Thompson), Tom Ramsbottom (Trevor Cherry), Alex Rogerson (Phil Boersma), John Savage (Gordon McQueen), Matthew Storton (Peter Lorimer), Danny Tomlinson (David Harvey), Keiran Waite (Ron Webster), Craig Williams (Joe Jordan)

The true story of how Brian Clough went from managing the Derby County soccer team to overseeing their rivals, Leeds United.

Colm Meaney

Jim Broadbent © Sony Pictures Classics

Timothy Spall, Michael Sheen

Peter McDonald, Stephen Graham, Mark Cameron

Lucy Punch (center) © NeoClassics Films

ST. TRINIAN'S

(NEOCLASSICS) Producers, Oliver Parker, Barnaby Thompson; Executive Producers, Nigel Green, Rupert Everett, James Spring; Co-Producer, Mark Hubbard; Directors, Oliver Parker, Barnaby Thompson; Screenplay, Piers Ashworth, Nick Moorcroft; Inspired by the original drawings of Ronald Searle and based on the motion picture *The Belles of St. Trinian's* directed by Frank Launder, with a screenplay by Launder, Sidney Gilliat, Val Valentine; Photography, Gavin Finney; Designer, Amanda McArthur; Costumes, Rebecca Hale; Music, Charlie Mole; Music Supervisor, Ian Neil; Editor, Alex Mackie; Special Effects Supervisor, Mark Holt; Casting, Lucy Bevan; an Entertainment Film, Ealing Studios, U.K. Film Council presentation of a Fragile Films production; British, 2007; Dolby; Technicolor; Rated PG-13; 100 minutes; American release date: October 9, 2009

CAST
Annabelle Fritton	**Talulah Riley**
Camilla Fritton/Carnaby Fritton	**Rupert Everett**
Beverly	**Jody Whittaker**
Kelly	**Gemma Arterton**
Taylor	**Kathryn Drysdale**
Celia	**Juno Temple**
Chloe	**Antonia Bernath**
Peaches	**Amara Karan**
Chelsea	**Tamsin Egerton**
Geoffrey Thwaites	**Colin Firth**
Miss Dickinson	**Lena Headey**

Lily Cole (Polly), Paloma Faith (Andrea), Holly Mackie (Tara), Cloe Mackie (Tania), Esme Thompson (1st Year Bookie), Bel Parker (Aerial Girl), Celia Imrie (Matron), Fenella Woolgar (Miss Cleaver), Theo Cross (Art Teacher), Russell Brand (Flash), Tereza Srbova (Anoushka), Toby Jones (Bursar), Caterina Murino (Miss Maupassant), James Rawlings (Press Secretary), Ben Willbond (Damaged Inspector), Emily Bevan, John Thompson (Inspectors), Lucy Punch (Verity Thwaites), Anna Chancellor (Miss Bagstock), Millie Foster (Saffron), Steve Furst (Bank Manager), Preston Thompson (Boy at the Party), Mischa Barton (JJ French), Stephen Fry (Himself), Cato Sandford, Jonathan Bailey (Bedales Pupils), Arthur Campbell (Eton Pupil), Denis Stephenson (Denise), Andrew Buckley, Jody Halse (Guards), Richard Glover (Floor Runner), Jeremy Thompson (Sky Newscaster), Nathaniel Parker (Chairman of the National Gallery), Cheryl Cole, Nadine Cole, Sarah Harding, Nicola Roberts, Kimberley Walsh (School Band Members)

Annabelle Fritton arrives at the unorthodox St. Trinian's girls school where she finds herself participating in a heist of a valuable painting in order to save the institution from bankruptcy. Previous films in the series: *The Belles of St. Triniain's* (1954), *Blue Murder at St. Trinian's* (1957), *The Pure Hell of St. Trinian's* (1960), *The Great St. Trinian's Train Robbery* (1966), and *The Wildcats of St. Trinian's* (1980).

BRONSON

(MAGNET) Producers, Rupert Preston, Danny Hansford; Executive Producers, Allan Niblo, James Richardson, Nick Love, Rob Morgan, Simon Fawcett, Suzanne Alizart, Kate Ogborn, Paul Martin, Thor Sigurjonsson; Director, Nicolas Winding Refn; Screenplay, Brock Norman Brock, Nicolas Winding Refn; Photography, Larry Smith; Music Supervisor, Lol Hammond; Editor, Mat Newman; Stunts, Julian Spencer; Casting, Des Hamilton; a Vertigo Films presentation in association with Aramid Entertainment, Str8jacket Creations, EM Media/4DH Film; British; Color; Rated R; 92 minutes; American release date: October 9, 2009

CAST
Michael Peterson ("Charles Bronson")	**Tom Hardy**
Paul Daniels	**Matt King**
Phil, Art Teacher	**James Lance**
Irene	**Kelly Adams**
Mum	**Amanda Burton**
Julie	**Katy Barker**
Brian	**Edward Bennett-Coles**

William Darke (Michael Peterson, age 13), Andrew Forbes (Joe Peterson), China-Black Black [aka Helen Grayson], June Bladon, Kate Hesketh, Leah Hinton-Fishlock, Jane McLennan (Uncle Jack's Party Guests), Anna Griffin (Train Girl), Mandy Kay (Boxing Crowd Member), Matt Legg, Brendan McCoy, Dean Spicksley (Prisoners), Juliet Oldfield (Alison), Hugh Ross (Uncle Jack), Mark Stocks (Gangster), Joe Tucker (John White)

The true story of how a robbery placed Michael Peterson behind bars for over 30 years, turning him from a rebellious youth into a brutal convict calling himself "Charles Bronson."

Tom Hardy © Magnet Releasing

Claudia Celedón

Catalina Saavedra

Catalina Saavedra © Elephant Eye Films

THE MAID

(ELEPHANT EYE) a.k.a. *La nana*; Producer, Gregorio Gonzalez; Director, Sebastián Silva; Screenplay, Sebastián Silva, Pedro Peirano; Photography, Sergio Armstrong; Art Director, Pablo Gonzalez; Editor, Danielle Fillios; a Forastero, Diroriro presentation, in association with Tiburón Filmes, Punto Guion Punto Prodcucciones; Chilean; Dolby; HD; Color; Not rated; 96 minutes; American release date: October 16, 2009

CAST
Raquel	Catalina Saavedra
Pilar	Claudia Celedón
Mundo	Alejandro Goic
Camila	Andrea Garcia-Huidobro
Lucy	Mariana Loyola
Lucas	Augustin Silva
Tomás	Darok Orellana
Gabriel	Sebastián La Rivera
Mercedes	Mercedes Villanueva
Sonia	Anita Reeves

Delfina Guzmán (Abuela), Luis Dubó (Eric), Luis Muñoz (Raúl), Andreina Olivari (Javiera), Gloria Canales (Lucy's Mother), Luis Wigdorsky (Lucy's Father), Juan Pablo Larenas (Rodrigo)

An efficient but emotionally reserved domestic takes charge of the household of a Latin American family, tolerating no interference in her desire to do things her way and her way only.

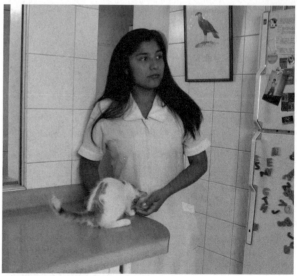

Mercedes Villanueva

THE LITTLE TRAITOR

(WESTCHESTER FILMS) Producers, Eitan Evan, Lynn Roth; Executive Producer, Marilyn Hall; Director/Screenplay, Lynn Roth; based on the novel *Panther in the Basement* by Amos Oz; Photography, Amnon Zalait; Art Director, Ido Dolev; Costumes, Inbal Shuki; Music, Deborah Lurie; Editors, Danny Shik, Michael Ruscio; Casting, Hila Yuval; an Evanstone Films/Panther production; Israeli-American; Color; Not rated; 89 minutes; American release date: October 16, 2009

CAST
Dunlop	**Alfred Molina**
Proffy	**Ido Port**
Proffy's Father	**Rami Heuberger**
Miriam	**Gilya Stern**
Security Officer	**Theodore Bikel**

Jake Barker (Chaim Zosoma), Vivian Brunstein (British Soldier), Levana Finkelstein (Grandmother Tykocinski), Anat Klausner (Yardena), Boris Reinis (Chita's Fatehr), Lior Sasson (Mr. Hochberg), Ofer Shechter (Sergeant)

A 12-year-old boy growing up in 1947 Palestine during the British occupation finds himself unexpectedly befriending an English sergeant.

Anat Klausner, Rami Heuberger, Ido Port, Gilya Stern

Alfred Molina, Ido Port © Westchester Films Inc.

Park Eun-hye, Kim Yeong-ho

Park Eun-hye, Kim Yeong-ho © IFC Films

NIGHT AND DAY

(IFC FILMS) a.k.a. *Bam gua nat*; Producers, Gang Dong-gu, Ellen Kim; Executive Producers, Michel Cho, Oh Jeong-wan; Director/Screenplay, Hong Sang-soo; Photography, Kim Hun-gwang; Music, Jeong Yong-jin; Editor, Ham Seong-weon; a KTB Investments, Korean Film Council, Cheongeoram presentation of a B.O.M. film Prods. production; South Korean, 2008; Dolby; Color; Not rated; 145 minutes; American release date: October 23, 2009

CAST
Kim Sung-nam	**Kim Yeong-ho**
Mr. Jang	**Kee Ju-bong**
Jang Minsun	**Kim Youjin**
Cho Hyunju	**Seo Min-jong**
Han Sungin	**Hwang Su-jeong**
Yoon Gyoungsu	**Lee Seon-gyun**
Lee Yujeong	**Park Eun-hye**
Jung Jihye	**Jung Jihye**

Fleeing from the Seoul police, Seong-nam ends up in Paris among other expatriate Koreans.

ANTICHRIST

(IFC FILMS) Producers, Meta Louise Foldager; Executive Producers, Peter Aalbaek Jensen, Peter Garde; Co-Producers, Lars Jonsson, Madeleine Ekman, Andrea Occipinti, Malorzata Szumowska, Ole Ostergaard; Executive Co-Producers, Bettina Brokemper, Marianne Slot; Director/Screenplay, Lars von Trier; Photography, Anthony Dod Mantle; Designer, Karl "Kalli" Juliusson; Costumes, Frauke Firl; Editor, Anders Refn; Visual Effects Supervisor, Peter Hjorth; a Zentropa Entertainments (Denmark) presentation of a Zentropa Intl. Köln (Germany)/ Slot Machine (France)/Memfis Film (Sweden)/Trollhättan Film AB (Sweden)/ Lucky Red (Italy)/Zentropa Intl. Poland co-production, presented in cooperation with Danmarks Radio, Filmstiftung Nordrhein-Westfalen, Arte France Cinéma, ZDF-Arte Group Grand Accord, ARTE, Film i Väst, Sveriges Television; Danish-German-French-Swedish-Italian-Polish; Dolby; Widescreen; Color; Not rated; 105 minutes; American release date: October 23, 2009

CAST
He   **Willem Dafoe**
She   **Charlotte Gainsbourg**

Devastated by the accidental death of their child, which occurred while they engaged in sex, a couple escapes to a cabin in the woods, where they proceed to exorcise their demons and address their guilt in a horrific and masochistic display of self-punishment.

Charlotte Gainsbourg © IFC Films

Charlotte Gainsbourg, Willem Dafoe

Willem Dafoe, Charlotte Gainsbourg

Tony Kgoroge, Sophie Okonedo

Sophie Okonedo, Tony Kgoroge © Jour de Fete

Ella Ramangwane

SKIN

(ELYSIAN FILMS) Producers, Anthony Fabian, Genevieve Hofmeyr, Margaret Matheson; Executive Producers, Simon Fawcett, Robbie Little, Laurence Paltiel, Alasdair MacCuish, Moses Silinda, Hellen Kalenga; Director, Anthony Fabian; Screenplay, Helen Crawley, Jessie Keyt, Helena Kriel; Photography, Dewald Aukema, Jonathan Partridge; Designer, Billy Keam; Costumes, Fotini Dimou; Music, Helene Muddiman; Editor, St. John O'Rorke; Casting, Christa Schamberger, Ana Feyder; an Elysian, Bard (U.K.)/Moonlighting (South Africa) production, in association with Aramid Entertainment, Industrial Development Corp. of South Africa, National Film & Video Foundation of South Africa, Lip Sync Prods.; British-South African, 2008; Dolby; Widescreen; Color; Rated PG-13; 107 minutes; American release date: October 30, 2009

CAST

Sandra Laing	**Sophie Okonedo**
Abraham Laing	**Sam Neill**
Sannie Laing	**Alice Krige**
Petrus Zwane	**Tony Kgoroge**
Young Sandra	**Ella Ramangwane**
Nora Molefe	**Faniswa Yisa**
Leon Laing	**Hannes Brummer**

Zoea Alberts (Shower Girl), Nomathamsanga Baleka (Factory Worker's Friend), Graeme Bloch (Bailiff), Ruaan Bok (Young Henry), Ben Botha (Dawie), Charlotte Butler (Woman #2), Tongai Arnold Chirisa (Young Priest), Onida Cowan (Miss Uys), Jeremy Crutchely (WNN Reporter), Lauren Das Neves (Elize), Jose Domingos, Nicole Regelous, Danie Struwig (Journalists), Terri Ann Eckstein (Elsie Laing), Nomkhosi Gidigidi (Maid in Pretoria), Jacques Gombault (Bearded Teacher), Kyle Grant (French Boy), Jakkie Groenewald (White Foreman), Lourens Groenewald (Willy Meyer), Nicole Holme (Miss Ludik), Danny Keogh (Van Tonder), Charmaine Kweyama (Fat Civil Servant), Mpho Lekalakala, Hector Rabopaphe (Swazi Cops), Matthew Lotter (Abusive Teen), Gladys Mahlangu (Sangoma), Bongani Masondo (Henry Laing), Simon Mdokhi (Joseph), Stephen Mofokeng (Black Gardener), Tumi Morake (Thembi), Ivy Nkutha (Drunk Woman), Nomhlé Nkyonyeni (Jenny Zwane), Burger Nortje (Fat Boy), Jonathan Pienaar (Van Niekerk), Fiona Ramsey (Woman at Church), Tiaan Rautenbach (Tall Policeman), Roland Read (Classmate), Dan Robbertse (Factory Forman), Duan Saayman (Cobus), Stacey Sachs (Thin Secretary), Elizabeth Serunye (Woman in Shop), Saint Seseli (Black Clerk), Malusi Skenjana (Minivan Driver), Valesika Smith (Factory Worker), Andre Stoltz (White Clerk), Elriza Swanepoel (Tiny Woman), Jonathan Taylor (Sound Recordist), Carel Trichardt (Magistrate), Leana Truitsman (Annie), Anna-Mart van der Merwe (Anna Roux), Karien Van Der Merwe (Nurse Beukes), Gordon Van Rooyen (Judge Galgut), Cobus Venter (Johann), Morne Visser (Dr. Sparks), Drikus Volschenk (Forced Removal Policeman), Kate-Lyn Von Meyer (Young Elsie), Khalem Willet (Adriaan Laing)

The true story of Sandra Laing, a South African who was born with black pigmentation and features to a white couple.

Alice Krige, Ella Ramangwane, Sam Neill

PIRATE RADIO

(FOCUS) a.k.a. *The Boat That Rocked*; Producers, Tim Bevan, Eric Fellner, Hilary Bevan Jones; Executive Producers, Richard Curtis, Debra Hayward, Liza Chasin; Director/Screenplay, Richard Curtis; Photography, Danny Cohen; Designer, Mark Tildesley; Costumes, Joanna Johnston; Music Supervisor, Nick Angel; Editor, Emma E. Hickox; Make-up/Hair Designer, Christine Blundell; Casting, Fiona Weir; a Working Title (U.K.) production, in association with Medienproduktion Prometheus Filmgesellschaft, presented in association with StudioCanal; British-German-American-French; Dolby; Color; Rated R; 116 minutes; American release date: November 13, 2009

Gemma Arterton, Nick Frost

CAST

The Count	**Philip Seymour Hoffman**
Quentin	**Bill Nighy**
Gavin	**Rhys Ifans**
Doctor Dave	**Nick Frost**
Sir Alistair Dormandy	**Kenneth Branagh**
Carl	**Tom Sturridge**
Simple Simon	**Chris O'Dowd**
Thick Kevin	**Tom Brooke**
Angus Nutsford	**Rhys Darby**
News John	**Will Adamsdale**
Felicity	**Katherine Parkinson**
Charlotte	**Emma Thompson**
Marianne	**Talulah Riley**
Twatt	**Jack Davenport**
Desiree	**Gemma Arterton**
Eleonore	**January Jones**

Ralph Brown (Bob Silver), Tom Wisdom (Mark), Michael Hadley (Mr. Roberts), Charlie Rowe (James), Lucy Fleming (Mrs. Roberts), Ian Mercer (Transfer Boatman), Ike Hamilton (Harold), Stephen Moore (Prime Minister), Michael Thomas (Sandford), Bo Poraj (Fredericks), Sinead Matthews (Miss C), Olegar Fedoro (Rock Boat Captain), Duncan Foster, Tomas Andrisiunas, Guðmundur Auðunsson, Kristofer Gummerus (Swedish Crewmen), Amanda Fairbanks-Hynes (Jemima Dormandy), Francesca Longrigg (Mrs. Dormandy), Poppy Delvingne, Sarah Forster, Ocean Moon, Tuuli Shipster (Models), David Sterne (Marianne's Captain), Olivia Llewellyn (Margaret), William Ilkley (Commanding Officer), Edward Hancock (Policeman), Katie Lyons (Angus' Boat Girl), Kirsty Mather (John's Boat Girl), Lana Davidson (Simon's T-Shirt Girl)

Kenneth Branagh, Sinead Matthews, Jack Davenport

The true story of how a group of renegade DJs kept broadcasting rock 'n' roll from a boat off the shores of England, despite the government's efforts to ban such music from the airwaves.

Tom Sturridge, Rhys Darby, Will Adamsdale, Bill Nighy

Philip Seymour Hoffman © Focus Features

Issei Ogata

Issei Ogata © Lorber

THE SUN

(LORBER) a.k.a. *Solntse*; Producers, Igor Kalenov, Andrey Sigle, Marco Mueller; Co-Producers, Alexander Rodnyansky, Andrey Zertsalov, Antoine de Clermont-Tonnerre; Director/Photography, Alexander Sokurov; Screenplay, Yuri Arabov; Designer, Yury Kuper; Costumes, Lidia Krukova; Music, Andrey Sigle; Editor, Sergey Ivanov; a Nikola Film, Proline Film (Russia), Downtown Pictures (Italy), MACT Productions (France), Riforma Film (Switzerland) production in association with RAI Cinema, Istituto Luce, with the participation of Cinema & Television Company, Lenfilm Studio, with the support of the Russian Ferderation of Cinematography and France's CNC (Centre National de la Cinématographie); Russian-Italian-French-Swiss, 2005; Dolby; Color; Not rated; 110 minutes; American release date: November 18, 2009

CAST
Emperor Hirohito	**Issei Ogata**
Gen. Douglas MacArthur	**Robert Dawson**
Empress Kojun	**Kaori Momoi**
The Chamberlain	**Shiro Sano**
Old Servant	**Shinmei Tsuji**

Taijiro Tamura (Director of the Institute), Georgi Pitskhelauri (MacArthur's Warrant Officer), Hiroya Morita (Suzuki, Prime Minister), Toshiaki Nishizawa (Yonai, Minister of the Navy), Naomasa Musaka (Anami, Minister of the War), Yusuke Tozawa (Kido), Kôjirô Kusanagi (Togo, Minister of Foreign Affairs), Tetsuro Tsuno (General Umezu), Rokuro Abe (General Toyoda), Jun Haichi (Abe, Minister of the Interior), Kojun Ito (Hironuma), Tôru Shinagawa (Sakomizu)

A look at Japanese Emperor Hirohito in the closing days of World War II.

RED CLIFF

(MAGNET) a.k.a. *Chi bi*; Producers, Terence Chang, John Woo; Executive Producers, Han Sanping, Wu Kebo, Masato Matsuura, Ryuhei Chiba, Dennis Wu, Jeonghun Ryu, John Woo; Director, John Woo; Screenplay, John Woo, Chan Khan, Kuo Cheng, Sheng Heyu; Photography, Lu Yue, Zhang Li; Designer/ Costumes, Tim Yip; Music, Taro Iwashiro; Editors, Angie Lam, Yang Hongyu, David Wu; Visual Effects Supervisor, Craig Hayes; Stunts, Guo Jianyong; 2nd Unit Directors, Zhang Jinzhan (Army Battles), Patrick Leung (Naval Battle); Action Director, Corey Yuen; a China Film Group Corp. (China)/Avex Entertainment (Japan)/ /Chengtian International Holdings, Ltd., CMC Entertainment (Taiwan)/ Showbox Entertainment and a John Woo presentation of a Lion Rock Prods. production; Chinese-Japanese-Tai-South Korean-American, 2008; Dolby; Color; Rated R; 148 minutes; American release date: November 18, 2009

CAST
Zhou Yu	**Tony Leung**
Zhuge Liang	**Takeshi Kaneshiro**
Cao Cao	**Zhang Fengyi**
Sun Quan	**Chang Chen**
Sun Shangxxaign	**Vicki Zhao**
Zhao Yun	**Hu Jun**
Gan Xing	**Shido Nakamura**
Xiao Qiao	**Lin Chi-ling**
Liu Bei	**You Yong**
Lu Su	**Hou Yong**
Sun Shucai	**Tony Dawei**

Song Jia (Li Ji), Ba Sen Za Bu (Guan Yu), Zang Jinsheng (Zhang Fei), Zhang Shan (Huang Gai), Wang Hui (Cao Hong), Shi Xiaohong (Jiang Gan), Wang Qingxiang (Kong Rong), Wang Ning (Emperor Xian), He Yin (Lady Mi)

Prime Minister Cao Cao leads his forces to do battle with a pair of rebellious warlords, leading to the collapse of the 400-year-old Han dynasty.

Fengyi Zhang

Tony Leung Chin-wai © Magnet Releasing

Blanca Portillo, Lluís Homar

Carmen Machi, Penélope Cruz

Lluis Homar, Blanca Portillo, Carlos Sampedro

Penélope Cruz © Sony Pictures Classics

Alejo Sauras, Tamar Novas

Tamar Novas, Rubén Ochandiano, Lluís Homar

Lola Dueñas, José Luis Gómez

BROKEN EMBRACES

(SONY CLASSICS) a.k.a. *Los abrazos rotos*; Producers, Esther García, Agustin Almodóvar; Director/Screenplay, Pedro Almodóvar; Photography, Rodrigo Prieto; Art Director, Antxon Gómez; Costumes, Sonia Grande; Music, Alberto Iglesias; Editor, José Salcedo; Casting, Luis San Narciso; an El Deseo, Universal Intl. Pictures Spain production, with the participation of Canal Plus; Spanish; Dolby; Panavision; Color; Rated R; 128 minutes; American release date: November 20, 2009

CAST

Lena	**Penélope Cruz**
Mateo Blanco (Harry Caine)	**Lluís Homar**
Judit	**Blanca Portillo**
Ernesto Martel	**José Luis Gómez**
Ray X (Ernesto Martel Jr.)	**Rubén Ochandiano**
Diego	**Tamar Novas**
Lena's Mother	**Ángela Molina**
Concierge	**Chus Lampreave**
Madame Mylene	**Kiti Manver**
Lip Reader	**Lola Dueñas**
Edurne	**Mariola Fuentes**
Chon	**Carmen Machi**
Model	**Kira Miró**
Julieta	**Rossy De Palma**
Alex	**Alejo Sauras**
Young Diego	**Carlos Sampedro**
Lena's Father	**Ramón Pons**
Maribel	**Marta Aledo**
Dr. Blasco	**Chema Ruiz**
Waiter	**Asier Etxeandia**
Luis	**Javier Coll**
Avid Editor	**Fernando Lueches**

Blind screenwriter Harry Caine reveals the secrets of his past to a young associate, from his former life as a filmmaker working under his given name, to the accident which claimed his sight and led to a break-up with Lena, a now-famous actress who lives in a gilded cage with her wealthy older partner.

Tamar Novas, Blanca Portillo

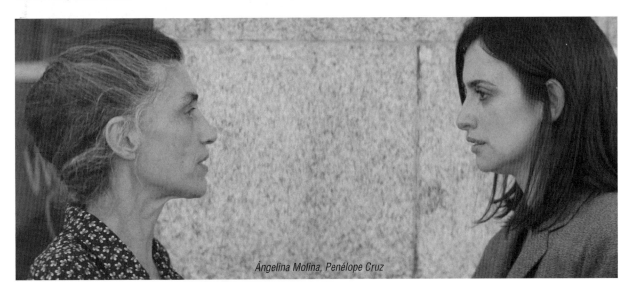

Ángelina Molina, Penélope Cruz

ME AND ORSON WELLES

(FREESTYLE) Producers, Richard Linklater, Marc Samuelson, Ann Carli; Executive Producers, Steve Christian, John Sloss, Steve Norris; Co-Producers, Holly Gent Palmo, Vince Palmo, Andrew Fingret; Screenplay, Holly Gent Palmo, Vince Palmo; Based on the novel by Robert Kaplow; Director, Richard Linklater; Photography, Dick Pope; Designer, Laurence Dorman; Costumes, Nic Ede; Music, Michael J. McEvoy; Music Supervisor, Marc Marot; Editor, Sandra Adair; Visual Effects Supervisor, Rob Duncan; Line Producer, Richard Hewitt; Associate Producers, Jessica Parker, Sara Greene; Casting, Lucy Bevan; a CinemaNX and Isle of Man Film, in association with Framestore Features, and Hart/Lunsford Pictures presentation of a CinemaNX, and Detour Filmproduction; British-American; Dolby; Widescreen; HD; Deluxe color; Rated PG-13; 114 minutes; American release date: November 25, 2009

CAST

Richard Samuels (Lucius)	**Zac Efron**
Sonja Jones	**Claire Danes**
Orson Welles (Brutus)	**Christian McKay**
George Coulouris (Mark Antony)	**Ben Chaplin**
Gretta Adler	**Zoe Kazan**
John Houseman	**Eddie Marsan**
Muriel Brassler (Portia)	**Kelly Reilly**
Joseph Cotten (Publius)	**James Tupper**
Norman Lloyd (Cinna the Poet)	**Leo Bill**
Sam Leve	**Al Weaver**
Vakhtangov	**Iain McKee**
Walter Ash	**Simon Lee Phillips**
Joe Holland (Julius Caesar)	**Simon Nehan**
Lorelei Lathrop	**Imogen Poots**
Grover Burgess (Ligarius)	**Patrick Kennedy**
Mrs. Samuels	**Janie Dee**
Grandmother Samuels	**Marlene Sidaway**
Dr. Mewling	**Garrick Hagon**
Evelyn Allen (Calpurnia)	**Megan Maczko**
Longchamps Kids	**Aaron Brown, John Young**
John Hoyt (Decius)	**Travis Oliver**
Radio Announcer	**Nathan Osgood**
Radio Director	**Robert Wilfort**
Les Tremayne	**Michael Brandon**
Barbara Luddy	**Saskia Reeves**
Martin Gabel (Cassius)	**Aidan McArdle**
I.L. Epstein	**Michael J. McEvoy**
George Duthie (Artemidorus)	**Thomas Arnold**
Jeannie Rosenthal	**Jo McInnes**
William Mowry (Flavius)	**Daniel Tuite**
Virginia Welles	**Emily Allen**

Eddi Reader (Singer), Jools Holland (Band Leader), Steven Parry (Mercury Trumpet Player), Jay Irving (Mercury Percussion Player), David Garbutt (Mercury French Horn Player)

A 17-year-old theater aficionado gets the opportunity of a lifetime when he is chosen to appear in Orson Welles' modern-dress version of *Julius Caesar*.

Al Weaver, Simon Lee Phillips, James Tupper, Simon Nehan, Iain McKee

Ben Chaplin, Christian McKay

Leo Bill

Christian McKay, Claire Danes © Freestyle Releasing

Zac Efron, Claire Danes

Christian McKay

Eddie Marsan

Zac Efron, Christian McKay, Leo Bill

Zoe Kazan, Zac Efron

THE LAST STATION

(SONY CLASSICS) Producers, Chris Curling, Jens Meurer, Bonnie Arnold; Executive Producers, Andrei Konchalovsky, Phil Robertson, Judy Tossell, Robbie Little; Co-Producers, Ewa Karlstrom, Andreas Ulmke-Smeaton; Director/ Screenplay, Michael Hoffman; Based on the novel by Jay Parini; Photography, Sebastian Edschmid; Designer, Patrizia von Brandenstein; Costumes, Monika Jacobs; Music, Sergey Yevtushenko; Editor, Patricia Rommel; Casting, Leo Davis, Lissy Holm; an Egoli Tossell Film/Zephyr Films presentation of an Egoli Tossell Film Halle production in co-production with the Andrei Konchalovsky Production Center and Samfilm; German-Russian-British; Dolby; Widescreen; Color; Rated R; 110 minutes; American release date: December 4, 2009

CAST

Sofya Tolstoy	**Helen Mirren**
Leo Tolstoy	**Christopher Plummer**
Vladimir Chertkov	**Paul Giamatti**
Valentin Bulgakov	**James McAvoy**
Sasha Tolstoy	**Anne-Marie Duff**
Masha	**Kerry Condon**
Dushan	**John Sessions**
Sergeyenko	**Patrick Kennedy**
Andrey Tolstoy	**Tomas Spencer**
Reporter	**David Masterson**
Vanja	**Nenad Lucic**
Kind	**Maximilian Gärtner**

Consenting to become the personal assistant to Leo Tolstoy, Valentin Bulgakov finds himself in the midst of a heated dispute over the future of the writer's estate, which the great author's wife hopes to keep from falling into the hands of the Russian people.

This film received Oscar nominations for actress (Helen Mirren) and supporting actor (Christopher Plummer).

Anne-Marie Duff, Paul Giamatti, Helen Mirren, Christopher Plummer

Kerry Condon, James McAvoy © Sony Pictures Classics

Helen Mirren, James McAvoy

Anne-Marie Duff, Helen Mirren

Aisling, Brendan © GKIDS

Brendan, Aisling

Aisling

THE SECRET OF KELLS

(GKIDS) formerly *Brendan and the Secret of Kells*; Producers, Didier Bruner, Viviane Vanfleteren, Paul Young; Executive Producer, Ian Rouveure; Director, Tomm Moore; Co-Director, Nora Twomey; Screenplay, Fabrice Ziolkowski; Editor, Fabienne Alvarez-Giro; Art Director, Ross Stewart; Music, Bruno Coulais; Animation Supervisor, Fabian Erlinghauser; Creative Supervisor, Anton Roebben; Storyboard, Remi Chaye; Character Designers, Tomm Moore, Barry Reynolds; Background Designers, Aurelie Bernard, Adrien Meringeau; a Les Armateurs, France 2 Cinema (France)/Vivi Film (Belgium)/Cartoon Saloon (Ireland) production; French-Belgian-Irish; Dolby; Color; Not rated; 78 minutes; American release date: December 4, 2009

VOICE CAST

Abbot Cellach	**Brendan Gleeson**
Brendan	**Evan McGuire**
Brother Tang/Leonardo	**Liam Hourican**
Aidan	**Mick Lally**
Adult Brendan	**Michael McGrath**
Aisling	**Christen Mooney**
Brother Assoua	**Paul Tylack**
Brother Square	**Paul Young**

A young boy living behind the walls of the abbey in Kells hopes to help a Scottish illustrator finish his Book of Iona.

This film received an Oscar nomination for animated feature.

A TOWN CALLED PANIC

(ZEITGEIST) a.k.a. *Panique au village*; Producers, Philippe Kaufmann, Vincent Tavier; Co-Producers, Marc Bonny, Xavier Diskeuve, Vincent Eches, Stephan Roelants, Pilar Torres Villodre, Arlette Zylberberg; Directors/Screenplay, Stéphane Aubier, Vincent Patar; Photography, Jan Vandenbussche; Designer, Gilles Cuvelier; Editor, Anne-Laure Guégan; Animation Manager, Steven de Beul; Animation, Stéphane Aubier, Marion Charrier, Zoe Goetgheluck, Florence Henrard, Vincent Patar; Creation of Plastic and Resin Figures, Marion Charrier, Zoe Goetgheluck; a La Parti Production, Beast Prods., Les Films du Grognon, RTBF Belgium Television/Made in Prods., Gebeka Films (France)/Melusine Productions (Luxembourg) production; Belgian-French-Luxembourg; Dolby; Color; Not rated; 75 minutes; American release date: December 16, 2009

VOICE CAST

Cowboy	**Stéphane Aubier**
Indian	**Bruce Ellison**
Cheval, Horse	**Vincent Patar**
Steven	**Benoît Poelvoorde**
Madame Longrée	**Jeanne Balibar**
Mouton/Jean-Paul	**Nicolas Buysse**
Janine	**Veronique Dumont**
Cow	**Christine Grulois**
Policeman/Gérard	**Frédéric Jannin**
Simon/Cow	**Bouli Lanners**
Rocky	**Eric Muller**
Ours	**Franco Piscopo**

Cowboy and Indian are beleaguered by a series of mishaps as they try to throw a surprise birthday party for Horse. Based on the Canal Plus series.

Indian, Cowboy, Horse © Zeitgeist Films

POLICE, ADJECTIVE

(IFC FILMS) a.k.a. *Politist, adjectiv*; Executive Producer, Marcela Urus; Producer/Director/Screenplay, Corneliu Porumboiu; Photography, Marius Panduru; Designer, Mihaela Poenaru; Costumes, Giorgiana Bostan; Editor, Roxana Szel; Romanian; Dolby; Color; Not rated; 113 minutes; American release date: December 23, 2009

CAST
Cristi	**Dragos Bucur**
Anghelache	**Vlad Ivanov**
Anca	**Irina Saulescu**
Nelu	**Ion Stoica**
The Prosecutor	**Marian Ghenea**
Costi	**Cosmin Selesi**
Sica	**Serban Georgevici**
Vali	**George Remes**
Dana	**Adina Dulcu**
Vic	**Dan Cogalniceanu**
Office on Duty	**Costi Dita**
Alex	**Alexandru Sabadac**
Doina	**Anca Diaconu**
Victor	**Radu Costin**

Viorel Nebunu (Alex's Father), Emanoela Tigla (Alex's Mother), Daniel Barsan (Bartender), Bungeanu Mioara (Shopkeeper), Cerasela Trandafir (Gina)

Officer Cristi challenges the law when he refuses to arrest a young man who is selling pot to his school mates.

Dragos Bucur © IFC Films

Dragos Bucur, Vlad Ivanov, Ion Stoica

Dragos Bucur

Irina Saulescu, Dragos Bucur

THE IMAGINARIUM OF DOCTOR PARNASSUS

(SONY CLASSICS) Producers, Terry Gilliam, Samuel Hadida, Amy Gilliam, William Vince; Executive Producers, Dave Valleau, Victor Hadida; Director, Terry Gilliam; Screenplay, Terry Gilliam, Charles McKeown; Photography, Nicola Pecorini; Designer, Anastasia Masaro; Costumes, Monique Prudhomme; Original Design and Art Direction, Dave Warren, Terry Gilliam; Music, Mychael Danna, Jeff Danna; Editor, Mick Audsley; Makeup and Hair Design, Sarah Monzani; Visual Effects Supervisors, John Paul Docherty, Richard Bain; Casting, Irene Lamb; an Infinity Features Entertainment (Canada) production in association with Poo Poo Pictures, Davis Films (France), and Grosvenor Park Productions & Parnassus Productions (U.S.); British-Canadian-French; Dolby; Color; Rated PG-13; 122 minutes; American release date: December 25, 2009

Lily Cole, Andrew Garfield

CAST

Tony Shepard	**Heath Ledger**
Imaginarium Tony #1	**Johnny Depp**
Imaginarium Tony #2	**Jude Law**
Imaginarium Tony #3	**Colin Farrell**
Doctor Parnassus	**Christopher Plummer**
Anton	**Andrew Garfield**
Percy	**Verne Troyer**
Valentina	**Lily Cole**
Mr. Nick	**Tom Waits**
LV Woman	**Maggie Steed**
Sally	**Paloma Faith**
Vladimir	**Ray Cooper**
Martin	**Richard Riddell**
Martin's Girlfriend	**Katie Lyons**
Friend of Martin	**Richard Shanks**
Face Changed Martin	**Bruce Crawford**
Policeman	**Johnny Harris**
Mum	**Lorraine Cheshire**
Dad	**Mark Benton**
Diego	**Lewis Gott**
Linda	**Sian Scott**
Uncle Bob	**Simon Daye**
Aunty Flo	**Moya Brady**
The President	**Peter Stormare**

Jude Law

Mackenzie Gray, Yurij Kis, Ian Wallace (Monks), Amanda Walker, Joann Condon, Carolyn Pickles (Shoppers), Montserrat Lombard (Sally's Friend), Craig Fraser (Debonair Gent), Amy Marston, Gwendoline Christie, Lucy Russell (Classy Shoppers), Ben Cartwright, Gavin Rolph (Policemen), Bobby Bysouth (LV Woman's Reflection), Vitaliy Kravchenko (Piotr), Emil Hostina (Serge), Igor Ingelsman (Gregor), Sarah Groundwater (Sales Girl), Dean Moen (Smiling Policeman), Fraser Aitcheson, Michael Bean, Jase-Anthony Griffith, Scott McGillivray, John Stewart, Chris Cochrane, Pearce Visser, Patrick Bahrich (Dancing Policemen), Georgina Hegedos (Baboushka), Cassandra Sawtell (Olga), Carrie Genzel, Mark Oliver (Journalists), Donna Lysell (President's Wife), Michael Eklund (Tony's Assistant), Raahul Singh (Security Guard), D. Harlan Cutshall, Deni Delory, Lisa Bunting (Charity Guests), Peter New, Michael Jonsson (Paramedics), Emma Karwandy (Valentina's Daughter), Quinn Lord (Young Boy), Bart Anderson (Young Boy's Father), Erika Conway (Young Boy's Mother), Wendy Carson, Christine McMahon (Nuns), Ryan Grantham (Little Anton)

Dr. Parnassus, the head of a traveling troupe, offers audiences a chance to step through a magic mirror to experience a world of limitless imagination, all the while dreading the Devil's promise to collect the doctor's daughter Valentina as her 16th birthday approaches. This was the final film appearance of actor Heath Ledger who died January 22, 2008 during production.

This film received Oscar nominations for art direction and costume design.

Heath Ledger, Verne Troyer

Lily Cole, Colin Farrell

Verne Troyer, Andrew Garfield, Christopher Plummer, Lily Cole, Heath Ledger

Heath Ledger © Sony Pictures Classics

Christopher Plummer, Lily Cole, Andrew Garfield

Maggie Steed, Johnny Depp

Tom Waits, Christopher Plummer

Burghart Klaussner

Kristina Kneppek, Stephanie Amarell, Bianca Mey, Mika Ahrens

Leonard Proxauf

Fion Mutert, Enno Trebs, Theo Trebs

Ursina Lardi

Fion Mutert

Miljan Chatelain

Thibault Serie © Sony Pictures Classics

Ulrich Tukur

THE WHITE RIBBON

(SONY CLASSICS) a.k.a. *Das weisse Band: Eine deutche Kindergeschichte*; Producers, Stefan Arndt, Veit Heiduschka, Margaret Menegoz, Andrea Occhipinti; Executive Producer, Michael Katz; Director/Screenplay, Michael Haneke; Photography, Christian Berer; Designer, Christoph Kanter; Costumes, Moidele Bickel; Editor, Monika Willi; an X Filme Creative Pool (Germany)/Les Films du Losange (France)/Wega Film (Austria)/Lucky Red (Italy) presentation; German-French-Austrian-Italian; Dolby; Black and white; Rated R; 144 minutes; American release date: December 30, 2009

CAST

The Schoolteacher	**Christian Friedel**
Eva	**Leonie Benesch**
The Baron	**Ulrich Tukur**
Marie-Louise, the Baroness	**Ursina Lardi**
The Pastor	**Burghart Klaussner**
Anna, the Pastor's Wife	**Steffi Kühnert**
The Steward	**Josef Bierbichler**
Emma, the Steward's Wife	**Gareila Maria Schmeide**

Rainer Bock (The Doctor), Susanne Lothar (The Midwife), Maria-Victoria Dragus (Klara), Leonard Proxauf (Martin), Janina Fautz (Erna), Eddy Grahl (Karli), Ernst Jacobi (Narrator), Fion Mutert (Sigi), Michael Kranz (The Home Teacher), Levin Henning (Adolf), Johanna Busse (Margarete), Thibault Sérié (Gustav), Enno Trebs (Georg), Theo Trebs (Ferdinand), Branko Samarovski (The Farmer), Klaus Manchen (Farmer's Voice), Birgit Minichmayr (Frieda), Sebastian Hülk (Max), Kai-Peter Malina (Karl), Kristina Kneppek (Else), Stephanie Amarell (Sophie), Binaca Mey (Paula), Aaron Denkel (Kurti),), Mika Ahrens (Willi), Detlev Buck (Eva's Father), Anne-Kathrin Gummich (Eva's Mother), Luzie Ahrens, Gary Bestla, Leonard Boes, Felix Boettcher, Sophie Czech, Paraschiva Dragus, Selina Ewald, Nora Gruler, Tim Guderjahn, Jonas Jennerjahn, Ole Joensson, Gerrit Langentepe, Lena Pankow, Sebastian Pauli, Franz Rewoldt, Kevin Schmolinski, Alexander Sedl, Nino Seide, Marvin Ray Spey, Malina Steffen, Lilli Trebs, Paul Wolf, Margarete Zimmermann (Schoolchildren), Carmen-Maja Antoni (Bathing Midwife), Christian Klischat (Gendarme), Michael Schenk, Hanus Polak Jr. (Detectives), Sara Schivazappa (The Italian Nanny), Marisa Growaldt (The Maid), Vincent Krüger (Fritz), Rüdiger Hauffe (Workman), Arndt Schwering-Sohnrey, Florian Köhler (Farmers), Sebastian Lach, Marcin Tyrol, Sebastian Badurek, Krysiek Zarzecki, Sebastian Pawlak (Foreign Harvesters), Lili Fichtner, Ameli Litwin, Paula Kalinski (Girls at Harvest Feast), Matthias Linke, Vladik Otaryan, Peter Mörike, Hans-Matthias Glassmann, Nikita Vaganov (Band Musicians)

A small German village is beset by a series of unfortunate events and tragic occurrences on the brink of World War I.

This film received Oscar nominations for foreign language film and cinematography.

Christian Friedel, Leonie Benesch

FOREIGN FILMS B

2009 Releases / January 1–December 31

CARGO 200 (The Disinformation Company) a.k.a. *Gruz 200*; Producer, Sergei Selyanov; Executive Producer, Maxim Ukhanov; Director/Screenplay, Alexei Balabanov; Photography, Alexander Simonov; Art Director, Pavel Parchomenko; Costumes, Nadezda Vasileva; Editor, Tatjana Kuzmyceva; a CTB Film Co. production; Russian, 2007; Dolby; Color; Not rated; 89 minutes; American release date: January 2, 2009. **CAST:** Alexei Serebryakov (Aleksey), Leonid Gromov (Artem), Yuri Stepanov (Mikhail), Agniya Kuznetsova (Angelika), Alexei Poluyan (Capt. Zhurov), Natalya Akimova (Tonya), Leonid Bicevin (Valera), Mikhail Skryabin (Sunka)

JUST ANOTHER LOVE STORY (Koch Lorber) a.k.a. *Kaerlighed pa film*; Producer, Michael Obel; Director/Screenplay, Ole Bornedal; Photography, Dan Laustsen; Designer, Anders Engelbrecht; Music, Joachim Holbek; Editor, Anders Villadsen; a Thura Film presentation; Danish, 2007; Dolby; Widescreen; Color; Not rated; 104 minutes; American release date: January 9, 2009. **CAST:** Anders W. Berthelsen (Jonas), Rebecka Hemse (Julia), Nikolaj Lie Kaas (Sebastian), Charlotte Fich (Mette), Dejan Cukic (Frank), Karsten Jansfort (Poul), Flemming Enevold (Dichmann), Bent Mejding (Mr. Castlund), Ewa Fröling (Mrs. Castlund), Josephine Raahauge (Monica Castlund), Timm Vladimir (Magnus Castlund), Ditte Hansen (Kirsten), Fanny Bornedal (Clara), Daniel Stampe (Frederik), Niels Anders Torn (Dr. Henriques), Desmond Boateng (Receptionist), Lin Kun Wu (Dr. Chen), Jannie Faurschou (Irma)

Anders W. Berthelsen, Charlotte Fich in Just another Love Story © *Koch Lorber Films*

THE PERVERT'S GUIDE TO CINEMA (Lone Star) Producers, Martin Rosenbaum, Georg Misch, Ralph Wiesler, Sophie Fiennes; Executive producers, Jan Younghusband, Reinhard Wulf; Director/Screenplay, Sophie Fiennes; Photography, Remko Schnorr; Designer, Ben Zuydwijk; Costumes, Hedi Legerstee; Music, Brian Eno; Editor, Ethel Shepherd; Narrator, Slavoj Zizek; a P Guide presentation of a Lone Star (U.K.)/Mischief Films (Austria)/Amoeba Films (Netherlands) production in association with Kasander Film; British-Austrian-Dutch; Dolby; Color; DigiBeta; Not rated; 150 minutes; American release date: January 16, 2009. Documentary in which philosopher Slavoj Zizek analyzes several notable movies.

BALLERINA (First Run Features) Producers, Frederic Podetti, Yann Brolli; Director, Bertrand Normand; Photography, Bertrand Normand, Franck Laniel, Isabelle Saunois, Edward Oleschak; Editor, Antonela Bevenja; Narrator, Diane Baker; an Adesif Prods./Les films du Tamarin production, in collaboration with TV5/Cityzen TV, with the participation of CNC (Centre National de la Cinematographie); French, 2006; Color; DV; Not rated; 77 minutes; American release date: January 16, 2009. Documentary on five members of the Kirov Ballet.

WITH: Uliana Lopetkina, Diana Vishneva, Svetlana Zakharova, Evgenia Obraztsova, Alina Somova, Valery Gergiev, Manuel Legris, Cedric Klapisch

Slavoj Zizek in The Pervert's Guide to Cinema © *Lone Star Prods.*

Uliana Lopatkina in Ballerina © *First Run Features*

CHANDNI CHOWK TO CHINA (Warner Bros.) Producers, Ramesh Sippy, Mukesh Talreja, Rohan Sippy; Director, Nikhil Advani; Screenplay, Shridhar Raghavan; Photography, Himman Dhamija; Costumes, Jaimal Odedra; Choreographer, Pony Verma; Fight Choreographer, Huan-Chiu Ku; Editor, Aarif Sheikh; a Ramesh Sippy Entertainment presentation of a People Tree Films production; Indian; Dolby; Color; Rated PG-13; 154 minutes; American release date: January 16, 2009. **CAST:** Akshay Kumar (Sidhu/Liu Sheuyn), Deepika Padukone (Sakhi/Suzy "Meow Meow" Miss TSM), Mithun Chakraborty (Dada), Ranvir Shorey (Chopstick), Gordon Liu (Hojo), Roger Yuan (Inspector Chiang Kohung), Kiran Juneja (Mrs. Kohung), Jun Li (Wong), Chang En Lu (Han), Conan Stevens (Joey), Kevin Wu (Frankie)

Akshay Kumar in Chandni Chow to China © *Warner Bros.*

CHERRY BLOSSOMS (Strand) a.k.a. *Kirschblüten – Hanami*; Producers, Molly von Fuerstenberg, Harald Kuegler; Director/Screenplay, Doris Dörrie; Photography, Hanno Lentz; Designer, Bele Schneider; Costumes, Sabine Greunig; Music, Claus Bantzer; Editors, Inez Regnier, Frank Mueller; a Bavaria Film Intl. presentation of an Olga Film production; German-French, 2008; Dolby; Color; HD; Not rated; 127 minutes; American release date: January 16, 2009. **CAST:** Elmar Wepper (Rudi Angermeier), Hannelore Elsner (Trudi Angemeier), Aya Irizuki (Yu), Maximilian Brückner (Karl Angermeier), Nadja Uhl (Franzi), Birgit Minichmayr (Karolin Angermeier), Felix Eitner (Klaus Angermeier), Floriance Daniel (Emma Angermeier), Celine Tanneberger (Celine Angermeier), Robert Döhlert (Robert Angermeier), Tadashi Endo (Butoh Dancer), Sarah Camp (Butcher), Gerhard Wittman, Veith von Fürstenberg (Doctors)

Hannelore Elsner, Elmar Wepper in Cherry Blossoms © *Strand Releasing*

OF TIME AND THE CITY (Strand) Producers, Sol Papadopoulos, Roy Boulter; Executive Producers, Christopher Moll, Lisa Marie Russo; Director/Screenplay, Terence Davies; Photography, Tim Pollard; Music, Ian Neil; Editor, Liza Ryan-Carter; a Northwest Vision and Media & Digital Departures presentation in association with the Liverpool Culture Co., BBC Films of a Hurricane Films production; British, 2008; Dolby; Color; Not rated; 77 minutes; American release date: January 21, 2009. Documentary on filmmaker Terence Davies' hometown of Liverpool, England.

Of Time and the City © *Strand Releasing*

DEALING AND WHEELING IN SMALL ARMS (Sander Francken Film) Producer/Director, Sander Francken; Screenplay, Josh Lacey, Joost Schrickx; Photography, Sander Snoep, Pieter Groeneveld, Edwin Donders, Jan-Dries Groenendijk, Maarten Kramer, Sander Francken; Music, Rainer Michel; Editor, Gys Zevenbergen; Narrator, Vanessa Redgrave; a co-production of Llink; Dutch, 2006; Color; Not rated; 75 minutes; American release date: January 21, 2009. Documentary about the small arms trade.

Dealing and Wheeling in Small Arms © *Sander Francken Film*

THE PHOTOGRAPH (Global Film Initiative) Producers, Nan Achnas, Shanty Harmayn, Paquita Widjaja-Afief, Natacha Devillers; Director/Screenplay, Nan Triveni Achnas; Photography, Yadi Sugandi; Music, Aksan Hanadyani, Titi Sjuman; Editor, Sastha Sunu; a Sintesa Group presentation of a Triximages, Salto Films (Indonesia)/Les Petites Lumieres (France) co-production; Indonesian-French, 2007; Color; Not rated; 98 minutes; American release date: January 21, 2009. **CAST:** Lim Kay Tong (Johan), Shanty (Sita), Lukman Sardi (Surosos), Indy Barends (Rosi)

DOG EAT DOG (IFC Films) a.k.a. *Perro come perro*; Producer, Diego F. Ramirez; Executive Producers, Diego F. Ramirez, Carolina Barrera, Rodrigo Guerrero; Director, Carlos Moreno; Screenplay, Carlos Moreno, Alonso Torres; Photography, Juan Carlos Gil; Designer, Jaime Luna; Costumes, Luz H. Cardenas; Music, Sultana; Editors, Felipe Guerrero, Santiago Palau, Marlon Moreno; an Antorcha Films/Patofeo Films/Dynamo presentation; Colombian, 2008; Deluxe color; Super 16mm; Not rated; 102 minutes; American release date: January 23, 2009. **CAST:** Marlon Moreno (Victor Peñaranda), Oscar Borda (Eusebio), Blas Jaramillo (El Orejon), Eusbeio Benitez, Alvaro Rodriguez

Oscar Borda in Dog Eat Dog © *IFC Films*

DONKEY PUNCH (Magnet) Producers, Angus Lamont, Robin Gutch, Mark Herbert; Executive Producers, Peter Carlton, Lizzie Francke, Hugo Heppell, Will Clarke; Director, Olly Blackburn; Screenplay, Olly Blackburn, David Bloom; Story, David Bloom; Photography, Nanu Segal; Designer, Delarey Wagener; Music, François-Eudes Chanfrault; Editor, Kate Evans; a U.K. Film Council, Film4 presentation, in association with Screen Yorkshire & EM Media, of a Warp X production; British, 2008; Dolby; Color; Not rated; 99 minutes; American release date: January 23, 2009. **CAST:** Robert Boulter (Sean), Sian Breckin (Lisa), Tom Burke (Bluey), Nichola Burley (Tammi), Julian Morris (Josh), Jay Taylor (Marcus), Jaime Winstone (Kim)

Tom Burke, Jay Taylor, Julian Morris in Donkey Punch © *Magnet Films*

LUCK BY CHANCE (Independent) Producers, Farhan Akhtar, Ritesh Sidhwani; Executive Producers/Director/Story, Zoya Akhtar; Screenplay, Javed Akhtar; Photography, Carlos Catalán; Editor, Anand Subaya; Indian; Color; Not rated; 156 minutes; American release date: January 30, 2009. **CAST:** Hrithik Roshan (Zaffar Khan), Juhi Chawla (Minty Rolly), Farhan Akhtar (Vikram Jaisingh), Rishi Kapoor (Rommy Rolly), Konkona Sen Sharma (Sona Mishra), Alyy Khan (Chaudhary), Isha Sharvani (Niki Walia), Sanjay Kapoor (Ranjit Rolly), Boman Irani (Dinaz Aziz), Arjun Mathur (Abhimanyu)

SHADOWS (Mitropoulos Films) a.k.a. *Senki*; Producers, Milcho Manchevski, Amedeo Pagani, Corinna Mehner; Director/Screenplay, Milcho Manchevski; Photography, Fabio Cianchetti; Designer, David Munns; Music, Ryan Shore; Editors, David Ray, Martin Levenstein; a Senka Dooel Film production, in association with Classic SRL, Blue Eyes Fiction; Macedonian, 2008; Dolby; Color; Not rated; 130 minutes; American release date: January 30, 2009. **CAST:** Borce Nacev (Dr. Lazare Perkov), Vesna Stanojevska (Menka), Ratka Radmanovic (Kalina), Salaetin Bilal (Gerasim), Sabina Ajrula-Tozija (Dr. Vera Perkova), Filareta Atanasova (Gordana), Dime Ilijev (Ignjat Perkov), Petar Mircevski (Blagojce), Vladimir Jacev (Siskin), Goce Vlahov (Prof. Kokale), Ana Kostovska (Radmila), Zaklina Stefkovska (Paca), Izabela Novotni (Izabela), Ilko Stefankovski (Dr. Karpuzovski), Vanja Radmilovic (Ivana)

THE COLOR OF MAGIC (Aquarius) Producers, Rod Brown, Ian Sharples; Director/Screenplay, Vadim Jean; Based on the novels by Terry Pratchett; Photography, Gavin Finney; Designer, Ricky Eyres; Costumes, Jane Spicer; Music, Paul E. Francis, David A. Hughes; Editors, Joe McNally, Liz Webber; a RHI Entertainment production; Color/Black and white; HD; Not rated; 137 minutes; American release date: January 30, 2009. **CAST:** David Jason (Rincewind), Sean Astin (Twoflower), Tim Curry (Trymon), Jeremy Irons (Patrician), Brian Cox (Narrator), James Cosmo (Galder Weatherwax), Christopher Lee (Voice of Death), Janet Suzman (Ninereeds), David Bradley (Cohen the Barbarian), Nigel Planer (Arch Astronomer), Stephen Marcus (Broadman), Laura Haddock (Bethan), Liz May Brice (Herrena), Karen David (Liessa), Geoffrey Hutchings (Picture Imp), Marnix Van Den Broeke (Death), Nicholas Tennant (Head Librarian), Michael Mears (Jiglad Wert), Roger Ashton-Griffiths (Lumuel Panter), Will Keen (Ganmack Treehallett), Peter Copley (Greyhald Spold), Ian Puleston-Davies (Wizard Leader), James Greene (Narrowbolt), Ian Burfield (Ymor), Arthur White (Rerpf), Miles Richardson (Zlorf), Terry Pratchett (Astrozoologist #1)

CHOCOLATE (Magnet) a.k.a. *Chokgohlaet*; Producers, Prachya Pinkaew, Panna Rittikrai, Sukanya Vongsthapat; Executive Producer, Somask Techarataprasert; Director, Prachya Pinkaew; Screenplay, Napalee, Chukiat Sakveerakul; Photography, Decha Srimatra; Designer, Nopporn Kirdsapa; Editor, Rashan Limtrakul; a Sahamongkol Film Intl. presentation of a Baa-Ram-Ewe production; Thai, 2008; Dolby; Color; Rated R; 92 minutes; American release date: February 6, 2009. **CAST:** Yanin Vismitananda (Zen), Hiroshi Abe (Masahi), Ammara Siripong (Zin), Tarphon Phopwandee (Mang Moom), Pongpat Wachirabunjong (No. 8), Dechawut Chuntakaro (Priscilla), Hirokazu Sano (Ryo), Aroon Wanatsabadeewong (Ice Man/Factory Owner), Anusuk Jangajit (Candy Man/Shop Owner), Nattakit Teachachevagpong (Pork Man/Slaughterhouse Owner), Kittitat Kowahagul (Epileptic Boxer), Thanyathon Seekhiaw (Fur), Pirom Ruangkitjakan (Petch), Su-jeong Lim, Abalhaja Soumia (Boxer's Henchwomen), Silpakorn Mongkolnimite (Masahashi, 3 years old), Sasisorn Fanyapathomwong, Thunchalaporn Chewcharm (Zen, 3 years old), Patsorn Koncameesuk (Zen, 8 years old), Amornpol Jeamwongsarijul, Thanakorn Sajlutikriangkri, Jirawat Silakis, Wirate Kemklad (Teenage Gang Boys), Wanda Sangboonkro, Apitchaya Spuanchat (Teenage Gang Girls), Thaweesilp Wisanuyotin (Zen's Doctor), Sompoi Ritdumrongkul (Zin's Doctor)

Yanin Vismitananda in Chocolate © *Magnet Films*

ABSURDISTAN (First Run Features) Producer/Director, Veit Helmer; Executive Producer, Linda Kornemann; Screenplay, Veit Helmer, Zaza Buadze, Gordan Mihic, Ahmet Golbol; Photography, George Beridze; Designer, Erwin Prib; Music, Shigeru Umebayashi; Editor, Vincent Assmann; a Veti Helmer Filmproduktion (Germany) production, in co-production with SWR (Südwestrundfunk – Germany), BR (Bayerischer Rundfunk – Germany), Arte France; German-French, 2008; Color; Not rated; 88 minutes; American release date: February 6, 2009. **CAST:** Kristyna Malérová (Aya), Maximilian Mauff (Temelko), Nino Chkheidze (Grandmotehr), Ivane Ivantbelidze (Shooting Gallery Guy), Ani Amiridze (Shooting Gallery Guy's Daughter), Ilko Stefanovski (Guri , Temelko's Father), Assun Planas (Temelko's Motehr), Otto Kuhnle (Barber), Hijran Nasirova (Barber's Wife), Hendrik Arnst (Landlord), Olha Nefjodova (Landlord's Wife), Adalet Zyadhanov (Policeman), Matanat Atakishiyeva (Policeman's Wife), Azelarab Kaghat (Baker), Michaela Bandi (Baker's Wife), Blagoja Spirkovski (Cobbler), Dace Bonate (Cobbler's Wife), Elhan Guliyev (Bus Driver), Julietta Koleva (Bus Driver's Wife), Helder Costa (Doctor), Mónica Calle (Doctor's Wife), Kazim Abdullayev (Shepherd), Firangiz Babyeva (Shepherd's Wife), László Németh (Postman), Sarah Bensoussan (Postman's Wife), Mubariz Alixanli (Watchmaker), Khatuna Ioseliani (Watchmaker's Wife), Nurradin Guliyev (Beekeeper), Elena Spitsina (Beekeeper's Wife), Radomil Uhlir (Butcher), Suzana Petricevic (Butcher's Wife), Rafiq Azimov (Carpenter), Nelli Cozaru (Carpenter's Wife), Vlasta Velisavljevic (Veteran)

Maximilian Mauff, Kristyna Malérová in Absurdistan
© *First Run Features*

DELHI-6 (UTV Motion Pictures) Producers, Ronnie Screwvala, Rakeysh Omprakash Mehra; Director/Co-Screenplay, Rakeysh Omprakash Mehra; Co-Screenplay, Prasoon Joshi, Kamlesh Pandev; Photography, Binod Pradhan; Lyrics & Dialogue, Prasoon Joshi; Editor, PS Bharathi; Choreographers, Vaibhavi Merchant, Saroj Khan; Costumes, Arjun Bhasin, Anamika Khanna; a Rakeysh Omprakash Mehra production; Indian; Dolby; Color; Not rated; 140 minutes; American release date: February 20, 2009. **CAST:** Waheeda Rehman (Dadi), Abhishek Bachchan (Roshan), Sonam Kapoor (Bittu), Om Puri (Madan Gopal), Rishi Kapoor (Ali), Prem Chopra (Lala Bhairam), Pawan Malhotra (Jai Gopal), Atul Kulkarni (Gobar), Supriya Pathak (Vimla), Tanvi Azmi (Fatima), Divya Dutta (Jalebi), Vijay Raaz (Inspector Ranvijay), Deepak Dobriyal (Mamdu), KK Raina (Haji Suleman), Akhilendra Mishra (Baba Bandarmaar), Sheeba Chaddha (Rajjo), Cyrus Shahukar (Suresh), Aditi Rao (Rama), Indrajeet Sarkar (Rajan Mehra), Daya Shankar Pandey (Kumar), Rajat Dholakia (Pagal Fakir), Khaalid Mohammad (Lala Lahorilal), Geeta Agarwal (Maitri Devi), Rajiv Mathur (Ganpat), Geeta Bisht (Shashi), Vinayak Doval (Bobby), Hussan Saad (Bhisham)

EXAMINED LIFE (Zeitgeist) Producers, Bill Imperial, Lea Marin; Executive Producers, Ronn Mann, Silva Basmajian; Director/Screenplay, Astra Taylor; Photography, John M. Tran; Editor, Robert Kennedy; a Sphynx and National Film Board of Canada production, in association with Ontario Media Development Corp., TVO and Knowledge Network; Canadian; Color; HD; Not rated; 88 minutes; American release date: February 25, 2009. Documentary on several professional philosophers. **WITH:** Cornel West, Avital Ronell, Peter Singer, Kwame Anthony Appiah, Martha Nussbaum, Michael Hardt, Slavoj Zizek, Judith Butler, Sunaura Taylor

Kwame Anthony Appiah in Examined Life © *Zeitgeist Films*

STREET FIGHTER: THE LEGEND OF CHUN-LI (20th Century Fox) Producers, Ashok Amritraj, Patrick Aiello; Executive Producers, Haruhiro Tsujimoto, Keiji Infaune, Toshiro Tokumaru; Director, Andrzej Bartkowiak; Screenplay, Justin Marks; Based on videogames by Capcom; Photography, Geoff Boyle; Designer, Michael Z. Hanan; Costumes, Shirley Chan Ku Fang; Music, Stephan Endleman; Editors, Derek G. Brechin, Niven Howie; Visual Effects Supervisor, Marc Kolbe; Action Choreographer/Supervising Stunt Coordinator, Dion Lam; a Hyde Park Entertainment, Capcom presentation, in association with AdLabs Films, of an Ashok Amritraj/Capcom production; Canadian-Indian-American-Japanese; Dolby; Arri Widescreen; Color; Rated PG-13; 96 minutes; Release date: February 27, 2009. **CAST:** Kristin Kreuk (Chun-Li), Chris Klein (Charlie Nash), Neal McDonough (Bison), Robin Shou (Gen), Moon Bloodgood (Det. Maya Sunee), Josie Ho (Cantana), Taboo (Vega), Michael Clarke Duncan (Balrog), Pei-pei Cheng (Zhilan), Edmund Chen (Xiang), Inez Yan (Chun-Li, 5 years), Elizaveta

Kiryukhina (Rose), Emilze Junqueira (Jeanne Xiang), Katherine Pemberton (Chun-Li, 10 years), Siri Sirijane (Liu), Krystal Vee (Lucy), Thamapat Seengamrat (Secretary Tong), Tim Man (Yung), Jeremy Thana (Korean Boss), Sami Vayrynen (European Boss), Jean-Jacques Vélicitat (Russian Bos), Arash Sharifi, Chuchok Ritnok (Pakistani Bosses), Norio Suzuki (Japanese Boss), Anis Cheurfa (Thug #1 in Alley), Kulnadda Pachimsawat (Thai News Reporter), Brahim Achabbakhe (Thug in Tenement House), Sahajak Boonthanakit (Thai Detective), Brendan Miller (Young Bison)

Kristin Kreuk in Street Fighter: The Legend of Chun-Li © *Capcom Co.*

DILLINGER IS DEAD (Janus Films) a.k.a. *Dillinger è morto*; Producers, Alfred Levy, Ever Haggiag; Director/Story, Marco Ferreri; Screenplay, Marco Ferreri, Sergio Bazzini; Photography, Mario Vulpiani; Designer, Nicola Tamburro; Music, Teo Usuelli; Editor, Mirella Mercio; Italian,1969; Eastmancolor; Not rated; 90 minutes; American release date: February 27, 2009. **CAST:** Michel Piccoli (Glauco), Anita Pallenberg (Ginette), Gigi Lavagetto (The Sailor), Mario Jannilli (The Captain of the Yacht), Annie Girardot (Sabine)

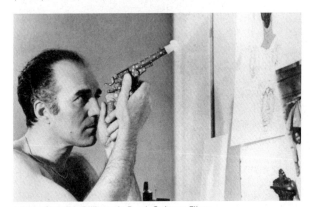

Michel Piccoli in Dillinger is Dead © *Janus Films*

13B: FEAR HAS A NEW ADDRESS (Adlabs) Producer, Rajesh Sawhney; Executive Producer, Sunir Kheterpal; Director/Screenplay, Vikram K. Kumar; Photography, P.C. Sreeram; Costumes, Anu Sundaram; Indian; Color/Black and white; Not rated; 146 minutes; American release date: March 6, 2009. **CAST:** R. Madhavan (Manohar), Neetu Chandra (Priya), Poonam Dhillon (Manohar's Mother), Sachin Khedekar (Dr. Shinde), Dhrithiman Chaterjee (Kamdar), Deepak Dobriyal (Ashok), Murali Sharma (Cop), Sampath (Adv. Ram Charan)

FADOS (New Yorker) Producers, Ivan Dias, Luis Galvao Teles, Antonio Saura; Executive Producers, Saura Medrano, Francois Gonot; Director/Screenplay/Designer, Carlos Saura; Based on an idea by Ivan Dias; Photography, Jose Luis Lopez-Linares; Music Advisor, Carlos do Carmo; Editor, Julia Juaniz; a Duvideo/Fado Filmes/Zebra Prods. production; Spanish-Portuguese, 2007; Dolby; Color; Not rated; 90 minutes; American release date: March 6, 2009. Documentary about Fado, a 19th century Portuguese song style. **WITH:** Chico Buarque de Hollanda, Camané, Carlos do Carmo, Lila Downs, Cesária Évora, Toni Garrido, Lura, Mariza, Miguel Poveda, Argentina Santos, Ana Sofia Varela, Caetano Veloso

TOKYO! (Liberation Entertainment) a Comme des Cinemas production, in co-production with Kansai Television Corp., Bitters End, Sponge Entertainment, Arte France Cinema, Cion Film, WDR/Arte, in association with Backup Films, Wild Bunch, Champion Top Investment, Vap, Hakuhodo DY Media Partners, Wowow, Asahi Broadcasting Corp, Picnic; French, 2008; Color; Not rated; 112 minutes; Release date: March 6, 2009. *Interior Design*: Executive Producers, Yuji Sadai, Hiroyuki Negishi; Director, Michel Gondry; Screenplay, Gabrielle Bell, Michel Gondry; Adapted from the comic *Cecil and Jordan in New York* by Gabrielle Bell, from an idea by Sadie Hales; Photography, Masami Inomoto; Designer, Yuji Hayashida; Music, Etienne Charry; Editor, Jeff Buchanan. **CAST:** Ayako Fujitani (Hiroko), Ryo Kase (Akira), Ayumi Ito (Akemi), Nao Omori (Hiroshi), Satoshi Tsumabuki (Takeshi); *Merde*: Executive Producer: Kenzo Horikoshi; Director/Screenplay, Leos Carax; Photography, Caroline Champetier; Designer, Toshihiro Isomi; Costumes, Céline Guignard, Editor, Nelly Quettier. **CAST:** Denis Lavant (Merde), Jean-Francois Balmer (Voland); *Shaking Tokyo*: Executive Producer, Yuji Sadai; Director/Screenplay, Bong Joon-ho; Photography, Jun Fukumoto; Designer, Mitsuo Harada; Music, Lee Byung Woo. **CAST:** Teruyuki Kagawa (Man), Yu Aoi (Pizza Delivery Girl), Naoto Takenaka (Pizza Delivery Man).

WAITING FOR DUBLIN (Cinema Libre) Producers, Paul Breuls, Catherine Vandeleene; Co-Producers, Kieran Corrigan, Jeff Abberley, Julia Blackman; Executive Producers, Martin DeWitte, Guy Collins, Keith Cousins, Michael Ryan; Director, Roger Tucker; Screenplay, Chuck Conaway; Photography, Marc Felperlaan; Designers, Crispin Sallis, Alan Farquharson; Costumes, Aisling Byrne, Maggie Reyish; Music, Alfred Van Acker; Editor, Les Healey; a Corsan presentation; British-Irish; Dolby; Color; Not rated; 83 minutes; American release date: March 13, 2009. **CAST:** Andrew Keegan (Lt. Mike Clarke), Jade Yourell (Maggie), Hugh O'Conor (Twickers), Frank Kelly (Thaddius McCafferty), Jenne Decleir (Otto "Dinky" Dinkelgruber), Guido De Craene (Dieter Kluge), Britta Smith (Mrs. Kelleher), Kevin Flood (Dr. Mahoney), David Wilmot (Heneghan), Don Foley (Eamonn), Pat Laffan (Paddy O'Dea), Des Braiden (Father Quinlan), Sheila Flitton (Old Crone), Tristan Hickey (Major Forbes), Maria Anastacia Keogh (Swing Dancer), Jack Lynch (Mr. Kelleher), Karl Sheils (Vito Massucci)

Andrew Keegan, Jade Yourell in Waiting for Dublin © *Cinema Libre*

TOKYO SONATA (Regent/Here!) Producers, Yukie Kito, Wouter Barendrecht; Executive Producers, Yasushi Kotani, Michael J. Werner; Director, Kiyoshi Kurosawa; Screenplay, Max Mannix, Kiyoshi Kurosawa, Sachiko Tanaka; Photography, Akiko Ashizawa; Music, Kazumasa Hashimoto; Editor, Koichi Takahashi; an Entertainment Farm (Japan)/Fortissimo Films (Netherlands-Hong Kong) production; Japanese-Netherlands-Hong Kong, 2008; Dolby; Color; Not rated; 119 minutes; American release date: March 13, 2009. **CAST:** Teruyuki Kagawa (Ryûhei Sasaki), Kyôko Koizumi (Megumi Sasaki), Yû Koyanagi (Takashi Sasaki), Kai Inowaki (Kenji Sasaki), Haruka Igawa (Kaneko-san), Kanji Tsuda (Kurosu), Kazuya Kojima (Kobayashi-san), Kôji Yakusho (Dorobô)

Askhat Kuchencherekov in Tulpan © *Zeitgeist Film*

Yû Koyanagi, Kyôko Koizumi in Tokyo Sonata © *Regent Releasing*

MÁNCORA (Maya Entertainment) Producer, Diego Ojeda; Executive Producers, Antonio Gijon, Enrique Murciano; Director, Ricardo de Montreuil; Screenplay, Oscar Torres, Angel Ibarguren, Juan Luis Nugent; Story, Ricardo de Montreuil, Diego Ojeda; Photography, Leandro Filloy; Designer, Miguel Ángel Álvarez; Music, Angelo Milli; Editor, Luis Carballar; a Napolit Pictures & Hispafilms presentation; Spanish-Peruvian; Color; HD-to-35mm; Rated R; 100 minutes; American release date: March 20, 2009. **CAST:** Jason Day (Santiago Pautrat), Elsa Pataky (Ximena Saavedra), Enrique Murciano (Iñigo), Phellipe Haagensen (Batú), Liz Gallardo (Mexican), Andres Arellano (Chester Creek), Anahí de Cárdenas (Ana Maria), Lucia Ojeda (Cuchi Cuchi), Ramsay Ross (jean Pautrat), Angelita Velásquez (Secretary)

TULPAN (Zeitgeist) Producers, Karl Baumgartner, Valerie Fischer, Gulnara Sarsenova, Bulat Galimgereyev, Sergey Melkumov, Elena Yatsoura, Sergei Selyanov, Henryk Romanowski, Thanassis Karathanos, Raimond Goebel; Director/ Screenplay, Sergei Dvortsevoy, Gennady Ostrovsky; Photography, Jola Dyleska; Art Director, Roger Martin; Costumes, Gaziza Korshiyeva; Editors, Isabel Meier, Petar Markovic; a Pandora Films (Germany)/Cobra Film (Switzerland)/Eurasia Film (Kazakhstan)/Film Co. Slovo (Russia)/CTB Filmproduction (Russia)/Filmcontract (Poland)/Pallas Film (Germany) production; German-Swiss-Kazakhstanian-Russian-Polish, 2008; Dolby; Color; Not rated; 100 minutes; American release date: April 1, 2009. **CAST:** Askhat Kuchencherekov (Asa), Samal Yeslavmova (Samal), Ondasyn Besikbasov (Ondas), Tulepbergen Baisakalov (Boni), Bereke Turganbayev (Beke), Mahabbat Turganbayeva (Maha)

ALIEN TRESPASS (Roadside Attractions) Producer/Director, R.W. Goodwin; Executive Producer, James Swift; Screenplay, Steve P. Fisher; Story, James Swift, Steve P. Fisher; Photography, David Moxness; Designer, Ian D. Thomas; Costumes, Jenni Gullett; Music, Louis Febre; Editors, Vaune Kirby Frechette, Michael Jablow; Casting, Susan Edelman; a Rangeland presentation; Canadian; Color; Rated PG; 90 minutes; American release date: April 3, 2009. **CAST:** Eric McCormack (Ted Lewis/Urp), Jenni Baird (Tammy), Robert Patrick (Vernon), Jody Thompson (Lana Lewis), Dan Lauria (Chief Dawson), Aaron Brooks (Cody), Sarah Smyth (Penny), Andrew Dunbar (Dick), Sage Brocklebank (Stu), Jonathan Young (Lloyd), Michael Roberds (Bubba), Tom McBeath (Wilson), Jerry Wasserman (Sam), Vincent Gale (Styles), Christina Schild (Darlene), Laura Konechny (Laura), Darren Rizzolo (Tommy), James Swift (TV Reporter), Chelah Horsdal (Betsy's Mom), Dayna Reid (Betsy), Dee Jay Jackson, Dean Moen (Workers), Aaron Craven (Car Owner), Daniella Evangelista (Greaser's Girlfriend), Justin Dickinson (Greaser), Julia Arkos (Panicked Woman), Jovan Nenadic (Ghota), Roy Campsall (Alien Urp), Tom Braidwood (Ed Sanders), Doolittle (Merlin the Dog)

Jenni Baird, Eric McCormack in Alien Trespass © *Roadside Attractions*

THE SONG OF SPARROWS (Regent) a.k.a. *Avaz-e gonjesk-ha*; Producer/ Director, Majid Majidi; Screenplay, Majid Majidi, Mehran Kashani; Photography, Tooraj Mansoouri; Designer/Costumes, Asghar Nezhad-Imani; Music, Hossein Alizadeh; Editor, Hassan Hassandoost; a Majidi Film production; Iranian; Color; Rated PG; 96 minutes; American release date: April 3, 2009. **CAST:** Reza Naji (Karim), Maryam Akbari (Narges), Kamran Dehgan (Abbas), Hossein Aghazi (Hussein), Shabnam Akhlaghi (Haniyeh), Neshat Nazari (Zahra), Hasan Rezai, Puya Sakhi, Ismael Azizi, Seyeed Reza Imami, Seyyed Peyman Imami, Hassan Rostampour, Saied Razavi, Ali Karam Shakrian (Boys from the Village), Akram Najafi (Mrs. Kokab), Zeinab Sohrabi (Abbas' Wife)

Maryam Akbari, Hamed Aghazi in The Song of Sparrows
© *Regent Releasing*

FORBIDDEN LIE$ (Roxie Releasing) Producer, Sally Regan; Executive Producer, Antonio Zeccola; Director/Screenplay, Anna Broinowski; Photography, Kathryn Milliss, Toby Oliver; Designer, Robert Webb; Costumes, Marriott Kerr; Editors, Alison Croft, Vanessa Milton; a Film Finance Corp. Australia, Liberty Prods. production; Australian, 2008; Dolby; Color; HD; Not rated; 106 minutes; American release date: April 3, 2009. Documentary on author Norma Khouri who pretended her friend was killed for falling in love with a Christian soldier, as recounted in her 2003 book *Honor Lost.* **WITH:** Norma Khouri, Malcolm Knox, Rana Husseini, Caroline Overington, Jon Yates, Ed Torian, Frank Bochte, Dawn Lawkowski, Rachel Richardson, Kara Elliot, Maree Elliot, John Toliopoulos, Majid Bagain, Asma Bayain, Cousin Faris, Larry Finlay, David Leser, Dr. Amal A. Sabbagh, Nadia Shamroukh, Charles V. Ford, Dr. Mu'men S. Hadidi, Dr. Hani Jahshan, Dr. Nasri Khoury, Jeremy Lackowski, John Akdikman, Mansour Ayyad

Norma Khouri in Forbidden Lie$ © *Roxie Releasing*

THE POPE'S TOILET (Film Movement) a.k.a. *El baño del papa*; Producer, Elena Roux; Executive Producers, Sandino Saravia Vinay, Claudia Buschel; Directors/Screenplay, Enrique Fernández, César Charlone; Based on the screenplay and idea by Enrique Fernández; Photography, César Charlone; Designer, Ines Olmedo; Costumes, Alejandra Rosasco; Music, Luciano Supervielle, Gabriel Casacuberta; Editor, Gustavo Giani; a Laroux Cine presentation in association with O2 Filmes, Chaya Films; Uruguayan, 2007; Dolby; Color; Not rated; 97 minutes; American release date: April 8, 2009. **CAST:** César Troncoso (Beto), Virginia Méndez (Carmen), Mario Silva (Valvulina), Virginia Ruiz (Silivia), Nelson Lence (Meleyo), Henry De Leon (Nacente), Jose Arce (Tica), Rosario Dos Santos (Teresa), Hugo Blandamuro (Tartamudo)

Virginia Mendéz, César Troncoso in The Pope's Toilet © *Film Movement*

OBLIVION (Icarus Films) a.k. a. *El olvido*; Producer, Carmen Cobos, Director, Heddy Honigmann; Screenplay, Heddy Honigmann, Judith Vreriks, Sonia Goldenberg; Photography, Adri Schover; Editors, Danniel Danniel, Jessica de Koning; a Cobos Films presentation of Cobos Films (Netherlands)/IKON, ZDF (Germany) production, in cooperation with Arte; Dutch-German, 2008; Color; Not rated; 94 minutes; American release date: April 15, 2009. Documentary about Peru's corrupt and disinterested government's effect on the population. **WITH:** Jorge Kanashiro, Luis Cerna, Mauro Gomez, David Gutierrez, Adolfo Chavez, Lucia Ruiz, Dulovina Cordoba, Daniel Gutierrez Grados, Anibal Cotrina

MUTANT CHRONICLES (Magnet) Producers, Edward R. Pressman, Tim Dennison, Peter La Terriere, Stephen Belafonte, Pras Michel; Executive Producers, Steve Christian, Alessandro Camon, Frederik Malmberg, Lee Solomon, Christian Halsey Solomon, Charles Finch, Stephen Bibeau, Jon Katz; Director, Simon Hunter; Screenplay, Philip Eisner; Photography, Geoff Boyle; Designer, Caroline Greville-Morris; Costumes, Yves Barre; Music, Richard Wells; Editors, Sean Barton, Alison Lewis; Visual Effects Supervisor, Simon Carr; Stunts, Rod Woodruff; Casting, Jeremy Zimmerman, Andrea Clark; an Isle of Man (U.K.) presentation of an Edward R. Pressman (U.S.) production, in association with Grosvenor Park, Remag Guerrilla Films; British-American; Dolby; Technicolor; HD; Rated R; 111 minutes; American release date: April 24, 2009. **CAST:** Thomas Jane (Maj. Mitch Hunter), Ron Perlman (Brother Samuel), Devon Aoki (Cpl. Valerie Duval), Sean Pertwee (Capt. Nathan Rooker), Benno Fürmann (Lt. Maximillian von Steiner), John Malkovich (Constantine), Anna Walton (Severian), Tom Wu (Cpl. Juba Kim Wu), Steve Toussaint (Capt. John McGuire), Luis Echegaray (Cpl. Jesus "El Jesus" de Barrera), Pras Michel (Capt. Michaels), Shauna Macdonald (Adelaide), Roger Ashton-Griffiths (Science Monk), Christopher Adamson (Hodge), Nicholas Ball (Plutocrat), Georgina Berriman (Grace), Georgina Bryce (Dorothy), Richard Buddle (Soldier), Jacqui Chan (Mishima Ambassador), Tim Daniel Clark, David Hewitt, Farhan Khan, Andrew Nixon, Thomas Power, Sanjay Prabhakar, Rafiq Richard (Principal Mutants), Vyelle Croom (Bartender), Dez Drummond (Padre), Christopher Dunne (Medic), Jack Finney (Peter), Nicholas Gecks (Bauhaus Ambassador), Simon Hunter (Transport Pilot), Mark Holloway (Skinny), Barry McCormick (Capitol Ambassador), Scott Joseph (Corporate Guard), Andre Mackay (Science Monk's Assistant), Alfred Mather (Messenger Boy), Neji Nejah (Imperial Ambassador), Don Rae (Grey Faced Sentry), Curtis Walker (Big Boy)

Thomas Jane, Ron Perlman, Benno Fürmann in Mutant Chronicles
© *Magnolia Pictures*

EMPTY NEST (Outsider) a.k.a. *El nido vacío*; Producers, Diego Dubcovsky, Daniel Burman; Executive Producer, Sebastian Ponce; Director/Screenplay, Daniel Burman; Photography, Hugo Colace; Designer, Aili Chen; Costumes, Roberta Pesci; Music, Nico Cota, Santiago Rios; Editor, Alejandro Brodersohn; a Burman Dubcovsky Cine production, in association with Wanda Visión/Paradis Films/Classic Film; Argentine, 2008; Dolby; Color; Not rated; 91 minutes; American release date: April 24, 2009. **CAST:** Oscar Martinez (Leonardo), Cecilia Roth (Martha), Inés Efron (Julia), Arturo Goetz (Dr. Sprivak), Jean Pierre Noher (Fernando), Eugenia Capizzano (Violeta), Ron Richter (Ianib), Carlos Bermejo (Marchetti)

Oscar Martínez, Cecilia Roth in Empty Nest © *Outsider Pictures*

LEON MORIN, PRIEST (Rialto) a.k.a. *Léon Morin, prêtre* and *The Forgiven Sinner*; Producers, Carlo Ponti, Georges de Beauregard; Director/Screenplay, Jean-Pierre Melville; Based on the novel by Béatrix Beck; Photography, Henri Decaë; Designer, Daniel Guéret; Music, Martial Solal; Editors, Jacqueline Meppiel, Nadine Trintignant, Marie-Josèphe Yoyotte; French-Italian, 1961; Black and white; Not rated; 117 minutes; American release date: April 17, 2009. **CAST:** Jean-Paul Belmondo (Leon Morin), Emmanuelle Riva (Barny), Irène Tunc (Christine Sangredin), Nicole Mirel (Sabine Levy), Gisèle Grimm (Lucienne), Marco Behard (Edelman), Monique Bertho (Marion)

GOOBY (Monterey Media) Producer/Director/Screenplay, Wilson Coneybeare; Photography, Michael Storey; Designer, Wendy Morrow; Editor, Ellen Fine; a Coneybeare Stories Inc. presentation; Canadian; Color; Rated PG; 99 minutes; American release date: April 17, 2009. **CAST:** Robbie Coltrane (Voice of Gooby), David James Elliott (Jack Dandridge), Ingrid Kavelaars (Elize), Eugene Levy (Mr. Nerdlinger), Matthew Knight (Willy), Derek Scott (Gooby), Mary Haney (Mrs. Williams), Len Doncheff (Mr. Ogilvey), Paula Boudreau (Mrs. Deacon), Elle Downs (Mrs. Donnelly), Ricky Hegarty (Colin), Luke Bilyk (Cute Kid), Alexander Conti (Eric), Christina Bilyk (Rona Cashier), Tyler Khan (Kid on Bench), Matthew Peart (Big Bruce), Jack Duffy (Grocery Store Manager), Judy Sinclair (Grocery Store Lady), Scott Montgomery (Ticket Booth Clerk), Daniel DeSanto (Crane), Martin Roach (Younger Cop), Tom Farr (Fork Lift Driver), Brad Borbridge (Young Dad), Avery Bisbee (Little Girl)

THREE MONKEYS (Zeitgeist) a.k.a. *Üç maymun*; Producer, Zeynep Ozbatur; Director, Nuri Bilge Ceylan; Screenplay, Ebru Ceylan, Ercan Kesal, Nuri Bilge Ceylan; Photography, Gokhan Tiryaki; Art Director, Ebru Ceylan; Editors, Ayhan Ergursel, Bora Goksingol, Nuri Bilge Ceylan; a Zeynofilm, NBC Film (Turkey)/Pyramide Prods. (France)/Bim Distribuzion (Italy) production; Turkish-French-Italian, 2008; Dolby; Widescreen; Color; HD; Not rated; 109 minutes; American release date: May 1, 2009. **CAST:** Yavuz Bingol (Eyüp), Hatice Aslan (Hacer), Rifat Sungar (Ismail), Ercan Kesal (Servet), Cafer Köser (Bayram), Gürkan Aydin (The Child)

Hatice Aslan, Yavuz Bingol in Three Monkeys © *Zeitgeist Films*

THE WINDOW (Film Movement) a.k.a. *La Ventana*; Producer, José María Morales; Director, Carlos Sorín; Screenplay, Carlos Sorín, Pedro Maizal; Photography, Julián Apezteguia; Music, Nicolás Sorín; Designer, Rafael Neville; Editor, Mohamed Rajid; a Guacamole Films and Wanda Visión production; Argentine-Spanish, 2008; Dolby; Color; Not rated; 85 minutes; American release date: May 6, 2009. **CAST:** Antonio Larreta (Antonio), María del Carmen Giménez (María del Carmen), Emilse Roldán (Emilse), Roberto Rovira (Afinador), Alberto Ledesma (Alberto), Marta Hermida, Victoria Herrera (Women), Arturo Goetz (Doctor Tomás), Marcos Lezama (Marcos), Marina Glazer (Ana), Luis Luque (Farina), Jorge Diez (Pablo), Carla Peteson (Claudia)

María del Carmen Jiménez, Antonio Larreta in The Window © *Film Movement*

REVUE (Icarus) a.k.a. *Predstavleniye*; Producers, Vyacheslav Telnov, Heino Deckert; Director/Editor, Sergei Loznitsa; a Ma.Ja. De Filmprodukton; German-Russian-Urkanian-Finnish, 2008; Black and white: Not rated; 82 minutes; American release date: May 13, 2009. Montage of archive clips documenting the lives of Soviet citizens during the 1950s and 1960s.

BEING JEWISH IN FRANCE (National Center for Jewish Film) a.k.a. *Comme un juif en France*; Producers, Michel Rotman, Marie Helene Ranc; Director/Screenplay, Yves Jeuland; Photography, Jerome Mignard; Music, Eric Slabiak; Editor, Sylvie Bourget; Narrator, Mathieu Amalric; French; Black and white/Color; Not rated; 185 minutes; American release date: May 13, 2009. Documentary on the varying history of the acceptance of Jews in France. **WITH:** Robert Badinter, Elie Barnavi, Jean Benguigui, Paul Bernard, Rachel Cohen, Daniel Farhi, Bruno Fiszon, Raphael Drai

BIG MAN JAPAN (Magnet) a.k.a. *Dai-Nihonjin;* ; Producer, Akihiko Okamoto; Executive Producers, Isao Yoshino, Hiroshi Osaki; Director, Hitoshi Matsumoto; Screenplay, Hitoshi Matsumoto, Mitsuyoshi Takasu; Photography, Hideo Yamamoto; Designer, Yuji Hayashida, Etsuko Aikou; Music, Towa Tei; Visual Effects Director, Hiroyuki Seshita; a Yoshimoto Kogyo Productions & Magnet Releasing presentation; Japanese; Color; Rated PG-13; 113 minutes; American release date: May 15, 2009. **CAST:** Hitoshi Matsumoto (Dai-Nihonjin, /Masaru Daisatou), Riki Takeuchi (Hanerunojyuu), Ua [a.k.a Kaori Murakami] (Manager Kobori), Ryunosuke Kamiki (Dounojyuu), Itsuji Itao (Female Niounojyuu)

Hitoshi Matsumoto in Big Man Japan © *Magnet Releasing*

99 (Showcase) Producers, Anupam Mittal, Aditya Shastri; Directors, Krishna D.K., Raj Nidimoru; Story/Screenplay, Krishna D.K. Raj Nidimoru, Sita Menon; Dialogue, Raja Sen; Photography, Prakash Kutti, Rajeev Ravi; Music, Roshan Machado; Editor, Cheragh Todiwala; Indian; Dolby; Color; Not rated; 135 minutes; American release date: May 15, 2009. **CAST:** Kunal Khemu (Sachin), Boman Irani (Rahul), Soha Ali Khan (Pooja), Cyrus Broacha (Zaramud), Simone Singh (Jahnavi), Mahesh Manjrekar (AGM), Amit Mistry (Kuber), Vinod Khanna (JC), Sudesh Berry (Sunil Mehta), Raja Kapse (Kewal Pandey), Rajesh Singh (Dimple)

JERICHOW (The Cinema Guild) Producers, Florian Koerner von Gustorf, Michael Weber; Director/Screenplay, Christian Petzold; Photography, Hans Fromm; Designer, Anette Guther; Music, Stefan Will; Editor, Bettina Böhler; a Schramm Film Koerner + Weber production, in association with BR, Arte; German; Dolby; Color; Not rated; 91 minutes; American release date: May 15, 2009. **CAST:** Benno Fürmann (Thomas), Nina Hoss (Laura), Hilmi Sözer (Ali), André M. Hennicke (Leon), Claudia Geisler (Administrator), Marie Gruber (Cashier), Knut Berger (Policeman)

Benno Fürmann, Nina Hoss, Hilmi Sözer in Jerichow © *Cinema Guild*

BURMA VJ: REPORTING FROM A CLOSED COUNTRY (Oscilloscope Pictures) a.k.a. *Reporter I et lukket land*; Producer, Lise Lense-Moller; Director, Anders Østergaard; Screenplay, Jan Krogsgaard, Anders Østergaard; Photography, Simon Plum; Music, Conny Malmqvist; Editors, Thomas Papapetros, Janus Billeskov; a Magic Hour Films production, in association with WG Film, Mediamente, Kamoli Films, with the participation of SVT, DR TV, Channel 4, NRK, Danish Film Institute, Danida; Danish; Color; HD; Not rated; 84 minutes; American release date: May 22, 2009. Documentary about the Democratic Voice of Burma, a group of underground journalist who covered the 2007 uprising against the junta. This film received an Oscar nomination for documentary feature.

Burma VJ © *Oscilloscope Pictures*

KABEI: OUR MOTHER (Strand) a.k.a. *Kâbê*; Producers, Hiroshi Fukasawa, Takashi Yajima; Director, Yoji Yamada; Screenplay, Yoji Yamada, Emiko Hiramatsu; Based on the story *Requiem for a Father* by Teruyo Nogami; Photography, Mutsuo Naganuma; Designer, Mitsuo Degawa; Music, Isao Tomita; Editor, Iwao Ishii; Japanese; Dolby; Color; Not rated; 133 minutes; American release date: May 22, 2009. **CAST:** Tadanobu Asano (Yamazaki Toru), Mirai Shida (Hatsuko Nogami),

Sayuri Yoshinaga (Kayo Nogami), Keiko Toda (Teruyo Nogami, Adult), Shôfukutei Tsurubei (Senkichi Fujioka), Miku Sato (Teruyo Nogami)

Miku Sato, Sayuri Yoshinaga, Mirai Shida in Kabei: Our Mother
© Strand Releasing

LAILA'S BIRTHDAY (Kino) a.k.a. *Eid milad Laila*; Producers, Mohamed Habib Attia, Peter van Vogelpool, Rashid Masharawi; Co-Producers, Wouter Barendrecht, Michael J. Werner; Director/Screenplay, Rashid Masharawi; Photography, Tarek Ben Abdallah, Nestor Sanz; Designer, Al'a Abu Ghosh; Music, Kais Sellami; Editor, Pascale Chavance; a Cinema Production Center (Palestine)/CineTeleFilms (Tunisia)/Sweetwater Pictures, Fortissimo Films (Netherlands) production; Palestinian-Tunisian-Dutch; Dolby; Color; HD; Not rated; 71 minutes; American release date: May 27, 2009. **CAST:** Mohammed Bakri (Abu Laila), Areen Omari (Um Laila), Nour Zoubi (Laila)

Nour Zoubi in Laila's Birthday © Kino Intl.

PONTYPOOL (IFC Films) Producers, Jeffrey Coghlan, Ambrose Roche; Executive Producers, Jasper Graham, Henry Cole, J. Miles Dale; Director, Bruce McDonald; Screenplay, Tony Burgess, based on his novel *Pontypool Changes Everything*; Photography, Miroslaw Baszak; Designer, Lea Carlson; Costumes, Sarah Armstrong; Music, Claude Foisy; Editor, Jeremiah Munce; a Maple Pictures presentation, in association with Crescent Road Films, of a Shadow Shows Entertainment/Ponty Up Pictures production; Canadian; Color; HD; Widescreen; Not rated; 96 minutes; American release date: May 29, 2009. **CAST:** Stephen McHattie (Grant Mazzy), Lisa Houle (Sydney Briar), Georgina Reilly (Laurel Ann), Hrant Alianak (Dr. Mendez), Rick Roberts (Keny Loney), Boyd Banks (Jay/Osama), Tony Burgess (Tony/Lawrence), Rachel Burns (Colin/Daud), Raffaele Carniato, Diane Gordon, Yvonne Moore, Louis Negin, Daniel Park (Conversationalists), Daniel Fathers (Nigel Healing), Hannah Fleming (Maureen/Faraj), Laura Nordin (Spooky Woman), Derek Scott (Fish Hut Man), Beatriz Yuste (Nancy Freethy)

Lisa Houle, Stephen McHattie in Pontypool © IFC Films

MUNYURANGABO (Film Movement) Producer/Director/Photography/Editor, Lee Isaac Chung; Screenplay, Lee Isaac Chung, Samuel Gray Anderson; Music, Claire Wibabara; Rwandan-American, 2008; Color; Not rated; 97 minutes; American release date: May 29, 2009. **CAST:** Jeff Rutagengwa (Munyurangabo), Eric Ndorunkundiye (Sangwa), Jean Marie Vianney Nkurikiyinka (Papa Sangwa), Jean Pierre Harerimana (Gwiza), Narcicia Nyirabucyeye (Mama Sangwa), Eduard B. Uwayo (Poet), Pierre Claver Kayitsinga (Killer), Etienne Rugazora (Munyurangabo's Father)

Jeff Rutagengwa, Eric Ndorunkundiye in Munyurangabo © Film

OWL AND THE SPARROW (Wave Releasing) a.k.a. *Cu va chim se se*; Producers, Quan Van Nguyen, Nam Nhat Doan; Executive Producers, Timothy Linh Bui, Ham Tran; Director/Screenplay/Photography, Stephane Gauger; Art Director, Nguyen Van Hoa; Music, Pete Nguyen; Editor, Ricardo Javier; an Annam Pictures production; Vietnamese-American, 2008; Color; DV-to-35mm; Rated PG; 97 minutes; American release date: May 29, 2009. **CAST:** Cat Ly (Lan), The Lu Le (Hai), Han Thi Pham (Thuy), Trong Hai (The Captain), Pham Thi Han (Thuy), Nguyen Hau (Uncle Minh), Teresa Michelle Lee (Bartender), Hoang Long (Soup Boy), Bui Thi Noan (Orphan Director), Danvy Pham (Dancer), Thi Han Phan (Thuy), Nguyen Kim Phuong (Phuong), Le Nguyen Vu (The Magician)

Han Thi Pham in Owl and the Sparrow © *Wave Releasing*

OFFSHORE (A Plus Entertainment) Producer, Marty Shea; Director/Editor, Diane Cheklich; Screenplay, Diane Cheklich, Peg Bogema, Chetana Kowshik; Photography, Gregg McNeill; Designer, Tushar Unadkat; Indian, 2007; Color; Rated PG-13; 92 minutes; American release date: May 29, 2009. **CAST:** Diane Allemon (Iris), Ratnabali Bhattacharjee (Anjali), Neil Bhoopalam (Nikhil), Robert C. Bonnell (Godfrey), Marty Bufalini (Derek Abernathy), Brent Cassidy (Limo Driver), Pauline V. Cheek (Office Profesional), Alison Crockett (Amanda Case), Phil Cuthbertson (Jason), Jesse Dean (Office Worker), Jason Endres (Office Mailboy), Geoff Ernst (Jerry), Axel Harney (Disgruntled Employee), Siddharth Makkar (Ajay Tiwari), Emily Rose Merrell (Bridgette Mars), Jaime Moyer (Marge), Leanor Reizen (Mrs. Fairfax), Emily Rose (Bridgette Mars), David Rumble (Denzel), Adam Schomer (Mark Jamison), Satish Shah (Devendra Tiwari), Malaika Shenoy (Reva), Deb Tunis (Carol Silvers), Gaurang Vyas (Satish Reddy)

Alison Crockett, Deb Tunis in Offshore © *Big Pictures*

UNMISTAKEN CHILD (Oscilloscope) Producers, Arik Bernstein, Ilil Alexander, Nati Baratz; Director, Nati Baratz; Screenplay, Nati Baratz; Photography, Yaron Orbach; Music, Cyril Morin; Editor, Ron Goldman; a Samsara Films, Alma Films production; Israeli, 2008; Color; Not rated; 102 minutes; American release date: June 3, 2009. Documentary on Nepalese monk Tenzin Zopa's search for the reincarnation of deceased Buddhist master Geshe Lama Konchong. **WITH:** Tenzin Zopa, Tenzin Ngodrup

Tenzin Zopa in Unmistaken Child © *Oscilloscope Films*

24 CITY (Cinema Guild) a.k.a. *Er shi si cheng ji*; Producers, Jia Zhangke, Shozo Ichiyama, Wang Hong; Executive Producers, Chow Keung, Ren Zhonglun, Tang Yong; Director, Jia Zhangke, Screenplay, Jia Zhangke, Zhai Yongming; Photography, Yu Lik-wai; Designer, Liu Qiang; Music, Yoshihro Hanno, Lim Giong; Editors, Lin Xudong, Kong Jinlei; an Xstream Pictures, Shanghai Film Group, China Resources Holdings Co. presentation; Japanese; Color; HD; Not rated; 112 minutes; American release date: June 5, 2009. **CAST:** Joan Chen (Gu Minhua/Xiao Hua), Lu Liping (Hao Dali), Zhao Tao (Su Na), Chen Jianbin, Jiang Shanshan, Chen Rui, Zhai Yongming, Yang Mengyue, Lui Xiangquan, Luo Gonghe; He Xikun, Wang Zhiren, Guan Fengjiu, Hou Lijun, Zhao Gang (Interviewees)

24 City © *Cinema Guild*

LE COMBAT DANS L'ILE (Rialto) a.k.a. *Fire and Ice*; Director/Screenplay, Alain Cavalier; Dialgoue, Jean-Paul Rappeneau; Photography, Pierre Lhomme; Designer, Bernard Evein; Music, Serge Nigg; Editor, Pierre Gillette; French, 1962; Black and white; Not rated; 104 minutes; American release date: June 12, 2009. **CAST:** Romy Schneider (Anne), Jean-Louis Trintignant (Clement Lesser), Henri Serre (Paul), Diana Lepvrier (Cécile) Robert Bousquet (Lucien), Jacques Berlioz (Father), Armand Meffre (André), Maurice Garrel (Terrasse), Pierre Asso (Serge)

THE END OF THE LINE (New American Vision) Producers, Claire Lewis, George Duffield; Director/Photography, Rupert Murray; Based on the book by Charles Clover; Underwater Photography, John Mcintyre, David Groundwater, Scubazoo; Music, Srdjan Kurpjel, Marios Takoushis; Editor, Claire Ferguson; Color; Not rated; 82 minutes; Release date: June 19, 2009. Documentary on the increasingly dangerous shortage of fish in the world. **WITH:** Charles Clover, John Crosbie, Brian Mulroney, Jeffrey Hutchings, Callum Roberts, Daniel Pauly, Boris Worm, Manolo Pacheco Luis, Ray Hilborn, Roberto Mielgo Bragazzi, Serge Tudela, Ben Bradshaw, Masanori Miyahara, Rashid Sumaila, Adama Mbergaul, Haidar El Ali, Yvonne Saovy, Chef Maxwell, Pete Petersen, Steve Palumbi, Richie Nota, Jamie Oliver, Ted Stevens, Matthew Moir, Patricia Majluf, Hardy McKinney

AFGHAN STAR (Zeitgeist) Producer, Havana Marking; Executive Producers, Mike Lerner, Martin Herring, Saad Mohensi, Jahid Moheni; Director, Havana Marking; Photography, Phil Stebbing; Music, Simon Russell; Editor, Ash Jenkins; a Channel 4 Documentary Foundation production in association with Tolo TV; British; Color; Not rated; 87 minutes; Documentary on Afghanistan's popular *American Idol*-like television show *Afghan Star*. **WITH:** Setara Hussainzada, Rafi Nabaazda, Hameed Sahkizada, Lema Sahar, Daoud Sediqi, Habib Amiri, Massoud Sanjer, Tahir Shaqi

Lema Sahar in Afghan Star © Zeitgeist

QUIET CHAOS (IFC Films) a.k.a. *Caos calmo*; Producer, Domenico Procacci; Executive Producer, Eric Abraham; Director, Antonello Grimaldi; Screenplay, Nanni Moretti, Laura Paolucci, Francesco Piccolo; Based on the novel by Sandro Veronesi; Photography, Alessandro Pesci; Designer, Giada Calabria; Costumes, Alexandra Toesca; Music, Paolo Buonvino; Editor, Angelo Nicolini; a Fandango production; Dolby; Color; Not rated; 112 minutes; American release date: June 29, 2009. **CAST:** Nanni Moretti (Pietro Paladini), Valeria Golino (Marta), Alessandro Gassman (Carlo Paladini), Isabella Ferrari (Eleanora Simoncini), Silvio Orlando (Samuele), Blu Yoshimi (Claudia Paladini), Hippolyte Girardot (Jean-Claude), Roberto Nobile (Taramanni), Alba Rohrwacher (Annalisa), Manuela Morabito (Maria Grazia), Kasia Smutniak (Jolanda), Beatrice Bruschi (Benedetta), Sara D'Amico (Francesca), Babak Karimi (Mario), Tatiana Leopre (Mamma di Matteo), Anna Gigante, Valentina Carnelutti (Amica di Maria Grazia), Denis Podalydès (Thierry), Charles Berling (Boesson), Antonella Attili (Gloria), Cloris Brosca

(Psicoterapeuta), Stefano Guglielmi (Matteo), Nestor Saied (Simoncini), Dina Braschi (Donna Anziana), Ester Cavallari (Lara Paladini), Roman Polanski (Steiner)

Blu Yoshimi, Alessandro Gassman in Quiet Chaos © IFC Films

TONY MANERO (Lorber) Producer, Juan de Dios Larraín; Director, Pablo Larraín; Screenplay, Pablo Larraín, Alfredo Castro, Mateo Iribarren; Photography, Sergio Armstrong; Designer, Polin Garbisu; Editor, Andrea Chignoli; a Fabula Prods. (Chile), Prodigital (Brazil) production; Chilean-Brazilian, 2008; Dolby; Color; 16-to-35mm; Not rated; 97 minutes; American release date: July 3, 2009. **CAST:** Alfredo Castro (Raúl Peralta), Amparo Noguera (Cony), Héctor Morales (Goyo), Paola Lattus (Pauli), Elsa Poblete (Wilma)

Alfredo Castro in Tony Manero © Lorber Films

EVANGELION: 1.0 YOU ARE (NOT) ALONE (Eleven Arts) a.k.a. *Evangelion Shin-Geki jo Ban*; Producer, Toshimichi Otsuki; Directors, Hideaki Anno, Masayuki, Kazuya Tsurumaki; Screenplay, Hideaki Anno; Photography, Toru Fukushi; Character Designer, Yushiyuki Sadamoto; Animation Director, Hiroshi Haraguchi; Music, Shiro Sasigu; Editor, Hiroshi Okuda; a Khara Corp. production; Japanese, 2007; Dolby; Color; Rated PG-13; 95 minutes; American release date: July 3, 2009.

KAMBAKKHT ISHQ (Eros) a.k.a. *Incredible Love*; Producer, Sajid Nadiadwala; Executive Producer, Prachi Thadani; Director, Sabbir Khan; Screenplay, Sabbir Khan, Ishita Moitra, Kiran Kotrial, Anvita Dutt Guptan; Photography, Vikas Sivaraman; Designer, Acropolis; Music, Any Malik; Lyrics, Anvita Dutt Guptan; Costumes, Aki Narula, Shabina Khan; Score, Salim-Sulaiman; Editor, Nitin Rokade; Choreographer, Vaibhavi Merchant; a Madiadwala Grandson Entertainment production; Indian; Dolby; Widescreen; Color; Not rated; 139 minutes; American release date: July 3, 2009. **CAST:** Ashay Kumar (Viraj), Kareena Kapoor (Simrita Rai, Slim), Aftab Shivdasani (Lucky Shergill), Amirta Arora (Kamini), Denise Richards, Sylvester Stallone, Brandon Routh (Themselves), Akshay Kumar (Viraj Shergill), Diane Sellers (Judge), Ashwin Mushran (Parmeet), Bayli Johnston (Flower Girl), Raeann Giles (Model), Vindu Dara Singh (Tiger), Sheridan Crist (Deacon), Tony Alameda (Fedora Gangster), Mikandrew Perdaris (Matt)

LION'S DEN (Strand) a.k.a. *Leonora*; Producers, Pablo Trapero, Youngjoo Suh; Co-Producer, Walter Salles; Executive Producer, Martina Gusman; Director, Pablo Trapero; Screenplay, Alejandro Fadel, Martín Mauregui, Santiago Mitre, Pablo Trapero; Photography, Guillermo Nieto; Editors, Ezequiel Borovinsky, Pablo Trapero; Argentine, 2008; Dolby; Color; Not rated; 113 minutes; American release date: July 3, 2009. **CAST:** Martina Gusman (Julia), Elli Medeiros (Sofia), Rodrigo Santoro (Ramiro), Laura Garcia (Marta), Tomas Plotinsky (Tomas VI), Leonardo Sauma (Ugo Casman), Walter Cignoli (Pcrito Psicólogo), Clara Sajnovetszky (Elsa)

Martina Gusman in Lion's Den © *Strand Releasing*

BLOOD: THE LAST VAMPIRE (Goldwyn) Producers, Bill Kong, Abel Nahimas; Director, Chris Nahon; Screenplay, Chris Chow; Based on the 2001 anime film by Kenji Kamiyama, Katsuya Terada; Photography, Poon Hang-sang; Designer, Nathan Amondson; Costumes, Constanza Balduzzi, Shandy Lui Fun Shan; Music, Clint Mansell; Editor, Marco Cave; Action Director, Corey Yuen; Creature and Makeup Effects, Spectral Motion; an East Wing Holdings Corp. (Hong Kong)/ SAJ (France) presentation in association with Beijing Happy Pictures Cultural

Communications; Hong Kong-French; Dolby; Widescreen; Color; Rated R; 89 minutes; American release date: July 10, 2009. **CAST:** Gianna Jun (Saya), Allison Miller (Alice McKee), Liam Cunningham (Michael), JJ Feild (Luke), Koyuki (Onigen), Yasuaki Kurata (Kato Takatora), Larry Lamb (Gen. McKee), Andrew Pleavin (Frank Nielsen), Michael Byrne (Elder), Colin Salmon (Powell), Masiela Lusha (Sharon), Ailish O'Connor (Linda), Constantine Gregory (Mr. Henry), Joey Anaya, Khary Payton (Creatures), Liu Lei (One-Eye), Santiago Alonso, Hector Alonso, Mercela Kawashita (Cleaners), Chun Yihe (Saya at 8), Lai Ziyang (Boy at 8), Alberto Silva, Luis Sabatini, Nathan Amondson, Julio Fries, Sergio Carelli (Organization Men), Matthew Walz (George), Laura Bugnoni (Liz), Xu Yang (Young Man), Shui Xian (Drag Queen Bartender), Jacques Eberhard, Keith Wyatt (Snipers), Johnny Lee (Bellhop)

Gianna Jun, Yasuaki Kurata in Blood: The Last Vampire © *Samuel Goldwyn Co.*

VANISHED EMPIRE (Kino) a.k.a. *Ischeznuvshaya imperiya*; Producers/Director, Karen Shakhnazarov; Executive Producer, Galina Shadur; Screenplay, Sergei Rokotov, Yevgeni Nikishov; Photography, Sandor Berkeshi; Designer, Lyudmila Kusakova; Music, Konstantin Shevelv; Editor, Irina Kozhhemyakina; a Mosfilm production; Russian, 2008; Dolby; Color; Not rated; 104 minutes; American release date: July 10, 2009. **CAST:** Aleksandr Lyapin (Sergei Narbekov), Lidiya Milyuzina (Lyuda Beletskaya), Yegor Baranovsky (Stepan Molodtsov), Ivan Kupreyenko (Kostya Denisov), Armen Dzhigarkhanyan (Sergei's Grandfaterh), Olga Tumajkina (Sergei's Mother), Vladimir Ilyin (Stepan, 30 years later), Tatyana Yakovenko (Lyuda's Motehr), Yanina Kalganova (Katya), Vasya Shahkhnazarov (Misha), Yekaterina Kasparova (Folklore Teacher)

Armen Dzhigarkhanyan, Aleksandr Lyapin in Vanished Empire © *Kino Intl.*

LAKE TAHOE (Film Movement) Producer, Christian Valdelievre; Executive Producer, Jaime Bernardo Ramos; Director, Fernando Eimbcke; Screenplay, Fernando Eimbcke, Paula Markovitch; Photography, Alexis Zabe; Art Director, Diana Quiroz; Editor, Mariana Rodriguez; a Cinepantera production, in association with Instituto Mexicano de Cinematografica (Mexico)/Sundance Institute (U.S.)/NHK (Japan); Mexican-American-Japanese; Color; Widescreen; Not rated; 81 minutes; American release date: July 10, 2009. **CAST:** Diego Cataño (Juan), Hector Herrera (Don Heber), Daniela Valentine (Lucia), Juan Carlos Lara II (David), Yemil Sefani (Joaquin), Olda López (David's Mother), Mariana Elizondo (Mother of Juan and Joquin), Joshua Habid (Fidel), Raquel Araujo (Arturo's Mother), Enrique Albor (Owner of Blue Bar)

Juan Carlos Lara II, Diego Cataño in Lake Tahoe © *Film Movement*

DIED YOUNG, STAYED PRETTY (Norotomo) Producer/Director/Photography/Editor, Eileen Yaghoobian; Music, Mark Greenberg; Visual Effects, Pete Dionne; a Norotomo Prods. presentation in association with Canadian Council for the Arts; Canadian; Color; DV; Not rated; 95 minutes; American release date: July 17, 2009. Documentary on rock poster artists. **WITH:** Ames Brothers, Art Chantry, Brian Chippendale, Clayton Hayes, Ron Hazelmyer, Rob Jones, Print Mafia, Bryce McCloud, Jay Ryan

Died Young, Stayed Pretty © *Notorama*

THE AGE OF STUPID (Spanner Films) Producer, Lizzie Gillett; Executive Producers, John Battsek, Andrew Ruhemann, Emily James, Paul Goodison; Director/Screenplay/Photography, Franny Armstrong; Designer, David Bryan; Costumes, Heidi Miller; Music, Chris Brierley; Editor, David G. Hill; Visual Effects Supervisor, Katie Roberts; Animation Director, Jonathan Hodgson; Presented in association with Passion Pictures; British; Color; HD/HDV-to-35mm; Not rated; 89 minutes; American release date: July 17, 2009. Documentary on the dangers of Earth's climate change. **WITH:** Pete Postlethwaite (The Archivist), Jamila Bayyoud, Adnan Bayyoud, Alvin DuVernay, Piers Guy, Layefa Malini, Fernand Pareau, Jeh Wadia

Pete Postlethwaite in The Age of Stupid © *Spanner/Passion*

THE ENGLISH SURGEON (Eyeline Films/Storyville) Producers, Geoffrey Smith, Rachel Wexler; Executive Producers, Greg Sanderson, Nick Fraser, Sally Jo Fifer; Director, Geoffrey Smith; Photography, Graham Day; Music, Nick Cave, Warren Ellis; Editor, Kathy O'Shea; an Eyeline Films/Bungalow Town production; British; Color; HD; Not rated; 94 minutes; American release date: July 24, 2009. Documentary about London brain surgeon Dr. Henry Marsh and his effort to improve the arcane medical conditions in the Ukraine. **WITH:** Henry Marsh, Igor Kurilets, Marian Dolishny

SURVIVING CROOKED LAKE (NeoClassics) a.k.a. *Crooked Lake*; Producers, Nicholas D. Tabarrok, Jaty Tam, Matthew Miller; Executive Producers, Uwe Feuersenger, Henry Gerstel; Directors/Screenplay, Sascha Drews, Ezra Krybus, Matthew Miller; Photography, Sascha Drews, Ezra Krybus; Music, Sascha Drews; Editor, Kathy Weinkauf; a Darius Films production, in association with Common Films, with the participation of Telefilm Canada; Canadian; Color; DVD; Not rated; 87 minutes; American release date: July 24, 2009. **CAST:** Alysha Aubin (Alysha), Candice Mausner (Candice), Morgan McCunn (Morgan), Stephannie Richardson (Steph), Guy Yarkoni (Jonah), Grant Palmer (Thumbs Up Dude)

YOU, THE LIVING (Palisades/Tartan) a.k.a. *Du levande*; Producers, Roy Andersson, Philippe Bober, Susanne Marian, Carsten Brandt, Hakon Overas; Director/Screenplay, Roy Andersson; Photography, Gustav Danielsson; Designers, Magnus Renfors, Elin Segerstedt; Costumes, Fredrik Borg; Music, Robert Hefter; Editor, Anna Marta Waern; a Studio 24 presentation; Swedish-French-Danish-Norwegian-German-Japanese, 2007; Color; Not rated; 92 minutes; American release date: July 29, 2009. **CAST:** Jessika Lundberg (Anna), Elisabeth Helander (Mia), Björn Englund (Tuba Player), Leif Larsson (Carpenter), Ollie Olson (Consultant), Birgitta Persson (Tuba Player's Wife), Kemal Sener (The Barber), Håkan Angser (The Psychiatrist), Rolf Engström (Trumslagaren), Gunnar Ivarsson (The Businessman), Eric Bäckman (Micke Larsson), Patrik Edgren (Professor), Lennart Eriksson (Man on Balcony), Pär Fredriksson (The Carpet Dealer), Jessica Nilsson (The Teacher), Jörgen Nohall (Uffe), Waldemar Nowak (The Pick-Pocket), Jan Wikbladh (The Fan), Bengt C.W. Carlsson (CEO)

Björn Englund in You, the Living © *Palisades Tartan*

GHOSTED (First Run Features) a.k.a. *Ai Mei*; Producer/Director, Monika Treut; Screenplay, Astrid Ströher, Monika Treut; Photography, Bernd Meiners; Designers, Isolde Rueter, Yang Cheng-yi; Costumes, Petra Kilian; Music, Uwe Haas; Editor, Renate Ober; a Hyena Films (Germany)/Chi & Co. (Taiwan) production; German-Tai; Color; HD-to-35mm; Not rated; 89 minutes; American release date: July 31, 2009. **CAST:** Inga Busch (Sophie Schmitt), Ke Huan-ru (Chen Ai ling), Hu Ting-ting (Wang Mei-li), Jana Schulz (Katrin Bendersen), Marek Hartoff (Leon), Jack Kao (Chen Fu), Lu Yi-ching (Ya-ching), Kevin Chen (Patrick), Nick Dong-Sik (Herr Lee)

Ting-ting Hu, Inge Busch in Ghosted © *First Run Features*

NOT QUITE HOLLYWOOD: THE WILD, UNTOLD STORY OF OZPLOITATION! (Magnolia) Producers, Michael Lynch, Craig Griffin; Executive Producers, Bruno Charlesworth, Jonathan Shteinman, Paul Weigard, Nick Batzias; Director/Screenplay, Mark Hartley; Photography, Kart von Moller; Music, Stephen Cummings, Billy Miller; Editors, Jamie Blanks, Sara Edwards, Mark Hartley; a Film Finance Corp. Australia, City Films Worldwide, Madman Films presentation; Australian; Dolby; Color; HD-and-35mm; Rated R; 102 minutes; American release date: July 31, 2009. Documentary on Australia's exploitation action films of the 1970s and '80s. **WITH:** Phillip Adams, Christine Amor, Glory Annen, Victoria Anoux, Ian Barry, Briony Behets, Steve Bisley, Jamie Blanks, Graeme Blundell, Russell Boyd, Richard Brennan, Dan Burstall, Tom Burstall, Robin Copping, Barry Crocker, Lynette Currant, Jamie Lee Curtis, Cassandra Delaney, Everett De Roche, Ross Dimsey, David Eggby, Bob Ellis, Alan Finney, Richard Franklin, Belinda Giblin, Rebecca Gilling, Antony I. Ginnane, Deborah Gray, David Hannay, Sandy

Harbutt, Rod Hardy, Gregory Harrison, Rod Hay, Carla Hoogeveen, Alan Hopgood, Dennis Hopper, John Michael Howson, Wendy Hughes, Barry Humphries, John Jarratt, Barry Jones, Brian Jones, Stacy Keach, Ted Kotcheff, John D. Lamond, Nina Landis, George Lazenby, Chris Löfvén, Greg Lynch, William Margold, Ross Matthews, Donald McAlpine, Bob McCarron, Hal McElroy, Greg Mclean, George Miller, Vincent Monton, Philippe Mora, Judy Morris, Russell Mulcahy, Rod Mullinar, Grant Page, Susan Penhaligon, Steve Railsback, Candy Raymond, Cheryl Rixon, Joanne Samuel, Fred Schepisi, John Seale, Ken Shorter, Lynda Stoner, Quentin Tarantino, Rod Taylor, Henry Thomas, Jeremy Thomas, Jack Thompson, Sigrid Thornton, Brian Trenchard-Smith, James Wan, Garry Wapshott, Roger Ward, John Waters, Heigh Whannell, David Williamson, Tony Williams, Simon Wincer, Arna-Maria Winchester, Uri Windt, Norman Yemm, Susannah York

Not Quite Hollywood © *Magnet*

IMPORT/EXPORT (Palisades/Tartan) a.k.a. *Import Eksport*; Producer, Egil Odegard; Director/Screenplay, Khalid Hussain; Photography, Kjell Vassdal; Art Director, Terje Lind Bjorsvik; Costumes, Ingun Ronesen; Music, Oistein Boassen; Editors, Bodil Kjaerhauge, Anders Refn; a Filmhuset Produksjoner production; Norwegian, 2005; Color; Not rated; 89 minutes; American release date: July 31, 2009. **CAST:** Iram Haq (Jasmin), Bjørnar Teigen (Jan), Assad Siddique (Yousuf), Talat Hussain (Allahditta), Niklas Gundersen (Nicolay), Janicke Holden (Mona), Kim Kolstad (Marius), Harald Lönnbro (Robert), Anne Marie Ottersen (Jan's Mother), Anita Uberoi (Nadia)

LUCK (Studio 18) Producer, Shree Ashtavinayak; Director/Story, Soham Shah; Screenplay, Renzil D'Silva; Photography, Santosh Thundiiayil; Indian; Color; Not rated; 155 minutes; American release date: July 31, 2009. **CAST:** Imran Khan (Ram Mehra), Danny Denzongpa (Lakhaan Tamaang), Mithun Chakraborty (Major Jabbar Pratap Singh), Sanjay Dutt (Karim Moussa), Shruti K. Haasan (Ayesha), Ravi Kishan (Raghav), Chritrashi Rawat (Shortcut)

BLISS (First Run Features) a.k.a. *Mutluluk*; Producer/Director, Abdullah Oguz; Screenplay, Kubilay Tuncer, Elif Ayan, Abdullah Oguz; based on the novel by Zülfü Livaneli; Photography, Mirsad Herovic; Art Director, Tolunay Turkoz; Music, Zülfü Livaneli; Editors, Levent Celebi, Abdullah Oguz; an ANS presentation; Turkish-Greek, 2007; American release date: August 7, 2009. **CAST:** Özgü Namal (Meryem), Talat Bulut (Irfan), Murat Han (Cemal), Mustafa Avkiran (Ali Riza), Emin Gursoy (Tahsin), Meral Çetinkaya (Münewer), Lale Mansur (Aysel), Sebnem Köstem (Döne), Leyla Basak (Serap), Idil Yener (Nazik), Erol Babaoglu (Yakup)

Talat Bulut, Özgü Namal, Murat Han in Bliss © *First Run Features*

I'M GONNA EXPLODE (IFC Films) a.k.a. *Voy a explotar*; Producers, Pablo Cruz, Gerardo Naranjo, Hunter Gray, Alain de la Mata; Executive Producers, Gael Garcia Bernal, Diego Luna, Tyler Brodie, Alex Orlovsky, Rafa Ley, Hector Ley, Kyzza Terrazas, Geminiano Pineda, Yibran Asuad, Gabriel Garcia Nava, Gabriel Nuncio; Director/Screenplay, Gerardo Naranjo; Photography, Tobias Datum; Designer, Claudio Castelli; Costumes, Annai Ramos Maza, Amanda Carcamo; Music, Georges Delerue; ; Editor, Yibran Asuad; a Canana Films, Cinematografica Revolcadero, Verisimilitiude, Fondo de Inversion y Estimulos al Cine production; Mexican, 2008; Dolby; Color; Widescreen; Not rated; 103 minutes; American release date: August 12, 2009. **CAST:** Maria Deschamps (Maru), Juan Pablo de Santiago (Roman), Daniel Gimenez Cacho (Eugenio), Martha Claudia Moreno (Helena), Rebecca Jones (Eva), Pedro González (Cantante)

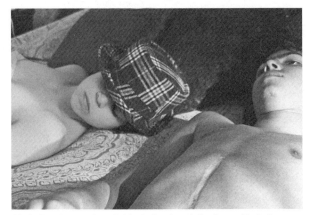

Maria Deschamps, Juan Pablo de Santiago in I'm Gonna Explode © *IFC Films*

YASUKUNI (The Film Library) Producers, Zhang Yuhui, Zhang Huijun, Hu Yun; Director/Screenplay, Li Ying; Photography, Yasuhiro Hotta, Li Ying; Editors, Yuji Oshige, Li Ying; a Dragon Films presentation; Japanese-Chinese, 2008; Color; Not rated; 123 minutes; American release date: August 12, 2009. Documentary on Tokyo's controversial Yasukuni monument to the Japanese war dead.

MY FÜHRER (First Run Features) a.k.a. *Mein Fuehrer: Die wirklich wahrste Wahrheit über Adolf Hitler*; Producer, Stefan Arndt; Director/Screenplay, Dani Levy; Photography, Carl-Friedrich Koschnick, Carsten Thiele; Designer, Christian Eisele; Costumes, Nicole Fischnaller; Music, Niki Reiser; Editor, Peter R. Adam; Casting, Simone Baehr; an X Verleih AG presentation of a Y Filme Directors

Kariya Naoharu in Yasukuni © *Dragon Films*

Pool, X Filme Creative Pool production; German, 2007; Dolby; Color; Not rated; 95 minutes; American release date: August 14, 2009. **CAST:** Helge Schneider (Adolf Hitler), Ulrich Mühe (Prof. Adolf Grünbaum), Sylvester Groth (Dr. Joseph Goebbels), Adriana Altaras (Elsa Grünbaum), Stefan Kurt (Albert Speer), Ulrich Noethen (Heinrich Himmler), Lambert Hamel (Lieutenant-Gernal Rattenhuber), Udo Kroschwald (Martin Bormann), Ilja Richter (Kurt Gerheim), Katja Reimann (Eva Braun), Meret Becker (Secretary), Axel Werner (Erich Kempka)

Helge Schneider in My Führer © *First Run Features*

CAPTAIN ABU RAED (NeoClassics) Producers, Kenneth Kokin, Nadine Toukan, Laith Al-Majali, Amin Matalqa, David Pritchard; Director/Screenplay, Amin Matalqa; Photography, Reinhart Peschke; Designer, Gerald Sullivan; Costumes, Jamila Alaeddin; Music, Austin Wintory; Editor, Laith Al-Majali; a Paper & Pen Films presentation, in association with Gigpix Studios, of a David Pritchard production; Jordanian, 2008; Color; Not rated; 104 minutes; American release date: August 14, 2009. **CAST:** Nadim Sawalha (Abu Raed), Rana Sultan (Nour), Hussein Al-Sous (Murad), Udey Al-Qiddissi (Tareq), Ghandi Saber (Abu Murad), Dina Raad-Yaghnam (Um Murad), Mohammad Qteshat (Hilal), Nadim Mushahwar (Sameh), Faisal Majali (Ziad), Khaled Al-Safi (Ali), Rami Samara (Chubby Boy), Ayat Najah Abd Al-Sadeq (Petra), Lara Sawalha (Girlfriend at Party), Khuloud Khaled Issa (Khuloud), Phaedra Dahdaleh (Nour's Friend), Claire Naber (Lady Writing Name), Fawaz Zoubi (Pilot)

Nadim Sawalha, Udey Al-Qiddisi in Captain Abu Raed © *Gigapix*

TAXIDERMIA (Regent) Producers, Péter Miskolczi, Gábor Váradi, Gabriele Kranzelbinder, Alexander Dumreicher-Ivanceanu, Alexandre Mallet-Guy, Emilie George; Director, György Pálfi; Screenplay, Zsófia Ruttkay, György Pálfi; Based on stories by Lajos Parti Nagy; Photography, Gergely Pohárnok; Designer, Adrien Asztalos; Costumes, Júlia Patkós; Music Supervisor, Amon Tobin; Editor, Réka Lemhényi; a Fortissimo Films presentation; Hungarian-Austrian-French, 2006; 91 minutes; American release date: August 14, 2009. **CAST:** Csaba Czene (Vendel Morosgoványi), Gergõ Trócsányi (Kálmán Balatony), Marc Bischoff (Lajos Balatony), Adél Stanczel (Gii Aczél), István Gyuricza (Hadnagy, Young Lieutenant), Piroska Molnár (Hadnagyné, Lieutenant's Wife), Gábor Máté (Old Kálmán), Géza Hegedžs (Dr. Andor Regõczy), István Hunyadkürti (Jenõ Bá), Zoltán Koppány (Béla Miszlényi)

Zoltán Koppány in Taxidermia © *Regent Releasing*

CASI DIVAS (Maya Entertainment) Producer, Luz Maria Rojas; Executive Producer/Original Idea, Ignacio Darnaude; Director/Screenplay, Issa Lopez; Photography, Carlos Aguilera; Designer, Carlos Herrera; Costumes, Bertha Romero; Casting, Andrea Abbiati, Isabel Cortazar; a Columbia Pictures Mexico production; Mexican, 2008; Dolby; Color; HD; Rated PG-13; 106 minutes; American release date: August 21, 2009. **CAST:** Patricia Llaca (Eva), Julio Bracho (Alejandro), Maya Zapata (Francisca), Ana Layevska (Ximena), Daniela Schmidt (Yesenia), Diana Garcia (Catailna), Mónica Huarte (Karen Trigo), Dario T. Pie (Jurado), Daniel Figueroa (Jonathan Armando), Ianis Guerrero (Osiris), Gustavo Sánchez Parra (Satán), Uriel del Toro (Conductor), Pedro Izquierdo (Adrián), Adrian Alonso (Patricks), Keiko Durán (Guiomar Lizárraga), Miriana Moro (Gladys), Marina de Tavira (Model), Arturo Barba (Director of Escena), Julian Sedgwick (Ted)

SIKANDAR (Big Pictures) a.k.a. *Foot Soldier*; Producer, Sudhir Mishra; Executive Producer, Anwar Jamal; Director/Screenplay, Piyush Jha; Photography, Somak Mukherjee; Designer, Shruti Gupte; Music, Justin-Uday, Sandesh Shandilya; Editor, Dev Jadhav; Indian; Dolby; Color; Not rated; 110 minutes; American release date: August 21, 2009. **CAST:** Parzan Dastur (Sikandar), Ayesha Kapoor (Nasreen), Sanjay Suri (Mukhtar Masoodi), Madhavan (Lt. Col. Rao), Arunoday Singh (Zehgeer Quadir)

LIVERPOOL (The Match Factory) Producers, Lisandro Alonso, Ilse Hughan, Marianne Slot, Louis Minarro; Director, Lisandro Alonso; Screenplay, Salvador Roselli; Photography, Luico Bonelli; Designer, Gonzalo Delgado; Music, Flor Maleva; Editors, Lisandro Alonso, Fernando Epstein, Martin Mainoli, Sergi Dies; a 4L (Argentina) production, in co-production with Fortuna Films, Slot Machine, Eddie Saeta, Black Forest Films; Argentine, 2008; Dolby; Color; Not rated; 85 minutes; American release date: September 2, 2009. **CAST:** Nieves Cabrera (Trujillo), Giselle Irrazabal (Analia), Juan Fernández (Farrel)

SANDSTORM (Wildcat Releasing) Producers, Rebecca Boudreau, Michael Mahonen; Executive Producer, Joe Wang; Directors/Screenplay/Casting, Michael Mahonen; Photography, David Chai; Costumes, Ni Mingda; Music, Carlos Campos, Susan Liu; Editors, Danielle Zhu, David Chai, Corban Hu; an NTD Films/Requisite Films production; Canadian, 2004; Color; Not rated; 75 minutes; American release date: September 4, 2009. **CAST:** Rong Tian (He Tian Ying), Lili Li (The Practitioner), Angela Huang (Young Policewoman), Steve Hong (Supervisor), Cheng Guang (Young Policeman), Annie Li (Daughter)

Annie Li in Sandstorm © *Requisite*

AMREEKA (National Geographic) Producers, Christina Piovesan, Paul Barkin; Executive Producers, Alicia Sams, Cherien Dabis; Director/Screenplay, Cherien Dabis; Photography, Tobias Datum; Designer, Aidan Leroux; Costumes, Patricia J. Henderson; Music, Kareem Roustom; Editor, Keith Reamer; an E1 Films Canada, Maximum Films Intl. (Canada)/Cinergy Prods. (U.S.) presentation; Canadian-American-Kuwait; Color; Widescreen; Not rated; 96 minutes; American release date: September 4, 2009. **CAST:** Nisreen Faour (Muna Farah), Melkar Muallem (Fadi Farah), Hiam Abbass (Raghda Halaby), Alia Shawkat (Salma), Jenna Kawar (Rana Halaby), Selena Haddad (Lamis Halaby), Yussuf Abu-Warda (Nabeel Halaby), Joseph Ziegler (Nr. Novatski), Andrew Sannie (James), Daniel Boiteau (Mike), Brodie Sanderson (Matt), Aaron Hughes, Craig Matthews (Police Officers), Arne MacPherson (Mike's Dad), Vanessa Mayberry (Sammy), Mike O'Brien, Adriana O'Neill (Bank Managers), Bradley Sawatzky (Parkton Bank Manager), Kristen Sawtzky (Official), Glen Thompson (Nelson), Will Woytowich (US Airport Customs Official)

RASHEVSKI'S TANGO (Menemsha) Producer, Diana Elbaum; Executive Producer, Benedicte Bellocq; Director, Sam Garbarski; Screenplay, Philippe Blasband, from an idea by Sam Garbarski; Photography, Virginie Saint-Martin; Designer, Veronique Sacrez; Music, Michael Galasso; Editor, Ludo Troch; an Entre Chien et Loup production; Belgian, 2003; Dolby; Color; Not rated; 90 minutes; American release date: September 11, 2009. **CAST:** Natan Cogan (Dolfo), Hippolyte Girardot (Antoine), Ishai Golan (Youval), Moscu Alcalay (Rabbi Shmouel), Daniel Mesguich (David Rashevski), Rudi Rosenberg (Ric Rashevski), Michel Jonasz (Simon Rashevski), Jonathan Zaccaï (Jonathan Rashevski), Tania Garbarski (Nina), Ludmila Mikaël (Isabelle), Michel Wouters (Morgue Employee), Selma Kouchy (Khadija), Laurent Capelluto (Rabin Elie), Alexander Wajnberg (Le Shammes), Sheriff Scouri (Mr. Benali), Henri Wajnberg (Mr. Litvak)

Rudi Rosenberg, Selma Kouchy in Rashevski's Tango
© Menemsha Films

GIVE ME YOUR HAND (Strand) a.k.a. *Donne-moi la main*; Producers, Nicolas Breviere, Markus Halberschmidt, Marcelo Busse; Director, Pascal-Alex Vincent; Screenplay, Pascal-Alex Vincent, Martin Druout, Story, Olivier Nicklaus, Pascal-Alex Vincent; Photography, Alexis Kavyrchine; Music, Bernd Jestram, Ronald Lippock; Editor, Dominique Petrot; Animation, 2 Minutes, Trickstudio Lutterbeck; a Local Films production, in co-production with Adam Prods./Busse & Halberschmidt Filmproduktion; French; Dolby; Widescreen; Color; Not rated; 77 minutes; American release date: September 11, 2009. **CAST:** Alexandre Carril (Antoine), Victor Carril (Quentin), Anaïs Demoustier (Clémentine), Samira Harrag (Hakim), Katrin Sass (Woman on Train), Fernando Ramallo (Angel), Patrick Hauthier (Man at Train Station), Maya Borker (Woman), Michel Grateau (Julian), Oswaldo Parma (Man with Car), Elsa Malterre (Nadège), Eldoie Meurlarger (Mélody), Jean-Pascal Abribat (Clémentine's Father), Franck Guilbot (Farmhouse Owner), Joël Pyrene (Vendor)

Victor Carril, Samir Harrag in Give Me Your Hand © Stand Releasing

BROKEN HILL (Audience Alliance) Producers, Chris Wyatt, Julie Ryan; Director/Screenplay, Dagen Merrill; Photography, Nick Matthews; Designer, Robert Webb; Costumes, Marriott Kerr; Music, Christopher Brady; Editors, David Ngo, Mike Saenz; Australian-American; Color; Rated PG; 102 minutes; American release date: September 11, 2009. **CAST:** Luke Arnold (Tommy McAlpine), Alexa Vega (Kat), Rhys Wakefield (Scott Price), Timothy Hutton (George McAlpine), Che Timmins (Kalai), John Clarke (Maestro Pindari), Leo Taylor (Warden), Andy McPhee (Bear), George Kapiniaris (Ricardo), Ebony Ween (Ricardo's Daughter), Luke O'Laughlin (Fuzz), Adam Grocke (Jock Boy), Peter Lamb (Officer Jack Taylor), Todd Telford (Jeffrey, Bells Player), Hung Le (Cho the Violin Player), Maude Davey (Dinnattee, Social Worker), Emma Rancie (Sharon), Dennis Noble (Sr. Sgt. Brady), Roger Newcombe (Mr. Woolley), Adam Morgan (Curious Guard), Wayne Mattie (The Maniac)

IN SEARCH OF BEETHOVEN (Seventh Art) Producer/Director/Screenplay/Photography, Phil Grabsky; Executive Producer, John Cassy; Editor, Phil Reynolds; Narrators, Juliet Stevenson, Davis Dawson; a Seventh Art production in association with Sky Arts; British; Color; Not rated; 139 minutes; American release date: September 23, 2009. Documentary on the life and work of composer Ludwig van Beethoven. **WITH:** Jonathan Bliss, Louis Langree, Gianandrea Noseda, Sir Roger Norrington, Lars Vogt, Emanuel Ax, Ronald Brautigam, Hélène Grimaud

INTIMATE ENEMIES (Outsider) a.k.a. *L'Ennemi Intime*; Producers, Francois Kraus, Denis Pineau-Valencienne; Director, Florent-Emilio Siri; Screenplay, Patrick Rotman; Inspired by his book and documentary; Photography, Giovanni Fiore Coltellacci; Designer, William Abello; Costumes, Mimi Lempicka; Editors, Olivier Gajan, Christophe Danilo; Casting, Stephane Foenkinos; a Les Films du Kiosque, SND, France 2 Cinema production; French; Dolby; Super 35 Widescreen; Color; Not rated; 110 minutes; American release date: October 2, 2009. **CAST:** Benoît Magimel (Lt. Terrien), Albert Dupontel (Sgt. Dougnac), Aurélien Recoing (Vesoul), Marc Barbé (Capt. Berthaut), Eric Slavin (Torturing Sergeant), Fellag (Idir Danoun, Prisoner), Vincent Rottiers (Lefranc), Lounès Tazairt (Saïd), Abdelhafid Metalsi (Rachid), Lounès Machene (Amar), Adrien Saint-Joré (Lacroix), Guillaume Gouix (Delmas), Ange Ruzé (Théron), Salem Aït-Ali-Belkacem (Ouramdam), Antoine Laurent (Maheu), Anthony Decadi (Rougier), Xavier Rothmann (Blois), Timothée Manesse (Zunino), Jeremy Azencott (Toto), Kamel Machene (Lounès), Abdelhafid Danoun (Ali), Saïd Djili (Nassim), Malik Bouarrar (Mahoud), Hassib Boukhellal (Hassib)

ARAYA (Milestone) Producer, Henry Nadler; Director, Margot Benacerraf; Screenplay, Margot Benacerraf, Pierre Seghers; Photography, Giuseppe Nisoli; Music, Guy Bernard; Editor, Pierre Jalluad; Narrators, Laurent Terzieff, José Ignacio Cabrujas; Venezuelan-French, 1959; Black and white; Not rated; 82 minutes; American release date: October 7, 2009. Documentary on Araya, a peninsula in northeastern Venezuela not for producing salt.

PASSPORT TO LOVE (Variance) a.k.a. *Chuyen tinh xa xu*; Producers, Victor Vu, Binh Le, Irene Trinh; Director, Victor Vu; Screenplay, Victor Vu, Nguyen Hoang Nam; Photography, Peter Soto; Costumes, Michelle Ngo, Nguyen Thi Kim Ngoc; Music, Christopher Wong; Editor, Vu Duc Thang; an Everest Productions presentation in association with In Focus Media Group and Wonderboy Entertainment; Vietnamese-American; Color; Rated PG-13; 100 minutes; Release date: October 9, 2009. **CAST:** Ngoc Diep (Jennifer), Mario E. Garcia (Cop), Huy Khanh (Hieu), Binh Minh (Khang), Tim Otholt (Casino Patron), Bao Quyen Tang (Thao), Kathy Uyen (Tiffany), Phuc Van Nguyen (Ong Hoang)

ADELA (MoMA) Producer, Arleen Cuevas; Director, Adolfo Borinaga Alix Jr.; Screenplay, Adolfo Borinaga Alix Jr., Nick Olanka; Photography, Albert Banzon; Designers, Adolfo Borinaga Alix Jr., Jerome Zamora; Filipino; Color; Not rated; 88 minutes; American release date: October 14, 2009. **CAST:** Anita Linda (Adela), Joem Bascon (Benlu), Jason Abalos (PJ), Angeli Bayani (Mercy), Perla Bautista (Glenda), Iza Calzado (Tina)

FOOD BEWARE: THE FRENCH ORGANIC REVOLUTION (First Run Features) a.k.a. *Nos enfants nous accuseront*; Producers, Jean-Paul Jaud, Beatric Jaud; Director, Jean-Paul Jaud; Photography, Joel Pierron, Ammar Arhab; Music, Gabriel Yared; Editor, Isabella Szumny; a J+B Sequences production; French; Color; HD; Not rated; 112 minutes; American release date: October 16, 2009. Documentary about how the French village of Barjac decided to go organic in order to reduce the health risks of its residents. **WITH:** John Peterson Myers, Perico Lagasse, Dominique Belpomme

Food Beware © *First Run Features*

OPA! (Cinedigm) Producers, Thierry Cagianut, Jeffery Bloom; Executive Producer, George Pappas; Director, Udayan Prasad; Screenplay, Raman Singh, Christina Concetta; Photography, Haris Zambarloukos; Designer, Dimitris Ziakis; Costumes, Bianca Nicolareisis, Despina Giavridi; Music, Stephen Warbeck; Editor, Barie Vince; an Elliott Kastner, George Pappas presentation in association with UFFP of a Cinema Seven production; British-Greek, 2005; Dolby; Deluxe color; Rated PG-13; 97 minutes; American release date: October 16, 2009. **CAST:** Matthew Modine (Eric), Richard Griffiths (Tierney), Agni Scott (Katerina), Christos Valavanidis (Mayor), Panayota Aravantzi (Agapoula), Mihalis Giannatos (Hektor), Shuler Hensley (Big Mac McLaren), Stahis Nikolaidis, Costas Xikominos, Alexandros Koliopoulos (Bureaucrats), Eirini Koumarianou (Yaya Adriana), Zozo

Zarpa, Titika Sarigouli, Efi Papatheodorou (Yayas), Grigoris Pimenidis (Yorgos), Stavros Sioulis (Kostas), Hristos Valavanidis (Mayor), Alki David (Spiros)

REMBRANDT'S J'ACCUSE (Independent) Producers, Femke Wolting, Bruno Felix; Director/Screenplay, Peter Greenaway; Photography, Reinier van Brummelen; Designer, Maarten Piersma; Costumes, Marrit van der Burgt; Music, Giovanni Sollima, Marco Robino; Editor, Elmer Leupen; a Content Intl. (U.K.) presentation of a Submarine (Netherlands) production, in association with Kasander Film, VPRO, WDR, YLE, in association with Arte France; British-Dutch, 2008; Dolby; Color; HD-to-35mm; Not rated; 90 minutes; American release date: October 21, 2009. **CAST:** Martin Freeman (Rembrandt van Rijn), Eva Birthistle (Saskia), Jodhi May (Geertje), Emily Holmes (Hendrickje), Jonathan Holmes (Ferdinand Bol), Michael Teigen (Carel Fabritius), Natalie Press (Marieke), Peter Greenaway (Himself/Public Prosecutor)

Jodhi May in Rembrandt's J'Accuse © *Submarine*

ONG BAK 2 (Magnet) Directors, Tony Jaa, Panna Rittikrai; Producer/Screenplay/Fight Choreographer, Panna Rittikrai; Photography, Nattawut Kittikhun; a Sahamongkol Film International presentation from Iyara Films; Thai; Dolby; Color; Rated R; 98 minutes; American release date: October 23, 2009. **CAST:** Tony Jaa (Tien), Sorapong Chatree (Chernang), Sarunyu Wongkrachang (Rajasena Lord), Nirut Sirijanya (Master Bua), Dance Chupong (Crow Ghost), Santisuk Promsiri (Nobleman Siha Decho), Primorata Dejudom (Pim), Natdanai Kongthong (Young Tien), Pattama Panthong (Lady Plai), Petchtai Wongkamlao (Mhen)

Tony Jaa in Ong Bak 2 © *Magnet*

Re

Re

Re

Re

Re

Re

THE WEDDING SONG (Strand) a.k.a. *Le Chant des Mariées*; Producers, Laurent Lavole, Isabelle Pragier; Director/Screenplay, Karin Albou; Photography, Laurent Brunet; Designer, Khaled Joulak; Costumes, Tania Shebabo-Cohen; Music, Francois-Eudes Chanfrault; Editor, Camille Cotte; Casting, Maya Serulla; a Gloria Films presentation and production, in association with France 3 Cinema, with the participation of Cinetelefilms; French, 2008; DTS Digital; Color; Not rated; 100 minutes; American release date: October 23, 2009. **CAST:** Lizzie Brocheré (Myriam), Olympe Borval (Nour), Najib Oudghiri (Khaled), Simon Abkarian (Raoul), Karin Albou (Tita)

Lizzie Brocheré, Olympe Borval in The Wedding Song © *Strand Releasing*

STORM (Film Movement) Producers, Britta Knoeller, Hans-Christian Schmid; Executive Producer, Maria Koepf; Director, Hans-Christian Schmid; Screenplay, Bernd Lange, Hans-Christian Schmid; Photography, Bogumil Godfrejow; Costumes, Steffi Bruhn; Music, The Notwist; Editor, Hansjoerg Weissbrich; a 23/5 Filmproduktion production; German-Danish-Dutch; Color; Not rated; 105 minutes; American release date: October 30, 2009. **CAST:** Kerry Fox (Hannah Maynard), Anamaria Marinca (Mira Arendt), Stephen Dillane (Keith Haywood), Rolf Lassgård (Jonas Dahlberg), Alexander Fehling (Patrick Faerber), Tarik Filipovic (Mladen Banovic), Kresimir Mikic (Alen Hajdarevic), Steven Scharf (Jan Arendt), Joel Eisenblätter (Simon Arendt), Wine Dierickx (Jule Svensson), Reinout Bussemaker (Carl Mathijsen), Bent Mejding (Judge Lars Andersen), Alexis Zegerman (Daliah Sofer), Arturo Venegas (Arnold Michaels), Drazen Kühn (Goran Duric), Nadezda Perisic-Nola (Biljana Duric), Arijana Cigura (Ana Duric), Sara Dazibarjric (Sofija Duric), Jadranka Djokic (Belma Sulic), Emina Muftic (Hotel Employee Vilina Kosa), Izudin Bajrovic (Branco Stanic), Leon Lucev (Milorad Alic), Marinko Prga (Photographer), Monique Wilsterman (Debbie Armstrong), Marijn Nieuwerf (VWU Agent), Dimme Treurniet (Policeman), Jesper Christensen (Anthony Weber)

Anamaria Marinca, Kerry Fox in Storm © *Film Movement*

ACT OF GOD (Zeitgeist) Producers, Nick de Pencier, Daniel Iron, Jennifer Baichwal; Director, Jennifer Baichwal; Screenplay, Jennifer Baichwal, James O'Reilly; Photography, Nick de Pencier; Music, Martin Tielli, Dave Bidini, Selina Martin; Editor, Roland Schlimme; a Mercury Films, Foundry Films production in association with Documentary, Channel 4, Arte France; Canadian-British-French; Dolby; Color; Not rated; 75 minutes; American release date: November 4, 2009. Documentary on lightning, including those struck by it. **WITH:** Paul Auster, Fred Frith, Chris Frith, Jean Ivens, Alex Hermant, Dalila Hermant, Dannion Brinkley, Juan Gonzalez Hernandez, Maria de Los Angeles Peredo, Salome Perez Morales, Nancy Gonzales, James O'Reilly

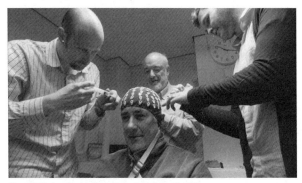

Fred Frith (center) in Act of God © *Zeitgeist Films*

LE DANSE: THE PARIS OPERA BALLET (Zipporah Films) Producers, Pierre-Olivier Bardet (Idéale Audience), Frederick Wiseman (Zipporah Films); Director/Editor, Frederick Wiseman; Photography, John Davey; French-American; Color; Not rated; 158 minutes; American release date: November 4, 2009. Documentary which looks behind the scenes and at some of the stage productions of the Paris Opera Ballet. **WITH:** Émilie Cozette, Aurélie Dupont, Dorothée Gilbert, Marie-Agnès Gillot, Agnès Letestu, Delphine Moussin, Clairemarie Osta, Laetitia Pujol, Kader Belarbi, Jérémie Belingard, Mathieu Ganio, Manuel Legris, Nicolas le Riche, José Martinez, Hervé Moreau, Benjamin Pech, Wilfried Romoli, Isabelle Ciaravola, Mathias Heymann, Nolwenn Daniel, Éve Grinsztajn, Mélanie Hurel, Myriam Ould-Braham, Stéphane Bullion, Christopher Duquenne, Karl Paquette, Stéphanie Phavorin, Emmanuel Thibault

La Danse: The Paris Opera Ballet © *Zipporah Films*

ENDGAME (Monterey Media) Producers, Hal Vogel, David Aukin; Executive Producers, Liza Marshall, Arwel Rees, Ian Jones, Alison Rayson, Rebecca Eaton; Director, Pete Travis; Screenplay, Paula Milne; Based on the book *Apartheid* by Robert Harvey; Photography, David Odd; Designer, Chris Roope; Costumes, Dinah Collin; Music, Martin Phipps, Ruth Barrett; Editors, Clive Barrett, Dominic Strevens; Casting, Celestia Fox; a Channel 4, Target Entertainment Group and Masterpiece presentation of a Daybreak Pictures production; British; Dolby; Color; Rated PG-13; 109 minutes; American release date: November 6, 2009. **CAST:** William Hurt (Prof. Will Esterhuyse), Chiwetel Ejiofor (President Thabo Kbeki), Jonny Lee Miller (Michael Young), Mark Strong (Dr. Niel Barnard), Clarke Peters (Nelson Mandela), John Kani (Oliver Tambo), Derek Jacobi (Rudolf Agnew), Amelia Bullmore (Gill), Dominik Danielewicz (Street Protestor), Kas Graham (Protestor), David Henry (Prof. Marinus Wiechers), Langley Kirkwood (W/O Jack Swart), Matthew Marsh (F.W. de Klerk), Danny Scheinmann (Albie Sachs), Jacques Strydom (Roadblock Policeman), Karl Thaning (De Klerk's Agent), Ramon Tikaram (Aziz Pahad), Lizanne Tulip (High Profile Banker), Timothy West (P.W. Botha), Mike Huff (Willem de Klerk), Faith Ndukwana (Winnie Mandela), Trevor

Sellers (Tony Trew)

Jonny Lee Miller in Endgame © *Endgame Film, Ltd.*

OH MY GOD (Mitropoulos Films) Producer/Director/Screenplay/Photography, Peter Rodger; Executive Producers, Horacio Altamirano, Metin Anter, Adam Krentzman; Music, Alexander van Bubenheim; Editor, John Hoyt; a Gussi Films (Mexico)/Mitropoulos Films (U.S.) presentation; Mexican-American; Dolby; Color; HD; Not rated; 93 minutes; Release date: November 13, 2009. Documentary that hopes to answer the question "what is God?". **WITH:** David Copperfield, John F. Demartini, Bob Geldof, Hugh Jackman, Baz Luhrmann, Princess Michael of Kent, Seal, Ringo Starr, Jack Thompson, Peter Rodger

Oh My God © *Mitropoulos Films*

MAMMOTH (IFC Films) Producer, Lars Jonsson; Executive Producers, Lena Borglum, Peter Garde, Vibeke Windelov; Co-Producers, Peter Aalbaek Jensen, Maria Kopf, Gunnar Carlsson, Tomas Eskilsson; Director/Screenplay, Lukas Moodysson; Photography, Marcel Zyskind; Designer, Josefin Asberg; Costumes, Denise Ostholm; Music, Jesper Kurlandsky, Erik Holmquist, Linus Gierta; Editor, Michal Leszczylowski; a Memfis Film (Sweden)/Zentropa Entertainments Berlin (Germany)/Zentropa Entertainments 5 ApS (Denmark) production; Swedish-German-Danish; Dolby; Super 35 Widescreen; Color; Not rated; 125 minutes; American release date: November 20, 2009. **CAST:** Gael Garcia Bernal (Leo Vidales), Michelle Williams (Ellen Vidales), Marife Necesito (Gloiria), Sophie Nyweide (Jackie Vidales), Run Srinikornchot (Cookie), Tom McCarthy (Bob), Jan David G. Nicado (Salvador), Martin Delos Santos (Manuel), Maria Esmeralda del Carmen (Grandmother), Perry Dizon (Uncle Fernando), Rudina Hatipi (Linda, Air Hostess), Joseph Mydell (Ben Jackson), Doña Croll (Alice), Caesar Kobb (Anthony), Pasakorn Mahakanok (Pom), Raul Morit (Man finding Salvador)

Michelle Williams, Gael Garcia Bernal, Sophie Nyweide in Mammoth © *IFC Films*

DEFAMATION (First Run Features) a.k.a. *Hashmatsa*; Producers, Karoline Leth, Sandra Itkoff, Philippa Kowarsky, Knut Ogris; Director/Screenplay/Photography, Yoav Shamir; Music, Mischa Krausz; Editor, Morten Hojbjerg; a Cinephil (Israel)/Ogris Films (Austria)/Reveal Prods. (U.S.)/SF Film Production (Denmark) production; Israeli-Austrian-American-Danish; Dolby; Color; Not rated; 91 minutes; American release date: November 20, 2009. Documentary in which filmmaker Yoav Shamir sets out to determine whether anti-Semitism is still prevalent. **WITH:** Abraham Foxman, Norman Finkelstein, Stephen M. Walt, John L. Mearsheimer

Defamation © *First Run Features*

FIX (E1 Entertainment) Producer, Nat Dinga; Executive Producers, Christopher Redlich, Giancarlo Canavesio, Cher Helina, Robert Kandle; Director, Tao Ruspoli; Screenplay, Tao Ruspoli, Jeremy C. Fels; Based on a story by Tao Ruspoli, Paul Duran, Charles Castaldi; Photography, Christopher Gallo, Tao Ruspoli; Designers, Sarah Osbourne, Erin Eagleton; Music Supersivor, Bryan Ling; Editor, Paul Forte; a LAFCO and Mangusta production; Color; HD; Not rated; 90 minutes; Release date: November 20, 2009. **CAST:** Shawn Andrews (Leo), Olivia Wilde (Bella), Megalyn Echikunwoke (Carmen), Tao Ruspoli (Milo), Dedee Pfeiffer (Daphne), Frank Alvarez (Diego), Aesop Aquarian (Bill), Christopher Cronin (Repo Man), Ian Duncan (Max), Rodney Eastman (Crackhead), Andrew Fiscella (Harry K. Rothstein), Aldo Gonzalez (Biker), Milauna Jemai (Lawyers Receptionist), Tarajia Morrell (Ivan's Assistant), Randall Park (Sam), Polly Brown (Jessica), Ric Sarabia (Ivan), Douglas Spain (Perez), Jakob Von Eichel (Shasta)

WARD NO. 6 (Mosfilm) a.k.a. *Palata No. 6*; Producer/Director, Karen Shakhnarazov; Executive Producer, Galina Shadur; Co-Director, Alexander Gornovsky; Screenplay, Alexander Borodyansky, Karen Shakhnazarov; Photography, Alexander Kuznetsov; Art Director, Ludmila Kusakova; Costumes, Alla Oleneva; Music, Evgeny Kadimsky; Editor, Irina Kozhemyakina; a Mosfilm/Courier Studio production; Russian; Dolby; Color; Not rated; 83 minutes; American release date: November 27, 2009. **CAST:** Vladimir Ilyin (Dr. Ragin), Yevgeni Stychkin (Dr. Khobotov), Aleksandr Pankratov-Chyorny (Mikhail Averyanovich), Viktor Solovyov (Nikita), Aleksei Vertkov (Gronov), Aleksei Zharkov (Old Chief Physician)

HOME (Lorber) Producers, Elena Tatti, Thierry Spicher, Denis Freyd, Denis Delcampe; Director, Ursula Meier; Screenplay, Ursula Meier, Antoine Jaccoud, Raphaelle Valbrune, Gilles Taurand, Olivier Lorelle, in collaboration with Alice Winocour; Photography, Agnes Godard; Editors, Susana Rossberg, Francois Gedigier, Nelly Quettier; a Box Prods. (Switzerland)/Archipel 35 (France)/Need Prods. (Belgium) presentation, in co-production with France 3 Cinema, Television Suisse Romande, SRG SSR Idee Suisse, RTBF, with the support of Eurimages; Swiss-French-Belgian, 2008; Color; Not rated; 98 minutes; American release date: November 27, 2009. **CAST:** Isabelle Huppert (Marthe), Olivier Gourmet (Michel), Adélaïde Leroux (Judith), Madeleine Budd (Marion), Kacey Mottet Klein (Julien), Renaud Rivier, Kilian Torrent, Nicolas Del Sordo, Hugo Saint-James, Virgil Berset (Julien's Friends)

Isabelle Huppert, Madeleine Budd, Kacey Mottet Klein in Home
© *Lorber*

BEFORE TOMORROW (Igloolik Isuma Prods.) a.k.a. *Le jour avant le lendemain*; Producer, Stephane Ritui; Executive Producers, Norman Cohn, Zacharias Kunuk; Director, Marie-Hélène Cousineau, Madeline Ivalu; Screenplay, Marie-Hélène Cousineau, Madeline Ivalu, Susan Avingaq; Based on the novel *For Morgendagen* by Jørn Riel; Photography, Norman Cohn, Felix Lajeunesse; Designer, Susan Avingaq; Costumes, Attuat Akkitirq; Music, Kate McGaggile, Anna McGarrigle; Editors, Norman Cohn, Marie-Helen Cousineau, Felix Lajeunesse, Louise Dugal; a Kunuk Cohn, Igloolik Isuma production; Canadian; Dolby; Color; HD-to-35mm; Not rated; 93 minutes; American release date: December 2, 2009. **CAST:** Peter-Henry Arnatsiaq (Apak), Madeline Ivalu (Ninioq), Paul-Dylan Ivalu (Maniq), Mary Qulitalik (Kuutujuk), Tumasie Sivuarapik (Kukik)

Paul-Dylan Ivalu, Madeline Ivalu in Before Tomorrow
© *Igloolik Isuma Prods.*

FILM IS A GIRL & A GUN (Sixpack Film) a.k.a. *Film Ist a Girl & a Gun*; Producer, Manfred Neuwirth; Director/Screenplay/Editor, Gustav Deutsch; a Loop Media production; Austrian; Black and white/16mm/35mm; Not rated; 93 minutes; American release date: December 3, 2009. Documentary examining sex and violence in the early years of cinema.

GIGANTE (Film Movement) Executive Producers, Agustina Chiarino, Fernando Epstein; Director/Screenplay, Adrián Biniez; Photography, Arauco Hernández; Art Director, Alejandro Castiglioni; Costumes, Emilia Carlevaro; Editor, Fernando Epstein; a Control Z Films (Motevideo), Rizoma Films (Buenos Aires), Pandorama Film (Cologone) production; Uruguayan-Argentine-German-Spanish, 2008; Dolby; Color; Not rated; 84 minutes; American release date: December 4, 2009. **CAST:** Horacio Camandule (Jara), Leonor Svarcas (Julia), Fernando Alonso (Julio), Diego Artucio (Omar), Ariel Caldarelli (Jaras Chef), Fabiana Charlo (Mariela), Andrés Gallo (Fidel), Federico García (Matias), Néstor Guzzini (Tomás), Esteban Lago (Gustavo), Ernesto Liotti (Danilo), Carlos Lissardy (Kennedy), Nacho Mendy (Miguel), Augusto Peloso (Rojas), Rafael Sosa Zeballos (Roquero)

Leonor Svarcas in Gigante
© *Film Movement*

PAA (Reliance Big Pictures) Producer, Sunil Manchanda; Executive Producers, Jitendra Bagga, Amitabh Bachchan; Director/Screenplay, R. Balki; Photography, P.C. Sreeram; Art Director, Sunil Babu; Prosthetics, Christien Tinsley, Dominie Till; Music, Ilaiyaraja; Lyrics, Swanand Kirkire; an AB Corp. production; Indian; Dolby; Widescreen; Color; Rated ; 133 minutes; American release date: December 4, 2009. **CAST:** Amitabh Bachchan (Auro), Abhishek Bachchan (Amol Arte), Vidya Balan (Vidhya Kumari), Paresh Rawal (Mr. Arte), Arundathi Nag (Vidya's Mother)

Amitabh Bachchan, Abhishek Bachchan in Paa © Big Pictures

TENDERNESS (Lionsgate) Producers, Howard Meltzer, John Penotti, Charles Randolph; Executive Producers, John Allen, Jana Edelbaum, Scott Hanson, Fisher Stevens, Tim Williams; Co-Producer, Sam Hoffman; Director, John Polson; Screenplay, Emil Stern; Based on the novel by Robert Cormier; Photography, Tom Stern; Designer, Mark Friedberg; Music, Jonathan Goldsmith; Editors, Lisa Zeno Churgin, Andrew Marcus, Beatrice Sisul; a GreeneStreet Films, iDeal Partners, Hanson-Allen presentation of a GreeneStreet Films, Turtleback production; Australian; Dolby; Panavision; Color; Rated R; 101 minutes; American release date: December 11, 2009. **CAST:** Russell Crowe (Det. Cristofuoro), Jon Foster (Eric Poole), Sophie Traub (Lori), Laura Dern (Aunt Teresa), Arija Bareikis (Marsha), Alexis Dziena (Maria), Michael Kelly (Gary), Vivienne Benesch (Lisa Komenko), Tanya Clarke (Jackie Cristufuoro), Tim Hopper (Dan Komenko), Brian Patrick Russell (Facility Director), Lee Sellars (Sam), Lou Sumrall (Cafeteria Guard), Matt Pepper (Ben), Saul Stein (Another Guard), Dan Fountain (Driver), C.S. Lee (Asian Cop), Scott Robertson (Highway Patrolman #2), Brian McCormack (Local Cop at Restaurant), Randy Cherkas (Playland Cop), Jane Fergus (TV Anchor), David Larosa (Paul), Alicia Harding (Debbie), Catherine Cox (Bowling Waitress), Ben Rauch (Nice Guy), Glenn Wein (Manager), Wade Mylius (Brakeman), Lauren Stewart (Young Lori), Mark Havlis (State Trooper)

Laura Dern, Jon Foster in Tenderness © Lionsgate

ROCKET SINGH: SALESMAN OF THE YEAR (Yash Raj Films) Producer, Aditya Chopra; Director, Shimit Amin; Screenplay/Lyrics, Jaideep Sahni; Music, Salim-Sulaiman; Photography, Vikash Nowlakha; Costumes, Niharika Khan; Editor, Arindam S. Ghatak; a Yash Chopra presentation; Indian; Color; Not rated; 150 minutes; American release date: December 11, 2009. **CAST:** Ranbir Kapoor (Harpeet Singh Bedi), Prem Chopra (P.S. Bedi), Mukesh Bhatt (Chhotelal Mishra), D. Santosh (Giri Reddy), Gauhar Khan (Koena Shaikh), Naveen Kaushik (Nitin Rathore), Manish Chaudhary (Sunil Puri), Bikramjeet Kanwarpal (Inamdar), Neeraj Sood (Lalwani)

RICKY (IFC Films) Producers, Claudie Ossard, Chris Bolzli; Director, François Ozon; Screenplay, François Ozon, Emmanuelle Bernheim; Inspired by the short story *Moth* by Rose Tremain; Photography, Jeanne Lapoirie; Designer, Katia Wyszkop; Costumes, Pascaline Chavanne; Music, Philippe Rombi; Editor, Muriel Breton; Visual Effects Supervisor, Georges Bouchelagehm; a Eurowide and Foz presentation and production, in association with Teodora Film; French; Dolby; Color; Not rated; 89 minutes; American release date: December 16, 2009. **CAST:** Alexandra Lamy (Katie), Sergi López (Paco), Mélusine Mayance (Lisa), Arthur Peyret (Ricky), André Wilms (Doctor), Jean-Claude Bolle-Reddat (Journalist), Maryilne Even (Odile), Véronique Joly (Social Worker), Martin Vandeville (Nurse), Myriam Azencot (Factory Supervisor), Diego Tosi (Waiter), Julien Haurant (Librarian), Eric Forterre (Butcher)

OLD PARTNER (Shcalo Media Group) a.k.a. *Wonangsori*; Producer, Young-jae Goh; Director/Screenplay/Editor, Chung-ryoul Lee; Photography, Jae-woo Ji; Music, Hoon Heo, So-yun Min; South Korean, 2008; Color; Not rated; 77 minutes; American release date: December 30, 2009. **CAST:** *Won-kyun Choi* (Elderly Farmer), Sam-soon Lee (Farmer's Wife)

Won-kyun Choi in Old Partner © Shcalo Media Group

THE CHASER (IFC Films) a.k.a. *Chugyeogja*; Producer, Su-jin Kim, In-beom Yoon; Director/Screenplay, Hong-jin Na; Photography, Sung-je Lee; Designer, Min-bog Lee; Music, Jun-seok Kim, Yong-rock Choi; Editor, Sun-min Kim; a Big House/Vantage Holdings presentation of a Bidangil Pictures production; Korean; Dolby; Cinemascope; Color; Not rated; 123 minutes; American release date: December 30, 2009. **CAST:** Yoon-suk Kim (Jung-ho), Jung-woo Ha (Young-min), Young-hee Seo (Mi-jin), You-jung Kim (Eun-jee), In-gi Jeong (Det. Lee), Jung-woo Choi (Chief), Kyoung-jin Min (Squad Leader), Hyo-ju Park (Det. Oh), Bon-woong Koo (Meathead), Woo-jung Oh (Sung-hee), Ji-yeon Yoo (Hee-jung), Sun-young Kim (Ji-young), Yo-sep Song (Det. Kang) Sung-kwang Ha (Det. Park), Deuk-je Cho (Det. Choi), Jae-sung Hong (Det. Kim), Gi-sup Jung (Prosecutor), Chan-guk Park (Identification Judge), Moo-young Ye (Inspector General)

PROMISING NEW ACTORS

2009

QUINTON AARON *(The Blind Side)*

NICOLE BEHAIRE *(American Violet)*

ZOE KAZAN *(I Hate Valentine's Day, It's Complicated, Me and Orson Welles, The Private Lives of Pippa Lee)*

SHARLTO COPLEY *(District 9)*

JONATHAN GROFF *(Taking Woodstock)*

MÉLANIE LAURENT *(Inglourious Basterds, Paris)*

CAREY MULLIGAN *(Brothers, An Education, Public Enemies)*

CHRISTIAN McKAY *(Me and Orson Welles)*

NATURI NAUGHTON *(Fame, Notorious)*

MAX RECORDS *(The Brothers Bloom, Where the Wild Things Are)*

SAM WORTHINGTON *(Avatar, Terminator Salvation)*

GABOUREY SIDIBE *(Precious: Based on the Novel 'Push' by Sapphire)*

ACADEMY AWARD

Winners and Nominees 2009

BEST PICTURE
THE HURT LOCKER

(SUMMIT) Producers, Kathryn Bigelow, Mark Boal, Nicolas Chartier, Greg Shapiro; Executive Producer, Tony Mark; Co-Producer, Donall McCusker; Director, Kathryn Bigelow; Screenplay, Mark Boal; Photography, Barry Ackroyd; Designer, Karl Júlíusson; Costumes, George Little; Music, Marco Beltrami, Buck Sanders; Music Supervisor, John Bissell; Editors, Bob Murawski, Chris Innis; Special Effects Supervisor, Richard Stutsman; Stunts, Robert Young; Casting, Mark Bennett; a Voltage Pictures presentation, in association with Grosvenor Park Media and FCEF, of a Voltage Pictures, First Light, Kingsgate Films production; Dolby; Color; Rated R; 130 minutes; Release date: June 29, 2009

Anthony Mackie

CAST

Staff Sgt. William James	**Jeremy Renner**
Sgt. J.T. Sanborn	**Anthony Mackie**
Specialist Owen Eldridge	**Brian Geraghty**
Staff Sgt. Matt Thompson	**Guy Pearce**
Contractor Team Leader	**Ralph Fiennes**
Col. Reed	**David Morse**
Connie James	**Evangeline Lilly**
Col. John Cambridge	**Christian Camargo**
Black Suit Man	**Suhail Al-Dabbach**
"Beckham"	**Christopher Sayegh**
Professor Nabil	**Nabil Koni**
Contractor Charlie	**Sam Spruell**
Contractor Jimmy	**Sam Redford**
Contractor Feisal	**Feisal Sadoun**
Contractor Chris	**Barrie Rice**
Iraqi Police Captain at UN	**Imad Dadudi**
Mortuary Affairs Officer	**Erin Gann**
Sgt. Carter	**Justin Campbell**
Sgt. Foster	**Malcolm Barrett**
Soldier at Intersection	**Kristoffer Winter**
Guard at Camp Liberty Market	**J.J. Kandel**
Guard at Liberty Gate	**Ryan Tramont**
Iraqi Translator	**Michael Desante**
DVD Merchant	**Hasan Darwish**
Insurgent in the Stairwell	**Wasfi Amour**
Nabil's Wife	**Nibras Quassem**
US Army Medic	**Ben Thomas**
Insurgent Sniper	**Nader Tarawneh**
Soldier at UN	**Anas "Tipsy" Wellman**
Butcher	**Omar Mario**
Soldier at Airfield	**Fleming Campbell**

Anthony Mackie, Jeremy Renner

Sgt. William James joins an elite U.S. bomb squad in Baghdad, where he finds a certain reckless thrill in his job of defusing deadly explosives.

2009 Academy Award Winner for Best Picture, Best Director, Best Original Screenplay, Best Film Editing, Best Sound Mixing, and Best Sound Editing.

This film received additional Oscar nominations for actor (Jeremy Renner), cinematography, and music.

Evangeline Lilly, Jeremy Renner © Summit Entertainment

Brian Geraghty

Jeremy Renner, Anthony Mackie

Brian Geraghty, Guy Pearce

Jeremy Renner

Jeremy Renner

Jeremy Renner

Carl Fredricksen, Dug, Russell

Russell, Carl Fredricksen

Dug, Russell, Kevin, Carl Fredricksen

Carl Fredricksen © Disney/Pixar

Dug, Carl Fredricksen, Russell

Ellie, Carl Fredricksen

Charles Muntz

Russell

BEST ANIMATED FEATURE
UP

(WALT DISNEY STUDIOS) Producer, Jonas Rivera; Executive Producers, John Lasseter, Andrew Stanton; Director, Pete Docter; Co-Director, Bob Peterson; Screenplay, Bob Peterson, Pete Docter; Story, Pete Docter, Bob Peterson, Thomas McCarthy; Photography, Patrick Lin; Designer, Ricky Nierva; Music, Michael Giacchino; Editor, Kevin Nolting; Supervising Technical Director, Steve May; Supervising Animator, Scott Clark; Casting, Kevin Reher, Natalie Lyon; a Pixar Animation Studios production; Dolby; Technicolor; 3-D; Rated PG; 89 minutes; Release date: May 29, 2009

VOICE CAST

Carl Fredricksen	**Ed Asner**
Charles Muntz	**Christopher Plummer**
Russell	**Jordan Nagai**
Dug/Alpha	**Bob Peterson**
Beta	**Delroy Lindo**
Gamma	**Jerome Ranft**
Construction Foreman Tom	**John Ratzenberger**
Newsreel Announcer	**David Kaye**
Young Ellie	**Elie Docter**
Young Carl	**Jeremy Leary**
Police Officer Edith	**Mickie T. McGowan**
Construction Worker Steve	**Danny Mann**
Nurse George	**Don Fullilove**
Nurse AJ	**Jess Harnell**
Omega	**Josh Cooley**
Campmaster Strauch/Kevins	**Pete Docter**

A senior citizen decides it is time to fulfill a lifelong dream and journeys to South America by hoisting his house afloat with balloons, inadvertently bringing along an eager-to-please Eagle Scout.

2009 Academy Award Winner for Best Animated Feature and Best Original Score.

This film received additional Oscar nominations for picture, original screenplay, and sound editing.

Russell, Carl Fredricksen

BEST FEATURE DOCUMENTARY
THE COVE

(ROADSIDE ATTRACTIONS) Producers, Paula DuPre Pesmen, Fisher Stevens; Executive Producer, Jim Clark; Co-Producer, Olivia Ahnemann; Director, Louie Psihoyos; Screenplay, Mark Monroe; Photography, Brook Aitken; Music, J. Ralph; Editor, Geoffrey Richman; an Oceanic Preservation Society presentation of a Jim Clark production; Color/black and white; HD; Rated ; 94 minutes; Release date: July 31, 2009

WITH
Richard O'Barry, Louis Psihoyos, Simon Hutchins, Mandy-Rae Cruickshank, Kirk Krack, David Rastovich, Joe Chisholm, Charles Hambleton, Isabel Lucas, Hayden Panettiere, Roger Payne, John Potter, Paul Watson.

Documentary in which marine crusader Richard O'Barry faces opposition as he tries to end the slaughter of dolphins in Taiji, Japan.

2009 Academy Award Winner for Best Documentary Feature.

Mandy-Rae Cruikshank © Lionsgate

ACADEMY AWARD FOR BEST ACTOR: Jeff Bridges in *Crazy Heart*

ACADEMY AWARD FOR BEST ACTRESS: Sandra Bullock in *The Blind Side*

ACADEMY AWARD FOR BEST SUPPORTING ACTOR : Christoph Waltz in *Inglourious Basterds*

ACADEMY AWARD FOR BEST SUPPORTING ACTRESS: Mo'Nique in *Precious*

ACADEMY AWARD NOMINEES FOR BEST ACTOR

George Clooney in *Up in the Air*

Colin Firth in *A Single Man*

Morgan Freeman in *Invictus*

Jeremy Renner in *The Hurt Locker*

ACADEMY AWARD NOMINEES FOR BEST ACTRESS

Helen Mirren in *The Last Station*

Carey Mulligan in *An Education*

Gabourey Sidibe in *Precious:* Based on the Novel *Push* by Sapphire

Meryl Streep in *Julie & Julia*

ACADEMY AWARD NOMINEES FOR BEST SUPPORTING ACTOR

Matt Damon in *Invictus*

Woody Harrelson in *The Messenger*

Christopher Plummer in *The Last Station*

Stanley Tucci in *The Lovely Bones*

ACADEMY AWARD NOMINEES FOR BEST SUPPORTING ACTRESS

Penélope Cruz in *Nine*

Vera Farmiga in *Up in the Air*

Maggie Gyllenhaal in *Crazy Heart*

Anna Kendrick in *Up in the Air*

TOP BOX OFFICE

Stars and Films 2009

1

TOP
BOX OFFICE
STARS OF 2008

1. *Sandra Bullock*
2. *Johnny Depp*
3. *Matt Damon*
4. *George Clooney*
5. *Robert Downey, Jr.*
6. *Tom Hanks*
7. *Meryl Streep*
8. *Brad Pitt*
9. *Shia LaBeouf*
10. *Denzel Washington*

3

4

2

5

6

8

9

7

10

TOP 100 BOX OFFICE FILMS OF 2009

1. Avatar (20th) $748,470,000
2. Transformers: Revenge of the Fallen (DW/Par) $402,120,000
3. Harry Potter and the Half-Blood Prince (WB) $301,960,000
4. New Moon (Summit) $296,620,000
5. Up (Disney) $293,100,000
6. The Hangover (WB) $277,330,000
7. Star Trek (Paramount) $257,730,000
8. The Blind Side (WB) $255,960,000
9. Alvin and the Chipmunks: The Squeakquel (20th) $219,100,000
10. Sherlock Holmes (WB) $208,400,000
11. Monsters vs. Aliens (DW) $198,360,000
12. Ice Age: Dawn of the Dinosaurs (20th) $196,580,000
13. X-Men Origins: Wolverine (20th) $179,890,000
14. Night at the Museum: Battle of the Smithsonian (20th) $177,180,000
15. The Proposal (Touchstone) $163,960,000
16. 2012 (Columbia) $163,740,000
17. Fast & Furious (Universal) $155,100,000
18. G.I. Joe: The Rise of Cobra (Paramount) $150,210,000
19. Paul Blart: Mall Cop (Columbia) $146,340,000
20. Taken (20th) $145,100,000
21. A Christmas Carol (Disney) $137,570,000
22. Angels & Demons (Columbia) $133,380,000

Daniel Radcliffe, Matthew Lewis, Emma Watson in
Harry Potter and the Half-Blood Prince

Stephen Lang, Sam Worthington in Avatar

23. Terminator Salvation (WB) $125,330,000
24. Cloudy with a Chance of Meatballs (Columbia) $124,190,000
25. Inglourious Basterds (Weinstein/Universal) $120,550,000
26. G-Force (Disney) $119,440,000
27. District 9 (TriStar) $115,650,000
28. It's Complicated (Universal) $112,710,000
29. Couples Retreat (Universal) $108,730,000
30. Paranormal Activity (Paramount) $107,910,000
31. Watchmen (WB/Par) $107,510,000
32. The Princess and the Frog (Disney) $104,380,000
33. Public Enemies (Universal) $97,110,000
34. Julie & Julia (Columbia) $94,130,000
35. He's Just Not That into You (New Line) $93,960,000
36. Tyler Perry's Madea Goes to Jail (Lionsgate) $90,510,000
37. The Ugly Truth (Columbia) $88,920,000
38. Up in the Air (Paramount) $83,780,000
39. Knowing (Summit) $79,960,000
40. Hannah Montana: The Movie (Disney) $79,560,000
41. Where the Wild Things Are (WB) $76,570,000
42. Zombieland (Columbia) $75,600,000
43. Coraline (Focus) $75,290,000
44. Law Abiding Citizen (Overture) $73,110,000
45. Hotel for Dogs (DW/Paramount) $73,100,000
46. Michael Jackson's This Is It (Columbia) $72,100,000
47. I Love You, Man (DW) $71,450,000
48. Obsessed (Screen Gems) $68,270,000
49. Race to Witch Mountain (Disney) $67,180,000
50. The Final Destination (New Line/WB) $66,480,000
51. The Taking of Pelham 123 (Columbia/MGM) $65,550,000
52. Friday the 13th (New Line/Par/WB) $65,100,000
53. 17 Again (New Line) $64,170,000
54. The Time Traveler's Wife (New Line) $63,420,000
55. Bruno (Universal) $60,100,000
56. Bride Wars (20th) $58,720,000
57. The Haunting in Connecticut (Lionsgate) $55,390,000
58. Ghosts of Girlfriends Past (New Line) $55,260,000
59. Funny People (Universal/Columbia) $51,860,000
60. I Can Do Bad All by Myself (Lionsgate) $51,740,000
61. My Bloody Valentine 3D (Lionsgate) $51,550,000
62. Land of the Lost (Universal) $49,440,000
63. My Sister's Keeper (New Line) $49,210,000
64. Old Dogs (Disney) $48,730,000
65. Precious: Based on the Novel "Push" by Sapphire (Lionsgate) $47,550,000
66. Underworld: Rise of the Lycans (Screen Gems) $45,810,000
67. Confessions of a Shopaholic (BV) $44,280,000
68. The Lovely Bones (DW/Par) $43,990,000
69. Year One (Columbia) $43,340,000
70. The Unborn (Rogue) $42,680,000
71. Drag Me to Hell (Universal) $42,110,000
72. Planet 51 (Screen Gems) $41,990,000
73. Orphan (WB) $41,600,000
74. Duplicity (Universal) $40,580,000
75. Crazy Heart (Fox Searchlight) $39,440,000
76. Surrogates (Disney) $38,580,000
77. Invictus (WB) $37,120,000
78. State of Play (Universal) $37,100,000
79. Notorious (Fox Searchlight) $36,850,000
80. The Pink Panther 2 (Col/MGM) $34,930,000
81. All About Steve (20th) $33,870,000
82. The Informant! (WB) $33,320,000
83. The Last House on the Left (Rogue) $32,760,000
84. (500) Days of Summer (Fox Searchlight) $32,400,000
85. Halloween II (Weinstein) $32,390,000

Jesse Eisenberg (left) in Zombieland

86. The Men Who Stare at Goats (Overture) $32,160,000
87. Earth (Disney) $32,100,000
88. Push (Summit) $31,790,000
89. 9 (Focus) $31,750,000
90. The Soloist (DW/Univ) $31,730,000
91. Toy Story/Toy Story 2 (Disney) $30,710,000
92. Did You Hear About the Morgans? (Columbia) $29,800,000
93. The Stepfather (Screen Gems) $29,100,000
94. The Uninvited (DW/Paramount) $28,600,000
95. Saw VI (Lionsgate) $26,700,000
96. Brothers (Lionsgate) $28,520,000
97. Dance Flick (Paramount) $25,670,000
98. The International (Columbia) $25,460,000
99. Aliens in the Attic (20th) $25,210,000
100. The Fourth Kind (Universal) $24,620,000

Amy Adams in Night at the Museum: Battle of the Smithsonian

Zac Efron in 17 Again

Saoirse Ronan in The Lovely Bones

Michael Cera, Jack Black in Year One

BIOGRAPHICAL DATA

2009

Aames, Willie (William Upton) Los Angeles, CA, July 15, 1960.
Aaron, Caroline Richmond, VA, Aug. 7, 1952. Catholic U.
Aaron, Quinton Bronx, NY, Aug. 15, 1984.
Abbott, Diahnne New York, NY, 1945.
Abraham, F. Murray Pittsburgh, PA, Oct. 24, 1939. U Texas.
Ackland, Joss London, England, Feb. 29, 1928.
Adams, Amy Vicenza, Italy, Aug. 20, 1975.
Adams, Brooke New York, NY, Feb. 8, 1949. Dalton.
Adams, Catlin Los Angeles, CA, Oct. 11, 1950.
Adams, Jane Washington, DC, April 1, 1965.
Adams, Joey Lauren Little Rock, AR, Jan. 9, 1968.
Adams, Julie (Betty May) Waterloo, IA, Oct. 17, 1926.
    Little Rock Junior College.
Adams, Maud (Maud Wikstrom) Lulea, Sweden, Feb. 12, 1945.
Adjani, Isabelle Paris, France, June 27, 1955.
Affleck, Ben Berkeley, CA, Aug. 15, 1972.
Affleck, Casey Falmouth, MA, Aug. 12, 1975.
Aghdashloo, Shohreh Tehran, Iran, May 11, 1952.
Agutter, Jenny Taunton, England, Dec. 20, 1952.
Aiello, Danny New York, NY, June 20, 1933.
Aiken, Liam New York, NY, Jan. 7, 1990.
Aimee, Anouk (Dreyfus) Paris, France, April 27, 1932. Bauer Therond.
Akerman, Malin Stockholm, Sweden, May 12, 1978.
Akers, Karen New York, NY, Oct. 13, 1945, Hunter College.
Alba, Jessica Pomona, CA, April 28, 1981.
Alberghetti, Anna Maria Pesaro, Italy, May 15, 1936.
Albright, Lola Akron, OH, July 20, 1925.
Alda, Alan New York, NY, Jan. 28, 1936. Fordham U.
Aleandro, Norma Buenos Aires, Argentina, Dec. 6, 1936.
Alejandro, Miguel New York, NY, Feb. 21, 1958.
Alexander, Jane (Quigley) Boston, MA, Oct. 28, 1939. Sarah Lawrence.
Alexander, Jason (Jay Greenspan) Newark, NJ, Sept. 23, 1959. Boston U.
Alice, Mary Indianola, MS, Dec. 3, 1941.
Allen, Debbie (Deborah) Houston, TX, Jan. 16, 1950. Howard U.
Allen, Joan Rochelle, IL, Aug. 20, 1956. East Illinois U.
Allen, Karen Carrollton, IL, Oct. 5, 1951. U Maryland.
Allen, Nancy New York, NY, June 24, 1950.
Allen, Tim Denver, CO, June 13, 1953. Western Michigan U.
Allen, Woody (Allan Stewart Konigsberg) Brooklyn, NY, Dec. 1, 1935.
Alley, Kirstie Wichita, KS, Jan. 12, 1951.
Alonso, Maria Conchita Cuba, June 29, 1957.
Alt, Carol Queens, NY, Dec. 1, 1960. Hofstra U.
Alvarado, Trini New York, NY, Jan. 10, 1967.
Amalric, Mathieu Neuilly-sur-Seine, France, Oct. 25, 1965.
Ambrose, Lauren New Haven, CT, Feb. 20, 1978.
Amis, Suzy Oklahoma City, OK, Jan. 5, 1962. Actors Studio.
Amos, John Newark, NJ, Dec. 27, 1939. Colorado U.
Anderson, Anthony Los Angeles, CA, Aug. 15, 1970.
Anderson, Gillian Chicago, IL, Aug. 9, 1968. DePaul U.
Anderson, Kevin Waukeegan, IL, Jan. 13, 1960.
Anderson, Loni St. Paul, MN, Aug. 5, 1946.
Anderson, Melissa Sue Berkeley, CA, Sept. 26, 1962.
Anderson, Melody Edmonton, Canada, Dec. 3, 1955. Carlton U.
Anderson, Michael, Jr. London, England, Aug. 6, 1943.
Anderson, Richard Dean Minneapolis, MN, Jan. 23, 1950.
Andersson, Bibi Stockholm, Sweden, Nov. 11, 1935. Royal Dramatic School.
Andress, Ursula Bern, Switzerland, March 19, 1936.
Andrews, Anthony London, England, Dec. 1, 1948.
Andrews, Julie (Julia Elizabeth Wells) Surrey, England, Oct. 1, 1935.
Andrews, Naveen London, England, Jan. 17, 1969.
Angarano, Michael Brooklyn, NY, Dec. 3, 1987.
Anglim, Philip San Francisco, CA, Feb. 11, 1952.
Aniston, Jennifer Sherman Oaks, CA, Feb. 11, 1969.

Ann-Margret (Olsson) Valsjobyn, Sweden, April 28, 1941. Northwestern.
Ansara, Michael Lowell, MA, April 15, 1922. Pasadena Playhouse.
Anspach, Susan New York, NY, Nov. 23, 1942.
Anthony, Lysette London, England, Sept. 26, 1963.
Anthony, Marc New York, NY, Sept. 16, 1968.
Anthony, Tony Clarksburg, WV, Oct. 16, 1937. Carnegie Tech.
Anton, Susan Yucaipa, CA, Oct. 12, 1950. Bemardino College.
Antonelli, Laura Pola, Italy, Nov. 28, 1941.
Anwar, Gabrielle Lalehaam, England, Feb. 4, 1970.
Applegate, Christina Hollywood, CA, Nov. 25, 1972.
Archer, Anne Los Angeles, CA, Aug. 25, 1947.
Ardant, Fanny Monte Carlo, Monaco, Mar 22, 1949.
Arkin, Adam Brooklyn, NY, Aug. 19, 1956.
Arkin, Alan New York, NY, March 26, 1934. LACC.
Armstrong, Bess Baltimore, MD, Dec. 11, 1953.
Arnaz, Desi, Jr. Los Angeles, CA, Jan. 19, 1953.
Arnaz, Lucie Hollywood, CA, July 17, 1951.
Arness, James (Aurness) Minneapolis, MN, May 26, 1923. Beloit College.
Arnett, Will Toronto, ON, Canada, May 5, 1970.
Arquette, David Winchester, VA, Sept. 8, 1971.
Arquette, Patricia New York, NY, April 8, 1968.
Arquette, Rosanna New York, NY, Aug. 10, 1959.
Asher, Jane London, England, April 5, 1946.
Ashley, Elizabeth (Elizabeth Ann Cole) Ocala, FL, Aug. 30, 1939.
Ashton, John Springfield, MA, Feb. 22, 1948. USC.
Asner, Edward Kansas City, KS, Nov. 15, 1929.
Assante, Armand New York, NY, Oct. 4, 1949. AADA.
Astin, John Baltimore, MD, March 30, 1930. U Minnesota.
Astin, MacKenzie Los Angeles, CA, May 12, 1973.
Astin, Sean Santa Monica, CA, Feb. 25, 1971.
Atherton, William Orange, CT, July 30, 1947. Carnegie Tech.
Atkins, Christopher Rye, NY, Feb. 21, 1961.
Atkins, Eileen London, England, June 16, 1934.
Atkinson, Rowan Consett, England, Jan. 6, 1955. Oxford.
Attenborough, Richard Cambridge, England, Aug. 29, 1923. RADA.
Auberjonois, Rene New York, NY, June 1, 1940. Carnegie Tech.
Audran, Stephane Versailles, France, Nov. 8, 1932.
Auger, Claudine Paris, France, April 26, 1941. Dramatic Conservatory.
Aulin, Ewa Stockholm, Sweden, Feb. 14, 1950.
Auteuil, Daniel Alger, Algeria, Jan. 24, 1950.
Avalon, Frankie (Francis Thomas Avallone) Philadelphia, PA, Sept. 18, 1939.
Aykroyd, Dan Ottawa, Canada, July 1, 1952.
Azaria, Hank Forest Hills, NY, April 25, 1964. AADA, Tufts U.
Aznavour, Charles (Varenagh Aznourian) Paris, France, May 22, 1924.
Azzara, Candice Brooklyn, NY, May 18, 1945.

Bacall, Lauren (Betty Perske) New York, NY, Sept. 16, 1924. AADA.
Bach, Barbara Queens, NY, Aug. 27, 1947.
Bach, Catherine Warren, OH, March 1, 1954.
Backer, Brian New York, NY, Dec. 5, 1956. Neighborhood Playhouse.
Bacon, Kevin Philadelphia, PA, July 8, 1958.
Bain, Barbara Chicago, IL, Sept. 13, 1931. U Illinois.
Baio, Scott Brooklyn, NY, Sept. 22, 1961.
Baker, Blanche New York, NY, Dec. 20, 1956.
Baker, Carroll Johnstown, PA, May 28, 1931. St. Petersburg Junior College.
Baker, Diane Hollywood, CA, Feb. 25, 1938. USC.
Baker, Dylan Syracuse, NY, Oct. 7, 1959.
Baker, Joe Don Groesbeck, TX, Feb. 12, 1936.
Baker, Kathy Midland, TX, June 8, 1950. UC Berkley.
Baker, Simon Launceston, Tasmania, July 30, 1969.
Bakula, Scott St. Louis, MO, Oct. 9, 1954. Kansas U.
Balaban, Bob Chicago, IL, Aug. 16, 1945. Colgate.
Baldwin, Adam Chicago, IL, Feb. 27, 1962.

Baldwin, Alec Massapequa, NY, April 3, 1958. NYU.
Baldwin, Daniel Massapequa, NY, Oct. 5, 1960.
Baldwin, Stephen Massapequa, NY, May 12, 1966.
Baldwin, William Massapequa, NY, Feb. 21, 1963.
Bale, Christian Pembrokeshire, West Wales, Jan. 30, 1974.
Balk, Fairuza Point Reyes, CA, May 21, 1974.
Ballard, Kaye Cleveland, OH, Nov. 20, 1925.
Bana, Eric Melbourne, Australia, Aug. 9, 1968.
Banderas, Antonio Malaga, Spain, Aug. 10, 1960.
Banerjee, Victor Calcutta, India, Oct. 15, 1946.
Banes, Lisa Chagrin Falls, OH, July 9, 1955. Juilliard.
Banks, Elizabeth Pittsfield, MA, Feb. 19, 1974. U Pennsylvania.
Baranski, Christine Buffalo, NY, May 2, 1952. Juilliard.
Barbeau, Adrienne Sacramento, CA, June 11, 1945. Foothill College.
Bardem, Javier Gran Canaria, Spain, May 1, 1969.
Bardot, Brigitte Paris, France, Sept. 28, 1934.
Barkin, Ellen Bronx, NY, April 16, 1954. Hunter College.
Barnes, Christopher Daniel Portland, ME, Nov. 7, 1972.
Barnett, Samuel Whitby, No. Yorkshire, England, April 25, 1980.
Baron Cohen, Sacha London, England, Oct. 13, 1971.
Barr, Jean-Marc Bitburg, Germany, Sept. 27, 1960.
Barr, Roseanne Salt Lake City, UT, Nov. 3, 1952.
Barrault, Marie-Christine Paris, France, March 21, 1944.
Barraza, Adriana Toluca, Mexico, March 5, 1956.
Barrie, Barbara Chicago, IL, May 23, 1931.
Barry, Gene (Eugene Klass) New York, NY, June 14, 1919.
Barry, Neill New York, NY, Nov. 29, 1965.
Barrymore, Drew Los Angeles, CA, Feb. 22, 1975.
Bart, Roger Norwalk, CT, Sept. 29, 1962.
Bartha, Justin West Bloomfield, MI, July 21, 1978.
Baruchel, Jay Ottawa, Canada, April 9, 1982.
Baryshnikov, Mikhail Riga, Latvia, Jan. 27, 1948.
Basinger, Kim Athens, GA, Dec. 8, 1953. Neighborhood Playhouse.
Bassett, Angela New York, NY, Aug. 16, 1958.
Bateman, Jason Rye, NY, Jan. 14, 1969.
Bateman, Justine Rye, NY, Feb. 19, 1966.
Bates, Kathy Memphis, TN, June 28, 1948. Southern Methodist U.
Bauer, Steven (Steven Rocky Echevarria) Havana, Cuba, Dec. 2, 1956. U Miami.
Baxter, Keith South Wales, England, April 29, 1933. RADA.
Baxter, Meredith Los Angeles, CA, June 21, 1947. Interlochen Academy.
Baye, Nathalie Mainevile, France, July 6, 1948.
Beach, Adam Winnipeg, Manitoba, Canada, Nov. 11, 1972.
Beacham, Stephanie Casablanca, Morocco, Feb. 28, 1947.
Beals, Jennifer Chicago, IL, Dec. 19, 1963.
Bean, Orson (Dallas Burrows) Burlington, VT, July 22, 1928.
Bean, Sean Sheffield, Yorkshire, England, April 17, 1959.
Beard, Matthew London, England, March 25, 1989.
Béart, Emmanuelle Gassin, France, Aug. 14, 1963.
Beatty, Ned Louisville, KY, July 6, 1937.
Beatty, Warren Richmond, VA, March 30, 1937.
Beck, John Chicago, IL, Jan. 28, 1943.
Beck, Michael Memphis, TN, Feb. 4, 1949. Millsap College.
Beckinsale, Kate London, England, July 26, 1974.
Bedelia, Bonnie New York, NY, March 25, 1948. Hunter College.
Begley, Ed, Jr. New York, NY, Sept. 16, 1949.
Belafonte, Harry New York, NY, March 1, 1927.
Bell, Jamie Billingham, England, March 14, 1988.
Bell, Kristen Huntington Woods, WI, July 18, 1980.
Bell, Tobin Queens, NY, Aug. 7, 1942.
Beller, Kathleen New York, NY, Feb. 10, 1956.
Bello, Maria Norristown, PA, April 18, 1967.
Bellucci, Monica Citta di Castello, Italy, Sept. 30, 1964.

Bellwood, Pamela (King) Scarsdale, NY, June 26, 1951.
Belmondo, Jean Paul Paris, France, April 9, 1933.
Belushi, James Chicago, IL, June 15, 1954.
Belzer, Richard Bridgeport, CT, Aug. 4, 1944.
Benedict, Dirk (Niewoehner) White Sulphur Springs, MT, March 1, 1945. Whitman College.
Benigni, Roberto Tuscany, Italy, Oct. 27, 1952.
Bening, Annette Topeka, KS, May 29, 1958. San Francisco State U.
Benjamin, Richard New York, NY, May 22, 1938. Northwestern.
Bennent, David Lausanne, Switzerland, Sept. 9, 1966.
Bennett, Alan Leeds, England, May 9, 1934. Oxford.
Bennett, Hywel Garnant, South Wales, April 8, 1944.
Benson, Robby Dallas, TX, Jan. 21, 1956.
Bentley, Wes Jonesboro, AR, Sept. 4, 1978.
Berenger, Tom Chicago, IL, May 31, 1949, U Missouri.
Berenson, Marisa New York, NY, Feb. 15, 1947.
Berg, Peter New York, NY, March 11, 1964. Malcalester College.
Bergen, Candice Los Angeles, CA, May 9, 1946. U Pennsylvania.
Bergen, Polly Knoxville, TN, July 14, 1930. Compton Junior College.
Berger, Helmut Salzburg, Austria, May 29, 1944.
Berger, Senta Vienna, Austria, May 13, 1941. Vienna School of Acting.
Bergerac, Jacques Biarritz, France, May 26, 1927. Paris U.
Bergin, Patrick Dublin, Ireland, Feb. 4, 1951.
Berkley, Elizabeth Detroit, MI, July 28, 1972.
Berkoff, Steven London, England, Aug. 3, 1937.
Berlin, Jeannie Los Angeles, CA, Nov. 1, 1949.
Berlinger, Warren Brooklyn, NY, Aug. 31, 1937. Columbia U.
Bernal, Gael García Guadalajara, Mexico, Oct. 30, 1978.
Bernhard, Sandra Flint, MI, June 6, 1955.
Bernsen, Corbin Los Angeles, CA, Sept. 7, 1954. UCLA.
Berridge, Elizabeth Westchester, NY, May 2, 1962. Strasberg Institute.
Berry, Halle Cleveland, OH, Aug. 14, 1968.
Berry, Ken Moline, IL, Nov. 3, 1933.
Bertinelli, Valerie Wilmington, DE, April 23, 1960.
Best, James Corydon, IN, July 26, 1926.
Bettany, Paul London, England, May 27, 1971.
Bey, Turhan Vienna, Austria, March 30, 1922.
Beymer, Richard Avoca, IA, Feb. 21, 1938.
Bialik, Mayim San Diego, CA, Dec. 12, 1975.
Biehn, Michael Anniston, AL, July 31, 1956.
Biel, Jessica Ely, MN, March 3, 1982.
Biggerstaff, Sean Glasgow, Scotland, March 15, 1983.
Biggs, Jason Pompton Plains, NJ, May 12, 1978.
Bikel, Theodore Vienna, Austria, May 2, 1924. RADA.
Billingsley, Peter New York, NY, April 16, 1972.
Binoche, Juliette Paris, France, March 9, 1964.
Birch, Thora Los Angeles, CA, March 11, 1982.
Birkin, Jane London, England, Dec. 14, 1946.
Birney, David Washington, DC, April 23, 1939. Dartmouth, UCLA.
Birney, Reed Alexandria, VA, Sept. 11, 1954. Boston U.
Bishop, Kevin Kent, England, June 18, 1980.
Bisset, Jacqueline Waybridge, England, Sept. 13, 1944.
Black, Jack (Thomas Black) Edmonton, Alberta, Canada, April 7, 1969.
Black, Karen (Ziegler) Park Ridge, IL, July 1, 1939. Northwestern.
Black, Lewis Silver Spring, MD, Aug. 30, 1948.
Black, Lucas Speake, AL, Nov. 29, 1982.
Blackman, Honor London, England, Aug. 22, 1927.
Blades, Ruben Panama City, FL, July 16, 1948. Harvard.
Blair, Linda Westport, CT, Jan. 22, 1959.
Blair, Selma Southfield, MI, June 23, 1972.
Blake, Robert (Michael Gubitosi) Nutley, NJ, Sept. 18, 1933.
Blakely, Susan Frankfurt, Germany, Sept. 7, 1948. U Texas.
Blakley, Ronee Stanley, ID, 1946. Stanford U.

Blanchett, Cate Melbourne, Australia, May 14, 1969.
Bledel, Alexis Houston, TX, Sept. 16, 1981.
Blethyn, Brenda Ramsgate, Kent, England, Feb. 20, 1946.
Blonsky, Nikki Great Neck, NY, Nov. 9, 1988.
Bloom, Claire London, England, Feb. 15, 1931. Badminton School.
Bloom, Orlando Canterbury, England, Jan. 13, 1977.
Bloom, Verna Lynn, MA, Aug. 7, 1939. Boston U.
Blount, Lisa Fayettville, AR, July 1, 1957. U Arkansas.
Blum, Mark Newark, NJ, May 14, 1950. U Minnesota.
Blunt, Emily London, England, Feb. 23, 1983.
Blyth, Ann Mt. Kisco, NY, Aug. 16, 1928. New Waybum Dramatic School.
Bochner, Hart Toronto, ON, Canada, Oct. 3, 1956. U San Diego.
Bogosian, Eric Woburn, MA, April 24, 1953. Oberlin College.
Bohringer, Richard Paris, France, Jan. 16, 1942.
Bolkan, Florinda (Florinda Soares Bulcao) Ceara, Brazil, Feb. 15, 1941.
Bologna, Joseph Brooklyn, NY, Dec. 30, 1934. Brown U.
Bonet, Lisa San Francisco, CA, Nov. 16, 1967.
Bonham-Carter, Helena London, England, May 26, 1966.
Boone, Pat Jacksonville, FL, June 1, 1934. Columbia U.
Boothe, Powers Snyder, TX, June 1, 1948. Southern Methodist U.
Borgnine, Ernest (Borgnino) Hamden, CT, Jan. 24, 1917. Randall School.
Bosco, Philip Jersey City, NJ, Sept. 26, 1930. Catholic U.
Bosley, Tom Chicago, IL, Oct. 1, 1927. DePaul U.
Bostwick, Barry San Mateo, CA, Feb. 24, 1945. NYU.
Bosworth, Kate Los Angeles, CA, Jan. 2, 1983.
Bottoms, Joseph Santa Barbara, CA, Aug. 30, 1954.
Bottoms, Timothy Santa Barbara, CA, Aug. 30, 1951.
Boulting, Ingrid Transvaal, South Africa, 1947.
Boutsikaris, Dennis Newark, NJ, Dec. 21, 1952. Catholic U.
Bowie, David (David Robert Jones) Brixton, South London, England, Jan. 8, 1947.
Bowker, Judi Shawford, England, April 6, 1954.
Boxleitner, Bruce Elgin, IL, May 12, 1950.
Boyd, Billy Glasgow, Scotland, Aug. 28, 1968.
Boyle, Lara Flynn Davenport, IA, March 24, 1970.
Bracco, Lorraine Brooklyn, NY, Oct. 2, 1954.
Bradford, Jesse Norwalk, CT, May 27, 1979.
Braeden, Eric (Hans Gudegast) Kiel, Germany, April 3, 1941.
Braff, Zach South Orange, NJ, April 6, 1975.
Braga, Alice São Paolo, Brazil, April 15, 1983.
Braga, Sonia Maringa, Brazil, June 8, 1950.
Branagh, Kenneth Belfast, Northern Ireland, Dec. 10, 1960.
Brandauer, Klaus Maria Altaussee, Austria, June 22, 1944.
Brandon, Clark New York, NY, Dec. 13, 1958.
Brandon, Michael (Feldman) Brooklyn, NY, April 20, 1945.
Brantley, Betsy Rutherfordton, NC, Sept. 20, 1955. London Central School of Drama.
Bratt, Benjamin San Francisco, CA, Dec. 16, 1963.
Brennan, Eileen Los Angeles, CA, Sept. 3, 1932. AADA.
Brenneman, Amy Glastonbury, CT, June 22, 1964.
Breslin, Abigail New York, NY, April 14, 1996.
Brialy, Jean-Claude Aumale, Algeria, 1933. Strasbourg Conservatory.
Bridges, Beau Los Angeles, CA, Dec. 9, 1941. UCLA.
Bridges, Chris "Ludacris" Champaign, IL, Sept. 11, 1977.
Bridges, Jeff Los Angeles, CA, Dec. 4, 1949.
Bright, Cameron Victoria, BC, Canada, Jan. 26, 1993.
Brimley, Wilford Salt Lake City, UT, Sept. 27, 1934.
Brinkley, Christie Malibu, CA, Feb. 2, 1954.
Britt, May (Maybritt Wilkins) Stockholm, Sweden, March 22, 1933.
Brittany, Morgan (Suzanne Cupito) Los Angeles, CA, Dec. 5, 1950.
Britton, Tony Birmingham, England, June 9, 1924.
Broadbent, Jim Lincoln, England, May 24, 1949.
Broderick, Matthew New York, NY, March 21, 1962.

Brody, Adrien New York, NY, Dec. 23, 1976.
Brolin, James Los Angeles, CA, July 18, 1940. UCLA.
Brolin, Josh Los Angeles, CA, Feb. 12, 1968.
Bron, Eleanor Stanmore, England, March 14, 1934.
Brookes, Jacqueline Montclair, NJ, July 24, 1930. RADA.
Brooks, Albert (Einstein) Los Angeles, CA, July 22, 1947.
Brooks, Mel (Melvyn Kaminski) Brooklyn, NY, June 28, 1926.
Brosnan, Pierce County Meath, Ireland. May 16, 1952.
Brown, Blair Washington, DC, April 23, 1946. Pine Manor.
Brown, Bryan Panania, Australia, June 23, 1947.
Brown, Georg Stanford Havana, Cuba, June 24, 1943. AMDA.
Brown, Jim St. Simons Island, NY, Feb. 17, 1936. Syracuse U.
Browne, Leslie New York, NY, June 29,1957.
Bruckner, Agnes Hollywood, CA, Aug. 16, 1985.
Brühl, Daniel (Daniel Domingo) Barcelona, Spain, June 16, 1978.
Buckley, Betty Big Spring, TX, July 3, 1947. Texas Christian U.
Bujold, Genevieve Montreal, Quebec, Canada, July 1, 1942.
Bullock, Sandra Arlington, VA, July 26, 1964.
Burghoff, Gary Bristol, CT, May 24, 1943.
Burgi, Richard Montclair, NJ, July 30, 1958.
Burnett, Carol San Antonio, TX, April 26, 1933. UCLA.
Burns, Catherine New York, NY, Sept. 25, 1945. AADA.
Burns, Edward Valley Stream, NY, Jan. 28, 1969.
Burrows, Darren E. Winfield, KS, Sept. 12, 1966.
Burrows, Saffron London, England, Oct. 22,, 1972.
Burstyn, Ellen (Edna Rae Gillhooly) Detroit, MI, Dec. 7, 1932.
Burton, Kate Geneva, Switzerland, Sept. 10, 1957.
Burton, LeVar Los Angeles, CA, Feb. 16, 1957. UCLA.
Buscemi, Steve Brooklyn, NY, Dec. 13, 1957.
Busey, Gary Goose Creek, TX, June 29, 1944.
Busfield, Timothy Lansing, MI, June 12, 1957. East Tennessee State U.
Butler, Gerard Glasgow, Scotland, Nov. 13, 1969.
Buzzi, Ruth Westerly, RI, July 24, 1936. Pasadena Playhouse.
Bygraves, Max London, England, Oct. 16, 1922. St. Joseph's School.
Bynes, Amanda Thousand Oaks, CA, April 3, 1986.
Byrne, David Dumbarton, Scotland, May 14, 1952.
Byrne, Gabriel Dublin, Ireland, May 12, 1950.
Byrnes, Edd New York, NY, July 30, 1933.

Caan, James Bronx, NY, March 26,1939.
Caesar, Sid Yonkers, NY, Sept. 8, 1922.
Cage, Nicolas (Coppola) Long Beach, CA, Jan. 7, 1964.
Cain, Dean (Dean Tanaka) Mt. Clemens, MI, July 31, 1966.
Caine, Michael (Maurice Micklewhite) London, England, March 14, 1933.
Caine, Shakira (Baksh) Guyana, Feb. 23, 1947. Indian Trust College.
Callan, Michael (Martin Calinieff) Philadelphia, PA, Nov. 22, 1935.
Callow, Simon London, England, June 15, 1949. Queens U.
Cameron, Kirk Panorama City, CA, Oct. 12, 1970.
Camp, Colleen San Francisco, CA, June 7, 1953.
Campbell, Bill Chicago, IL, July 7, 1959.
Campbell, Glen Delight, AR, April 22, 1936.
Campbell, Neve Guelph, ON, Canada, Oct. 3, 1973.
Campbell, Tisha Oklahoma City, OK, Oct. 13, 1968.
Cannon, Dyan (Samille Diane Friesen) Tacoma, WA, Jan. 4, 1937.
Capshaw, Kate Ft. Worth, TX, Nov. 3, 1953. U Misourri.
Cara, Irene New York, NY, March 18, 1959.
Cardellini, Linda Redwood City, CA, June 25, 1975.
Cardinale, Claudia Tunis, North Africa. April 15, 1938. College Paul Cambon.
Carell, Steve Concord, MA, Aug. 16, 1962.
Carey, Harry, Jr. Saugus, CA, May 16, 1921. Black Fox Military Academy.
Cariou, Len Winnipeg, Manitoba, Canada, Sept. 30, 1939.
Carlyle, Robert Glasgow, Scotland, April 14, 1961.
Carmen, Julie Mt. Vernon, NY, April 4, 1954.

Carmichael, Ian Hull, England, June 18, 1920. Scarborough College.
Carne, Judy (Joyce Botterill) Northampton, England, 1939. Bush-Davis Theatre School.
Caron, Leslie Paris, France, July 1, 1931. National Conservatory, Paris.
Carpenter, Carleton Bennington, VT, July 10, 1926. Northwestern.
Carradine, Keith San Mateo, CA, Aug. 8, 1950. Colo. State U.
Carradine, Robert San Mateo, CA, March 24, 1954.
Carrel, Dany Tourane, Indochina, Sept. 20, 1932. Marseilles Conservatory.
Carrera, Barbara Managua, Nicaragua, Dec. 31, 1945.
Carrere, Tia (Althea Janairo) Honolulu, HI, Jan. 2, 1965.
Carrey, Jim Jacksons Point, ON, Canada, Jan. 17, 1962.
Carriere, Mathieu Hannover, West Germany, Aug. 2, 1950.
Carroll, Diahann (Johnson) New York, NY, July 17, 1935. NYU.
Carroll, Pat Shreveport, LA, May 5, 1927. Catholic U.
Carsten, Peter (Ransenthaler) Weissenberg, Bavaria, April 30, 1928. Munich Akademie.
Cartwright, Veronica Bristol, England, Apr 20, 1949.
Caruso, David Forest Hills, NY, Jan. 7, 1956.
Carvey, Dana Missoula, MT, April 2, 1955. San Francisco State U.
Casella, Max Washington D.C, June 6, 1967.
Casey, Bernie Wyco, WV, June 8, 1939.
Cassavetes, Nick New York, NY, 1959, Syracuse U, AADA.
Cassel, Seymour Detroit, MI, Jan. 22, 1935.
Cassel, Vincent Paris, France, Nov. 23, 1966.
Cassidy, David New York, NY, April 12, 1950.
Cassidy, Joanna Camden, NJ, Aug. 2, 1945. Syracuse U.
Cassidy, Patrick Los Angeles, CA, Jan. 4, 1962.
Castellaneta, Dan Chicago, IL, Oct. 29, 1957.
Cates, Phoebe New York, NY, July 16, 1963.
Cattrall, Kim Liverpool, England, Aug. 21, 1956. AADA.
Caulfield, Maxwell Glasgow, Scotland, Nov. 23, 1959.
Cavani, Liliana Bologna, Italy, Jan. 12, 1933. U Bologna.
Cavett, Dick Gibbon, NE, Nov. 19, 1936.
Caviezel, Jim Mt. Vernon, WA, Sept. 26, 1968.
Cedric the Entertainer (Cedric Kyles) Jefferson City, MO, April 24, 1964.
Cera, Michael Brampton, ON, Canada, June 7, 1988.
Chakiris, George Norwood, OH, Sept. 16, 1934.
Chamberlain, Richard Beverly Hills, CA, March 31, 1934. Pomona.
Champion, Marge (Marjorie Belcher) Los Angeles, CA, Sept. 2, 1919.
Chan, Jackie Hong Kong, April 7, 1954.
Chandler, Kyle Buffalo, NY, Sept. 17, 1965
Channing, Carol Seattle, WA, Jan. 31, 1921. Bennington.
Channing, Stockard (Susan Stockard) New York, NY, Feb. 13, 1944. Radcliffe.
Chapin, Miles New York, NY, Dec. 6, 1954. HB Studio.
Chaplin, Ben London, England, July 31, 1970.
Chaplin, Geraldine Santa Monica, CA, July 31, 1944. Royal Ballet.
Charles, Josh Baltimore, MD, Sept. 15, 1971.
Charles, Walter East Strousburg, PA, April 4, 1945. Boston U.
Chase, Chevy (Cornelius Crane Chase) New York, NY, Oct. 8, 1943.
Chatwin, Justin Nanaimo, BC, Canada, Oct. 31, 1982.
Chaves, Richard Jacksonville, FL, Oct. 9, 1951. Occidental College.
Chaykin, Maury Brooklyn, NY, July 27, 1949.
Cheadle, Don Kansas City, MO, Nov. 29, 1964.
Chen, Joan (Chen Chung) Shanghai, China, April 26, 1961. Cal State.
Chenoweth, Kristin Broken Arrow, OK, July 24, 1968.
Cher (Cherilyn Sarkisian) El Centro, CA, May 20, 1946.
Chiklis, Michael Lowell, MA, Aug. 30, 1963.
Chiles, Lois Alice, TX, April 15, 1947.
Cho, John Seoul, Korea, June 16, 1972.
Cho, Margaret San Francisco, CA, Dec. 5, 1968.
Chong, Rae Dawn Vancouver, BC, Canada, Feb. 28, 1961.
Chong, Thomas Edmonton, Alberta, Canada, May 24, 1938.

Christensen, Erika Seattle, WA, Aug. 19, 1982.
Christensen, Hayden Vancouver, BC, Canada, April 19, 1981.
Christian, Linda (Blanca Rosa Welter) Tampico, Mexico, Nov. 13, 1923.
Christie, Julie Chukua, Assam, India, April 14, 1941.
Christopher, Dennis (Carrelli) Philadelphia, PA, Dec. 2, 1955. Temple U.
Christopher, Jordan Youngstown, OH, Oct. 23, 1942. Kent State.
Church, Thomas Haden El Paso, TX, June 17, 1961.
Cilento, Diane Queensland, Australia, Oct. 5, 1933. AADA.
Clark, Candy Norman, OK, June 20, 1947.
Clark, Dick Mt. Vernon, NY, Nov. 30, 1929. Syracuse U.
Clark, Matt Washington, DC, Nov. 25, 1936.
Clark, Petula Epsom, England, Nov. 15, 1932.
Clark, Susan Sarnid, ON, Canada, March 8, 1940. RADA.
Clarkson, Patricia New Orleans, LA, Dec. 29, 1959.
Clay, Andrew Dice (Andrew Silverstein) Brooklyn, NY, Sept. 29, 1957, Kingsborough College.
Clayburgh, Jill New York, NY, April 30, 1944. Sarah Lawrence.
Cleese, John Weston-Super-Mare, England, Oct. 27, 1939, Cambridge.
Clooney, George Lexington, KY, May 6, 1961.
Close, Glenn Greenwich, CT, March 19, 1947. William & Mary College.
Cochrane, Rory Syracuse, NY, Feb. 28, 1972.
Cody, Kathleen Bronx, NY, Oct. 30, 1953.
Coffey, Scott Honolulu, HI, May 1, 1964.
Cole, George London, England, April 22, 1925.
Coleman, Dabney Austin, TX, Jan. 3, 1932.
Coleman, Gary Zion, IL, Feb. 8, 1968.
Coleman, Jack Easton, PA, Feb. 21, 1958. Duke U.
Colin, Margaret New York, NY, May 26, 1958.
Collet, Christopher New York, NY, March 13, 1968. Strasberg Institute.
Collette, Toni Sydney, Australia, Nov. 1, 1972.
Collins, Clifton, Jr. Los Angeles, CA, June 16, 1970.
Collins, Joan London, England, May 21, 1933. Francis Holland School.
Collins, Pauline Devon, England, Sept. 3, 1940.
Collins, Stephen Des Moines, IA, Oct. 1, 1947. Amherst.
Colon, Miriam Ponce, PR., Aug. 20, 1936. UPR.
Coltrane, Robbie Ruthergien, Scotland, March 30, 1950.
Combs, Sean "Puffy" New York, NY, Nov. 4, 1969.
Comer, Anjanette Dawson, TX, Aug. 7, 1939. Baylor, Texas U.
Conant, Oliver New York, NY, Nov. 15, 1955. Dalton.
Conaway, Jeff New York, NY, Oct. 5, 1950. NYU.
Connelly, Jennifer New York, NY, Dec. 12, 1970.
Connery, Jason London, England, Jan. 11, 1963.
Connery, Sean Edinburgh, Scotland, Aug. 25, 1930.
Connick, Harry, Jr. New Orleans, LA, Sept. 11, 1967.
Connolly, Billy Glasgow, Scotland, Nov. 24, 1942.
Connors, Mike (Krekor Ohanian) Fresno, CA, Aug. 15, 1925. UCLA.
Conrad, Robert (Conrad Robert Falk) Chicago, IL, March 1, 1929. Northwestern.
Considine, Paddy Burton-on-Trent, England, Sept. 5, 1974.
Constantine, Michael Reading, PA, May 22, 1927.
Conti, Tom Paisley, Scotland, Nov. 22, 1941.
Converse, Frank St. Louis, MO, May 22, 1938. Carnegie Tech.
Conway, Gary Boston, MA, Feb. 4, 1936.
Conway, Kevin New York, NY, May 29, 1942.
Conway, Tim (Thomas Daniel) Willoughby, OH, Dec. 15, 1933. Bowling Green State.
Coogan, Keith (Keith Mitchell Franklin) Palm Springs, CA, Jan. 13, 1970.
Coogan, Steve Manchester, England, Oct. 14, 1965.
Cook, Dane Boston, MA, March 18, 1972.
Cook, Rachael Leigh Minneapolis, MN, Oct. 4, 1979.
Coolidge, Jennifer Boston, MA, Aug. 28, 1963.
Cooper, Ben Hartford, CT, Sept. 30, 1930. Columbia U.
Cooper, Chris Kansas City, MO, July 9, 1951. U Misourri.

Cooper, Dominic London, England, June 2, 1978.
Cooper, Jackie Los Angeles, CA, Sept. 15, 1922.
Copeland, Joan New York, NY, June 1, 1922. Brooklyn, NY College, RADA.
Copley, Sharlto Johannesburg, So. Africa, Nov. 27, 1973.
Corbett, Gretchen Portland, OR, Aug. 13, 1947. Carnegie Tech.
Corbett, John Wheeling, WV, May 9, 1961.
Corbin, Barry Dawson County, TX, Oct. 16, 1940. Texas Tech. U.
Corcoran, Donna Quincy, MA, Sept. 29, 1942.
Cord, Alex (Viespi) Floral Park, NY, Aug. 3, 1933. NYU, Actors Studio.
Corday, Mara (Marilyn Watts) Santa Monica, CA, Jan. 3, 1930.
Corri, Adrienne Glasgow, Scotland, Nov. 13, 1930. RADA.
Cort, Bud (Walter Edward Cox) New Rochelle, NY, March 29, 1948. NYU.
Cortesa, Valentina Milan, Italy, Jan. 1, 1923.
Cosby, Bill Philadelphia, PA, July 12, 1937. Temple U.
Coster, Nicolas London, England, Dec. 3, 1933. Neighborhood Playhouse.
Costner, Kevin Lynwood, CA, Jan. 18, 1955. California State U.
Cotillard, Marion Paris, France, Sept. 30, 1975.
Courtenay, Tom Hull, England, Feb. 25, 1937. RADA.
Courtland, Jerome Knoxville, TN, Dec. 27, 1926.
Cox, Brian Dundee, Scotland, June 1, 1946. LAMDA.
Cox, Charlie London, England, Dec. 21, 1982.
Cox, Courteney Birmingham, AL, June 15, 1964.
Cox, Ronny Cloudcroft, NM, Aug. 23, 1930.
Coyote, Peter (Cohon) New York, NY, Oct. 10, 1941.
Craig, Daniel Chester, England, March 2, 1968. Guildhall.
Craig, Michael Poona, India, Jan. 27, 1928.
Craven, Gemma Dublin, Ireland, June 1, 1950.
Crawford, Michael (Dumbel-Smith) Salisbury, England, Jan. 19, 1942.
Cremer, Bruno Saint-Mande, Val-de-Varne, France, Oct. 6, 1929.
Cristal, Linda (Victoria Moya) Buenos Aires, Argentina, Feb. 25, 1934.
Cromwell, James Los Angeles, CA, Jan. 27, 1940.
Crosby, Denise Hollywood, CA, Nov. 24, 1957.
Crosby, Harry Los Angeles, CA, Aug. 8, 1958.
Crosby, Mary Frances Los Angeles, CA, Sept. 14, 1959.
Cross, Ben London, England, Dec. 16, 1947. RADA.
Cross, Joseph New Brunswick, NJ, May 28, 1986.
Crouse, Lindsay New York, NY, May 12, 1948. Radcliffe.
Crowe, Russell New Zealand, April 7, 1964.
Crowley, Pat Olyphant, PA, Sept. 17, 1933.
Crudup, Billy Manhasset, NY, July 8, 1968. UNC, Chapel Hill.
Cruise, Tom (T. C. Mapother, IV) July 3, 1962, Syracuse, NY.
Cruz, Penélope (P.C. Sanchez) Madrid, Spain, April 28, 1974.
Cruz, Wilson Brooklyn, NY, Dec. 27, 1973.
Cryer, Jon New York, NY, April 16, 1965, RADA.
Crystal, Billy Long Beach, NY, March 14, 1947. Marshall U.
Culkin, Kieran New York, NY, Sept. 30, 1982.
Culkin, Macaulay New York, NY, Aug. 26, 1980.
Culkin, Rory New York, NY, July 21, 1989.
Cullum, John Knoxville, TN, March 2, 1930. U Tennessee.
Cullum, John David New York, NY, March 1, 1966.
Culp, Robert Oakland, CA, Aug. 16, 1930. U Washington.
Cumming, Alan Perthshire, Scotland, Jan. 27, 1965.
Cummings, Quinn Hollywood, CA, Aug. 13, 1967.
Cummins, Peggy Prestatyn, North Wales, Dec. 18, 1925. Alexandra School.
Curry, Tim Cheshire, England, April 19, 1946. Birmingham U.
Curtin, Jane Cambridge, MA, Sept. 6, 1947.
Curtis, Jamie Lee Los Angeles, CA, Nov. 22, 1958.
Curtis, Tony (Bernard Schwartz) New York, NY, June 3, 1925.
Curtis-Hall, Vondie Detroit, MI, Sept. 30, 1956.
Cusack, Joan Evanston, IL, Oct. 11, 1962.
Cusack, John Chicago, IL, June 28, 1966.
Cusack, Sinead Dalkey, Ireland, Feb. 18, 1948.
Cyrus, Miley Franklin, TN, nov. 23, 1992.

Dafoe, Willem Appleton, WI, July 22, 1955.
Dahl, Arlene Minneapolis, MN, Aug. 11, 1928. U Minnesota.
Dale, Jim Rothwell, England, Aug. 15, 1935.
Dallesandro, Joe Pensacola, FL, Dec. 31, 1948.
Dalton, Timothy Colwyn Bay, Wales, March 21, 1944. RADA.
Daltrey, Roger London, England, March 1, 1944.
Daly, Tim New York, NY, March 1, 1956. Bennington College.
Daly, Tyne Madison, WI, Feb. 21, 1946. AMDA.
Damon, Matt Cambridge, MA, Oct. 8, 1970.
Damone, Vic (Vito Farinola) Brooklyn, NY, June 12, 1928.
Dance, Charles Plymouth, England, Oct. 10, 1946.
Dancy, Hugh Stoke-on-Trent, England, June 19, 1975.
Danes, Claire New York, NY, April 12, 1979.
D'Angelo, Beverly Columbus, OH, Nov. 15, 1951.
Daniels, Jeff Athens, GA, Feb. 19, 1955. Central Michigan U.
Daniels, William Brooklyn, NY, March 31, 1927. Northwestern.
Danner, Blythe Philadelphia, PA, Feb. 3, 1943. Bard College.
Danning, Sybil (Sybille Johanna Danninger) Vienna, Austria, May 4, 1947.
Dano, Paul Wilton, CT, June 19, 1983.
Danson, Ted San Diego, CA, Dec. 29, 1947. Stanford, Carnegie Tech.
Dante, Michael (Ralph Vitti) Stamford, CT, 1931. U Miami.
Danza, Tony Brooklyn, NY, April 21, 1951. U Dubuque.
D'arbanville, Patti New York, NY, May 25, 1951.
Darby, Kim (Deborah Zerby) North Hollywood, CA, July 8, 1947.
Darcel, Denise (Denise Billecard) Paris, France, Sept. 8, 1925. U Dijon.
Darren, James Philadelphia, PA, June 8, 1936. Stella Adler School.
Darrieux, Danielle Bordeaux, France, May 1, 1917. Lycee LaTour.
Davenport, Jack Suffolk, England, March 1, 1973.
Davenport, Nigel Cambridge, England, May 23, 1928. Trinity College.
David, Keith New York, NY, June 4, 1956. Juilliard.
David, Larry Brooklyn, NY, July 2, 1947.
Davidovich, Lolita Toronto, ON, Canada, July 15, 1961.
Davidson, Jaye Riverside, CA, March 21, 1968.
Davidson, John Pittsburgh, PA, Dec. 13, 1941. Denison U.
Davidtz, Embeth Lafayette, IN, Aug. 11, 1965.
Davies, Jeremy (Boring) Rockford, IA, Oct. 28, 1969.
Davis, Clifton Chicago, IL, Oct. 4, 1945. Oakwood College.
Davis, Geena Wareham, MA, Jan. 21, 1957.
Davis, Hope Tenafly, NJ, March 23, 1964.
Davis, Judy Perth, Australia, April 23, 1955.
Davis, Mac Lubbock, TX, Jan. 21,1942.
Davis, Nancy (Anne Frances Robbins) New York, NY, July 6, 1921. Smith College.
Davis, Sammi Kidderminster, Worcestershire, England, June 21, 1964.
Davis, Viola Saint Matthews, SC, Aug. 11, 1965.
Davison, Bruce Philadelphia, PA, June 28, 1946.
Dawber, Pam Detroit, MI, Oct. 18, 1951.
Dawson, Rosario New York, NY, May 9, 1979.
Day, Doris (Doris Kappelhoff) Cincinatti, OH, April 3, 1924.
Day-Lewis, Daniel London, England, April 29, 1957. Bristol Old Vic.
Dayan, Assi Israel, Nov. 23, 1945. U Jerusalem.
Deakins, Lucy New York, NY, 1971.
Dean, Jimmy Plainview, TX, Aug. 10, 1928.
Dean, Loren Las Vegas, NV, July 31, 1969.
De Bankole, Isaach Abidjan, Ivory Coast, Aug. 12, 1957.
Dee, Joey (Joseph Di Nicola) Passaic, NJ, June 11, 1940. Patterson State College.
Dee, Ruby Cleveland, OH, Oct. 27, 1924. Hunter College.
DeGeneres, Ellen New Orleans, LA, Jan. 26, 1958.
DeHaven, Gloria Los Angeles, CA, July 23, 1923.
DeHavilland, Olivia Tokyo, Japan, July 1, 1916. Notre Dame Convent School.
Delair, Suzy (Suzanne Delaire) Paris, France, Dec. 31, 1917.

Delany, Dana New York, NY, March 13, 1956. Wesleyan U.
Delon, Alain Sceaux, France, Nov. 8, 1935.
Delorme, Daniele Paris, France, Oct. 9, 1926. Sorbonne.
Delpy, Julie Paris, France, Dec. 21, 1969.
Del Toro, Benicio Santurce, Puerto Rico, Feb. 19, 1967.
DeLuise, Peter New York, NY, Nov. 6, 1966.
Demongeot, Mylene Nice, France, Sept. 29, 1935.
DeMornay, Rebecca Los Angeles, CA, Aug. 29, 1959. Strasberg Institute.
Dempsey, Patrick Lewiston, ME, Jan. 13, 1966.
DeMunn, Jeffrey Buffalo, NY, April 25, 1947. Union College.
Dench, Judi York, England, Dec. 9, 1934.
Deneuve, Catherine Paris, France, Oct. 22, 1943.
De Niro, Robert New York, NY, Aug. 17, 1943. Stella Adler.
Dennehy, Brian Bridgeport, CT, July 9, 1938. Columbia U.
Depardieu, Gérard Chateauroux, France, Dec. 27, 1948.
Depp, Johnny Owensboro, KY, June 9, 1963.
Derek, Bo (Mary Cathleen Collins) Long Beach, CA, Nov. 20, 1956.
Dern, Bruce Chicago, IL, June 4, 1936. UPA.
Dern, Laura Los Angeles, CA, Feb. 10, 1967.
DeSalvo, Anne Philadelphia, PA, April 3, 1949.
Deschanel, Zooey Los Angeles, CA, Jan. 17, 1980.
Devane, William Albany, NY, Sept. 5, 1939.
Devine, Loretta Houston, TX, Aug. 21, 1949.
DeVito, Danny Asbury Park, NJ, Nov. 17, 1944.
Dey, Susan Pekin, IL, Dec. 10, 1952.
DeYoung, Cliff Los Angeles, CA, Feb. 12, 1945. California State U.
Diamond, Neil New York, NY, Jan. 24, 1941. NYU.
Diaz, Cameron Long Beach, CA, Aug. 30, 1972.
DiCaprio, Leonardo Hollywood, CA, Nov. 11, 1974.
Dickinson, Angie (Angeline Brown) Kulm, ND, Sept. 30, 1931. Glendale College.
Diesel, Vin (Mark Vincent) New York, NY, July 18, 1967.
Diggs, Taye (Scott Diggs) Rochester, NY, Jan. 2, 1972.
Dillahunt, Garrett Castro Valley, CA Nov. 24, 1964.
Diller, Phyllis (Driver) Lima, OH, July 17, 1917. Bluffton College.
Dillman, Bradford San Francisco, CA, April 14, 1930. Yale.
Dillon, Kevin Mamaroneck, NY, Aug. 19, 1965.
Dillon, Matt Larchmont, NY, Feb. 18, 1964. AADA.
Dillon, Melinda Hope, AR, Oct. 13, 1939. Goodman Theatre School.
Dinklage, Peter Morristown, NJ, June 11, 1969.
Dixon, Donna Alexandria, VA, July 20, 1957.
Dobson, Kevin New York, NY, March 18, 1944.
Doherty, Shannen Memphis, TN, April 12, 1971.
Dolan, Michael Oklahoma City, OK, June 21, 1965.
Donat, Peter Nova Scotia, Canada, Jan. 20, 1928. Yale.
Donnelly, Donal Bradford, England, July 6, 1931.
D'Onofrio, Vincent Brooklyn, NY, June 30, 1959.
Donohoe, Amanda London, England, June 29 1962.
Donovan, Martin Reseda, CA, Aug. 19, 1957.
Donovan, Tate New York, NY, Sept. 25, 1963.
Dooley, Paul Parkersburg WV, Feb. 22, 1928. U West Virginia.
Dorff, Stephen Atlanta, GA, July 29, 1973.
Doug, Doug E. (Douglas Bourne) Brooklyn, NY, Jan. 7, 1970.
Douglas, Donna (Dorothy Bourgeois) Baywood, LA, Sept. 26, 1935.
Douglas, Illeana Quincy, MA, July 25, 1965.
Douglas, Kirk (Issur Danielovitch) Amsterdam, NY, Dec. 9, 1916. St. Lawrence U.
Douglas, Michael New Brunswick, NJ, Sept. 25, 1944. U California.
Douglass, Robyn Sendai, Japan, June 21, 1953. UC Davis.
Dourif, Brad Huntington, WV, March 18, 1950. Marshall U.
Down, Lesley-Anne London, England, March 17, 1954.
Downey, Robert, Jr. New York, NY, April 4, 1965.
Drake, Betsy Paris, France, Sept. 11, 1923.

Drescher, Fran Queens, NY, Sept. 30, 1957.
Dreyfuss, Richard Brooklyn, NY, Oct. 19, 1947.
Drillinger, Brian Brooklyn, NY, June 27, 1960. SUNY-Purchase.
Driver, Minnie (Amelia Driver) London, England, Jan. 31, 1971.
Duchovny, David New York, NY, Aug. 7, 1960. Yale.
Dudikoff, Michael Torrance, CA, Oct. 8, 1954.
Duff, Hilary Houston, TX, Sept. 28, 1987.
Dugan, Dennis Wheaton, IL, Sept. 5, 1946.
Duhamel, Josh Minot, ND, Nov. 14, 1972.
Dukakis, Olympia Lowell, MA, June 20, 1931.
Duke, Bill Poughkeepsie, NY, Feb. 26, 1943. NYU.
Duke, Patty (Anna Marie) New York, NY, Dec. 14, 1946.
Dullea, Keir Cleveland, OH, May 30, 1936. San Francisco State College.
Dunaway, Faye Bascom, FL, Jan. 14, 1941, Florida U.
Duncan, Lindsay Edinburgh, Scotland, Nov. 7, 1950.
Duncan, Sandy Henderson, TX, Feb. 20, 1946. Len Morris College.
Dunne, Griffin New York, NY, June 8, 1955. Neighborhood Playhouse.
Dunst, Kirsten Point Pleasant, NJ, April 30, 1982.
Duperey, Anny Paris, France, June 28, 1947.
Durbin, Deanna (Edna) Winnipeg, Manitoba, Canada, Dec. 4, 1921.
Duris, Romain Paris, France, May 28, 1974.
Durning, Charles Highland Falls, NY, Feb. 28, 1923. NYU.
Dushku, Eliza Boston, MA, Dec. 30, 1980.
Dussollier, André Annecy, France, Feb. 17, 1946.
Dutton, Charles Baltimore, MD, Jan. 30, 1951. Yale.
DuVall, Clea Los Angeles, CA, Sept. 25, 1977.
Duvall, Robert San Diego, CA, Jan. 5, 1931. Principia College.
Duvall, Shelley Houston, TX, July 7, 1949.
Dysart, Richard Brighton, ME, March 30, 1929.
Dzundza, George Rosenheim, Germany, July 19, 1945.

Easton, Robert Milwaukee, WI, Nov. 23, 1930. U Texas.
Eastwood, Clint San Francisco, CA, May 31, 1930. LACC.
Eaton, Shirley London, England, Jan. 12, 1937. Aida Foster School.
Eckemyr, Agneta Karlsborg, Sweden, July 2, 1950 Actors Studio.
Eckhart, Aaron Santa Clara, CA, March 12, 1968.
Edelman, Gregg Chicago, IL, Sept. 12, 1958. Northwestern.
Eden, Barbara (Huffman) Tucson, AZ, Aug. 23, 1934.
Edwards, Anthony Santa Barbara, CA, July 19, 1962. RADA.
Edwards, Luke Nevada City, CA, March 24, 1980.
Efron, Zac San Luis Obispo, CA, Oct. 18, 1987.
Eggar, Samantha London, England, March 5, 1939.
Eichhorn, Lisa Reading, PA, Feb. 4, 1952. Queens Ont. U RADA.
Eikenberry, Jill New Haven, CT, Jan. 21, 1947.
Eilber, Janet Detroit, MI, July 27, 1951. Juilliard.
Eisenberg, Jesse New York, NY, Oct. 5, 1983.
Ejiofor, Chiwitel London, England, July 10, 1974.
Ekberg, Anita Malmo, Sweden, Sept. 29, 1931.
Ekland, Britt Stockholm, Sweden, Oct. 6, 1942.
Eldard, Ron Long Island, NY, Feb. 20, 1965.
Elfman, Jenna (Jennifer Mary Batula) Los Angeles, CA, Sept. 30, 1971.
Elise, Kimberly Minneapolis, MN, April 17, 1967.
Elizondo, Hector New York, NY, Dec. 22, 1936.
Elliott, Alison San Francisco, CA, May 19, 1970.
Elliott, Chris New York, NY, May 31, 1960.
Elliott, Patricia Gunnison, CO, July 21, 1942. U Colorado.
Elliott, Sam Sacramento, CA, Aug. 9, 1944. U Oregon.
Elwes, Cary London, England, Oct. 26, 1962.
Ely, Ron (Ronald Pierce) Hereford, TX, June 21, 1938.
Embry, Ethan (Ethan Randall) Huntington Beach, CA, June 13, 1978.
Englund, Robert Glendale, CA, June 6, 1949.
Epps, Mike Indianapolis, IN, Nov. 18, 1970.
Epps, Omar Brooklyn, NY, July 23, 1973.

Erbe, Kathryn Newton, MA, July 2, 1966.
Erdman, Richard Enid, OK, June 1, 1925.
Ericson, John Dusseldorf, Germany, Sept. 25, 1926. AADA.
Ermey, R. Lee (Ronald) Emporia, KS, March 24, 1944.
Esposito, Giancarlo Copenhagen, Denmark, April 26, 1958.
Estevez, Emilio New York, NY, May 12, 1962.
Estrada, Erik New York, NY, March 16, 1949.
Etel, Alex Manchester, England, Sept. 19, 1994.
Evans, Chris Sudbury, MA, June 13, 1981.
Evans, Josh New York, NY, Jan. 16, 1971.
Evans, Linda (Evanstad) Hartford, CT, Nov. 18, 1942.
Everett, Chad (Ray Cramton) South Bend, IN, June 11, 1936.
Everett, Rupert Norfolk, England, May 29, 1959.
Evigan, Greg South Amboy, NJ, Oct. 14, 1953.

Fabares, Shelley Los Angeles, CA, Jan. 19, 1944.
Fabian (Fabian Forte) Philadelphia, PA, Feb. 6, 1943.
Fabray, Nanette (Ruby Nanette Fabares) San Diego, Oct. 27, 1920.
Fahey, Jeff Olean, NY, Nov. 29, 1956.
Fairchild, Morgan (Patsy McClenny) Dallas, TX, Feb. 3, 1950. UCLA.
Falco, Edie Brooklyn, NY, July 5, 1963.
Falk, Peter New York, NY, Sept. 16, 1927. New School.
Fallon, Jimmy Brooklyn, NY, Sept. 19, 1974.
Fanning, Dakota Conyers, GA, Feb. 23, 1994.
Farentino, James Brooklyn, NY, Feb. 24, 1938. AADA.
Fargas, Antonio Bronx, NY, Aug. 14, 1946.
Farina, Dennis Chicago, IL, Feb. 29, 1944.
Faris, Anna Baltimore, MD, Nov. 29, 1976. U Washington.
Farmiga, Vera Passaic, NJ, Aug. 6, 1973.
Farr, Felicia Westchester, NY, Oct. 4. 1932. Penn State College.
Farrell, Colin Castleknock, Ireland, March 31, 1976.
Farrow, Mia (Maria) Los Angeles, CA, Feb. 9, 1945.
Faulkner, Graham London, England, Sept. 26, 1947. Webber-Douglas.
Favreau, Jon Queens, NY, Oct. 16, 1966.
Feinstein, Alan New York, NY, Sept. 8, 1941.
Feldman, Corey Encino, CA, July 16, 1971.
Feldon, Barbara (Hall) Pittsburgh, PA, March 12, 1941. Carnegie Tech.
Feldshuh, Tovah New York, NY, Dec. 27, 1953, Sarah Lawrence.
Fellows, Edith Boston, MA, May 20, 1923.
Fenn, Sherilyn Detroit, MI, Feb. 1, 1965.
Ferrell, Conchata Charleston, WV, March 28, 1943. Marshall U.
Ferrell, Will Irvine, CA, July 16, 1968.
Ferrer, Miguel Santa Monica, CA, Feb. 7, 1954.
Ferrera, America Los Angeles, CA, April 18, 1984.
Ferris, Barbara London, England, July 27, 1942.
Fey, Tina (Elizabeth Stamatina Fey) Upper Darby, PA, May 18, 1970.
Field, Sally Pasadena, CA, Nov. 6, 1946.
Field, Shirley-Anne London, England, June 27, 1938.
Field, Todd (William Todd Field) Pomona, CA, Feb. 24, 1964.
Fiennes, Joseph Salisbury, Wiltshire, England, May 27, 1970.
Fiennes, Ralph Suffolk, England, Dec. 22, 1962. RADA.
Fierstein, Harvey Brooklyn, NY, June 6, 1954. Pratt Institute.
Finch, Jon Caterham, England, March 2, 1941.
Finlay, Frank Farnworth, England, Aug. 6, 1926.
Finney, Albert Salford, Lancashire, England, May 9, 1936. RADA.
Fiorentino, Linda Philadelphia, PA, March 9, 1960.
Firth, Colin Grayshott, Hampshire, England, Sept. 10, 1960.
Firth, Peter Bradford, England, Oct. 27, 1953.
Fishburne, Laurence Augusta, GA, July 30, 1961.
Fischer, Jenna Ft. Wayne, IN, March 7, 1974.
Fisher, Carrie Los Angeles, CA, Oct. 21, 1956. London Central School of Drama.
Fisher, Eddie Philadelphia, PA, Aug. 10, 1928.

Fisher, Frances Milford-on-the-Sea, England, May 11, 1952.
Fisher, Isla Muscat, Oman, Feb. 3, 1976.
Fitzgerald, Tara London, England, Sept. 17, 1968.
Flagg, Fannie Birmingham, AL, Sept. 21, 1944. U Alabama.
Flanagan, Fionnula Dublin, Ireland, Dec. 10, 1941.
Flannery, Susan Jersey City, NJ, July 31, 1943.
Fleming, Rhonda (Marilyn Louis) Los Angeles, CA, Aug. 10, 1922.
Fletcher, Louise Birmingham, AL, July 22 1934.
Flockhart, Calista Stockton, IL, Nov. 11, Rutgers U.
Fogler, Dan Brooklyn, NY, Oct. 20, 1976.
Foley, Dave Toronto, ON, Canada, Jan. 4, 1963.
Follows, Megan Toronto, ON, Canada, March 14, 1968.
Fonda, Bridget Los Angeles, CA, Jan. 27, 1964.
Fonda, Jane New York, NY, Dec. 21, 1937. Vassar.
Fonda, Peter New York, NY, Feb. 23, 1939. U Omaha.
Fontaine, Joan Tokyo, Japan, Oct. 22, 1917.
Foote, Hallie New York, NY, 1953. U New Hampshire.
Ford, Harrison Chicago, IL, July 13, 1942. Ripon College.
Forlani, Claire London, England, July 1, 1972.
Forrest, Frederic Waxahachie, TX, Dec. 23, 1936.
Forrest, Steve Huntsville, TX, Sept. 29, 1924. UCLA.
Forslund, Connie San Diego, CA, June 19, 1950. NYU.
Forster, Robert (Foster, Jr.) Rochester, NY, July 13, 1941. Rochester U.
Forsythe, John (Freund) Penns Grove, NJ, Jan. 29, 1918.
Forsythe, William Brooklyn, NY, June 7, 1955.
Fossey, Brigitte Tourcoing, France, March 11, 1946.
Foster, Ben Boston, MA, Oct. 29, 1980.
Foster, Jodie (Alicia Christian Foster) Los Angeles, CA, Nov. 19, 1962. Yale.
Foster, Meg Reading, PA, May 14, 1948.
Fox, Edward London, England, April 13, 1937. RADA.
Fox, James London, England, May 19, 1939.
Fox, Megan Rockwood, TN, May 16, 1986.
Fox, Michael J. Vancouver, BC, Canada, June 9, 1961.
Fox, Vivica A. Indianapolis, July 30, 1964.
Foxworth, Robert Houston, TX, Nov. 1, 1941. Carnegie Tech.
Foxx, Jamie Terrell, TX, Dec. 13, 1967.
Frain, James Leeds, England, March 14, 1969.
Frakes, Jonathan Bethlehem, PA, Aug. 19, 1952. Harvard.
Francis, Anne Ossining, NY, Sept. 16, 1930.
Francis, Connie (Constance Franconero) Newark, NJ, Dec. 12, 1938.
Francks, Don Vancouver, BC, Canada, Feb. 28, 1932.
Franco, James Palo Alto, CA, April 19, 1978.
Franklin, Pamela Tokyo, Japan, Feb. 4, 1950.
Franz, Dennis Chicago, IL, Oct. 28, 1944.
Fraser, Brendan Indianapolis, IN, Dec. 3, 1968.
Frazier, Sheila New York, NY, Nov. 13, 1948.
Frechette, Peter Warwick, RI, Oct. 1956. U Rhode Island.
Freeman, Al, Jr. San Antonio, TX, March 21, 1934. CCLA.
Freeman, Martin Aldershot, England, Sept. 8, 1971.
Freeman, Mona Baltimore, MD, June 9, 1926.
Freeman, Morgan Memphis, TN, June 1, 1937. LACC.
Frewer, Matt Washington, DC, Jan. 4, 1958, Old Vic.
Fricker, Brenda Dublin, Ireland, Feb. 17, 1945.
Friel, Anna Rochdale, England, July 12, 1976.
Friels, Colin Glasgow, Scotland, Sept. 25, 1952.
Friend, Rupert Oxfordshire, England, Oct. 1, 1981.
Frost, Nick Essex, England, March 28, 1972.
Fry, Stephen Hampstead, London, England, Aug. 24, 1957.
Fuller, Penny Durham, NC, July 21, 1940. Northwestern.
Funicello, Annette Utica, NY, Oct. 22, 1942.
Furlong, Edward Glendale, CA, Aug. 2, 1977.
Furneaux, Yvonne Lille, France, May 11, 1928. Oxford U.
Futterman, Dan Silver Spring, MD, June 8, 1967.

Gable, John Clark Los Angeles, CA, March 20, 1961. Santa Monica College.
Gabor, Zsa Zsa (Sari Gabor) Budapest, Hungary, Feb. 6, 1917.
Gail, Max Derfoil, MI, April 5, 1943.
Gaines, Boyd Atlanta, GA, May 11, 1953. Juilliard.
Gainsbourg, Charlotte London, England, July 21, 1971.
Galecki, Johnny Bree, Belgium, April 30, 1975.
Galifianakis, Zach Wilkesboro, NC, Oct. 1, 1969.
Gallagher, Peter New York, NY, Aug. 19, 1955. Tufts U.
Galligan, Zach New York, NY, Feb. 14, 1963. Columbia U.
Gallo, Vincent Buffalo, NY, April 11, 1961.
Gam, Rita Pittsburgh, PA, April 2, 1927.
Gamble, Mason Chicago, IL, Jan. 16, 1986.
Gambon, Michael Dublin, Ireland, Oct. 19, 1940.
Gandolfini, James Westwood, NJ, Sept. 18, 1961.
Ganz, Bruno Zurich, Switzerland, March 22, 1941.
Garai, Romola Hong Kong, Aug. 6, 1982.
Garber, Victor Montreal, Quebec, Canada, March 16, 1949.
Garcia, Adam Wahroonga, New So. Wales, Australia, June 1, 1973.
Garcia, Andy Havana, Cuba, April 12, 1956. FIaInt.
Garfield, Allen (Allen Goorwitz) Newark, NJ, Nov. 22, 1939. Actors Studio.
Garfield, Andrew Los Angeles, CA, Aug. 20, 1983.
Garfunkel, Art New York, NY, Nov. 5, 1941.
Garlin, Jeff Chicago, IL, June 5, 1962.
Garner, James (James Baumgarner) Norman, OK, April 7, 1928. Oklahoma U.
Garner, Jennifer Houston, TX, April 17, 1972.
Garner, Kelli Bakersfield, CA, Aprl. 11, 1984.
Garofalo, Janeane Newton, NJ, Sept. 28, 1964.
Garr, Teri Lakewood, OH, Dec. 11, 1949.
Garrel, Louis Paris, June 14, 1983.
Garrett, Betty St. Joseph, MO, May 23, 1919. Annie Wright Seminary.
Garrison, Sean New York, NY, Oct. 19, 1937.
Gary, Lorraine New York, NY, Aug. 16, 1937.
Gavin, John Los Angeles, CA, April 8, 1928. Stanford U.
Gaylord, Mitch Van Nuys, CA, March 10, 1961. UCLA.
Gaynor, Mitzi (Francesca Marlene Von Gerber) Chicago, IL, Sept. 4, 1931.
Gazzara, Ben New York, NY, Aug. 28, 1930. Actors Studio.
Geary, Anthony Coalsville, UT, May 29, 1947. U Utah.
Gedrick, Jason Chicago, IL, Feb. 7, 1965. Drake U.
Geeson, Judy Arundel, England, Sept. 10, 1948. Corona.
Gellar, Sarah Michelle New York, NY, April 14, 1977.
Geoffreys, Stephen (Miller) Cincinnati, OH, Nov. 22, 1959. NYU.
George, Susan West London, England, July 26, 1950.
Gerard, Gil Little Rock, AR, Jan. 23, 1943.
Geraghty, Brian Toms River, NJ, May 13, 1974.
Gere, Richard Philadelphia, PA, Aug. 29, 1949. U Mass.
Gerroll, Daniel London, England, Oct. 16, 1951. Central.
Gershon, Gina Los Angeles, CA, June 10, 1962.
Gertz, Jami Chicago, IL, Oct. 28, 1965.
Gervais, Ricky Reading, England, June 25, 1961.
Getty, Balthazar Los Angeles, CA, Jan. 22, 1975.
Gholson, Julie Birmingham, AL, June 4, 1958.
Giamatti, Paul New York, NY, June 6, 1967. Yale.
Giannini, Giancarlo Spezia, Italy, Aug. 1, 1942. Rome Academy of Drama.
Gibb, Cynthia Bennington, VT, Dec. 14, 1963.
Gibson, Mel Peekskill, NY, Jan. 3, 1956. NIDA.
Gibson, Thomas Charleston, SC, July 3, 1962.
Gibson, Tyrese Los Angeles, CA, Dec. 30, 1978.
Gift, Roland Birmingham, England, May 28 1962.
Gilbert, Melissa Los Angeles, CA, May 8, 1964.
Giles, Nancy New York, NY, July 17, 1960, Oberlin College.
Gillette, Anita Baltimore, MD, Aug. 16, 1936.
Gilliam, Terry Minneapolis, MN, Nov. 22, 1940.
Gillis, Ann (Alma O'Connor) Little Rock, AR, Feb. 12, 1927.

Ginty, Robert New York, NY, Nov. 14, 1948. Yale.
Girardot, Annie Paris, France, Oct. 25, 1931.
Gish, Annabeth Albuquerque, NM, March 13, 1971. Duke U.
Givens, Robin New York, NY, Nov. 27, 1964.
Glaser, Paul Michael Boston, MA, March 25, 1943. Boston U.
Glass, Ron Evansville, IN, July 10, 1945.
Gleason, Joanna Winnipeg, Manitoba, Canada, June 2, 1950. UCLA.
Gleeson, Brendan Belfast, Northern Ireland, Nov. 9, 1955.
Glenn, Scott Pittsburgh, PA, Jan. 26, 1942. William and Mary College.
Glover, Crispin New York, NY, Sept 20, 1964.
Glover, Danny San Francisco, CA, July 22, 1947. San Francisco State U.
Glover, John Kingston, NY, Aug. 7, 1944.
Glynn, Carlin Cleveland, OH, Feb. 19, 1940. Actors Studio.
Goldberg, Adam Santa Monica, CA, Oct. 25, 1970.
Goldberg, Whoopi (Caryn Johnson) New York, NY, Nov. 13, 1949.
Goldblum, Jeff Pittsburgh, PA, Oct. 22, 1952. Neighborhood Playhouse.
Golden, Annie Brooklyn, NY, Oct. 19, 1951.
Goldstein, Jenette Beverly Hills, CA, Feb. 4, 1960.
Goldthwait, Bob Syracuse, NY, May 1, 1962.
Goldwyn, Tony Los Angeles, CA, May 20, 1960. LAMDA.
Golino, Valeria Naples, Italy, Oct. 22, 1966.
Gonzalez, Cordelia San Juan, PR, Aug. 11, 1957. UPR.
Good, Meagan Panorama City, CA, Aug. 8, 1981.
Goodall, Caroline London, England, Nov. 13, 1959. Bristol U.
Goode, Matthew Exeter, England, April 3, 1978.
Gooding, Cuba, Jr. Bronx, NY, Jan. 2, 1968.
Goodman, John St. Louis, MO, June 20, 1952.
Gordon, Keith New York, NY, Feb. 3, 1961.
Gordon-Levitt, Joseph Los Angeles, CA, Feb. 17, 1981.
Gortner, Marjoe Long Beach, CA, Jan. 14, 1944.
Gosling, Ryan London, ON, Canada, Nov. 12, 1980.
Goss, Luke London, England, Sept. 28, 1968.
Gossett, Louis, Jr. Brooklyn, NY, May 27, 1936. NYU.
Gould, Elliott (Goldstein) Brooklyn, NY, Aug. 29, 1938. Columbia U.
Gould, Harold Schenectady, NY, Dec. 10, 1923. Cornell.
Gould, Jason New York, NY, Dec. 29, 1966.
Grace, Topher New York, NY, July 12, 1978.
Graff, Todd New York, NY, Oct. 22, 1959. SUNY-Purchase.
Graham, Heather Milwauke, WI, Jan. 29, 1970.
Grammer, Kelsey St. Thomas, Virgin Islands, Feb. 21, 1955.
Granger, Farley San Jose, CA, July 1, 1925.
Grant, David Marshall Westport, CT, June 21, 1955. Yale.
Grant, Hugh London, England, Sept. 9, 1960. Oxford.
Grant, Kathryn (Olive Grandstaff) Houston, TX, Nov. 25, 1933. UCLA.
Grant, Lee New York, NY, Oct. 31, 1927. Juilliard.
Grant, Richard E. Mbabane, Swaziland, May 5, 1957. Cape Town U.
Graves, Peter (Aurness) Minneapolis, MN, March 18, 1926. U Minnesota.
Graves, Rupert Weston-Super-Mare, England, June 30, 1963.
Gray, Coleen (Doris Jensen) Staplehurst, NB, Oct. 23, 1922. Hamline.
Gray, Linda Santa Monica, CA, Sept. 12, 1940.
Grayson, Kathryn (Zelma Hedrick) Winston-Salem, NC, Feb. 9, 1922.
Green, Eva Paris, France, July 5, 1980.
Green, Kerri Fort Lee, NJ, Jan. 14, 1967. Vassar.
Green, Seth Philadelphia, PA, Feb. 8, 1974.
Greene, Ellen New York, NY, Feb. 22, 1950. Ryder College.
Greene, Graham Six Nations Reserve, ON, Canada, June 22, 1952.
Greenwood, Bruce Quebec, Canada, Aug. 12, 1956.
Greer, Michael Galesburg, IL, April 20, 1943.
Greist, Kim Stamford, CT, May 12, 1958.
Grenier, Adrian Brooklyn, NY, July 10, 1976.
Grey, Jennifer New York, NY, March 26, 1960.
Grey, Joel (Katz) Cleveland, OH, April 11, 1932.
Grieco, Richard Watertown, NY, March 23, 1965.

Grier, David Alan Detroit, MI, June 30, 1955. Yale.
Grier, Pam Winston-Salem, NC, May 26, 1949.
Griffin, Eddie Kansas City, MO, July 15, 1968.
Griffith, Andy Mt. Airy, NC, June 1, 1926. U North Carolina.
Griffith, Melanie New York, NY, Aug. 9, 1957. Pierce Collge.
Griffith, Thomas Ian Hartford, CT, March 18, 1962.
Griffiths, Rachel Melbourne, Australia, June 4, 1968.
Griffiths, Richard Tornaby-on-Tees, England, July 31, 1947.
Grimes, Gary San Francisco, CA, June 2, 1955.
Grimes, Scott Lowell, MA, July 9, 1971.
Grimes, Tammy Lynn, MA, Jan. 30, 1934. Stephens College.
Grint, Rupert Watton-at-Stone, England, Aug. 24, 1988.
Grodin, Charles Pittsburgh, PA, April 21, 1935.
Groh, David New York, NY, May 21, 1939. Brown U, LAMDA.
Gross, Mary Chicago, IL, March 25, 1953.
Gross, Michael Chicago, IL, June 21, 1947.
Gruffud, Ioan Cardiff, Wales, Oct. 6, 1973.
Guest, Christopher New York, NY, Feb. 5, 1948.
Guest, Lance Saratoga, CA, July 21, 1960. UCLA.
Gugino, Carla Sarasota, FL, Aug. 29, 1971.
Guillaume, Robert (Williams) St. Louis, MO, Nov. 30, 1937.
Guiry, Thomas Trenton, NJ, Oct. 12, 1981.
Gulager, Clu Holdenville, OK, Nov. 16 1928.
Guttenberg, Steve Massapequa, NY, Aug. 24, 1958. UCLA.
Guy, Jasmine Boston, MA, March 10, 1964.
Guzman, Luis Cayey, Puerto Rico, Jan. 1, 1957.
Gyllenhaal, Jake Los Angeles, CA, Dec. 19, 1980.
Gyllenhaal, Maggie Los Angeles, CA, Nov. 16, 1977.

Haas, Lukas West Hollywood, CA, April 16, 1976.
Hack, Shelley Greenwich, CT, July 6, 1952.
Hackman, Gene San Bernardino, CA, Jan. 30, 1930.
Hader, Bill Tulsa, OK, June 7, 1978.
Hagerty, Julie Cincinnati, OH, June 15, 1955. Juilliard.
Hagman, Larry (Hageman) Weatherford, TX, Sept. 21, 1931. Bard.
Haid, Charles San Francisco, CA, June 2, 1943. Carnegie Tech.
Haim, Corey Toronto, ON, Canada, Dec. 23, 1972.
Hale, Barbara DeKalb, IL, April 18, 1922. Chicago Academy of Fine Arts.
Haley, Jackie Earle Northridge, CA, July 14, 1961.
Hall, Albert Boothton, AL, Nov. 10, 1937. Columbia U.
Hall, Anthony Michael Boston, MA, April 14, 1968.
Hall, Arsenio Cleveland, OH, Feb. 12, 1959.
Hall, Philip Baker Toledo, OH, Sept. 10, 1931.
Hamel, Veronica Philadelphia, PA, Nov. 20, 1943.
Hamill, Mark Oakland, CA, Sept. 25, 1952. LACC.
Hamilton, George Memphis, TN, Aug. 12, 1939. Hackley.
Hamilton, Josh New York, NY, June 9, 1969.
Hamilton, Linda Salisbury, MD, Sept. 26, 1956.
Hamlin, Harry Pasadena, CA, Oct. 30, 1951.
Hampshire, Susan London, England, May 12, 1941.
Hampton, James Oklahoma City, OK, July 9, 1936. Northern Texas State.
Han, Maggie Providence, RI, 1959.
Handler, Evan New York, NY, Jan. 10, 1961. Juilliard.
Hanks, Colin Sacramento, CA, Nov. 24, 1977.
Hanks, Tom Concord, CA, July 9, 1956. California State.
Hannah, Daryl Chicago, IL, Dec. 3, 1960. UCLA.
Hannah, Page Chicago, IL, April 13, 1964.
Harden, Marcia Gay La Jolla, CA, Aug. 14, 1959.
Hardin, Ty (Orison Whipple Hungerford, II) New York, NY, Jan. 1, 1930.
Harewood, Dorian Dayton, OH, Aug. 6, 1950. U Cinncinatti.
Harmon, Mark Los Angeles, CA, Sept. 2, 1951. UCLA.
Harper, Jessica Chicago, IL, Oct. 10, 1949.
Harper, Tess Mammoth Spring, AR, 1952. Southwestern Misourri State.

Harper, Valerie Suffern, NY, Aug. 22, 1939.
Harrelson, Woody Midland, TX, July 23, 1961. Hanover College.
Harrington, Pat New York, NY, Aug. 13, 1929. Fordham U.
Harris, Barbara (Sandra Markowitz) Evanston, IL, July 25, 1935.
Harris, Ed Tenafly, NJ, Nov. 28, 1950. Columbia U.
Harris, Jared London, England, Aug. 24, 1961.
Harris, Julie Grosse Point, MI, Dec. 2, 1925. Yale School of Drama.
Harris, Mel (Mary Ellen) Bethlehem, PA, 1957. Columbia U.
Harris, Neil Patrick Albuquerque, NM, June 15, 1973.
Harris, Rosemary Ashby, England, Sept. 19, 1930. RADA.
Harrison, Gregory Catalina Island, CA, May 31, 1950. Actors Studio.
Harrison, Noel London, England, Jan. 29, 1936.
Harrold, Kathryn Tazewell, VA, Aug. 2, 1950. Mills College.
Harry, Deborah Miami, IL, July 1, 1945.
Hart, Ian Liverpool, England, Oct. 8, 1964.
Hart, Roxanne Trenton, NJ, July 27, 1952. Princeton.
Hartley, Mariette New York, NY, June 21, 1940.
Hartman, David Pawtucket, RI, May 19, 1935. Duke U.
Hartnett, Josh San Francisco, CA, July 21, 1978.
Hassett, Marilyn Los Angeles, CA, Dec. 17, 1947.
Hatcher, Teri Sunnyvale, CA, Dec. 8, 1964.
Hathaway, Anne Brooklyn, NY, Nov. 12, 1982.
Hatosy, Shawn Fredrick, MD, Dec. 29, 1975.
Hauer, Rutger Amsterdam, Holland, Jan. 23, 1944.
Hauser, Cole Santa Barbara, CA, March 22, 1975.
Hasuer, Wings (Gerald Dwight Hauser) Hollywood, CA, Dec. 12, 1947.
Havoc, June (Hovick) Seattle, WA, Nov. 8, 1916.
Hawke, Ethan Austin, TX, Nov. 6, 1970.
Hawn, Goldie Washington, DC, Nov. 21, 1945.
Hayek, Salma Coatzacoalcos, Veracruz, Mexico, Sept. 2, 1968.
Hayes, Sean Chicago, IL, June 26, 1970.
Hays, Robert Bethesda, MD, July 24, 1947. South Dakota State College.
Haysbert, Dennis San Mateo, CA, June 2, 1954.
Headey, Lena Bermuda, Oct. 3, 1973.
Headly, Glenne New London, CT, March 13, 1955. American College of Switzerland.
Heald, Anthony New Rochelle, NY, Aug. 25, 1944. Michigan State.
Heard, John Washington, DC, March 7, 1946. Clark U.
Heatherton, Joey New York, NY, Sept. 14, 1944.
Heche, Anne Aurora, OH, May 25, 1969.
Hedaya, Dan Brooklyn, NY, July 24, 1940.
Heder, Jon Fort Collins, CO, Oct. 26, 1977.
Hedison, David Providence, RI, May 20, 1929. Brown U.
Hedren, Tippi (Natalie) Lafayette, MN, Jan. 19, 1931.
Hegyes, Robert Metuchen, NJ, May 7, 1951.
Heigl, Katherine Washington, DC, Nov. 24, 1978.
Helmond, Katherine Galveston, TX, July 5, 1928.
Helms, Ed Atlanta, GA, Jan. 24, 1974.
Hemingway, Mariel Ketchum, ID, Nov. 22, 1961.
Hemsley, Sherman Philadelphia, PA, Feb. 1, 1938.
Henderson, Florence Dale, IN, Feb. 14, 1934.
Hendry, Gloria Winter Haven, FL, March 3, 1949.
Henley, Georgie Ikley, England, July 9, 1995.
Henner, Marilu Chicago, IL, April 6, 1952.
Henriksen, Lance New York, NY, May 5, 1940.
Henry, Buck (Henry Zuckerman) New York, NY, Dec. 9, 1930. Dartmouth.
Henry, Justin Rye, NY, May 25, 1971.
Henson, Taraji P. Washington, DC, Sept. 11, 1970. Howard U.
Henstridge, Natasha Springdale, Newfoundland, Canada, Aug. 15, 1974.
Hernandez, Jay (Javier Hernandez, Jr.) Montebello, CA, Feb. 20, 1978.
Herrmann, Edward Washington, DC, July 21, 1943. Bucknell, LAMDA.
Hershey, Barbara (Herzstein) Hollywood, CA, Feb. 5, 1948.
Hesseman, Howard Lebanon, OR, Feb. 27, 1940.

Hewitt, Jennifer Love Waco, TX, Feb. 21, 1979.
Hewitt, Martin Claremont, CA, Feb. 19, 1958. AADA.
Heywood, Anne (Violet Pretty) Birmingham, England, Dec. 11, 1932.
Hickey, John Benjamin Plano, TX, June 25, 1963.
Hickman, Darryl Hollywood, CA, July 28, 1933. Loyola U.
Hickman, Dwayne Los Angeles, CA, May 18, 1934. Loyola U.
Hicks, Catherine New York, NY, Aug. 6, 1951. Notre Dame.
Higgins, Anthony (Corlan) Cork City, Ireland, May 9, 1947. Birmingham Dramatic Arts.
Higgins, John Michael Boston, MA, Feb. 12, 1963.
Higgins, Michael Brooklyn, NY, Jan. 20, 1921. American Theatre Wing.
Highmore, Freddie London, England, Feb. 14, 1992.
Hill, Bernard Manchester, England, Dec. 17, 1944.
Hill, Jonah Los Angeles, CA, Dec. 20, 1983.
Hill, Steven Seattle, WA, Feb. 24, 1922. U Washington.
Hill, Terrence (Mario Girotti) Venice, Italy, March 29, 1941. U Rome.
Hillerman, John Denison, TX, Dec. 20, 1932.
Hinds, Ciaran Belfast, Northern Ireland, Feb. 9, 1953.
Hirsch, Emile Topanga Canyon, CA, March 13, 1985.
Hirsch, Judd New York, NY, March 15, 1935. AADA.
Hobel, Mara New York, NY, June 18, 1971.
Hodge, Patricia Lincolnshire, England, Sept. 29, 1946. LAMDA.
Hoffman, Dustin Los Angeles, CA, Aug. 8, 1937. Pasadena Playhouse.
Hoffman, Philip Seymour Fairport, NY, July 23, 1967. NYU.
Hogan, Jonathan Chicago, IL, June 13, 1951.
Hogan, Paul Lightning Ridge, Australia, Oct. 8, 1939.
Holbrook, Hal (Harold) Cleveland, OH, Feb. 17, 1925. Denison.
Hollander, Tom Oxford, England, Aug. 25, 1967.
Holliman, Earl Tennass Swamp, Delhi, LA, Sept. 11, 1928. UCLA.
Holm, Celeste New York, NY, April 29, 1919.
Holm, Ian Ilford, Essex, England, Sept. 12, 1931. RADA.
Holmes, Katie Toledo, OH, Dec. 18, 1978.
Homeier, Skip (George Vincent Homeier) Chicago, IL, Oct. 5, 1930. UCLA.
Hooks, Robert Washington, DC, April 18, 1937. Temple.
Hopkins, Anthony Port Talbot, So. Wales, Dec. 31, 1937. RADA.
Hopper, Dennis Dodge City, KS, May 17, 1936.
Horne, Lena Brooklyn, NY, June 30, 1917.
Horrocks, Jane Rossendale Valley, England, Jan. 18, 1964.
Horsley, Lee Muleshoe, TX, May 15, 1955.
Horton, Robert Los Angeles, CA, July 29, 1924. UCLA.
Hoskins, Bob Bury St. Edmunds, England, Oct. 26, 1942.
Houghton, Katharine Hartford, CT, March 10, 1945. Sarah Lawrence.
Hoult, Nicholas Wokingham, England, Dec. 7, 1989.
Hounsou, Djimon Benin, West Africa, April 24, 1964.
Houser, Jerry Los Angeles, CA, July 14, 1952. Valley Junior College.
Howard, Arliss Independence, MO, 1955. Columbia College.
Howard, Bryce Dallas Los Angeles, CA, March 2, 1981.
Howard, Ken El Centro, CA, March 28, 1944. Yale.
Howard, Ron Duncan, OK, March 1, 1954. USC.
Howard, Terrence Chicago, IL, March 11, 1969. Pratt Inst.
Howell, C. Thomas Los Angeles, CA, Dec. 7, 1966.
Howes, Sally Ann London, England, July 20, 1930.
Howland, Beth Boston, MA, May 28, 1941.
Hubley, Season New York, NY, May 14, 1951.
Huddleston, David Vinton, VA, Sept. 17, 1930.
Hudson, Ernie Benton Harbor, MI, Dec. 17, 1945.
Hudson, Jennifer Chicago, IL, Sept. 12, 1981.
Hudson, Kate Los Angeles, CA, April 19, 1979.
Huffman, Felicity Bedford, NY, Dec. 9, 1962. NYU.
Hughes, Kathleen (Betty von Gerkan) Hollywood, CA, Nov. 14, 1928. UCLA.
Hulce, Tom Plymouth, MI, Dec. 6, 1953. North Carolina School of Arts.
Hunnicut, Gayle Ft. Worth, TX, Feb. 6, 1943. UCLA.
Hunt, Helen Los Angeles, CA, June 15, 1963.

Hunt, Linda Morristown, NJ, April 1945. Goodman Theatre.
Hunt, Marsha Chicago, IL, Oct. 17, 1917.
Hunter, Holly Atlanta, GA, March 20, 1958. Carnegie-Mellon.
Hunter, Tab (Arthur Gelien) New York, NY, July 11, 1931.
Huntington, Sam Peterborough, NH, April 1, 1982.
Huppert, Isabelle Paris, France, March 16, 1955.
Hurley, Elizabeth Hampshire, England, June 10, 1965.
Hurt, John Lincolnshire, England, Jan. 22, 1940.
Hurt, Mary Beth (Supinger) Marshalltown, IA, Sept. 26, 1948. NYU.
Hurt, William Washington, DC, March 20, 1950. Tufts, Juilliard.
Huston, Anjelica Santa Monica, CA, July 9, 1951.
Huston, Danny Rome, Italy, May 14, 1962.
Hutcherson, Josh Union, KY, Oct. 12, 1992.
Hutton, Lauren (Mary) Charleston, SC, Nov. 17, 1943. Newcomb College.
Hutton, Timothy Malibu, CA, Aug. 16, 1960.
Hyer, Martha Fort Worth, TX, Aug. 10, 1924. Northwestern.

Ice Cube (O'Shea Jackson) Los Angeles, CA, June 15, 1969.
Idle, Eric South Shields, Durham, England, March 29, 1943. Cambridge.
Ifans, Rhys Ruthin, Wales, July 22, 1968.
Ingels, Marty Brooklyn, NY, March 9, 1936.
Ireland, Kathy Santa Barbara, CA, March 8, 1963.
Irons, Jeremy Cowes, England, Sept. 19, 1948. Old Vic.
Ironside, Michael Toronto, ON, Canada, Feb. 12, 1950.
Irving, Amy Palo Alto, CA, Sept. 10, 1953. LADA.
Irwin, Bill Santa Monica, CA, April 11, 1950.
Isaak, Chris Stockton, CA, June 26, 1956. U of the Pacific.
Ivanek, Zeljko Lujubljana, Yugoslavia, Aug. 15, 1957. Yale, LAMDA.
Ivey, Judith El Paso, TX, Sept. 4, 1951.
Izzard, Eddie Aden, Yemen, Feb. 7, 1962.

Jackson, Anne Allegheny, PA, Sept. 3, 1926. Neighborhood Playhouse.
Jackson, Glenda Hoylake, Cheshire, England, May 9, 1936. RADA.
Jackson, Janet Gary, IN, May 16, 1966.
Jackson, Joshua Vancouver, BC, Canada, June 11, 1978.
Jackson, Kate Birmingham, AL, Oct. 29, 1948. AADA.
Jackson, Samuel L. Atlanta, GA, Dec. 21, 1948.
Jackson, Victoria Miami, FL, Aug. 2, 1958.
Jacobi, Derek London, England, Oct. 22, 1938. Cambridge.
Jacobs, Lawrence-Hilton Virgin Islands, Sept. 14, 1953.
Jacoby, Scott Chicago, IL, Nov. 19, 1956.
Jagger, Mick Dartford, Kent, England, July 26, 1943.
James, Clifton New York, NY, May 29, 1921. Oregon U.
James, Kevin Stony Brook, NY, April 26, 1965.
Jane, Thomas Baltimore, MD, Jan. 29, 1969.
Janney, Allison Dayton, OH, Nov. 20, 1960. RADA.
Janssen, Famke Amsterdam, Holland, Nov. 5, 1965.
Jarman, Claude, Jr. Nashville, TN, Sept. 27, 1934.
Jean, Gloria (Gloria Jean Schoonover) Buffalo, NY, April 14, 1927.
Jeffreys, Anne (Carmichael) Goldsboro, NC, Jan. 26, 1923. Anderson College.
Jeffries, Lionel London, England, June 10, 1926. RADA.
Jenkins, Richard Dekalb, IL, May 4, 1947. Wesleyan U.
Jillian, Ann (Nauseda) Cambridge, MA, Jan. 29, 1950.
Johansen, David Staten Island, NY, Jan. 9, 1950.
Johansson, Scarlett New York, NY, Nov. 22, 1984.
John, Elton (Reginald Dwight) Middlesex, England, March 25, 1947. RAM.
Johns, Glynis Durban, S. Africa, Oct. 5, 1923.
Johnson, Don Galena, MO, Dec. 15, 1949. U Kansas.
Johnson, Dwayne (a.k.a. The Rock) Hayward, CA, May 2, 1972.
Johnson, Page Welch, WV, Aug. 25, 1930. Ithaca.
Johnson, Rafer Hillsboro, TX, Aug. 18, 1935. UCLA.
Johnson, Richard Essex, England, July 30, 1927. RADA.

Johnson, Robin Brooklyn, NY, May 29, 1964.
Jolie, Angelina (Angelina Jolie Voight) Los Angeles, CA, June 4, 1975.
Jones, Cherry Paris, France, TN, Nov. 21, 1956.
Jones, Christopher Jackson, TN, Aug. 18, 1941. Actors Studio.
Jones, Dean Decatur, AL, Jan. 25, 1931. Actors Studio.
Jones, Grace Spanishtown, Jamaica, May 19, 1952.
Jones, Jack Bel Air, CA, Jan. 14, 1938.
Jones, James Earl Arkabutla, MS, Jan. 17, 1931. U Michigan
Jones, Jeffrey Buffalo, NY, Sept. 28, 1947. LAMDA.
Jones, Jennifer (Phyllis Isley) Tulsa, OK, March 2, 1919. AADA.
Jones, L.Q. (Justice Ellis McQueen) Beaumont, TX, Aug 19, 1927.
Jones, Orlando Mobile, AL, April 10, 1968.
Jones, Sam J. Chicago, IL, Aug. 12, 1954.
Jones, Shirley Smithton, PA, March 31, 1934.
Jones, Terry Colwyn Bay, Wales, Feb. 1, 1942.
Jones, Toby Oxford, England, Sept. 7, 1967.
Jones, Tommy Lee San Saba, TX, Sept. 15, 1946. Harvard.
Jourdan, Louis Marseilles, France, June 19, 1919.
Jovovich, Milla Kiev, Ukraine, Dec. 17, 1975.
Joy, Robert Montreal, Quebec, Canada, Aug. 17, 1951. Oxford.
Judd, Ashley Los Angeles, CA, April 19, 1968.

Kaczmarek, Jane Milwaukee, WI, Dec. 21, 1955.
Kane, Carol Cleveland, OH, June 18, 1952.
Kaplan, Marvin Brooklyn, NY, Jan. 24, 1924.
Kapoor, Shashi Calcutta, India, March 18, 1938.
Kaprisky, Valerie (Cheres) Paris, France, Aug. 19, 1962.
Karras, Alex Gary, IN, July 15, 1935.
Kartheiser, Vincent Minneapolis, MN, May 5, 1979.
Karyo, Tcheky Istanbul, Oct. 4, 1953.
Kassovitz, Mathieu Paris, France, Aug. 3, 1967.
Katt, Nicky South Dakota, May 11, 1970.
Katt, William Los Angeles, CA, Feb. 16, 1955.
Kattan, Chris Mt. Baldy, CA, Oct. 19, 1970.
Kaufmann, Christine Lansdorf, Graz, Austria, Jan. 11, 1945.
Kavner, Julie Burbank, CA, Sept. 7, 1950. UCLA.
Kazan, Lainie (Levine) Brooklyn, NY, May 15, 1940.
Kazurinsky, Tim Johnstown, PA, March 3, 1950.
Keach, Stacy Savannah, GA, June 2, 1941. U California, Yale.
Keaton, Diane (Hall) Los Angeles, CA, Jan. 5, 1946. Neighborhood Playhouse.
Keaton, Michael Coraopolis, PA, Sept. 9, 1951. Kent State U.
Keegan, Andrew Los Angeles, CA, Jan. 29, 1979.
Keener, Catherine Miami, FL, March 26, 1960. Wheaton College.
Keeslar, Matt Grand Rapids, MI, Oct. 15, 1972.
Keitel, Harvey Brooklyn, NY, May 13, 1939.
Keith, David Knoxville, TN, May 8, 1954. U Tennessee.
Keller, Marthe Basel, Switzerland, 1945. Munich Stanislavsky School.
Kellerman, Sally Long Beach, CA, June 2, 1937. Actors Studio West.
Kelley, Elijah LaGrange, GA, Aug. 1, 1986.
Kelly, Moira Queens, NY, March 6, 1968.
Kemp, Jeremy (Wacker) Chesterfield, England, Feb. 3, 1935. Central School.
Kendrick, Anna Portland, ME, Aug. 9, 1985.
Kennedy, George New York, NY, Feb. 18, 1925.
Kennedy, Jamie Upper Darby, PA, May 25, 1970.
Kennedy, Leon Isaac Cleveland, OH, Jan. 1, 1949.
Kensit, Patsy London, England, March 4, 1968.
Kerr, John New York, NY, Nov. 15, 1931. Harvard, Columbia.
Kerwin, Brian Chicago, IL, Oct. 25, 1949.
Keynes, Skandar London, Sept. 5, 1991.
Kidder, Margot Yellow Knife, Canada, Oct. 17, 1948. U British Columbia.
Kidman, Nicole Honolulu, HI, June 20, 1967.
Kiel, Richard Detroit, MI, Sept. 13, 1939.

Kier, Udo Koeln, Germany, Oct. 14, 1944.
Kikuchi, Rinko Kanagawa, Japan, Jan. 6, 1981.
Kilmer, Val Los Angeles, CA, Dec. 31, 1959. Juilliard.
Kincaid, Aron (Norman Neale Williams, III) Los Angeles, CA, June 15, 1940. UCLA.
Kind, Richard Trenton, NJ, Nov. 22, 1956.
King, Perry Alliance, OH, April 30, 1948. Yale.
Kingsley, Ben (Krishna Bhanji) Snaiton, Yorkshire, England, Dec. 31, 1943.
Kinnear, Greg Logansport, IN, June 17, 1963.
Kinski, Nastassja Berlin, Germany, Jan. 24, 1959.
Kirk, Justin Salem, OR, May 28, 1969.
Kirk, Tommy Louisville, KY, Dec. 10 1941.
Kirkland, Sally New York, NY, Oct. 31, 1941. Actors Studio.
Klein, Chris Hinsdale, IL, March 14, 1979.
Klein, Robert New York, NY, Feb. 8, 1942. Alfred U.
Kline, Kevin St. Louis, MO, Oct. 24, 1947. Juilliard.
Klugman, Jack Philadelphia, PA, April 27, 1922. Carnegie Tech.
Knight, Michael E. Princeton, NJ, May 7, 1959.
Knight, Shirley Goessel, KS, July 5, 1937. Wichita State U.
Knightley, Keira Teddington, England, March 26, 1985.
Knox, Elyse Hartford, CT, Dec. 14, 1917. Traphagen School.
Knoxville, Johnny (Phillip John Clapp) Knoxville, TN, March 11, 1971.
Koechner, David Tipton, MO, Aug. 24, 1962.
Koenig, Walter Chicago, IL, Sept. 14, 1936. UCLA.
Kohner, Susan Los Angeles, CA, Nov. 11, 1936. U California.
Korsmo, Charlie Minneapolis, MN, July, 20, 1978.
Koteas, Elias Montreal, Quebec, Canada, 1961. AADA.
Kotto, Yaphet New York, NY, Nov. 15, 1937.
Kozak, Harley Jane Wilkes-Barre, PA, Jan. 28, 1957. NYU.
Krabbe, Jeroen Amsterdam, The Netherlands, Dec. 5, 1944.
Krasinski, John Newton, MA, Oct. 20, 1979.
Krause, Peter Alexandria, MN, Aug. 12, 1965.
Kretschmann, Thomas Dessau, East Germany, Sept. 8, 1962.
Krige, Alice Upington, South Africa, June 28, 1954.
Kristel, Sylvia Amsterdam, The Netherlands, Sept. 28, 1952.
Kristofferson, Kris Brownsville, TX, June 22, 1936. Pomona College.
Kruger, Diane Algermissen, Germany, July 15, 1976.
Kruger, Hardy Berlin, Germany, April 12, 1928.
Krumholtz, David New York, NY, May 15, 1978.
Kunis, Mila Kiev, Ukraine, Aug. 14, 1983.
Kudrow, Lisa Encino, CA, July 30, 1963.
Kurtz, Swoosie Omaha, NE, Sept. 6, 1944.
Kutcher, Ashton (Christopher Ashton Kutcher) Cedar Rapids, IA, Feb. 7, 1978.
Kwan, Nancy Hong Kong, May 19, 1939. Royal Ballet.

LaBelle, Patti Philadelphia, PA, May 24, 1944.
LaBeouf, Shia Los Angeles, CA, June 11, 1986.
Lacy, Jerry Sioux City, IA, March 27, 1936. LACC.
Ladd, Cheryl (Stoppelmoor) Huron, SD. July 12, 1951.
Ladd, Diane (Ladner) Meridian, MS, Nov. 29, 1932. Tulane U.
Lahti, Christine Detroit, MI, April 4, 1950. U Michigan
Lake, Ricki New York, NY, Sept. 21, 1968.
Lamas, Lorenzo Los Angeles, CA, Jan. 28, 1958.
Lambert, Christopher New York, NY, March 29, 1957.
Landau, Martin Brooklyn, NY, June 20, 1931. Actors Studio.
Lane, Abbe Brooklyn, NY, Dec. 14, 1932.
Lane, Diane New York, NY, Jan. 22, 1963.
Lane, Nathan Jersey City, NJ, Feb. 3, 1956.
Lang, Stephen New York, NY, July 11, 1952. Swarthmore College.
Lange, Jessica Cloquet, MN, April 20, 1949. U Minnesota
Langella, Frank Bayonne, NJ, Jan. 1, 1938. Syracuse U.
Lansbury, Angela London, England, Oct. 16, 1925. London Academy of Music.

LaPaglia, Anthony Adelaide, Australia. Jan 31, 1959.
Larroquette, John New Orleans, LA, Nov. 25, 1947.
Lasser, Louise New York, NY, April 11, 1939. Brandeis U.
Lathan, Sanaa New York, NY, Sept. 19, 1971.
Latifah, Queen (Dana Owens) East Orange, NJ, March 18, 1970.
Laughlin, John Memphis, TN, April 3, 1953.
Laughlin, Tom Milwaukee, WI, Aug. 10, 1931
Lauper, Cyndi Astoria, Queens, New York, NY, June 20, 1953.
Laure, Carole Montreal, Quebec, Canada, Aug. 5, 1948.
Laurent, Mélanie Paris, France, Feb. 21, 1983.
Laurie, Hugh Oxford, England, June 11, 1959.
Laurie, Piper (Rosetta Jacobs) Detroit, MI, Jan. 22, 1932.
Lauter, Ed Long Beach, NY, Oct. 30, 1940.
Lautner, Taylor Grand Rapids, MI, Feb. 11, 1992.
Lavin, Linda Portland, ME, Oct. 15 1937.
Law, Jude Lewisham, England, Dec. 29, 1972.
Lawrence, Barbara Carnegie, OK, Feb. 24, 1928. UCLA.
Lawrence, Carol (Laraia) Melrose Park, IL, Sept. 5, 1932.
Lawrence, Martin Frankfurt, Germany, April 16, 1965.
Lawrence, Vicki Inglewood, CA, March 26, 1949.
Lawson, Leigh Atherston, England, July 21, 1945. RADA.
Leachman, Cloris Des Moines, IA, April 30, 1926. Northwestern.
Leal, Sharon Tuscon, AZ, Oct. 17, 1972.
Leary, Denis Boston, MA, Aug. 18, 1957.
Léaud, Jean-Pierre Paris, France, May 5, 1944.
LeBlanc, Matt Newton, MA, July 25, 1967.
Lee, Christopher London, England, May 27, 1922. Wellington College.
Lee, Jason Huntington Beach, CA, April 25, 1970.
Lee, Mark Sydney, Australia, 1958.
Lee, Michele (Dusiak) Los Angeles, CA, June 24, 1942. LACC.
Lee, Sheryl Augsburg, Germany, Arp. 22, 1967.
Lee, Spike (Shelton Lee) Atlanta, GA, March 20, 1957.
Legge, Michael Newry, Northern Ireland, Dec. 11, 1978.
Legros, James Minneapolis, MN, April 27, 1962.
Leguizamo, John Colombia, July 22, 1965. NYU.
Leibman, Ron New York, NY, Oct. 11, 1937. Ohio Wesleyan.
Leigh, Jennifer Jason Los Angeles, CA, Feb. 5, 1962.
Le Mat, Paul Rahway, NJ, Sept. 22, 1946.
Lemmon, Chris Los Angeles, CA, Jan. 22, 1954.
Leno, Jay New Rochelle, NY, April 28, 1950. Emerson College.
Lenz, Kay Los Angeles, CA, March 4, 1953.
Lenz, Rick Springfield, IL, Nov. 21, 1939. U Michigan.
Leo, Melissa NYC, Sept. 14, 1960. SUNY-Purchase.
Leonard, Robert Sean Westwood, NJ, Feb. 28, 1969.
Leoni, Téa (Elizabeth Téa Pantaleoni) New York, NY, Feb. 25, 1966.
Lerman, Logan Beverly Hills, Jan. 19, 1992.
Lerner, Michael Brooklyn, NY, June 22, 1941.
Leslie, Joan (Joan Brodell) Detroit, MI, Jan. 26, 1925. St. Benedict's.
Lester, Mark Oxford, England, July 11, 1958.
Leto, Jared Bossier City, LA, Dec. 26, 1971.
Leung, Tony Hong Kong, June 27, 1962.
Levels, Calvin Cleveland. OH, Sept. 30, 1954. CCC.
Levin, Rachel (Rachel Chagall) New York, NY, Nov. 24, 1954. Goddard College.
Levine, Jerry New Brunswick, NJ, March 12, 1957, Boston U.
Levy, Eugene Hamilton, Canada, Dec. 17, 1946. McMaster U.
Lewis, Charlotte London, England, Aug. 7, 1967.
Lewis, Damian London, England, Feb. 11, 1971. Guildhall.
Lewis, Geoffrey San Diego, CA, Jan. 1, 1935.
Lewis, Jerry (Joseph Levitch) Newark, NJ, March 16, 1926.
Lewis, Juliette Los Angeles, CA, June 21, 1973.
Li, Jet Beijing, China, April 26, 1963.
Ligon, Tom New Orleans, LA, Sept. 10, 1945.

Lillard, Matthew Lansing, MI, Jan. 24, 1970.
Lilly, Evangline Fort Saskatchewan, Canada, Aug. 3, 1979.
Lincoln, Abbey (Anna Marie Woolridge) Chicago, IL, Aug. 6, 1930.
Linden, Hal Bronx, NY, March 20, 1931. City College of NY.
Lindo, Delroy London, England, Nov. 18, 1952.
Lindsay, Robert Ilketson, Derbyshire, England, Dec. 13, 1951, RADA.
Linn-Baker, Mark St. Louis, MO, June 17, 1954, Yale.
Linney, Laura New York, NY, Feb. 5, 1964.
Liotta, Ray Newark, NJ, Dec. 18, 1955. U Miami.
Lisi, Virna Rome, Italy, Nov. 8, 1936.
Lithgow, John Rochester, NY, Oct. 19, 1945. Harvard.
Liu, Lucy Queens, NY, Dec. 2, 1967.
Livingston, Ron Cedar Rapids, IA, June 5, 1968.
LL Cool J (James Todd Smith) Queens, NY, Jan. 14, 1968.
Lloyd, Christopher Stamford, CT, Oct. 22, 1938.
Lloyd, Emily London, England, Sept. 29, 1970.
Locke, Sondra Shelbyville, TN, May, 28, 1947.
Lockhart, June New York, NY, June 25, 1925. Westlake School.
Lockwood, Gary Van Nuys, CA, Feb. 21, 1937.
Loggia, Robert Staten Island, NY, Jan. 3, 1930. U Missouri.
Lohan, Lindsay New York, NY, July 2, 1986.
Lohman, Alison Palm Springs, CA, Sept. 18, 1979.
Lollobrigida, Gina Subiaco, Italy, July 4, 1927. Rome Academy of Fine Arts.
Lom, Herbert Prague, Czech Republic, Jan. 9, 1917. Prague U.
Lomez, Celine Montreal, Quebec, Canada, May 11, 1953.
Lone, John Hong Kong, Oct 13, 1952. AADA.
Long, Justin Fairfield, CT, June 2, 1978.
Long, Nia Brooklyn, NY, Oct. 30, 1970.
Long, Shelley Ft. Wayne, IN, Aug. 23, 1949. Northwestern.
Lopez, Jennifer Bronx, NY, July 24, 1970.
Lords, Tracy (Nora Louise Kuzma) Steubenville, OH, May 7, 1968.
Loren, Sophia (Sophia Scicolone) Rome, Italy, Sept. 20, 1934.
Louis-Dreyfus, Julia New York, NY, Jan. 13, 1961.
Louise, Tina (Blacker) New York, NY, Feb. 11, 1934, Miami U.
Love, Courtney (Love Michelle Harrison) San Francisco, CA, July 9, 1965.
Lovett, Lyle Klein, TX, Nov. 1, 1957.
Lovitz, Jon Tarzana, CA, July 21, 1957.
Lowe, Chad Dayton, OH, Jan. 15, 1968.
Lowe, Rob Charlottesville, VA, March 17, 1964.
Lucas, Josh Little Rock, AR, June 20, 1971.
Luckinbill, Laurence Fort Smith, AR, Nov. 21, 1934.
Luft, Lorna Los Angeles, CA, Nov. 21, 1952.
Luke, Derek Jersey City, NJ, April 24, 1974.
Lulu (Marie Lawrie) Glasgow, Scotland, Nov. 3, 1948.
Luna, Barbara New York, NY, March 2, 1939.
Luna, Diego Mexico City, Mexico, Dec. 29, 1979.
Lundgren, Dolph Stockolm, Sweden, Nov. 3, 1959. Royal Institute.
LuPone, Patti Northport, NY, April 21, 1949. Juilliard.
Lydon, James Harrington Park, NJ, May 30, 1923.
Lynch, Jane Dolton, IL, July 14, 1960.
Lynch, Kelly Minneapolis, MN, Jan. 31, 1959.
Lynley, Carol (Jones) New York, NY, Feb. 13, 1942.
Lynskey, Melanie New Plymouth, New Zealand, May 16, 1977.
Lyon, Sue Davenport, IA, July 10, 1946.
Lyonne, Natasha (Braunstein) New York, NY, April 4, 1979.

MacArthur, James Los Angeles, CA, Dec. 8, 1937. Harvard.
Macchio, Ralph Huntington, NY, Nov. 4, 1961.
MacCorkindale, Simon Cambridge, England, Feb. 12, 1952.
Mackie, Anthony New Orleans, LA, Sept. 23, 1979.
Macdonald, Kelly Glasgow, Scotland, Feb. 23, 1976.
MacDowell, Andie (Rose Anderson MacDowell) Gaffney, SC, April 21, 1958.
MacFadyen, Angus Glasgow, Scotland, Oct. 21, 1963.

MacGraw, Ali New York, NY, April 1, 1938. Wellesley.
MacLachlan, Kyle Yakima, WA, Feb. 22, 1959. U Washington.
MacLaine, Shirley (Beaty) Richmond, VA, April 24, 1934.
MacLeod, Gavin Mt. Kisco, NY, Feb. 28, 1930.
MacNaughton, Robert New York, NY, Dec. 19, 1966.
Macnee, Patrick London, England, Feb. 6, 1922.
MacNicol, Peter Dallas, TX, April 10, 1954. U Minnesota.
MacPherson, Elle Sydney, Australia, March 29, 1963.
MacVittie, Bruce Providence, RI, Oct. 14, 1956. Boston U.
Macy, William H. Miami, FL, March 13, 1950. Goddard College.
Madigan, Amy Chicago, IL, Sept. 11, 1950. Marquette U.
Madonna (Madonna Louise Veronica Cicone) Bay City, MI, Aug. 16, 1958. U Michigan.
Madsen, Michael Chicago, IL, Sept. 25, 1958.
Madsen, Virginia Winnetka, IL, Sept. 11, 1963.
Magnuson, Ann Charleston, WV, Jan. 4, 1956.
Maguire, Tobey Santa Monica, CA, June 27, 1975.
Maharis, George Astoria, NY, Sept. 1, 1928. Actors Studio.
Mahoney, John Manchester, England, June 20, 1940. Western Illinois U.
Mailer, Stephen New York, NY, March 10, 1966. NYU.
Majors, Lee Wyandotte, MI, April 23, 1940. Eastern Kentucky State College.
Makepeace, Chris Toronto, ON, Canada, April 22, 1964,
Malkovich, John Christopher, IL, Dec. 9, 1953, Illinois State U.
Malone, Dorothy Chicago, IL, Jan. 30, 1925.
Malone, Jena Lake Tahoe, NV, Nov. 21, 1984.
Mann, Leslie San Francisco, CA, March 26, 1972.
Mann, Terrence Kentucky, July 1, 1951. NC School Arts.
Manoff, Dinah New York, NY, Jan. 25, 1958. Cal Arts.
Mantegna, Joe Chicago, IL, Nov. 13, 1947. Goodman Theatre.
Manz, Linda New York, NY, Aug. 20, 1961.
Marceau, Sophie (Maupu) Paris, France, Nov. 17, 1966.
Marcovicci, Andrea New York, NY, Nov. 18, 1948.
Margulies, Julianna Spring Valley, NY, June 8, 1966.
Marin, Cheech (Richard) Los Angeles, CA, July 13, 1946.
Marinaro, Ed New York, NY, March 31, 1950. Cornell.
Mars, Kenneth Chicago, IL, April 14, 1936.
Marsden, James Stillwater, OK, Sept. 18, 1973.
Marsh, Jean London, England, July 1, 1934.
Marshall, Ken New York, NY, June 27, 1950. Juilliard.
Marshall, Penny Bronx, NY, Oct. 15, 1943. U New Mexico.
Martin, Andrea Portland, ME, Jan. 15, 1947.
Martin, George N. New York, NY, Aug. 15, 1929.
Martin, Millicent Romford, England, June 8, 1934.
Martin, Pamela Sue Westport, CT, Jan. 15, 1953.
Martin, Steve Waco, TX, Aug. 14, 1945. UCLA.
Martin, Tony (Alfred Norris) Oakland, CA, Dec. 25, 1913. St. Mary's College.
Martindale, Margo Jacksonville, TX, July 18, 1951.
Martinez, Olivier Paris, France, Jan. 12, 1966.
Mason, Marsha St. Louis, MO, April 3, 1942. Webster College.
Masters, Ben Corvallis, OR, May 6, 1947. U Oregon.
Masterson, Mary Stuart Los Angeles, CA, June 28, 1966, NYU.
Masterson, Peter Angleton, TX, June 1, 1934. Rice U.
Mastrantonio, Mary Elizabeth Chicago, IL, Nov. 17, 1958. U Illinois.
Masur, Richard New York, NY, Nov. 20, 1948.
Matheson, Tim Glendale, CA, Dec. 31, 1947. Cal State.
Mathis, Samantha New York, NY, May 12, 1970.
Matlin, Marlee Morton Grove, IL, Aug. 24, 1965.
Matthews, Brian Philadelphia, PA, Jan. 24. 1953. St. Olaf.
Maura, Carmen Madrid, Spain, Sept. 15, 1945.
May, Elaine (Berlin) Philadelphia, PA, April 21, 1932.
Mayron, Melanie Philadelphia, PA, Oct. 20, 1952. AADA.
Mazursky, Paul Brooklyn, NY, April 25, 1930. Brooklyn, NY College.
Mazzello, Joseph Rhinebeck, NY, Sept. 21, 1983.

McAdams, Rachel London, ON, Canada, Oct. 7, 1976.
McAvoy, James Glasgow, Scotland, Jan. 1, 1979.
McBride, Chi Chicago, IL, Sept. 23, 1961.
McBride, Danny Statesboro, GA, Dec. 29, 1976.
McCallum, David Scotland, Sept. 19, 1933. Chapman College.
McCarthy, Andrew New York, NY, Nov. 29, 1962, NYU.
McCarthy, Kevin Seattle, WA, Feb. 15, 1914. Minnesota U.
McCartney, Paul Liverpool, England, June 18, 1942.
McClanahan, Rue Healdton, OK, Feb. 21, 1934.
McClure, Marc San Mateo, CA, March 31, 1957.
McClurg, Edie Kansas City, MO, July 23, 1951.
McCormack, Catherine Alton, Hampshire, England, Jan. 1, 1972.
McCowen, Alec Tunbridge Wells, England, May 26, 1925. RADA.
McCrane, Paul Philadelphia, PA, Jan. 19. 1961.
McCrary, Darius Walnut, CA, May 1, 1976.
McDermott, Dylan Waterbury, CT, Oct. 26, 1962. Neighborhood Playhouse.
McDonald, Christopher New York, NY, Feb. 15, 1955.
McDonnell, Mary Wilkes Barre, PA, April 28, 1952.
McDonough, Neal Dorchester, MA, Feb. 13, 1966.
McDormand, Frances Illinois, June 23, 1957. Yale.
McDowell, Malcolm (Taylor) Leeds, England, June 19, 1943. LAMDA.
McElhone, Natascha (Natasha Taylor) London, England, March 23, 1971.
McEnery, Peter Walsall, England, Feb. 21, 1940.
McEntire, Reba McAlester, OK, March 28, 1955. Southeastern Oklahoma State U.
McGill, Everett Miami Beach, FL, Oct. 21, 1945.
McGillis, Kelly Newport Beach, CA, July 9, 1957. Juilliard.
McGinley, John C. New York, NY, Aug. 3, 1959. NYU.
McGovern, Elizabeth Evanston, IL, July 18, 1961. Juilliard.
McGovern, Maureen Youngstown, OH, July 27, 1949.
McGowan, Rose Florence, Italy, Sept. 5, 1973.
McGraw, Tim Delhi, LA, May 1, 1967.
McGregor, Ewan Perth, Scotland, March 31, 1971.
McGuire, Biff New Haven, CT, Oct. 25. 1926. Mass. State College.
McHattie, Stephen Antigonish, Nova Scotia, Feb. 3, 1947. Acadia U, AADA.
McKay, Christian Bury, Lancashire, England, 1973.
McKean, Michael New York, NY, Oct. 17, 1947.
McKee, Lonette Detroit, MI, July 22, 1954.
McKellen, Ian Burnley, England, May 25, 1939.
McKenna, Virginia London, England, June 7, 1931.
McKenzie, Ben (Benjamin Schenkkan) Austin, TX, Sept. 12, 1978. U Virginia.
McKeon, Doug Pompton Plains, NJ, June 10, 1966.
McLerie, Allyn Ann Grand Mere, Canada, Dec. 1, 1926.
McMahon, Julian Sydney, Australia, July 27, 1968.
McNamara, William Dallas, TX, March 31, 1965.
McNichol, Kristy Los Angeles, CA, Sept. 11, 1962.
McQueen, Armelia North Carolina, Jan. 6, 1952. Brooklyn Conservatory.
McQueen, Chad Los Angeles, CA, Dec. 28, 1960. Actors Studio.
McRaney, Gerald Collins, MS, Aug. 19, 1947.
McShane, Ian Blackburn, England, Sept. 29, 1942. RADA.
McTeer, Janet York, England, May 8, 1961.
Meadows, Jayne (Jayne Cotter) Wuchang, China, Sept. 27, 1920. St. Margaret's.
Meaney, Colm Dublin, Ireland, May 30, 1953.
Meara, Anne Brooklyn, NY, Sept. 20, 1929.
Meat Loaf (Marvin Lee Aday) Dallas, TX, Sept. 27, 1947.
Mechlowicz, Scott New York, NY, Jan. 17, 1981.
Medwin, Michael London, England, July 18, 1923. Instut Fischer.
Mekka, Eddie Worcester, MA, June 14, 1952. Boston Conservatory.
Melato, Mariangela Milan, Italy, Sept. 18, 1941. Milan Theatre Academy.
Mendes, Eva Los Angeles, CA, March 5, 1974.
Menzel, Idina Syosset, NY, May 30, 1971. NYU.
Meredith, Lee (Judi Lee Sauls) River Edge, NJ, Oct. 22, 1947. AADA.

Merkerson, S. Epatha Saganaw, MI, Nov. 28, 1952. Wayne State U.
Merrill, Dina (Nedinia Hutton) New York, NY, Dec. 29, 1923. AADA.
Messina, Chris New York, NY, Aug. 11, 1974.
Messing, Debra Brooklyn, NY, Aug. 15, 1968.
Metcalf, Laurie Edwardsville, IL, June 16, 1955. Illinois State U.
Metzler, Jim Oneonta, NY, June 23, 1951. Dartmouth.
Meyer, Breckin Minneapolis, MN, May 7, 1974.
Michell, Keith Adelaide, Australia, Dec. 1, 1928.
Midler, Bette Honolulu, HI, Dec. 1, 1945.
Mihok, Dash New York, NY, May 24, 1974.
Mikkelsen, Mads Copenhagen, Denmark, Nov. 22, 1965.
Milano, Alyssa Brooklyn, NY, Dec. 19, 1972.
Miles, Joanna Nice, France, March 6, 1940.
Miles, Sarah Ingatestone, England, Dec. 31, 1941. RADA.
Miles, Sylvia New York, NY, Sept. 9, 1932. Actors Studio.
Miles, Vera (Ralston) Boise City, OK, Aug. 23, 1929. UCLA.
Miller, Barry Los Angeles, CA, Feb. 6, 1958.
Miller, Dick New York, NY, Dec. 25, 1928.
Miller, Jonny Lee Surrey, England, Nov. 15, 1972.
Miller, Linda New York, NY, Sept. 16, 1942. Catholic U.
Miller, Penelope Ann Santa Monica, CA, Jan. 13, 1964.
Miller, Rebecca Roxbury, CT, Sept. 15, 1962. Yale.
Miller, Sienna New York, NY, Dec. 28, 1981.
Mills, Donna Chicago, IL, Dec. 11, 1940. U Illinois.
Mills, Hayley London, England, April 18, 1946. Elmhurst School.
Mills, Juliet London, England, Nov. 21, 1941.
Milner, Martin Detroit, MI, Dec. 28, 1931.
Mimieux, Yvette Los Angeles, CA, Jan. 8, 1941. Hollywood High.
Minnelli, Liza Los Angeles, CA, March 19, 1946.
Miou-Miou (Sylvette Henry) Paris, France, Feb. 22, 1950.
Mirren, Helen (Ilynea Mironoff) London, England, July 26, 1945.
Mistry, Jimi Scarborough, England, 1973.
Mitchell, James Sacramento, CA, Feb. 29, 1920. LACC.
Mitchell, John Cameron El Paso, TX, April 21, 1963. Northwestern.
Mitchell, Radha Melbourne, Australia, Nov. 12, 1973.
Mitchum, James Los Angeles, CA, May 8, 1941.
Modine, Matthew Loma Linda, CA, March 22, 1959.
Moffat, Donald Plymouth, England, Dec. 26, 1930. RADA.
Moffett, D. W. Highland Park, IL, Oct. 26, 1954. Stanford U.
Mohr, Jay Verona, NJ, Aug. 23, 1971.
Mol, Gretchen Deep River, CT, Nov. 8, 1972.
Molina, Alfred London, England, May 24, 1953. Guildhall.
Moll, Richard Pasadena, CA, Jan. 13, 1943.
Monaghan, Dominic Berlin, Germany, Dec. 8, 1976.
Monaghan, Michelle Winthrop, IA, March 23, 1976.
Mo'Nique (Monique Imes) Woodland, MD, Dec. 11, 1967.
Monk, Debra Middletown, OH, Feb. 27, 1949. Frostburg State.
Montenegro, Fernanda (Arlete Pinheiro) Rio de Janiero, Brazil, 1929.
Montgomery, Belinda Winnipeg, Manitoba, Canada, July 23, 1950.
Moody, Ron London, England, Jan. 8, 1924. London U.
Moore, Demi (Guines) Roswell, NM, Nov. 11, 1962.
Moore, Dick Los Angeles, CA, Sept. 12, 1925.
Moore, Joel David Portland, OR, Sept. 25, 1977.
Moore, Julianne (Julie Anne Smith) Fayetteville, NC, Dec. 30, 1960. Boston U.
Moore, Mandy Nashua, NH, April 10, 1984.
Moore, Mary Tyler Brooklyn, NY, Dec. 29, 1936.
Moore, Roger London, England, Oct. 14, 1927. RADA.
Moore, Stephen Campbell (Stephen Thorpe) London, England, 1979.
Moore, Terry (Helen Koford) Los Angeles, CA, Jan. 7, 1929.
Morales, Esai Brooklyn, NY, Oct. 1, 1962.
Moranis, Rick Toronto, ON, Canada, April 18, 1954.
Moreau, Jeanne Paris, France, Jan. 23, 1928.

Moreno, Catalina Sandino Bogota, Colombia, April 19, 1981.
Moreno, Rita (Rosita Alverio) Humacao, P.R., Dec. 11, 1931.
Morgan, Harry (Henry) (Harry Bratsburg) Detroit, MI, April 10, 1915. U Chicago.
Mogran, Jeffrey Dean Seattle, WA, April 22, 1966.
Morgan, Michele (Simone Roussel) Paris, France, Feb. 29, 1920. Paris Dramatic School.
Morgan, Tracy Bronx, NY, Nov. 10, 1968.
Moriarty, Cathy Bronx, NY, Nov. 29, 1960.
Moriarty, Michael Detroit, MI, April 5, 1941. Dartmouth.
Morison, Patricia New York, NY, March 19, 1914.
Morris, Garrett New Orleans, LA, Feb. 1, 1937.
Morrow, Rob New Rochelle, NY, Sept. 21, 1962.
Morse, David Hamilton, MA, Oct. 11, 1953.
Morse, Robert Newton, MA, May 18, 1931.
Mortensen, Viggo New York, NY, Oct. 20, 1958.
Mortimer, Emily London, England, Dec. 1, 1971.
Morton, Joe New York, NY, Oct. 18, 1947. Hofstra U.
Morton, Samantha Nottingham, England, May 13, 1977.
Mos Def (Dante Beze) Brooklyn, NY, Dec. 11, 1973.
Moseley, William Sheepscombe, England, April 27, 1987.
Moses, William Los Angeles, CA, Nov. 17, 1959.
Moss, Carrie-Anne Vancouver, BC, Canada, Aug. 21, 1967.
Mostel, Josh New York, NY, Dec. 21, 1946. Brandeis U.
Mouchet, Catherine Paris, France, 1959. National Conservatory.
Moynahan, Bridget Binghamton, NY, Sept. 21, 1972.
Mueller-Stahl, Armin Tilsit, East Prussia, Dec. 17, 1930.
Muldaur, Diana New York, NY, Aug. 19, 1938. Sweet Briar College.
Mulgrew, Kate Dubuque, IA, April 29, 1955. NYU.
Mulhern, Matt Philadelphia, PA, July 21, 1960. Rutgers U.
Mull, Martin N. Ridgefield, OH, Aug. 18, 1943. RI School of Design.
Mulligan, Carey London, England, May 28, 1985.
Mulroney, Dermot Alexandria, VA, Oct. 31, 1963. Northwestern.
Mumy, Bill (Charles William Mumy, Jr.) San Gabriel, CA, Feb. 1, 1954.
Muniz, Frankie Ridgewood, NJ, Dec. 5, 1985.
Murphy, Cillian Douglas, Ireland, March 13, 1974.
Murphy, Donna Queens, NY, March 7, 1958.
Murphy, Eddie Brooklyn, NY, April 3, 1961.
Murphy, Michael Los Angeles, CA, May 5, 1938. U Arizona.
Murray, Bill Wilmette, IL, Sept. 21, 1950. Regis College.
Murray, Don Hollywood, CA, July 31, 1929.
Musante, Tony Bridgeport, CT, June 30, 1936. Oberlin College.
Myers, Mike Scarborough, Canada, May 25, 1963.

Nabors, Jim Sylacauga, GA, June 12, 1932.
Nader, Michael Los Angeles, CA, Feb. 19, 1945.
Namath, Joe Beaver Falls, PA, May 31, 1943. U Alabama.
Naughton, David Hartford, CT, Feb. 13, 1951.
Naughton, James Middletown, CT, Dec. 6, 1945.
Neal, Patricia Packard, KY, Jan. 20, 1926. Northwestern.
Neeson, Liam Ballymena, Northern Ireland, June 7, 1952.
Neill, Sam Northern Ireland, Sept. 14, 1947. U Canterbury.
Nelligan, Kate London, ON, Canada, March 16, 1950. U Toronto.
Nelson, Craig T. Spokane, WA, April 4, 1944.
Nelson, David New York, NY, Oct. 24, 1936. USC.
Nelson, Judd Portland, ME, Nov. 28, 1959. Haverford College.
Nelson, Lori (Dixie Kay Nelson) Santa Fe, NM, Aug. 15, 1933.
Nelson, Tim Blake Tulsa, OK, Nov. 5, 1964.
Nelson, Tracy Santa Monica, CA, Oct. 25, 1963.
Nelson, Willie Abbott, TX, April 30, 1933.
Nemec, Corin Little Rock, AR, Nov. 5, 1971.
Nero, Franco (Francisco Spartanero) Parma, Italy, Nov. 23, 1941.
Nesmith, Michael Houston, TX, Dec. 30, 1942.

Neuwirth, Bebe Princeton, NJ, Dec. 31, 1958.
Newhart, Bob Chicago, IL, Sept. 5, 1929. Loyola U.
Newman, Barry Boston, MA, Nov. 7, 1938. Brandeis U.
Newman, Laraine Los Angeles, CA, March 2, 1952.
Newman, Nanette Northampton, England, May 29, 1934.
Newmar, Julie (Newmeyer) Los Angeles, CA, Aug. 16, 1933.
Newton, Thandie Zambia, Nov. 16, 1972.
Newton-John, Olivia Cambridge, England, Sept. 26, 1948.
Nguyen, Dustin Saigon, Vietnam, Sept. 17, 1962.
Nicholas, Denise Detroit, MI, July 12, 1944.
Nicholas, Paul Peterborough, Cambridge, England, Dec. 3, 1945.
Nichols, Nichelle Robbins, IL, Dec. 28, 1932.
Nicholson, Jack Neptune, NJ, April 22, 1937.
Nicholson, Julianne Medford, MA, July 1, 1971.
Nickerson, Denise New York, NY, April 1, 1957.
Nielsen, Brigitte Denmark, July 15, 1963.
Nielsen, Connie Elling, Denmark, July 3, 1965.
Nielsen, Leslie Regina, Saskatchewan, Canada, Feb. 11, 1926.
   Neighborhood Playhouse.
Nighy, Bill Caterham, England, Dec. 12, 1949. Guildford.
Nimoy, Leonard Boston, MA, March 26, 1931. Boston College,
   Antioch College.
Nivola, Alessandro Boston, MA, June 28, 1972. Yale.
Nixon, Cynthia New York, NY, April 9, 1966. Columbia U.
Noble, James Dallas, TX, March 5, 1922, SMU.
Nolan, Kathleen St. Louis, MO, Sept. 27, 1933. Neighborhood Playhouse.
Nolte, Nick Omaha, NE, Feb. 8, 1940. Pasadena City College.
Norris, Bruce Houston, TX, May 16, 1960. Northwestern.
Norris, Christopher New York, NY, Oct. 7, 1953. Lincoln Square Academy.
Norris, Chuck (Carlos Ray) Ryan, OK, March 10, 1940.
North, Heather Pasadena, CA, Dec. 13, 1950. Actors Workshop.
Northam, Jeremy Cambridge, England, Dec. 1, 1961.
Norton, Edward Boston, MA, Aug. 18, 1969.
Norton, Ken Jacksonville, IL, Aug. 9, 1943.
Noseworthy, Jack Lynn, MA, Dec. 21, 1969.
Nouri, Michael Washington, DC, Dec. 9, 1945.
Novak, Kim (Marilyn Novak) Chicago, IL, Feb. 13, 1933. LACC.
Novello, Don Ashtabula, OH, Jan. 1, 1943. U Dayton.
Nuyen, France (Vannga) Marseilles, France, July 31, 1939.
   Beaux Arts School.

O'Brian, Hugh (Hugh J. Krampe) Rochester, NY. April 19, 1923. Cincinnati U.
O'Brien, Clay Ray, AZ, May 6, 1961.
O'Brien, Margaret (Angela Maxine O'Brien) Los Angeles, CA, Jan. 15, 1937.
O'Connell, Jerry (Jeremiah O'Connell) New York, NY, Feb. 17, 1974.
O'Connor, Glynnis New York, NY, Nov. 19, 1956. NYSU.
O'Donnell, Chris Winetka, IL, June 27, 1970.
O'Donnell, Keir Sydney, Australia, Nov. 8, 1978.
O'Donnell, Rosie Commack, NY, March 21, 1961.
Oh, Sandra Nepean, ON, Canada, Nov. 30, 1970.
O'Halloran, Brian New York, NY, Sept. 1, 1969.
O'Hara, Catherine Toronto, ON, Canada, March 4, 1954.
O'Hara, Maureen (Maureen Fitzsimons) Dublin, Ireland, Aug. 17, 1920.
O'Hare, Dennis Kansas City, MO, Jan. 17, 1962.
O'Keefe, Michael Larchmont, NY, April 24, 1955. NYU, AADA.
Okonedo, Sophie London, England, Jan. 1, 1969.
Oldman, Gary New Cross, South London, England, March 21, 1958.
O'Leary, Matt Chicago, IL, July 6, 1987.
Olin, Ken Chicago, IL, July 30, 1954. U Pennsylvania.
Olin, Lena Stockholm, Sweden, March 22, 1955.
Olmos, Edward James Los Angeles, CA, Feb. 24, 1947. CSLA.
O'Loughlin, Gerald S. New York, NY, Dec. 23, 1921. U Rochester.
Olson, James Evanston, IL, Oct. 8, 1930.

Olson, Nancy Milwaukee, WI, July 14, 1928. UCLA.
Olyphant, Timothy Honolulu, HI, May 20, 1968.
O'Neal, Griffin Los Angeles, CA, Oct. 28, 1964.
O'Neal, Ryan Los Angeles, CA, April 20, 1941.
O'Neal, Tatum Los Angeles, CA, Nov. 5, 1963.
O'Neil, Tricia Shreveport, LA, March 11, 1945. Baylor U.
O'Neill, Ed Youngstown, OH, April 12, 1946.
O'Neill, Jennifer Rio de Janeiro, Brazil, Feb. 20, 1948.
   Neighborhood Playhouse.
Ontkean, Michael Vancouver, BC, Canada, Jan. 24, 1946.
O'Quinn, Terry Newbury, MI, July 15, 1952.
Ormond, Julia Epsom, England, Jan. 4, 1965.
O'Shea, Milo Dublin, Ireland, June 2, 1926.
Osment, Haley Joel Los Angeles, CA, April 10, 1988.
Oswalt, Patton Portsmouth, VA, Jan. 27, 1969.
O'Toole, Annette (Toole) Houston, TX, April 1, 1952. UCLA.
O'Toole, Peter Connemara, Ireland, Aug. 2, 1932. RADA.
Otto, Miranda Brisbane, Australia, Dec. 16, 1967.
Overall, Park Nashville, TN, March 15, 1957. Tusculum College.
Owen, Clive Keresley, England, Oct. 3, 1964.
Oz, Frank (Oznowicz) Hereford, England, May 25, 1944.

Pace, Lee Chickasha, OK, March 25, 1979.
Pacino, Al New York, NY, April 25, 1940.
Pacula, Joanna Tamaszow Lubelski, Poland, Jan. 2, 1957. Polish National
   Theatre School.
Page, Ellen Hallifax, Nova Scotia, Feb. 21, 1987.
Paget, Debra (Debralee Griffin) Denver, CO, Aug. 19, 1933.
Paige, Janis (Donna Mae Jaden) Tacoma, WA, Sept. 16, 1922.
Palin, Michael Sheffield, England, May 5, 1943, Oxford.
Palmer, Betsy East Chicago, IN, Nov. 1, 1926. DePaul U.
Palmer, Gregg (Palmer Lee) San Francisco, CA, Jan. 25, 1927. U Utah.
Palminteri, Chazz (Calogero Lorenzo Palminteri) New York, NY,
   May 15, 1952.
Paltrow, Gwyneth Los Angeles, CA, Sept. 28, 1973.
Pampanini, Silvana Rome, Italy, Sept. 25, 1925.
Panebianco, Richard New York, NY, 1971.
Pankin, Stuart Philadelphia, PA, April 8, 1946.
Pantoliano, Joe Jersey City, NJ, Sept. 12, 1951.
Papas, Irene Chiliomodion, Greece, March 9, 1926.
Paquin, Anna Winnipeg, Manitoba, Canada, July, 24, 1982.
Pardue, Kip (Kevin Ian Pardue) Atlanta, GA, Sept. 23, 1976. Yale.
Pare, Michael Brooklyn, NY, Oct. 9, 1958.
Parker, Corey New York, NY, July 8, 1965. NYU.
Parker, Eleanor Cedarville, OH, June 26, 1922. Pasadena Playhouse.
Parker, Fess Fort Worth, TX, Aug. 16, 1925. USC.
Parker, Jameson Baltimore, MD, Nov. 18, 1947. Beloit College.
Parker, Mary-Louise Ft. Jackson, SC, Aug. 2, 1964. Bard College.
Parke, Nate Norfolk, VA, Nov. 18, 1979.
Parker, Nathaniel London, England, May 18, 1962.
Parker, Sarah Jessica Nelsonville, OH, March 25, 1965.
Parker, Trey Auburn, AL, May 30, 1972.
Parkins, Barbara Vancouver, BC, Canada, May 22, 1942.
Parks, Michael Corona, CA, April 4, 1940.
Parsons, Estelle Lynn, MA, Nov. 20, 1927. Boston U.
Parton, Dolly Sevierville, TN, Jan. 19, 1946.
Pascal, Adam Bronx, NY, Oct. 25, 1970.
Patel, Dev London, April 23, 1990.
Patinkin, Mandy Chicago, IL, Nov. 30, 1952. Juilliard.
Patric, Jason New York, NY, June 17, 1966.
Patrick, Robert Marietta, GA, Nov. 5, 1958.
Pattinson, Robert London, May 13, 1986.
Patton, Paula Los Angeles, CA, Dec. 5, 1975.

Patton, Will Charleston, SC, June 14, 1954.
Paulik, Johan Prague, Czech Republic, March 14, 1975.
Paulson, Sarah Tampa, FL, Dec. 17, 1975.
Pavan, Marisa (Marisa Pierangeli) Cagliari, Sardinia, June 19, 1932. Torquado Tasso College.
Paxton, Bill Fort Worth, TX, May. 17, 1955.
Paymer, David Oceanside, NY, Aug. 30, 1954.
Pays, Amanda Berkshire, England, June 6, 1959.
Peach, Mary Durban, South Africa, Oct. 20, 1934.
Pearce, Guy Ely, England, Oct. 5, 1967.
Pearson, Beatrice Dennison, TX, July 27, 1920.
Peet, Amanda New York, NY, Jan. 11, 1972.
Pegg, Simon Gloucester, England, Feb. 14, 1970.
Peña, Elizabeth Elizabeth, NJ, Sept. 23, 1961.
Peña, Michael Chicago, IL, Jan. 13, 1976.
Pendleton, Austin Warren, OH, March 27, 1940. Yale.
Penhall, Bruce Balboa, CA, Aug. 17, 1957.
Penn, Kal Montclair, NJ, April 23, 1977.
Penn, Sean Burbank, CA, Aug. 17, 1960.
Pepper, Barry Campbell River, BC, Canada, April 4, 1970.
Perabo, Piper Toms River, NJ, Oct. 31, 1976.
Perez, Jose New York, NY, 1940.
Perez, Rosie Brooklyn, NY, Sept. 6, 1964.
Perkins, Elizabeth Queens, NY, Nov. 18, 1960. Goodman School.
Perkins, Millie Passaic, NJ, May 12, 1938.
Perlman, Rhea Brooklyn, NY, March 31, 1948.
Perlman, Ron New York, NY, April 13, 1950. U Minnesota.
Perreau, Gigi (Ghislaine) Los Angeles, CA, Feb. 6, 1941.
Perrine, Valerie Galveston, TX, Sept. 3, 1943. U Arizona.
Perry, Luke (Coy Luther Perry, III) Fredricktown, OH, Oct. 11, 1966.
Perry, Tyler New Orleans, LA, Sept. 13, 1969.
Pesci, Joe Newark, NJ. Feb. 9, 1943.
Pescow, Donna Brooklyn, NY, March 24, 1954.
Peters, Bernadette (Lazzara) Jamaica, NY, Feb. 28, 1948.
Petersen, Paul Glendale, CA, Sept. 23, 1945. Valley College.
Petersen, William Chicago, IL, Feb. 21, 1953.
Peterson, Cassandra Colorado Springs, CO, Sept. 17, 1951.
Pettet, Joanna London, England, Nov. 16, 1942. Neighborhood Playhouse.
Petty, Lori Chattanooga, TN, March 23, 1963.
Pfeiffer, Michelle Santa Ana, CA, April 29, 1958.
Phifer, Mekhi New York, NY, Dec. 12, 1975.
Phillippe, Ryan (Matthew Phillippe) New Castle, DE, Sept. 10, 1975.
Phillips, Lou Diamond Phillipines, Feb. 17, 1962, U Texas.
Phillips, MacKenzie Alexandria, VA, Nov. 10, 1959.
Phillips, Michelle (Holly Gilliam) Long Beach, CA, June 4, 1944.
Phillips, Sian Bettws, Wales, May 14, 1933. U Wales.
Phoenix, Joaquin San Juan, Puerto Rico, Oct. 28, 1974.
Picardo, Robert Philadelphia, PA, Oct. 27, 1953. Yale.
Picerni, Paul New York, NY, Dec. 1, 1922. Loyola U.
Pidgeon, Rebecca Cambridge, MA, Oct. 10, 1965.
Pierce, David Hyde Saratoga Springs, NY, April 3, 1959.
Pigott-Smith, Tim Rugby, England, May 13, 1946.
Pike, Rosamund London, England, Jan. 28, 1979.
Pinchot, Bronson New York, NY, May 20, 1959. Yale.
Pine, Chris Los Angeles, Aug. 26, 1980.
Pinsent, Gordon Grand Falls, Newfoundland, July 12, 1930.
Piscopo, Joe Passaic, NJ, June 17, 1951.
Pisier, Marie-France Dalat, Vietnam, May 10, 1944. U Paris.
Pitillo, Maria Elmira, NY, Jan. 8, 1966.
Pitt, Brad (William Bradley Pitt) Shawnee, OK, Dec. 18, 1963.
Pitt, Michael West Orange, NJ, April 10, 1981.
Piven, Jeremy New York, NY, July 26, 1965.
Place, Mary Kay Tulsa OK, Sept. 23, 1947. U Tulsa.

Platt, Oliver Windsor, ON, Canada, Oct. 10, 1960.
Playten, Alice New York, NY, Aug. 28, 1947. NYU.
Plimpton, Martha New York, NY, Nov. 16, 1970.
Plowright, Joan Scunthorpe, England, Oct. 28, 1929. Old Vic.
Plumb, Eve Burbank, CA, April 29, 1958.
Plummer, Amanda New York, NY, March 23, 1957. Middlebury College.
Plummer, Christopher Toronto, ON, Canada, Dec. 13, 1927.
Podesta, Rossana Tripoli, Libya, June 20, 1934.
Poehler, Amy Burlington, MA, Sept. 16, 1971.
Poitier, Sidney Miami, FL, Feb. 27, 1927.
Polanski, Roman Paris, France, Aug. 18, 1933.
Polito, Jon Philadelphia, PA, Dec. 29, 1950. Villanova U.
Polito, Lina Naples, Italy, Aug. 11, 1954.
Pollak, Kevin San Francisco, CA, Oct. 30, 1957.
Pollan, Tracy New York, NY, June 22, 1960.
Pollard, Michael J. Passaic, NJ, May 30, 1939.
Polley, Sarah Toronto, ON, Canada, Jan. 8, 1979.
Popplewell, Anna London, Dec. 16, 1988.
Portman, Natalie Jerusalem, Israel, June 9, 1981.
Posey, Parker Baltimore, MD, Nov. 8, 1968.
Postlethwaite, Pete London, England, Feb. 7, 1946.
Potente, Franka Dulmen, Germany, July 22, 1974.
Potter, Monica Cleveland, OH, June 30, 1971.
Potts, Annie Nashville, TN, Oct. 28, 1952. Stephens College.
Powell, Jane (Suzanne Burce) Portland, OR, April 1, 1928.
Powell, Robert Salford, England, June 1, 1944. Manchester U.
Power, Taryn Los Angeles, CA, Sept. 13, 1953.
Power, Tyrone, IV Los Angeles, CA, Jan. 22, 1959.
Powers, Stefanie (Federkiewicz) Hollywood, CA, Oct. 12, 1942.
Prentiss, Paula (Paula Ragusa) San Antonio, TX, March 4, 1938. Northwestern.
Presle, Micheline (Micheline Chassagne) Paris, France, Aug. 22, 1922. Rouleau Drama School.
Presley, Priscilla Brooklyn, NY, May 24, 1945.
Preston, Kelly Honolulu, HI, Oct. 13, 1962. USC.
Price, Lonny New York, NY, March 9, 1959. Juilliard.
Priestley, Jason Vancouver, BC, Canada, Aug, 28, 1969.
Primus, Barry New York, NY, Feb. 16, 1938. CCNY.
Prince (P. Rogers Nelson) Minneapolis, MN, June 7, 1958.
Principal, Victoria Fukuoka, Japan, Jan. 3, 1950. Dade Junior College.
Prinze, Freddie, Jr., Los Angeles, CA, March 8, 1976.
Prochnow, Jurgen Berlin, Germany, June 10, 1941.
Proval, David Brooklyn, NY, May 20, 1942.
Provine, Dorothy Deadwood, SD, Jan. 20, 1937. U Washington.
Pryce, Jonathan Holywell, North Wales, June 1, 1947, RADA.
Pucci, Lou Taylor Seaside Heights, NJ, July 27, 1985.
Pullman, Bill Delphi, NY, Dec. 17, 1953. SUNY-Oneonta, U Mass.
Purcell, Lee Cherry Point, NC, June 15, 1947. Stephens.
Pyle, Missi Houston, TX, Nov. 16, 1972.

Quaid, Dennis Houston, TX, April 9, 1954.
Quaid, Randy Houston, TX, Oct. 1, 1950. U Houston.
Qualls, DJ (Donald Joseph) Nashville, TN, June 12, 1978.
Quinlan, Kathleen Mill Valley, CA, Nov. 19, 1954.
Quinn, Aidan Chicago, IL, March 8, 1959.
Quinto, Zachary Pittsburgh, PA, June 2, 1977.

Radcliffe, Daniel London, England, July 23, 1989.
Raffin, Deborah Los Angeles, CA, March 13, 1953. Valley College.
Ragsdale, William El Dorado, AR, Jan. 19, 1961. Hendrix College.
Railsback, Steve Dallas, TX, Nov. 16, 1945.
Rainer, Luise Vienna, Austria, Jan. 12, 1910.
Ramis, Harold Chicago, IL, Nov. 21, 1944. Washington U.

Rampling, Charlotte Surmer, England, Feb. 5, 1946. U Madrid.
Rapaport, Michael New York, NY, March 20, 1970.
Rapp, Anthony Chicago, IL, Oct. 26, 1971.
Rasche, David St. Louis, MO, Aug. 7, 1944.
Rea, Stephen Belfast, Northern Ireland, Oct. 31, 1946.
Reason, Rex Berlin, Germany, Nov. 30, 1928. Pasadena Playhouse.
Reddy, Helen Melbourne, Australia, Oct. 25, 1941.
Redford, Robert Santa Monica, CA, Aug. 18, 1937. AADA.
Redgrave, Corin London, England, July 16, 1939.
Redgrave, Lynn London, England, March 8, 1943.
Redgrave, Vanessa London, England, Jan. 30, 1937.
Redman, Joyce County Mayo, Ireland, Dec. 9, 1918. RADA.
Redmayne, Eddie London, Jan. 6, 1982.
Reed, Nikki W. Los Angeles, CA, May 17, 1988.
Reed, Pamela Tacoma, WA, April 2, 1949.
Rees, Roger Aberystwyth, Wales, May 5, 1944.
Reese, Della Detroit, MI, July 6, 1931.
Reeves, Keanu Beiruit, Lebanon, Sept. 2, 1964.
Regehr, Duncan Lethbridge, Canada, Oct. 5, 1952.
Reid, Elliott New York, NY, Jan. 16, 1920.
Reid, Tara Wyckoff, NJ, Nov. 8, 1975.
Roid, Tim Norfolk, VA, Dec. 19, 1944.
Reilly, John C. Chicago, IL, May 24, 1965.
Reiner, Carl New York, NY, March 20, 1922. Georgetown.
Reiner, Rob New York, NY, March 6, 1947. UCLA.
Reinhold, Judge (Edward Ernest, Jr.) Wilmington, DE, May 21, 1957. NC School of Arts
Reinking, Ann Seattle, WA, Nov. 10, 1949.
Reiser, Paul New York, NY, March 30, 1957.
Remar, James Boston, MA, Dec. 31, 1953. Neighborhood Playhouse.
Renner, Jeremy Modesto, CA, Jan.7, 1971.
Reno, Jean (Juan Moreno) Casablanca, Morocco, July 30, 1948.
Reubens, Paul (Paul Reubenfeld) Peekskill, NY, Aug. 27, 1952.
Revill, Clive Wellington, NZ, April 18, 1930.
Rey, Antonia Havana, Cuba, Oct. 12, 1927.
Reynolds, Burt Waycross, GA, Feb. 11, 1936. Florida State.
Reynolds, Debbie (Mary Frances Reynolds) El Paso, TX, April 1, 1932.
Reynolds, Ryan Vancouver, BC, Can, Oct. 23, 1976.
Rhames, Ving (Irving Rhames) New York, NY, May 12, 1959.
Rhoades, Barbara Poughkeepsie, NY, March 23, 1947.
Rhodes, Cynthia Nashville, TN, Nov. 21, 1956.
Rhys, Paul Neath, Wales, Dec. 19, 1963.
Rhys-Davies, John Salisbury, England, May 5, 1944.
Rhys Meyers, Jonathan Cork, Ireland, July 27, 1977.
Ribisi, Giovanni Los Angeles, CA, Dec. 17, 1974.
Ricci, Christina Santa Monica, CA, Feb. 12, 1980.
Richard, Cliff (Harry Webb) India, Oct. 14, 1940.
Richards, Denise Downers Grove, IL, Feb. 17, 1972.
Richards, Michael Culver City, CA, July 14, 1949.
Richardson, Joely London, England, Jan. 9, 1965.
Richardson, Miranda Southport, England, March 3, 1958.
Rickles, Don New York, NY, May 8, 1926. AADA.
Rickman, Alan Hammersmith, England, Feb. 21, 1946.
Riegert, Peter New York, NY, April 11, 1947. U Buffalo.
Rifkin, Ron New York, NY, Oct. 31, 1939.
Rigg, Diana Doncaster, England, July 20, 1938. RADA.
Ringwald, Molly Rosewood, CA, Feb. 16, 1968.
Rivers, Joan (Molinsky) Brooklyn, NY, June 8, 1933.
Roache, Linus Manchester, England, Feb. 1, 1964.
Robards, Sam New York, NY, Dec. 16, 1961.
Robb, AnnaSophia Denver, CO, Dec. 8, 1993.
Robbins, Tim New York, NY, Oct. 16, 1958. UCLA.
Roberts, Dallas Houston, TX, May 10, 1970.

Roberts, Eric Biloxi, MS, April 18, 1956. RADA.
Roberts, Julia Atlanta, GA, Oct. 28, 1967.
Roberts, Tanya (Leigh) Bronx, NY, Oct. 15, 1955.
Roberts, Tony New York, NY, Oct. 22, 1939. Northwestern.
Robertson, Cliff La Jolla, CA, Sept. 9, 1925. Antioch College.
Robertson, Dale Oklahoma City, OK, July 14, 1923.
Robinson, Chris West Palm Beach, FL, Nov. 5, 1938. LACC.
Robinson, Jay New York, NY, April 14, 1930.
Robinson, Roger Seattle, WA, May 2, 1940. USC.
Rochefort, Jean Paris, France, April 29, 1930.
Rochon, Lela Los Angeles, CA, April 17, 1964.
Rock, Chris Brooklyn, NY, Feb. 7, 1966.
Rockwell, Sam Daly City, CA, Nov. 5, 1968.
Rodriguez, Freddy Chicago, IL, Jan. 17, 1975.
Rodriguez, Michelle Bexar County, TX, July 12, 1978.
Rogen, Seth Vancouver, BC, Canada, April 14, 1982.
Rogers, Mimi Coral Gables, FL, Jan. 27, 1956.
Rogers, Wayne Birmingham, AL, April 7, 1933. Princeton.
Romano, Ray Queens, NY, Dec. 21, 1957.
Romijn, Rebecca Berkeley, CA, Nov. 6, 1972.
Ronan, Saoirse New York, NY, April 12, 1994.
Ronstadt, Linda Tucson, AZ, July 15, 1946.
Rooker, Michael Jasper, AL, April 6, 1955.
Rooney, Mickey (Joe Yule, Jr.) Brooklyn, NY, Sept. 23, 1920.
Rose, Reva Chicago, IL, July 30, 1940. Goodman.
Ross, Diana Detroit, MI, March 26, 1944.
Ross, Justin Brooklyn, NY, Dec. 15, 1954.
Ross, Katharine Hollywood, CA, Jan. 29, 1940. Santa Rosa College.
Rossellini, Isabella Rome, Italy, June 18, 1952.
Rossovich, Rick Palo Alto, CA, Aug. 28, 1957.
Rossum, Emmy New York, NY, Sept. 12, 1986.
Roth, Tim London, England, May 14, 1961.
Roundtree, Richard New Rochelle, NY, Sept. 7, 1942. Southern Illinois.
Rourke, Mickey (Philip Andre Rourke, Jr.) Schenectady, NY, Sept. 16, 1952.
Routh, Brandon Des Moines, IA, Oct. 9, 1979.
Rowe, Nicholas Edinburgh, Scotland, Nov. 22, 1966, Eton.
Rowlands, Gena Cambria, WI, June 19, 1930.
Rubin, Andrew New Bedford, MA, June 22, 1946. AADA.
Rubinek, Saul Fohrenwold, Germany, July 2, 1948.
Rubinstein, John Los Angeles, CA, Dec. 8, 1946. UCLA.
Ruck, Alan Cleveland, OH, July 1, 1956.
Rucker, Bo Tampa, FL, Aug. 17, 1948.
Rudd, Paul Boston, MA, May 15, 1940.
Rudd, Paul Passaic, NJ, April 6, 1969.
Rudner, Rita Miami, FL, Sept. 17, 1953.
Rudolph, Maya Gainesville, FL, July 27, 1972.
Ruehl, Mercedes Queens, NY, Feb. 28, 1948.
Ruffalo, Mark Kenosha, WI, Nov. 22, 1967.
Rupert, Michael Denver, CO, Oct. 23, 1951. Pasadena Playhouse.
Rush, Barbara Denver, CO, Jan. 4, 1927. U California.
Rush, Geoffrey Toowoomba, Australia, July 6, 1951. U Queensland.
Russell, Jane Bemidji, MI, June 21, 1921. Max Reinhardt School.
Russell, Keri Fountain Valley, CA, March 23, 1976.
Russell, Kurt Springfield, MA, March 17, 1951.
Russell, Theresa (Paup) San Diego, CA, March 20, 1957.
Russo, James New York, NY, April 23, 1953.
Russo, Rene Burbank, CA, Feb. 17, 1954.
Rutherford, Ann Toronto, ON, Canada, Nov. 2, 1920.
Ryan, Amy Queens, NY, Nov. 30, 1969.
Ryan, Meg Fairfield, CT, Nov. 19, 1961. NYU.
Ryder, Winona (Horowitz) Winona, MN, Oct. 29, 1971.

Sacchi, Robert Bronx, NY, 1941. NYU.
Sägebrecht, Marianne Starnberg, Bavaria, Aug. 27, 1945.
Saint, Eva Marie Newark, NJ, July 4, 1924. Bowling Green State U.
Saint James, Susan (Suzie Jane Miller) Los Angeles, CA, Aug. 14, 1946. Connecticut College.
St. John, Betta Hawthorne, CA, Nov. 26, 1929.
St. John, Jill (Jill Oppenheim) Los Angeles, CA, Aug. 19, 1940.
Saldana, Theresa Brooklyn, NY, Aug. 20, 1954.
Saldana, Zoe NJ, June 19, 1978.
Salinger, Matt Windsor, VT, Feb. 13, 1960. Princeton, Columbia.
Salt, Jennifer Los Angeles, CA, Sept. 4, 1944. Sarah Lawrence College.
Samms, Emma London, England, Aug. 28, 1960.
San Giacomo, Laura Orange, NJ, Nov. 14, 1962.
Sanders, Jay O. Austin, TX, April 16, 1953.
Sandler, Adam Bronx, NY, Sept. 9, 1966. NYU.
Sands, Julian Yorkshire, England, Jan 15, 1958.
Sands, Tommy Chicago, IL, Aug. 27, 1937.
Sara, Mia (Sarapocciello) Brooklyn, NY, June 19, 1967.
Sarandon, Chris Beckley, WV, July 24, 1942. U West Virginia., Catholic U.
Sarandon, Susan (Tomalin) New York, NY, Oct. 4, 1946. Catholic U.
Sarrazin, Michael Quebec City, Canada, May 22, 1940.
Sarsgaard, Peter Scott Air Force Base, Illinois, March 7, 1971. Washington U St. Louis
Savage, Fred Highland Park, IL, July 9, 1976.
Savage, John (Youngs) Long Island, NY, Aug. 25, 1949. AADA.
Saviola, Camille Bronx, NY, July 16, 1950.
Savoy, Teresa Ann London, England, July 18, 1955.
Sawa, Devon Vancouver, BC, Canada, Sept. 7, 1978.
Saxon, John (Carmen Orrico) Brooklyn, NY, Aug. 5, 1935.
Sbarge, Raphael New York, NY, Feb. 12, 1964.
Scacchi, Greta Milan, Italy, Feb. 18, 1960.
Scalia, Jack Brooklyn, NY, Nov. 10, 1951.
Scarwid, Diana Savannah, GA, Aug. 27, 1955, AADA. Pace U.
Schell, Maximilian Vienna, Austria, Dec. 8, 1930.
Schlatter, Charlie Englewood, NJ, May 1, 1966. Ithaca College.
Schneider, John Mt. Kisco, NY, April 8, 1960.
Schneider, Maria Paris, France, March 27, 1952.
Schneider, Paul Asheville, NC, March 16, 1976.
Schreiber, Liev San Francisco, CA, Oct. 4, 1967.
Schroder, Rick Staten Island, NY, April 13, 1970.
Schuck, John Boston, MA, Feb. 4, 1940.
Schultz, Dwight Baltimore, MD, Nov. 24, 1947.
Schwartzman, Jason Los Angeles, CA, June 26, 1980.
Schwarzenegger, Arnold Austria, July 30, 1947.
Schwimmer, David Queens, NY, Nov. 12, 1966.
Schygulla, Hanna Katlowitz, Germany, Dec. 25, 1943.
Sciorra, Annabella New York, NY, March 24, 1960.
Scoggins, Tracy Galveston, TX, Nov. 13, 1953.
Scolari, Peter Scarsdale, NY, Sept. 12, 1955. City College NY.
Scott, Campbell South Salem, NY, July 19, 1961. Lawrence.
Scott, Lizabeth (Emma Matso) Scranton, PA, Sept. 29, 1922.
Scott, Seann William Cottage Grove, MN, Oct. 3, 1976.
Scott Thomas, Kristin Redruth, Cornwall, England, May 24, 1960.
Seagal, Steven Detroit, MI, April 10, 1951.
Sedgwick, Kyra New York, NY, Aug. 19, 1965. USC.
Segal, George New York, NY, Feb. 13, 1934. Columbia U.
Segel, Jason Los Angeles, Jan. 18, 1980.
Seinfeld, Jerry Brooklyn, NY, April 29, 1954.
Selby, David Morganstown, WV, Feb. 5, 1941. U West Virginia.
Sellars, Elizabeth Glasgow, Scotland, May 6, 1923.
Selleck, Tom Detroit, MI, Jan. 29, 1945. USC.
Sernas, Jacques Lithuania, July 30, 1925.
Seth, Roshan New Delhi, India, Aug. 17, 1942.

Sevigny, Chloë Springfield, MA, Nov. 18, 1974.
Sewell, Rufus Twickenham, England, Oct. 29, 1967.
Seyfried, Amanda Allentown, PA, Dec. 3, 1985.
Seymour, Jane (Joyce Frankenberg) Hillingdon, England, Feb. 15, 1951.
Shalhoub, Tony Green Bay, WI, Oct. 9, 1953.
Shandling, Garry Chicago, IL, Nov. 29, 1949.
Shannon, Michael Lexington, KY, Aug. 7, 1974.
Shannon, Molly Shaker Heights, OH, Sept. 16, 1964.
Sharif, Omar (Michel Shalhoub) Alexandria, Egypt, April 10, 1932. Victoria College.
Shatner, William Montreal, Quebec, Canada, March 22, 1931. McGill U.
Shaver, Helen St. Thomas, ON, Canada, Feb. 24, 1951.
Shaw, Fiona Cork, Ireland, July 10, 1958. RADA.
Shaw, Stan Chicago, IL, July 14, 1952.
Shawn, Wallace New York, NY, Nov. 12, 1943. Harvard.
Shea, John North Conway, NH, April 14, 1949. Bates, Yale.
Shearer, Harry Los Angeles, CA, Dec. 23, 1943. UCLA.
Sheedy, Ally New York, NY, June 13, 1962. USC.
Sheen, Charlie (Carlos Irwin Estevez) Santa Monica, CA, Sept. 3, 1965.
Sheen, Martin (Ramon Estevez) Dayton, OH, Aug. 3, 1940.
Sheen, Michael Newport, Wales, Feb. 5, 1969.
Sheffer, Craig York, PA, April 23, 1960. E. Stroudsberg U.
Sheffield, John Pasadena, CA, April 11, 1931. UCLA.
Shelley, Carol London, England, Aug. 16, 1939.
Shelton, Marley Los Angeles, CA, April 12, 1974.
Shepard, Dax Milford, MI, Jan. 2, 1975.
Shepard, Sam (Rogers) Ft. Sheridan, IL, Nov. 5, 1943.
Shepherd, Cybill Memphis, TN, Feb. 18, 1950. Hunter, NYU.
Sher, Antony Cape Town, South Africa, June 14, 1949.
Sherbedgia, Rade Korenica, Croatia, July 27, 1946.
Sheridan, Jamey Pasadena, CA, July 12, 1951.
Shields, Brooke New York, NY, May 31, 1965.
Shire, Talia Lake Success, NY, April 25, 1946. Yale.
Short, Martin Toronto, ON, Canada, March 26, 1950. McMaster U.
Shue, Elisabeth S. Orange, NJ, Oct. 6, 1963. Harvard.
Sidibe, Gabourey Brooklyn, NY, May 6, 1983.
Siemaszko, Casey Chicago, IL, March 17, 1961.
Sikking, James B. Los Angeles, CA, March 5, 1934.
Silva, Henry Brooklyn, NY, Sept. 15, 1928.
Silverman, Jonathan Los Angeles, CA, Aug. 5, 1966. USC.
Silverman, Sarah Bedford, NH, Dec. 1, 1970.
Silverstone, Alicia San Francisco, CA, Oct. 4, 1976.
Silverstone, Ben London, England, April 9, 1979.
Simmons, J.K. (Jonathan Kimble) Detroit, MI, Jan. 9, 1955. U Montana.
Simmons, Jean London, England, Jan. 31, 1929. Aida Foster School.
Simon, Paul Newark, NJ, Nov. 5, 1942.
Simpson, O.J. (Orenthal James) San Francisco, CA, July 9, 1947. UCLA.
Sinbad (David Adkins) Benton Harbor, MI, Nov. 10, 1956.
Sinden, Donald Plymouth, England, Oct. 9, 1923. Webber-Douglas.
Singer, Lori Corpus Christi, TX, May 6, 1957. Juilliard.
Sinise, Gary Chicago, IL, March 17, 1955.
Sizemore, Tom Detroit, MI, Sept. 29, 1961.
Skarsgård, Stellan Gothenburg, Sweden, June 13, 1951.
Skerritt, Tom Detroit, MI, Aug. 25, 1933. Wayne State U.
Skye, Ione (Leitch) London, England, Sept. 4, 1970.
Slater, Christian New York, NY, Aug. 18, 1969.
Slater, Helen New York, NY, Dec. 15, 1963.
Slattery, John Boston, MA, Aug. 13, 1962.
Smart, Amy Topanga Canyon, CA, March 26, 1976.
Smith, Charles Martin Los Angeles, CA, Oct. 30, 1953. Cal State U.
Smith, Jaclyn Houston, TX, Oct. 26, 1945.
Smith, Jada Pinkett Baltimore, MD, Sept. 18, 1971.
Smith, Kerr Exton, PA, March 9, 1972.

Smith, Kevin Red Bank, NJ, Aug. 2, 1970.
Smith, Kurtwood New Lisbon, WI, July 3, 1943.
Smith, Lewis Chattanooga, TN, 1956. Actors Studio.
Smith, Lois Topeka, KS, Nov. 3, 1930. U Washington.
Smith, Maggie Ilford, England, Dec. 28, 1934.
Smith, Roger South Gate, CA, Dec. 18, 1932. U Arizona.
Smith, Will Philadelphia, PA, Sept. 25, 1968.
Smithers, William Richmond, VA, July 10, 1927. Catholic U.
Smits, Jimmy Brooklyn, NY, July 9, 1955. Cornell U.
Smollett, Jurnee New York, NY, Oct. 1, 1986.
Snipes, Wesley New York, NY, July 31, 1962. SUNY-Purchase.
Snoop Dogg (Calvin Broadus) Long Beach, CA, Oct. 20, 1971.
Snow, Brittany Tampa, FL, March 9, 1986.
Sobieksi, Leelee (Liliane Sobieski) New York, NY, June 10, 1982.
Solomon, Bruce New York, NY, Aug. 12, 1944. U Miami, Wayne State U.
Somerhalder, Ian Covington, LA, Dec. 8, 1978.
Somers, Suzanne (Mahoney) San Bruno, CA, Oct. 16, 1946.
    Lone Mt. College.
Sommer, Elke (Schletz) Berlin, Germany, Nov. 5, 1940.
Sommer, Josef Greifswald, Germany, June 26, 1934.
Sorvino, Mira Tenafly, NJ, Sept. 28, 1967.
Sorvino, Paul New York, NY, April 13, 1939. AMDA.
Soto, Talisa (Miriam Soto) Brooklyn, NY, March 27, 1967.
Soul, David Chicago, IL, Aug. 28, 1943.
Spacek, Sissy Quitman, TX, Dec. 25, 1949. Actors Studio.
Spacey, Kevin So. Orange, NJ, July 26, 1959. Juilliard.
Spade, David Birmingham, MI, July 22, 1964.
Spader, James Buzzards Bay, MA, Feb. 7, 1960.
Spall, Timothy London, England, Feb. 27, 1957.
Spano, Vincent Brooklyn, NY, Oct. 18, 1962.
Spenser, Jeremy London, England, July 16, 1937.
Spinella, Stephen Naples, Italy, Oct. 11, 1956. NYU.
Springfield, Rick (Richard Spring Thorpe) Sydney, Australia, Aug. 23, 1949.
Stadlen, Lewis J. Brooklyn, NY, March 7, 1947. Neighborhood Playhouse.
Stahl, Nick Dallas, TX, Dec. 5, 1979.
Stallone, Frank New York, NY, July 30, 1950.
Stallone, Sylvester New York, NY, July 6, 1946. U Miami.
Stamp, Terence London, England, July 23, 1939.
Stanford, Aaron Westford, MA, Dec. 18, 1977.
Stanton, Harry Dean Lexington, KY, July 14, 1926.
Stapleton, Jean New York, NY, Jan. 19, 1923.
Starr, Ringo (Richard Starkey) Liverpool, England, July 7, 1940.
Statham, Jason London, England, Sept. 12, 1972.
Staunton, Imelda London, England, Jan. 9, 1956.
Steele, Barbara England, Dec. 29, 1937.
Steele, Tommy London, England, Dec. 17, 1936.
Steenburgen, Mary Newport, AR, Feb. 8, 1953. Neighborhood Playhouse.
Stern, Daniel Bethesda, MD, Aug. 28, 1957.
Sternhagen, Frances Washington, DC, Jan. 13, 1930.
Stevens, Andrew Memphis, TN, June 10, 1955.
Stevens, Connie (Concetta Ann Ingolia) Brooklyn, NY, Aug. 8, 1938.
    Hollywood Professional School.
Stevens, Fisher Chicago, IL, Nov. 27, 1963. NYU.
Stevens, Stella (Estelle Eggleston) Hot Coffee, MS, Oct. 1, 1936.
Stevenson, Juliet Essex, England, Oct. 30, 1956.
Stevenson, Parker Philadelphia, PA, June 4, 1952. Princeton.
Stewart, Alexandra Montreal, Quebec, Canada, June 10, 1939. Louvre.
Stewart, Elaine (Elsy Steinberg) Montclair, NJ, May 31, 1929.
Stewart, French (Milton French Stewart) Albuquerque, NM, Feb. 20, 1964.
Stewart, Jon (Jonathan Stewart Liebowitz) Trenton, NJ, Nov. 28, 1962.
Stewart, Kristen Los Angeles, CA, April 9, 1990.
Stewart, Martha (Martha Haworth) Bardwell, KY, Oct. 7, 1922.
Stewart, Patrick Mirfield, England, July 13, 1940.

Stiers, David Ogden Peoria, IL, Oct. 31, 1942.
Stiles, Julia New York, NY, March 28, 1981.
Stiller, Ben New York, NY, Nov. 30, 1965.
Stiller, Jerry New York, NY, June 8, 1927.
Sting (Gordon Matthew Sumner) Wallsend, England, Oct. 2, 1951.
Stockwell, Dean Hollywood, CA, March 5, 1935.
Stockwell, John (John Samuels, IV) Galveston, TX, March 25, 1961. Harvard.
Stoltz, Eric Whittier, CA, Sept. 30, 1961. USC.
Stowe, Madeleine Eagle Rock, CA, Aug. 18, 1958.
Strassman, Marcia New York, NY, April 28, 1948.
Strathairn, David San Francisco, CA, Jan. 26, 1949.Williams College.
Strauss, Peter New York, NY, Feb. 20, 1947.
Streep, Meryl (Mary Louise) Summit, NJ, June 22, 1949 Vassar, Yale.
Streisand, Barbra Brooklyn, NY, April 24, 1942.
Stritch, Elaine Detroit, MI, Feb. 2, 1925. Drama Workshop.
Strong, Mark London, England, Aug. 1963.
Stroud, Don Honolulu, HI, Sept. 1, 1943.
Struthers, Sally Portland, OR, July 28, 1948. Pasadena Playhouse.
Studi, Wes (Wesley Studie) Nofire Hollow, OK, Dec. 17, 1947.
Summer, Donna (LaDonna Gaines) Boston, MA, Dec. 31, 1948.
Sumpter, Jeremy Monterey, CA, Feb. 5, 1989.
Sutherland, Donald St. John, New Brunswick, Canada, July 17, 1935.
    U Toronto.
Sutherland, Kiefer Los Angeles, CA, Dec. 18, 1966.
Suvari, Mena Newport, RI, Feb. 9, 1979.
Svenson, Bo Goreborg, Sweden, Feb. 13, 1941. UCLA.
Swank, Hilary Bellingham, WA, July 30, 1974.
Sweeney, D. B. (Daniel Bernard Sweeney) Shoreham, NY, Nov. 14, 1961.
Swinton, Tilda London, England, Nov. 5, 1960.
Swit, Loretta Passaic, NJ, Nov. 4, 1937, AADA.
Sykes, Wanda Portsmouth, VA, March 7, 1964.
Syms, Sylvia London, England, June 1, 1934. Convent School.
Szarabajka, Keith Oak Park, IL, Dec. 2, 1952. U Chicago.

T, Mr. (Lawrence Tero) Chicago, IL, May 21, 1952.
Tabori, Kristoffer (Siegel) Los Angeles, CA, Aug. 4, 1952.
Takei, George Los Angeles, CA, April 20, 1937. UCLA.
Talbot, Nita New York, NY, Aug. 8, 1930. Irvine Studio School.
Tamblyn, Amber Santa Monica, CA, May 14, 1983.
Tamblyn, Russ Los Angeles, CA, Dec. 30, 1934.
Tambor, Jeffrey San Francisco, CA, July 8, 1944.
Tarantino, Quentin Knoxville, TN, March 27, 1963.
Tate, Larenz Chicago, IL, Sept. 8, 1975.
Tatum, Channing Cullman, AL, April 26, 1980.
Tautou, Audrey Beaumont, France, Aug. 9, 1978.
Taylor, Elizabeth London, England, Feb. 27, 1932. Byron House School.
Taylor, Lili Glencoe, IL, Feb. 20, 1967.
Taylor, Noah London, England, Sept. 4, 1969.
Taylor, Renée New York, NY, March 19, 1935.
Taylor, Rod (Robert) Sydney, Australia, Jan. 11, 1929.
Taylor-Young, Leigh Washington, DC, Jan. 25, 1945. Northwestern.
Teefy, Maureen Minneapolis, MN, Oct. 26, 1953, Juilliard.
Temple, Shirley Santa Monica, CA, April 23, 1927.
Tennant, Victoria London, England, Sept. 30, 1950.
Tenney, Jon Princeton, NJ, Dec. 16, 1961.
Terzieff, Laurent Paris, France, June 25, 1935.
Tewes, Lauren Braddock, PA, Oct. 26, 1954.
Thacker, Russ Washington, DC, June 23, 1946. Montgomery College.
Thaxter, Phyllis Portland, ME, Nov. 20, 1921. St. Genevieve.
Thelen, Jodi St. Cloud, MN, June 12, 1962.
Theron, Charlize Benoni, South Africa, Aug. 7, 1975.
Thewlis, David Blackpool, England, March 20, 1963.
Thierot, Max Los Altos Hills, CA, Oct. 14, 1988.

Thomas, Henry San Antonio, TX, Sept. 8, 1971.
Thomas, Jay New Orleans, LA, July 12, 1948.
Thomas, Jonathan Taylor (Weiss) Bethlehem, PA, Sept. 8, 1981.
Thomas, Marlo (Margaret) Detroit, MI, Nov. 21, 1937. USC.
Thomas, Philip Michael Columbus, OH, May 26, 1949. Oakwood College.
Thomas, Richard New York, NY, June 13, 1951. Columbia.
Thompson, Emma London, England, April 15, 1959. Cambridge.
Thompson, Fred Dalton Sheffield, AL, Aug. 19, 1942.
Thompson, Jack (John Payne) Sydney, Australia, Aug. 31, 1940.
Thompson, Lea Rochester, MN, May 31, 1961.
Thompson, Rex New York, NY, Dec. 14, 1942.
Thompson, Sada Des Moines, IA, Sept. 27, 1929. Carnegie Tech.
Thornton, Billy Bob Hot Spring, AR, Aug. 4, 1955.
Thorson, Linda Toronto, ON, Canada, June 18, 1947. RADA.
Thurman, Uma Boston, MA, April 29, 1970.
Ticotin, Rachel Bronx, NY, Nov. 1, 1958.
Tierney, Maura Boston, MA, Feb. 3, 1965.
Tiffin, Pamela (Wonso) Oklahoma City, OK, Oct. 13, 1942.
Tighe, Kevin Los Angeles, CA, Aug. 13, 1944.
Tilly, Jennifer Los Angeles, CA, Sept. 16, 1958.
Tilly, Meg Texada, Canada, Feb. 14, 1960.
Timberlake, Justin Memphis, TN, Jan. 31, 1981.
Tobolowsky, Stephen Dallas, TX, May 30, 1951. Southern Methodist U.
Todd, Beverly Chicago, IL, July 1, 1946.
Todd, Richard Dublin, Ireland, June 11, 1919. Shrewsbury School.
Todd, Tony Washington, DC, Dec. 4, 1954.
Tolkan, James Calumet, MI, June 20, 1931.
Tomei, Marisa Brooklyn, NY, Dec. 4, 1964. NYU.
Tomlin, Lily Detroit, MI, Sept. 1, 1939. Wayne State U.
Topol (Chaim Topol) Tel Aviv, Israel, Sept. 9, 1935.
Torn, Rip Temple, TX, Feb. 6, 1931. U Texas.
Torres, Liz New York, NY, Sept. 27, 1947. NYU.
Totter, Audrey Joliet, IL, Dec. 20, 1918.
Towsend, Robert Chicago, IL, Feb. 6, 1957.
Townsend, Stuart Dublin, Ireland, Dec. 15, 1972.
Trachtenberg, Michelle New York, NY, Oct. 11, 1985.
Travanti, Daniel J. Kenosha, WI, March 7, 1940.
Travis, Nancy Astoria, NY, Sept. 21, 1961.
Travolta, Joey Englewood, NJ, Oct. 14, 1950.
Travolta, John Englewood, NJ, Feb. 18, 1954.
Trejo, Danny Los Angeles, CA, May 16, 1944.
Trintignant, Jean-Louis Pont-St. Esprit, France, Dec. 11, 1930. Dullin-Balachova Drama School.
Tripplehorn, Jeanne Tulsa, OK, June 10, 1963.
Tsopei, Corinna Athens, Greece, June 21, 1944.
Tubb, Barry Snyder, TX, 1963. Am Consv Th.
Tucci, Stanley Katonah, NY, Jan. 11, 1960.
Tucker, Chris Decatur, GA, Aug. 31, 1972.
Tucker, Jonathan Boston, MA, May 31, 1982.
Tucker, Michael Baltimore, MD, Feb. 6, 1944.
Tudyk, Alan El Paso, TX, March 16, 1971.
Tune, Tommy Wichita Falls, TX, Feb. 28, 1939.
Tunney, Robin Chicago, IL, June 19, 1972.
Turner, Janine (Gaunt) Lincoln, NE, Dec. 6, 1963.
Turner, Kathleen Springfield, MO, June 19, 1954. U Maryland.
Turner, Tina (Anna Mae Bullock) Nutbush, TN, Nov. 26, 1938.
Turturro, John Brooklyn, NY, Feb. 28, 1957. Yale.
Tushingham, Rita Liverpool, England, March 14, 1940.
Twiggy (Lesley Hornby) London, England, Sept. 19, 1949.
Twomey, Anne Boston, MA, June 7, 1951. Temple U.
Tyler, Liv Portland, ME, July 1, 1977.
Tyrrell, Susan San Francisco, CA, March 18, 1945.

Tyson, Cathy Liverpool, England, June 12, 1965. Royal Shakespeare Company.
Tyson, Cicely New York, NY, Dec. 19, 1933. NYU.

Uggams, Leslie New York, NY, May 25, 1943. Juilliard.
Ulliel, Gaspard Boulogne-Billancourt, France, Nov. 25, 1984.
Ullman, Tracey Slough, England, Dec. 30, 1959.
Ullmann, Liv Tokyo, Japan, Dec. 10, 1938. Webber-Douglas Academy.
Ulrich, Skeet (Bryan Ray Ulrich) North Carolina, Jan. 20, 1969.
Underwood, Blair Tacoma, WA, Aug. 25, 1964. Carnegie-Mellon U.
Unger, Deborah Kara Victoria, BC, Canada, May 12, 1966.
Union, Gabrielle Omaha, NE, Oct. 29, 1973.

Vaccaro, Brenda Brooklyn, NY, Nov. 18, 1939. Neighborhood Playhouse.
Van Ark, Joan New York, NY, June 16, 1943. Yale.
Van Damme, Jean-Claude (J-C Vorenberg) Brussels, Belgium, April 1, 1960.
Van De Ven, Monique Zeeland, Netherlands, July 28, 1952.
Van Der Beek, James Chesire, CT, March 8, 1977.
Van Devere, Trish (Patricia Dressel) Englewood Cliffs, NJ, March 9, 1945. Ohio Wesleyan.
Van Dien, Casper Ridgefield, NJ, Dec. 18, 1968.
Van Doren, Mamie (Joan Lucile Olander) Rowena, SD, Feb. 6, 1933.
Van Dyke, Dick West Plains, MO, Dec. 13, 1925.
Van Houten, Clarice Leiderdorp, Netherlands, Sept. 5, 1976.
Vanity (Denise Katrina Smith) Niagara, ON, Can, Jan. 4, 1959.
Van Pallandt, Nina Copenhagen, Denmark, July 15, 1932.
Van Patten, Dick New York, NY, Dec. 9, 1928.
Van Patten, Joyce New York, NY, March 9, 1934.
Van Peebles, Mario New York, NY, Jan. 15, 1958. Columbia U.
Van Peebles, Melvin Chicago, IL, Aug. 21, 1932.
Vance, Courtney B. Detroit, MI, March 12, 1960.
Vardalos, Nia Winnipeg, Manitoba, Canada, Sept. 24, 1962.
Vartan, Michael Boulogne-Billancourt, France, Nov. 27, 1968.
Vaughn, Robert New York, NY, Nov. 22, 1932. USC.
Vaughn, Vince Minneapolis, MN, March 28, 1970.
Vega, Isela Hermosillo, Mexico, Nov. 5, 1940.
Veljohnson, Reginald New York, NY, Aug. 16, 1952.
Vennera, Chick Herkimer, NY, March 27, 1952. Pasadena Playhouse.
Venora, Diane Hartford, CT, Aug. 10, 1952. Juilliard.
Vereen, Ben Miami, FL, Oct. 10, 1946.
Victor, James (Lincoln Rafael Peralta Diaz) Santiago, D.R., July 27, 1939. Haaren HS/New York, NY.
Vincent, Jan-Michael Denver, CO, July 15, 1944. Ventura.
Violet, Ultra (Isabelle Collin-Dufresne) Grenoble, France, Sept. 6, 1935.
Visnjic, Goran Sibenik, Yugoslavia, Sept. 9, 1972. .
Voight, Jon Yonkers, NY, Dec. 29, 1938. Catholic U.
Von Bargen, Daniel Cincinnati, OH, June 5, 1950. Purdue.
Von Dohlen, Lenny Augusta, GA, Dec. 22, 1958. U Texas.
Von Sydow, Max Lund, Sweden, July 10, 1929. Royal Drama Theatre.

Wagner, Lindsay Los Angeles, CA, June 22. 1949.
Wagner, Natasha Gregson Los Angeles, CA, Sept. 29, 1970.
Wagner, Robert Detroit, MI, Feb. 10, 1930.
Wahl, Ken Chicago, IL, Feb. 14, 1954.
Waite, Genevieve Cape Town, South Africa, Feb. 19, 1948.
Waite, Ralph White Plains, NY, June 22, 1928. Yale.
Waits, Tom Pomona, CA, Dec. 7, 1949.
Wallace, Dee (Deanna Bowers) Kansas City, KS, Dec. 14, 1948.
Walken, Christopher Astoria, NY, March 31, 1943. Hofstra.
Walker, Clint Hartfold, IL, May 30, 1927. USC.
Walker, Paul Glendale, CA, Sept. 12, 1973.
Wallach, Eli Brooklyn, NY, Dec. 7, 1915. CCNY, U Texas.

Wallach, Roberta New York, NY, Aug. 2, 1955.
Wallis, Shani London, England, April 5, 1933.
Walsh, Dylan Los Angeles, CA, Nov. 17, 1963.
Walsh, M. Emmet Ogdensburg, NY, March 22, 1935. Clarkson College, AADA.
Walter, Jessica Brooklyn, NY, Jan. 31, 1944 Neighborhood Playhouse.
Walter, Tracey Jersey City, NJ, Nov. 25, 1942.
Walters, Julie London, England, Feb. 22, 1950.
Walton, Emma London, England, Nov. 1962. Brown U.
Waltz, Christoph Vienna, Austria, Oct. 4, 1956.
Wanamaker, Zoë New York, NY, May 13, 1949.
Ward, Burt (Gervis) Los Angeles, CA, July 6, 1945.
Ward, Fred San Diego, CA, Dec. 30, 1942.
Ward, Rachel London, England, Sept. 12, 1957.
Ward, Sela Meridian, MS, July 11, 1956.
Ward, Simon London, England, Oct. 19, 1941.
Warner, David Manchester, England, July 29, 1941. RADA.
Warner, Malcolm-Jamal Jersey City, NJ, Aug. 18, 1970.
Warren, Jennifer New York, NY, Aug. 12, 1941. U Wisconsin.
Warren, Lesley Ann New York, NY, Aug. 16, 1946.
Warren, Michael South Bend, IN, March 5, 1946. UCLA.
Washington, Denzel Mt. Vernon, NY, Dec. 20, 1954. Fordham U.
Washington, Kerry Bronx, NY, Jan. 31, 1977.
Wasson, Craig Ontario, OR, March 15, 1954. U Oregon.
Watanabe, Ken Koide, Japan, Oct. 21, 1959.
Waterston, Sam Cambridge, MA, Nov. 15, 1940. Yale.
Watson, Emily London, England, Jan. 14, 1967.
Watson, Emma Oxford, England, April 15, 1990.
Watts, Naomi Shoreham, England, Sept. 28, 1968.
Wayans, Damon New York, NY, Sept. 4, 1960.
Wayans, Keenen Ivory New York, NY, June 8, 1958. Tuskegee Institute.
Wayans, Marlon New York, NY, July 23, 1972.
Wayans, Shawn New York, NY, Jan. 19, 1971.
Wayne, Patrick Los Angeles, CA, July 15, 1939. Loyola.
Weathers, Carl New Orleans, LA, Jan. 14, 1948. Long Beach CC.
Weaver, Fritz Pittsburgh, PA, Jan. 19, 1926.
Weaver, Sigourney (Susan) New York, NY, Oct. 8, 1949. Stanford, Yale.
Weaving, Hugo Austin, Nigeria, April 4, 1960. NIDA.
Webber, Mark Minneapolis, MN, July 19, 1980.
Weber, Steven Queens, NY, March 4, 1961.
Wedgeworth, Ann Abilene, TX, Jan. 21, 1934. U Texas.
Weisz, Rachel London, England, March 7, 1971. Cambridge.
Welch, Raquel (Tejada) Chicago, IL, Sept. 5, 1940.
Weld, Tuesday (Susan) New York, NY, Aug. 27, 1943. Hollywood Professional School.
Weldon, Joan San Francisco, CA, Aug. 5, 1933. San Francisco Conservatory.
Weller, Peter Stevens Point, WI, June 24, 1947. American Theatre Wing.
Welling, Tom New York, NY, April 26, 1977.
Wendt, George Chicago, IL, Oct. 17, 1948.
West, Adam (William Anderson) Walla Walla, WA, Sept. 19, 1928.
West, Dominic Sheffield, England, Oct. 15, 1969.
West, Shane Baton Rouge, LA, June 10, 1978.
Westfeldt, Jennifer Guilford, CT, Feb. 2, 1971.
Wettig, Patricia Cincinatti, OH, Dec. 4, 1951. Temple U.
Whaley, Frank Syracuse, NY, July 20, 1963. SUNY-Albany.
Whalley, Joanne Manchester, England, Aug. 25, 1964.
Wheaton, Wil Burbank, CA, July 29, 1972.
Whishaw, Ben Clifton, England, Oct. 14, 1980.
Whitaker, Denzel Torrance, CA, June 15, 1990.
Whitaker, Forest Longview, TX, July 15, 1961.
Whitaker, Johnny Van Nuys, CA, Dec. 13, 1959.
White, Betty Oak Park, IL, Jan. 17, 1922.
White, Julie San Diego, CA, June 4, 1961.

Whitelaw, Billie Coventry, England, June 6, 1932.
Whitman, Stuart San Francisco, CA, Feb. 1, 1928. CCLA.
Whitney, Grace Lee Detroit, MI, April 1, 1930.
Whitton, Margaret Philadelphia, PA, Nov. 30, 1950.
Widdoes, Kathleen Wilmington, DE, March 21, 1939.
Wiest, Dianne Kansas City, MO, March 28, 1948. U Maryland.
Wiig, Kristen Canandaigua, NY, Aug. 22, 1973.
Wilby, James Burma, Feb. 20, 1958.
Wilder, Gene (Jerome Silberman) Milwaukee, WI, June 11, 1933. U Iowa.
Wilkinson, Tom Leeds, England, Dec. 12, 1948. U Kentucky.
Willard, Fred Shaker Heights, OH, Sept. 18, 1939.
Williams, Billy Dee New York, NY, April 6, 1937.
Williams, Cara (Bernice Kamiat) Brooklyn, NY, June 29, 1925.
Williams, Cindy Van Nuys, CA, Aug. 22, 1947. KACC.
Williams, Clarence, III New York, NY, Aug. 21, 1939.
Williams, Esther Los Angeles, CA, Aug. 8, 1921.
Williams, Jobeth Houston, TX, Dec 6, 1948. Brown U.
Williams, Michelle Kalispell, MT, Sept. 9, 1980.
Williams, Olivia London, England, Jan. 1, 1968.
Williams, Paul Omaha, NE, Sept. 19, 1940.
Williams, Robin Chicago, IL, July 21, 1951. Juilliard.
Williams, Treat (Richard) Rowayton, CT, Dec. 1, 1951.
Williams, Vanessa Tarrytown, NY, March 18, 1963.
Williamson, Fred Gary, IN, March 5, 1938. Northwestern.
Williamson, Nicol Hamilton, Scotland, Sept. 14, 1936.
Willis, Bruce Penns Grove, NJ, March 19, 1955.
Willison, Walter Monterey Park, CA, June 24, 1947.
Wilson, Demond New York, NY, Oct. 13, 1946. Hunter College.
Wilson, Elizabeth Grand Rapids, MI, April 4, 1925.
Wilson, Lambert Neuilly-sur-Seine, France, Aug. 3, 1958.
Wilson, Luke Dallas, TX, Sept. 21, 1971.
Wilson, Owen Dallas, TX, Nov. 18, 1968.
Wilson, Patrick Norfolk, VA, July 3, 1973.
Wilson, Rainn Seattle, WA, Jan. 20, 1966.
Wilson, Scott Atlanta, GA, March 29, 1942.
Wilson, Stuart Guildford, England, Dec. 25, 1946.
Wincott, Jeff Toronto, ON, Canada, May 8, 1957.
Wincott, Michael Toronto, ON, Canada, Jan. 6, 1959. Juilliard.
Windom, William New York, NY, Sept. 28, 1923. Williams College.
Winfrey, Oprah Kosciusko, MS, Jan. 29, 1954. Tennessee State U.
Winger, Debra Cleveland, OH, May 17, 1955. Cal State.
Winkler, Henry New York, NY, Oct. 30, 1945. Yale.
Winn, Kitty Washington, DC, Feb, 21, 1944. Boston U.
Winningham, Mare Phoenix, AZ, May 6, 1959.
Winslet, Kate Reading, England, Oct. 5, 1975.
Winslow, Michael Spokane, WA, Sept. 6, 1960.
Winstone, Ray London, England, Feb. 19, 1957.
Winter, Alex London, England, July 17, 1965. NYU.
Winters, Jonathan Dayton, OH, Nov. 11, 1925. Kenyon College.
Withers, Googie Karachi, India, March 12, 1917. Italia Conti.
Withers, Jane Atlanta, GA, April 12, 1926.
Witherspoon, Reese (Laura Jean Reese Witherspoon) Nashville, TN, March 22, 1976.
Wolf, Scott Newton, MA, June 4, 1968.
Wong, B.D. San Francisco, CA, Oct. 24,1962.
Wong, Russell Troy, NY, March 1, 1963. Santa Monica College.
Wood, Elijah Cedar Rapids, IA, Jan 28, 1981.
Wood, Evan Rachel Raleigh, NC, Sept. 7, 1987.
Woodard, Alfre Tulsa, OK, Nov. 2, 1953. Boston U.
Woodlawn, Holly (Haroldo Danhakl) Juana Diaz, PR, Oct. 26, 1946.
Woods, James Vernal, UT, April 18, 1947. MIT.
Woodward, Joanne Thomasville, GA, Feb. 27, 1930. Neighborhood Playhouse.

Woronov, Mary Brooklyn, NY, Dec. 8, 1943. Cornell.
Worthington, Sam Goldalming, Surrey, England, Aug. 2, 1976. NIDA.
Wright, Amy Chicago, IL, April 15, 1950.
Wright, Jeffrey Washington, DC, Dec. 7, 1965. Amherst College.
Wright, Max Detroit, MI, Aug. 2, 1943. Wayne State U.
Wright, Robin Dallas, TX, April 8, 1966.
Wuhl, Robert Union City, NJ, Oct. 9, 1951. U Houston.
Wyle, Noah Los Angeles, CA, June 2, 1971.
Wymore, Patrice Miltonvale, KS, Dec. 17, 1926.
Wynn, May (Donna Lee Hickey) New York, NY, Jan. 8, 1928.
Wynter, Dana (Dagmar) London, England, June 8. 1927. Rhodes U.

Yelchin, Anton St. Petersburg, Russia, March 11, 1989.
Yoba, Malik Bronx, NY, Sept. 17, 1967.
York, Michael Fulmer, England, March 27, 1942. Oxford.
York, Susannah London, England, Jan. 9, 1939. RADA.
Young, Alan (Angus) North Shield, England, Nov. 19, 1919.

Young, Burt Queens, NY, April 30, 1940.
Young, Chris Chambersburg, PA, April 28, 1971.
Young, Sean Louisville, KY, Nov. 20, 1959. Interlochen.
Yulin, Harris Los Angeles, CA, Nov. 5, 1937.
Yun-Fat, Chow Lamma Island, Hong Kong, May 18, 1955.

Zacharias, Ann Stockholm, Sweden, Sept. 19, 1956.
Zadora, Pia Hoboken, NJ, May 4, 1954.
Zahn, Steve Marshall, MN, Nov. 13, 1968.
Zegers, Kevin Woodstock, ON, Canada, Sept. 19, 1984.
Zellweger, Renée Katy, TX, April 25, 1969.
Zerbe, Anthony Long Beach, CA, May 20, 1936.
Zeta-Jones, Catherine Swansea, Wales, Sept. 25, 1969.
Zimbalist, Efrem, Jr. New York, NY, Nov. 30, 1918. Yale.
Zuniga, Daphne Berkeley, CA, Oct. 28, 1963. UCLA.

OBITUARIES
2009

Gene Barry

David Carradine

Dom DeLuise

Farrah Fawcett

Henry Gibson

John Hughes

Lou Jacobi

Jennifer Jones

Karl Malden

Patrick McGoohan

Ricardo Montalban

Brittany Murphy

Harve Presnell

Natasha Richardson

Arnold Stang

Patrick Swayze

Richard Todd

James Whitmore

Joseph Wiseman

ROBERT ANDERSON, 91, New York City-born screenwriter-playwright died on February 9, 2009 in Manhattan. He earned Oscar nominations for *The Nun's Story* and for adapting his play *I Never Sang for My Father* to the screen. He also adapted his breakthrough work *Tea and Sympathy* for film and wrote the script for *The Sand Pebbles*. Survived by his two stepchildren from his marriage to the late actress Teresa Wright.

ARMY ARCHERD (Armand Archerd), 87, Bronx-born writer, a major columnist with *Daily Variety* for more than half a century, died of cancer on September 8, 2009 in Los Angeles. He also appeared in such films as *Teacher's Pet, What a Way to Go!, The Oscar, Planet of the Apes* (1968), *Wild in the Streets,* and *Won Ton Ton the Dog Who Saved Hollywood.* He is survived by his wife, actress Selma Archerd; a son; two stepsons; and five grandchildren.

KEN ANNAKIN, 94, British director of such films as Disney's *Swiss Family Robinson* and *Those Magnificent Men in Their Flying Machines* (for which he earned an Oscar nomination for co-writing), died of natural causes on April 22, 2009 at his home in Beverly Hills, CA. His other credits include *Miranda, The Story of Robin Hood, The Sword and the Rose, Across the Bridge, Third Man on the Mountain, The Longest Day* (co-director), *Battle of the Bulge, The Biggest Bundle of Them All, Those Daring Young Men in Their Jaunty Jalopies (Monte Carlo or Bust), Cheaper to Keep Her,* and *The Pirate Movie.* He is survived by his wife of 49 years, his daughter, two grandchildren, and two great-grandchildren.

BEATRICE ARTHUR (Bernice Frankel), 86, New York City-born actress, best known for her Emmy-winning roles on the series *Maude* and *The Golden Girls,* died of cancer on April 25, 2009 at her Los Angeles home. She was also seen in a handful of films including *That Certain Woman, Lovers and Other Strangers, Mame* (repeating her Tony-winning role), and *History of the World Part 1.* Survivors include her two sons from her thirty-year marriage to director-actor Gene Saks, whom she divorced in 1980.

VAL AVERY, 85, Philadelphia-born character actor died in New York City on December 12, 2009. His many films include *Last Train from Gun Hill, The Magnificent Seven, Hud, Nevada Smith, Hombre, The Traveling Executioner, The Anderson Tapes, Minnie and Moskowitz, Papillon, Up in Smoke, The Amityville Horror* (1979), *Brubaker, Easy Money, The Pope of Greenwich Village,* and *Donnie Brasco.*

JILL BALCON, 84, London-born actress died there on July 19, 2004. Her handful of films include *Nicholas Nickleby* (1947 debut; as Madeline Bray), *Saraband (for Dead Lovers), Highly Dangerous, Edward II,* and *An Ideal Husband.* She is survived by her son, actor Daniel Day-Lewis, and her daughter.

CARL BALLANTINE (Meyer Kessler), 92, Chicago-born comedian-magician, most familiar for his role as Lester Gruber on the series *McHale's Navy,* died of age-related causes no November 3, 2009 at his home in Hollywood. He was seen in such movies as *McHale's Navy* (the 1964 theatrical spin-off), *Penelope, Speedway, The World's Greatest Lover, The North Avenue Irregulars, Just You and Me Kid, The Best of Times, Mr. Saturday Night,* and *My Giant.* Survived by a sister and two daughters.

GENE BARRY (Eugene Klass), 90, who starred in the 1953 sci-fi classic *The War of the Wars,* died of congestive heart failure on December 9, 2009 in Los Angeles. His other films include *The Atomic City, The Girls of Pleasure Island, Those Redheads from Seattle, Red Garters, Soldier of Fortune, The Purple Mask, The Houston Story, Forty Guns, Hong Kong Confidential, Thunder Road, Maroc 7,* and *The Second Coming of Suzanne* (which he also executive produced). On television he was known for starring in such series as *Bat Masterson, Burke's Law,* and *The Name of the Game.* He is survived by his three children, three grandchildren, and two great-grandchildren.

MOLLY BEE (Mollie Beachboard), 69, Oklahoma City-born country music singer died on February 7, 2009 in Oceanside, CA of complications related to a stroke. She was seen in the motion pictures *Going Steady, Summer Love, Chartroose Caboose, The Young Swingers,* and *Hillbillys in a Haunted House.* Survived by her three children.

CLAUDE BERRI, 74, French director-producer-writer-actor, best known in America for such films as *The Two of Us* and *Jean de Florette,* died of a stroke on January 12, 2009 in Paris. In addition to winning an Academy Award for the short *The Chicken (Le Poulet),* he also earned an Oscar nomination as one of the producers of *Tess.* Among his other films as director-writer are *Marry Me! Marry Me!, Le Sex Shop, Manon of the Spring, Uranus,* and *Lucie Aubric.* Survived by two sons.

BETSY BLAIR (Elizabeth Winifred Boger), 85, New Jersey-born actress, best known for her Oscar-nominated performance as Clara Snyder in the 1955 Academy Award-winner for Best Picture, *Marty,* died of cancer in London on March 13, 2009. Her other movies include *The Guilt of Janet Ames, A Double Life, Another Part of the Forest, The Snake Pit, Kind Lady, The Halliday Brand, A Delicate Balance,* and *Betrayed* (1988). She is survived by her daughter from her first marriage, to actor-dancer Gene Kelly, as well as eight grandchildren and four great-grandchildren. She was married to director Karel Reisz from 1963 until his death in 2002.

JIMMY BOYD, 70, Mississippi-born singer-actor, best known for the 1952 novelty hit "I Saw Mommy Kissing Santa Claus," died of cancer in Santa Monica on March 7, 2009. He also acted in such movies as *Racing Blood, The Second Greatest Sex, Platinum High School, High Time, Inherit the Wind, The Two Little Bears,* and *Norwood.* Survived by his son.

PAUL BURKE, 83, New Orleans-born actor, who starred in the TV series adaptations of *The Naked City* and *Twelve O'Clock High,* died of leukemia and non-Hodgkin's lymphoma on September 13, 2009 at his home in Palm Springs, CA. His movie credits include *Fearless Fagan, Francis in the Navy, Valley of the Dolls, The Thomas Crown Affair* (1968), *Daddy's Gone A-Hunting,* and *Once You Kiss a Stranger* … Survived by second wife; three children from his first marriage; six grandchildren, one of whom is actress Alia Shawkat; and two great-grandchildren.

JACK CARDIFF, 94, British cinematographer and director, who won an Academy Award for photographing *Black Narcissus,* died at his home in Ely, England, on April 22, 2009. He earned additional nominations for photographing *War and Peace* (1956) and *Fanny,* as well as directing *Sons and Lovers.* His other cinematography credits include *Stairway to Heaven (A Matter of Life and Death), The Red Shoes, Scott of the Antarctic, The Black Rose, The African Queen, The Brave One* (1956), *Death on the Nile, Ghost Story,* and *Rambo: First Blood Part II.* He also directed such films as *Scent of Mystery, The Lion, My Geisha, The Long Ships, Dark of the Sun (The Mercenaries;* also cinematographer*), The Girl on a Motorcycle* (also cinematographer), and *The Mutations.* He is survived by his third wife and three sons.

PHIL CAREY (Eugene Joseph Carey), 83, New Jersey-born screen and television actor, best known for his role as Asa Buchanan which he played for 27 years on the daytime serial *One Life to Live,* died on February 6, 2009 after a long battle with lung cancer. His movies include *Operation Pacific, Cattle Town, Springfield Rifle, Calamity Jane, The Nebraskan, Massacre Canyon, Mister Roberts, County Three and Pray, The Long Gray Line, Screaming Mimi, Tonka, Dead Ringer, The Rebel Rousers, The Seven Minutes,* and *Fighting Mad.* He is survived by his second wife and their two children, plus three children from his previous marriage.

DAVID CARRADINE (John Arthur Carradine), 72, Hollywood-born actor, best remembered for his starring role on the 1970's series *Kung Fu*, was found dead on June 4, 2009 in his Bangkok hotel room, having accidentally hanged himself. His many films include *Bus Riley's Back in Town, The Violent Ones, Young Billy Young, The Good Guys and the Bad Guys, Macho Callahan, Boxcar Bertha, Mean Streets, Death Race 2000, Cannonball, Bound for Glory* (as Woody Guthrie), *The Serpent's Egg, Gray Lady Down, Circle of Iron, The Long Riders, Q, Lone Wolf McQuade, Sonny Boy, Bird on a Wire, Roadside Prophets, Kill Bill: Vol. 2, How to Rob a Bank, The Golden Boys,* and *Crank: High Voltage*. The eldest son of the late actor John Carradine, his survivors includes his fifth wife; seven children; four half-brothers, including actors Keith and Robert Carradine; several grandchildren and great-grand children.

SYDNEY CHAPLIN, 82, Los Angeles-born screen, stage, and television actor, best known for his Broadway roles in *Bells are Ringing* (for which he won a Tony Award) and *Funny Girl*, died at his home in Rancho Mirage, CA, on March 3, 2009, following a stroke. In addition to appearing in two movies directed by his father, Charles Chaplin, *Limelight* and *A Countess from Hong Kong*, he was seen in the films *Land of the Pharaohs, Four Girls in Town, The Adding Machine, The Sicilian Clan,* and *Satan's Cheerleaders*. He is survived by his third wife, a son from his first marriage, and a granddaughter.

FRANK COGHLAN, JR. (Junior Coghlan), 93, New Haven-born actor, who starred in the 1940's serial *Adventures of Captain Marvel*, died of natural causes on Sept. 7, 2009 at his home in Saugus, CA. Starting as a child actor in silent films (where he was billed as "Junior"), he went on to appear in such movies as *A Woman of Paris, The Darling of New York, Rubber Tires, The Yankee Clipper, The Public Enemy, Penrod and Sam, The Last of the Mohicans* (1932), *Hell's House, In the Money, Pardon My Pups, Alibi Ike, Service de Luxe, Off the Record, It's a Wonderful World, Gone with the Wind, The Fighting 69th, Those Were the Days!, Henry Aldrich for President, Presenting Lily Mars,* and *Valley of the Dolls*. He is survived by his son; three daughters; and six grandchildren.

WARD COSTELLO (Edward Costello), 89, Boston-born character actor died in Redlands, CA, on June 4, 2009, of complications from a stroke. His films include *The Gallant Hours, MacArthur, Goldengirl, Whose Life is it Anyway?,* and *Missing*. He is survived by his wife, three sons, a daughter, two brothers and a sister.

VIRGINIA DAVIS, 90, Kansas City-born child actress, who starred in Walt Disney's *Alice in Cartoonland* shorts during the early 1920s, died on Aug. 15, 2009 at her home in Corona, CA. As a chorus girl she was later seen in such films as *Murder at the Vanities, Week-End in Havana,* and *The Harvey Girls*. She is survived by her two daughters, and three grandchildren.

DOM DeLUISE, 75, Brooklyn-born actor-comedian, who appeared in such Seventies comedies as *Blazing Saddles* and *The End*, died in his sleep at his Los Angeles home on May 4, 2009, following a long illness. His other film credits include *Fail-Safe, The Glass Bottom Boat, The Twelve Chairs, Every Little Crook and Nanny, The Adventure of Sherlock Holmes' Smarter Brother, Silent Movie, The World's Greatest Lover, The Cheap Detective, Sextette, The Muppet Movie, Hot Stuff* (which he also directed), *Fatso, History of the World Part 1, The Cannonball Run, The Best Little Whorehouse in Texas, Johnny Dangerously, Haunted Honeymoon,* and *Baby Geniuses*. Survivors include his wife and his three sons, all of whom became actors.

DICK DUROCK, 72, Indiana-born actor/stuntman, who played the title role in the 1982 cult horror film *Swamp Thing*, died of pancreatic cancer in Oak Park, CA, on September 17, 2009. His other films include *The Enforcer* (1976), *The Nude Bomb, Any Which Way You Can, Silverado, Stand by Me, Mr. North,* and *Delirious*.

FARRAH FAWCETT (Farrah Leni Fawcett), 62, Texas-born screen, stage, and television star, who came to prominence with the seventies cop series *Charlie's Angels*, died on June 25, 2009 in Santa Monica, CA, following a long battle with anal cancer. Her films include *Myra Breckinridge, Logan's Run, Somebody Killed Her Husband, Sunburn, Saturn 3, The Cannonball Run, Extremities, See You in the Morning, The Apostle, Dr. T and the Women,* and *The Cookout*. Survivors include her father and her son from her long term relationship with actor Ryan O'Neal.

HORTON FOOTE, 92, Texas-born screen, stage, and television writer, who won Academy Awards for his screenplays for *To Kill a Mockingbird* and *Tender Mercies*, died in his sleep on March 4, 2009 in Hartford, CT. His other film scripts are *Storm Fear, Baby the Rain Must Fall, The Chase* (1966), *Hurry Sundown, Tomorrow, 1918, The Trip to Bountiful* (Oscar nomination), *On Valentine's Day, Convicts,* and *Of Mice and Men* (1992). His other awards include the Pulitzer Prize for the 1995 play *The Young Man from Atlanta*. He is survived by his daughters, actresses Hallie and Daisy Foote, and his two sons.

SUSANNA FOSTER (Susanna DeLee Flanders Larson), 84, Chicago-born actress-singer, best remembered for playing Christine in the 1943 version of *Phantom of the Opera*, died on January 17, 2009 in Englewood, NJ. She made such other films as *The Great Victor Herbert, There's Magic in Music, Top Man, The Climax, Bowery to Broadway,* and *That Night with You*, before quitting the business in 1945. She is survived by her son and two grandchildren.

LORENA GALE, 51, Canadian actress died on June 21, 2009 in Vancouver of cancer. Her films include *The Hotel New Hampshire, Cousins, Snow Day, The Butterfly Effect,* and *Slither*.

DON GALLOWAY, 71, Kentucky-born actor, best known for playing Sgt. Ed Brown on the series *Ironside*, died on January 8, 2009 in Reno, NV, after suffering a stroke. He was seen in such films as *The Rare Breed, Rough Night in Jericho, The Big Chill, Two Moon Junction,* and *Clifford*. He is survived by his wife; two daughters; two stepchildren; and three grandchildren.

LARRY GELBART, 81, Chicago-born writer, who earned Oscar nominations for scripting the hit comedies *Oh, God!* and *Tootsie*, died of cancer on September 11, 2009 at his home in Beverly Hills. In addition to writing the Broadway musical *A Funny Thing Happened on the Way to the Forum* and helping to produce, create, and write the series adaptation of *M*A*S*H*, he worked on such other screenplays as *The Notorious Landlady, The Thrill of it All, The Wrong Box, Not with My Wife You Don't!, Movie Movie, Blame it on Rio,* and *Bedazzled* (2000). He is survived by his wife of 53 years; two children; two stepsons; six grandchildren; and two great-grandchildren.

HENRY GIBSON (James Bateman), 73, Pennsylvania-born actor, who appeared on television as cast regular on *Rowan & Martin's Laugh-In* and as part of the ensemble of Robert Altman's classic *Nashville*, died of cancer on September 14, 2009 at his home in Malibu, CA. He was seen in such other movies as *The Nutty Professor* (1963), *Kiss Me, Stupid, The Outlaws is Coming, The Long Goodbye, The Last Remake of Beau Geste, A Perfect Couple, The Blues Brothers, The Incredible Shrinking Woman, Innerspace, Switching Channels, The 'burbs, Magnolia,* and *Wedding Crashers*. He is survived by three sons; two sisters; and two grandchildren.

PAT HINGLE, 84, Denver-born screen, stage, and television character actor, died at his home in Carolina Beach, NC, on Jan. 3, 2009, of blood cancer. Following his 1954 debut in *On the Waterfront*, he was seen in such motion pictures as *The Strange One, No Down Payment, Splendor in the Grass, The Ugly American, All the Way Home, Hang 'em High, Bloody Mama, WUSA, The Carey Treatment, The Super Cops, The Gauntlet, When You Comin' Back Red Ryder?, Norma Rae, Sudden Impact, The Falcon and the Snowman, Baby Boom, Batman* (1989), *The Grifters, The Quick and the Dead, Muppets in Space, Shaft* (2000), and *Talladega Nights: The Ballad of Ricky Bobby*. Survived by his wife; five children; 11 grandchildren; and two sisters.

JOHN HUGHES, 59, Michigan-born filmmaker, best known for such seminal teen comedies of the 1980s as *The Breakfast Club* and *Ferris Bueller's Day Off*, died of a heart attack while walking in Manhattan on August 6, 2009. His other films as director-writer include *Sixteen Candles, Planes Trains & Automobiles, She's Having a Baby*, and *Uncle Buck*, while he also wrote such movies as *National Lampoon's Vacation, Pretty in Pink, Some Kind of Wonderful, Home Alone, Beethoven* (as "Edmond Dantes"), *Dennis the Menace*, and *Reach the Rock*. He is survived by his wife, two sons, and four grandchildren.

MICHAEL JACKSON, 50, Indiana-born singer, who became one of pop music's superstars through such hit songs as "Got to Be There," "Beat It," and "Thriller," died of a heart attack on June 25, 2009 in Los Angeles. He was seen in the movies *Save the Children, The Wiz, Men in Black II*, and the posthumously released *Michael Jackson's This is It*. He is survived by his parents, his five brothers, three sisters, and three children.

LOU JACOBI (Louis Harold Jacobovitch), 95, Toronto-born character actor, who played the philosophical bar owner "Moustache" in the 1963 comedy hit *Irma La Douce*, died of natural causes on October 23, 2009 at his Manhattan home. His other films include *A Kid for Two Farthings, The Diary of Anne Frank* (repeating his Broadway role), *The Last of the Secret Agents?, Little Murders, Everything You Always Wanted to Know about Sex* But Were Afraid to Ask, Next Stop Greenwich Village, Roseland, Arthur, My Favorite Year, Amazon Women on the Moon, Avalon*, and *I.Q.* He is survived by a brother and a sister.

MAURICE JARRE, 84, French composer, who won Oscars for his memorable themes from *Lawrence of Arabia* and *Doctor Zhivago*, died of cancer in Los Angeles on March 29, 2009. His many other scores include *Sundays and Cybele* (Oscar nomination), *The Longest Day, The Train, The Collector, Grand Prix, The Fixer, Ryan's Daughter, The Life and Times of Judge Roy Bean* (Oscar nomination for the song "Marmalade, Molasses and Honey"), *Mandingo, The Last Tycoon, Mohammed – Messenger of God* (Oscar nomination), *The Year of Living Dangerously, A Passage to India* (Academy Award), *Witness* (Oscar nomination), *Enemy Mine, Fatal Attraction, Gorillas in the Mist* (Oscar nomination), *Dead Poets Society, Ghost* (Oscar nomination), *Fearless*, and *I Dreamed of Africa*. He is survived by his two sons and a daughter.

JENNIFER JONES (Phyllis Isley), 90, Tulsa-born actress, one of the major film names of the 1940s and the winner of the 1943 Academy Award for her breakthrough performance in *The Song of Bernadette*, died on December 17, 2009 at her home in Malibu. She received additional Oscar nominations for the films *Since You Went Away* (opposite her first husband, Robert Walker, and working for her second husband, producer David O. Selznick), *Love Letters, Duel in the Sun*, and *Love is a Many-Splendored Thing*. Her other movies include *New Frontier* (her 1939 debut, under her real name), *Cluny Brown, Portrait of Jennie, We Were Strangers, Madame Bovary, Carrie* (1952), *Ruby Gentry, Indiscretion of an American Wife* (*Termini Statione*), *Beat the Devil, The Man in the Grey Flannel Suit, A Farewell to Arms* (1957), *Tender is the Night, Angel Angel Down We Go*, and her last, *The Towering Inferno*. She is survived by one of her children from her first husband, actor Robert Walker Jr., her grandchildren and great grandchildren.

BRENDA JOYCE (Betty Leabo), 92, Missouri-born actress, who played "Jane" in several *Tarzan* features, died on July 4, 2009 in Santa Monica. Her other films include *The Rains Came, Here I am a Stranger, Little Old New York, Maryland, I'll Tell the World, The Enchanted Forest, Pillow of Death, Little Giant*, and *Danger Woman*. She retired from acting in the late 1940's and later joined the U.S. Immigration Department, working under the name Betty Ward. She is survived by two daughters and a son.

EDWARD JUDD, 76, Shanghai-born British actor, who starred in such early sixties sci-fi films as *The Day the Earth Caught Fire* and *First Men in the Moon*, died of bronchial pneumonia on Feb. 24, 2009 in Mitcham, Surrey, England. His other films include *The Good Die Young, I Was Monty's Double, The Long Ships,*

Strange Bedfellows, O Lucky Man!, The Vault of Horror, The Incredible Sarah, and *The Kitchen Toto*. He is survived by his second wife, actress Norma Ronald, and two daughters.

MILLARD KAUFMAN, 92, Baltimore-born screenwriter died of complications of open heart surgery on March 14, 2009 in Los Angeles. Among his credits are *Take the High Ground* (Oscar nomination), *Bad Day at Black Rock* (Oscar nomination), *Raintree County, Never So Few, Convicts 4, The War Lord*, and *Living Free*. Survivors include his wife of 66 years.

HUGH LEONARD (John Joseph Byrne), 82, Dublin-born writer, who won the Tony Award for the play *Da*, died on Feb. 12, 2009 in Dalkey, Ireland. In addition to much work on television he is the credit screenwriter on such films as *Interlude, Great Catherine, Percy, Da*, and *Widow's Peak*. Survived by hi second wife and his daughter.

KARL MALDEN (Mladen Sekulovich), 97, Chicago-born actor, who won the Academy Award for repeating his Broadway role of "Mitch" in *A Streetcar Named Desire*, died of natural causes at his Brentwood, CA, home on July 1, 2009. Following his debut in *They Knew What They Wanted*, he was seen in such movies as *Winged Victory, Kiss of Death* (1947), *Boomerang!* (1947), *The Gunfighter, Halls of Montezuma, Where the Sidewalk Ends, I Confess, Ruby Gentry, Phantom of the Rue Morgue, On the Waterfront* (Oscar nomination), *Baby Doll, Fear Strikes Out, The Hanging Tree, Pollyanna* (1960), *Parrish, One-Eyed Jacks, All Fall Down, Birdman of Alcatraz, Gypsy, How the West Was Won, Dead Ringer, Cheyenne Autumn, The Cincinnati Kid, Nevada Smith, Murderers' Row, Hotel, The Adventures of Bullwhip Griffin, Hot Millions, Patton* (as Gen. Omar N. Bradley), *Wild Rovers, Twilight Time*, and *Nuts*. He also directed the 1957 film *Time Limit*. He is survived by his wife of 70 years, his two daughters, three granddaughters, and four great grandchildren.

ZENA MARSHALL, 83, Kenya-born actress died in London of cancer on July 10, 2009. Her films include *So Evil My Love, Miranda, Sleeping Car to Trieste, So Long at the Fair, Bermuda Affair, Dr. No*, and *Those Magnificent Men in Their Flying Machines*.

JODY McCREA, 74, Los Angeles-born actor, best known for appearing in several "Beach Party" movies, died of cardiac arrest on April 4, 2009 in Roswell, NM. The son of actors Joel McCrea and Frances Dee, his films included *The First Texan, The Monster That Challenged the World, Lafayette Escadrille, The Restless Years, All Hands on Deck, Beach Party, Muscle Beach Party, Pajama Party, Young Fury, Major Dundee, How to Stuff a Wild Bikini*, and *The Glory Stompers*. He retired from acting in the early 1970s to become a rancher. Survivors include his two brothers.

PATRICK McGOOHAN, 80, Astoria, New York-born actor, who established his career in the U.K., becoming a star with the series *Danger Man* (*Secret Agent*) and *The Prisoner* (which he also produced and directed), died in Los Angeles on January 13, 2009 following a short illness. His motion picture credits include *I am a Camera, Hell Drivers, The Three Lives of Thomasina, Ice Station Zebra, Mary Queen of Scots, Silver Streak, Brass Target, Escape from Alcatraz, Scanners, Baby: Secret of the Lost Legend, Braveheart*, and *A Time to Kill*. On television he won Emmys for directing episodes of *Columbo*. He is survived by his wife of 57 years; his three daughters; five grandchildren; and a great grandson.

ED McMAHON, 86, Detroit-born announcer-host-actor, who served as Johnny Carson's sidekick on *The Tonight Show* for thirty years, died in Los Angeles on June 23, 2009. In addition to his varied television work, he was seen in such motion pictures as *The Incident, Slaughter's Big Rip-Off, Fun with Dick and Jane* (1977), *Butterfly, Love Affair* (1994), and *The Weather Man*. Survivors include his third wife.

DANIEL MELNICK, 77, New York City-born film and television producer died at his home in Los Angeles on October 13, 2009. He had recently undergone surgery for lung cancer. His motion picture credits include *Straw Dogs, That's Entertainment!, All That Jazz, Altered States, Making Love, Footloose, Roxanne, Punchline, Air America,* and *L.A. Story.* He is survived by his son, his daughter, and two grandchildren.

ZAKES MOKAE, 75, South African actor, best known for his collaborations with playwright Athol Fugard including *The Blood Knot* and *Master Harold … and the Boys,* died on September 11, 2009 in Las Vegas from complications of a stoke. He was seen in such films as *The Comedians, The River Niger, The Island* (1980), *Cry Freedom, The Serpent and the Rainbow, A Dry White Season, Dad, A Rage in Harlem, Outbreak,* and *Waterworld.* He is survived by his wife; two sisters; two brothers; a daughter; and grandchildren.

RICARDO MONTALBAN, 88, Mexico-born American screen, stage, and television actor, whose long career included roles in such films as *Battleground* and *Sayonara,* as well as the lead on the hit series *Fantasy Island,* died of natural causes on Jan. 14, 2009 at his Los Angeles home. Following a career in Mexican films he made his Hollywood debut in *Fiesta* in 1947. His other films include *On an Island with You, The Kissing Bandit, Neptune's Daughter* (in which he helped introduce the Oscar-winning song "Baby, It's Cold Outside"), *Border Incident, Right Cross, Two Weeks with Love, Across the Wide Missouri, Sombrero, Latin Lovers, Queen of Babylon, Let No Man Write My Epitaph, Love is a Ball, Cheyenne Autumn, Madame X* (1966), *The Singing Nun, Sol Madrid, Sweet Charity, Escape from the Planet of the Apes, Won Ton Ton the Dog Who Saved Hollywood, Star Trek II: The Wrath of Khan, The Naked Gun: From the Files of Police Squad,* and *Spy Kids 2: The Island of Lost Dreams.* His wife of 63 years died in 2007. He is survived by his four children and six grandchildren.

JOHN MORTIMER, 85, British writer-lawyer, best known for his television work, including *Rumpole of the Bailey* and *Brideshead Revisited,* died on January 16, 2009 in Oxfordshire, England. His few screenplays include *Trial and Error* (*The Dock Brief*), *The Running Man* (1963), *Bunny Lake is Missing, John and Mary,* and *Tea with Mussolini.* He is survived by his second wife and five children, one of whom is actress Emily Mortimer.

BRITTANY MURPHY, 32, Atlanta-born actress who appeared in such films as *Clueless* and *8 Mile,* died of pneumonia and drug intoxication at her home in Los Angeles on December 20, 2009. Her other films include *Drop Dead Gorgeous; Girl, Interrupted; Sidewalks of New York; Don't Say a Word; Riding in Cars with Boys; Just Married; Uptown Girls; Little Black Book; Sin City; Happy Feet* (voice); and *Across the Hall.* She is survived by her husband, her parents, and a brother.

DAN O'BANNON, 63, St. Louis-born screenwriter, who penned the script for the original *Alien,* died in Santa Monica, CA, on December 17, 2009 of Crohn's disease. His other credits include *Dark Star, Blue Thunder, Lifeforce, Invaders from Mars* (1986), *The Return of the Living Dead,* and *Total Recall.* Survived by his wife and his son.

TULLIO PINELLI, 100, Italian writer, known for his frequent collaborations with Federico Fellini, died in Rome on March 7, 2009. He earned Oscar nominations for his work on *La Strada, I Vitelloni, La Dolce Vita,* and *8 ½.* His other scripts include *Variety Lights, The White Sheik, Nights of Cabiria, Juliet of the Spirits,* and *Ginger and Fred.*

HARVE PRESNELL (George Harvey Presnell), 75, California-born singer-actor, best known for his role as "Leadville" Johnny Brown in the original Broadway production of *The Unsinkable Molly Brown* and its film adaptation, died of pancreatic cancer on June 30, 2009 in Santa Monica, CA. His other movies include *When the Boys Meet the Girls, The Glory Guys, Paint You Wagon, Fargo, The Chamber, The Whole Wide World, Face/Off, Saving Private Ryan, Patch Adams, Old School, Flags of Our Fathers,* and *Evan Almighty.* He is survived by his second wife and his three children from his previous marriage.

EDMUND PURDOM, 84, British screen and television actor, died on Jan. 1, 2009 in Rome. His films include *Titanic* (1953), *Julius Caesar* (1953), *The Student Prince* (1954), *The Egyptian, Athena, The Prodigal, The King's Thief, Herod the Great, Queen of the Nile, The Yellow Rolls-Royce, A Matter of Time,* and *Pieces.* He is survived by his fourth wife and two daughters.

ROBERT QUARRY, 83, California-born character actor, best known for playing the title role in *Count Yorga – Vampire* and its sequel, *The Return of Count Yorga,* died on Feb. 20, 2009 in Woodland Hills, CA. He had been in declining health for years, suffering from heart trouble. His other films include *A Kiss Before Dying* (1956), *Agent for H.A.R.M., WUSA, Dr. Phibes Rises Again, The Midnight Man, Rollercoaster,* and *Commando Squad.*

JANE RANDOLPH (Jane Roermer), 93, Ohio-born actress, best remembered for her ingénue role in *Abbott and Costello Meet Frankenstein,* died on May 4, 2009 in Gstaad, Switzerland of complications following hip surgery. During the 1940s she was seen in such other movies as *Cat People, The Falcon Strikes Back, In the Meantime Darling, Jealousy, Railroaded!,* and *Open Secret* before retiring following her marriage in 1949.

NATASHA RICHARDSON, 45, London-born actress died in New York on March 18, 2009 from head injuries caused by a skiing accident in Mont Tremblant, Canada. Her film credits include *Gothic, A Month in the Country, Patty Hearst, Fat Man and Little Boy, The Handmaid's Tale, The Comfort of Strangers, The Favor, the Watch and the Very Big Fish, Nell, The Parent Trap* (1998), *Chelsea Walls, Maid in Manhattan,* and *Evening.* She is survived by her second husband, actor Liam Neeson; her two sons; her mother, actress Vanessa Redgrave; and her sister, actress Joely Richardson.

SHIRLEY JEAN RICKERT, 82, Seattle-born child star, who appeared in several *Our Gang* and *Mickey Maguire* shorts, died in Saratoga Springs, NY on Feb. 6, 2009 after a long illness. She was later an uncredited dancer in such movies as *Best Foot Forward, Good News* (1947), and *Singin' in the Rain.* Survivors include a daughter.

MARC ROCCO, 46, Los Angeles-born filmmaker died on May 1, 2009 in Northridge, CA. He directed and wrote the films *Dream a Little Dream, Where the Day Takes You,* and *Murder in the First.* Survivors include his adoptive father, actor Alex Rocco.

JAN RUBES, 89, Czech-born actor and former opera singer died on June 29, 2009 in Toronto. A founding member of the Canadian Opera Company, he appeared in such films as *The Incredible Journey, The Amateur, Witness, One Magic Christmas* (as Santa Claus), *Dead of Winter, Something about Love, The Kiss, Class Action, Deceived, Roommates,* and *Snow Falling on Cedars.* He is survived by his wife, two sons, and three grandsons.

SOUPY SALES (Milton Supman), 83, North Carolina-born comedian, best known for his outlandish children's series of the 1960's, *The Soupy Sales Show,* died on October 22, 2009 in the Bronx, following a long illness. He was seen in such films as *Two Little Bears, Critics' Choice, Birds Do It,* and *The Making of '… And God Spoke.'* Survived by his wife and two sons.

OLGA SAN JUAN, 81, Brooklyn-born actress-dancer, who danced with Fred Astaire in the 1946 musical *Blue Skies,* died on Jan. 3, 2009 in Burbank, CA, from kidney failure following a long illness. Her other movies include *Duffy's Tavern, Variety Girl, One Touch of Venus, The Beautiful Blonde from Bashful Bend,* and *The 3ʳᵈ Voice* (which also starred her husband at the time, Edmond O'Brien). She is survived by her three children with O'Brien, her sister, and three grandchildren.

ROSANNA SCHIAFFINO, 69, Italian actress died of breast cancer in Milan on October 17, 2009. Her films include *Minotaur: Wild Beast of Crete, Two Weeks in Another Town, The Victors, The Long Ships, The Cavern, Mandragola (The*

Mandrake), El Greco, and *Arrivederci Baby! (Drop Dead Darling).* She retired from acting in the 1970s. She is survived by her son and her daughter.

BUDD SCHULBERG, 95, New York City-born writer, who won an Academy Award for the 1954 classic *On the Waterfront,* died in Westhampton, NY, on August 5, 2009. His other screenplays include *Winter Carnival, A Face in the Crowd* and *Wind Across the Everglades.* He is survived by his daughter from his first marriage; a son from his second marriage; two children from his fourth marriage; and two grandchildren.

RON SILVER, 62, New York City-born actor, who portrayed attorney Alan Dershowitz in the 1990 Oscar-winning film *Reversal of Fortune,* died of esophageal cancer on March 15, 2009 in Manhattan. His other film credits include *Semi-Tough, The Entity, Best Friends, Silkwood, Romancing the Stone, Garbo Talks, Enemies – A Love Story, Blue Steel, Mr. Saturday Night, Married to It, Ali, Find Me Guilty,* and *The Ten.* On Broadway he won a Tony for *Speed-the-Plow.* Survived by his parents; two brothers; a son; and a daughter.

MELVIN SIMON, 82, Brooklyn-born producer-entrepreneur, who was instrumental in developing the concept of the shopping mall, died on September 15, 2009 in Carmel, IN of unspecified causes. For a brief period he dabbled in the film business, serving as executive producer on such movies as *When You Comin' Back Red Ryder?, When a Stranger Calls* (1979), *My Bodyguard, The Stunt Man, The Man with Bogart's Face,* and *Porky's.* Survived by his two brothers; his second wife; three daughters; a son; and 10 grandchildren.

ARNOLD STANG, 91, New York-born character player, instantly recognizable by his horn-rimmed glasses and his squawking voice, died of pneumonia in Newton, MA on December 20, 2009. In addition to many TV and radio roles and voice work (including the animated series *Top Cat*) he could be seen in such motion pictures as *Seven Days Leave, So This is New York, The Man with the Golden Arm, Dondi, The Wonderful World of the Brothers Grimm, It's a Mad Mad Mad Mad World, Skidoo, Hello Down There, Ghost Dad,* and *Dennis the Menace.* He is survived by his wife of 61 years, his son, his daughter, and two grandchildren.

GALE STORM (Josephine Cottle), 87, Texas-born actress-singer, best remembered for the 1950's sitcoms *My Little Margie* and *The Gale Storm Show,* died on June 27, 2009 in Danville, CA. Her films include *Tom Brown's School Days* (1940), *Let's Go Collegiate, Red River Valley, Man from Cheyenne, Revenge of the Zombies, Campus Rhythm, It Happened on Fifth Avenue, The Dude Goes West, The Kid from Texas, Curtain Call at Cactus Creek,* and *Woman of the North Country.* She is survived by her three sons; her daughter; eight grandchildren; and four great-grandchildren.

PATRICK SWAYZE, 57, Texas-born actor, who starred in such hit films as *Dirty Dancing* and *Ghost,* died on September 14, 2009 in Los Angeles after a battle with pancreatic cancer. His other movies include *Skatetown U.S.A., The Outsiders, Grandview U.S.A., Red Dawn, Youngblood, Road House* (1989), *City of Joy, Point Break, Tall Tale, To Wong Foo Thanks for Everything Julie Newmar, Three Wishes, Donnie Darko, Waking Up in Reno,* and *Keeping Mum.* He is survived by his wife; his brother; and his mother.

NED TANEN, 77, Los Angeles born producer-executive died of natural causes on January 5, 2009 in Santa Monica, CA. In addition to serving as president of Universal (1976-82) and Paramount (1984-88), he produced such films as *Sixteen Candles, The Breakfast Club, St. Elmo's Fire,* and *Guarding Tess.* He is survived by his partner; two daughters; and three grandchildren.

CHARLES "BUD" TINGWELL, 92, Australian actor died of complications from prostate cancer in Melbourne on May 15, 2009. He could be seen in such films as *Kangaroo, The Desert Rats, Murder She Said* (and 3 other "Miss Marple" films, as Inspector Craddock), *Dracula: Prince of Darkness, Nobody Runs Forever, Breaker Morant, A Cry in the Dark, The Castle, The Dish, Ned Kelly* (2004), and *Jindabyne.*

RICHARD TODD (Richard Andrew Palethorpe-Todd), 90, Dublin-born actor, who earned an Oscar nomination for repeating his stage role as a belligerent, dying Scotsman in *The Hasty Heart,* died in his sleep on December 3, 2009 at his home in Little Humby, England. He had been suffering with cancer for some time. His other motion pictures include *Stage Fright, Lightning Strikes Twice, The Story of Robin Hood and His Merrie Men, The Sword and the Rose, Rob Roy the Highland Rogue, A Man Called Peter, The Virgin Queen, The Dam Busters, D-Day the Sixth of June, Saint Joan, Chase a Crooked Shadow, The Long and the Short and the Tall* (*Jungle Fighters*), *The Longest Day, The Battle of the Villa Fiorita, Operation Crossbow, The Love-Ins, Asylum,* and *The Big Sleep* (1978). He is survived by a daughter from his first marriage and a son from his second.

HARRY ALAN TOWERS, 88, British producer died on July 31, 2009 in Toronto. His credits include *Code 7 Victim 5, The Face of Fu Manchu, Psycho Circus, Bang! Bang! You're Dead!, Those Fantastic Flying Fools (Blast-Off!),* and three different versions of *Ten Little Indians.*

KARL MICHAEL VOGLER, 80, German actor, who portrayed Field Marshal Rommel in the 1970 Oscar-winning *Patton,* died in Bavaria on June 9, 2009. His other English-language films include *Those Magnificent Men in Their Flying Machines, The Blue Max, How I Won the War, Downhill Racer,* and *Deep End.*

KEITH WATERHOUSE, 80, British writer, who created the title character of daydreaming *Billy Liar* for novel, stage, and screen, died on September 4, 2009 in London. Among his other screenplay credits are *Whistle Down the Wind, A Kind of Loving,* and *Man in the Middle.* Survivors include his second wife.

JAMES WHITMORE, 87, New York-born screen, stage, and television character actor, who received Oscar nominations for his performances in *Battleground* and *Give 'em Hell, Harry!* (recreating his one-man stage role), died of lung cancer at his home in Malibu on Feb. 6, 2009. Following his motion picture debut in *The Undercover Man,* he was seen in such other films as *The Outriders, The Asphalt Jungle, The Next Voice You Hear …, Mrs. O'Malley and Mr. Malone, It's a Big Country, Above and Beyond, All the Brothers Were Valiant, Kiss Me Kate, Them!, Battle Cry, Oklahoma!, The Eddy Duchin Story, The Young Don't Cry, The Deep Six, Who Was That Lady?, Black Like Me, Planet of the Apes* (1968), *Madigan, Tora! Tora! Tora!, Where the Red Fern Grows, The Serpent's Egg, The First Deadly Sin, Nuts, The Shawshank Redemption,* and *The Majestic.* He is survived by his third wife, three sons, and eight grandchildren.

COLLIN WILCOX, 74, Ohio-born actress best known for playing "Mayella Euella" in the classic film *To Kill a Mockingbird,* died on October 14, 2009 in Highlands, NC. Acting also as Collin Wilcox-Horne and Collin Wilcox Paxton she was seen in such other films as *Catch-22, The Revolutionary, The Baby Maker; September 30, 1955;* and *Marie.* She is survived by her husband a two children.

JOSEPH WISEMAN, 91, Montreal-born screen, stage, and television actor, who created an indelible impression playing the title role in the first James Bond feature, *Dr. No,* died at his home in Manhattan on October 19, 2009. His other movies include *Detective Story* (repeating his Broadway role), *Les Misérables* (1952), *Viva Zapata!, The Silver Chalice, The Garment Jungle, The Unforgiven, Bye Bye Braverman, The Night They Raided Minsky's, Lawman, The Valachi Papers, The Apprenticeship of Duddy Kravitz,* and *The Betsy.* His second wife passed away in February. He is survived by his daughter from his first marriage and a sister.

EDWARD WOODWARD, 79, British actor, best known in America for his starring role on the CBS series *The Equalizer* and the 1973 cult horror film *The Wicker Man,* died in Truro, Cornwall, England on November 16, 2009 after suffering from a series of illnesses. He was seen in such other motion pictures as *Becket, The File of the Golden Goose, Young Winston, Breaker Morant, King David, Mister Johnson,* and *Hot Fuzz.* He is survived by his second wife, their daughter, and two sons and a daughter from his first marriage.

HOWARD ZIEFF, 81, Los Angeles-born director, best known for the 1980 hit *Private Benjamin*, died in Los Angeles on Feb. 22, 2009. Following a career in commercials, his other films included *Hearts of the West, House Calls, The Main Event, Unfaithfully Yours* (1984), *The Dream Team*, and *My Girl.* He is survived by his wife and his sister.

Index